The History Of The Reformation Of The Church Of England

A

COLLECTION

OF

RECORDS,

AND

ORIGINAL PAPERS;

WITH OTHER

INSTRUMENTS

REFERRED TO IN THE FORMER HISTORY.

COLLECTION OF RECORDS,

&c.

I.

The Record of Card. Adrian's Oath of Fidelity, to Henry VII.
for the Bishopric of Bath and Wells.

BOOK
I.

Treat.
Rolls.

HENRICUS REX, &c. Reverend. in Christo Patri Domino Sylvestro Episcop. Wigorn. venerabili viro Domino Roberto Sherbourn Ecclesiæ Sancti Pauli London. decano, nostris in Romana curia oratoribus, ac Magistro Hugoni Yowng Sacræ Theologiæ Professori, salutem. Cum omnes et singuli Archiepiscopi et Episcopi hujus nostri inclyti Regni, quorum omnium nominationes, et promotiones, ad ipsas supremas dignitates, nobis attinent ex regali et peculiari quadam Prærogativa, jureq; municipali, ac inveterata consuetudine, hactenus in hoc nostro Regno inconcusse et inviolabiliter observata, teneantur et astringantur, statim et immediate post impetratas Bullas Apostolicas, super eorundem promotionē ad ipsam nostram nominationem, coram nobis et in præsentia nostra, si in hoc Regno nostro fuerunt, vel coram Commissariis nostris, ad hoc sufficienter et legittime deputatis, si alibi moram traxerunt, non solum palam, publice, et expresse, totaliter cedere, et in manus nostras renunciare omnibus, et quibuscunq; verbis, claůsulis, et sententiis in ipsis Bullis Apostolicis contentis, et descriptis, quæ sunt, vel quovis modo in futurum esse poterunt, præjudicialia, sive damnosa, nobis, hæredibusq; de corpore nostro legittime procreatis Angliæ regibus, Coronæ

A

aut Regno nostro, juribus vel consuetudinibus aut Prærogativis ejusdem Regni nostri, et quoad hoc totaliter seipsos
submittere et ponere in nostra bona venia et gratia ; sed
etiam juramentum fidelitatis et homagii ad Sancta Dei
Evangelia, per eosdem respective corporaliter tacta, nobis
facere et præstare : Cumq ; nos ob præclara merita eximi-
asq ; virtutes quibus Reverendissimum in Christo Patrem,
Dominum Adrianum tituli Sancti Chrisogoni Presbyterum
Cardinalem, abunde refertum conspicimus, obq ; diuturnum et fidele obsequium per ipsum Cardinalem nobis factum et impensum, eundem ad Ecclesias Bathon. et Wellen.
invicem unitas nominavimus et promovimus, qui idcirco et
ob id quod in curia Romana continue moram trahit, non
potest commode hujusmodi renunciationem et juramentum
coram nobis personaliter facere et præstare : Hinc est quod
nos de fidelitatibus vestris et provida circumspectione, ad
plenum confidentes, dedimus, et concessimus, ac per præsentes damus et concedimus, vobis, tribus aut duobus
vestrum, quorum præfatum Episcopum Wigorn. unicum
esse volumus, plenam potestatem et autoritatem, vice et
nomine nostris, hujusmodi renunciationem in manus vestras, et juramentum ad Sancta Dei Evangelia corporaliter
tacta, juxta formam et verum tenorem, de verbo in verbum
inferius descriptum, ab eodem Reverendissimo Domino
Cardinali recipiendi, exigendi, et cum effectu præstari videndi ; ipsumq ; Cardinalem, ut hujusmodi renunciationem
et juramentum per ipsum sic ut permittatis fiendum, et
præstandum, manu et subscriptione suis signet, et muniat,
requirendi, et ut ita fiat cum effectu videndi, literas quoq ;
et instrumenta publica super hujusmodi renunciatione, et
juramento fieri petendi, et notarium sive notarios publicos,
unum vel plures, ut ipsa instrumenta conficiant : Necnon
testes qui tunc præsentes erunt, ut veritati testimonium per-
hibeant rogandi et requirendi, ipsaq ; juramentum vel instrumenta taliter fienda, verum ordinem rei gerendæ, et
renunciationis ac juramenti tenores in se continens vel con-
tinentia, nobis destinandi et transmittendi : Et generaliter
omnia et singula faciendi, gerendi, et exercendi, quæ in
prædictis et quolibet prædictorum necessaria fuerint, seu
quomodolibet opportuna, ac quæ rei qualitas exigit et requirit, et quæ nosipsi facere et exercere possemus si præ-

sens et personaliter interessemus, etiam si talis forent quæ
de se mandatum exigant magis speciale. Tenor Renunciationis sequitur et est talis : Ego Adrianus miseratione divina tituli Sancti Chrisogoni Presbyt. Cardinalis Episcopus
Bathon. et Wellen. coram vobis Reverendo Patre Episcopo Wigorn. Domino Roberto Shurborno decano Sancti
Pauli London. et Hugone Yowng in Theologia Professore,
Commissariis ad hoc a serenissimo atq; excellentissimo
Principe Domino Henrico Dei Gratia Rege Angliæ, et
Franciæ, et Domino Hiberniæ, ejus nominis septimo, Domino meo supremo, sufficienter et legittime deputatis, expresse renuncio, et in his scriptis manu et sigillo meis in
præsentia notariorum et testium subscriptorum munitis,
totaliter cedo omnibus et quibuscunq; verbis, clausulis et
sententiis, in bullis Apostolicis mihi factis de prædict. Episcopat. Bathon. et Wellen. contentis et descriptis, quæ sunt
vel quovis modo in futurum esse poterint præjudicialia sive
damnosa præfato serenissimo Regi, Domino meo supremo,
et hæredibus suis de corpore suo legittime procreatis Angl.
Regibus, Coronæ aut Regno, sive Majestatis Juribus vel
consuetudinibus, aut Prærogativis ejusdem Regni: et
quoad hoc me integraliter submitto et pono in gratia suæ
Celsitudinis, humillime supplicans suam Majestatem, dignetur mihi concedere temporalia dicti Episcopatus Bathon.
et Wellen. quæ recognosco tenere a sua Majestate tanquam a Domino meo supremo. Tenor Juramenti sequitur et est talis: Et ego idem Adrianus Cardinalis prædictus Juro ad hæc Sancta Dei Evangelia per me corporaliter tacta, quod ab hac die et in antea, vita mea naturali
durante, ero fidelis et verus ligens, ac fidelitatem in ligen-
cia mea pure et sincere servabo, fideleq; et verum obsequium secundum optimum posse meum faciam et impend-
am serenissimo Principi Henrico ejus nominis septimo,
Dei Gratia Angl. et Fran. Regi ac Domino Hiber. Domino meo supremo, et hæredibus suis de corpore suo legittime procreatis Angl. Regibus, contra quascunq; personas,
cujuscunq; status, gradus, præeminentiæ aut conditionis
extiterint: nec quicquam faciam aut attemptabo fieri, ne
aut attemptari consentiam, quod in damnum, incommodum,
aut præjudicium, ipsius serenissimi Regis aut hæredum
suorum prædictorum, jurium, libertatum, Prærogativarum,

privilegiorum et consuetudinum sui incliti Regni, quovis modo cedere poterit; sed omne id quod jam scio, vel imposterum cognoscam inhonorabile, damnosum aut præjudiciale, suæ Serenitati, aut Regno suo, seu contrarium honori aut Serenitati suæ Majestatis, aut hæredum suorum prædictorum, non solum impediam ad extremum potentiæ meæ, sed etiam cum omni possibili diligentia id ostendam et significabo, ostendive aut significari faciam eidem serenissimo Regi, omni favore, metu, promisso aut Jurejurando cuicunq; personæ aut quibuscunq: personis cujuscunq; status, gradus, ordinis, præeminentiæ, conditionisve extiterunt, quod antehac per me factum aut interpositum seu imposterum fiendum aut interponendum, penitus sublato et non obstantibus. Honorem insuper suæ Majestati ad extremum potentiæ meæ servabo, Parliamentis quoq; et aliis Consiliis suæ Celsitudinis cum in ejus Regno fuero diligenter attendam; Consilium quod sua Serenitas per se ceu literas aut nuncium suum mihi manifestabit, nemini pandam, nisi iis quibus ipse jusserit: et si consilium meum super aliquo facto Majestas sua postulaverit, fideliter sibi consulam, et quod magis suæ Serenitati videbitur expedire, et conducere juxta opinionem et scire meum, dicam et aperiam, atque id si sua Serenitas mandaverit pro posse meo diligenter faciam. Causas insuper et negotia omnia suæ Serenitatis mihi commissa, seu imposterum committenda, in Curia Romana prosequenda, pertractanda et solicitanda, fideliter, accurate et diligenter, cum omnimoda dexteritate prosequar, pertractabo et solicitabo: Bullasq; et alias Literas Apostolicas validas et efficaces, in debita Juris forma, super eisdem causis et negotiis impetrare et obtinere absq; fraude, dolo aut sinistra quavis machinatione quantum in me erit, cum omni effectu enitar, operam dabo et conabor: ac easdem taliter expeditas, cum ea quam res expostulat diligentia, suæ Serenitati, transmittam aut per alios transmitti, tradi et liberari curabo, et faciam. Servitia quoq; et homagia pro temporalibus dicti Episcopatus, quæ recognosco tenere a sua Celsitudine tanquam a Domino meo supremo, fideliter faciam et implebo. Ita me Deus adjuvet et hæc Sancta Dei Evangelia. In cujus, &c. T. R. apud Westm. 13 die Octob.

Per ipsum Regem.

II.

Pope Julius's Letter to Archbishop Warham, for giving King Henry VIII. the Golden Rose.

Julius Secundus Papa venerabili Fratri Guilielmo Archiepiscop. Cantuarien.

VENERABILIS Frater, salutem et Apostolicam Benedictionem. Charissimum in Christo Filium nostrum Henricum Angliæ Regem Illustrissimum, quem peculiari charitate complectimur, aliquo insigni Apostolico munere in hoc Regni sui primordio, decorandum putantes, mittimus nunc ad eum Rosam Auream, Sancto Chrismate delibutam, et odorifero Musco aspersam, nostrisq; manibus de more Romanorum Pontificum benedictam, quam ei a tua Fraternitate inter Missarum solemnia per te celebranda, cum cæremoniis in notula alligata contentis, dari volumus nostra et Apostolica benedictione. Datum Romæ apud Sanctum Petrum sub Annulo Piscatoris, 5 April. 1510. Pontificatus nostri Anno septimo.

Registrum Warhami Fol. 26.

Sigismundus.

The Note of the Ceremonies of delivering the Rose, referred to in the Letter, was not thought worthy to be put in the Register.

III.

A Writ for Summoning Convocations.

REX, &c. Reverendissimo in Christo Patri Cantuarien. Archiepis. totius Angliæ Primati et Apostolicæ sedis Legato, salutem. Quibusdam arduis et urgentibus negotiis, Nos, defensionem et securitatem Ecclesiæ Anglicanæ, ac pacem, tranquillitatem, et bonum publicum, et defensionem Regni nostri et subditorum nostrorum ejusdem concernentibus, vobis in fide et dilectione quibus nobis tenemini rogando mandamus, quatenus præmissis debito intuitu attentis et ponderatis, universos et singulos Episcopos vestræ

Tonst. Regist. Fol. 33.

Provinciæ, ac Decanos et Priores Ecclesiarum Cathedralium, Abbates, Priores et alios Electivos, exemptos et non
exemptos, necnon Archidiaconos, Conventus, Capitula, et
Collegia, totumq; Clerum, cujuslibet Dioceseos ejusdem
Provinciæ, ad conveniendum coram vobis in Ecclesia Sancti
Pauli London. vel alibi prout melius expedire videritis,
cum omni celeritate accommoda, modo debito convocari
faciatis ad tractandum, consentiendum, et concludendum
super præmissis, et aliis quæ sibi clarius proponentur, tunc
et ibidem ex parte nostra. Et hoc, sicut Nos et statum
Regni nostri, et honorem et utilitatem Ecclesiæ prædictæ
diligitis, nullatenus omittatis. Teste meipso, &c. apud
Westminst. 6 Feb. Anno Regni 14.

*Warham in his Writ of executing this Summons, prefixes the
20th of April for the day of their meeting.*

IV.

*A Writ for a Convocation summoned by Warham on an
Ecclesiastical Account.*

WILLIELMUS permissione divina Cantuar. Archiepiscopus, totius Angliæ Primas et Apostolicæ sedis Legatus,
venerabili confratri nostro Domino Ricardo Dei Gratia
London. Episcopo, salutem et fraternam in Domino cari-
tatem. Cum nuper Ecclesia Anglicana, quæ majorum nostrorum temporibus, multis ac magnis libertatibus et immu-
nitatibus gaudere solebat, quorundam iniquorum hominum
malitiis, et nequitiis fortiter fuerit inquietata et perturbata,
qui omnia quæ a majoribus nostris sancte et pie, ob tranquillitatem dictæ Ecclesiæ, fuerunt ordinata ac sancita, vel
prava et sinistra interpretatione prope subvertentes, vel
personas Ecclesiasticas male tractantes, ac eas contemptui
habentes, dictam Ecclesiam pene prostraverunt ac pedibus
conculcarunt: Ne igitur dicta Ecclesia Anglicana ad cala-
mitatem insignem seu ruinam ac jacturam, et quod absit,
desolationem perveniat, quas diu eadem Ecclesia Anglica-

na per diversas personas, ut præfertur præ oculis suis Deum non habentes, nec censuras Sanctæ Matris Ecclesiæ timentes, sustinuit et sustinebat, prout de verisimili Reformatione non habita in futurum sustinere debeat; Nos prout tenemur, congruum remedium in hac parte providere cupientes, et ob id ipsum Prælatos et Clerum nostræ Cantuar. Provinciæ convocare volentes; Fraternitati vestræ igitur committimus et mandamus, quatenus omnes et singulos dictæ nostræ Cant. Ecclesiæ Suffraganeos infra nostram Provinciam constitutos, et absentium Episcoporum si qui fuerunt Vicarios in Spiritualibus generales, ac Diocesium vacantium Custodes Spiritualitatis, et Officiales citetis seu citari faciatis, peremptorie, et per eos Decanos et Priores Ecclesiarum Cath. ac singula Capitula eorundum, Archidiaconos, Abbates et Priores, Conventus sub se habentes, et alios Ecclesiarum Prælatos exemptos, et non exemptos, Clerumq; cujuslibet Dioceseos Provinciæ nostræ antedictæ, citari peremptorie et præmoneri volumus et mandamus, Quod iidem Episcopi Suffraganei, nostri Vicarii Generales, Decani et Custodes sive Officiales, Abbates, Priores, Archidiaconi ac cæteri Ecclesiarum Prælati, exempti et non exempti, personaliter, et quodlibet Capitulum Ecclesiarum Cath. per unum de Capitulo graduatum, vel magis idoneum, dictiq; singuli Abbates, sive Priores, Conventus sub se habentes, nullo obstante impedimento legittimo, per unam Religiosam personam de Conventu graduatam si quæ sit, ceu alias per unam magis idoneam de eodem Conventu, Clerusq; cujuslibet Dioc. Provinciæ antedictæ per duos procuratores graduato ejusdem Dioc. seu alias si non fuerunt, per duos sufficientiores et habiliores Dioc. in eorum Beneficiis realiter residentes, compareant coram nobis aut nostris in hac parte locumtenentibus, vel Commissariis si nos tunc (quod absit) impediri contigerit in Ecclesia Cathed. Sancti Pauli London. die Sabbat. viz. 26. mensis Januarii &c. Dat. in Manerio nostro de Lambeth. primo die mensis Novembris Anno Domini millesimo quingentesimo nono, et nostræ Translat. Anno sexto.

V.

The Preamble of the Act of Subsidy granted by the Clergy.

Anno
Dom.
1523.
Regist.
Cuth-
berti
Tou-
stall.
Folio
40.

Quum Illustrissimus et Potentissimus Dominus noster Rex Angliæ et Franciæ, Defensor Fidei et Dominus Hibern. semper extitit constantissimus Ecclesiæ Protector et Patronus optime meritus, atq; superioribus annis, in diebus fœlicis recordationis Julii ejus nominis Papæ secundi, grave Schisma in Ecclesia Romana exortum pacavit et extinxit; et postea ipsam Ecclesiam Romanam contra vim et potentiam Gallorum, qui tunc Italiam et Urbem Romanam in servitutem redigere moliebantur, validissimo excercitu et bello longe omnium sumptuosissimo fœliciter defendit, et securam reddidit: Ac præterea postremis his diebus Lutheranas Hæreses, in Ecclesiæ Sacramenta Ecclesiæq; statum furiose debaccantes doctissimo et nunquam satis laudato libello contudit et superavit; vicissim tam gladio quam calamo hostes Ecclesiæ strenuissime profligans, quibus meritis suam clarissimam famam immortali gloriæ pariter consecravit, tales laudes et gratias sua incomparabili bonitate ab Ecclesia promeruit, quales nunquam satis dignas quisquam mortalium referre poterit, sed Deus affatim persolvet præmia digna. Quumq; idem Rex noster et Protector illustrissimus a Rege Gallorum per Mare et per Terras, incolas hujus Regni contra percussum fœdus, promissam fidem, et suum ipsius salvum conductum assidue infestante, et Scotos contra Regnum hoc instigante ac suis stipendiis conducente, atq; ducem Albaniæ in perniciem principis Scotorum nostri Regis ex sorore Nepotis impellente, aliasq; injurias multas et graves contra Regiam Majestatem suosq; amicos et subditos quotidie multiplicante, provocatur, irritatur atq; urgetur ut bellum suscipiat, suumq; Regnum tam contra Gallos quam contra Scotos ut decet imvictissimum Principem potenter defendat; non enim ultra pacem colere vel pacem longius expectare convenit postquam Rex Gallorum summum Pontificem bene moventem, et quæ pacis sunt suadentem, audire recusat, exercitum instruens et bellum apparans, fortassis in multos annos duraturum: dignissimum est ob præfata tam præclara facinora, ut sicut

Rex noster illustrissimus plus cæteris Regibus antecessoribus suis pro Ecclesiæ defensione, utilitate et honore insudavit, et plus expensarum sustinuit ; ita ad sustinenda bellorum onera imminentia, pro Ecclesiæ et totius Regni hujus defensione, per Ecclesiam tali subsidio adjuvetur quale anterioribus Regibus nunquam antehac concessum est, nec fortassis posterioribus Regibus unquam simile, nisi ob talia benefacta vel extremam bellorum necessitatem postea concedetur. Quocirca ut Regia Majestas ad fovendam et protegendam Ecclesiam, et Clerum Angliæ, magis indies animetur, et ut jura, libertates et privilegia Ecclesiæ concessa benigne Ecclesiæ servet, et ab aliis servari faciat, et ne præfata benefacta in ingratos contulisse videatur.

Nos Prælati et Clerus Cant. Provinciæ in hac Sacra Synodo Provinciali sive Prælatorum et Cleri ejusdem Convocatione, in Ecclesia Cathed. Divi Pauli London. vicesimo die mensis Aprilis Anno Dom. millesimo quingentesimo vicesimo tertio inchoata, ac usq; ad et in decimum quartum diem mensis Augusti proxime ex tunc sequentis de diebus in dies continuata, congregati, Illustrissimo Domino Regi perpetuo et potentissimo Fidei et Ecclesiæ defensori, subsidium dare et concedere Decrevimus, quam nostram Benevolentiam ut gratam et acceptam habeat humillime deprecamur, protestantes expresse, quod per præsentem concessionem, quam tanquam novam et ante insolitam pro nostra singulari et personali in Regiam Majestatem observantia sine exemplo donamus, omnino nolumus Ecclesiæ Anglicanæ aut successoribus nostris in aliquo præjudicium generari, nec casum hunc singularem ad sequen. trahi : Quod si præsentem Concessionem pro exemplo et (ut vocant) pro Præsidente ad similes unquam Concessiones exigendas accipiendam fore præsentiremus, certe in eam omnino consentire recusassemus ; quandoquidem subsidium sub modis, formis, conditionibus, exceptionibus ac provisionibus, et protestatione super et infrascriptis, et non aliter, neq ; alio modo, Damus et Concedimus, viz. Subsidium se extendens ad Medietatem sive mediam partem valoris omnium fructuum reddituum, et proventuum, possessionum, unius anni, omnium et singulorum Episcopatuum, Ecclesiarum Cathed. et Collegiatarum, Dignitatum, Hospita-

lium, Monast. Abbaciarum, Prioratuum aliarumq; domorum Religiosarum, necnon quorumcunq; beneficiorum et
Possessionum Ecclesiasticarum, &c.

VI.

*Bishop Tonstal's Licence to Sir Thomas More for reading
Heretical Books.*

Regist.
Tonst.
Fol.
138.
CUTHBERTUS permissione Divina London. Episcopus
Clarissimo et Egregio viro Domino Thomæ More fratri et
amico Charissimo Salutem in Domino et Benedict. Quia
nuper, postquam Ecclesia Dei per Germaniam ab hæreticis
infestata est, juncti sunt nonnulli iniquitatis Filii, qui veterem et damnatam hæresim Wycliffianam et Lutherianam,
etiam hæresis Wycliffianæ alumni transferendis in nostra-
tem vernaculam linguam corruptissimis quibuscunq; eorum opusculis, atque illis ipsis magna copia impressis, in
hanc nostram Regionem inducere conantur; quam sane
pestilentissimis dogmatibus Catholicæ fidei veritati repug-
nantibus maculare atq; inficere magnis conatibus moliun-
tur. Magnopere igitur verendum est ne Catholica veritas
in totum periclitetur nisi boni et eruditi viri malignitati
tam prædictorum hominum strenue occurrant, idquod nulla
ratione melius et aptius fieri poterit, quam si in lingua Catholica veritas in totum expugnans hæc insana dogmata
simul etiam ipsissima prodeat in lucem. Quo fiet ut Sacrarum Literarum imperiti homines in manus sumentes novos
istos Hæreticos Libros, atq; una etiam Catholicos ipsos re-
fellentes, vel ipsi per se verum discernere, vel ab aliis quorum perspicacius est judicium recte admoneri et doceri possint. Et quia tu, Frater Clarissime, in lingua nostra vernacula, sicut etiam in Latina, Demosthenem quendam
præstare potes, et Catholicæ veritatis assertor acerrimus in
omni congressu esse soles, melius subcisivas horas, si quas
tuis occupationibus suffurari potes, collocare nunquam poteris, quam in nostrate lingua aliqua edas quæ simplicibus
et ideotis hominibus subdolam hæreticorum malignitatem

aperiant, ac contra tam impios Ecclesiæ supplantatores red-
dant eos instructiores: habes ad id exemplum quod imi-
teris præclarissimum, illustrissimi Domini nostri Regis
Henrici octavi, qui Sacramenta Ecclesiæ contra Lutherum
totis viribus ea subvertentem asserere aggressus, immortale
nomen Defensoris Ecclesiæ in omne ævum promeruit. Et
ne Andabatarum more cum ejusmodi larvis lucteris, igno-
rans ipse quod oppugnes, mitto ad te insanas in nostrate
lingua istorum nænias, atque una etiam nonnullos Lutheri
Libros ex quibus hæc opinionum monstra prodierunt. Quibus abs te diligenter perlectis, facilius intelligas quibus lati-
bulis tortuosi serpentes sese condant, quibusq; anfractibus
elabi deprehensi studeant. Magni enim ad victoriam momenti est hostium Consilia explorata habere, et quid sentiant quove tendant penitus nosse: nam si convellere pares
quæ isti se non sensisse dicent, in totum perdas operam.
Macte igitur virtute, tam sanctum opus aggredere, quo et
Dei Ecclesiæ præsis, et tibi immortale nomen atq; æternam
in Cœlis gloriam pares: quod ut facias atque Dei Ecclesiam tuo patrocinio munias, magnopere in Domino obse-
cramus, atq; ad illum finem ejusmodi libros et retinendi et
legendi facultatem atq; licentiam impertimur et concedimus. Dat. 7 die Martii, Anno 1527 et nostræ Cons. sexto.

AD LIBRUM SECUNDUM.

———

I.

The Bull for the King's Marriage with Queen Katherine.

BOOK
II.

Cott.
libr.
Vitel.
B. 12.

JULIUS Episcopus servus servorum Dei, dilecto Filio Henrico Carissimi in Christo Filii Henrici Angliæ Regis illustriss. Nato, et dilectæ in Christo Filiæ Catharinæ, Carissimi in Christo Filii nostri Ferdinandi Regis, ac Carissimæ in Christo Filiæ nostræ Elizabeth. Reginæ Hispaniarum et Siciliæ Catholicorum natæ, illustribus, salutem et Apostolicam Benedictionem. Romani Pontificis præcellens Autoritas concessa sibi desuper utitur potestate, prout personarum, negotiorum et temporum qualitate pensata, id in Domino conspicit salubriter expedire. Oblatæ nobis nuper pro parte vestra petitionis series continebat, Quod cum alias tu Filia Catharina, et tunc in humanis agens quondam Arthurus, Carissimi in Christo Filii nostri Henrici Angliæ Regis illustrissimi primogenitus, pro conservandis pacis et amicitiæ nexibus et fæderibus inter Carissimum in Christo Filium nostrum Ferdinandum, et Carissimam in Christo Filiam nostram Elizabeth. Hispaniarum et Siciliæ Catholicos, ac præfatum Angliæ Reges et Reginam, matrimonium per verba legi time de præsenti contraxissetis, illudq; carnali Copula forsan consummavissetis, Dominus Arthurus prole ex hujusmodi Matrimonio non suscepta decessit ; Cum autem, sicut eadem petitio subjungebat, ad hoc ut hujusmodi vinclum Pacis et Amicitiæ inter præfatos Reges et Reginam diutius permaneat, cupiatis Matrimonium inter vos per verba legitime de præsenti contrahere, supplicari nobis fecistis, ut vobis in præmissis de opportunæ Dispensationis gratia providere de benignitate Apostolica dignaremur: Nos igitur, qui inter singulos Christi fideles, præsertim Catholicos Reges et Principes, Pacis et Concordiæ amænitatem vigere intensis

desideriis affectamus, vosque et quemlibet vestrum a quibuscunque Excommunicationis, Suspensionis et Interdict.
aliisque Ecclesiasticis Sententiis, Censuris, Pænis, a jure
vel ab homine, quavis occasione vel causa latis, si quibus
quomodolibet innodati existitis, ad effectum præsentium
duntaxat consequendum, harum serie absolventes, et abso-
lutos fore censentes hujusmodi supplicationibus inclinati,
vobiscum, ut impedimento affinitatis hujusmodi ex præmissis proveniente, ac Constitutionibus et Ordinationibus
Apostolicis cæterisq; contrariis nequaquam obstantibus,
Matrimonium per verba legitime de præsenti inter vos contrahere, et in eo, postquam contractum fuerit, etiamsi jam
forsan hactenus de facto publice vel clandestine contraxeritis, ac illud Carnali Copula consummaveritis, licite
remanere valeatis, Auctoritate Apostolica tenore præsentium de specialis dono Gratiæ Dispensamus; ac vos et
quemlibet vestrorum si contraxeritis (ut præfertur) ab excessu hujusmodi, ac Excommunicationis Sententia quam
propterea incurristis, eadem Auctoritate Absolvimus, Prolem ex hujusmodi Matrimonio, sive contracto, sive contrahendo, susceptam forsan vel suscipiendam legitimam
decernendo. Proviso quod tu (Filia Catharina) propter
hoc rapta non fueris; volumus autem quod si hujusmodi
Matrimonium de facto contraxistis, Confessor, per vos
et quemlibet vestrum eligendus, pænitentiam salutarem
propterea vobis injungat, quam adimplere teneamini. Nulli
ergo omnino hominum liceat hanc paginam nostræ Absolutionis, Dispensationis et voluntatis infringere, vel ei ausu
temerario contraire; si quis autem hoc attemptare præsumpserit, indignationem Omnipotentis Dei ac Beatorum
Petri et Pauli Apostolorum ejus se noverit incursurum.
Dat. Romæ apud Sanctum Petrum, Anno Incarnationis
Dominicæ millesimo quingentesimo tertio, septimo Cal.
Januarii, Pontificatus nostri Anno primo.

II.

The King's Protestation against the Marriage.

Cotton
Libr.
Vitell.
B. 12.

In Dei Nomine, Amen. Coram vobis Reverendo in Christo
Patre et Domino, Domino Richardo Dei et Apostolicæ sedis
gratia Episcopo Wintoniensi, Ego Henricus Walliæ Princeps, Dux Cornubiæ et Comes Cestriæ, dico, allego et in
his Scriptis propono, Quod licet ego minorem ætatem agens,
et intra annos pubertatis notorie existens, cum Serenissima
Domina Katharina Hispaniarum Regis Filia, Matrimonium de facto contraxerim, qui quidem Contractus, quamvis obstante ipsa minore ætate mea de se jam invalidus, im-
perfectus, nullius efficaciæ aut vigoris extiterit; quia tamen
annis pubertatis et matura ætate jam superveniente, Contractus ipse per tacitum Consensum, mutuam cohabitationem, munerum aut intersignium dationem seu receptionem,
vel alium quemcunq; modum jure declaratum, forsan exist-
imari seu videri poterit apparenter validatus aut con-
firmatus; Ea-propter, Ego Henricus Walliæ Princeps
prædictus, jam proximus pubertati existens, et annos pubertatis attingens, Protestor, quod non intendo eundem
prætensum contractum per quæcunq; per me dicta seu di-
cenda, facta aut facienda, in aliquo approbare, validare,
seu ratum habere, sed nunc in præsenti, non vi, dolo, nec
prece inductus, sed sponte et libere, nullo modo coactus,
contra hujusmodi Contractum reclamo, et eidem dissentio,
voloq; et omnino intendo ab eodem contractu Matrimoniali prætenso, melioribus modo et forma, quibus de jure
melius, validius, aut efficacius potero vel possim, penitus
resilire, et eidem expresse dissentire, prout in præsenti
contra eundem reclamo, et eidem dissentio. Protestorq;
quod per nullum dictum, factum, actum, aut gestum per
me, aut nomine meo per alium quemcunque, quandocunq;
aut qualemcunque, imposterum faciendum, agendum, ge-
rendum, aut explicandum, volo aut intendo in præfatum
contractum Matrimonialem, aut in dictam Dominam Catharinam tanquam Sponsam aut Uxorem meam consentire.
Super quibus vos omnes testimonium perhibere volo, re-
quiro, rogo, atque obtestor.

Per me Henricum Walliæ Principem.

LECTA fuit et facta suprascripta Protestatio, per præfatum Serenissimum Principem Dominum Henricum, coram Reverendo in Christo Patre et Domino, Domino Richardo, permissione Divina Winton. Episcopo, Judicialiter pro tribunali sedent. Et me Notarium infra scriptum ad tunc præsentem in ejus Actorum Scribam in hac parte assumente, et Testium infrascriptorum præsentiis. Anno Dom. 1505. Indictione octava, Pontificatus Sanctissimi in Christo Patris et Domini nostri Julii, Divina Providentia eo nomine Papæ secundi Anno secundo, Mensis vero Junii die 27; quo die Dominus Serenissimus Princeps proximus pubertati, et annos pubertatis attingens erat, ut tunc ibidem asserebat, in quadam bassa Camera infra Palatium Regium Richemondiæ, in parte occidentali ejusdem Palatii situat. Super quibus omnibus et singulis, præfatus Serenissimus Princeps me Notarium præmemoratum Instrumentum conficere, et testes infra nominatos testimonium perhibere requisivit instanter, et rogavit. In quorum omnium et singulorum fidem et testimonium, præfatus Serenissimus Princeps supra, et testes, ut præmittitur, rogati et requisiti, sua nomina propriis manibus infra scripserunt. Ita est ut supra, quod ego Joannes Raed. manu et signo meo manuali Attestor.

BOOK II.

> Giles Daubney, C. Somerset.
> Thomas Rowthale.
> Nicholas West.
> Henry Marny.

III.

Cardinal Wolsey's first Letter to Sir Gregory Cassali, about the Divorce. Taken from the Original.

DOMINE GREGORI, Post meam cordatissimam Commendationem, post ultimum vestrum a me discessum ex Compendio ad vos scripsi, ut ob nonnullas maximi momenti causas procurare differetis quod de Regiæ Majestatis negotio in quibusdam nobis traditis Commissionibus con-

Cotton Libr. Vitellius B. 9.

tinebatur, quòad rursus vobis significarem quid ea in`re
fieri vellemus. Ubi verò ad Regiam Majestatem rediissem;
variis crebrisq; cum ea habitis sermonibus, adeo abunde ac
distincte illi aperui quam ex animo ac diligenter, et quam
sincere et ex fide, diu noctuque exoptetis eidem Regiæ
Majestati inservire; neque ullum unquam laborem, periculum aut molestiam vos velle recusare, ut omni studio ac
viribus id fideliter præstare possitis quod illi gratum aut
acceptum quoquo modo esse posse cognoveritis, omnemq;
industriam vos esse adhibituros quo vestræ fidei curæque
commissa optatum finem consequantur; quem vestrum
animum propensissima voluntate sic sub mea fide Regiæ
Majestati insinuavi, ut meam hanc relationem atque spon-
sionem pectori suo constantissime adfixerit, certissimaque
fiducia concepit, omnino futurum ut nostræ tunc expectationi quacunque in re et occasione respondeatis: Ex quo
fit ut vestræ operæ, curæ atque prudentiæ ea nunc tractanda et procuranda committat, quibus nihil magis cordi
habeat, nihil ardentius exoptet, aut majoris sit momenti
vel gravioris successus, nec ullum habet Consiliarium, ut-
cunque intimum, cui graviora possit committere. Quum
itaque, me intercedente et procurante, nunc vos Regia
Majestas præ cæteris ad hoc fidei adsciverit et elegerit, ut
in re tam gravi fidelissima vestra opera ac ministerio
utatur, fidemque illi meam de vobis jam ei adstrinxerim,
nihil ambigens quin postquam ejus animum ac voluntatem
cognoveritis, fueritisque abunde instructi quam maximi
hæc quæ nunc expono sunt momenti, utpote quæ potissimum concernunt Regiæ conscientiæ exonerationem ani-
mæque suæ salutem, vitæ conservationem et incolumitatem,
Regii Stemmatis continuationem, publicumque commodum
et quietem subditorum omnium, eorum pariter qui sub ejus
imperio nunc vivunt vel qui postea unquam in hoc suo
Regno vivent; quumque perspiciam sedulum vestrum Ministerium hoc in negotio impendendum omnino redunda-
turum esse in præcipuam vestram exaltationem et utilitatem, postquam infelices istos jam passos successus occasionem se obtulisse videtis, qua vestra familia hujusmodi
operam huic Serenissimo Principi navare possit, quod
statum omnem vestrum in longe meliorem quam antea sit
haud dubie restituturus et adaucturus, certissimum com-

pertissimumque habeo, quod ob has tam urgentes causas et
tam graves successuros effectus, adeo toto pectore vires
omnes vestras industria ac studio tantæ conficiendæ rei
addicetis, ut omnia queatis ad optatum exitum perducere;
atque ita promissum fidemque meam præstabitis, tam optimum Regiæ Majestatis institutum juvabitis, ejus desiderio
et expectationi omni ex parte satisfacietis, et præter bene
peractæ rei honorem et laudem comparandam, mercedem
quoque reportabitis tanti Principis liberalitate dignam,
quæ certissime cedet in perpetuum vestrum totiusque vestræ
familiæ commodum et incrementum: Et quum jam mihi
persuadeam futurum omnino ut officiis actionibusque
vestris sitis promissis sponsionibusque meis omnino satis-
facturi, ad id pluribus verbis neutiquam adhortabor, proinde
ad rem nunc ipsam venio.   Ante hoc tempus vobis aperui,
quemadmodum Regia Majestas, partim assiduo suo studio
et eruditione, partim relatu ac judicio multorum Theologorum, et in omni Doctrinæ genere doctorum virorum
asseveratione, existimans conscientiam suam non esse sufficienter exoneratam, quod in conjugio existeret cum Regina, Deumque primo et ante omnia ac animæ suæ quietem
et salutem respiciens, mox vero suæ Successionis securitatem, perpendensque accurate quam gravia hinc mala
provenirent, aperte sentit quam maxime futurum sit Deo
molestum, inhonorificum sibi, et ingratum apud homines,
suisque subditis periculosum, ex hoc non sufficienti conjugio, si deprehendatur dicta Majestas sciens ac volens in
eo perstare, et vivere præter modum debitum, juxtaque
ritum et legitima Ecclesiæ Statuta: quibus igitur ex causis
longo jam tempore, intimo suæ conscientiæ remorsu, sum-
mique Dei rationem habens, existimat animam suam læsam
et offensam, adeo quod, quum in suis conatibus actionibusque quibuscunque Deum potissimum sibi semper proponat,
ingenti cum molestia cordisque perturbatione in hoc Matrimonio degit; super qua re maturum sanumque judicium
consuluit clarissimorum celeberrimorumque; Doctorum
aliorumq; complurium in omni eruditionis genere excel-
lentiorum virorum ac Prælatorum, partim Theologorum,
partim Jurisperitorum, tum in suo Regno, tum alibi ex-
istentium, ut aperte vereq; cognosceret, an Dispensatio
antea concessa pro se et Regina, ex eo quod Regina Fratris

sui uterini Uxor antea extiterit, valida et sufficiens foret,
necne; demumq; a variis multisq; ex his Doctoribus
asseritur, quod Papa non potest dispensare in primo gradu
affinitatis, tanquam ex jure Divino, moraliter, naturali-
terq; prohibito, ac si potest, omnes affirmant et consen-
tiunt quod hoc non potest, nisi ex urgentissimis et arduis
causis, quales non subfuerunt, Bulla præterea Dispensationis fundatur et concessa est sub quibusdam rationibus
falso suggestis et enarratis, in ea namq; asseritur, quod,
hæc Regia Majestas Matrimonium hoc cum Regina percu-
piebat, pro bono pacis inter Henricum septimum Ferdinandum et Elizabetham, quum revera nulla tunc dissensio
aut belli suspicio esset inter dictos Principes, vel Regiam
Majestatem prædictam, quæ in teneris adhuc annis, nec in
discretione aut judicio constitutis agebat; nunquam deinde
assensit, aut quicquam cognovit de hujusmodi bullæ Impe-
tratione, nec unquam hoc Matrimonium optavit, aut aliquid
de eo accepit ante bullæ Impetrationem. Quocirca ab his
omnibus Doctoribus atq; Prælatis judicatur hujusmodi
Dispensationem non adeo validam et idoneam esse ac effi-
cacem, ut prædictum Matrimonium manifeste justum legi-
timumq; sit; sed potius quod multa possunt objici, magnis probabilibusq; fundata et corroborata rationibus, in non
leve periculum Regiæ prolis, totiusq; Regni ac subditorum gravem perturbationem. Adhæc, postquam Regia Majestas, qui Walliæ Princeps tunc erat, decimum quartum
annum attigisset, contractus Revocatio subsequuta est, Rege
Patre expresse nolente quod hujusmodi Matrimonium ullo
pacto sortiretur effectum. His causis Rex hic Serenissimus, tanquam bonus et Catholicus Princeps, timens ne ob
tam diuturnam cum Regina continuationem, indignatus et
iratus Deus citius ex humanis evocaverit Masculam e Regina susceptam prolem, graviusq; a Deo supplicium expa-
vescit si in Matrimonio hoc non-legitimo perseveraverit;
ex hac ideo occasione, intimis præcordiis hunc Conscientiæ
scrupulum concepit, in animo nihilominus habens, pro
animi conscientiæq; suæ quiete et salute, prolisq; securitate, ad Sanctam Domini nostri sedemq; Apostolicam confugere, tantæ rei remedium impetraturus confidens, quod
ob complura sua erga eam merita et officia tum calamo
ingeniiq; viribus, tum armis præstita, subsidia in Ecclesiæ

calamitatibus prompte subministrata, Sanctissimus Dominus
noster non gravabitur sua benignitate, Authoritate ac
facultate, intimum hunc Regiæ Majestatis cordi inhærentem
dolorem amovere, eumq; modum ac rationem inire qua
Regia Majestas prædicta Uxorem aliam ducere, et, Deo
volente, masculam prolem in suæ successionis securitatem
queat ex ea suscipere, et tam certam quietem in suo Regno
constituere: Quumq; ejus Sanctitas ab his nunc captiva
detineatur, qui pro virili sua forsan conabuntur impedire,
turbareq; hoc Regiæ Majestatis desiderium et Statutum,
ipsa præterea cogitur vias omnes excogitare, quibus dicta
Sanctitas de hac re dexterius et commodius instrui, et facilius adduci queat ad ea concedenda, quorum medio et vigore
Regiæ Majestatis animus et desiderium queat optatum sortiri
effectum: Proinde ipsa Regia Majestas de fide, industria,
dexteritate prudentiaq; vestra plenissime confidens, vult ut
statim bis literis acceptis, rebus aliis omnibus quibuscunq;
ab eo vel a quovis alio vobis commissis omnino posthabitis,
vias modosq; omnes possibiles excogitetis quibus potestis
secretissime, mutato habitu et tanquam alicujus Minister,
vel tanquam Commissionem habens a Duce Ferrariæ pro
nonnullis inter Pontificem et eum componendis controversiis, vel alia qua licuerit securiori via, ad Pontificis præsentiam et colloquium accedendi, omnibus arbitris semotis,
si fieri possit, pro vestris obeundis mandatis; quorum ob-
tinendorum gratia, si ita expedire judicaveritis, eam mercedem ac pecuniarum summam promittetis ac tradetis, his
qui revera volent atq; poterunt hoc negotium ad effectum
pertrahere, quam summam, et ejus limitationem, judicio,
prudentiæque vestræ integram Regia Majestas remittit;
etiam si his danda foret qui Pontificem asservant, vel cuicunq; alio qui vos tuto ad secretum cum sua Sanctitate
Sermonem adducere, in locumq; tutum reducere posset:
Cujus rei gratia, aliisq; ad hunc finem consequendum sus-
tinendis oneribus necessariis, pecuniæ ad summam decem
mille ducatorum, per Mensarios Venetias transmittentur,
qui illic in promptu aderunt, persolvendæ et consignandæ
Prothonotario Fratri vestro, Regio illic existenti Oratori;
per eumq; de tempore in tempus ad vos transmitti ea summa poterit quam huic obtinendo negotio conducere posse
existimaveritis, nihilq; ambigo quin dictam pecuniam fide-

liter collocetis, ex Regiæ Majestatis utilitate, expectatione,
atq; sententia. Atq; ubi ad Sanctum Dominum nostrum,
accesseritis, post filiales et cordatissimas Regiæ Majestatis.
measq; devotas et humillimas commendationes, et post.
exhibitas a Rege Credentiæ literas, in quibus in negotii
adjumentum clausula vehemens est propria ejus manu con-
scripta, ut ex earum exemplo cognoscetis, ejus Sanctitati.
exponetis quam grave, molestumq; Regiæ Majestati et,
mihi sit, audire infælicissimos eventus, calamitatemq;
miserandam, in qua nunc ejus Sanctitas cum Reverendiss.
Cardinalib. versatur, cum gravissimo detrimento irrepara-
biliq; sedis Apostolicæ illiusq; Patrimonii jactura, ad quæ
mala sublevanda et corrigenda nullum in Regia Majestate
officium desiderabitur, quod ab ullo erga Sanctam Domini nostri vel sedem Apostolicam observantissimo Principe queat excogitari; in eoq; omne meum ministerium ac.
studium non minus promptum aderit, quam si ex ea re solum
possem mihi cœlum comparare: quemadmodum experientia, aliqua in parte, jam docuit, et Deo duce posthac uberius
comprobabit: quam rem copiosius optimisq; verbis agetis,
præsertim, quum sciatis quanto et quam sincero affectu
Regia Majestas ejus Sanctitatem prosequatur, et quanta
mea sit in ipsam devotio, in hisque sermonibus insistetis
prout loci, temporis, negociique ratio videbitur judicio
vestro postulare.

    Secundo, Sanctissimo Domino nostro solita vestra dex-
teritate aperietis id quod in his ipsis literis ad vos scripsi
concernens hujus Matrimonii insufficientiam, ab hisq; rationibus et causis fundamentum capietis, quæ superius
enarrantur integrumq; discursum ejus Sanctitati declarabitis, non omittentes intrinsecum dolorem, conscientiæ
scrupulum, Dei rationem, Masculæ prolis respectum, hujus
Regni bonum, et alia omnia ut superius scripta sunt: addentes insuper, nihil vehementius optari a tota Regni
Nobilitate, subditisq; omnibus nullo discrimine, quam è
Regiæ Majestatis corpore Masculum hæredem a Deo sibi
dari, in perpetuam consolationem, gaudium, quietem, ac
totius Regni securitatem, posteritatisq; firmissimum colu-
men; prudentiorumq; opinionem esse, quod Deus omni-
potens a tanto bono concedendo divinam suam manum
substrahit, ob errorem, culpamq; in dicto Matrimonio

hactenus admissam, quæ nisi mature corrigatur, graviora
ex hac occasione in hoc Regno mala succedent, quam
antea unquam fuerunt audita; etenim si hoc negotium in
suspenso et indiscussum relinqueretur, hujusmodi possent
quæstiones, controversiæ et contentiones ac factiones post
defunctum Regem exoriri, ob Regni hæreditatem, quæ non
possent in multorum ævo restingui, ut antea olim ex causa
longe leviori accidit, neq; ex re tam ambigua, tam sævæ
olim depopulationes, bella, intestinæq; controversiæ exor-
tæ, et ad multum tempus continuatæ sunt, in extremum et
ferme ultimum Regni excidium; quæ quum tam gravia
sunt, Sanctissimus Dominus noster veluti pater et guberna-
tor Christianitatis prospicere ex officio debet, et quibuscunq; modis potest, pro viribus adniti et conari, ut hæc
Regna ac dominia quæ nunc super-sunt in fide et obedientia Ecclesiæ assidue contineat, inter quæ, Deo sit laus, hoc
Regnum haud recensendum est inter minima sed tanquam
illud quod hactenus juvavit, et posthac pro tuto præsidio
semper haberi poterit, adversus ea quæ cedere possent in
Ecclesiæ Catholicæ vel sanctæ fidei detrimentum.

Tertio, Sanctissimo Domino nostro proponetis præsentem
Ecclesiæ statum, rogabitisq; ut in mentem velit redigere,
quo nunc in statu suæ Sanctitatis res cum Christianis Principibus versentur, cumq; privatæ contentiones, quæ illi
sunt cum magna eorum principum parte, addita et ambi-
tione immoderatoq; regum appetitu et ex arbitrio suo,
Temporale jus omne atq; Spirituale tractandi, Ecclesiasti-
camq; Jurisdictionem et Authoritatem invertendi, eo certe
animo ut sedis Apostolicæ dignitatem extinguant; his omnibus in unum connexis ac bene consideratis, ejus Sanctitas
manifeste cognoscet, Principem nullum, neq; portum, aut
refugium tam tutum, cui in omnem eventum queat inhæ-
rere, sibi relictum esse, quam hæc Regia Majestas est quæ
nihil sibi vendicat, nil ambit, quod præjudicio esse possit
dictæ Sanctitati, sed ejus, Apostolicæque sedis, semper fuit,
'est, esseq; decrevit firmissimum scutum, tutissimumq; pro-
pugnaculum, ita suas actiones cum cæteris Principibus fir-
mans et connectens, ut semper ex ea occasione in suam
hanc optimam sententiam reliquos possit attrahere, adeo
quod Regi tam optime in Sanctissimum Dominum nostrum
affecto nihil denegari debeat, utcumq; maximum quod

possit ab ejus Sanctitate præstari ordinaria vel absoluta sua
Authoritate; nam procul dubio, post vias modosq; omnes
tentatos, omnino perspicietur omnia alia amicitiæ officia,
si huic quod petitur comparentur, esse perquam exigua, et
hoc amicum officium hujusmodi futurum, ex quo reliqua
queant incrementum capere, sine eo futura alioquin parvi
ac nullius fere momenti.

Tertio, probe notandum est, quod res nunc aperta et
petita, a Regiaq; Majestate tantopere optata, ex tam magno conscientiæ scrupulo, cordisq; remorsu oritur, ut uni-
cuiq; debita sit, quantumcunq; minori quam Regia Majestas sit de Sanctissimo Domino nostro merito. Quocirca
judicat, et pro re comperta sibi persuadet, quod si ulla
meritorum vel officiorum ratio habeatur, nunc ipsius Sanctitas huic suo desiderio et petitioni benignissime liber-
rimeque adjuvet, nullo prorsus dubio, difficultate, contradictione aut mora injecta. Negotiumque hujusmodi est, ut
cognita Dispensationis insufficientia, quamvis id non re-
quisivisset Rex, ultro proponi offerrique debuisset ab eadem
Sanctitate tanquam a Patre Spirituali, in ejus salutis et
conscientiæ beneficium.

In gratiam igitur et contemplationem præmissorum omnium instantissime vehementissimèq; a Sanctissimo Domino
nostro requiretis et contendetis, ut dubio, metuq; omni
seposito, respicere velit ad causæ statum, et ad ea quæ
subsequutura videantur, rationemq; habere infinitorum
commodorum, quæ ex hac re suæ Sanctitati Apostolicæq;
sedi inde provenient, rem hanc statim, absq; temporis
tractu, et causæ circumstantia, nemini eam aperiens, libere concedere et indulgere nulliq; communicata specialem
Commissionem ad hunc effectum et finem confestam in
forma Brevis concedere, et ad me dirigere, Facultatem
addens, ut mihi liceat quoscunq; voluero ad me vocare,
mihiq; asciscere ad procedendum in hac causa, et inquirendum de dictæ Bullæ ac Dispensationis sufficientia,
juxta formam ac tenorem expressum in quodam libello
hujus rei gratia confecto; quem cum his ad vos mitto, sic
in debita forma conscriptum et digestum ut non sit futurum
opus quo denuo ab ullo alio exscribatur, si forsan periculosum putaretur eam rem cuiq; patefacere vel in dubium
aut dilationem protractum iri negotium, si ulli ex Sanctis-

simi Domini nostri officiariis committeretur rursus con-
scribendum; sed quod in hujusmodi periculi eventum possit
ejus Sanctitas sine ullo discrimine vel alicujus cognitione
eam dicto libello signaturam, sigillumq; apponere, ut aperte inde constet, Pontificis meram voluntatem sic esse,
illiusq; Signaturæ ac Sigilli vigore, legitime et sufficienter
possim ego procedere ad inquisitionem de dictæ Dispensationis insufficientia, cognitionem et aliarum causarum et
rationum, quæ adduci possunt pro dicti Matrimonii invaliditate.

Item cum his ad vos mitto Dispensationem in debita
forma confectam et scriptam in modum Brevis, secreto
impetrandam et expediendam eidem Signaturam vel Sigillum apponendo, vel alio quovis modo valido: Et quamvis
ex hac re multa pendeant, ob quæ ista requiruntur, et quæ,
Deo favente, neutiquam timenda sunt; Attamen Regia
Majestas exemplo innitens, et recordationi complurium
rerum, quæ olim præteritis temporibus fuerunt injuste
asserta, vel adducta, in animo habens causas suas omnes
absq; ulla controversia aut difficultate ad perfectum finem
perducere, et ne ullo quovis prætextu, argumento aut colore, postmodum emergente perturbarentur, hoc a Sanctissimo Domino nostro requirit, veluti rem necessariam, qua
nullo pacto carere queat; firmiter confidens, quod Sanctitas sua, benigne atq; amanter isti ejus desiderio assentiet,
et concedet sine ullo obstaculo dictam Commissionem,
juxta formam quam Regia Majestas petit et eodem tempore, atq; hæc omnia ita benigne ac liberaliter expedire,
secretiori et validiori quo fieri possit modo, quo optatus
finis subsequi possit in eum effectum, laudabileque propositum, de quo superius dictum est; Qua ex occasione
Sanctissimum Dominum nostrum in perpetuum sibi ad-
stringet, indissolubiliq; amicitiæ vinculo hanc Regiam
Majestatem sibi alligabit, quæ nulli labori, periculo, opibus,
Regno, subditis, nec ipsi sanguini parcens, ab ejus Sanctitate nunquam divelletur aut eam deseret, sed totis suis
viribus constantissime semper illi adhærebit, tum in suæ
Sanctitatis et Cardinalium liberationem, tum in hostibus
persequendis; ad quem finem, magnam jam pecuniarum
summam ad Regem Christianissimum misit, pro illo Italiæ
exercitu continuando, et præter id in animo statutum habet,

quod nisi Cæsar de dicta Sanctitate liberanda consentire, et
ad pacem devenire voluerit, bellum gerere adversus has
inferiores Cæsaris Regiones et Dominia, quo vehementius
urgeat Sanctissimi Domini nostri liberationem, Ecclesiæq;
in pristinam suam dignitatem et authoritatem restitutionem,
eaq; de se indicia exhibebit ut universo orbi manifestum
sit futurum, dictam suam Majestatem esse solidum perfectum amicum, filium obsequentissimum et ejus devotissimum; a qua pectoris sui sententia, nullo thesauro, nullis
opibus, nullis Regnis, seu Ditionibus, vel occasione quacunq; unquam adducetur, sed ex filiali sua observantia et
in Christianam Religionem zelo, innatoq; erga sedem
Apostolicam studio, et præcipuo quodam affectu, quem
Sanctissimo Domino nostro gerit: in compensationem
quoq; gratitudinis, quam tam avide in hoc suo negotio ab
ejus Sanctitate expectat, decretum prorsus habet in con-
stantissimo hoc et indissolubili amicitiæ et conjunctionis
vinculo sincerissimo perstare, id quod dicta Regia Majestas
Sanctissimum Dominum nostrum vehementissime rogat, ut
probe velit in omnem partem librare, vicissimq; efficere,
ut ex Regiæ petitionis indulgentia palam constet parem
benevolentiam et humanitatem a Sanctissimo Domino nostro ex mutuo præstari.

Hac autem causa ipsius Sanctitati a vobis, ut dictum est,
exposita et declarata, neutiquam dubitandum est, quin
benevole atq; libenter statim adnuat Regiæ Majestatis
expectationi et quod huic assentiet, dictam Commissionem
secreto modo ipsa concedens, neminem de ea re ut dictum
est, participem faciens; qui modus servandus est, si videritis hæc effici non posse, nisi cum periculo quin hæc res
eis communicetur, qui eam sint interturbaturi, vel si id
præstare fuerit in Sanctissimi Domini nostri arbitrio, tunc
ejus Sanctitas non gravetur, per Brevia, vel per Bullas,
prout validius et magis sufficiens fore judicaverit, præmissa
omnia concedere, ad quod vestram omnem industriam,
prudentiam, studium, diligentiamq; adhibebitis: Sic omnia prudenter ac circumspecte agentes, ne in discrimen
deveniatur negotium hoc his detegendi, qui illud vel impedire vel retardare forsan voluerint aut potuerint, sed
potius quam ad id periculi res deducatur contenti eritis sola
dictorum libellorum Signatura, in eam formam confecta,

quum ex ea palam constet, Pontificis assensum in id actualiter concurrisse, qui postea recentioribus scriptis, si ita opus fuerit, firmius confirmari corroborariq; poterit.

Et quoniam incertum est, utrum ante vestrum ad Pontificem accessum, ejus Sanctitas fuerit in suam libertatem restituta, necne, quæ forsan libera non tanti faciet Regiæ Majestatis amicitiam et conjunctionem, vel allegabit, se nec audere nec posse, ex. suis cum Cæsare conventionibus ista concedere, nec secreto ullo modo, vel ullo colore, quod ea in re fecisset apud Cæsarem justificare, et potuisset antea in Regiæ Majestatis auxilio pro sua liberatione sperans, dum adhuc detineretur captivus; eo casu Sanctissimo Domino nostro in mentem redigetis, quam parum fidere possit ullis sibi factis a Cæsare promissis, quum nulla in parte redundare possit in commodum aut securitatem, sed solum in extremum excidium ac detrimentum sedis Apostolicæ; et licet ad breve tempus multa videretur Cæsar in ejus Sanctitatis gratiam facturus, compertissimum tamen semper Pontifici esse debet Cæsarianos ea facere, semperq; facturos, quæ Cæsarem possint exaltare, et tendant ad usurpationem potius et depressionem status Ecclesiastici, quam ad ejus continuationem, vel conservationem; et quotiens adversus Ecclesiam ista tentarentur, Regia Majestas in hac sua petitione passa repulsam, quæ alioquin ejus Sanctitati in omnem eventum firmissime adhæsisset, et alios suos confæderatos in eandem sententiam pertraxisset, quam, ea deficiente, in contrarium facile possent allici, quo animo futura sit, et quam bene suum affectum et observantiam collocasse existimatura : summæ est prudentiæ omnia considerare.

Haud incognitum præterea est Sanctissimum Dominum nostrum ad Cæsaris instantiam, quum non multam ab ejus Sanctitate gratiam promeritus esset, ei concessisse Dispensationem et Absolutionem a jurejurando ab illo præstito, de ducenda in Conjugem Domina Principissa, nullo ut par fuisset a Regia Majestate habito, seu petito consensu, non obstante quod Cæsar in validissima forma, non solum præstito jurejurando, sed cautione et Ecclesiasticarum censurarum et pænarum abhibita, quod perstringeretur de dicto Matrimonio perimplendo, ac si Pontifex contentus esse potuit, tantam ei ostendere gratitudinem, quum veluti ho-

tis indies certior tunc poterat haberi, et qui majora parabat
quam juste posset optare, suis petitionibus, Regia Majestate inconsulta, neutiquam parcens, quanto propensius
ejus Sanctitas adnuere debet ejus Principis voto, cujus
fidem et observantiam vere filialem sæpe experta est. Verum ta men si Sanctissimus Dominus noster difficulter vi-
sus fuerit posse adduci, ut in meam Personam dictæ Com-
missioni assentiat, allegans quod non sum indifferens, cui
ex suæ Sanctitatis honore hoc negotium committi possit,
cum Regiæ Majestati sum subditus et intimus Consiliarius, tunc tamdiu persistetis ea in re, quoad vobis visum
fuerit conveniens, negotii expeditionem non ideo protra-
hentes, aut differentes, sed instantes ut hujusmodi Commissio concedatur; affirmabitisq; me pro re nulla quantum-
libet grandi, nullo favore, aut commodo, quicquam effecturum esse, quod aversetur officio meo, et erga Christum
præstitæ professioni, neq; unquam a recto, vero, justoq;
tramite digressurum; Et quin Cardinalis sim et Apostolicæ sedis de latere Legatus, ejus Sanctitatis honor, integra-
que conscientia, a me omnino conservaretur, ex hujusmo-
dique concessa Commissione, omni ex parte exoneraretur.
Tandem si ad hoc, nullis rationibus Pontifex potuerit adduci, ab ejus Sanctitate requiretis, ut dictam velit Commissionem concedere in personam Domini Staphylei Decani
Rotæ, qui et vir indifferens est, et hujusmodi rei ob erudi-
tionem accommodatus, nullo pacto omittentes Dispensationis expeditionem, ut dictum est; et hujus rei gratia Commissionem nunc ad vos mitto, in debita forma confectam et
paratam, quæ signetur ad dictum Dominum Staphyleum
directa, quam Sanctissimo Domino nostro reddetis, casu
quo alia nequeat obtineri, rogabitisq; ut cum dicta Dispensatione eam velit concedere. Et quoniam fieri possit quod
dum fieret mentio de me excipiendo, forsitan ejus Sanctitas
aliquem alium quam Dominum Staphyleum nominaret, ad
quem Commissio hujusmodi dirigeretur, hoc vero in loco
tenacissime insistetis, firmiterq; inhærebitis ei rei, nec in
alium aliquem virum exterum ullo pacto consentientes, sed
solum pro eodem Domino Staphyleio instantes, ejus Sanctitatem summis precibus vehementissime rogantes, et rationibus omnibus suadentes, ne alium ullum nominare velit,
asserentes quod quum in Instructionibus vestris non conti-

neatur, nec de alio ullo fiat mentio, nisi illo, me recusato,
iterum atq ; iterum ab eadem Sanctitate petetis, ut nomine
hujus Aaditoris Rotæ hæc fiat et expediatur commissio, vos
nec audere nec posse vobis præscriptos fines transgredi.

De Regii vero desiderii ac petitionis frustratione super
dicta Commissione obtinenda, dicetis unum et idem esse,
hanc illi denegare, vel alii concedere quam in vestris Instructionibus contineatur, non quod Regia Majestas de aliorum rectitudine aut indifferentia quicquam suspicetur, vel
quod judicet eorum aliquem affectibus obnoxium ; sed quod
pro re certissima credidit, quod Sanctissimus Dominus noster in neminem tam facile condescenderet, quam in dictæ
Rotæ Decanum, ob idque de eo Instructionibus vestris
mentionem fecit : sed Commissiones in debita forma cum
his nominibus fieri et conscribi jussit, quod si hic credidis-
semus, Dom. Staphileum habitum istic iri pro suspecto,
affirmare potestis me fuisse omnino missurum consimilem
Commissionis formulam, spatio relicto pro aliquo alio in-
scribendo nomine, aliquamq ; aliam super ea re Instruc-
tionem me daturum fuisse, et haud dubie ; si de nominibus
duntaxat fuerit controversia, hæ rationes facile poterunt
Pontificem attrahere, ut in me consentiat, vel in Staphyleum.   De aliis vero neminem admittetis, nec tamen Pontifici aperietis vos, ne id faciatis habere in mandatis, sed
superius enarratas Causas in vestram excusationem alle-
gantes, omnino ut vobis injungitur ea in re insistetis.

Quod si nullis modis dictam Commissionem, et Dispensationem impetrare poteritis, ad idq ; nequiverit Pontifex
adduci, nisi rem prius alicui ex Cardinalibus vel Officiariis
communicaverit, in eo tunc casu, ejus Sanctitati in memoriam reducite, quot et quam gravia mala ex hujus negotii
propalatione possent provenire, si ex ea occasione aliquæ
contrarietates vel impedimentum suboriretur, unde Regiæ
Majestatis expectatio postmodum frustaretur : Quo igitur,
si ullæ injiciantur in hac re tractandæ difficultates, ut Pontifex etiam facilior ad Regium votum concedendum promp-
tiorq ; reddatur, alias etiam præter has literas seorsim ad
vos scripsi, quas una cum his accipietis, in quibus copiose
aggessi, quam multas magni momenti rationes, ob quas
sententia judiciumq ; meum est, ne ullo pacto Pontifex
hanc petitionem Regiæ Majestatis deneget ; quas literas,

quam in eis argumentum vehemens est, nee ob prolixitatem
tædiosum aut molestum quod legatur, modum aliquem ipsius Sanctitati legendi invenietis ; spemq ; certam habeo, si
earum summa, tenor, atq ; sententia profunde perpendatur, quam satis id esse poterit ad omnem tollendam difficultatem, quæ possit obversari in dicta Commissione Dispen-
sationeque obtinenda, in eis contenta sigillatim exponetis
adeo, quod hoc negotium confici queat, Arbitris aut Consi-
liaribus ad id neutiquam accitis, si fieri possit : si tamen
Pontifex speraverit se posse hæc omnia eos celare qui huic
rei forsan voluerint refragari, et omnino decreverit aliquos
Cardinales vel Officiarios istius causæ participes facere,
omnem tunc industriam statim adhibebitis, ut his cognitis
eorum gratiam et favorem ea in re vobis comparetis, partim eis respectus, et causas omnes in meis literis contentas,
etiam in causæ commodum facientes, uberius exponentes,
partim vero eam remunerationem illis dantes, quæ judicio
vestro conveniens habebitur, dummodo optatum res sortiatur effectum. Et ut omnia queatis præstare commodius
cum his, meas literas accipietis quas ad Cardinalem *Sanctorum Quatuor* et Collegium Cardinalium scribo, easque
reddetis ut expedire censueritis, plane confidens nihil a
vobis omissum iri, ut hac in re eorum gratiam atq; favorem
queatis obtinere, in quem eventum ea munera offeretis, quæ
convenientia visa fuerint, Regiaq; Majestas quicquid ejus
nomine promiseritis, id fidelissime, uberrimeq ; præstabit,
pro quarum rerum expeditione, illis pecuniis uti poteritis per
literas Cambii Venetias transmissis, quousq; suffecerint,
necessariumq ; vos existimaveritis rei impetrandæ. Et quum
ambiguum sit an vobis licuerit hoc tempore ad Pontificis
præsentiam accedere, hujusmodi accessus defectus, si aliæ
rem ad bonum exitum perducendi rationes non excogi-
tarentur, causa esse posset longioris moræ, et totius rei impedimento ; proinde Regia Majestas, ut modos omnes expe-
riatur, nec uni soli inhæreat, hæc eadem in mandatis dedit
Domino Secretario, quem non procul ab Urbe esse intelleximus, quemadmodum in his aliisq ; meis brevioribus
literis continentur, ita quod alter vestrum, vel uterque, si
fieri possit, ad Pontificis præsentiam accessum habeat ; nihil tamen, sub spe Domini Secretarii, vestræ vos diligentiæ aut industriæ omittetis, nec ille sub spe vestra, in re

hac modis omnibus promovenda, remissior erit, sed nihil conjunctim aut divisim intentatum relinquetis. Quod si uterq; vestrum ad Pontificem admittatur, alter de altero nescius, id non oberit, sed multum proficiet, etiam si ante alterius adventum negotium hoc alter impetrasset; sed si aliquis vestrum cognoverit causam hanc expeditam esse, omniaq; pro certo impetrata esse, tunc labori et sumptibus Pontificem pro eadem re accedendi parcere poteritis, neq; in eam amplius ingerere, neq; necessarium aut opportunum erit, ut pro ulla alia re in præsentia quam pro hac apud Sanctissimum Dominum nostrum agatis, sed solum nunc procurabitis de Commissione et Dispensatione juxta formam ad vos missam obtinenda, necnon de profestinatione illa, quam compendio ad vos dedi, in quibus omnibus et singulis apte tractandis Regia Majestas magnam fiduciam in vestra prudentia collocavit, in quibus, cum tam magni sint momenti, ex Regiæ Majestatis sententia nunc vobis maxime elaborandum est.

Deniq; quum intelligam Dominum Lautrek nonnihil mirari, quod Regiæ Majestatis istic agentes, nullam suorum mandatorum partem cum eo conferunt, ad eum nunc scribo, et nonnulla Domino Roberto Jernyngham ei exponenda committo concernentia actiones cum Ferrariæ Duce, et alia quædam eodem Domino Lautrek; significans, vos missos esse ad dictas causas juvandas, et Pontificis liberationem promovendam, quemadmodum ex literarum ad Dominum Jernyngham exemplo cognoscetis: expediens itaq; fuerit, ut præ se feratis, vos dictæ rei gratia missos esse, ne forsan Dominus Lautrek in falsam aliquam conjecturam aut suspicionem incideret, quæ communibus rebus nocere posset, et in vestrarum quoq; actionum impedimentum redundare.

Illud deinde reticere nolui, quod si ullo pacto vobis liceat ad Sanctissimi Domini nostri præsentiam accedere, nihil omittatis in favorem et gratiam Reverendi Domini Datarii, de cujus animo nihil dubitamus, comparandam, eiq; asseretis, quod quum in nostris omnibus occurrentiis illius opera ac Patrocinio semper usi fuerimus, ipse vero tanta semper fide ac sedulitate omnia effecerit quæ nobis grata et optata esse cognovit, ut nostram omnem operam suis rebus reddiderit, promptissimam, et suæ utilitatis et exaltationis.

cupidissimam. Quocirca hæc Regia Majestas hac in re, qua nullam magis cordi habet, nec gravioris momenti quicquam sibi accidere posse judicat, ex animi sui sententia conficienda, post Sanctissimum Dominum nostrum, in Domino Datario spem omnem collocavit, qui ex hac occasione, si operam suam ad optatum usq; exitum interponere non gravetur, Regiæ Majestatis animum et pectus, sic omni ex parte promerebitur, ut dicta Majestas non solum omnia curatura sit, quæ ex Domini Veronensis commodo et ornamento fuerint, sed eam etiam munificentiam et gratitudinem addet, quæ majorem vel integram partem, a captivitate Redemtionis persolvendæ compensabit; In me vero non aliam fidem et amicitiam experietur, quam ab ullo fratre posset expectare. Et bene valete. Londini ex meis Ædibus. Die quinto Decemb. M. D. XXVII.

Vester tanquam frater Amantiss.

T. Cardinalis Eborac.

Rome Jan. 1. 1528.

IV.

Two Letters of Secretary Knights to the Cardinal and the King, giving an account of his Conference with the Pope about his Divorce.   Taken from the Originals.

PLEASE it your Grace to understand, That immediately upon the receipt of your Graces Letters, severally directed unto Mr. Gregory and me ; he and I resorted unto the Pope his Holiness, making congratulation of his restitution unto liberty on yours and his behalf, to his singular comfort and consolation; and so much the more, because that I was the first that made like salutation in any great Princes Name ; He being well assured that I spake the same on the behalf of his two chief, sincere, and unfeigned Friends : Wherefore with great high thanks, and long discourse, with rehearsal of the King's and your Merits and Acts, in most vertuous and Catholick manner, employed

for his restitution, and your continual and effectual study BOOK
how the See Apostolique might recover the pristine Repu- II.
tation and Dignity; He confirmed as much as I had
spoken. After this Mr. Gregory and I entred into our
Charge, shewing at length the high deserts of the Princes
and Realm of England, the devotion of the same towards
the Church; how expedient it was, as well for the See
Apostolique, as for the said Realm, to foresee und provide
that all occasions of Dissension and War were extinct and
put away; which for lack of Heir Male of our Sovereign's
Line, and Stem, should undoubtedly follow, with other
considerations at length contained in our Instructions. We
desired his Holiness to commit the knowledg of the Dispensation that was obtained in time of Julius, of famous
memory, for Matrimony to be had between the King and
the Widow, Relict late of Prince Arthur; and that we
might have it in form as that was that your Grace sent
hither. His Holiness answered, That our sayings had
great likelihood of truth, for lacking of Issue Male of
the King's Stem, considering the nature of Men being
prone unto Novelties, and disposed unto Parties and Fac-
tions. The Realm of England would not only enter into
their accustomed Divisions, but also would owe or do small
devotion unto the Church; Wherefore his Holiness was
right well content and ready to adhibit all Remedy that in
him was possible as this time would serve. And because
he was not expert in making of Commissions, he would
consult with the Cardinal *Sanctorum Quatuor*, and use his
advice, which we should shortly know.

We perceiving that the obtaining of our Charges after
the King's and your Graces pleasure, depended much upon
the Advice of *Sanctorum Quatuor*, did prevent his going
unto the Pope and delivering your Grace's Letters with
Recommendations accordingly, we desired him to be good
and favourable unto our Requests in the King's behalf;
and for the better obtaining of our desires, we promised to
see unto him with a competent reward. And this communication had, we shewed unto him the Commission, which
he said could not pass without perpetual dishonour unto
the Pope, the King, and your Grace; and a great part of
such Clauses as be omitted, he hath touched and laid rea--

son for the same in a Writing, which I do send unto your Grace with this. Considering his great Experience, Wisdom, Learning, and the entire affection that he beareth unto the King and your Grace; and that it was far from the King's desire, and nothing for your purposes, that I should first have sent the said Cardinal's Sayings unto your Grace, and abide answer, and eft-soons prevent to do the same: Considering also that the said King desireth a Commission convenient and sufficient, we desired him to make the minute of one, which he gladly did: When it was made, the Pope said, That at his being in the Castle of St. Angelo, the General of the Observants in Spain, required his Holiness, in the Emperor's Name, not to grant unto any Act that might be preparative, or otherwise, to Divorce to be made between the King and the Queen: and moreover desired an Inhibition, that the said Cause should not come in knowledge before any Judg within the King's Dominions. The Pope answered that *Inhibitio non datur nisi post litem motam.* And as unto the first his Holiness was content, if any like thing were demanded, to advertise the Emperor before, that he did let it pass; and this was in a manner for his Holiness being in Captivity. But his Holiness being yet in Captivity, as your Grace reports, and esteemeth him to be as long as the Almaines and Spaniards continueth in Italy; he thought if he should grant this Commission, that he should have the Emperor his perpetual Enemy, without any hope of reconciliation: Notwithstanding he was content rather to put himself in evident ruine, and utter undoing, then the King, or your Grace, should suspect any point of ingratitude in him, heartily desiring *cum suspiriis & lachrimis,* that the King and your Grace, which have always been fast and good unto him, will not now suddenly precipitate him for ever; which should be done, if immediately upon delivering of the Commission your Grace should begin Process. He intendeth to save all upright thus: If Monsieur de Lautrech would set forwards, which he saith daily that he will do, but yet he doth not, at his coming the Pope's Holiness may have good colour to say, He was required by the Ambassadour of England of a like Commission. And denying the same, because of his promise unto the General, he was eft-soons by Monsieur de Lautrech, to grant the said Commission, inasmuch as it was but a Letter of Justice. And by this colour he would cover the Matter, so that it might appear unto the Emperor, That the Pope did it not as he that would gladly do displeasure unto the Emperor, but as an indifferent Prince that could not nor might deny Justice, specially being required by such Personages! and immediately he would dispatch a Commission, bearing date after the time that Monsieur Lautrech had been with him or nigh unto him. The Pope most instantly beseecheth your Grace, to be a mean that the King's Highness may accept this in a good part, and that he will take patience for this little time, which as it is supposed will be but short, and (*in omnem eventum*) I do bring a Commission with me, and a Dispensation, which I trust the King and your Grace will like well.

We have given unto my Lord Cardinal *Sanctorum Quatuor* 4000 Crowns, and unto the Secretary 30 Crowns.

With this Your Grace shall receive a Letter from the Pope's Holiness, Item, a Counsel of Oldrand. that giveth light unto the King's Cause. I shall make the most diligence homeward that I can. Our Lord Jesus preserve Your Grace.

At Orvieto, this first
  day of January.

Your most humble Servant
  and Chaplain,
      W. Knight.

Rome Jan. 1. 1528.

TO THE KING.

PLEASE it your Highness to understand, That as soon as the Pope was at liberty, and came unto Orvieto, I resorted unto his Holiness with all diligence; and at my coming unto him, did make congratulation on your Highness behalf; forasmuch as he was restored unto his Liberty, which he accepted very joyfully and thankfully, giving unto your High-

ness manifold and high thanks for your great goodness, as
well proved in his adversity, as when he was in his most felicity. After this he rehearsed my being at Rome, how dangerous it was, inasmuch as when my being there was detect, es-
pial was made, and I was not passed out of Rome by the space
of two hours, or two hundred Spaniards invaded and searched the House. He shewed also that he had received all such
Letters as I at my being in Rome did send unto his Holiness; whereby he did perceive the Effect of your Highness
desire concerning your Dispensation: And albeit he did
send me word that I should depart, and his Holiness would
send unto me the said Dispensation fully speed. Nevertheless he trusted that your Highness would be content to
tarry for a time: for the General of the Observants in
Spain being lately in Rome, had required him, according unto his Instructions, that he should suffer nothing to
pass that might be prejudicial or against the Queen, directly or indirectly, but that the Pope should first advertise
thereof certain of the Cæsarians here. And forasmuch as
this Dispensation might encourage your Grace to cause my
Lord Legate *Auctoritate Legationis* to hear and decern
in the Cause that your Highness intendeth, and his Holiness standeth as yet in manner in captivity and perplexity:
His Holiness therefore besought your Grace to have patience for a time, and it should not be long e're your Highness should have, not only that Dispensation, but any thing
else that may lie in his power. I replied unto this, That
his Holiness had once granted it, and that I had dispatched
a Post, and made relation thereof, by my Writings, unto
your Highness; so that I could not imagine by what reason I might perswade unto you that he would perform the
promise that he had once broken. In conclusion; He was
content that your Highness should have it, but he would
have it delivered with this condition; That the Prothonotary Gambora and I, should beseech your Highness
not to attempt any thing in your Cause against the Queen,
till such time as the Pope were frankly at his Liberty; which
could not be as long as the Almaynes and Spaniards did
thus reign in Italy; and promise made, we should deliver
the Dispensation: and in my poor judgment, it was best always to be in possession of this Dispensation. After this he

shewed the Minute unto the Cardinal *Sanctorum Quatuor*, willing him to reform it according to the stile of this Court; which done, he shewed it unto me, and after said, That he thought good I should depart, because I rode but competent Journies, and the Prothonotary Gambora should follow by Post and bring the Bull with him, which is of the same form and substance that your Highness's Minute is of: And if there be any thing omitted, or to be added, his Holiness is always content to reform it, and to put it under the same date that the same Dispensation now beareth; the Copy whereof I do send unto your Highness with this, the Commission General and Protestation being void, because they were conceived *durante captivitate* only. And here, on my behalf, none other thing being to be done, I took my leave of the Pope and departed. At my coming unto Scarperii near unto Bonony, I did meet with Thadeus this Courier, which brought certain Expeditions Triplicat; the one unto the Prothonotar Gambora, the other unto Gregory de Cassali, and the third unto me; among which was a general Commission Triplicat, the one to be committed to my Lord Legate; and if that could not be obtained, because my Lord Legate might be thought partial, then the same to be committed unto Staphileius. Item; There was a Copy of a Dispensation, where I perceived, by your Grace's Letter, that your pleasure was to have your Dispensation in form, after the minute that Barlow brought, which was then sped, and already passed; so remained nothing to be sped, but the Commission your Highness pleases. This knowing, I caused my Servants to continue their Journey, and with one Servant and this Courier, I returned unto Orvieto with Post-Horses; where Mr. Gregory and I, with much Business, have obtained a Commission directed unto my Lord Legate, not in the form that was conceived in England, but after such manner as is sufficient for the Cause, and as I trust shall content your Highness; wherein the Lord Cardinal *Sanctorum Quatuor*, hath taken great pains to pen, as well your Dispensation as the Commission; for which, and that hereafter he may do unto your Highness the better service, Mr. Gregory and I have rewarded him with 4000 Crowns, of such Money as your Highness hath caused to be made unto

Venice for the furtherance of your Causes. But albeit that every thing is passed according to your Highness pleasure, I cannot see, but in case the same be put in execution at this time, the Pope is utterly undone, and so he saith himself. The Imperialists do daily spoil Castles and Towns about Rome; Monsieur de Lautrek is yet at Bonony, and small hope is of any great Act that he intends. The Cæsarians have taken within these three days, two Castles lying within six miles of this: and the Pope being in this perplexity, not assured of any one Friend but of your Highness, that lieth too far off; if he do at this time any displeasure unto the Emperor, he thinketh he is undone for ever; wherefore he puts his Honour and Health wholly into your Highness Power and Dispostion. This morning I return homewards, and Gregory de Cassali goeth in my Company as far as unto Florence; and from thence he goeth unto Monsieur de Lautrek, to sollicit him forwards, if it may be. The Holy Ghost send your Highness a prosperous New Year, and many.

At Orvieto, the first   Your most humble Subject,
   day of January.   Servant, and Chaplain.

W. Knight.

V.

Rome 10. Jan. 1528.

A part of an Original Letter from the same Person to Cardinal Wolsey, by which it appears that the Dispensation was then granted and sent over.

Your Grace commandeth, That I should send the Commission and Dispensation with diligence, in case they were sped, before the receit of your Graces Letters sent at this time. Wherefore the Prothonotar Gambora and I being commanded *sub pœna Excommunicationis* to deliver the same, with a certain Request to be made to the King's Highness and his Grace, at the time of delivery; I send

the same at this time unto Gambora, requiring him in any
wise to make diligence towards the King's Highness, and
not to abide my coming; the Request and Cause thereof
your Grace shall perceive by mine other Letters adjoined
herewith. And supposing that when your Grace hath seen
my Letters, and the Dispensations, and considered this
time well, it may chance that the King and your Grace will
be rather well content with that that is passed, without
suing for any other thing that could not be obtained without long tract, and peradventure not so. Your Grace hath
committed as much unto Gregory de Cassali at this time,
as unto me, which being near unto the Pope, will without
fail do his best diligence: And if it shall be thought good
unto the King's Highness, and your Grace, that I do return unto Orvieto, I shall do as much as my poor Carcase
may endure, and thereby at Turine I shall abide the knowledge of your Grace's pleasure. The Datary hath clean
forsaken the Court, and will serve no longer but only God
and his Cure. The Cardinal Campegius continueth in
Rome sore vexed with the Gout; The Cardinals Pisane,
Triuulcis, Ursine, Gadis and Cesis, remaineth for Host-
ages. The Cardinals Monte, *Sanctorum Quatuor*, Ri-
dulph, Ravenna, and Perusino, be with the Pope; the rest
abides absent. Our Lord Jesus preserve your Grace.

At Aste, the 10th   Your most humble Beadsman
 day of January.   and Servant,

             W. Knight.

VI.

Orvieto the 13th of January.

*Gregory Cassali's Letter about the Method in which the Pope
desired the Divorce should be managed. Taken from a
Copy written by Cardinal Wolsey's Secretary.*

Cotton
Libr.
Vitel.
B. 10.

HERI et hodie ad multam diem sum alloquutus Sanctum
Dominum nostrum de mittendo legato, insequens ordinem a

Reverendissimo Domino Eboracen. suis literis 27 Decembᵣ mibi præscriptum.　Pontifex ostendit se cupidissimum satisfaciendi Regiæ Excellentiæ, cui omnia se debere fatetur, et nunc habuit mecum longum de hac re colloquium, ut inveniatur modus omnia, bene, firme et secure faciendi, quo facto et tueri possit; ideoq; consulere voluit judicium Cardinalis *Sanctorum Quatuor* et Symonettæ, qui excellentior et Doctior Auditor Rotæ est, cum quibus sub sigillo Confessionis egit, ut ex eorum consilio inveniatur modus, ad moram tollendam, et causam secure peragendam: Atq; ita Pontifex cum illis, in hoc quod sequitur, se revolvit, videturq; optimus, verus et securus modus, et me rogavit, ut nullo pacto dicam hoc obtinuisse ab ejus Sanctitate sicuti revera obtinui, nam Cæsariani eum statum pro suspecto allegarent, sed quod dicam me habuisse a Cardinali *Sanctorum Quatuor*, et a dicto Auditore.　Dicunt quod Rex deberet committere istic causam Cardinali, ratione Commissionis quam attulit Secretarius, vel propria Authoritate Legationis, quod facere potest; et ubi causa fuerit commissa, si Rex conscientiam suam persentiat coram Deo exoneratam, et quod recte possit facere quod quærit, quia nullus Doctor in mundo est, qui de hac re melius decernere possit quam ipse Rex, itaq; si in hoc se resolverit, ut Pontifex credit, statim causam committat, aliam Uxorem ducat, litem sequatur, mittatur publice pro Legato, qui Consistorialiter mittetur, ita enim maxime expediret: nam Cardinalis *Sanctorum Quatuor* et Symonetta dicunt hoc certum esse, quod si Regina citetur illa nihil volet respondere, nisi quod protestabitur locum et judices suspectos esse, et Cæsariani petent a Pontifice per viam Signaturæ, justitiæ Inhibitionem, qua Rex aliam nullam possit Uxorem capere, et si capiat proles non sit legitima donec causa non definiatur, et petent Commissionem qua Causa audiatur in Curia; de Inhibitione vero Pontifex non potest negare, neq; et Commissionem nisi injustitia et mera vis inferatur, adversus quam omnis mundus exclamaret.　Quod si Rex aliam Uxorem ceperit hoc non possunt petere, et si petant, negabit Pontifex quod jure possit, nec aliud dicere poterunt vel allegare, nisi quod Cardinalis Eboracen. et Cardinalis mittendus et locus sit suspectus, et petere quod Causa videatur hic, in quo si deducatur, statim

feretur sententia quam Pontifex maturabit, non servatis
terminis propter momentum negotii et alias rationes, quas
sciet Pontifex adducere, et ita hic obtinebuntur sententiæ
quæ per totum Orbem approbabuntur, quibus nullus His-
panus aut Germanus poterit contradicere, et mittentur in
Angliam declarandæ per Cardinales prout Rex voluerit, et
hoc etiam non obstante Pontifex mittet Cardinalem.

Tandem hic est modus rebus omnibus secure medendi,
ad quem sequendum vos Pontifex hortatur, et rogat ut nihil dicatur quod ab eo procedat. Iste modus non videtur
inutilis, quia hic Auditor asserit, non aliter esse faciendum
si bene volumus; et quia Reverendissimus Cardinalis Dominus Eboracen. instat pro celeritate, interim accersiri
poterit qualiscunq; Legatus Rex voluerit, et magis satis-
fiet vulgo in mittendo Legato, veluti ad definiendam causam, et hic etiam ut dixi omnia fient quæ super id Rex
petierit.

Præterea Pontifex, id quod fecit ut me resolverem ad
has literas scribendum, contentus est mittere quemcunq;
Cardinalem ego petiero, sed ait oportere ut aliquis mittatur habilis, id est Doctor in Jure, vel in Theologia, qui
sunt isti Campegius, Cæsarinus, Senensis, Cæsis, Araceli,
Monte, qui senex est et immobilis; Cæsis in obsidem ivit
Neapolim, Cæsarinus Episcopatum habet in Hispania,
Araceli podagra laborat et Frater est, Senensis est Impe-
rialis et non valde prudens, Campegius esset maxime ad
propositum, sed Romæ est locum tenens Pontificis, unde
non posset discedere, continuantibus discordiis inter Germanos et Hispanos, neq; auderet egredi a castro; sed hoc
periculum et dubium brevi expedietur, nam intra octo dies
Cæsariani cogentur sibi consulere ut eant in Regnum, si
Dominus Lautrek eo progrediatur, vel ibunt Senas per
iter Florentiæ, et tunc Campegius poterit exire, et si Rex
ita jusserit statim accingetur itineri. Pontifex jussit ut
scribam, quod nunquam ingenio aut studio deerit in exco-
gitando ut adimpleat desiderium et voluntatem Regis, et
quod solum ista proponit pro meliori securitate, ne ista
fiant quæ postea referri debeant, quod pareret dilationem
et difficultatem, et quantum ego possim conjicere Pontifex
exoptat satisfacere Regiæ voluntati. Pontifex denuo re-
plicavit quod se totum rejicit in Brachia Regiæ Majestatis,

et quod certus est quod Cæsar nunquam hoc illi ignoscet,
et quod ex hac occasione vocabit eum ad Concilium, vel
nihil aliud quæret nisi ut eum omni statu et vita privet; et
dicta Sanctitas parvam spem habet in Gallis, nisi quantum
operabitur per Regiam Majestatem et Reverendissimum
Dominum Eboracen. Ad quod Respondi, illum ex præteritis et præsentibus posse judicare futura. Tandem affirmo, quod si semel tollatur Cæsarianorum metus, poteritis
ex arbitrio vestro disponere de sede Apostolica.

Cardinalis Campegius ad Pontificem scripsit, quod sunt
tres dies ex quo frater Generalis communicaverat secum
negotium Regiæ Majestatis, et quod dixerat ut ad ejus
Sanctitatem scriberet, ut omnino faceret aliquam Inhibitionem ne causa istic tractaretur. Ad quod Pontifex non
respondit, sed respondebit, se nihil de eo posse facere, quia
non pendet causa.

VII.

Januar. 1528. ad Collegium.

*A Duplicat. The King's Letter to the Colledg of Cardinals;
from which it appears how much they favoured his Cause.*

Cotton
Libr.
Vitel.
B. 10.
HENRICUS REX, Reverendissimis in Christo Patribus Dominis Episcopis Patribus et Diaconis S. R. E. Cardinalibus
et Amicis nostris Charissimis salutem. Nihil unquam tam
grande esse posse putavimus, quin de ista Sancta sede,
vestrarumq; Reverendissimarum Dominat. summa erga nos
benignitate, illud semper audacter nobis fuerimus polliciti,
quod certe S. Sanctum istud Collegium, quotiens ullam
nobis gratificandi occasionem oblatam habuit, cumulatis-
sime præstitit : Cæterum benevolentiam istam vestram, et
singulare in nos studium, nunc longe superavit, alacritas,
quam in nostra omnium gravissima causa, juvanda ac promovenda, in publico Consistorio, amantissime omnes exhi-
buistis, quo certe beneficio sic Sacro isti Collegio Sanctis-
simæq; isti sedi adstrictos nos fatemur, ut vehementissime

optemus gratiam, vel sanguine ipso, publice ac privatim BOOK
II.
Reverendissimis Dominat. vestris quoq; posse referre.
Quocirca iterum eas impense rogamus, ut in suo erga nos
affectu perseverare non graventur, efficiemusq; (Deo bene
juvante) ut brevi perspiciant, apud gratum et memorem
Principem, Sanctæq; Rom. Ecclæsiæ observantissimum,
sua se beneficia et officia collocasse. Interim vobis quas
possumus ex animo, tum his literis, tum per Oratorem
istic nostrum immortales gratias Reverendissimis vestris
Dominis agimus, existimetisq; quicquid a nobis præstari
queat, id suo ornamento et commodo promptissimum futuram.

VIII.

Febr. 10. 1528.

*A duplicate of the Cardinal's Letter to the Pope, about the
Divorce; corrected with his own hand.*

BEATISSIME Pater, post humillimam Commendationem, Cotton
Libr.
Vitel.
B. 10.
et Sanctissimorum pedum oscula, doleo atq; gravissime ex-
crucior, quod ea quæ tanta solicitudine, literis et nunciis
apud Beatitudinem vestram ago, nequeam, ut unice et rerum omnium maxime vellem, prius tractare, hoc est, negotium Potentissimi Domini mei Regis, negotium inquam
rectissimum, honestissimum ac sanctissimum, in quo pro-
curando non aliter me interpono, quam in ejus Regiæ Majestatis salute tuenda, in hoc Regno conservando, in publica tranquillitate fovenda, in Apostolica Autoritate, in
mea deniq; vita et anima protegenda debeo. Beatissime
Pater, ad vestræ Sanctitatis genua provolutus, obsecro et
obtestor, ut si me Christianum virum, si bonum Cardinalem, si S. Sancto isto Senatu dignum, si Apostolicæ sedis
membrum non stupidum et inutile, si recti, justitiæq; cul-
torem, si fidelem Creaturam suam, si demum æternæ salutis cupidum me existimet, nunc velit mei Consilii et inter-
cessionis rationem habere, et pientissimis hujus Regis precibus, benigne, prompteq; adnuere: quas nisi rectas, sanc-

tas ac justas esse scirem, omne prius supplicii genus ultro,
subirem, quam eas promoverem, pro hisq ; ego vitam meam et animam spondeo. Alioquin vereor (quod tamen ne-
queo tacere) ne Regia Majestas humano, divinoq; jure
(quod habet ex omni Christianitate suis his actionibus ad-
junctum) freta, postquam viderit sedis Apostolicæ gratiam,
et Christi in terris Vicarii clementiam desperatam, Cæsaris
intuitu, in cujus manu neutiquam est tam Sanctos conatus
reprimere, ea tunc moliatur, ea suæ causæ perquirat remedia, quæ et non solum huic Regno, sed etiam aliis Christianis Principibus, occasionem subministrarent, sedis Apostolicæ Autoritatem et Jurisdictionem imminuendi, et vili-
pendendi, non absq ; Christianæ Reip. perturbatione : Quibus malis potest vestra Sanctitas sua autoritate et prudentia
mederi. Hæc loquor ut Christianus, et ut devotissimum
istius Sedis membrum sincere suadeo ; non affectus, non
Principis amor, non servitutis vinculum me impellit, sed
sola rectitudine ad id adducor. Cæterum animi solicitudo
non sinit plura exprimere. Vestra Sanctitas in tam justo
Regis voto adnuendo, sic ejus Majestatis animum sibi devinciet et conservabit, ut non solum ipse et ego, sed omnes ejus
subditi sint ad omnem occasionem, opes, vires, et sanguinem in Sanctitatis vestræ, Apostolicæ Sedis beneficium,
libentissime profusuri Mitto ad Beatitudinem vestram
hujus rei gratia, Dominum Stephanum Gardinerum, Pri-
marium Secretissimorum Consiliorum Secretarium, mei di-
midium, et quo neminem habeo cariorem ; referet ille cuncta distinctius, meum pectus aperiet. Vestram igitur Sanctitatem humillime rogo, ut eum loquentem me loqui existi-
mares, et eam fidem quam præsenti mihi haberet, illi et Domino Edwardo Foxo Regio familiari in omnibus præstare,
et me a tam anxia expectatione liberare dignetur.

IX.

*Cardinal Wolsey's Letter to Gregory Cassali, directing him
to make Presents at Rome.*

TANTA deinde sunt, tamq; magna officia, quæ Reveren- Cotton
Libr.
Vitell.
B. 10.
dissimus Dominus Sanctorum Quatuor, tum erga Regiam
Majestatem, tum erga me, nunquam non amantissime exhi-
buit, ut quum ea in agendis gratiis assequi conamur, id animo facilius complecti, quam exteriori ullo propensæ nostræ in eum voluntatis testimonio indicare queamus : ad nostriq; in eum summum studii et affectionis cumulum, nunc
tantum accessit, quantum vix unquam possit a nobis ex-
solvi ; licetq; de ejus Reverendissim. Dominat. ingenti
Regiæ Majestati, et mihi gratificandi ardore nunquam addu-
bitaverim, sic tamen pectus suum, in Regiæ Majestatis promovenda juvandaq; causa, sic in meis seorsim curandis ex-
pediendisq; negotiis, operam, fidem, autoritatemq; suam
interposuit, ut non minora semper efficeret, quam nos optare potuerimus: quo certe nomine, ita utrumq; nostrum,
suo suorumq; omnium commodo et ornamento devinxit, ut
non prius conquieturi sumus quam aliquo indicio rebus ipsis nostram vicissim gratitudinem fuerimus testati ; quot
enim modis et quanta sollicitudine Reverendissimus Sanctorum Quatuor de nobis sit optime meritus, res præstita
indicat, et Dominus Stephanus Secretarius meus suo Sermone ac relatu assidue prædicat; et quamvis minusculum
illud olim oblatum recusaverit, non tamen Regiæ Majestati
satisfactum esse potest, nisi memoris sui animi pignus aliquod exhibuerit. Quocirca cum eodem Reverendissimo Domino dexterime agite, ut in familiari aliquo colloquio elicia-
tis, quibus rebus ille maxime oblectetur, mihiq; quam primum significate, num illi, aulea, Vasa aurea, aut equi maxime probentur, efficiamq; ne putet apud Principem inhuma-
num aut ingratum sua se officia collocasse. Intellexi quoq;
ex eodem Domino Stephano, quam ardentur idem Dominus
Sanctorum Quatuor cupiat ædificium Sancti Petri absolvi,
veluti monumentum illud Religionis ac pietatis perpetuo futurum, quod certe ejus animi consilium, ut Sanctum ita dignissimum censeo, ut Christianorum Principum liberalitatem
quam plurimum mereatur ; meo igitur nomine affirmabitis,

sic meam me esse operam apud hunc Serenissimum Regem
interpositurum, ut palam constet omnibus, me Ecclesiæ
membrum non omnino inutile aut stupidum esse.

De aliis vero rebus, in quibus S. D. N. benignitatem et
Reverendissimi Domini Sanctorum Quatuor opera et Patrocinio Regiæ Majestati et mihi in præsentia est opus, per
Dominum Stephanum copiose vos instruo, iterum atq;
iterum impense rogans, ut solita vestra diligentia et sedu
litate ex nostra expectatione eas curare conficereq; velitis.

X.

Rome Feb. 1527.

The Decretal Bull that was desired in the King's Cause.

DILECTO, &c. Salutem et Apostolicam Benedict. Sedis
Apostolicæ Suprema Autoritas potestatis suæ copiam sic
omnibus exhibet, ut pro causarum, personarum et temporum qualitate remedia singulis ad ædificationem subministrare, et causas ad Canonum Sanctiones expensas æquissi-
mâ certisimaq; lance trutinans, laborantibus conscientiis
et fluctuantibus consulere, summamq; ipsis tranquillitatem statuere contendat. Cum itaq; Clarissimus in Christo
Filius noster Henricus Octavus Angliæ Rex, Fidei Defensor, et Dominus Hiberniæ, sua nobis conquestione monstra-
verat, quod cum Annos ab hinc decem et octo nobilem Mu-
lierem Catharinam Ferdinandi quondam Hispaniarum Regis Filiam, Illustris Principis Arthuri Fratris sui defuncti
quondam Uxorem, hortatu, suasu, ac consiliis eorum, quibus se totum in prima Regni sui Administratione credide-
rat, quadam sedis Apostolicæ Dispensatione prætensa sibi
bona fide Matrimonio copulasset, ac ab eo tempore hactenus cum eadem tanquam cum Uxore cohabitasset, prole
interim fœmina suscepta et superstite ex eadem, ac jam
tandem post desperatam prolem Masculam, de stabilienda
et confirmanda ejusdem Filiæ suæ successione cogitaret,
lustratisq; Scriniis dictam super Matrimonio præfato Dis-

pensationem faceret proferri, doctorumq; Virorum judicia examinari, cujus quidem Dispensationis tenor sequitur, et est talis, &c.

Quidam Sanctionum et Canonum Ecclesiasticorum consulti, datam dictæ cum narratis ejusdem conferentes, aliasq; nonnullas circumstantias quæ tum ante dictæ Dispensationis impetrationem, quæ etiam post eandem impetratam intervenerunt, ponderantes, tum quod causa quæ in Bulla pretensa est pacis continuandæ, viz. quæ ipsa tum coaluerat, fœderibus percussis firma constiterat, mutuis etiam populorum commerciis aucta, nullum suæ violationis timorem incutiens, qui justus et non omnino vanus dici posset, nec urgentissima proinde nec evidentissima videretur, qualem prohibitionis relaxatio exigat et requirat; tum quod preces falsæ erant dum narrabatur Prædecessori nostro, eundem Charissimum Filium nostrum tum cupere cum dicta charissima Domina Catharina contrahere Matrimonium, ad hoc ut pacis fœdera diutius continuarentur, cum eo tempore, ut asserit, impetrationem prorsus ignoraret, et per ætatis immaturitatem, duodecimum, viz. annum non excedentis, affectum hujusmodi inducere non potuerat; tum quod Protestatione postmodum interveniente et vim Renunciationis habente, Dispensatio tunc per Renunciationem extincta videretur; Deniq; quod principes inter quos fœdera conservarentur, ante mandatam executioni Bullam fatis concesserant; Bullam ipsam, tum ex surreptionis et obreptionis vitiis, quam aliis etiam de Causis minus validam et inefficacem esse renunciarunt et retulerunt, scrupulum dicti Regis animo conscientiæq; gravem injicientes, eamq; illi opinionem inducentes, ut Matrimonium prædictum non consistere neq; hactenus jure constitisse judicaret. · Porro autem cum frequentius apud se, ut asserit, animo volveret ac meditaretur, quales exitus hujusmodi nuptiæ præfatæ habuerunt, ex quibus, viz. aliquot partus masculi imperfecti parumq; vitales prodiere, atq; ideo se omni spe successoris prorsus destitui, quo suam familiam ad paucos redactam conservaret, occurente simul memoriæ Divina interminatione quæ Fratris sui turpitudinem revelanti, et illius Uxorem contra S. Sancta Dei præcepta accipienti inscribitur, præsertim ubi Dispensatio non interveniat, quæ ex omni sua parte valeat et consistat,

nonnullis etiam affirmantibus nostram non eatenus pro-
testatem patere ut in ea specie gratiam faciamus, etiamsi ut
scribit de nostræ potestatis plenitudine non dubitet, juste
duntaxat legitimeq; interpositæ, quam summam in terris
agnoscit et veneratur, ad improbandas illas nuptias tantum
undiq; videt consensum ut illas animo abhorreat, nec aliorum rationibus posset dissuaderi quin abominandas eas
judicet, et Divinæ Majestati odiosas. Deniq; idem Caris-
simus Filius noster debita cum instantia nos precibus solli-
citaverit, quatenus personæ suæ et Regni nobis semper devotissimi rationem habentes, maturo judicio ab angustiis li-
beremus, quibus se usu præsentis Matrimonii per legem
conscientiæ privatum, nec ad aliud per leges publicas ante
sententiam admissum, vehementer conqueritur comprehen-
sum esse. Nos igitur considerantes quot, quanta, tum in
Sedem Apostolicam, tum in fidem Christianam officia præ
cæteris exhibuerit, promeritus eo nomine ut nostræ vicissim potestatis gratiam uberrimam et promptissimam referat, aliamq; illius causam atq; privati esse, ex qua nimirum pendeat salus plurimorum, nec posse dictæ causæ decisionem diutius proferri et protelari sine gravi discriminis
periculo, dicti vero Principis cruciatu maxima quæ nos ex
gratitudinis vicissitudine minueret debeamus, qua decet
festinatione procedi facientes ut ad finem celerrime per-
ducatur, de Consilio Fratrum nostrorum, quorum in hac
causa tam gravi atq; urgenti judicium adhibuimus, ac
etiam eorum quos et Sacræ Theologiæ peritissimos et juris
Ecclesiastici callentissimos desuper consulendos audien-
dosq; putavimus, quoniam vitia et defectus prædictos ejusmodi esse comperimus, quæ pensata præfatæ Prohibitionis
natura, vires ipsius Bullæ merito enervarent; quo magis,
viz. attestemur et palam faciamus, quanta animi cura et
solicitudine præfati Carissimi Filii nostri conscientiam
hujusmodi scrupulis et difficultatibus impediri, implicari
atq; vexari sustineamus, cum alioquin te dilectum Filium
nostrorum Cardin. Eboracen. in illa Provincia et Apostolicæ Sedis Legatum, a præclaris animi tui virtutibus, ad
justitiam vero et æquitatem propensissimo sincerissimoq;
affectu nobis sic commendatum et cognitum habeamus, ut
tibi merito soli omnem nostram Autoritatem, cum in hac
Causa expedienda, tum etiam in reliquis committendam

putaverimus, dignissimus quidem nobis existimatus, qui
partes nostras tractes et vices absentis posses supplere: Te
tamen Dilectum Filium——— a nobis specialiter istuc destin-
andum duximus, ut conjunctim in hac causa procedere possitis, ita nihilomimus propter incertum casuum eventum
mandatam Authoritatem temperantes, ut altero vestrum
nolente aut impedito alter omnia exequi et causam fine debito valeat terminare. Vobis ut præfertur conjunctim et
ut præfertur divisim, ad cognoscendum et procedendum
summarie et de plano, sine strepitu et figura judicii, ac de
et super viribus dictæ Bullæ sive Dispensationis inquirendum, ipsamq; Bullam sive Dispensationem, si de vitiis
prædictis aut eorum aliquo tali probatione constiterit, quæ
licet aliis minus clara videatur, animo tamen Religioso,
conscientiæq; vestræ, aut ejus vestrum qui in hac Causa
processerit, divisim ut præfertur, satisfecerit, et verisimile
apparuerit, vel pacem quæ in Bulla prætenditur sine hujus
Matrimonii contractu consistere potuisse et continuari, vel
dictum Charissimum Filium nostrum, ut allegabatur, non
cupiisse contrahere Matrimonium ad hoc ut pacis fœdera
conservarentur, vel deniq; Principes in Bulla nominatos,
inter quos fœdera per illud Matrimonium continuatum iri
allegabatur, ante mandatam executioni Bullam fatis concessisse, ipsam nullam, minus validam, ex surreptione et
obreptione inefficacem, irritam et inanem fuisse, semper et
esse pronuntiandam et declarandam ; Matrimonium autem
prædictum, quod ejusdem virtute consistere videtur, nullam simul ac minus legitimum esse, ac pro nullo minusq; legitimo haberi deberi decernendum ; ipsos porro contrahentes
ab omni contractu Matrimoniali hujusmodi liberos, a con-
sortio conjugali quod hactenus observarunt separari deberi,
sententiendum et autoritate nostra separandum. Deniq; utrumque ad contrahendum cum alio vel alia, novum conjugium ineundi, licentiam et facultatem tribuendum et concedendum, citra omnem recusationem, aut appellationis inter-
positionem, committimus et demandamus vices nostras ; ac
vos conjunctim, et altero vestrum nolente ut præfertur aut
impedito, divisim, ad præmissa exercenda et expedienda,
plenæ finaliq; executioni demandanda, Vicarios nostros et
nostrum Vicarium, aut si quo alio nomine uti poterimus,
quod demandatam in prædictis Autoritatem ampliaret, cum

omni potestatis plenitudine tam absolutæ quam ordinariæ,
quatenus vel ad præfati Matrimonii congruam dissolutionem, vel novi contrahendi firmam Constitutionem, expedire
videbitur aut pertinere ; ita etiam ut Autoritate præsentis
Commissionis nostræ, cum omnibus illis Canonibus, ad validiorem efficacioremq ; processus vestri firmitatem poteritis
dispensare, quæcunq ; eidem obstare putabuntur, omnemq ;
defectum quacunq; ex causa contingentem nostræ Autoritatis interpositione, Dispensatione Apostolica supplere possitis
et valeatis, tam prolem ex primo Matrimonio susceptam propter bonam fidem Parentum, si ita expedire visum fuerit,
legitimam decernendo, pronuntiando et promulgando, quam ex secundo Matrimonio suscipiendam ; legitimitatem
etiam utriusq ; prolis, censuris et pœnis Ecclesiasticis quibuscunque, per modum decreti aut Sanctionis perpetuæ
muniendo et vallando, omnibus validioribus et efficacióribus modis et formis quæ de jure concipi et excogitari
poterunt, facimus, constituimus et ordinamus per præsentes : et quicquid per vos conjunctim, ut præfertur, aut
divisim procedentes, per cognitionem judiciariam et summariam, aut extra judiciariam, processus quoscunq ; faciendo, pronunciando aut promulgando, eosdemve executioni mandando, Dispensationes quascunq ; aut gratias in
præmissis concedendo et faciendo, et generaliter in aliquibus prædictorum potestatem nostram vel ordinariam vel
absolutam exercendo, ut præfertur, actum, gestum, decretum, dispensatum, pronuntiatum, mandatum, aut executum
fuerit, id omne et totum, cum primum poterimus, ratum,
gratum et firmum habentes, in validissima et efficacissima
forma confirmabimus, nec eorum aliqua unquam infirmabimus aut infringemus, aut eorum alicui contraveniemus,
nec interim revocabimus ; declarantes etiam et protestantes
per præsentes, nostræ intentionis esse, ut præsens Commissio, sive Delegatio Autoritatis nostræ, perpetuo effectu
gaudeat, et usq ; ad finalem prædictorum conclusionem
extremumq ; terminum duret et consistat, non obstantibus
quibuscunq ; decretis, sententiis, mandatis, rescriptis, literis
aut Brevibus in contrarium, deinceps per nos tanquam irritatoriis, derogatoriis aut revocatoriis præsentis Concessionis
nostræ, emittendis, destinandis aut promulgandis ; quibus
omnibus expresse per præsentes derogantes, et illa omnia

pro nullis, cassis, irritis et inanibus reputantes, ac talia esse
et haberi, istisq; omnino anteriora judicari, præsentia vero
semper posteriora, et post illa repetita, emissa et destinata,
censeri ac tanquam ultima et posteriora contrariis sic deinceps emittendis derogare debere, et cæteris contrariis
non obstantibus quibuscunque.

BOOK
II.

XI·

The Cardinal's Letter to John Cassali about it; Taken from a Duplicate written by his Secretary.

REVERENDE Domine Protonotari, tanquam Frater Amantissime, cum aliis meis literis copiose ad vos perscripsi Regiæ Majestatis animum, et desiderium super his rebus quas
vobis in præsentia commisit, suo nomine S. D. N. decla-
randas.

Cotton
Libr.
Vitel.
B. 10.

Nunc vero ob humillimam sinceramq; meam Devotionem, quæ ex jure et officio non solum ejus Sanctitati, sed
miseris Ecclesiæ sublevandis rebus, dignitatiq; Apostolicæ
restituendæ adstringor, his literis vos instruam super quibusdam rebus, præcipue et accurate notandis et considerin-
dis, quas post humillimam, reverentissimamq; meam Commendationem dictæ Sanctitati, meo nomine sigillatim, spe-
ciatim declarabitis; et cum causam concernant, quam Regia Majestas nunc maxime optat et requirit, eandem Sanctitatem vehementissime rogabitis, ut cuncta legere et bene
notare non gravetur.

Primo itaq; indolens infælicem adversumq; præsentium
rerum successum, in quo S. D. N. Cardinaliumq: Collegium versatur, diuq; ac noctu mente volvens, quo pacto
quibusve modis, totis meis viribus, omni sumptu molestiaq;
neglecta, et cum proprii sanguinis vitæq: effusione, ministerium aliquod impendere, tantæq; afflictioni solamen afferre, et Ecclesiæ Sanctissimi Domini nostri collapso statui
opitulari, in quam rem haud dubie quoadq; vita suppetet
incumbam; mihiq; in hac cogitatione versanti, in mentem
recordationemq; subiit, mirus quidem et grandis affectus,

qui Divina sic disponente Providentia, ex instanti assiduaq;
mea opera provenit, ut hunc optimum Dominum meum
Regem inducerem, eique persuaderem quod ad arctissimam
istam intimamq; cordis et animi conjunctionem deveniret
erga, S. D. N. Ecclesiæq; et sedis Apostolicæ tutelam ac
patrocinium suscipiendum, memoriæq; succurrunt innu-
meræ rationes a me adductæ, ut Regiam Majestatem, quæ
Cæsari tenacissime inhærebat, adducerem, ad S. D. N. defensionem, rerumq; Italicarum tutelam amplectendam, ac
inter omnes allegatas rationes, nulla fuit validior aut vehe-
mentior, vel quæ Regiæ Majestatis pectus magis permo-
veret, quam intima securitas, perfectaq; constantia, quam
ei assidue indesinenterq; insinuavi de ejus Sanctitatis vera
optimaq; et flagranti correspondentia in amore perpetuo
indissolubiliq; amicitia, animo et voluntate, petitionibus
semper suæ R. Majest. et desideriis concedendis, quoad
Ecclesiæ Thesaurus et Autoritas ejus Sanctitati Christi
Vicario concessa permittit, vel quoad se extendit, seu possit
extendere; super idq; omnia uberrime promisi, meam etiam
salutem, fidem, honorem animamque adstringens, quod
omnia ex ipsius Regiæ Majestatis votis, in omne tempus
præstarentur, absq; ulla prorsus occasione aut scrupulo,
ab hujusmodi indulgendis petitionibus digrediendi, adeo
quod Regia Majestas, ex hoc meo asseveranti relatu, hunc
propensum S. D. N. in se animum perspiciens, mihiq; ejus
Sanctitatis nomine, veluti Legato, et Sedis Apostolicæ
membro loquenti, firmam, certamq; fidem adhibens, periculis omnibus posthabitis, laboribus sumptibusq; spretis,
nullaq; sui Regni aut subditorum habita ratione, animum
adfixit, prorsusq; statutum et decretum in omnibus se adjungere, atq; perpetuo et constanter cum S. D. N. in affectu concurrere, in eoq; certum habeo velle decrevisseq;
perstare, ad mortem usque, nisi forsan ex eventibus, longe
diversis a meo promisso et ejus expectatione, occasio sub-
ministretur suam Regiam Majestatem ab hoc animi sui decreto amovendi. Id si illi accideret (quod avertat Deus)
merito mihi posset adscribere perfidiam, levitatem, viola-
tionemq; promissionis, quo casu quid mox officii aut mi-
nisterii possem Sanctissimo Domino nostro præstare, aut
quæ fides in Ecclesiæ rebus mihi haberetur, singulari ejus
Sanctitatis prudentiæ judicandum relinquo: nunquam enim

meo in arbitrio posthac esset, quicquam alicujus momenti hinc efficere, in ejus Sanctitatis commodum, hac nunc in re Regiæ Majestatis concepta spe, aut expectatione frustrata.

Est secundo accurate considerandum quantopere hoc negotium Regiæ Majestati intersit, et quanti sit momenti, unde namque, præter Conscientiæ Regiæ exonerationem, omnis quoq; Regiæ lineæ, et stemmatis continuatio pendet; huic adnectitur totius Regni fælicitas, vel excidium, hic securitas et salus eorum consistit, qui sub Regis sunt Imperio, et qui ullo unquam tempore nascentur in ejus Regno, qua ex re oriri potest occasio, et fomes tranquillitatis perpetuæ, aut discordiæ belliq; atrocissimi in universum Christianum orbem, quæ omnia majoris sunt momenti, et vigilantius prospicienda quam cujusq; Principis vel Principissæ gratia, favor et expectatio.

Tertio, Causa ex se est hujusmodi ut in animam meam spondere ausim, ejus concessionem, futuram non solum in conscientiæ, honorisq; Pontificis exonerationem coram Deo et hominibus, sed in Cœlis quoq; gratam, acceptamq; extituram: In hac deinde re secreta insunt nonnulla, secreto S. D. N. exponenda, et non credenda literis, quas ob causas, morbosq; nonnullos, quibus absq; remedio Regina laborat, et ob animi etiam conceptum scrupulum, Regia Majestas nec potest, nec vult ullo unquam posthac tempore, ea uti, vel ut Uxorem admittere, quodcunque advenerit. Non exigua præterea habenda est ratio eorum, quæ aliis meis literis continentur, concernentia, quæ pro ingenti thesauro S. D. N. habere queat, tam certam Regiæ Majestatis amicitiam, cum ejus Sanctitate constantissime conjunctam futuram in prosperis et adversis, in quas etiam partes amicos suos omnes pertraxit, et assidue pertrahit: ad Ecclesiæ defensionem, Sanctissimi Domini nostri conservationem, causas omnes suas et actiones dirigens; possentq; hi omnes, Regia Majestate deficiente, in contrarium verti, et, ut vera loquar, nullum Principem video in quo S. D. N. possit, quam in Regia Majestate plenius aut perfectius confidere, vel cujus medio Apostolicæ sedis status in pristinam suam dignitatem queat certius restitui, cum absq; ejus subsidio, nisi solus Deus ex immensa sua bonitate manum citissime apponat, omnino imminutus iri videatur. Quod si Sanctissimus Dominus noster nunc (quod

absit) in his Regiis petitionibus durum se, aut difficilem se
exhibuerit, mihi certe molestissimum est futurum vivere
diutius, ob innumera mala, quæ inde subsecutura videntur,
hoc præsertim firmo, tutoq; Regio subsidio tam ingrate
abjecto; hocq : solum, et certum, et salubre remedium videtur tantæ corrigendæ calamitati superesse, quo neglecto
omnia corruant necesse est. Hac autem in re S. D. N. sua
erga Regiam Majestatem animi gratitudine comprobata,
poterit de illius amicitia et conjunctione quæcunq; volet
sibi polliceri, adversus eos omnes, qui ejus Autoritatem aut
dignitatem voluerint oppugnare. Tandem his causis ra-
tionibusq; omnibus in unum congestis, mecum ipse repu-
tans, quam multa gravissimi momenti in hujus conjugii
Dissolutione occurrant, in tanta æquitate justoq; fundamento posita, ob quæ hæc Dissolutio nec possit absq; gravissimo detrimento, nec debeat diutius protrahi aut inter-
mitti; videns quoq: quid allegari possit et allegabitur
omnino ad Regiæ Majestatis conscientiam coram Deo pur-
gandam, etiamsi id a S. D. N. neutiquam admittatur, quæ
in hujusmodi allegationibus confisa, vereor ne in tanta rerum extremitate constitûta, potius quam ingentia mala, quæ
hinc apertissime imminent, succedant, dicta Regia Majestas
ex duobus malis minus malum eligat, et soli suæ puræq;
conscientiæ innitens, id agat, quod nunc tam reverenter a
Sedis Apostolicæ Authoritate exigit, unde Sedis contempt-
us indies gravior excresceret, hoc præsertim tempore admodum periculoso : quæ omnia sunt a S. D. N. summa sua
prudentia alte consideranda, nullo prorsus dubio aut difficultate in re tam gravi mature concedenda interjecta; nec
eam retardare debet cujusquam mortalis instantia, con-
templatio vel satisfactio, præsertim quum in multis aliis rebus, forsan non tam manifestis et apparentibus, Sanctitas
sua liberalem, facilemq; erga alios se sæpe præstiterit ;
cui humillima reverentia præmissa meo nomine dicetis,
quod hæc loquor tamquam fidele, utcunq; Ecclesiæ indignum membrum, omnia excogitans quæ possent in Ecclesiæ
augmentum et existimationem cedere, ea etiam admovens
et consulens ut evitentur, quæ cessura videantur in contrarium. Quocirca Sanctissimo Domino nostro affirmabitis,
quod præmissis omnibus tam maximi momenti existentibus
probe consideratis, non veluti Mediator aut Intercessor, ob

privatum illum affectum quem Regiæ Majestatis causis, ut
mei juris est, promovendis gero, sed tanquam is qui in re
tanta et ex tam certa scientia et cognitione, velim Sanctissimo Domino nostro suadere, ut quod nunc petitur omnino
concedat, idque suaderem etiam si in hoc Regnum nunquam
venissem, neq; hic commune quicquam haberem; rogoque,
precor, et obtestor ejus Sanctitatem, ut omni dubio, respectu, metuq; deposito, nullo pacto neget aut differat ea
concedere aut adnuere, quæ Regia Majestas urgentissimas
ob causas tanta nunc animi sollicitudine exposcit; sed his
potius benignius liberaliterq; adnuat, et omnia concedere
non gravetur in pleniorem modum qui hujus rei gratia possit excogitari, compertissimumq; sibi sua Sanctitas habeat,
se id effecturum, quod coram Deo et hominibus justum omnino habebitur, actissimeque Regiam Majestatem devinciet
ad suæ Sanctitatis, Ecclesiæ Apostolicæque Sedis, causas-
que omnes pro viribus juvandas protegendasque, nec ea in
re, ulli labori, sumptui, Regno vel subditis parcet nec (si
opus fuerit) propriam Personam exponere recusabit, in ea
opinione constantissime permansura, in eandemque sententiam Gallorum Regem et alios confæderatos attrahet,
tum pro suæ Sanctitatis et Cardinalium liberatione, tum
pro Sedis Apostolicæ Authoritatis et dignitatis restitu-
tione; et præterquam quum dicta Sanctitas mei humil-
limæ suæ Creaturæ fidem et existimationem conservabit,
quo in omnem eventum et necessitatem ea possim hic facilius commodiusq; tractare quæ in Ecclesiæ commodum,
beneficium et securitatem cessura videbuntur, in quæ officia omnem meam industriam, zelum, studiumq; adhibe-
bo, hunc quoq; Serenissimum Regem in perpetuum sibi
lucrifaciet. Quod si harum rerum rationem non habuerit,
vereor ne sit futurum in mea potestate, ut ullo modo hanc
Regiam Majestatem vel alium ullum Principem ad ea ad-
ducam, quæ Sanctissimo Domino nostro solatio aut subsidio esse possunt. Sed confido ab ipsius Sanctitate tantam
malorum occasionem sublatam iri, gratissimo, benignissimo,
liberrimoq; animo, omnia ut petuntur concessuram esse,
nullo objecto impedimento, contradictione aut mora.

XII.

Romæ Jan. 20. 1528.

*Staphileus's Letter to the Cardinal, that shews how much
he was persuaded of the Justice of the King's Cause. The
Original.*

Cotton
Libr.
Vitell.
B. 10.

REVERENDISSIME et illustrissime Domine D. mihi colendissime, post humillimam commendationem D. V. Reverend. dignabitur intelligere, qualiter quintadecima die
post recessum nostrum a Londino conscendimus navem,
retenti interim in portu ob tempestatem Maris et contrarios
ventos: interim in itinere fui cum Reverendo Domino
Roffen. et disputavimus materiam multum, copiose, et satis
prolixe, in præsentia Domini Doctoris Marmeduci, qui
intellexit omnia ex utraq; parte ab utroque dicta et sæpius
replicata; penes quem autem steterit victoria, vel saltem,
uter nostrum validius certaverit, D. V. Reverend. perci-
piet ex fideli relatione præfati D. Marmeduci. Unum cer-
tifico D. V. Reverend. quod pro uno mediocri Episcopatu
desiderassem quod huic nostræ Disputationi interfuisset
Serenissimus Rex noster et D. V. et Regina, pro intelligentia veritatis et pro modo disputandi: etenim commendo
humiliter D. V. Reverend. istum bonum virum, bonum ser-
vitorem ac diligentem Serenissimæ Regiæ Majestatis et
D. V. Reverendiss. Quibus me quoq; humillimum ac ex
toto devotissimum eorum servum quam humillime possum
ex toto corde meo semper commendo, præstiturus utriq;
fideliss. et amantiss. obsequium in rebus et negotiis mihi
commissis et committendis. Bene valeat D. V. Reverendiss. quæ dignabitur tenere me semper in bona gratia Serenissimi Regis nostri, qui est decus et ornamentum Regiæ Dignitatis. Ex Bononia 20 Jan. 1528.

D. V. Reverendiss.

Humillimus Servitor Episcopus
Staphileus.

XIII.

Ad Campegium, 1528.

The Cardinal's Letter to Campegius, taken from the Draught of it; Corrected with his own hand.

REVERENDISSIME in Christo Pater, grata semper huic Regiæ Majestati extiterunt Vestræ Reverend. Dominat. officia, sed gratissimum omnium illud fuit, quod tanta fide et sedulitate in ipsius promovenda causa ab ea fuisse præstitum ex Reverendi Domini Jerdonen. sermone cognovit: quam optimi amoris significationem toto pectore amplexatur, jussitq; ut suis nominibus ingentes vestræ Reverendissimæ D. gratias haberemus : Cui ego eo quoq; nomine maxime quoq; me debere fateor, nulla enim in re magis obnoxium me sibi potest efficere, quam si totis suis viribus, omni gratia et Authoritate adnitatur, quo negotium hoc ex Regiæ Majestatis sententia quam citissime conficiatur ; hujusmodi enim est ut nullum gravius possit accidere, dilationem nullam patitur, utpote quod totius hujus Regni conservationem, Regiæ sobolis continuationem et ejus animi salutem in se contineat: causa quidem manifestior est quam disputatione egeat, et sanctior quam debeat in controversiam adduci, hanc unam gratiam et nunc primum a Sede Apostolica votis omnibus petit, et eam tum ex rei justitia, tum ex sua in S. D. N. filiali devotione, spem concepit, ut nullo pacto sibi persuadeat unquam fieri posse ut sua expectatione frustretur, quam scit vestræ R. D. opera ac pio patrocinio maxime posse juvari.

Iterum igitur atq; iterum Reverendissimam D. vestram obsecro, ut postquam recenti et claro hoc testimonio purgavit quicquid antea in Regiam Majestatem fide sinistre fuerat ad nos delatum, et nostrum animum sibi totum devinxit, non gravetur nunc strenue in hoc Regio promovendo negotio ad optatum usq; finem perseverare, quod ita cor nostrum premit, ut vel proprio sanguine id vellemus posse a S. D. N. impetrare. Cætera, vestra Reverendissima D. uberius ac distinctius cognoscet ex Reverendo Domino Episcopo Jerdonensi, et ex Domino Stephano Gardinero intimo meo servo, et Domino Edwardo Foxo Regio familiari, quibus rogo ut certissimam in omnibus fidem velit habere. Et fælicissime valeat.

Cotton
Libr.
Vitell.
B. 10.

XIV.

Maii 7. 1528.

*The Cardinal's Letter to G. Cassali, desiring a Decretal
Bull to be sent over. A Duplicate.*

MAGNIFICE Domine Gregori, &c. Ingentem Serenissima Regia Majestas et ego lætitiam concepimus, quum tum ex Domini Stephani literis, tum vero ex Domini Foxi relatu cognovimus, quanta fide, industria, ac vigilantia. usi sitis in ejusdem Regiæ Majestatis conficiendo negotio, quem vestrum animum, etsi sæpe antea arduis in rebus exploratissimum certissimumq; haberemus, hoc tamen tam claro testimonio nihil a vobis omissum perspicimus, quod votum nostrum utcunq; juvare potuisset. Cæterum quum nonnulla adhuc meo aliorumq; Doctiss. virorum judicio superesse videantur, ad Regiæ Majestatis causam securissime stabiliendam finiendamq; de quibus ad D. Stephanum in præsentia perscribo; Vos iterum atq; iterum rogo, ut de illis impetrandis apud S. D. N. una cum Domino Stephano vestram gratiam et Authoritatem, quam apud ejus Sanctitatem maximam esse et audio et gaudeo, pro viribus interponatis, maxime autem ut in Commissione illa Decretali a S. D. N. nullis Arbitris seu consultoribus admissis concedenda, et secreto ad me mittenda, omnes vires ingenii, prudentiæ diligentiæq; vestræ adhibeatis, affirmabitisq; et in salutem animamq; meam eidem S. D. N. spondebitis, quod dictam Bullam secretissime nullis mortalium oculis conspiciendam apud me asservabo, tanta fide et cautione, ut ne minimum quidem ex ea re periculum, vel periculi metum ejus Sanctitas sit sensura; non enim eo consilio aut animo eam Commissionem impetrari tam vehementer cupio, ut vel illius vigore ullius processus aut aliud præterea quicquid ageretur, vel eadem publice privatimve legere illa ulli exhiberetur, sed ut hac quasi arrha et pignore summæ paternæq; S. D. N. erga Regiam Majestatem benevolentiæ apud me deposito, quum videat nihil illi denegaturum quod petiverit, perspiciatq; tantum fidei ejus Sanctitatem in me reposuisse, sic mea apud dictam Majestatem augeatur Authoritas, ut quanquam vires omnes suas opesq; Apostolicæ Sedis conservationi et in pristinum statum reparationi sic sponte dicaverit, me tamen suasore et consultore omnia in posterum, et in sanguinis effusionem sit concessura, et effectura, quæ in ejusdem Sedis et suæ Beatitudinis securitatem, tranquillitatem et commodum, quaquam ratione cedere poterunt.

XV.

The Brieve of Pope Julius for the King's Marriage ;
suspected to be forged.

JULIUS Papa Secundus. Dilecte Fili et dilecta in Christo Cotton Libr. Vitel. B. 12. Filia, salutem et Apostolicam Benedictionem. Romani Pontificis præcellens Authoritas concessa sibi desuper utitur potestate, prout (personarum, negotiorum et temporum qualitate pensata) id in Domino conspicit expedire. Oblatæ nobis nuper pro parte vestra petitionis series continebat, quod cum alias tu Filia Catharina, et tunc in humanis agens quondam Arthurus Carissimi in Christo Filii nostri Henrici Angliæ Regis illustrissimus primogenitus, pro conservandis pacis et amicitiæ nexibus et fœderibus inter præfatum Angliæ Regem, et Carissimum in Christo Filium nostrum Ferdinandum Regem, et Carissimam in Christo Filiam nostram Elizabeth. Reginam Catholicos Hispaniarum et Siciliæ, Matrimonium per verba legitime de præsenti contraxeritis, *illudque carnali copula consummaveritis,* quia tamen Dominus Arthurus, prole ex hujusmodi Matrimonio non suscepta, decessit, et hujusmodi vinculum pacis et connexitatis inter præfatos Reges et Reginam ita firmiter verisimiliter non perduraret, nisi etiam illud alio affinitatis vinculo confoveretur et confirmaretur, ex his et certis aliis causis, desideratis Matrimonium inter vos per verba legitime de præsenti contrahere : Sed quia desiderium vestrum in præmissis adimplere non potestis, Dispensatione Apostolica desuper non obtenta, nobis propterea humiliter supplicari fecistis, ut vobis providere in præmissis de Dispensationis gratia et benignitate Apostolica dignaremur. Nos igitur qui inter singulos Christi fideles, præsertim Catholicos Reges et Principes, pacis et concordiæ

BOOK
II. amænitatem vigere intensis desideriis affectamus, his et aliis
causis animum nostrum moventibus, hujusmodi supplicationibus inclinati, vobiscum, ut aliquo impedimento affinitatis hujusmodi ex præmissis proveniente non obstante Matrimonium inter vos contrahere, et in eo postquam contractum fuerit, remanere, libere et licite valeatis, Authoritate
Apostolica per præsentes Dispensamus; et quatenus forsan
jam Matrimonium inter vos de facto publice vel clandestine
contraxeritis, ac carnali copula consummaveritis, vos et
quemlibet vestrum ab excessu hujusmodi, ac Excommunicationis sententia quam propterea incurristis, eadem Authoritate absolvimus, ac etiam vobiscum ut in hujusmodi Matrimonio sic de facto contracto remanere, seu illud de novo
contrahere, inter vos libere et licite valeatis, similiter Dispensamus, prolem ex hujusmodi Matrimonio sive contracto
sive contrahendo suscipiendam legitimam decernendo. Volumus autem, si hujusmodi Matrimonium de facto contraxistis, Confessor, per vos et quemlibet vestrum eligendus,
pænitentiam, quam adimplere teneamini, propterea vobis
injungat. Dat. Romæ apud Sanctum Petrum sub annulo
Piscatoris, die 26 Decemb. millesimo quingentesimo tertio.
Pont. nostri Anno primo.

Sigismundus.

XVI.

*A part of the Cardinal's Letter to G. Cassali, desiring leave
to shew the Decretal Bull to some of the King's Council.
A Duplicate.*

Cott.
Libr.
Vitel.
B. 10. ILLUD igitur video maxime necessarium superesse ut Decretalis Bulla, quam Reverendissimus Dominus Legatus
secum defert, secreto legenda exhibeatur nonnullis exRegis
Consultoribus, eo quidem consilio, non ut in judicium proferatur, vel ad causam definiendam adhibeatur, sed solum
ut perspicientes illi, quorum prudentia et Autoritas non parva est, nihil a me fuisse omissum, quod causam Regis possit securissimam redere, omniaq; fuisse a S. D. N. concessa, quæ in causæ firmamentum ullo pacto queant exco-

gitari facilius, ubi Regiæ Majestatis securitati, Regni quieti, et perpetuo totius rei stabilimento undiq; consultum
viderint, in sententiam nostram deveniant, summaq; cum
diligentia in AutoritateApostolica ad Dei gloriam conjuncta
rectissime absolvantur. Proinde, Domine Gregori, iterum
atq; iterum vos impense rogo, quod ad S. D. N. genua de-
voluti ejus Beatitudinem meo nomine obsecretis, ut hoc reliquum meæ fidei meæq; dexteritati de BullaDecretali ostend-
enda committere velit, quam rem sic moderabor, ut nullum
prorsus periculum, nullum damnum, nullum odium queat
unquam sibi, vel Sedi Apostolicæ provenire; hocq; tam
instanter precor, ut pro salute mea conservanda petere
queam ardentius nihil.

XVII.

*John Cassali's Letter about a Conference he had with the
Pope. An Original.*

*Reverendissime ac Illustrissime Domine D. mi Colendissime,
&c.*

Quum Tabellarius D. Vestræ Reverendissimæ cum ejus
mandatis literisq; die 2. Novemb. datis Bononiam ad Equitem fratrem pervenisset, neq; ipse tunc posset præ debili-
tate properatis itineribus Romam venire, ne ad eam rem
longioris temporis moram interponeret, misit per dispositos
equos D. Vicentium Cassalium fratrem nostrum patruelem,
volens ipsum statim subsequi; venit igitur D. Vincentius
Cassalius. At ego Vestræ Dominationis Reverendissimæ
literis lectis ac perpensis, S. D. N. adivi, et ea quæ D. V.
Reverendissima scripserat, diligenter ejus Sanctitati exposui, ipsasq; etiam literas recitavi, quæ prudentissime et
efficacissime omnia explicabant. Atq; hujusmodi verbis
sum loquutus.

Non locus hic nec tempus postulat, Beatissime Pater, ut
ego nunc commemorem, quanto amore, quanto animi affectu, quibusq; officiis illa Regia Majestas Apostolicam
Sedem Sanctitatemq; Vestram sit ubique omni tempore

prosequuta, quantaq; observantia et fide Reverendissimus
Dominus Eboracen. semper coluerit; nec recensendum hic
videtur, quot labores, quot incommoda subiverint, quæ officia, quas multoties impensas effecerint, quærentes Ecclesiasticum statum, Christianam Religionem, et Catholicam
Fidem protegere ac conservare: Nec vestra Sanctitas ig-
norare debet, quibus laboribus, quantis precibus, quot ta-
bellariis, quot oratoribus missis, quot non dicam literis,
sed voluminibus conscriptis, post multa insuper Jurisperitorum consilia, tum ex Anglia allata, tum hic etiam for-
mata, fuerit tandem a vestra Sanctitate impetratum, ut res
eo, quo fuit pacto, componeretur: Qua ratione Regiæ Majestatis desiderio indulgebatur, et Beatitudinis vestræ honori ac conscientiæ, justitiæq; et æquitati consulebatur:
At nunc Sanctitas Vestra animadvertit illos, præter omnium nostrum spem et opinionem, omni auxilio penitus esse
destitutos: Reverendiss. Campegius non modo non ostendit, se adeo urgentibus precibus Serenissimi Regis obtemperare velle, sed ut primum ad Colloquium venit, rem totam pervertit, Regiam Majestatem a Divortio dissuasit,
perinde ac si ei Legatio demandata fuerit, ut Serenissimo
Regi ex parte Reginæ persuadere debeat, ut se a Divortio
abstineat, adeo ut non possit Regia Majestas stimulum
hunc Conscientiæ ex suo pectore evellere, semperq; in ea
mentis perturbatione illi sit permanendum, ut omnibus
horis cogitet successorem sui Regni ex suo sanguine defu-
turum.   Neq; adhuc Reverendissimus Campegius ullam
significationem dedit, velle se ad id exequendum descendere, quod priore illa generali Commissione continetur;
verum, quod pejus etiam est, quum multis precibus Bulla
Decretalis in hac causa Regia impetrata fuerit, promise-
ritq; Vestra Sanctitas se permissurum ut Serenissimo Regi
ac Reverendiss. D. Eboracen. ostenderetur, et eorum manibus crederetur, quam ipsi aliquibus ex Secretissimis Consiliariis ostenderent, ut Serenissimus Rex de totius negotii
æquitate instructior fieret, noluit Reverendissimus Campegius eam credere Serenissimo Regi, aut Reverendissimo
Domino Eboracen. suo in ea causa Collegæ. Cur autem
velit Vestra Sanctitas Regiam Majestatem in eam spem
adduxisse, ut deinde hoc pacto illam frustretur ac deludat.
Tunc S. D. N. injecta in meum brachium manu, me ulteri-

us loqui prohibuit, se ira accensum non abscondens, dixit,
Non parum sibi de D. V. Reverendissima conquerendum
esse, atque sub ejus fide se deceptum esse; Bullam Decretalem dedisse, ut tantum Regi ostenderetur, concremare-
turq; statim: ad hoc me (inquit) multis ille magnisque precibus protraxit, ostendens, si id non daretur, manifestam
suæ saluti ruinam impendere; nunc autem eam Bullam,
quæ debuit esse Secretissima, vult divulgare, neq; unquam
se promisisse concessurum ut Consiliariis ostendatur: literas (inquit) ipsas Reverendissimi Eboracen. proferre possum, quibus id tantum, quod dixi, petit, et ipsum Equitem Cassalium testem volo, quod Dominus Stephanus Gardinerus et ipse nil aliud a me postulaverunt, nec si postu-
lassent, quicquam amplius obtinuissent; atq; utinam aliter
rem petissent, eam namq; facile denegassem, nec ad hanc
pœnitentiam venissem, ex qua vel unius digiti jactura (modo fieri possit) quod factum fuit revocarem, video enim
quantum mali ex eo mihi subeundum sit. Quum S. D. N.
hæc et similia contra suum morem dixisset, ego in eam sententiam subsequutus, sciendum esse, quod D. V. Reverendissima petit, non esse ab eo, quod ejus Sanctitas constitutum fuisse dicit alienum, nec D. V. Reverendissima hanc
rem divulgari velle, aut secundum eam Bullam sententiam
ferri: Cæterum Regiæ Majestati et sibi tradi, ut possent
aliquibus fidelioribus carioribusq; Consiliariis ostendere,
ut ipsi de re tota fiant instructiores, quod perinde arcanum
erit, ac si in nullius notitiam devenisset. An non (inquam)
Sanctitas Vestra plerosq; habet, quibus quum aliquid arcanum crediderit, putet id non minus celatum esse, quam si
uno tantum pectore contineretur, quod multo magis Serenissimo Angliæ Regi evenire debet, cui singuli in suo Regno sunt subjecti, neq; etiamsi velint, possunt Regi non esse
fidelissimi: Væ namq; illis si vel parvo momento ab illius
voluntate recederent, quid hoc præterea obesse potest? an
non sic petitum, sic constitutum fuit? quæ ratio Sanctitatem Vestram propositum mutare cogit? Ibi Pontifex ira-
cundus, et concitatior etiam quam paulo ante; Haud (inquit) ita fuit constitutum, nec me latet, quid de ea Bulla
facere cogitent et cujusmodi ex eo mihi damnum redunda-
turum sit; firmum igitur illud habeatis, me decrevisse,
neq; sententiam muto, nolle quicquam amplius hac in re

permittere. At ego, nolit (quæso) Vestra Sanctitas sic ex
certa animi sententia loqui, ac potius in his literis Reverendissimi Domini Eboracen. consideret damna, ruinas,
hæreses, quæ Vestræ Sanctitatis culpa in illo Regno ori-
rentur: Regia enim Majestas male a Vestra Beatitudine
tractata, injuria, et ignominia affecta, studium et voluntatem, quam semper optimam in Sedem Apostolicam habuit,
in contrariam partem convertere posset, hoc est Domina-
tioni Vestræ toto pectore considerandum. Esto quod de
hujus negotii æquitate disceptatum non sit, concedamus
etiam hanc rem malam, et mali exempli futuram (quod
quidem secus esse judicaverunt omnes) an non Vestra Sanctitas novit pleraq; quæ non bona sunt præferri nonnunquam a nobis solere, no pejora patiamur; atq; hoc tum
aliis in rebus, tum imprimis hæresium evitandarum causa
providendum est, quas videmus, quum semel altiores radices egerint, non posse amplius extirpari: atq; ibi ad illius pedes genibus flexis, eam precibus omnibus sum obtes-
tatus, ut amicitiam potentissimi Regis conservare, observantiam Dominationis Vestræ Reverendissimæ erga ejus
Sanctitatem, nostramq; servitutem respicere vellet; relicta namq: Regiæ Majestatis amicitia, religionis immi-
nutio subsequeretur, et Regni illius a tam antiqua cum
Sede Apostolica conjunctione dissolutio, ac Dominationis
Vestræ Reverendissimæ gratia et Autoritas apud Sereniss.
Regem non suo merito deficeret ejusq; fortasse salus pe-
riclitaretur; Nos autem qui semper Beatitudini Vestræ
inservivimus, pro qua tot bonis officiis functi sumus, et tantum operæ perfecimus, ad integram amicitiam inter Regiam Majestatem et Vestram Sanctitatem conservandam,
in medio nostrarum actionum, Regni illius damna et cala-
mitatem, nostramq; certissimam ruinam conspiceremus.
Ad hæc S. D. N. et brachiorum et totius corporis agita-
tione, animum commotum ostendens, Volo (inquit) ego
ruinam, quæ mihi modo immineat considerare, et idipsum
quod feci valde me angit; Si hæreses, vel alia mala ori-
tura sunt, quænam in eo mea culpa erit, satis meæ conscientiæ fuerit me vacasse culpa, cui essem obnoxius, si hoc
etiam quod nunc ex me petitur concederem: Nec Reverendissimus Dominus Eboracensis, nec vos ullam causam
de me conquerendi habetis, quicquid nunc pollicitus sum

præstiti, neq; aliud unquam, etsi mihi faciendi esset facultas, Regia Majestas et Reverendissimus Dominus Eboracen. a me petierunt, quod non promptissime concesserim, ut quisq; facile intelligat, quanti eos semper fecerim; ad aliqua etiam Vestri causa faciliorem me præbui. Cæterum ubi vertitur meæ conscientiæ integritas omnia posthabenda censeo, agant per se ipsi quod volunt, Legatum remittant eo prætextu, quod in causam ulterius procedi nolint, et deinceps ut ipsi volent rem conficiant, modo ne me autore injuste quicquam agatur. Tunc ego, Nonne Vestra Sanctitas vult, ut ex vigore Commissionis procedatur? quod quum velle affirmasset, dixi, igitur Reverendissimus Campegius Sanctitatis Vestræ voluntati adversatur, Divortium enim Regi dissuasit; At Pontifex, ego (inquit) illi imposui, ut Divortium Regi dissuaderet, persuaderet Reginæ; quod autem ad Commissionem pertinet, si requiratur, exequetur. Sumus ergo (inquam) concordes, Beatissime Pater, quod quum ita sit, quid nocere poterit Decretalem Bullam aliquibus secretissimis ac juramento addactis Consiliariis ostendisse: Tum quassans caput, Scio (inquit) quid de ea facere constituant, verum nondum Campegii literas ex Anglia legi, quapropter die crastino ad me redibitis. Hoc pacto S. D. N. primo die me dimisit. Adfuit his sermonibus Dominus Vincentius Cassalius, quem ob equitem fratrem huc missum dixi, qui equitem ipsum excusavit, quod quamvis ille animadverteret negotium hoc tanti momenti esse, ut etiam cum vitæ discrimine Romam per dispositos equos sibi properandum esse videret, nihilominus supersedisse videns quod si id fecisset necesse sibi futurum domi, et in lectulo permanere potius, quam de re tanta coram ejus Sanctitate agere. Atque interim Dominus Vincentius multas rationes ad persuadendum, equitis Cassalii nomine adhibuit, quas eodem pacto ejus Sanctitas in sequentem diem rejecit.

Postridie ejus diei signatura habita est, cui ego tanquam referendarius interfui, in vesperumq; est protracta, nec judicavi opportunum Pontificem signaturæ munere defessum aggredi, quum præsertim ejus Sanctitas diceret se nondum Campegii literas perlegisse. Res igitur iterum in diem proximum rejecta fuit, quo postea horam commodam nactus Pontificem adivi, quumq; omnium Capitum, quæ D.V.

Reverendissimæ literis continebantur, quasi summam effecissem, ne quicquam per oblivionem præterirem, ab ea primum parte cœpi, in qua dicitur suam Sanctitatem concessisse Commissionem generalem in amplissima forma, et promisisse ferendam sententiam, se ratificaturum. Pontifex hoc verum esse affirmavit, dicens se contentum esse, ut ad sententiam procedatur; Qua vero parte est, ejus Sanctitatem Bullam Decretalem concessisse, ut secretiores Regiæ Majestatis Consiliarios instrueret, id a veritate longe remotum dixit, posseq; ad id se literas D. V. Reverendissimæ ostendere: Atque ea repetivit, quæ priore die super hoc dixerat, viz. Dominum Stephanum Gardinerum et Equitem Cassalium se testes habere, hanc Bullam non ea conditione petitam fuisse ut ostenderetur cuiquam, præterquam Serenissimo Regi et D. V. Reverendissimæ, et Campegium nunc ad se scribere tantundem effecisse, quo facto ex conventione Bullam comburi debere, promissurum quoq; se dixit, ut si quæ allegantur, probentur, ad sententiam ferendam procedatur, se id ratum habiturum. Quumq; ego quæsissem an vellet, quæ fierent per eam Bullam comprobare, minime id oportere dixit; negavit quoq; eam Consiliariis ostendendam esse, qui tametsi rem bonam non judicarent, approbarent tamen super ejus Sanctitatis Conscientiam; ac sæpius interim repetivit, non esse amplius in ea re commorandum. Ad aliam igitur partem deveni, in qua D. V. Reverendissima dicit, Reverendissimum Campegium Divortium inter Regem Serenissimum et Reginam conatum dissuadere: Tum Pontifex Campegium scribere dixit, eo se etiam functurum officio, ut Reginæ Divortium persuaderet, quam ab eo alienam invenerit; modeste tamen eam, ait, locutam fuisse, et Consiliarios petiisse, qui ex Hispania denegati fuerint, ex Flandria autem concessi. Dixit etiam S. D. N. se literas ad Regem, Reverendissimo Campegio ex suo Chirographo dedisse, ut Regia Majestas fidem his haberet quæ Reverendissimus Campegius suæ Sanctitatis nomine diceret. Ad illam deinde partem deveni, ubi est: Causam Regis perinde differt, ac si nolit ad judicium, sententiamq; in partem suæ Majestatis ferendam descendere, donec S. D. N. certiorem prius effecerit, de his ad hanc causam concernentibus, quæ ibi vidit et audivit. Ad hæc respondit, Campegium quandocunq; requisitus fuerit, processurum, neq; de supersedendo Commissionem habere; se tantum injunxisse, ut quum procedi cœptum esset, se certiorem faceret, ne tamen interim moræ aliquid interponeretur. At ubi est nullo pacto adduci vult, ut mihi suo Collegæ Commissionem hanc Decretalem credat: Dixit verum id esse, ideo factum ne pluribus palam fieret, eaque conditione qua petitum fuit, ostensam nequicquam amplius expectandum, ea repetens, quæ prius etiam circa hoc dixerat. At ego, videat Sanctitas vestra quod ex his verbis, quæ hic scripta sunt loquor, quæ dicunt Sanctitatem Vestram Commissionem Decretalem concessisse, ea conditione ut aliquibus Regiis Consiliariis ostenderetur. Tum Pontifex iterum excandescens; Ostendam (inquit) literas ipsius Reverendissimi Eboracen. nec loquor mendacia, et non minus meis verbis, literisq; prioribus Reverendissimi Eboracen. fides est habenda, quam his quas nunc affertis. Tum ejus Sanctitatem mitigari quæsivi, si minus urgenter mandata exequerer, quoniam id a me fieri oportet. Quod ad Regni ruinas, damna, calamitates, scandala, et diminutionem Religionis, multa in eandem sententiam dixit, in quam primo die locutus fuit; quum diceret, Egregium vero decus Serenissimo huic Regi fuerit, si ipse, qui Fidei Defensor et sit et appelletur, qui libros etiam pro ejus defensione ediderit, eandem nunc impugnare cogatur; Ad hæc quam recte sint venturi, viderint ipsi. Eo autem loco, in quo dicebatur aliquid de Regio negotio, inter Generalem Fatrum de observantia, et ejus Sanctitatem convenisse, et eo autore fœdus inter ejus Sanctitatem et Cæsarianos componendum, Dixit, id ostendere, quod de Regio negotio nihil promiserit, quod quicunq; pollicitus sit, et quin poterit habita ratione suæ conscientiæ, re ipsa præstare velit: In eo autem quod de Pace tractanda affertur, dixit, se nullum modum in tali negotio invenire, neq; se adhuc scire, quod iste Generalis ullas pacis conditiones sit allaturus; atq; ea insuper addidit, quæ meis literis die 15 Novemb. datis D. V. Reverendissimæ significavi.

Aliis deinde diebus S. D. N. sæpissime sum alloquutus, qui decrevit cum Reverendissimis de Monte et Sanctorum Quatuor Cardinalibus de his rebus omnibus loqui, præterquam de Bulla Decretali, de qua cum nemine vult ullam fieri mentionem, jussitq; ex omni Scriptura ejus memoriam eximi. De reliquis itaq; rebus omnibus loquutus sum cum his duobus Cardinalibus qui dixerunt Pontificem contentum fore, ut ad sententiam procedatur, tametsi id plerisq; alienum videatur, deque eo nonnulli ex Cardinalibus cum obtrectatione loquuntur, et Cæsaris Orator ne procedatur Protestatur, voluntq; fieri in Curia Causæ advocationem, Commissionemq; cum Inhibitione ad partes; dicuntq; hi duo Reverendissimi, quod quæ postulant illi, justa sunt, nec minimo cuiq; denegari possent, nolle tamen Regiæ Majestatis causa S. D. N. quicquam ex eo quod factum sit, immutare.

Quum alio etiam die Pontificem otiosum nactus essem, multa cum ejus Sanctitate, de rebus præteritis disserui, deque eo, quod ego ad ejus utilitatem cum Venetis egissem, quoniam scirem Serenissimi Regis, et D. V. Reverendissimæ voluntatem esse, ut quotiescunq; occasio daretur, pro suæ Sanctitatis commodo omnia fierent : Exposui deinde quantopere elaborassem pro negotio Cerviæ et Ravennæ, utq; multa Gallici Oratores egissent a D. V. Reverendissima potissimum instigati ; Addidi etiam efficacissima verba, quibus usus est Dominus Stephanus Gardinerus. Ad omnia S. D. N. respondit, se ea de re Regiæ Majestati, ac D. V. Reverendissimæ gratias habere, et mihi quoque gratias egit ; dixitque, non tamen omnes simul tantum efficere potuistis, ut mihi meæ civitates redderentur. Scitis autem conditiones fœderis in quo ego quoque eram, fuisse, ut quum quis nostrum injuria afficeretur, ab eo cæteri confœderati injuriam propulsarent, quod multo magis pro me faciendum erat, quum qui in ipso fœdere essent mihi injuriarentur ; Et inde Cæsariani volunt mihi persuadere Venetos non fuisse id facturos, si putassent Regi Angliæ aut Christianissimo displiciturum : Neque interim desistunt, multa, magnaq; mihi polliceri, unde ego, quod alias etiam dixi, id quod affertur, quum aliter facere nequeam, accipere cogar. Illudq; etiam vos scire volo promissum mihi fuisse, si legatus hic in Angliam mitteretur, futurum ut mihi civitates a Venetis restituerentur. Tum ego, non omnia, Beatissime Pater, adhuc sunt perfecta, Rex enim potentissimus omnino operam dabit, ut illæ civitates Beatitu-

dini Vestræ restituantur : An non, quæ ejus Majestas scribit Vestra Sanctitas animadvertit? . Cui videndum imprimis est, ne de ipsa Serenissimo Regi sit conquerendum ;
et ex hac occasione iterum ad Regiam Causam redii. At
ejus Sanctitas dixit, se omnia quæ potuisset pro Regia Majestate et D. V. Reverendissima fecisse, facturamq; etiam
libenter.

Nonne igitur (inquam) posset ratio aliqua inveniri qua
concederetur eam Bullam aliquibus ex Secretioribus Consiliariis ostendi posse? Tum Pontifex, non (inquit) Non
potest hoc fieri, nec a me impetrari ; quod si ullo modo fieri
potuisset, minime tam multas magnasq; preces a Serenissimo Rege, et Reverendissimo Domino Eboracen. expec-
tassem ; quumq; quibusdam validis Argumentis instarem,
prohibuit me ulterius de hujusmodi re loqui. Nolui ego
unquam dicere, equitem fratrem brevi esse venturum, ne
Pontifex rem in illius adventum protraheret, ea tantum de
causa, ut moram interponeret.

Omnibus deinde aliis diebus super eodem negotio institi,
nunquam tamen Pontifex sententiam suam ulla ex parte
immutare voluit ; tantum illud decrevit, Nuntium mittere
velle, qui suam sententiam verbis explicaret : quumq; nulla mihi amplius spes relinqueretur quicquam amplius impe-
trandi, tum demum dixi, Equitem fratrem Romæ futurum
sequenti die, qui quum adeo gravis momenti rem, cerneret,
noluerit suæ valetudini consulere, et quod is minime pu-
tasset, suæ servitutis in ejus Sanctitatem merita hoc modo
male tractanda fuisse. Gratum sibi dixit Pontifex Equitis
adventum fore, quodq; cum ipso et constituerentur omnia,
negans tamen se ullo pacto id quod nunc petitur concessurum. Venit itaq; Eques frater, qui non secus ac si nunquam quisquam de hac re cum Pontifice egisset, singula de
integro tractavit, omnibus his modis et rationibus tentatis
quæ excogitari poterunt. Quæ omnia minutim Dominus
Vincentius Cassalius noster patruelis, quem ad ipsum mittimus, verbis coram explicabit, egoque ne D. V. Reverendissimæ jam nimis molestus sim, de hac ulterius non
scribam.

Quod ad Wintoniensem Expeditionem spectat, multum
hi Reverendissimi Domini Cardinales offendebantur, nunc

ab ipsis pecuniarum remissiones postulari, quum deprædata eorum bona siat, ipsiq; propter id ad Paupertatem redacti. Quibus ego ostendi, majus emolumentum ad ipsos venturum, si D. V. Reverendissima unam Ecclesiam acciperet, alteram deponeret, quam si alter tantum Wintoniensis Ecclesiæ expeditionem faceret; neque D. V. Reverendissimam nimis hanc permutationem optare dixi, quum Wintoniensis non multo Ecclesiæ Dunelmensi sit ditior. Ad hæc dixerunt, quod libentius D. V. Reverendissimæ quam cuiquam alteri erunt gratificaturi, quoniam ipsa de sede Apostolica sit semper bene merita, non tamen se vereri, quin D. V. Reverendissima Wintoniensem Ecclesiam illius Regni primariam sit acceptura. Ego quum Pontificem, et deinde Cardinales eos qui magis rebus nostris student ambissem, effeci ut Pontifex, de ea re in Consistorio referret, quod ejus Sanctitas effecit, multis etiam additis laudibus D. V. Reverendissimæ, quibus aliqui Cardinales, et maxime Neapolitani, responderunt ea quæ superius dixi. Illud tandem decreverunt, quod quum D. V. Reverendissima solvere debeat, pro expeditione Wintoniensis Ecclesiæ, et pro retentione Ecclesiæ Eboracensis et Abbatiæ Sancti Albani, habita ratione totius summæ, ejus pars dimidia V. D. Reverendissimæ condonaretur, et ut ad 13 vel 14 millia aureorum remittant, et non multo plus eo, quod pro Wintonien. tum Ecclesia deberet solvere. Id Reverendissimis Cardinalibus ideo displicebat, quoniam nollent res hujusmodi in exemplum trahi, quum præsertim Magnus Franciæ Cancellarius, ipse quoque in magna quadam Expeditione, idipsum in præsentia flagitat, quod isti concedere nolunt.

Cætera ex Domini Vincentio D. V. Reverendissima copiosius coram intelligat; Quæ bene valeat. Dat. Romæ die 17 Decemb. 1528.

Humillimus servus

Jo. Cassalius

Prothonotar.

XVIII.

The Pope's Letter to the Cardinal, giving Credence to Campana. An Original.

Dilecto Filio nostro Thomæ Sanctæ Ceciliæ Presbytero, Cardinali Eboracen. In Regno Angliæ, nostro et Sedis de Latere Legato.

DILECTE Fili noster, salutem et Apostolicam Benedictionem. Existimavimus non tam commdeo per literas responderi posse his, de quibus postremo Oratores Carissimi in Christo Filii nostri istius Regis nobiscum egerunt; Itaq; proprium hominem Franciscum Campanam familiarem nostrum istuc mittimus, ex quo sua Serenitas ac Circumspectio tua plenius intelligent quæ nobis occurrant, tam de rebus ad pacem et publice ad universam Christianitatem spectantibus, quam super privatis Serenitatis suæ, de quibus nobis per literas et Oratores vestros significastis, quas quidem summopere cordi habemus. Circumspectionem tuam hortamur, ut sibi ac Serenitati suæ persuadeat nos paternam benevolentiam atq; animum gessisse et gerere erga Serenitatem suam, ab eodemq; amore proficisci omni quæcunq; illi significamus, ut pluribus Circumspectionem tuam, quam merito multum amamus, exponet Dilect. Fil. Card. Campegius, Legatus una tecum noster, ac dictus Franciscus, quibus plenissimam fidem habebitis. Datum Romæ 15. Decembris M. D. XXVIII.

Cotton
Libr.
Vitell.
B. 10.

J.

Clemens manu propria.

XIX.

Decemb. 1. 1528.

A Part of Peter Vannes his Instructions, directing him to threaten the Pope. An Original.

——AND Peter, as of himself, shall a-part say unto his Holiness; Sir, I being an Italian, cannot but with a more

fervent zeal and mind than any other, study and desire the
Weal, Honour, and Safety of your Holiness and the See
Apostolick; which compelleth me to shew unto your Holiness, frankly, what I see in this matter. Surely, Sir, in case
your Holiness continuing this particular respect of fear of
the Emperor, do thus delay, protract, and put off the accomplishment of the King's so instant desire in this Matter,
and not impart to his Majesty therein bounteously of the
Treasure and Goods of the Church, and the See Apostolick, *quantum potestis ex Thesauro Ecclesiæ et ex plenitudine Potestatis ac Autoritate a Deo vel ab Ecclesia collata*. I
see assuredly, that it will be a means so to alienate the fast
and entire mind which his Highness beareth to your said
Holiness, as not only thereby his Grace, Nobles, and
Realm, but also many other Princes his Friends and Confederates, with their Nobles and Realms, shall withdraw
their Devotion and Obedience from your Holiness, and the
See Apostolick, studying how they may acquite this your
Ingratitude, in the highest cause that can be devised,
shewed, and so long continued with the semblable. And
therefore, Sir, at the reverence of Almighty God, cast not
from you the heart of this noble virtuous Prince, who finally cannot fail, the Peace had, which Christendom may not
long forbear, to have in his puissance, such a stay as may
be able, in the highest and largest manner, to recompence
his Friends, and to acquite the contrary.

HENRY R.

XX.

*The Cardinal's Letter to the Ambassadors about his Pro-
motion to the Popedom. An Original.*

*Magnifico Equiti Domino Gregorio Cassalio ac Domino
Petro Vanni, Serenissimi Domini Angliæ et Franciæ
Regis in Rom. Curia oratoribus.*

Cotton
Libr.
Vitel.
B. 10. MAGNIFICE Domine Gregori et Domine Petre salutem.
Sicuti incommodissimus totius Reipublicæ Christianæ, ac
potissimum Regis Majestatis negotiis S. D. N. obitus acci-

dit, ita etiam vos non latere puto quantum periculi et discriminis hujus Serenissimi Regis saluti et honori, ac Regni
sui quieti ab hac futuri Pontificis Electione immineat, et
quantopere vobis adnitendum, ac vestro studio, diligentia,
industria et prudentia occurrendum et obstandum sit, ne
aliquis eligatur Pontifex alienus ab hac Regia Majestate;
et quid pro me promovendo facere ac tractare debeatis, cu-
mulate per communes meas literas vos admonui: nec oportet per has quicquid aliud replicare, quas solum ad vos scribere volui, ut significem vobis me totum hoc gravissimum
et omnium maximum negotium, de quo acturi estis, vestræ
prudentiæ, fidei, et dexteritati, quam longo temporis usu
exploratissimam habeo, committere et credere, speroq; vos
spei et opinioni meæ de vobis conceptæ omnino respon-
suros, et bene valete. Londini die 6 Feb. 1528.

Vester amantissimus Frater,

T. Cardin. Eborac.

XXI.

*An Information given to the Pope about the Divorce.
An Original.*

*Adnotatio Summaria eorum quæ aliis libellis fusius explicata
S. D. N. tum licere, tum expedire, persuadent, ut in Causa Regiæ Majestatis Sententiam divortii ferat.*

PRIMUM licet atque etiam expedit dirimere hoc Matrimonium, quod juri tum divino tum humano repugnat.

Divinum enim jus duci prohibet Uxorem fratris, quin hic
fratris Uxorem ductam fuisse sit notorium.

Humanum vero jus, duo hujus Matrimonii impedimenta
continet, alterum Affinitatis, quod divino jure inductum se-
verissime sancivit; alterum publicæ Honestatis, et justitiæ,
quod promulgavit Deus, si ex definitione Matrimonii, divini, humaniq; juris commutatio interveniret, quibusnam
auspiciis hoc Matrimonium constare dicemus, quod utroque
jure adversante ac repugnante, contractum est, coit, et ut-
cumque consistit?

Sed cessavit, inquiunt, in hac specie juris utriusq; prohibitio per gratiam et Dispensationem summi Pontificis.

Respondetur quidem istis multis modis. Primo non esse
videri, quod nullum est, nullum autem haberi quod sine
Autoritate legitima fiat; deniq; Pontificis Autoritatem non
eatenus pertinere, ut in gradibus divina lege prohibitis dispensare possit: non opinionibus Scripturientium, qui Pontificis Authoritatem imminutam velint, sed ipsius Pontificis sententia constat, quem suæ Jurisdictionis modum, et
optime novisse et ampliare velle potius quam restringere
credendum est; quæ quum ita sint, etiam si humani juris
prohibitio per Dispensationem sublata videatur, manet nihilominus immotum, quod divinum est, si ipsis contra seipsos credimus Pontificibus.

Deinde, ut posse Pontifices dispensare fateamur, et in ea
parte tribuamus plus Authoritatis quam ipsi sibiipsis au-
deant arrogare, tamen non passim, non quocunq; modo,
non temere, et sine omni consideratione, posse eos dispensare; atq; fatendum est ne suo testimonio Dissipatores
verius, quam Dispensatores appellentur. Itaque ut causam urgentissimam et evidentissimam, tum etiam manifes-
tissimam debet habere Dispensatio, precibus deniq; veris,
non ementitis atq; confictis inniti.

In Dispensatione autem, quo constat hoc Matrimonium,
verbis quidem pacis causa proponitur, sed non ideo quia
sic refertur, re ipsa subsistit, Pontificis facta non ad verborum superficiem, sed rei ipsius solidam veritatem expendi
convenit.

Certum est, pacem multis modis, tum firmissimam fuisse
unoq; Matrimonio conciliatam, pactorum deniq; ac fæde-
rum vi constantem, istud necessario Matrimonium non de-
siderasse, et jam Dispensationem sine causa intervenisse
dicimus, et consequenter nullam esse, manereq; adhuc divinam prohibitionem atq; adeo et humanam.

Porro etiam, si aliqua sit, et causam haberet, tum men-
daciis conflata est, subreptitia et obreptitia merito appel-
landa, jure tum divino, tum humano reprobata.

Nam quum quod alioqui Canonibus cautum sit, ipsius
etiam Dispensationis proœmium contineat, "Romani Pontificis Autoritatem concessa sibi desuper uti potestate,
prout personarum, causarum, et temporum qualitate pen-

ata, id in Domino salubriter conspicit expedire;" Quomodo potuit S. D. N. hujus Serenissimi Regis qualitates pensare quas ignoravit ? Neque enim de ætate quicquam, quæ
in contrahendo hoc Matrimonio præcipua qualitas erat,
narrabatur, et tamen illum annum eo tempore duodecimum non excessisse notorium est; et tacita ad hunc modum ætate, mendacium pro causa suggestum est manifestis-
simum; Cupisse, viz. tunc Serenissimum Regem contrahere Matrimonium, ad hoc ut pacis fœdera continuarentur: facti veritas est, tum quid ageretur ignorasse, et etiamsi tum scivisset, tamen non fuisse verum quod cuperet
ad hoc ut pacis fœdera continuarentur, ætas ostendit, quæ
per communis juris dispositionem discretionem non admittit; cupere quidem affectus est, cæterum cupere contrahere
Matrimonium, ad hoc ut pacis fœdera continuarentur, judicii est et discretionis. Porro autem, quum de continu-
andis inter duos Principes fœderibus ageretur, alter ante
mandatam exequutioni Bullam satis concessit, et re integra, causa, si quæ fuit, cessavit.

Sed producitur aliud Breve tenoris tam efficacis ut istas
 Objectiones non admittat.

Sed manet nihilominus eorum sententia, qui Pontificem
non posse dispensare affirmant, secundum quos nec Breve
nec Bulla consistit; deinde Breve falsum esse, et pro falso
judicari deberi, multis rationibus convincitur; denique falsum cum sit, et tamen prioris Bullæ errores corrigat, illam
opinionem merito confirmet, ne prior Dispensatio efficax
videatur, vel eorum judicio, qui hoc Matrimonium defendere studuerunt, viz. qui veris allegationibus diffisi, ad fal-
sas et confictas Dispensationes, vitia objecta removentes
confugere coacti sunt.

Ista, si singula minus sufficiant, saltem collata, obtineant
et persuadeant licere. Illa vero opinio multis persuasa,
Pontificem, viz. non potuisse dispensare, ut sola infirmet
Dispensationem, non petitur, sed habet nihilominus aliquid
considerationis; quanquam enim refellatur a quibusdam et
reprobetur, manet tamen scripta, atque adeo testimonio
ipsius Pontificis comprobata. Perpendatur deinde causa
et suggestionis veritas, si mendacium intervenisse apparet,
et quod est notorium, illam Dispensationem adversariorum

factis in novi Brevis fabricatione tacite reprobari, quis non videt ex his causis licere ut sententia Divortii proferatur?

Postremo expedit ut id pronuntietur, quod in omnium sententias consentiat, Reprobatio autem Dispensationis cum omnibus convenit opinionibus, sive quia Authoritas abfuit, sive quia non recte interposita dicatur; Approbatio vero cum istis dissentit omnibus.

Expedit ut firma sit et inconcussa Regni Successio, quæ contra has opiniones confirmari non potest.

Expedit ut conscientia Serenissimi Regis his scrupulis impedita, et turbata, expedita et tranquilla reddatur.

Breviter, expedit votis Serenissimi Regis satisfieri, qui pro genuinis et innatis suis virtutibus, non nisi optima cupit, et modo etiam optimo votorum suorum compotem effici laborat; si non virtutem spectaret, cætera nihil haberent difficultatis, sed omnium virtutum cogitationem quandam esse animadvertens, suum justitiæ decorum, quod temperantia est, quærit, ut justum, justo modo, obtineat et assequatur. Itaq; expedit ne auxilium denegetur, vel differatur ei qui id juste implorat.

XXII.

The second part of a long Dispatch of the Cardinals concerning the Divorce. An Original.

To my loving Friends Master Stephen Gardiner Doctor of both Laws; Sir Francis Brian, and Sir Gregory Cassalis, Knights; and Mr. Peter Vannes Secretary to the King's Highness for the Latin Tongue; His Graces Orators, Residents in the Court of Rome.

——ANOTHER part of your Charge consisteth in expedition of the King's great and weighty Cause of Matrimony, whereupon depend so many high Consequences, as for no earthly Cause to suffer or tolerate, tract or delay, in what case soever the Pope's Holiness be of amendment or danger of life; nor as is aforesaid, oweth to be by his Holiness preteromitted, whether the same be in the state of Recovery, or in any doubt or despair thereof: for one assured and principal fundamental and ground is to be regarded, whereupon the King's Highness doth plant and build his Acts and Cogitations in this behalf, which is from the reasonable favour and justice, being the things from the which the Pope's Holiness, *in prosperis nec adversis*, may lawfully and honestly digress ; and when the plainness of his Cause is well considered, with the manifest Presumptions, Arguments, and Suspitions, both of the insufficiency of the Bull, and falsity of the Brief, such as may lead any Man of reason or intendment, well to perceive and know, that no sufficiency or assured truth can be therein; How may the Pope's Holiness, *ex æquo et justo*, refuse or deny to any Christian Man, much less to a Prince of so high merits, and in a Cause whereupon depend so many consequences, to his Holiness well known, for a vain respect of any Person, or by excuse of any Sickness, justifie, colour, or defend any manner refusal, tract, or delay, used in declaration of the truth in so great a Matter, which neither for the infinite conveniences that thereby might ensue, admitteth or suffereth to be delaied, nor by other than himself, his Act or Authority, may lawfully be declared. And well may his Holiness know, That to none it appertaineth more to look unto the justness of the King's desire in this behalf, than to his Highness his self, whose Interest, whose Cause, with the same of his Realm and Succession resteth herein ; for if his Grace were minded, or would intend to do a thing inique or unjust, there were no need to recur unto the Pope's Holiness for doing thereof. But because his Highness and his Council, who best know the whole of this Matter, and to whose part it belongeth most profoundly to weigh and ponder every thing concerning the same, be well assured of the truth of the Matter, needing none other thing but for observance of his Duty towards God and his Church, to have the same Truth also approbate and declared by him to whom the doing thereof appertaineth ; his Grace therefore seeing an untruth alledged, and that so craftily as by undue and perverse ways, the same, without good reason adhibited, may for a season bring things into confusion, doth communicate unto the Pope's Holiness presumptions and evidences enough, and sufficient to in-

BOOK
II.

form the Conscience of his Holiness of the very truth:
which then, if his Holiness will not see, but either for affection, fear, or other private cause, will hearken to every
dilatory and vain allegation of such as led upon undue
grounds would colour the Truth; What doth his Holiness
less therein, than under a right vain colour expresly deny
and refuse the said Justice, which to be done either in
health or sickness, in a matter of so great moment, is in no
wise tolerable? But for the same reasons that he before
mentioned, is the thing, whether the Pope's Holiness be
in hope or despair of life, without further tract to be absolved and determined; for if Almighty God grant his
Holiness life, this Act is, and always shall be, able to bear
it self, and is meet to be an Example, a President, and a
Law, in all like Cases emerging, the Circumstances and
Specialities of the same in every part concurring as they do
in this; nor can the Emperor make exceptions at the same,
when he best knowing, percase, the untruth shall see the
grounds and occasions, that of necessity and meer Justice
have enforced and constrained the Pope's Holiness thereunto; which he could not refuse to do, unless he would
openly and manifestly commit express injury and notorious
injustice. For be it that the Pope's Holiness hearkning
to the said frivolous and vain Allegations, would refuse to
declare the Law herein to the King's purpose, then must
his Holiness, either standing in doubt, leave and suffer the
Cause to remain in suspence to the extream danger of the
King's Realm and Succession for ever, or else declare the
Bull or Breve, or both to be good, which I suppose neither
his Holiness nor any true Christian Man can do, standing
the manifest occasions, presumptions, and apparent evidences to the contrary. Then if the matter be not to be
left in suspence, no judgment can be truly given to the approbation of the Bull or Breve; how can the Pope's Holiness of Conscience, Honour or Vertue, living or dying,
thus procrastinate or put over the immediate finishing
thereof, according to the King's desire? or how may his
Holiness find his Conscience towards God exonerate, if
either living he should be the cause of so many evils as
hereof may arise; or dying, wilfully leave this so great a
Matter, by his own default, in this confusion, incertainty

and perplexity? It is not to be supposed, that ever Prince most devout to the See Apostolick, could so long tolerate so high an Injury, as being so merited towards the said See, is both unacquitted for his kindness with any special Grace, and also denied upon his petition of that, which is evident to be plain Justice. This thing is otherwise to be looked upon, than for the Pope's Sickness, where most need were to put an end unto it, to be delaied, seeing that living and amending, it is of it self expedient and justifiable, and dying, it shall be an act both necessary, meritorious and honourable. For this cause ye now knowing the King's mind in this behalf, shall, if ye have not already before this time spoken with the Pope's Holiness at length in these Matters, as the King's Grace trusteth ye have done, sollicite as well by the means of Messiere Jacobo Salviati, as by the Bishop of Verone, and otherwise as ye can think best, to have such commodious access unto his Holiness, as ye may declare the Premises unto him; which by your wisdoms, in as effectual and vive manner as ye can open it unto his Holiness. It is undoubtedly to be thought the same shall rather be to his comfort and encrease of Health, than to any his trouble or unquietness; and that his Holiness hearing these Reasons not evitable, will, whether he be in way and hope of amendment, or otherwise, both proceed to the said indication, and also to the Declaration of the Law, and passing of a sufficient and ample Decretal, as hath been devised in the King's said Cause, with other such things, as by former Letters and Instructions, by the Decrees mentioned in the same, that failing have been committed unto you, to be solicited and procured there; in the labouring whereof, albeit since your departures from hence, the things have, by reasons of the Pope's sore sickness, otherwise chanced than was here supposed, by means whereof ye not instructed what to do in any such case, were peradventure not over-hasty or importune to labour these Matters, till the Pope's Holiness might be better amended, nor could percase find the means to have convenient access unto his presence for the same, ye must nevertheless adhibit such diligence, as howsoever the sickness of his Holiness shall cease, amend, or continue, these things be not for the same, or any other cause, tracted or left in

longer suspense; but finding possible means to come unto
the Pope's presence, to declare all such things unto the
same, mentioned both in the former Letters and Instructions given unto you, and also in these presents, as may
make to the purpose: and failing of often access in your
own Persons to his Holiness, ye cause the Bishop of Verone,
and other such assured Friends as ye can attain, being
about him at such times as they may have with his Holiness, to inculcate unto him the said Points and Considerations, and all other that ye can excogitate and devise to
the furtherance and advancement of these Matters, not
forbearing or sparing also, if ye shall see difficulty at the
Pope's hand, or in audience to be given to you or your
Friends there, being about his Person, to break and open
after a good fashion and manner the same unto such of the
Cardinals, as ye may perceive assuredly and constantly to
favour the King's Highness, and the French King in Election of a future Pope, in case (as God forbid) the Pope's
Holiness should decease; and to shew unto the same Cardinals, all such things as you shall think meet, both for
their more ample instructions in the truth and specialities
of the Matters, as well concerning the Indication of Truce,
as the King's said Cause, and the presumptuous Reasons,
and plainer Evidences, leading to the insufficiency of the
Bull, and apparent falsity of the said Breve; to the intent,
that as many of the said Cardinals as ye can win, made
sure in those Matters, they may, both in time of sickness,
and also of amendment, move and induce the Pope's Holiness thereunto, laying before him as well the Merits and
Honour that may ensue by the perfection of the premises,
as the danger imminent by the contrary: and semblably
it shall be expedient that ye win and make sure to the
same purpose, as many of the Officers of the Rota and
other as ye can, who as ye write be not accustomed, nor
will give counsel to any Person but the Pope's Holiness;
for albeit, ye cannot have them to be of the King's Council, yet nevertheless they may do as much good, or more,
in training and counselling the Pope's Holiness, upon the
great Reasons that you can shew unto them, to hearken
unto your Overtures in this behalf. To which purpose
you shall adjure, make, and win, as many Friends of the

Cardinals, of them, and other, as ye possibly may, as for the thing which the King's Highness and I more esteem than twenty Papalities ; and amongst other, ye shall insist, by all means and good persuasions ye can, for the continuance there of the said Bishop of Verone, so as he may countervail the Arch-Bishop of Capuan; who, as it seemeth, is continually about the Pope's Person, and were necessary to be met with in the labours and persuasions, which by likelihood he maketh to the hindrance of the King's Purpose: For the better continuing of the which Bishop of Verone, not only the King's Highness and I write unto him at this time, as by the Copy of the same several Letters being herewith ye shall perceive, but also the French King will do the semblable. And furthermore, to the intent that the Pope's Holiness may well perceive, that not only the said French King mindeth the King's said Cause, and taketh it to heart as much as it were his own, and will effectually join and concur with the King's Highness therein, but that also he is and will be conformable to the said Indication ; He will send thither, with all speed, the Bishop of Bayon to further, sollicite, and set forth the same; who, before his departure from hence, which was a good season passed, was and is sufficiently and amply instructed in all things requisite to this purpose; and not only in these Matters, but also in such other as were written unto you by Vincent de Cassalis, and Hercules, upon advertisement given hither that the Pope's Holiness was deceased ; so as ye may be sure to have of him effectual concurrence and advice in the furtherance and sollicitation of your Charges, whether the Pope's Holiness amend, remain long sick, or (as God forbid) should fortune to die ; trusting, that being so well furnished by all ways that can be devised, ye will not fail to use such diligence as may be to the consecuting and attaining of the King's Purpose : wherein, tho ye be so amply and largely instructed, that more cannot be, yet nevertheless having lately received from the Bishop of Worcester a Memorial of divers great things to be well noted and considered, for trial of the falsity of the said Brieve, I send you herewith a Copy of the same Memorial, to the intent ye substantially visiting and perusing the same, may follow and put in execution such part thereof,

for better trial of the falsity, as is to be done there, like as
the rest meet to be done here, shall not fail to be executed
with diligence accordingly.

Thus be ye with these, and other former Writings, sufficiently instructed what is to be done by you there, whether the Pope's Holiness continue long in his sickness, or
whether the same fortune to decease, or soon, God willing, to amend. There resteth no more, but that ye always
take for a perfect ground, That tho to every new chance
not before known, sufficient Provision and Instruction
could not be given to you at your departure, ye always
note, remember, and regard, That this the King's Cause
admitteth nor suffereth any manner negative, tract, or delay; wherefore knowing that so well as ye do, and also how
much the Indiction of the Truce shall be commodious and
necessary, both to the King's Highness in particular, and
to all Christendom in general, by means whereof his Grace
shall avoid Contribution, and other Charges of the War,
ye must now, if ever you will have thanks, laud, or praise
for your Service, employ your selves *opportune et importune*, to put an end to the Points to the King's satisfaction
and desire; and in every difficulty to study, by your Wisdoms, the best and next Remedy, and not always to tract
your doings, till upon your Advertisement hither, ye shall
have new knowledg from hence: For thereby the matter it
self, and also your demur there, be of over-long a continuance, and infinite in conveniences by the same may ensue.
I therefore require you, according to the special trust and
confidence that the King's Highness and I have in you,
now for ever to acquit your selves herein with all effect
possible, accordingly so as the King's Highness be not longer kept in this perplexity and suspence, to his Graces intolerable inquietness, and the great heaviness of all those
that observe and love the same.

Furthermore, tho it so be that the King's Trust, and also
mine is, Ye will by your Wisdom find such good means
and ways as ye shall not fail, God willing, to open and declare unto the Pope's Holiness, the whole of the King's
Mind, and all and singular the Premisses, with the residue
above-mentioned in your former Instructions and Letters
sent unto you: Yet nevertheless considering what ye wrote

of the doubt of continuance of the Pope's sickness, and to make sure for all Events and Chances, in case his Holiness (as God forbid) should long remain in such state, as he might either take upon him the naming of the Peace, journeying and repairing to the sacre Diet, nor also hear the whole of the things by you to be opened and propounded touching the King's said Cause; It hath been thought to the King's Highness convenient, rather than these great and weighty Matters should hang in longer suspense, to excogitate some other good means and way how these Matters, so necessary, may by some ways be conduced and brought to an end: And it is this; That the Pope's Holiness not being able to travel to the place devised, where the Princes may be near him for Treaty, and managing of the Peace, he do depute me and my Lord Cardinal *Campegius, conjunctim et divisim,* as his Legats for that purpose, to do and execute all such things in his Holiness's Name, as the same should do in that behalf if he were there present; whereunto, for the well of Christendom, we shall be contented to condescend. So always, that as hath been written heretofore unto you, before I pass or set forth to any Convention or Place, to the intent before specified, the King's Highness be fully satisfied and pleased in his said matter of Matrimony, without which, neither with nor without the Pope's presence, I will ever begin or take that Voyage: for performance whereof, this Article following is of new devised, to be by you propounded unto his Holiness, if the Decretals cannot be obtained, or some other thing, that ye shall well know and perceive, by advice of expert Counsel there, to be better to the Kings purpose than this thing now devised, and that may without tract be passed or granted; that is to say, That his Holiness do enlarge, extend, and amplify his Commission given to me and my Lord Legate Campegius, whereby we jointly and severally may be sufficiently furnished and authorized, to do as much in this cause of Matrimony, with all the emergents and dependencies upon the same, as his Holiness may do of his ordinary and absolute Power, with sufficient and ample Clauses, *ad Decernend. et Interpretand. jura, leges, et Rescripta quæcunq; hoc Matrimonium concernentia, una cum omnibus et singulis dubiis in eadem causa emergentibus.* And further, to make out Compulsories to any Princes, or Persons of what preheminence, dignity, state, or condition soever they be, *Etiam si in Imperiali, Regali, vel alia quacunque dignitate perfulgeant, sub quibuscunq ; pœnis,* and in what Countries and places soever they be, to exhibit and produce any manner Witness, Records, Originals, Rescripts, or other thing, in what place, or time we, or the one of us shall require them, or any of them in this behalf, with all and singular the Circumstances re- quisite and necessary to such a Commission, after such ample and assured manner, as the same once had, we shall not need for any Objections, doubt, or other thing that might infringe or lack, to send of new to the Pope's Holi- ness for other provision, whereby the King's said Cause might hang in any longer tract or delay. In which case of coming to this Commission, ye Mr. Stevins must have spe- cial regard to see the same sufficiently and substantially penned, by advice of the most expert Men that ye can find to that purpose: For the better doing whereof, I send un- to you herewith a Copy of the said Commission to me and my Lord Campegius, with certain Additions thereunto noted in the Margin, such as have been here devised; and also a Copy of certain Clauses in a Bull, to the intent ye may see how amply the same be couched, to avoid appella- tions and other delays in Causes of far less moment and importance than the King's is. Nevertheless ye must, if it shall come to the obtaining of this new Commission, see to the penning and more fully perfecting thereof, so as the same may be in due perfection, without needing to send eftsoons for remedying of any thing therein, as is aforesaid; looking also substantially whether the Chirograph of Poli- citation, being already in your hands, be so couched, as the Date, and every thing considered, it may sufficiently oblige and astringe the Popes Holiness to confirm all that we, or one of us, shall do, by virtue of this New or the Old Com- mission: And if it be not of such efficacy so to do, then must ye in this case see, that either by sufficient and ample words to be put in this new Commission, if it may be so had, or by a new Chirograph the Pope's Holiness may be so astringed; which Chirograph, with the Commissions be- fore specified, if ye obtain the same, the King's pleasure is,

That ye Sir Francis Brian shall bring hither, in all possible diligence, after the having and obtaining thereof,
solliciting nevertheless, whether the Pope be to be facilly
spoken with, or not, the immediate Indication of the Truce,
as is aforesaid, without which in vain it were for me, either
with or without the Pope, to travel for labouring and conducing of the Peace. And so by this way should the
Pope's Holiness, with his merit and sufficient justification,
proceed for the Truce, as a fundament of Universal Peace,
satisfy the King's desires, and avoid any doubt of the Emperor; forasmuch as his Holiness might alledg, That being
so extreamly sick, that he was not able to know of the
Cause himself, he could no less do of justice, than to commit it unto other, seeing that the same is of such importance as suffereth no tract or delay. And finally, the King's
Highness, God willing, by this means, should have an end
of this Matter. One thing ye shall well note, which is
this; Albeit this new Device was now for doubt of the
Pope's long continuance of sickness, first excogitate; yet
is it not meant, nor ye be limited to this Device, in case
ye can obtain any other, nor ye be also commanded, to pre-
fer this before all the other Devices: but now that ye shall
see and understand what this Device is, and knowing what
thing is like or possible to be obtained there, without long
putting over of your pursuits, expend, consider, and regard
well with your self, what thing of this, or any other that
may best serve to the brief and good expedition of the
King's Cause. So always that it be a thing sure, sufficient,
and available to his Grace's Purpose, that may without
any further tract be there had; and then by your Wisdom
taking unto you the best Learned Counsel that ye can
have there, leave you to the expedition of that which so
may be most meet, as the times require and suffer, to the
brief furnishing of the King's said Cause to this purpose,
without tract or delay, and that ye may see is the thing,
which as the matter stands, can speedily be obtained and
sped, as is aforesaid. For whether the Decretal be better
than this, or this better than that, or which soever be best,
far it shall be from Wisdom to stick, and still to rest upon
a thing that cannot be obtained; but since ye know the
King's meaning, which is to have a way sufficient and good

for the speedy finishing of this Cause to his Grace's purpose, note ye now, and consider with your self, by advice
of Learned Counsel, as is aforesaid, how ye may bring that
to pass, and shall ye deserve as high thanks as can be possible. So always that it be so well provided and looked
upon, that in it be no such limitations or defaults, as shall
compel us any more to write or send for reformation thereof: And coming to this Commission, tho percase ye can by
no means or sticking have it in every point as the Copy,
which I send you with the Annotations do purport; yet
shall ye not therefore refuse it, but take it, or any other
thing as can be had, after such form as may substantially
serve, and as ye can by your wisdom and good sollicitations
obtain, for the speedy finishing of the King's Cause to his
purpose, as is aforesaid, which is the scope whereunto we
must tend at this time; and therefore ye be not limited or
coacted within any such bounds as ye should thereby be
compelled or driven, for lack of obtaining any thing or
point mentioned in these or other your Instructions, or former Writings, to send hither again for further knowledg
of the King's pleasure; but ye be put at liberty so to qua-
lify, so to add, detray, immix, change, chuse or mend as ye
shall think good; so always that ye take the thing that best
can be had, being such as may as effectually as ye can
bring about, serve to the King's purpose, and to put indelayed end to it, according to his Grace's desire, without
further tract, or sending thither, which is as much as here
can be said or devised. And therefore at the reverence of
Almighty God, bring us out of this perplexity, that this
Vertuous Prince may have this thing sped to the purpose
desired, which shall be the most joyous thing that this day in
Earth may chance and succeed to my heart; and therefore I
eftsoons beseech you to regard it accordingly: Howbeit if
the Pope's Holiness refusing all your desires, shall make
difficulty and delay therein, it is an evident sign and token,
that his Holiness is neither favourable to the King's reasonable Petitions, nor indifferent, but should thereby show
himself both partial, and expresly averse unto his Grace;
wherefore in that case finding in his Holiness such unrea-
sonableness, as it can in no wise be thought ye shall do,
The King's pleasure is, that ye proceed to the Protestations

mentioned in the first Instructions given to you Mr. Stevins, for you and the residue of your Collegues; and that ye not only be plain and round with the Pope's Holiness therein, if ye come to his speech, but also ye show and extend unto the Cardinals, and other that be your Friends, which may do any good with him, the great peril and danger imminent unto the Church and See Apostolick; thereby exhorting them, That they like vertuous Fathers have regard thereunto, and not to suffer the Pope's Holiness, if he would thus wilfully, without reason or discretion to precipitate himself and the said See, which by this refusal is like to suffer ten times more detriment, than it could do for any miscontentment that the Emperor could take with the contrary: for ye shall say, sure they may be, and so I for my discharge declare, both to the Pope's Holiness and to them, If this Noble and Vertuous Prince, in this so great and reasonable a Cause, be thus extreamly denied of the grace and lawful favour of the Church, the Pope's Holiness shall not fail for the same to lose Him and his Realm, the French King and his Realm, with many other their Confederates; besides those that having particular Quarrels to the Pope, and so aforesaid will not fail, with diverse other, as they daily seek occasions, and provoke the King's Highness thereunto, which will do the semblable, being a thing of another sort to be regarded, than the respect to the Emperor; for two Cities, which nevertheless shall be had well enough, and the Emperor neither so evil contented, nor so much to be doubted herein, as is there supposed, This, with other words mentioned in your Instructions concerning like matter, ye shall declare unto his Holiness, and to the said Cardinals, and other being your Friends, if it come to that point; whereby it is not to be doubted, but they perceiving the dangers aforesaid, shall be glad to exhort and induce his Holiness, for the well of himself and the Church, to condescend to the King's desire; which is as much as can be here thought or devised, to be by you done in all Events and Chances: And therefore I pray you, eft-soons, and most instantly require you, as afore, to handle this Matter with all effect possible. Coming to this new Commission, when you shall have once attained such thing as shall be sufficient for the King's purpose, as is aforesaid; and that ye have it in your

hands and custody, and not afore, lest thereby ye might
hinder the expedition thereof, ye shall by all ways and
means possible, labour and insist, That the King's Highness, as need shall be, may use and enjoy the benefit of the
Decretal, being already in my Lord Cardinal Campegius's
hands, whereunto his Highness and I desire you to put all
your effectual labour for the attaining of the Pope's consent thereunto accordingly.

Ye shall furthermore understand, That it is thought
here, in case, as God forbid, the Pope should die before
ye should have impetrate any thing that may serve to the
absolution of the King's Matter, That the Colledg of Cardinals have Authority, Power, and Jurisdiction, *sede vacante,* to inhibit, avoke, *et ex consequenti,* to pass and decide
the King's Matter, seeing that the same is of so high moment and importance, concerning the surety of a Prince
and his Realm, as more amply ye shall perceive in the
Chapters, *ubi Periculum de Electione, ne Romani, de Jurejurando, et capite primo de Scismaticis;* Wherefore the King's
pleasure is, That ye Mr. Stevins shall diligently weigh
and ponder the effect of the said Chapters, not only with
your self, but also with such the King's Learned Counsel
as ye and your Collegues have conducted there; and what
Jurisdiction, *sede vacante,* the Colledg of Cardinals have,
either by the Common Law, usage or prescription, which
may far better be known there than here: And if ye find
that the Cardinals have in this the King's Cause, and such
other like Authority and Jurisdictions to inhibite, avoke
and decern, then, *in casu mortis Pontificis, quod Deus avertat,* ye shall specially foresee and regard that for none Intercession or pursute made by the Emperor and his Adherents, they shall either inhibit or avoke: And also if before
such Death, ye shall not have obtained such thing to the
Kings desire and purpose, as these present Letters before
do purport, his Grace's pleasure is, That ye shall pursue
the effectual expedition of the same, at the hands of the said
Colledg, *Sede vacante, ne res quæ nullam dilationem exposcit,
tantopere usque ad Electionem novi Pontificis quoquam modo
differatur;* using for this purpose all such Reasons, Allegations, and Persuasions mentioned in those Letters, and
your former Instructions, as ye shall see and perceive to

serve to that effect; and so to endeavour and acquit your self, that such things may be attained there, as may absolve this the King's Matter, without any further tract or delay; whereby ye shall as afore highly deserve the King's and my special thanks, which shall be so acquitted, as ye shall have cause to think your pains and diligences therein in the best wise imployed, trusting in God that howsoever the World shall come, ye shall by one means or other bring the King's Matter, which so highly toucheth his Honour and quiet of Mind, unto the desired end and perfection.

Finally; Ye shall understand that the French King, among other things, doth commit at this time to the Bishop of Bayon, and Mr. John Joachim to treat and conclude the Confederation heretofore spoken of, between his Holiness and the King's Highness, the French King, the Venetians, and other Potentates of Italy, for a continual Army to be entertained to invade Spain in case it stand by the Emperor, that the Peace shall not take effect: Wherefore the King's pleasure is, That ye having conference with them at good length in that Matter, do also for your parts, sollicite, procure, and set forth the same; entring also on the King's behalf unto the Treaty, and conclusion thereof, after such manner as your former Instructions and Writings do purport. So as like as the French King is determined, that his Agents shall join and concur with you in the King's Pursuits and Causes.; So ye must also concur with them in advancement of their Affairs, the successes whereof, and of all other your doings there, it shall be expedient ye more often notify hitherto than ye do, for many times in one whole month no knowledg is had from you, which is not meet in those so weighty Matters, specially considering that sometime by such as pass to Lyons, ye might find the means to send your Letters, which should be greatly to the King's and my consolation, in hearing thereby from time to time, how the things succeed there; I pray you therefore to use more diligence therein, as the Kings and my special trust is in you. And heartily fare you well. From my Palace besides Westminster, the sixth day of April.

The French King hath sent hither an Ambassiate, Monsieur de Langes, Brother to the said Bishop of Bayon, with certain clauses in his Instructions, concerning the said

Treaty of Confederation, the Copy whereof ye shall receive herewith, for your better carrying on that Matter. Praying God to speed you well, and to give you grace to make a good and short end in your Matters. And eft-soons fare ye well,

Your Loving Friend,

T. Cardin. Eborac.

XXIII.

Another Dispatch to the Ambassadours to the same purpose.
A Duplicate.

RIGHT well beloved Friends, I commend me unto you in my hearty manner, letting you wit, that by the hands of Thadeus bearer hereof, the King's Highness hath received your several Letters to the same, directed with the Pope's Pollicitation mentioned in the same, and semblablie I have received your Conjunct and several Letters of the date of the 18 and 29 days of March; the 8, 19, 20, and 22 of April, to me directed, wherein ye at right good length have made mention of such Discourses, Conferences, Audiences and Communications as ye have had concerning your Charge, since the time of your former Advertisements made in that behalf, with all such Answers and Replications as have been made unto you by the Pope's Holiness, and other on his behalf concerning the same. In the Circumstances whereof ye have so diligently, discreetly, and substantially, acquitted your selves, as not only your firm and fervent desire, to do unto the King's Highness special and singular service in this his great and weighty Cause, but also your Wisdom, Learning, and perfect dexterities, heretofore well known, hath every one for his part thereby been largely of new shewed, comprobate and declared to the King's good contentment, my rejoice and gladness, and to your great laud and praise. For the which his Grace giveth unto you right hearty thanks, and I also for my part do the semblable; assuring you, in few words, though the time and state of things hath not suffered that your desires might at this time be brought unto effect, yet the King's Grace well knoweth, perceiveth, and taketh, that more could not have been done, excogitated, or devised, than ye have largely endeavoured your self unto for conducing the King's purpose, which his Grace accepteth, as touching your merits and acquittal in no less good and thankful part, than if ye finding the disposition of things in more direct state, had consecute all your pursuits and desires: Nor ye shall doubt or think, that either the King's Highness or I have conceived, or thought any manner negligence in you for such things as were mentioned, in the last Letters sent unto you by Alexander, Messenger, but that albeit his Highness had cause, as the same wrote, to marvel of your long demor, and lack of expedition of one or other of the things committed to your charge; yet did his Highness right well persuade unto himself the default not to be in you, but in some other cause, whereof his Grace not knowing the same, might justly and meritoriously be brought unto admiration, and marvel: And therefore be ye all of good comfort, and think your perfect endeavours used, and services done, to be employed there, as it can right well, in every part regarded and considered.

In effect coming to the Specialities of the things now to be answered, The King's Highness having groundly noted and considered the whole continue and circumstances of all your said Letters and Advertisements, findeth and perceiveth evidently, that whatsoever Pursuits, and Instances, and Requests have been, or shall be for this present time, made there by you on his Grace's behalf to the Pope's Holiness, for the furtherance of the said great and weighty Cause; and how much soever the necessity of Christendom for the good of Peace, the importance of the Matter, the justness of the thing it self, reason, duty, respect to good Merits, detecting of Falsities used, evident Arguments and Presumptions to the same, or other thing whatsoever it be, making for the King's purpose, do weigh; the Times be now such, as all that shall be done in any of the Premisses there, is apparent by such privy Intelligence and promise as is between the Pope and the Emperor, to hang and depend upon the Emperor's Will, Pleasure, and Arbitre, as whom the Pope's Holiness neither dare nor will in any part displease, offend, or miscontent, nor do by himself any thing notable therein, which he shall think or suppose to be of moment, the said Emperor first inconsulted, or not consenting thereunto. And for that cause, since the Emperor not only is the Adversary of Universal Peace, Letter, and Impeacher thereof, but also, as hath appeared by sundry Letters heretofore, and now of new sent out of Spain, doth shew himself adverse, and enterponing himself as a Party against the King's said great Matter; It were in manner all one to prosecute the same at the Emperor's hands, as at the Popes, which so totally dependeth upon the Emperor; and as much Fruit might be hoped of the one as of the other, so as far discrepant it were from any wisdom in a thing so necessary, and which as ye know must needs be brought unto an end without any further delay, to consume and spend the time, where such express contrariety and in manner dispair appeareth to do good therein, and where should be none other but continual craft, colour, abuses, refuses and delays, but rather to proceed unto the same in place, and after such form as may be a appearance of some good and brief effect to ensue. Wherefore to shew you in Counsel, and to be reserved unto your selves, The King's Highness finding this ingratitude in the Pope's Holiness, is minded for the time to dissemble the Matter, and taking as much as may be had and attained there to the benefit of his Cause, to proceed in the decision of the same here, by virtue of the Commission already granted unto me and my Lord Legate Campegius.

And for because that ye Mr. Stevins be largely ripened and acquainted in this Matter, and that both the King's Highness and I have right large experience of your entire zeal and mind to the studying and setting forth of such things concerning the Law, as may be to the furtherance hereof; considering also that for any great thing like to be done there herein, such Personages as be of good Authority, Wisdom, and Experience, tho they be not learned in the Law, may with such Counsel as ye have retained there, right well serve to the accomplishment of such other things as shall occur, or be committed unto them on the King's behalf, tho so many Ambassadors do not there remain and

continue: His Grace therefore willing and minding to revoke you all by little and little, except you Sir Gregory
being his Ambassadour there continually residing, willeth,
That after such things perfected and done, as hereafter
shall be mentioned, ye Mr. Stevins, and you Sir Francis
Brian, shall take your leave of the Pope's Holiness, and
with diligence return home. For if ne had been the absence of you Mr. Stevins, seeing that there is small appearance of any Fruit to be obtained there, the King's Highness would have entred into Process here before this Whitsuntide: But because his Grace would have you here present, as well for the forming of the said Process, and for
such things as be trusted that ye shall obtain and bring
with you, as also for the better knowledge to be had in
sundry Matters, wherein you may be the better ripened and
informed by means of your being in that Court: And otherwise his Highness will somewhat the longer defer the com-
mencement of the said Process, and respite the same, only
for your coming; which his Grace therefore desireth you
so much the more to accelerate, as ye know how necessary
it is, that all diligence and expedition be used in that Matter. And so ye all to handle and endeavour your selves
there, for the time of your demor, as ye may do the most
benefit and advantage that may be to the speedy furtherance of the said Cause.

And forasmuch as at the dispatch of your said last Letters, ye had not opened unto the Pope's Holiness, the last
and uttermost Device here conceived, and to you written
in my Letters sent by the said Alexander, but that ye intended, as soon as ye might have time and access, to set
forth the same; wherein it is to be trusted, since that thing
could by no colour or respect to the Emperor be reasonably denied, ye have before this time done some good, and
brought unto perfection; I therefore remitting you to such
Instructions as ye received at that time, advertise you that
the King's mind and pleasure is, ye do your best to attain
the Ampliation of the said Commission, after such form as
is to you, in the said last Letters and Instructions, prescribed; which if ye cannot in every thing bring to pass, at
the least to obtain as much to the King's purpose, and the
benefit of the Cause as ye can; wherein all good policy

and dexterity is to be used, and the Pope's Holiness by all perswasions to be induced thereunto; shewing unto the same how ye have received Letters from the King's Highness and me, responsives to such as ye wrote of the Dates before rehearsed; whereby ye be advertised that the King's Highness, perceiving the Pope's strange demeanour in this his great and weighty Cause, with the little respect that his Holiness hath, either to the importance thereof, or to do unto his Holiness at this his great necessity, gratuity and pleasure; not only cannot be a little sorry and heavy to see himself frustrate of the future hope and expectation that his Grace had, to have found the Pope's Holiness a most loving, fast, near and kind Father, and assured Friend, ready and glad to have done for his Grace, that which of his Power Ordinary or Absolute, he might have done in this thing, which so near toucheth the King's Conscience, Health, Succession, Realm, and Subjects; But also marvelleth highly, That his Holiness, both in Matters of Peace, Truce, in this the King's Cause, and in all other, hath more respect to please and content him of whom he hath received most displeasures, and who studieth nothing more than the detriment of the See, than his Holiness hath either to do that which a good common Father, for the well of the Church, Himself, and all Christendom, is bounden, and oweth to do, or also that which every thing well pondered, it were both of Congruence, Right, Truth, Equity, Wisdom, and conveniency for to do. Thinking verily that his Highness deserved to be far otherwise entreated, and that not at his most need in things nearest touching his Grace, and where the same had his chief and principal confidence, thus to have his just and reasonable Petitions rejected and totally to be converted, to the arbitre of his Enemy, which is not the way to win, acquire and conserve Friends to the Pope's Holiness and See Apostolick, nor that which a good and indifferent Vicar of Jesus Christ and common Father unto all Princes, oweth and is bound to observe. Nevertheless ye shall say the King's Highness, who always hath shewed, and largely comprobate himself a most devout Son unto the See Apostolick, must and will take patience; and shall pray to God to put in the Pope's mind, a more direct and vertuous intent, so to pro ceed in his acts and doing, as he may be found a very Father, upright, indifferent, loving and kind; and not thus for partial respect, fear, or other inordinate Affection, or cause, to degenerate from his best Children, showing himself unto them, as a Step-Father, nor the King's Highness ye shall say can persuade unto himself, that the Pope's Holiness is of that nature and disposition, that he will so totally fail his Grace in this Matter of so high importance, but that by one good mean or other, his Holiness will perfectly comprobate the intire love that always the same hath shewed to bear towards his Highness, wherein ye shall desire him now to declare by his Acts the uttermost of his intent and disposition; so as ye Mr. Stevins and Mr. Brian, who be revoked home, do not return with void hands, or bring with you things of such meagerness, or little substance, as shall be to no purpose: And thus by these, or like words, seconding to the same effect, which as the time shall require, and as he shall have cause, ye by your Wisdoms can qualifie and devise, It is not to be doubted, but that the Pope's Holiness perceiving how the King's Highness taketh this Matter, and that two of you shall now return, will in expedition of the said Ampliation of the Commission, and other things requisite, strain himself to do unto the King's Highness as much gratuity and pleasure as may be; for the better attaining whereof, ye shall also shew, how heavy and sorry I with my Lord Legate Campegius be, to see this manner of proceeding, and the large promises which he and I so often have made unto the King's Highness, of the Pope's fast and assured mind, to do all that his Holiness, *etiam ex plenitudine potestatis*, might do, thus to be diappointed; most humbly beseeching his Holiness on my behalf, by his high Wisdom to consider, what a Prince this is; the infinite and excellent gratitudes which the same hath exhibited to the Pope's Person in particular, and to the See Apostolick in the general; the magnitude and importance of this Cause, with the Consequences that may follow, by the good or ill entreating of the King's Highness in the same; wherein ye shall say, I have so largely written, so plainly for my discharge declared the truth unto his Holiness, and so humbly, reverently, and devoutly, made intercession, that more can I

not add or accumulate thereunto, but only pray unto God
that the same may be perceived, understood, and taken, as
the exigence of the Case, and the merits of this Noble
Prince doth require ; trusting always, and with fervent desire, from day to day, abiding to hear from his said Holiness some such thing as I shall now be able constantly to
justifie and defend, the great things which 1 and my said
Lord Legate have said and attested on his Holiness behalf.

This, with all other such matter as may serve to the purpose, ye shall extend as well as ye can, and by that means
get and attain as much to your purpose for the corroboration and surety of all things to be done here as is possible,
leaving to speak any more, or also to take or admit any rescripts for exhibition of the Brief, advocation of the Cause,
or other of the former degrees, seeing that all which shall
or can be done or attained there, shall hang meerly upon
the Emperor's Will, Consent, and Arbitre : and therefore
nothing is now or hereafter to be procured, that may tend
to any Act to be done, in decision of the Cause or otherwise there, or which may bring the adverse Party to any
advantage to be taken by the favour or partiality, that the
same may have in that Court ; but to convert and employ
all your suit, to that thing which may be to the most con-
validation and surety of the Process, and things to be done
here, as well by attaining, as ample, large, and sufficient
words, clauses and sentences as ye can get, for ampliation
of the new Commission.

As for the defeating of any thing that may be procured
to the impeachment of the Process thereof, and the corroboration of the things to be passed, and done, by virtue of
the same. And amongst other things, whereas ye with
these last Letters, sent the Pope's Pollicitation, for the
non-inhibition or avoking of the Cause, the ratifying and
confirming of the Sentence by us his Legates herein to be
given, and other things mentioned in the same, ye shall
understand, that the said Pollicitation is so couched and
qualified, as the Pope's Holiness whensoever he will may
resile ; like-as by certain Lines and Annotations, which in
the Margin of a Copy of the said Pollicitation I send you
herewith, ye shall perceive more at large : And therefore
after your other suits, for the ampliation of the new Com-

mission, if any such may be attained, brought unto as good a purpose as ye can, ye shall by some good way find the mean to attain a new Pollicitation, with such, or as many of the words and additions newly devised as ye can get; which ye may do under this form and colour, that is to say, to shew unto the Pope's Holiness, by way of sorrow and doleance, how your Courier, to whom ye committed the conveyance of the said Pollicitation, so chanced, in wet and water in the carriage thereof, as the Pacquet wherein it was, with such Letters as were with the same, and amongst other the Rescripts of Pollicitation, were totally wet, defaced, and not legible; so as the Pacquet and Rescript was and is detained by him to whom ye direct your Letters, and not delivered amongst the other unto the King's hands; and unless his Holiness, of his goodness unto you, will grant you a double of the said Pollicitation, ye see not but there shall be some notable blame imputed unto you for not better ordering thereof, to the conservation of it from such chance. And thus coming to a new Pollicitation, and saying, ye will devise it as near as ye can remember, according to the former, ye by your Wisdoms, and namely ye Mr. Stevins, may find the means to get as many of the new and other pregnant, fat, and available words as is possible, the same signed and sealed as the other is, to be written in Parchment; the politick handling whereof, the King's Highness and I commit unto your good discretions; for therein, as ye Mr. Stevins know, resteth a great strength and corroboration of all that shall be done there, in decision of the King's said Cause; and as ye write, may be in manner as beneficial to the King's purpose, as the Commission Decretal.

And to the intent ye may the better know how to proceed in this Business, I advertise you that the King's Highness hath now received fresh Letters out of Spain, answering to those sent by Curson jointly with a Servant of the Queens, for exhibition of the Original Brief here, of whose expedition you Mr. Stevins were privy before your departure. The Letters were of sundry dates, the last whereof is the 21 of April, at which time the Emperor was at Cæsar Augusta, upon his departure towards Barselona. In effect, the Emperor minding by his departure thither, and other

his Acts, to make a great demonstration of his coming into
Italy, who is to nothing, as the King's Ambassadours write,
more unmeet and unfurnished than to that voyage, not having any Gallies there but three, which lay on dry Land un-
rigged, as they have done a long time passed, none Assem-
bly of the States of that Land, none order, provision of
Victual, towardness in conscription of Men of War, or appearance of such thing, but that his going to Barselona, is
chiefly under pretext to attain certain old Treasure there
remaining, and to give the better reputation to his Affairs
in Italy. As to the matter of Peace and Truce, he seemeth
not so alien from it, but that he would, under colour thereof, be glad to separate and dis-join other from the sincerity
of confidence that is between them, working somewhat with
the French King, which he himself confesseth to be but
abuses. On the other side, he maketh overture of Peace
or Truce to be had with the King's Highness apart; and
in the mean time entertaineth the Pope's Holiness, as one
whom won from the residue of the Confederates, he thinketh himself most assured of: Howbeit in all this his Business, ye may constantly affirm, that his Compasses cannot
prevail in any thing that may be excogitate to the separation of the King's Highness and the French King, who so
entirely proceed together, that the Emperor coming or not
coming into Italy, the said French King intendeth to prosecute him in the place where his Person shall be. To
whom the King's Highness now sendeth the Duke of Suffolk, with the Treasurer of his honourable Houshold; who
if the Pope will not really and actually intend to the main-
taining of the Peace, coming to the convention of his Holiness, moved as the case shall require, shall be furnished of
a substantial number of Men of War out of his Realm to the
assistance of the said French King, if the Emperor happen
to descend in Italy. So as his things there, be not like to
be in such surety as might bring the Pope's Holiness to
this extremity of fear and respect. And all the Premisse
touching this knowledg had out of Spain, and the French
King's Interest with the King's Concurrence, as afore; I
shall be well done ye declare to the Pope's Holiness
whereby peradventure the same shall be removed from
some part of his said overmuch respect to that part.

As to sending of the Brief, the Emperor refusing to send it into England, sheweth some towardness of sending it to Rome, minding and intending to have the King's Matter decided there and not here; howbeit all be but vain Collusions: For as ye shall perceive by such things as be extracted out of the Letters of the King's Orators Resident in Spain, a Copy whereof I send you herewith, the more the said Breve cometh into light and knowledg, the more falsities be deprehended therein; and amongst other, one there is specially to be noted, making, if it be true, a clearer and manifest proof of the same Falsity; which because if it were perceived by the adverse Party, or any of their Friends, Counsellors, or Adherents, it might soon by a semblable falsity be reformed, is above all other things to be kept secret, both from the Pope, and all other there, except to your selves: for in computation of the Year of our Lord is a diverse order observed in the Court of Rome in Bulls and Breves; That is to say, in the Bull beginning at the Incarnation of our Lord, in the Brief at the Nativity; So as the thing well searched, it is thought it shall be found, that the date presupposed to be of the Breve, which is 26 *Decemb. Anno Dom.* 1503. *Pontificatus Julii anno primo,* well conferred with the manner and usages of that Court: He that counterfeited the Brieve, not knowing such diversity between the date of the Bull and Breves, and thinking to make both Dates of one day, dated the Breve at a day before Pope Julii was Pope; which ye shall more plainly perceive by the said Copy, and specially if under some good colour ye ripen your selves there, whether the year in the date of Breves change upon Christmass day, or upon New-years day, wherein the King's pleasure is, that ye ensearch and certifie here what ye shall know and perceive. And if ye shall by such inquiry find matter making to the purpose, as it is not doubted but ye shall do, then for the more sure justification and proof thereof before the Judges; It shall be expedient ye in writing make mention of such a doubt, finding the means that it may be answered and declared in the same Writing, by certain expert Persons of the Secretaries, and other Officers of that Court, with subscription of their Answer and Names; whereby it may appear here before us as Judges,

as a thing true and approved: Howbeit, great dexterity is
to be used for the secrecy thereof; for if such Exceptions
might come to the knowledg of the Adverse Party, they
might, as the said Orators write, soon reform that default by detrahing one Letter, or Title, or forging a new
Brief, alledging error in the Transumpts, which might be
the total disappointment of deprehension of the falsity in
that chief and principal point. I pray you therefore to regard that Matter substantially, and to order it by your
good Wisdoms accordingly.

XXIV.

*The two Legates Letter to the Pope, advising a Decretal
Bull. A Duplicate.*

Cotton
Libr.
Vitell.
B. 11.
PRIORIBUS nostris ad Sanctitatem Vestram literis quid
hic ageremus, quove in statu causa hæc esset exposuimus ;
postea quum, et res ipsa, et desiderium Regis admodum ur-
geret, ut ad Causæ ipsius merita agnoscenda accingere-
mur, quando in suspenso, non modo horum Regum vota,
sed nec hujus Regni firmandi ratio, diutius haberi potest,
omni suasionis genere horum animis prius adhibito, ut alterius voluntati alter cederet, eique morem gererent, cum
nihil profecerimus, ad Judicii institutionem accedentes, de
modo causam ipsam pertractandi, multa longioribus collo-
quiis inter nos commentati sumus ; qua in re, dum quæ necessaria sunt adornantur, exhibitûm est per Reginam exemplum Brevis Julii 2. eodem tempore quo et Bulla super
hac materia, dati et scripti, sed attentiore cura et longe
consideratiore mente confecti, quod, quia in substantiali-
bus etiam ab ipsa Bulla diversum est, non modo Regium,
sed nostrum quoq; animum, mire suspensum habuit, usq ;
adeo ut de ejus veritate plurimum suspicari libeat ; nam
præter insperatam in tanta opportunitate ejus apparitio-
nem, incredibile videtur, ut eodem tempore idem author,
eisdem partibus, in eadem Causa, diversa admodum ratione caverit, et permansuro Diplomati ejusq ; Decreto, ad
perpetuam rei memoriam, proferendo, et plumbeo caractere

excudendo dormitaverit, brevioribus vero literis, molli *BOOK*
cera communiendis exactissimi studii et sobriæ cogitationis *II.*
speciem impresserit : ne tamen Majestas hæc rem hanc
damnatam priusquam exploratam habeat, quippe quæ magis inveritate quam in voto suo, Causæ hujus eventum sus-
ceptura videtur, ad ipsius Brevis exhibitionem instat, quod,
quia honestum et rationi consonum videtur, a nobis etiam
probatur, propterea omni studio curamus, ut Breve ipsum,
quod in Hispaniis esse dicitur, et a quo exemplum hoc
effigiatum aiunt proferatur ; atque ut hoc expeditiore cura, et majore compendio assequamur, præter primam et
summam illam de Causa cognoscendi potestatem, quam a
Sanctitate Vestra habemus, aliam quoque ad hunc specialiter articulum habendam putamus, per quam possimus
etiam per censuras, omnes etiam Regia et Imperiali Authoritate fulgentes, monere et adigere ut dictum Breve nobis exhibeant, sine quo causa hæc nedum absolvi, sed nec
commode tractari queat. Atque hoc primum est, quod Majestas hæc, in tanta animi fluctuatione qua nunc æstuat, a
nobis curandum putat, quo impetrato, Judicii via insi-
stentes ad Causæ cognitionem procedemus ; quod si non
proferatur, vel inutile et vitiatum, et fide sua facile rejiciendum, prolatum fuerit, nihil prohibebit, hoc sublato ob-
ice, quin ex officio nostro reliqua prosequamur : sin vero
exhibeatur, et veritate sua, vel adeo scite conficta fallacia,
ita se tueatur ut acriori examine id inquiri debeat, patefacto jam patronorum cavillis et calumniis foro, quibus un-
dis et judicii fluctibus non solum articulum hunc Brevis, sed
universam Causam implicaturi simus, nullus non viderit ;
neque enim deerunt quæ suspectam ipsius Brevis fidem faciant, vel ex hoc maxime, quod cum maxime Regis et Regni hujus intersit, nihil prorsus de eo antehac auditum fuerit, nec ejus memoria aut ratio ulla extet in Scriniis Regiis, in quibus etiam minima quæque ad Regnum spectantia asservari solent : nam verisimile non est in Hispaniis
majorem Anglicæ rei curam fuisse quam in ipsa Anglia,
neq ; quempiam solerti et acri adeo ingenio fuisse, qui hu-
juscemodi dissidium vigesimo quinto ab hinc anno subori-
turum, et hac sola ratione sublatum iri posse divinaverit,
nulla ut diximus apud hunc Regem, et in hoc Regno talis
rei memoria extante. Porro si ex Brevi ad Bullam, et ex

Bulla ad Breve transitus fiat, atque illius jejunitatem et ari-
ditatem insectemur, hujus prægnantia verba, et ad omnes
fere exceptiones tollendas, superstitiosam quodammodo vi-
gilantiam conferamus, et quæ utrinq; deduci poterunt in
Rescriptis Apostolicis æquo animo audiamus, periclitaturi
certe sumus, ne, quod minime cupimus, Sedis Apostolicæ
Authoritatem patientia nostra in discrimen rapiamus, atque dum Regno, et Regni hinc suppetias ferre volumus,
rem dignitatemq; nostram multo minorem faciamus, cui
tum posita etiam anima, favere et adesse semper cupimus
et debemus. Propterea, Beatissime Pater, non solum pro
Regis et Causæ hujus commodo, sed pro dignitate quoq;
Ecclesiastica et Sanctitatis Vestræ Autoritate hic tuenda
et conservanda, nullo pacto committendum ducimus, ut nobis spectantibus et audientibus, de Potestate Romani Pontificis, de literarum Apostolicarum sub plumbo et sub annulo scriptarum fide, et repugnantia, deque juris divini
abrogatione disceptetur, maxime in Regum causa oppug-
nanda et defendenda, qui, ut sublimiore sunt fastigio collo-
cati, ita iniquiori animo patiuntur Causæ suæ casum, cum
qua et dignitatem et existimationem suam diminutam iri
intelligunt, quæ si ignobilium etiam animos quosq; exul-
cerare, ipsa rerum experientia docti cernimus, qualiter
quæso putamus Regios et generosos affectura. Itaq; quoniam hanc carybdim et hos scopulos evitasse semper tutum
erit, propterea hujusmodi incommoda quodammodo præter-
vecti, ubi ad litis molestias et incertas fori fluctuationes
causam deducendam perspicimus, suadere, rogare et summis precibus pariq; reverentia contendere non desinemus,
ut si exhibito Brevi pura veritas ita latitaverit, quod rec-
tumne an falsum, vitiatum ceu adulterinum fuerit judicare
ac decernere minime valeamus, Sanctitas Vestra Causam
hanc ad se avocet, non solum ut tanto discrimine, et per-
plexitate nos eximat, sed ut paterno affectu Causæ et Regi huic optimo subveniat et opem ferat, atque ex Potestatis
suæ plenitudine et summa prudentia finem huic rei optatum imponat, quæ non sine magno hujus Regni et Ecclesiasticæ dignitatis periculo diutius trahi potest: Speramus
autem Serenissimum hunc Regem in hujusmodi avocandæ
Causæ consilio facile quieturum, salebrosa hæc litium iti-
nera et labirinthos evitaturum, modo in fide Sanctitatis

Vestræ chyrographo manus suæ testata, cognoverit, se diutius suspenso in hac re animo detinendum non fore, atq; ab
hujusmodi Matrimonio se tandem liberandum, in quo nec
humano nec divino jure permanere se posse putat, ex causis Sanctitati Vestræ forsan notis, et per hos suos nuntios
longioribus verbis explicandis. Quod si SanctitasVestra commodius existimaverit, Avocatione hujusmodi posthabita, per
Decretalis unius concessionem huic causæ occurri et succurri
posse, in hanc quoque rationem Regis animum paratum dabimus; et propterea concepto quodam Decretalis módulo,
eum per hos ipsos Majestatis suæ nuntios mittimus, ex quibus abunde intelliget, quodque non absque exemplo istius-
modi auxilia proponantur, et quam non temere nec absque
ratione Majestas hæc desiderio huic suo inhæreat: interea
vero, dum hac vel illa ratione huic rei occurritur et Breve
ipsum perquiretur, posset utiq; Sanctitas Vestra iterum
Reginæ animum tentare, et ad Religionem emollire, curando (ut quod maxime apud eam gratia et Autoritate esse
debeant) et literis, et precibus, et nuntiis, omniq; alia ratione, hac ipsa via, sibi, suisq; rebus omnibus, atq; aliis
optime consulat. Cujusmodi multa, pro salute Regni et
publica cum dignitate, tum tranquillitate animo agitamus,
ut tandem optimo Regi præsidio simus, qui incredibili patientia et humanitate, nostram et Sanctitatis Vestræ opem
expectat, sed tanta obsessus cura, sollicitudine et anxi-
etate, ut nullus facile explicare possit, vix enim in hoc
ipso, oculis et auribus nostris credimus; cujus usque adeo
nos miseret, ut nihil ingrato magis animo audiamus quam
ejus de hac re verba, querelas et cruciatum: jure, an injuria liceat nobis hoc, Beatissime Pater, cum Sanctitate
Vestra tacere, ne præjudicium nobis aut aliis faciamus, sed
quem non excitet tot annorum Conscientiæ Carnificina,
quam ut transversum et modo in has et modo in illas partes
agant Theologorum disputationes, et Patrum decreta, nullus non videt; qua in re enucleanda ita ambiguo laboratur
sensu, ut jam non doctioris sed melioris hominis lumine et
pietate egeamus, et propterea factum est ut cum ab utraq;
parte stant assertores maximi, in illam magis Majestas sua
inclinat, quæ ab offensionibus et periculis magis remota videtur. Quem præterea non moveat dulcis illa insitaque
sobolis successio, in qua morientes et animam exhalaturi

conquiescere, natura ipsa, videmur omnes? quem insuper
non accendat, Regni atque imperii propagatio, et per solos
liberos continuata quædam fruitio? quem deniq; populorum fidei ac ejus curæ commissorum tranquillitas et securitas, quæ in designatis jam regibus et principibus nutritur
et vivit, non sollicitet? ita ut tanti adeoq; communis boni fundamenta nulla a se jacta, non doleat et suspiret, cum
in extremis ejus diebus, extrema quoque tempora eis ad-
ventare sentiat, atq; secum omnia quodammodo in ruinam
trahi? Majores habet, Beatissime Pater, Causa hæc an-
fractus et difficultates, quam superficie tenus inspectanti-
bus offerantur, in quo vel hæ potissimæ sunt quod nec moram patitur, et in alteram partem non inclinat quidem, sed
omnino cogit, ni velimus ab ea præcipites et maxima cum
privatæ tum publicæ rei jactura cadere; nam qui vel Reginæ odio, vel speratæ, nec dum forsan notæ, futuræ conjugis illecebra et titillatione Regem agi putant, ii excordes
plane et toto, quod aiunt, cœlo errare videntur: ut enim
credere dignum est, nullis illius quamlibet duris moribus
aut injccunda consuetudine, vel ulterioris sobolis spe des-
perata, Regium animo tanto periculo ad odium impelli posse; ita nec in hominis bene sani mente cadere debet, Regem
hunc imbecillo adeo esse animo, ut sensuum suadela eam
abrumpere cupiat consuetudinem, in qua adolescentiæ suæ
florentes annos exegerit persancte adeo, ut in hac quoq;
fluctuatione, non sine reverentia et honore versetur. Inest,
credite omnes, voluntati ejus non modo divinæ legis timor,
sed humani quoq; juris ratio eximia, hæcq; non privata
sed publica, ad quam cum ejus animum trahant, utriusq;
juris peritissimi, et Regni hujus sui proceres, et primates
omnes, nihil tamen suo, aut suorum tantum arbitrio constitutum habere cupit, sed Apostolicæ Sedis judicio; qua in
re quanta sit pietate, maxime ostendit, quum non ex mago-
rum carminibus, et circulatorum imposturis, aliisve malis
artibus, sed Sanctissima Pontificis manu, tanto huic vulneri suo opem petat, de quo vel plura forte quam licuisset
Sanctitati Vestræ subjecimus, quoniam hæc ipsa ulcera
manibus nostris contrectavimus, et quantum vitales spiritus
exhalent cognovimus: proinde Sanctitas Vestra, pii patris
et peritissimi medici more, dum virtus adhuc stat, dum salus non desperatur, dum æger ipse sese sustinet et legitima

petit auxilia, **Regem** de se et Apostolica sede optime me-
ritum in pietatis suæ sinu foveat, illudq; ei indulgeat quod
nec disputationum immortalia dissidia, nec litium immen-
sum chaos unquam dabit, nec sine maximo discrimine unquam tractabitur; atque illud etiam secum reputet, quam
injurium, et cum privatis tum publicis rebus incommodum
sit, extremos juris apices consectari, quanquam non expediat ex scripto jure semper judicari; cui, quia Pontifices
et Principes miro omnium consensu, a Deo ipso præfecti,
censentur Spiritus et animæ vice, merito in ambiguis, et
ubi multa periclitatur hominum salus, arbitrio suo ejus
duritiem moderari possunt et debent, in quo Sanctitas Vestra et **Regem** et **Regnum** hoc plane servaverit. Quod si
alia ratione vel aliunde paranda sibi fuerint auxilia, vere-
mur ne de **Regno** et **Rege** hoc actum sit, quicquid enim
alia manu huic vulneri impositum fuerit, nihil minus faciet
quam sanitatem, seditionibus enim et tumultibus omnia
exponentur, atq; imprimis Ecclesiastica **Dignitas** et Apostolicæ Sedis Authoritas hinc deturbabitur; quod non erit
difficile, aut ingratum quibusdam, qui **Rege** cum Sanctitate Vestra nunc conjunctissimo, impietatis suæ venenum
perbelle dissimulant; Cujusmodi jacturam si dura hæc
tempora nostra fecerunt, quod deinde sperandum sit, non
videmus. Conservandus itaq; **Rex** est, ejusq; eximia in
Apostolicam Sedem voluntas et fides, ne eo a nobis abali-
enato, non modo Angliæ **Regem**, sed Fidei quoq; Defensorem amittamus, cujus virtutes et **Religionem** tanto plau-
su orbi commendavimus. Brevitati studentes multa præ-
terimus, et præsertim quid **Regni** proceres, Nobiles æque
atque ignobiles dicant, qui fremunt et acerbissime indig-
nantur, se tamdiu suspensos haberi, atq; ab aliorum nutu
et voluntate exspectare, quid de fortunis eorum omnibus
et capitibus statuant, aut decernant: atq; hac potissimum
via insistunt, qui nullam aut certe diminutam hic **Romani**
Pontificis Authoritatem vellent, quorum pleriq; in his dis-
ceptationibus, quibus alter alteri, ut usu venire solet, re in
ambiguo posita, adversatur, ea dicunt quæ non absq; hor-
rore referri queant; nam inter cætera illud maxime in ore
obvium habent, et prædicant, se nunquam satis demirari,
aut ridere posse quorundam ignaviam, qui patienter audi-
unt, Pontificibus in Jure Divino figendo et refigendo li-

cere, Pontifici Pontificis ceram aut plumbum conflare non
permitti; nos, ut hos scopulos et has syrtes evitemus, nihil
non agimus, et ne præceps, huc vel illuc, Rex hic ruat, curamus, quem in officio vix contineri posse confidimus, dum
a Sanctitate Vestra his literis rescribatur: quibus si ut
speramus et cupimus aliquid rescriptum fuerit, per quod et
Regem et horum omnium animos quietiores reddere valeamus, accedet nobis quoq; vis aliqua cætera felicius perfi-
ciendi; sin minus, omnia in deterius itura non ambigimus.
Quæ ut celerius Majestas sua cognoscat, præsentes hos
nuntios suos per dispositos equos ad Sanctitatem Vestram
mittit, ex quorum sermone plura quoque intelligent quam
literæ ipsæ commode capere potuerunt. Ignoscet vero
Sanctitas Vestra literarum nostrarum prolixitati, quæ tametsi modum excedunt, rei tamen hujus difficultatem et periculum majori ex parte minime attingunt.

XXV.

May 21. 1529. Richmont.

Another Dispatch to Rome. An Original.

RIGHT well beloved Friends, I commend me unto you
in my most hearty manner, by the hands of Alexander,
Messenger; I have in good diligence received your Letters
of the 4th of this Month; and semblably the King's Highness hath received your other Letters, sent by the same
Messenger unto his Grace: By tenour whereof it well appeareth that the King's Highness is now, frustrate of the
good hope and expectation that his Grace and semblably I
were in of the Pope's determination, to have done for his
Highness in this great and weighty Cause of Matrimony,
as his Holiness by his Chamberlain promised; not only
that which might be done of power ordinary, but also of
absolute; and that ye be utterly in despair to consecute or
attain any thing to the purpose there, to the benefit of the
said Cause, with the strange demeanour that hath been

used in calling you to make answer, why the supplications presented by the Emperor's Ambassador for advocation of the Cause should not proceed; and how discreetly and substantially ye have answered and ordered your selves therein: Affirming finally, that as to that Matter, ye think it shall not serve to any purpose, but only to stop your suit in the obtaining of a new Commission, and desiring to be ascertained of the King's pleasure touching the Protestation mentioned in your Instructions, and how the same is meant and understood, with many other things comprised in your said Letters, right well and substantially couched and handled; for the which the Kings Highness giveth you hearty thanks, and I also thank you in most hearty manner for my part.

Ascertaining you, that by Thadeus, Courier, upon receipt of your former Letters sent by him, who I trust be arrived with you long before this time; I wrote unto you the King's mind and pleasure, as well to forbear any further pursuits of the Degrees committed unto your Charge, except only the expedition of a new Commission and Pollicitation mentioned in the same. As also that you Mr. Stevins, and Sir Francis Brian, should return home, like as my said Letters purported. And forasmuch as now it appeareth, that there is no hope for you to attain the said Commission and Pollicitation, the King's Highness supposing that ye the said Mr. Stevins and Sir Francis be on your way homeward; and perceiving that it should be necessary for his Grace to have there a substantial Counsellor of his, well learned in the Laws, as well to defend all such things as shall be procured or set forth by the Cæsareans, to the hindrance of the King's Cause, as to let and impeach any Advocations, Inhibitions, or other thing that may be dammageable thereunto, hath dispatched thither this Bearer and Mr. Bennet, who hath commandment to shew unto you, and every of you, wheresover he shall meet with or find you, his whole Instructions, by tenour whereof ye shall be advertised of the King's further mind and pleasure in that behalf; wherefore this shall be only to signifie unto you, how his Highness will that ye now forbear any pursuit, either for Commission, Pollicitation or Rescript to be sent to the Emperor for exhibition of the Brief,

either here or at Rome, but that following in every part
the tenor of the said Instructions, ye Mr. Stevins and Sir
Francis Brian use all the diligence possible in your Voyage
homeward, and the residue of you to intend to such things
as be mentioned in the said Instructions ; ascertaining you,
that whereas ye were in doubt what is meant by the Protestation spoken of in my former Letters and your Instructions, it was none other thing than in the same Instructions was plainly specified and declared; That is to say,
Failing of all your Requests and Pursuits touching the
King's great Matter, to have shewed unto his Holiness the
danger that might ensue, by losing the entire favour of this
Prince, by mean of his so strange and unkind dealing with
his Grace ; howbeit, considering in what state the things
now be, and how much the Pope's Holiness seemeth to be
inclined to the Emperors part. And yet as appeareth both
by your Letters, and by such other knowledg as the King
hath, his Holiness would gladly conserve the King's Love
and Favour, and is loth to do any thing to the prejudice of
his Cause : It is no time to come to any rigorous or extream words with his Holiness, but in gentle and modest
manner to shew himself in such words as he mentioned in
my said last Letters sent by Thadeus ; and so without irri-
tation of him, but with conservation of his favour to entertain his Holiness in the best manner that may be, without
medling in any other Protestation, but only to look what
may be done touching such Protestations apart, as is mentioned in the said Instructions given to Mr. Benet, which
with these Letters shall be a sufficient information of you
all what to do in the Causes to you committed, not doubting but in all other particular suits of Bulls, and other things
committed unto you, ye Mr. Stevins and Sir Francis Brian,
have or will do your best to bring the same with you ; the
expedition whereof, if they be not sped already, the King's
Highness committeth to the Wisdoms of such of you as
shall fortune to be in the Court of Rome at the receipt
hereof; wherein, and in all other things, his Highness
trusteth, and I do the semblable, that ye will order your
selves with all effectual diligence, as the special confidence
that is put in you doth appertain.

And forasmuch as the greatest thing that is to be looked

unto is the importune Suit of the Cæsareans, not only to
stop any further things to be granted to the King's Highness, but also to revoke the Commission given to the Lord
Legate Campegius and to me, which should be a clear disappointment and frustration of the King's Cause; ye shall
therefore look substantially by all politick means to with-
stand, that no such thing be granted; assuring the Pope
and all the Cardinals, and such other as have respect to the
well of the See Apostolick, that if he should do such an
high injury to the King and his Realm, and an Act so con-
tumelious to us his Legates, and so contrarious to his Faith
and Promise, he should thereby not fail so highly to irri-
tate the King and all the Nobles of this Realm, that undoubtedly they should decline from the obedience of the
See Apostolick, and consequently all other Realms should
do the semblable, forasmuch as they should find in the
Head of the same, neither justness, uprightness, nor truth;
and this shall be necessary, as the case shall require, well
to be inculked and put in his head, to the intent his Holiness by the same may be preserved from granting, passing,
or condescending to any such thing.

After these Letters perfected hither, and read unto the
King's Highness, albeit that mention is made in sundry
places heretofore, that as well ye Mr. Stevins, and Sir
Francis Brian, if ye be not returned from the Court of
Rome, as also the rest of the King's Ambassadors, which at
the arrival of Mr. Doctor Bennet shall fortune to be there,
shall forbear to make any further means or pursuit for the
New Commission and Pollicitation, but clearly to use silence
therein; yet nevertheless regarding, and more profoundly
considering the effect of your Letters last sent, it doth
plainly appear, that tho after the overture made to the
Pope's Holiness of the said New Commission, the Business
chanced to be made by the Emperor's Ambassador, upon pre-
ferring a Supplication for advocation of the Cause; which
thing by your writing, Mr. Stevins, to Capisuke was well
avoided; yet was there none express refusal made by the
Pope's Holiness to condescend unto the said New Commission, but order given that you should consult and confer with the Cardinal Anconitane and Symonette upon the
same; which Conference, by mean of the said Business,

was deferred and disappointed, without any final conclusion or resolution taken thereupon. Wherefore inasmuch
as yet there appeareth none utter despair of obtaining the
said New Commission and Pollicitation, with some more
fat, pregnant, and effectual Clauses than the other hath ;
The King's pleasure is, That notwithstanding any words
before mentioned, both ye the said Mr. Stevins, and Sir
Francis Brian, if ye be not departed from the Court of
Rome, do for the time of your demur there, which the
King's pleasure is, shall not be long, but only for taking of
your leave ; and also the rest of the King's said Orators,
after your departure, shall, as ye shall see the case require,
endeavour your selves as much as may be, to obtain the
said New Commission and Pollicitation, foreseeing always
that you handle the matter after such manner, as thereby
the Pope be not the rather induced to hearken and incline
to any persuites of the Imperials for advocation of the
Cause, which were a total frustration of all the King's intent, but so to use your selves, as ye shall see to be to the
benefit, and not to the hindrance thereof: Which done,
the King's Grace doth refer the good handling of this
thing to your wisdoms and discretions, neither to leave the
persuit for the said Commission and Pollicitation, if it may
without dammage be followed ; nor to follow it, if thereby
you shall see apparent danger of any such Advocation, or
advantage to ensue to the purpose of the Imperialists, like
as his Highness doubteth not, knowing now the King's
mind and pleasure, you will with wisdom and dexterity,
order your selves herein accordingly.

And furthermore, you shall in any wise dissuade the
Pope for sending either by his Nuntio, to be sent unto
Spain, or otherwise, for the Original Brief. And if the
Nuntio be already passed, having charge to speak for sending the same to the Court of Rome, then to find the means
that a Commandment be by the Pope's Holiness sent after
him, not to make any mention thereof: Which done to
you, the King's said Ambassador shall have a good colour
to induce the Pope's Holiness, saying, as of yourself, That
you have well considered your own pursuits for producing
the Brief at Rome; and because the Emperor might percase think that the Pope were about to arect unto him the

falsity of the said Brief, therefore you can be contented that that matter be put off, and no mention to be made thereof by his Nuntio, or otherwise; whereunto it is not to be doubted but the Pope's Holiness will have special regard, and facilly condescend to your desires in that behalf.

Finally; It appeareth also by certain your Letters sent, as well to the King's Highness as to me, that the Pope's Holiness is much desirous to study and find a mean and way to satisfy the King's Highness in this behalf: Amongst which one clause in his Letters to me is this; *Tametsi enim jurisperitorum consilium quæsiverimus, sed nihil reperimus, quod bonis oratoribus simul et justitiæ ac honori nostro satisfaceret; sed tamen agimus omnia, et tentamus omnes modos Regiæ suæ Serenitati, ac circumspectioni tuæ satisfaciendi.* (And it is added in the Margin, with Wolsey's hand;

Mi Petre, referas tuis literis pervelim quid tibi et mihi Pontifex dixerit de modis excogitandis, et quomodo subridens dicebat, In nomine Patris, &c.)

Wherefore since his Holiness so plainly declared, that he seeketh the ways and means to satisfie the King's Highness, it shall be in any wise expedient, that you the said Orators perceiving any towardness of Advocation, lay this to the Pope's Holiness, saying, That that is not the way to satisfy his Grace; and yet besides that, by your Wisdoms to find the means to understand and know of his Holiness what be the ways and means, which his Holiness hath studied or can study to satisfie the King according to his writing in this behalf, whereof they shall say his Grace is glad, and is very desirous to know and understand the same; and as you shall perceive any towardness or untowardness in the Pope in that behalf, so to set forth your pursuits to the best purpose accordingly. And thus heartily fare you well. From Richmond, the 21 day of May.

Your loving Friend,

T. Cardinalis Eborac.

XXVI,

May 31. Romæ 1529.

A Letter of the Popes to the Cardinal. An Original.

Dilecto Filio nostro Thomæ tituli Sanctæ Ceciliæ Presbytero Cardinali Eboracensi, nostro et sedis Apostolicæ Legato de latere.

Clemens manu propria.

Cotton Libr. Vitel. B. 11.

DILECTE Fili noster, salutem et Apostolicam benedictionem. Cum Angliæ Rex ac Circumspectio vestra, vetera erga nos et Sedem Apostolicam merita novis officiis augeretis, optabamus occasionem, in qua et vos nostrum amorem cognoscere possetis ; sed molestissime tulimus eam primum esse oblatam, in qua circumsepti angustis terminis Justitiæ, non possemus progredi quantum vellemus, studio vobis gratificandi, multis ac rationabilibus Causis desiderium vestrum impedientibus, quod quidem Regiis Oratoribus istuc redeuntibus demonstrare conati sumus. Sed super his et publicis negotiis copiosius vobiscum loquetur Dilectus Filius noster Cardinalis Campegius. Datum Romæ die ultima Maii, 1529.

J.

XXVII.

April 6. 1529.

The King's Letter to his Ambassadors, to hinder an Avocation of the Suit. An Original.

BY THE KING.

HENRY REX,

Cotton Libr. Vitel. B. 11.

TRUSTY and right well-beloved we greet you well. Since your departure from hence, we have received sundry your Letters to us directed, whereof the last beareth date at Rome, the 4th day of the last month ; and have also seen

such other as from time to time ye have sent to the most **BOOK**
Reverend Father in God, our most entirely well-beloved **II.**
Counsellor the Lord Legate, Cardinal, Archbishop of
York, Primate of England, and our Chancellour : By continue whereof, we have been advertised of the Successes,
as well of your Journey thitherwards, as of such things as
ye to that time had done in our Causes to you committed;
for the which your diligent advertisement, and good acquittal, we give unto you condign thanks : ascertaining you,
We do not a little marvel, that in your said last Letters
you shew so much desperation of any great favour to be
had at the Pope's hand in our said Causes; considering
that neither ye then had spoken with his Holiness in the
same, nor by such Conferences as ye had had with Mr.
Jacobo Salviati, or other on his behalf, we can perceive
but all good favour and towardness; tho per-case the su-
periority of the Imperials, and the common fame, led you
to think the contrary : Howbeit as you know no credence
is to be given unto such common report, nor we trust the
same shall prove more true, than hath done the Opinion
that was of the Lord Legate Campegius now here Resident, whom we find and certainly know to be of a far other
sort in his love and inclination towards us, than was spoken,
not having such affection towards the Emperor, as in him
was suspected. And to be plain with you, if ever he had been
of other mind, we have said somewhat to him after such
manner as might soon change that intention. So that little
Faith is to be given to the outward Sayings and Opinions
of such People as measure every thing at their pleasure;
which we doubt not but ye right wisely do consider, and
that ye have before this time, by your diligent sollicitation
made to speak with the Pope's Holiness for declaration of
your Charge, proved the contrary. Whereof we shall be
glad and joyous to hear; willing and desiring you therefore, according to the great and special confidence that we
have in you, to pretermit no time in the diligent handling
and execution of your said Charge, but by one good way
or other to find the mean, if you have not already done it,
to declare the same unto the Pope, wherein the good advice and address of the Bishop of Verone shall, We trust,
do you great furtherance; and by whose means, if ye for

the Pope's extreme debility or sickness might in no wise be often admitted unto his presence, ye may signify unto him at great length, our whole Mind, Desire, and Intent, after such form as your Instructions and Letters given and sent unto you in that behalf do purport: For sure ye may be, it shall highly confer unto the benefit of our Causes, that ye have there present one so fast and assured Friend unto us, as we trust the Bishop of Verone is, who shall be able right largely to countervail, and meet with the malicious practices of the Archbishop of Capua, who is thought to be one of the chief Authors and Contrivers of the Falsities, Crafts, and Abuses, set forth to the hindrance of our said Causes; which no Man shall more politickly and facilly deprehend, than the said Bishop of Verone may do: And therefore he is by you, with all good means and ways possible, to be entertained; as we doubt not but you will have special eye and regard to the making, winning, and conservation of as many Friends to our purpose as ye can possibly obtain; so handling your self, as now may appear your dexterity and perfect endeavour to conduce, with your diligent labour and policy, our Matters to the speedy, indelayed, and desired end and effect, which ye may be sure we shall not put in oblivion, but will have the same in remembrance accordingly. Marvelling nevertheless, that though ye Mr. Stevins could not bring hitherto our great Causes to perfection, ye had not in the mean season advertised us what is done touching such Bulls as were to be sped for our other particular Matters, whereof no mention is made in your said Letters; willing and desiring you therefore, by your next Letters, to advertise us in what state and train the same be; knowing right well that ye being not only by the former Letters and Writings, but also by such as be sent unto you, at this time sufficiently and amply instructed of our Mind and Pleasure, will now so acquit your self, as shall correspond to the perfect expectation, and firm opinion that we have of you, which we shall not fail to have in our tender consideration to your well, as is aforesaid. Ye shall also, in your Conferences with the said Bishop of Verone, understand and know of him, by what ways and means ye may best further his advancement to the Cardinality; exhorting him, for the manifold good

effects that thereof may ensue, to conform himself to the BOOK
acceptation thereof, if it may be obtained; for doubtless II.
his Vertue, Wisdom, Experience, Fidelity, and other great
and commendable merits well considered, we think no
Man more meet at this time to be preferred thereunto than
him: And therefore our express Mind and Pleasure is,
that ye do it by all the ways and means to you possible.
And finally we will that ye show unto him how effectually
we have written unto you in that behalf, to the intent, being advanced thereunto, he may give us the better thanks,
and in every way bear to us the more perfect affection. And
by your next Letters, We will that ye advertise us what
Advocates ye have on our part, with their Names and Qualities; finding the means also, if it be possible, to retain
some notable and excellent Divine, a Frier, or other that
may, can, or will firmly stick to our Causes, in leaning to
that, *Quod Pontifex ex Jure Divino non potest dispensare,*
&c. And of all the Successes to advertise us, as our special
trust is in you. Given under our Signet, at our Mannor of
Greenwich, the 6th of this April.

XXVIII.

The King's Letter to his Ambassadours, about his appear-
ance before the Legates. An Original.

June 23. 1529.

To our trusty and right well-beloved Counsellors, Mr. Wm.
Bennet, Doctor of both Laws; Sir Gregory de Cassalis,
Knight; and Mr. Peter Vannes our Secretary for the
Latin Tongue, our Ambassadours, resident in the Court of
Rome, and to every of them.

BY THE KING.

HENRY R.

TRUSTY and right well-beloved, we greet you well. By Cotton
former Letters and Writings sent to you Sir Gregory and Libr.
Mr. Peter, with other of your Collegues then being at B. 13.

Rome, and by such conference as was had with you Mr.
Benet before your departure, you were advertised in what
state then stood our Cause and Matter of Matrimony, and
how it was intended that the Process of the same should
with diligence be commenced before the Pope's Legates
here, being authorized for that purpose. Since that time,
ensuing the deliberation taken in that behalf, the said Legates, all due Ceremonies first observed, have directed
Citations both to us and to the Queen, for our and for her
appearing before them the 18th of this month; which appearance was duly on either Party kept, performed, and
all requisite Solemnities accomplished: At which time the
Queen trusting more in the power of the Imperialists, than
in any justness of her Cause, and thinking of likelyhood,
by frustratory allegations and delays, to tract and put over
the Matter to her advantage, did protest at the said day,
putting in Libels, Recusatories of the Judges; and also
made a provocation, alledging the Cause to be avoked by
the Pope's Holiness, *et litis pendentiam coram eodem;* desiring to be admitted for probation thereof, and to have a
term competent for the same: Whereupon day was given
by the Judges till the 21 of the same month, for declaration
of their minds and intentions thereunto; The Queen in
Person, and we by our Proctor enjoined to appear the same
day, to hear what the said Judges should determine in and
upon the same. At which time both we and the Queen
appeared in Person; and notwithstanding that the said
Judges amply and sufficiently declared, as well the sincerity of their minds directly, justly to proceed without favour, dread, affection, or partiality; as also that no such
Recusation, Appellation, or term for proving of *Litis pendentiam*, could or might be by them admitted: yet she nevertheless persisting in her former wilfulness, and in her
Appeal, which also by the said Judges was likewise re-
cused: And they minding to proceed further in the Cause,
the Queen would no longer make her abode to hear what
the said Judges would fully discern, but incontinently departed out of the Court; wherefore she was thrice precon-
nisate, and called eft-soons to return and appear; which
she refusing to do, was denounced by the Judges Contu-
max, and a Citation decerned for her appearance on Friday

next, to make answer to such Articles and Positions as should be objected unto her: So as now it is not to be doubted, but that she will use all the ways and means to her possible, to impetrate and attain such things, as well by her own pursute, as by her Friends, as may be to the impeachment of the rightful Process of this Cause, either by Advocation, Inhibition, or otherwise: Wherefore seeing now in what state this our Matter standeth and dependeth, necessary and requisite for the great Consequences hanging upon the same, not only for the exoneration of our Conscience, but also for the surety of our Succession, and the well of this our Realm and People, to be with all celerity perfected and observed. It was thought convenient to advertise you of the Premisses, to the intent ye being well and sufficiently instructed in all things concerning the same, shall by your wisdoms and diligences have special regard that nothing pass or be granted there by the Pope's Holiness, which may either give delay or disappointment to the direct and speedy process to be used in this Cause, neither by Advocation of the Cause, Inhibition, or otherwise; but that if any such thing shall, by the Cæsareans, or by her Agents, or other, be attempted, or desired, the like Men of Wisdom, good Zeal, Learning, and Experience, diligently procure the stopping thereof, as well upon such Reasons and Considerations as before have been signified unto you, as by inferring the high and extream dishonour, and intolerable prejudice that the Pope's Holiness thereof should do to his said Legates; and also the contrariety both of his Bull and Commission, and also of his Promise and Pollicitation passed upon the same; beside the notable and excellent displeasure thereby to be done by his Holiness to us, and our Realm, clear contrary to our merits and deserts; extending also the other dangers mentioned in the said former Writings, apparent to ensue thereby to his Holiness, and the See Apostolick, with the manifold, and in manner, infinite inconveniences like to follow of the same to all Christendom, and all other such reasons, introductions and perswasions ye can make and devise for that purpose: putting him also in remembrance of the great Commodity coming unto his Holiness herein, by reason that this Cause being here decided, the Pope not only is delivered from the pains that he should in this time of Disease and Sickness, to the extream peril of his Life sustain with the same, seeing that it is of such moment and importance, as suffereth no tract or delay; but also his Holiness shall by such decision here eschew and avoid all displeasure that he should not fail to have, if it were or should be passed elsewhere: which matter is no little wisdom well to foresee and consider, and not only to forbear to do or pass any thing derogatory or prejudical to his said Commission, but also by all means possible to corroborate and fortify the same, and all such Acts judicial as shall pass by his said Legates by virtue thereof. Like-as we doubt not but that the Pope's Holiness, of his Uprightness, Vertue, and perfect Wisdom will do; and rather like a most loving Father and Friend, tender and favour our good; just and reasonable Causes and Desires, putting thereunto all the furtherance he may do, than to do or consent to be done any thing hurtful, prejudical, dammageable, or displeasant unto us, or this our said Cause. And finally; If need shall be, we will ye also infer, as the case shall require, how inconvenient it were this our Matter should be decided in the Court of Rome; which now dependeth totally in the Emperor's Arbitre, having such puissance near thereunto, that, as hath been written by the Pope's own Letters, their State and Life there is all in the Emperor's hands, whose Armies may famish or relieve them at their pleasure. And semblably ye shall not forget the prerogative of our Crown and Jurisdiction Royal, by the ancient Laws of our Realm, which admitteth nothing to be done by the Pope to the prejudice thereof, and also what danger they should incur that would presume to bring or present any such thing unto the same, as in our last Letters sent by Alexander was touched at good length. Wherein since ye be already so well and amply instructed, knowing also how much the Matter imports and toucheth us, and what profit and agreeable service ye may do unto us herein, with the high thanks that ye may deserve for the same: We shall not be more prolix, but refer the substantial, perfect, and assured handling hereof to your circumspections, fidelities, and diligences, not doubting but that ye will now above all other things, look vigilantly hereunto, and so acquit your selves in the same, as it may well appear that your Acts shall be correspondent to our firm trust and expectation, and no less tender this thing than ye know it to be imprinted in the bottom of our Heart, nor than as ye know both the importance and high moment, and also the very necessity of the Matter doth require. In which doing, beside the laud and praise that ye shall consecute thereby of all good Men, we shall so have your acquittals in our remembrance, as ye shall have cause to think your travels, pains, and studies herein, in the best wise collocate and emploied. Given under our Signet, at our Palace of Bridewel, the 23d day of June.

XXIX.

Rome 9 July 1529.

Doctor Bennet's Letter to the Cardinal, shewing how little they might expect from the Pope. An Original.

PLEASE it your Grace to understand, that the 6th day of this month the Pope's Holiness send for us : Albeit we had made great sute for audience before to his Holiness, soon after that we had understanding that his Holiness was recovered of this his last Sickness, into the which he fell the second day, after I had my first audience of his Holiness, which was the 21 day of the last month : And after our long communication and reasoning in the King's Highness Cause, which, at length, we have written to your Grace in our common Letter, for a confirmation of many inconveniences and dangers which we perswaded to his Holiness, to follow both to himself and to the See Apostolick, in case his Holiness should avoke the cause ; I thought much convenient at that same time to deliver the King's familiar, and likewise your Grace's Letter, and so to shew your Grace's Credence to his Holiness. After the foresaid Letters delivered, and by his Holiness shewed me, that he perceived by your Grace's Letters, that I had certain Credence to shew unto him of great moment and importance, concerning him and the See Apostolick. I shewed to his Holiness

Cotton
Libr.
Vitel.
B. 11.

your Grace's Faith and observance, his Holiness doth best know; most humbly besought his Holiness to believe these undoubtedly to follow, That if his Holiness should, at the labours of the Cæsareans, avoke the Cause, he should not alonely offend the King's Highness, which hitherto hath been a stay, a help, and a defence of the See Apostolick; but also by reason of this injury, without remedy, shall alienate his Majesty and Realms, with others, from the devotion and obedience of the See Apostolick. This I shewed his Holiness, that your Grace doth evidently perceive to follow, in case his Holiness should incline to the Cæsareans desire on this behalf: Yea further, I said, that your Grace most clearly perceiveth also by that Act, the Church of England utterly to be destroyed, and likewise your Person; and that these your Grace, with weeping tears, most lamentably committed unto me to shew to his Holiness. Furthermore I shewed to his Holiness, that your Grace, howsoever you should proceed in this Cause, did intend to proceed so sincerely, indifferently, and justly, that you would rather suffer to be jointed, Joint by Joint, than either for affection or fear, do any act either against your Conscience or Justice. Furthermore I said, that seeing his Holiness may be so well assured, that your Grace will do nothing but according to Justice in this Cause, he may, the more boldly deny Avocations to the Cæsareans, seeing that the Queen and the Emperor can desire but Justice, which they may have at your Grace's hand, and my Lord Campegius, as well there as here; and by this means his Holiness should deliver himself from great pains and unquietness of mind, which he should sustain in case the Cause should be known here, where he should have the King's Highness on one part, and the Emperor on the other side, daily calling upon his Holiness. To this his Holiness most heavily, and with tears, answered and said, That now he saw the destruction of Christendom, and lamented that his fortune was such to live to this day, and not to be able to remedy it, (saying these words) For God is my Judg, I would do as gladly for the King, as I would for my self; and to that I knowledg my self most bounden, but in this case I cannot satisfy his desire, but that I should do manifestly against Justice to the charge of my Conscience, to my rebuke, and to the dishonour of the See Apostolick; affirming, that his Counsel shews him, that seeing the Cæsareans have a Mandate or Proxie of the Queen, to ask the Avocations in her Name, he cannot of Justice deny it, and the whole Signature be in that same opinion; so that though he would most gladly do that thing that might be to the King's pleasure, yet he cannot do it, seeing that Signature would be against him whensoever the Supplication should be up there: And so being late, we took our leave of his Holiness, and departed, seeing that we could obtain nothing of the Pope for stopping the Avocation, we consulted and devised for the deferring of it, till such time as your Grace might make an end in the Cause there. And so concluded upon a new Device, which at length we have written in our common Letter, wherein I promise your Grace, Mr. Gregory has used great diligence, and taken great labours at this time, we can do no more for our lives: And if your Grace saw the importune labour of the Ambassadors of the Emperor's and Ferdinandoes, you would marvel; I promise your Grace they never cease; wherefore in staying hitherto, as we have done, it is marvel, as God knoweth, whom I pray to preserve your Grace in health and prosperity *ad multos annos.* I beseech your Grace most humbly to commend me to the King's Highness; and likewise I beseech your Grace to pardon my ill writing. At Rome, the 9th day of July.

> Your daily Beadman
> and Servant,
> W. Benet.

XXX.

19 Julii, 1529.

A Letter of the Pope's to the Cardinal concerning the Avocation. An Original.

DILECTE Fili noster, salutem et Apostolicam Benedictionem. Difficile est nobis explicare literis, quâ nostrâ molestia seu potius dolore fuerimus coacti, ad Avocatio-

nem Causæ istic commissæ concedendam ; nam etsi res ita
fuit justa ut tanto tempore differri non debuerit, tamen nos
qui isti Serenissimo Regi pro ejus singularibus erga nos
et Apostolicam sedem meritis placere in omnibus cupimus,
sicut consuevimus, ægre nunc adducti sumus, ut quamquam
justitia cogente, quicquid contra ejus voluntatem concede-
remus. Nec vero minus, Fili, doluimus tua causa, cui rem
hanc tantæ curæ esse perspeximus quantum tua erga dictum Regem fides et amor postulat ; sed tamen quod datur
justitiæ minus esse molestum debet, cum præsertim id fuerit tam dilatum à nobis, omniaq ; antea pertentata ne ad
hoc descenderemus. Itaq ; optamus in hoc adhiberi à te
illam tuam singularem prudentiam et æquitatem, persua-
dereq ; te tibi id quod est, nos, qui semper vobis placere
quantum nobis licuit studuimus, id quod vestro maximo
merito fecimus, et semper facturi sumus, nunc non nisi in-
vitos et justitia coactos quod fecimus fecisse : Teq ; omni
studio et amore hortamur, ut dictum Regem in solita erga
nos benevolentia retinere velis, eique persuadere, nihil ex
hoc apud nos de benevolentia erga se veteri imminutum unquam fore, quod recipiemus à Circumspectione tua longe
gratissimum. Quemadmodum plenius dilectus Filius noster Cardinalis Campegius hæc Circumspectioni tuæ explicabit. Dat. Romæ apud Sanctum Petrum sub annulo Piscatoris die 19. Julii 1529. Pont. nostri anno sexto.

Blosius.

XXXI.

Act. 26. Anno Regni 21. Henr. 8.

*An Act for the releasing unto the King his Highness of such
Sums of Money as was to be required of him, by any his
Subjects, for any Manner of Loan, by his Letters Missives,
or other ways or manner whatsoever.*

ITEM *quædam alia billa formam cujusdam actus in se continens, exhibita est præfato Domino Regi in Parliamento prædicto, cujus quidem billæ tenor sequitur in hæc verba.* The King's

humble, faithful, and loving Subjects, the Lords Spiritual
and Temporal, and Commons in this present Parliament
assembled, considering and calling to their remembrances,
the inestimable Costs, Charges, and Expences, which the
King's Highness necessarily hath been compelled to support and sustain, since his assumption to his Crown, Estate,
and Dignity Royal; as well first for the extinction of a
right dangerous and damnable Schism sprung and risen in
the Church; which by the providence of the Almighty
God, and the high prudence, and provision, and assistance
of the King's Highness, was, to the great honour, laud,
and glory of his Majesty, repressed; the Enemies then
being of the Church reformed, returned, and restored to the
unity of the same, and peace over all componed and concluded, as also for the modifying of the insatiable and inordinate ambition of those which do aspire unto the Monarchy of Christendom, did put universal trouble, divisions
in the same, intending, if they might, not only to have subdued this Realm, but also all the rest unto their Power
and Subjection: For the resistance whereof, the King's
Highness was compelled, after the Universal Peace, by the
great study, labour, and travel of his Grace conduced, and
the same by some of the Contrahents newly violate and in-
fringed; in shewing the form of the Treaties thereupon
made again, to take Armour. And over and besides the
notable and excessive treasure and substance which his
Highness in his first Wars had emploied for the defence of
the Church, the Faith Catholick, and this his Realm, and
of the People and Subjects of the same, was eft-soons
brought of necessity to new, excellent, and marvellous
Charges, both for the supportation of sundry Armies by
Sea and by Land; and also for divers and manifold Contributions outward, to serve, keep, and contain his own
Subjects at home in rest and repose; which hath been so
politickly handled and conduced, that when the most part
of all religious Christians have been infested with cruel
Wars, Discords, Divisions, and Dissensions, the great
Heads and Princes of the World brought unto Captivity;
Cities, Towns, and Places, by force and sedition, taken,
spoiled, burnt, and sacked; Men, Women, and Children
found in the same slain and destroyed; Virgins, Wives,

Widows, and Religious Women, ravished and defloured;
Holy Churches and Temples polluted, and turned unto
prophane use; the Reliques of the Holy Saints irre-
verently treated; Hunger, Dearth, and Famine, by mean
thereof in the said outward Regions, insuing and generally
over all, was depopulation, destruction and confusion; the
King's said Subjects in all this time, were by the high providence and politick means of his Grace nevertheless preserved, defended, and maintained, from all these inconveniences and dangers; and such provisions taken, by one
way or other, so as reasonable commodity was always given
unto them to exercise their Traffiques of Merchandise, and
other their Crafts, Mysteries, and Occupations for their
living; which could not possibly have been brought about,
unless then the King's Highness, with continual studies,
travels, and pains, and with his infinite Charges and Expences, had converted the peril and danger of the Enter-
prises and Exploits, set forth for the reduction of the
Enemies unto Peace; from his own Subjects unto Strangers: Whereof finally such Fruit and Effect is ensued,
as by the King's policy, puissance, and means, general
and universal Peace is established amongst all Christian Princes; and this Realm now, thanked be God, constitute in free, better, and more assured and profitable
Amity with all outward Parties, than hath been at any
time whereof is memory or remembrance. Considering
furthermore, That his Highness, in and about the Premisses, hath been fain to employ, not only such sums of
Mony as hath risen and grown by any manner of contribution made unto his Grace by his said loving Subjects, but
also over and above the same, sundry other notable and
excellent Sums of his own Treasure, and yearly Revenues,
which else his Grace might have kept and reserved to his
own use; amongst which manifold great Sums so employed,
his Highness also, as is notoriously known, and as doth
evidently appear by the accompts of the same, hath to that
use and none other, converted all such Mony, as by any his
Subjects and People, Spiritual and Temporal, hath been
advanced unto his Grace by way of Prest and Loan, either
particularly, or by any Taxation made of the same; being
a thing so well collocate and bestowed; seeing the said high

and great Fruits and Effects thereof ensued, to the honour,
surety, weal, perfect commodity, and perpetual tranquillity of this said Realm, as nothing could better nor more
to the comfort of his said Subjects be desired, studied, or
imagined; Of one mind, consent and assent, and by Authority of this present Parliament, do for themselves, and
all the whole Body of the Realm whom they do represent,
freely, liberally, and absolutely, give and grant unto the
King's Highness, by Authority of this present Parliament,
all and every Sum and Sums of Mony, which to them, and
every of them, is, ought, or might be due, by reason of
any Mony, or any other thing, to his Grace at any time
heretofore advanced, or payed, by way of Prest or Loan,
either upon any Letter or Letters under the King's Privy
Seal, general or particular, Letter, Missive, Promise,
Bond, or Obligation of payment, or by any Taxation, or
other Assessing, by virtue of any Commission or Commissions, or by any other mean or means whatsoever it be
heretofore passed for that purpose, and utterly, frankly,
liberally, and most willingly and benevolently, for them,
their Heirs, Executors, and Successors, do remit, release,
and quit claim, unto his Highness, his Heirs and Successors for ever, all and every the same Sums of Money, and
every parcel thereof, and all and singular Suits, Petitions,
and Demands, which they, or any of them, their Heirs,
Successors, or Executors, or the Heirs, Executors, or Successors of any of them, have, had, or may have for the same,
or any parcel thereof; most humbly and lovingly, beseeching his Highness, for the more clear discharge for the same,
that it may be ordained and enacted by the King, our said
Sovereign Lord, the Lords Spiritual and Temporal, and
the Commons of this present Parliament assembled, and by
authority of the same, that all Promises, Bonds, Writings, Obligatory Letters, under the King's Privy Seal Signet, Sign Manual, or Great Seal passed, and other Bonds
or Promises, whatsoever they be, had, or made, to any
Person or Persons, Spiritual or Temporal, Shire, City,
Burrough, Waxentale, Tranship, Hamlet, Village, Monastry, Church, Cathedral, or Collegiat, or to any Guild, Fra-
ternity, or Body Corporate, Fellowship, or Company, or
other whatsoever, having capacity to take any Bond, espe-

cially and generally, jointly or severally, touching or concerning the same Prest or Loan, or every of them, or the
repaiment of any Sum or Sums of Mony for the same, be
from henceforth void and of none effect. *Cui quidem billæ
probe et ad plenum intellectæ per dictum Dominum Regem
ex assensu et Authoritate Parliamenti prædicti taliter est responsum. Le Roy remercie Les Seigneurs et ses communes
de leur bonne cueurs en faifant cest graunt, et icelle se Maje-
ste accepte et tout le contenu, et cest escriture a graunt et
aprove avecques tous les articles en ceste escripture specifies.*

XXXII.

*A Letter from Gardiner and Fox, about their Proceedings
at Cambridg. An Original.*

Feb. 1530. *from Cambridg by Stephen Gardiner.*

TO THE KING'S HIGHNESS.

PLEASETH it your Highness to be advertised, That ar-
riving here at Cambridg upon Saturday last past at noon,
that same night, and Sunday in the Morning, we devised
with the Vice-chancellour, and such other as favoureth
your Grace's Cause, how and in what sort to compass and
attain your Grace's Purpose and Intent; wherein we assure
your Grace, we found much towardness, good will, and diligence, in the Vice-Chancellour and Dr. Edmunds, being
as studious to serve your Grace as we could wish or desire:
Nevertheless there was not so much care, labour, study,
and diligence employed on our Party, by them, our self,
and other, for attaining your Grace's Purpose, but there
was as much done by others for the lett and empeachment
of the same; and as we assembled they assembled, as we
made Friends they made Friends, to lett that nothing
should pass as in the Universities Name; wherein the first
day they were Superiors, for they had put in the ears of
them, by whose Voices such things do pass, *multas fabulas*,
too tedious to write unto your Grace. Upon Sunday at
afternoon were assembled, after the manner of the Univer-

sity, all the Doctors, Batchellors of Divinity, and Masters BOOK
of Art, being in number almost two hundred: In that Con- II.
gregation we delivered.your Grace's Letters, which were
read openly by the Vice-Chancellor.   And for answer to
be made unto them, first the Vice-Chancellor calling apart
the Doctors, asked their Advice and Opinion ; whereunto
they answered severally, as their Affections led them, *et
res erat in multa confusione.*   *Tandem* they were content
Answer should be made to the Questions by indifferent
Men : But then they came to Exceptions against the Abbot of St. Benets, who seemed to come for that purpose ;
and likewise against Dr. Reppes, and Dr. Crome ; and also
generally against all such as had allowed Dr. Cranmer's
Book, inasmuch as they had already declared their Opinion. We said thereunto, That by that reason they might
except against all ; for it was lightly, that in a Question so
notable as this is, every Man Learned hath said to his
Friend as he thinketh in it for the time ; but we ought not
to judg of any Man, that he setteth more to defend that
which he hath once said, than Truth afterward known.
Finally ; The Vice-Chancellor, because the day was much
spent in those altercations, commanding every Man to resort to his Seat apart, as the manner is in those Assemblies, willed every Mau's mind to be known secretly, whether they would be content with such an Order as he had
conceived for answer to be made by the University to your
Grace's Letters ; whereunto that night they would in no
wise agree.   And forasmuch as it was then dark night, the
Vice-Chancellor continued the Congregation till the next
day at one of the Clock ; at which time the Vice-Chancellor proponed a Grace after the form herein inclosed ; and
it was first denied : When it was asked again, it was even
on both Parties, to be denied or granted ; and at the last,
by labour of Friends to cause some to depart the House
which were against it, it was obtained in such form as the
Schedule herein enclosed purporteth ; wherein be two
Points which we would have left out ; but considering by
putting in of them, we allured many, and that indeed they
shall not hurt the Determination for your Grace's part, we
were finally content therewith. The one Point is that
where it was first, that *quicquid major pars* of them that be

named *decreverit*, should be taken for the Determination of the University. Now it referred *ad duas partes*, wherein we suppose shall be no difficulty. The other Point is, That your Grace's Question shall be openly disputed, which we think to be very honourable; and it is agreed amongst us, That in that Disputation, shall answer, the Abbot of St. Benets, Dr. Reppes, and I Mr. Fox, to all such as will object any thing or reason against the conclusion to be sustained for your Grace's part. And because Mr. Doctor Cliff hath said, That he hath somewhat to say concerning the Canon-Law; I your Secretary shall be adjoined unto them for answer to be made therein. In the Schedule which we send unto your Grace herewith, containing the names of those who shall determine your Grace's Question, all marked with the Letter A. be already of your Grace's Opinion; by which we trust, and with other good means, to induce and obtain a great part of the rest Thus we beseech Almighty God to preserve your most Noble and Royal Estate. From Cambridg the   day of February.

Your Highness's most humble
Subjects and Servants,
Stephen Gardiner,
Edward Fox.

The Grace purposed and obtained, Feb. 1530.
Placet vobis ut

A. Vicecancellarius.

Doctores.

A. Salcot. The Abbot of St. Benet's.

Watson.

A. Repps.

Tomson.

Venetus, *de isto bene speratur.*

Magistri in Theologia.

Middleton.

A. Heynes.

Mylsent. *de isto bene speratur.*

A. Shaxton.

A. Latimer.

A. Simon.

Longford. *De isto bene speratur.*

Thyxtel.

Doctores.	Magistri in Theologia.
A. Edmunds.	Nicols.
Downes.	Hutton.
A. Crome.	A. Skip.
A. Wygan.	A. Goodrich.
A. Boston.	A. Heth.
	Hadway, de isto bene spe-
	ratur.
	Dey.
	Bayne.
	A. A. Duo Procuratores.

HABEANT plenam facultatem et Auctoritatem, nomine totius Universitatis, respondendi Literis Regiæ Majestatis in hac Congregatione lectis, ac nomine totius Universitatis definiendi et determinandi quæstionem in dictis literis propositam: ita quod quicquid duæ partes eorum præsentium inter se decreverint, respondendi dictis literis, et definierint ac determinaverint super quæstione proposita, in iisdem habeatur, et reputetur pro Responsione, Definitione et Determinatione totius Universitatis, et quod liceat Vicecancellario, Procuratoribus et Scrutatoribus, literis super dictarum duarum partium definitione et determinatione concipienda sigillum commune Universitatis apponere: sic quod disputetur Quæstio publice et antea legatur coram Universitate absq; ulteriori gratia desuper petenda aut obtinenda.

Your Highness may perceive by the Notes, that we be already sure of as many as be requisite, wanting only three; and we have good hope four; of which four if we get two, and obtain of another to be absent, it is sufficient for our purpose

XXXIII.

July 1. 1530.

A Letter from Crook out of Venice, concerning the Opinions of Divines about the Divorce. An Original.

PLEASE it your Highness to be advertised, That as this day I obtained the Common Seal of the University of Padua, in substantial and good form; for all the Doctors were assembled upon Sunday, and the Case was amongst them solemnly and earnestly disputed all Monday, Tuesday, Wednesday, and Thursday, and this present Friday in the morning again; and thereupon they concluded with your Highness, and desired a Notary to set his Sign and Hand unto an Instrument, by Leonicus and Simonetus devised, in corroboration of your Cause, and thereby to testify that this Instrument was their Deed, Device, Act, and Conclusion; and for the more credence to be given to the said Instrument, they caused the Chancellor of the Potestate here to set his Hand and Seal for the approbation of the Authority of the Notary: A Copy of all the which things I send unto your Highness by this Bearer, in most humble wise beseeching the same to be advertised, that the General of the Black-Friers hath given a Commandment, That no Black-Frier dispute the Pope's Power: Notwithstanding Prior Thomas Omnibonus procureth daily new Subscriptions, and will do till the Brief of contrary Commandment shall come unto his hands.

My fidelity bindeth me to advertise your Highness, that all Lutherans be utterly against your Highness in this Cause, and have letted as much with their wretched Power, Malice, without Reason or Authority, as they could and might, as well here, as in Padua and Ferrara, where be no small Companies of them. I doubt not but all Christian Universities, if they be well handled, will earnestly conclude with your Highness. And to obtain their assent, as well through Italy, France, Almagne, Austrich, Hungary, and Scotland, I think it marvellous expedient, for the preferment of this your most honourable and high Cause; As from the Seigniory and Dominion of Venice towards Rome, and beyond Rome, I think there can be no more done than is done already, albeit, gracious Lord, if that I had in time been sufficiently furnished with Mony. Albeit I have beside this Seal procured unto your Highness an hundred and ten Subscriptions, yet it had been nothing in comparison of that that I might easily and would have done; and at this hour I assure your Highness, that I have neither Provision nor Mony, and have borrowed an hundred Crowns, the which also are spent about the getting of this Seal; of the which my need, and divers impediments in your Highness's Cause here, I have advertised your Highness by many and sundry Letters, and with the same sent divers Books and Writings, part to Hierom Molins a Venetian, and factor to Mappheus Bernardus, by the hands of your Subject Edmund Herwell, part directed to Mr. Tuke, whereof I am nothing ascertained whether they be exhibited unto your Highness or not, to no little discomfort unto me; notwithstanding I have reserved a Copy of all things, Letters, and other, and herein enclosed a Bill, specifying by whom and to whom I directed my said Letters, in most humble wise, beseeching your most Royal Clemency, to ponder my true, sure, and good endeavours, and not to suffer me to be destitute of Mony, to my undoing, and utter loss of your most high Causes here; for of my self I have nothing whereby to help my self. And thus the most Blessed Trinity keep and preserve your Highness in his most Royal Estate. At Venice, the first day of July at night, Anno—30.

R. Crook.

XXXIV.

*The Judgment of the Universities concerning the King's
Marriage; taken from the Printed Edition of them. London, 1532.*

*Censura Facultatis Sacræ Theologiæ almæ Universitatis
Parisiensis.*

DECANUS et Facultas Sacræ Theologiæ almæ Universitatis Parisiensis, omnibus, ad quos præsens scriptum perve-
nerit, salutem in eo, qui est vera Salus. Cum nuper subor-
ta magnæ difficultatis controversia super invaliditate Matrimonii, inter Serenissimum Henricum Octavum Angliæ
Regem, Fidei Defensorem, et Dominum Hiberniæ, ac Illustrissimam Dominam Catharinam Angliæ Reginam, claræ
memoriæ Ferdinandi Regis Catholici Filiam contracti, et
carnali copula consummati, illa etiam nobis Quæstio in justitia et veritate discutienda et examinanda proposita fuerat, videlicet, Anducere relictam fratris mortui sine liberis
sic esset jure divino et naturali prohibitum, ut interveniente summi Pontificis Dispensatione, non posset fieri lici-
tum, ut quis Christianus relictam fratris ducat, et habeat
in Uxorem; Nos Decanus et Facultas antedicta, cogitantes, quam esset pium et sanctum, nec-non debito charitatis,
et nostræ Professioni consentaneum, ut his, qui in lege Domini secura, tranquillaq; conscientia vitam hanc ducere,
et transigere cupiant, viam justitiæ ostenderemus, nolui-
mus tam justis et piis votis deesse. Hinc more solito, apud
ædem S. Mathurini per juramentum convenientes, et solemni Missa cum Invocatione Spiritus Sancti ob hoc celebrata, nec-non præstito juramento de deliberando super
præfata quæstione, secundum Deum et Conscientiam; Post
varias et multiplices Sessiones, tam apud ædem S. Mathurini, quam apud Collegium Sobonæ, ab octava Junii usq;
ad secundum Julii habitas, et continuatas, perscrutatis prius
excussisq; quam diligentissime, ac ea qua decuit, reverentia et Religione, Sacræ Scripturæ Libris eorumq; proba-
tissimis interpretibus, nec-non Sacrosanctæ Ecclesiæ gene-
ralibus ac Synodalibus Concilii Decretis et Constitutionibus longo usu receptis et approbatis: Nos prædicti Deca-

nus et Facultas de prædicta Quæstione disserentes, et ad
eam respondentes, sequentes unanime judicium et consensum Majoris partis totius Facultatis, Asseruimus et Deter-
minavimus, prout et in his Scriptis per præsentes Asseri-
mus et Determinamus, quod prædictæ nuptiæ cum Relictis fratrum decedentium sine liberis, sic naturali jure pariter
et divino sunt prohibitæ, ut super talibus Matrimoniis con-
tractis, sive contrahendis, Summus Pontifex dispensare non
possit. In cujus nostræ Assertionis et Determinationis
fidem et testimonium, sigillum nostræ Facultatis cum signo nostri Notarii, seu Bedelli præsentibus apponi curavi-
mus. Datum in generali nostra Congregatione per juramentum celebrata apud S. Mathurinum. Anno Dom. Millesimo quingentesimo trigesimo, Mensis vero Julii die secundo.

Censura Facultatis Decretorum almæ Universitatis Pari-
siensis.

In Nomine Domini Amen. Cum proposita fuisset coram nobis Decano et Collegio Consultissimæ Facultatis
Decretorum Parisiensis Universitatis Quæstio ; An Papa
possit Dispensare, quod Frater possit in Uxorem ducere,
sive accipere relictam Fratris sui, Matrimonio consummato
per Fratrem præmortuum? Nos Decanus et Collegium
præfatæ Facultatis, post multas Disputationes et Argumenta hinc inde super hac materia facta ac habita, cum
magna et longa librorum, tam divini, quam Pontificii et
Civilis, jurium revolutione consulimus, et dicimus, Papam
non posse in facto proposito dispensare. In cujus rei testimonium, has præsentes Sigillo nostræ Facultatis, et signo
nostri scribæ primi Bedelli muniri fecimus. Datum in
Congregatione nostra apud Sanctum Joannem Lateranen-
sem, Parisiis die vicesima tertia mensis Maii, Anno Dom.
millesimo quingentesimo trigesimo.

Censura almæ Universitatis Aurelianensis.

Cum abhinc aliquod tempus nobis Collegio Doctorum
Regentium almæ Universitatis Aurelianensis propositæ fuerint, quæ sequuntur Quæstiones, videlicet ; Si jure divino
liceat fratri Relictam fratris (quam Fratriam vocant) acci-

pere Uxorem? Item et si hoc sit eo jure vetitum, utrum divinæ Legis prohibitio Pontificali Dispensatione remitti
possit? Nos prædictum Collegium, post multas ad prædictorum dubiorum Disputationem (de more nostro) factas
Sessiones et Congregationes, postque Juris tum Divini tum
Canonici locos (quod facere potuimus) examinatos, et omnibus mature atque exacte pensatis et consideratis : Definivimus, prædictas nuptias citra divinæ legis injuriam attentari non posse, etiamsi summi Pontificis accedat indulgentia, vel permissus. In cujus rei testimonium præsens publicum Instrumentum a Scriba præfatæ almæ Universitatis
subsignari fecimus, ejusdemq; Sigillo communiri. Actum
in Sacello Beatæ Mariæ Boninuncii Aurelianensis. Anno
Dom. Millesimo quingentesimo vigesimo nono, die quinto
Mensis Aprilis.

Censura Facultatum Juris Pontificii et legum Almæ Universitatis Andegavensis.

Cum certo abhinc tempore nobis Rectori et Doctoribus
Regentibus in Pontificia et legum disciplina almæ Universitatis Andegavensis sequentes Quæstiones propositæ fuerint, scilicet, Utrum Jure Divino pariter et naturali ll icitum sit homini Christiano Relictam fratris sui, etiam
absq; liberis, sed Matrimonio jam consummato defuncti,
ducere Uxorem? Et an Summo Pontifici liceat super hujusmodi nuptiis dispensare? Nos præfati Rector et Doctores, post plures ad Disputationem hujusmodi quæstionum,
et veritatem comperiendam factas, ex more, Congregationes et Sessiones, postq; varios Juris tam Divini, quam
humani locos, qui ad eam rem pertinere videbantur, discussos, multas quoq; rationes in utramq; partem adductas
et examinatas, omnibus fideliter consideratis, et matura deliberatione præhabita, Definimus neque Divino neque Naturali Jure permitti homini Christiano, etiam cum Sedis
Apostolicæ Authoritate seu Dispensatione super hoc adhibita, Relictam fratris, qui etiam sine liberis post consummatum Matrimonium decesserit, Uxorem accipere vel habere. In quorum omnium supradictorum fidem, præsens
publicum Instrumentum a Scriba seu Notario præfatæ Almæ Universitatis subsignari jussimus, ejusdemq; Universitatis Magno Sigillo muniri. Actum in æde sacra Divi

Petri Andegavensi, in Collegio nostro. Anno Domini Millesimo quingentesimo tricesimo, die septimo Maii.

Censura almæ Universitatis Bituricensis.

Nos cum Decano Theologiæ, Facultas in Universitate
Bituricensi (ut Doctoris Gentium Pauli exemplo plerisq;
locis auspicemur scriptum nostrum a precatione) omnibus
dilectis Dei in quibus vocati estis, Lectores Charissimi,
quiq; ad quos scribimus, Gratia vobis et pax a Deo Patre
et Domino nostro Jesu Christo. Dum complerentur dies
inter Octavas Pentecostes, et essemus omnes pariter in
eodem loco, corpore et animo congregati, sedentesq; in
domo dicti Decani; facta est nobis rursus Quæstio eadem,
quæ sæpius antea, non quidem parva, hunc in modum: An
rem faciat illicitam necne, frater accipiens Uxorem a præ-
mortuo fratre relictam, consummato etiam Matrimonio?
Tandem rei ipsius veritate disquisita et perspecta, multo
singulorum labore, et Sacrorum iterata atq; iterata revolutione codicum, unusquisq; nostrum non fascinatus, quo
minus veritati obediret, cæpit, prout Spiritus Sanctus dedit, suum hoc unum arbitrium eloqui, absq; personarum
acceptione, in veritate comperi, personas memoratas in
Capite Levitici octavo supra decimum prohibitas esse jure
ipso naturali, authoritate humana minime relaxabili, et ve-
titas, ne invicem Matrimonium contrahant, quo fit fraternæ
turpitudinis abominabilis Revelatio. Et hoc nobis signum
nostri Bedelli Notarii publici, cum Sigillo dictæ supra nostræ Facultatis præsentibus appenso. Die decimo Junii,
Anno vero a Christi Nativitate, Millesimo quingentesimo
tricesimo. Ut autem nostræ scriptionis pes et caput uni
reddantur formæ, quemadmodum sumus auspicati a precatione, ita claudamus illius quo utimur exemplo. Gratia
Domini nostri Jesu Christi, charitas Dei, et communicatio
Sancti Spiritus sit cum omnibus vobis. Amen.

Censura Almæ Universitatis Tholosanæ.

Tractabatur in nostra Tholosana Academia perquam
difficilis Quæstio, Liceatve fratri eam, quæ jam olim de-
functo fratri Uxor fuerat (nullis tamen relictis liberis) in
Matrimonio sibi conjungere? Accedebat et alius scrupulus, qui nos potissimum torquebat, Si Romanus Pontifex,

cui est commissa gregis Christiani cura, id sua, quam vocamus, Dispensatione permittat, tunc saltem liceat? Ad utramq; Quæstionem agitandam Doctores omnes Regentes,
qui tunc Tholosæ aderant, coegit Rector in Concilium, neque id semel tantum sed etjam iterum: Quippe existimavit
præcipitari non oportere Consilia, indigereq; nos tempore, ut aliquid maturius agamus. . Demum, cum in unum
locum convenissent omnes, tum Sacrarum Literarum dis-
ertissimi Interpretes, tum utriusq; Censuræ Consultissimi,
deniq; qui quavis in re et judicio et oratione viri fœlicibus
ingeniis non mediocriter exercitati essent, ac sese Sacro-
sanctis Conciliis parere velle, Sanctorumq; Patrum haud
quaquam piis animis violanda Decreta imitari jurassent, et
unusquisq; suam sententiam protulisset, atq; in utramq;
partem diffuse decertatum esset; tandem in eam Sententiam sic frequentius itum est, ut uno omnium ore Alma
nostra Universitas animis sincerissimis nulloq; fermento
vitiatis censuerit, Jure Divino pariter et Naturali Uxorem
relictam fratris sui nemini licere accipere. At postquam
id lege eadem non licet, responsum est, non posse Pontificem aliquem ea lege solvere. Nec huic sententiæ refragari potest, quod cogeretur olim frater Uxorem demortui
fratris accipere. Nam hoc figura erat, atque umbra futu-
rorum, quæ omnia adveniente luce et veritate Evangelii
evanuerunt. Hæc quoniam ita se habent, in hanc formam
redegimus, et per Notarium, qui nobis est a Secretis, signari, sigilliq; autentici ejusdem nostræ Almæ Universitatis jussimus Appensione Communiri. Tholosæ. Kal. Octob.
Ann. a Christo nato M. D. XXX.

*Censura Facultatis Sacræ Theologiæ Universitatis Bono-
niensis.*

Cum Deus Optimus Maximus veterem Legem ad morum
vitæque informationem ac institutionem ore suo tradiderit,
idemque humanitate sumpta, mortalium Redemptor Deus
novum condiderit Testamentum, sed ad dubia, quæ in multis emergebant, tollenda declarandaque contulerit, quæ ad
hominum perfectionem elucidata nonnihil conferunt; nostras partes semper fore duximus hujusmodi sanctissima Patris æterni documenta sectari, et in rebus arduis ac dubita-
bilibus, superno illustratos lumine, nostram ferre senten-

tiam, ubi causa mature consulta, multisq; hinc inde rationibus, scriptisq; Patrum dilucidata fuerit, nihil quod
possumus, in aliquo temere ferentes. Cum itaq; nos,
præstantes quidam et clarissimi viri, obnixe rogarint, ut
subsequentem casum maxima diligentia perscrutaremur,
nostrumq; subinde in eum judicium ferremus æquissime,
soli veritati innitentes, in unum omnes Almæ Universitatis hujus Doctores Theologi convenimus, casu prius per
unumquemq; nostrum sigillatim domibus propriis examina-
to, summaq; solertia per dies plurimos contracto: Illud
una mox vidimus, examinavimus, contulimus, ad amus-
simq; singula quæq; pertractantes ponderavimus, rationes
quascunq; contrarias, quas fieri posse censuimus, in me-
dium afferentes atq; solventes, etiam ipsius Reverendissimi D. D. Card. Cajetani, necnon Deuteronomicam Dispensationem de fratris suscitando semine, et reliquas tandem omnes sententias oppositas, quæ ad id negotii facere
viderentur. Quæsitum est igitur a nobis, An ex sola Ecclesiæ institutione vel etiam Jure Divino prohibitum fuerit, ne quis Relictam a fratre sine liberis in Uxorem ducere valeat? Quod si utraq; lege ne fieri possit, cautum
est; An quenquam possit Beatissimus Pontifex super ejusmodi contrahendo Matrimonio dispensare? Qua diligentissime (ut diximus) ac exactissime seorsim palamq; examinata, ac pro viribus nostris, optime discussa Quæstione,
Censemus, Judicamus, dicimus, constantissime Testamur
et indubie affirmamus, hujusmodi Matrimonium, tales nuptias, tale conjugium horrendum fore, execrabile, detestan-
dum, viroq; Christiano, immo etiam cuilibet infideli prorsus abominabile, esseque a Jure naturæ divino et humano,
diris pænis prohibitum. Nec posse Sanctissimum Papam
(qui tamen fere omnia potest) cui collatæ sunt a Christo
claves Regni Cœlorum: Non inquam posse aliqua ex causa super hujusmodi contrahendo Matrimonio, quenquam
dispensare. Ad hujus Conclusionis veritatem tutandam,
omnes in omnia loca et tempora parati sumus. In quorum
fidem has scripsimus, almæq; nostræ Universitatis ac Sacri
Venerabilium Theologorum Collegii Sigillo munivimus,
solita nostra generali subscriptione Signantes. Bononiæ in
Ecclesia Cathedrali, decima Junii, Anno Dom. M.D.XXX.
sub Divi Clementis 7. Pontificatu.

*Censura Facultatis Sacræ Theologiæ Almæ Universitatis
Pataviensis.*

TESTANTUR, qui Catholicam fidem astruunt, Deum
Optimum Maximum legis veteris præcepta filiis Israel ad
exemplar vitæ ac morum nostrorum institutionem ore proprio tradidisse, eundemq; trabea humanitatis indutum, Re-
demptorem omnium factum, Novum Testamentum condi-
disse, et nedum propter hoc, sed ad dubia quæcunq; emer-
gentia removenda, dilucidandaq; nobis misericorditer con-
donasse, quæ ad nostri perfectionem enucleata fructus ube-
res conferunt et salutares. Nostrum semper fuit eritq;
per sæcula (uti Christicolas decet) hujusmodi celebratissi-
ma Summi Pontificis instituta sectari, et in quibusq; du-
bitationibus, ac arduis Quæstionibus supernaturali lumine
freti, nostrum proferre Judicium, ubi res ipsa optime con-
siderata, multisq; hinc inde demonstrationibus, atq; Patrum Authoritatibus mature declarata fuerit, temere quoad
possumus nihil omnino judicantes. Cum igitur nos, quidam oratores clarissimi, suppliciter exorarint, ut subsequentem casum diligentissime perscrutari dignaremur, atq;
nostram ferremus exinde sententiam, soli veritati simpliciter attendentes: Qua ex re omnes hujus Almæ Universitatis Doctores Theologi in simul convenimus, re ipsa
prius per nostrum quemlibet particulariter propriis domibus examinata, summaq; cum solertia enucleata, mox in
unum redacti cuncta consideravimus, examinavimus, omniaq; sigillatim ponderavimus, Argumenta quæcunq; contraria, quæ fieri quoquomodo posse putavimus, adducentes,
atq; integerrime dissolventes, necnon Deuteronomicam
Dispensationem de Fratris suscitando semine, et reliquas
omnes rationes atq; sententias oppositas, quæ ad id facere
videbantur: Quæstio igitur talis fuit exposita, An ex sola
Sanctæ Matris Ecclesiæ institutione, vel etiam de Jure Divino prohibitum fuerit, ne quis Relictam fratris absq; liberis in Uxorem ducere valeat? Quod si utrobiq; fieri
nequeat cautum est, An Beatissimus Pontifex super hujusmodi contrahendo Matrimonio quenquam dispensare legitime possit? Quo exactissime (ut dictum est) seorsim pub-
liceq; discusso, ac pro viribus dilucidato quæsito, Dicimus, Judicamus, Decernimus, Attestamur, atque veridice
Affirmamus, Matrimonium hujusmodi, tale conjugium et

tales nuptias nullas esse, immo detestabiles, atque exe-crandas Christiano cuilibet esse, prophanas, et, ut scelus abominandas, crudelissimis pœnis, jure naturæ, divino et humano, clarissime esse prohibitas. Nec Beatissimum Pontificem, cui claves Regni cœlestis a Christo Dei Filio sunt collatæ, ulla ex causa posse super tali Matrimonio contrahendo quenquam juridice dispensare. Cum illa, quæ sunt a Jure Divino prohibita, non subsint ejus potestati, nec in illa gerit vicem Dei, sed solum super ea, quæ sunt commissa jurisdictioni hominum. Ad cujus Sententiæ ac Conclusionis veritatem tutandam et ejusdem certissimam defensionem, Nos omnes unanimes semper et ubique parati sumus. In quorum fidem has nostras fecimus, Almæ Universitatis nostræ, ac Sacri Reverendorum Theologorum Collegii Sigillo solito communivimus. Datum Paduæ in Ecclesia Hermitarum S. Augustini, dieprimo Julii, M.D.XXX.

XXXV.

The Judgment of the Lutheran Divines about the King's Marriage, ex MSS. R. Smith, London.

Ex hac Collatione in qua audivimus Argumenta de Controversia Divortii Serenissimi et Illustrissimi Regis Angliæ, Franciæ, &c. proposita et diligenter agitata a Reverendo D. D. Edwardo Hereford. Episcopo, D. Nicolao Archdiacono et D. D. Barnes, intelleximus Serenissimum Regem maximis et gravissimis Causis adductum, superatum et conclusum esse, ut in hoc negotio Matrimonii sui faceret quod fecit: Nam hoc manifestum est et negare nemo potest, quod Lex Levit. tradita Lev. 18. v. 20. prohibet ducere fratris Uxorem, &c. sed Divina, naturalis, et moralis Lex est intelligenda tam de vivi quam de mortui fratris Uxore, et quod contra hanc legem nulla contraria lex fieri aut constitui possit, sicut et tota Ecclesia semper hanc Legem retinuit, et judicavit hujusmodi nuptias incestas esse, sicut testantur Synodorum Decreta et Sanctissimorum Patrum Clarissimæ Sententiæ, et has nuptias prohibent et vocant incestas etiam jura Civilia. Proinde et nos sentimus, et hanc Legem de non ducenda Uxore fratris in omnibus Ecclesiis servandam esse veluti divinam, naturalem, et moralem Legem; Nec in nostris Ecclesiis vellemus dispensare aut permittere, præsertim ante factum, ut ejusmodi nuptiæ contraherentur, et hanc Doctrinam possumus et volumus Deo volente facile defendere. Cæterum quantum ad Divortium pertinet, nondum sumus plene persuasi ut sententiam nostram ferre possimus, An post Contractum Matrimonium in hoc casu Serenissimi Regis debuerit fieri Divortium. Rogamus igitur Seren. Regem ut æquo animo ferat, differri nostram Sententiam in hac re donec erimus certiores.

XXXVI.

An Abstract of the Grounds of the Divorce.

Written in the beginning, Thomas Cantuarien, *with his own hand.*

Articuli ex quibus plane admodum demonstratur Divortium inter Henr. 8. Angliæ Regem Invictiss. et Serenissimam Catharinam necessario esse faciendum.

Cotton
Libr.
Vesp.
B. 5.

1. AFFINITAS quæ Divino et Naturali Jure impedit ne Matrimonium contrahatur, et contractum dirimit, solo nuptiali fœdere inducitur.

2. Substantia Matrimonii, verum perfectumq; conjugium, sola conjugali pactione, et non carnali copula efficitur.

3. Vir et Uxor solo fœdere conjugali, Deo inprimis operante, una mens et una caro fiunt.

4. Carnalis Copula affinitatem solo Jure Ecclesiastico repertam inducit.

5. Affinitas sola Carnis concubitu orta Sanctione humana solum impedit, ne Matrimonium contrahatur, et contractum dissolvit.

6. Carnalis Copula Matrimonium necessario reddit consummatum.

7. Potest Matrimonium Carnali Copula consummari, etiam Uxoris Virginitate irrecuperabili non amissa.

8. Serenissimam Catharinam ab Illustrissimo Principe BOOK
Arthuro relictam Virginem non fuisse affirmamus. II.

9. Sereniss. Catharinam ex Judiciis quam plurimis attestantibus, et violentam praesumptionem inducentibus, ab
eodem Illustrissimo Principe Arthuro corruptam, atque
Matrimonium inter eos consummatum fuisse non dubitamus.

10. Serenissima Catharina, praesumptione violenta hujusmodi constante, Virginitatem suam Juramento praeser-
tim publico probare nequit.

11. Judex eandem Serenissimam Catharinam, super ea
causa jurare volentem, ad juramentum jure quidem admittere non potest.

12. Henrici octavi Angliae Regis Invictissimi et Serenis-
simae Catharinae praetensum Matrimonium, lege Divina et
naturali prohibente, nullum omnino fuisse neq; esse posse
Censemus.

XXXVII.

*A Bull sent to the Arch-Bishop of Canterbury, against the
Statutes of Provisors.*

MARTINUS Episcopus, Servus Servorum Dei, venerabili ExM.S.
Fratri Archiepiscopo Cantuariensi salutem et Apostolicam D. Po-
Benedictionem. Si quam districto Dei Judicio de com- tyti.
missis tibi ovibus rationem redditurus es, aliquando cogi-
tares, si meminisses et tu quae pastoralis officii cura esse debet, quantumq; Ecclesiae Romanae, a qua dignitatem et
auctoritatem vendicas, jus atque honorem tueri obligatus
es, in considerationem duceres; profecto non usque adeo
dormitares neque negligeres: Surrexisses jamdudum, et
post oves jam longe aberrantes inclamares, ac pro viribus
resisteres iis, qui jura ac privilegia a summo Ecclesiarum
capite omnium Christo, Ecclesiae Romanae tradita, sacri-
lego vel ausu violant atque contemnunt. Numquid ideo
Pontificalis Dignitas tibi commissa est ut hominibus praesis,
opes cumules, et quae tua sunt non quae Jesu Christi quae-
rere debeas? Si id existimas vehementer erras, et a

Christi intentione longe abes, qui cum Beato Petro oves
suas committeret, nil ei aliud nisi ut illas pasceret indixit,
priusque non semel, sed bis ac tertio, an ab eo diligeretur
expostulans. Estne hæc in Christum dilectio quam habes?
Estne hoc amare ac pascere oves? Itane debitum quo Ecclesiæ Romanæ astringeris, recte exsolvis? En ante oculos tuos ab ovili errantes in præcipitium labuntur oves, nec
illas revocas neque reducis. In conspectu tuo herbas per-
gunt pestiferas pascere, nec illas prohibes, immo (quod abominabile est) tuis quasi manibus hujusmodi præbes morti-
ferum cibum. Te vidente, lupus illas dispergit, et taces
tanquam canis mutus non valens latrare. Aspicis simul et
Christi et Ecclesiæ et sedis Apostolicæ mandata, auctoritatem, reverentiamque contemptui haberi, nec semel unum
murmuras verbum, clauculum saltem, si nolles palam. An
ignoras ante æterni tribunal judicis hujusmodi reatus et
culpæ usque ad minimum quadrantem redditurum te rationem? num credis, si qua tuo neglectu perierit ovium (pe-
reunt autem multæ) de tuis manibus sanguis earum exige-
tur? Quid per os Ezechielis Dominus comminatur, me-
mora et extimesce. Ipse, inquit, Speculatorem Domini
posuit te Deus, si videris gladium venientem, et non inso-
nueris buccina, et aliquis perierit, sanguinem ejus de manibus tuis requiram; hæc dicit Dominus. Qualis autem et
qualis iniquitatis et abominationis gladius in Angliæ Regnum, atque oves tuas descenderit, tuo judicio (si ratione
uteris) relinquimus. Perlege illud Statutum Regium, si tamen Statutum, si tamen Regium dici fas est. Nam quomodo Statutum, quod Statuta Dei et Ecclesiæ destruit? Quomodo Regium? quod Instituta peremit? contra illud quod
scriptum est, Honor Regis Judicium diligit. Et judica,
venerabilis Frater et Christiane Episcope, ac Catholice
Præsul, si justum, si æquum, si a Populo Christiano servari est. Imprimis per illud execrabile Statutum ita Rex
Angliæ de Ecclesin cum Provisionibus et Administrationi-
bus disponit, quasi Vicarium suum Christus eum instituis-
set. Legem condit super Ecclesias, beneficia, Clericos et
Ecclesiasticum statum, ad se suamq; laicalem Curiam nonnullas causas Spirituales et Ecclesiasticas jubet introduci;
et ut uno verbo concludamus, ita de Clericis statuit, de
Ecclesiis et Ecclesiastico Statu, quasi Ecclesiæ claves in

manibus haberet, et non Petro, sed sibi hujusmodi cura commissa foret. Præter hanc nefandam Dispositionem, vipereas quasdam contra Clericos adjecit pœnas, quæ ne quidem contra Judæos vel Saracenos, per ullum de Statutis suis, promulgatæ inveniuntur. Possunt ad Angliæ Regnum cujuslibet generis homines libere proficisci; soli acceptantes beneficia Auctoritate Summi Pontificis, Vicarii Jesu Christi, jubentur exulari, capi, incarcerari, omnibusq; bonis exui, executoresq; literarum Apostolicarum, Procuratores, Notarii, ac quicunq; alii Censuram seu Processum ab Apostolica sede in Regnum mittentes aut deferentes, ultimo supplicio deputantur, projectiq; extra protectionem Regis exponuntur ab omnibus captivandi. Vide si audita est unquam similis Statuti iniquitas: Consideret prudentia tua, si Regem aut Regnum hujusmodi Statuta decent: Cogita si te talia inspicientem silere oporteat, et non magis clamare, contradicere, et pro viribus resistere. Estne ista filialis Reverentia? Estne ista Christiana devotio quam Regnum Angliæ suæ Matri Ecclesiæ ac Sedi Apostolicæ exhibet? Potestne Catholicum Regnum dici, ubi hujusmodi statuuntur profanæ leges et observantur, ubi prohibetur adiri Vicarius Christi; ubi oves suas Successor Apostoli Petri pascere juxta mandatum Domini non permittitur? Christus dixit Petro suisq; Successoribus, Pasce oves meas; Statutum autem Regni pascere ipsas non sinit, sed vult ut Rex ipse pascat, devolvendo ad eum in certis casibus Apostolicam Auctoritatem. Christus ædificavit supra Petrum Ecclesiam; sed Regni Statutum, id prohibet: Nam non patitur Petri Cathedram de Ecclesia prout judicaverit, expedire, ordinare vel disponere. Christus voluit quod quicquid summus Pontifex in terris solverit aut ligaverit, solutum ligatumve esset in cœlis; Statutum huic divinæ voluntati non assentit: Nam si quos Sacerdotes ad ligandum solvendumq; animas Christi Vicarius in Regnum contra Statuti tenorem destinaret, non modo ipsos non admittit Statutum sed exulare jubet, bonis privari, aliisq; pœnis affligi, et censuram seu Processum Apostolicum in Regnum deferens, tanquam Sacrilegus capite punitur. Quid ad hoc tua Discretio respondebit? Estne hoc Catholicum Statutum? Potestne sine Christi injuria, sine Evangelii transgressione, sine animæ interitu tolerari aut ob-

servari? Cur igitur non clamas, et quasi tuba exaltas vocem tuam, annuncians populo tuo peccata sua, Domui Israel scelera eorum, ne sanguis eorum de manibus tuis requiratur. Quod et si omnes quibus populorum cura commissa est, facere teneantur, quanto magis id tibi erit necessarium exequi, cui populos et populorum ministros, oves
et ovium pastores, tuæ solicitudini Romana deputavit Ecclesia, a qua et Primatum et Sedis Apostolicæ legationem
super Anglicanas Ecclesias suscepisti, et ipsius gloriosissi-
mi Martyris Beati Thomæ olim Cantuariæ Archiepiscopi
Successor effectus es, qui adversus similia decertans Statuta, holocaustum se Deo offerens pro libertate Ecclesiastica occubuit. Tu certe ob hæc, omnium primus qui vexillo assumpto in aciem prodire deberes, et fratres Co-epis-
copos tuos tuo exemplo in certamine sistere, primus omnium terga vertis, et aliquos qui forte resistendi impetum
caperent, tua sive pusillanimitate, sive dissimulatione, sive
(ut omnes attestantur) evidenti prævaricatione a bono pro-
pòsito dejicis. Itaq; si de te queritur Ecclesia, si in te omnis culpa transfertur, non mirari sed dolere, immo potius
teipsum corrigere debes, et debitum quo ovium jure as-
trictus es audacter exolvere: pro qua re efficienda, si velis
quam potes operam adhibere, non magnum certamen subeundum est. Persuade tuo pro officio et Auctoritate tua,
secularibus, et eos veritatem instrue. Ostende eis peccatum quo observantes prædictum Statutum illaqueantur:
Et erunt (ut omnes asserunt) prava in directa, et aspera in
vias planas. Ne ergo, si tacueramus et nos, tuam aliorumq; desidiam dissimulantes similis apud omnipotentem
Deum culpæ reos efficiat, neve ovium nostrarum sanguis
(si neglexerimus) de manibus nostris exigatur, tuam frater-
nitatem qua possumus instantia, toto corde, totoq; affectu
hortamur, monemus, requirimus, et in virtute Sanctæ obedientiæ, et sub Excommunicationis pœna cui (si neglexeris)
ipso facto te subjicimus, districte præcipiendo mandamus,
quatenus quamprimum ad locum ubi Consiliarii Charissimi
in Christo Filii nostri Henrici Angliæ Regis Illustris conveniunt, personaliter accedas, eosq; tam Ecclesiasticos
quam Seculares pro sapientia tua, quam tibi Dominus in-
spiraverit, rationibus ac monitionibus reddas instructos, ut
prædictum Statutum in proximo Parliamento tollant peni-

tus et aboleant : Cum enim Divinæ et Humanæ rationi, veteris ac Novi Testamenti, Conciliorum, Sanctorum Patrum, Summorum Pontificum Decretis, ipsius denique
Universalis Ecclesiæ observantiæ evidentissime contradi-
cat, nec sine interitu salutis æternæ quovis modo servari
possit. Illudq.; inter alia dicere non omittas, qualiter Ecclesiasticæ libertatis violatores, facientesq ; Statuta aut
consuetudines contra libertatem servari, Officiales, Rec-
tores et Consiliarii, locorum ubi hujusmodi Statuta vel consuetudines editæ fuerunt vel servatæ, Ac etiam qui secundum prædicta judicaverint, ipso jure Excommunicationem
incurrunt, quæ quantum sit Christi fidelibus metuenda,
ipsis plene poteris declarare. Idem sub pœna eadem te
facere volumus cum Parliamentum inchoabitur, tam erga
prædictos Consiliarios quam Communitates, et alios qui
vocem in ipso habuerint Parliamento. Insuper ut pluribus
viis honori Dei et Sanctæ Matris Ecclesiæ, et animarum
saluti provideatur, sub simili pœna mandes ac præcipias
omnibus tam Rectoribus Ecclesiarum, quam aliis officium
prædicationis obtinentibus, Secularibus et Religiosis, ut
frequenter in sermonibus suis populos de prædicta materia
instruere non omittant. Volumus autem ut quicquid super prædictis feceris per tuas literas (quibus saltem duæ
graves personæ, quæ ipsis requisitionibus per te faciendis
interfuerint, se subscribant) nos certiores efficias. Dat.
Rom. apud Sanctos Apostolos quinto die Decembris, Pontificatus nostri Anno decimo.

XXXVIII.

A Letter to King Henry the Sixth for Repealing that Statute.

MARTINUS Episcopus, Servus Servorum Dei, Charissimo in Christo Filio Henrico Regi Angliæ Illustri, salutem
et Apostolicam Benedictionem. Quum post multos nuncios ad tuam Serenitatem pro abolitione illius detestabilis
Statuti contra libertatem Ecclesiasticam editi olim trans-

missos, postremo dilectum filium Magistrum Julianum causarum curiæ Cameræ Apostolicæ Auditorem, pro eadem
causa destinassemus; per ipsum tua Celsitudo tunc nobis
respondit, quod quamprimum commode possit, Parliamentum, sine quo idem nequit aboleri Statutum, convocaret,
et in eo quod sibi possibile foret pro nostræ requisitionis
implemento faceret, Protestans quod Sanctæ Romanæ Ecclesiæ sedisq; Apostolicæ Juribus ac Privilegiis nullo modo detrahere aut derogare intendebat: Nos ob hoc, sicut
deinde aliis literis tibi significavimus, usq; ad id tempus
cum patientia expectare decrevimus, sperantes quod in Verbo Regio nobis pollicitus fueris, id tempore suo exequi non
differres; itaq; quicquid ex parte nostra hactenus faciendum fuit, omnem mansuetudinis et patientiæ modum experientes jam fecimus. Et licet gravibus interim per aliquos de Regno tuo lacessiti sumus injuriis, volumus tamen
(ne quid contra promissum fieri videretur) usq; ad id tempus (non sine rubore Sedis Apostolicæ) expectare, ut merito
illud verbum Evangelicum jam dici possit, Quid debui
huic vineæ facere et non feci? Tu vero, Fili Charissime,
cum ipsius Parliamenti jam tempus instet, quod ex tua
parte agendum restat, juxta promissionem tuam ac verbum
Regium implere non omittas, ad quod et Jure Divino et
Humano tanquam Christianissimus Princeps obligatus, sine
cujusvis requisitione pro tua et tuorum subditorum salute
et honore facere teneris: præsertim quum talia obtuleramus, ob quæ nec tibi nec dicto Regno ex prædicti Statuti
abolitione præjudicium ullum redundare possit; providere
enim iis omnibus quæ causam Statuto dedisse dicuntur, jam
sæpe nostro nomine oblatum est, et nunc de novo offerimus. Jam igitur cum nulla quævis contradicendi occasio
prætendi possit, speramus in dicto Parliamento tuam Serenitatem ita facturam, ut prædictum tam execrabile Statutum penitus de eodem Regno tollatur. Quod si feceris,
salvabis primum tuam, tum vero multorum animas, quæ ob
dictum Statutum gravi crimine illa queatæ tenentur: Pro
videbis deinde tuo et ipsius Regni honori, quod utiq; prop
terea non modicum est notatum: Demum nos ac sedem ip
sam semper tuis justis desideriis obligabis. Super iis au
tem omnibus et de nostra intentione plene per literas nos
tras instructo, dilecto Filio magistro Joanni de Obizis i

dicto Regno Nuncio et Collectori nostro, dabis credentiæ
fidem plenam. Dat. Rom. die decimo tertio Octobris, Pontificatus nostri Anno decimo.

XXXIX.

A Letter to the Parliament upon the same occasion.

MARTINUS Episcopus, Servus Servorum Dei, venerabilibus Fratribus et dilectis Filiis, Nobilibus viris Parliamenti Regni Angliæ, salutem et Apostolicam Benedictionem. Multis nunciis ac frequentibus exhortationibus, pro
debito pastoralis officii, vos ac Regnum vestrum hactenus
admonuimus, ut pro salute animarum vestrarum, et ipsius
Regni honore, quoddam detestabile Statutum contra Divinum et Humanum Jus editum, quod sine interitu salutis
æternæ nullatenus servari potest, aboleretur. Et quoniam
id sine Parliamento tolli non posse, ex parte Charissimi in
Christo Filii nostri Henrici Regis Angliæ illustris, Dilecto Filio Magistro Juliano Causarum curiæ Cameræ Apostolicæ Auditori, tunc Nuncio nostro, responsum extitit, in
quo (quam primum posset) convocato, quod sibi possibile
foret pro nostræ Requisitionis executione se facturum,
idem Rex pollicitus est, protestans Juribus ac Privilegiis
Sanctæ Romanæ Ecclesiæ et Sedis Apostolicæ in nullo
velle detrahere aut derogare. Nos volentes solita erga vos
mansuetudine uti, decrevimus usq; ad ipsius Parliamenti
tempus expectare, sperantes quod tam Rex juxta suam
Regiam Promissionem, quam vos pro salute animarum vestrarum, Sancte ac Catholice secundum nostram Requisitionem concludetis. Itaq; cum Parliamentum (ut fertur) jam
instet, vos omnes, quorum animas nostræ curæ Dominus
noster Jesus Christus commisit, hortamur, monemus obse-
cramus, ut unanimes vestrarum animarum salutem, ac conscientiarum puritatem præ cæteris rebus amantes, prædictum abominabile Statutum (quod qui observat vel observari faciat salvari non potest) penitus tollatur, et de Regno
in perpetuum aboleatis. Quod si quis forsitan vobis contrarium persuadere audeat, quicunq; ille sit, Sæcularis vel

BOOK II.

Ecclesiastici Status tanquam hostem animarum vestrarum et honorum, nullatenus audite; nec eum virum Catholicum reputetis, qui adversus Romanæ Ecclesiæ Auctoritatem, Juraque et Privilegia Sedi Apostolicæ Divinitus concessa, aliquid machinari præsumpserit, quibus ipse Rex vester Illustris nolle ullatenus derogare publice protestatus est. Nos quidem ipsi sumus ab omnipotenti Deo Jesu Christo super vos et Universalem Ecclesiam constituti, cujus Doctrinæ ac persuasioni sine ulla contradictione omnimodam fidem vos et quilibet Christianus habere debetis: Nos tamen, etsi indignos, oves suas pascere Christus voluit, clavesq; aperiendi ac solvendi Cœlos tradidit. Et si quis nos audit, servi Christi testimonium Christianum audit; et si quis nos spernit, Christum spernere convincitur. Et quoniam de vobis ac singulis Christianis in districto Dei Judicio rationem reddituri sumus, ideo vos pro salute vestra tam sæpe tamq; efficaciter admonemus; et ne quisquam sub alicujus damni temporalis prætextu vos ab hac nostra Catholica Doctrina submoveat, ecce nos promptos paratosq; offerimus, omnibus causis, propter quas dictum Statutum conditum esse prætenditur, salubriter providere, ita ut nec Regno nec cuiquam privatæ personæ præjudicium aliquod ex ipsius Statuti abolitione possit accidere. Super his omnibus et nostra intentione plene instructo dilecto Filio Magistro Joanni de Obizis, in dicto Regno Nuntio et Collectori nostro, dabitis Credentiæ plenam fidem. Dat. Romæ apud Sanctos Apostolos tertio die Octobris, Pontificatus nostri Anno decimo.

XL.

An Instrument of the Speech the Arch-Bishop of Canterbury made to the House of Commons about it.

Die Veneris, penultimo mensis Januarii, Anno Domini secundum cursum et computationem Ecclesiæ Anglicanæ millesimo quadringentesimo decimo septimo, indictione sexta, Pontificatus Sanctissimi in Christo Patris et Domini nostri Domini Martini Divina Providentia Papæ quinti Anno undecimo, Reverendissimi in Christo Patres et Do-

mini, Domini, Henricus Dei Gratia Cantuariensis et
Johannes Eboracensis Archiepiscopi, necnon Reverendiss.
Patres W. Londinensis, Benedictus Menevensis, Philippus
Eliensis, Jochen et W. Norvicensis, Episcopi, et cum eis
venerabiles Patres et viri religiosi Westmonasterii et Ra-
dingiæ Abbates de palatio regio Westmonasteriensi de Camera, viz. Ubi tam Domini Spirituales quam Temporales
in Parliamento adtunc tento negotia Regni tractaverint et
tractare solebant, recedentes, et dimissis ibi Dominis Temporalibus, in simul transierunt ad viros illos' qui pro communitate Regni ad Parliamentum hujusmodi venerant in
loco solito, viz. in Refectorio Abbatiæ Westmonasteriensis
prædictæ personaliter existentes, et incontinenter eisdem
Dominis Spiritualibus cum reverentia debita, prout decuit
a viris hujusmodi communitatem Regni facientibus et repræsentantibus, receptis: Præfatus Reverendissimus Pater Archiepiscopus Cantuariensis causam adventus sui et
con-fratrum suorum ad tunc exponere cœpit in vulgari ;
Protestando primitus, et protestabatur idem Dominus Cantuariensis vice sua et confratrum suorum prædictorum,
quod pro dicendo tunc ibidem non intendebat ipse Reverendissimus Pater, aut aliquis confratrum suorum, Domino Regi Angliæ aut Coronæ suæ vel communitati Regni in
aliquo derogare, et sic adhærendo Protestationi suæ hujusmodi, idem Reverendissimus Pater prosequebatur et exposuit solemniter causam adventus sui et confratrum suorum, sumpto quasi pro themate, Reddite quæ sunt Cæsaris, Cæsari, et quæ sunt Dei Deo. Super quo proceden-
do, ea quæ ad Jurisdictionem Ecclesiasticam, et ea quæ ad
Cæaaream pertinebant, notabiliter et ad longum declaravit, materiam Provisionis et pro Statuti illius contra Pro-
visores editi abolitione, cum bona et matura deliberatione
prosequendo, et in processu declarationis hujusmodi jura
nonnulla et Sacræ Scripturæ Auctoritates convenientes al-
legavit, pro jure Domini nostri Papæ in Provisionibus ha-
bendis, sicut Sancti Prædecessores sui summi Pontifices in
Regno Angliæ et alibi per Universalem Christianitatem
habuerunt, ipseq; Dominus Papa modernus in cæteris Regnis habet et possidet in præsenti: Unde præmissis, Bul-
lisq; et literis Apostolicis, quas pro hac re idem Dominus
Papa jam tarde ad Regnum transmiserat, diligenter consi-

BOOK
II.

deratis, et quod dictus Dominus noster Papa tot Ambas-
siatas et nuncios solemnes ad prosequendum jus suum et
Ecclesiæ libertatem in præmissis, non absq; laboribus magnis, periculis et expensis, de Curia Romana ad Regnum
Angliæ destinavit, idem Reverendissimus Pater Cantuar.
Archiepiscopus, nomine suo et confratrum suorum ad tunc
ibidem præsentium, et absentium in dicto Parliamento per
Procuratores comparentium, ad quos ut asseruit divisim
saltem principalis cura animarum totius Communitatis Regni pertinere dignoscitur, dictos viros omnes et singulos
tunc præsentes, Communitatem (ut præmittitur) repræsentantes, requisivit et in Domino exhortabatur, quatenus ob
salutem animarum suarum totiusq; Regni prosperitatem
et pacem, materiam prædictam sic ponderarent, et taliter
in eodem Parliamento super eadem deliberarent, ut Sanctissimus Dominus noster Papa placari, ac Regis zelum ad
Sedem Apostolicam totiusq; Regni devotionem in hac
parte habere posset materiam commendandi. Et addidit ultra hujusmodi Requisitionem et Exhortationem præfatus
Reverendissimus Pater Archiepiscopus Cantuariensis; et
ex corde, ut apparuit, exposuit, lacrymando, pericula per
censurarum, viz. Ecclesiasticarum et etiam Interdicti ful-
minationem, et alias tam Regi quam Regno (quod absit)
verisimiliter eventura alia, in casu quo responsio Parliamenti illius, in materia tunc declarata, grata non foret Domino Papæ et accepta, sic dicendo; Forte videtur quibusdam vestrum, quod hæc quæ Regni Prælatos potissime
concernunt ex corde non profero, Sciatis pro certo, et in
fide, qua Deo teneor et Ecclesiæ, affirmo coram vobis, quod
magis mihi foret acceptum nunquam conferre aut etiam habere aliquod beneficium Ecclesiasticum quam aliqua talia
pericula seu processus meo tempore in Ecclesiæ Anglicanæ Scandalum venirent. Ulterius idem Reverendissimus
Pater expresse declaravit, qualiter dictus Dominus noster
Papa in diversis Bullis suis obtulit et promisit, se et Sedem
Apostolicam, ad quascunq; causas et occasiones editionis
Statuti prædicti rationabile, remedium apponere, et ma-
terias causarum et occasionum hujusmodi Statuti in toto
tollere et abolere; et sic Requisitione, Exhortatione et
periculorum hujusmodi expositione finitis, Reverendissimi
Patres Cantuar. et Eborac. Archiepiscopi, cum confratri-

bus suis Episcopis et Prælatis prædictis, recesserunt, Regni
Communitate, seu saltem dictis viris Communitatem Regni repræsentantibus remanentibus, et circa materiam eis
expositam tractantibus, præsentibus, et Declarationem, Requisitionem, et Exhortationem, hujusmodiq; periculorum
expositionem per dictum Dominum Archiepiscopum Cantuariensem (ut præmittitur) factas audientibus, venerabilibus viris Richardo Coudray Archidiacono Norwici in Ecclesia Norwicensi, Magistro Joanne Forster Canonico Lincol-
nensi, &c. et Johanne Boold Notario Publico et multis aliis.

XLI.

Act. 33. Anno Regni vicesimo tertio.

*An Act concerning Restraint of payment of Annates to the
See of Rome.*

FORASMUCH as it is well perceived, by long approved
experience, that great and inestimable Sums of Mony have
been daily conveyed out of this Realm, to the impoverishment of the same; and specially such sums of Mony as the
Pope's Holiness, his Predecessors, and the Court of Rome,
by long time have heretofore taken of all and singular those
Spiritual Persons which have been named, elected, presented, or postulated to be Arch-Bishops or Bishops within
this Realm of England, under the Title of Annates, otherwise called First-Fruits. Which Annates, or First-Fruits,
have been taken of every Arch-Bishoprick, or Bishoprick,
within this Realm, by restraint of the Pope's Bulls, for
Confirmations, Elections, Admissions, Postulations, Provisions, Collations, Dispositions, Institutions, Installa-
tions, Investitures, Orders, Holy Benedictions, Palles, or
other things requisite and necessary to the attaining of
those their Promotions; and have been compelled to pay,
before they could attain the same, great Sums of Mony, before they might receive any part of the Fruits of the said
Arch-Bishoprick, or Bishoprick, whereunto they were
named, elected, presented, or postulated; by occasion
whereof, not only the Treasure of this Realm hath been

greatly conveighed out of the same, but also it hath hapned many times, by occasion of death, unto such Arch-Bishops, and Bishops, so newly promoted, within two or three years after his or their Consecration, that his or their Friends, by whom he or they have been holpen to advance and make paiment of the said Annates, or First-Fruits, have been thereby utterly undone and impoverished. And for because the said Annates have risen, grown, and encreased, by an uncharitable Custom, grounded upon no just or good title, and the paiments thereof obtained by restraint of Bulls, until the same Annates, or First-Fruits, have been paied, or Surety made for the same; which declareth the said Paiments to be exacted, and taken by constraint, against all equity and justice. The Noble Men therefore of the Realm, and the Wise, Sage, Politick Commons of the same, assembled in this present Parliament, considering that the Court of Rome ceaseth not to tax, take, and exact the said great Sums of Mony, under the Title of Annates, or First-Fruits, as is aforesaid, to the great damage of the said Prelates, and this Realm; Which Annates, or First-Fruits, were first suffered to be taken within the same Realm, for the only defence of Christian People against the Infidels, and now they be claimed and demanded as mere duty, only for lucre, against all right and conscience. Insomuch that it is evidently known, that there hath passed out of this Realm unto the Court of Rome, sithen the second year of the Reign of the most Noble Prince, of famous memory, King Henry the Seventh, unto this present time, under the name of Annates, or First-Fruits, payed for the expedition of Bulls of Arch-Bishopricks and Bishopricks, the sum of eight hundred thousand Ducats, amounting in Sterling Mony, at the least, to eightscore thousand pounds, besides other great and intolerable Sums which have yearly been conveighed to the said Court of Rome, by many other ways and means, to the great impoverishment of this Realm. And albeit, that our said Sovereign the King, and all his natural Subjects, as well Spiritual as temporal, been as obedient, devout, Catholick and humble Children of God, and Holy Church, as any People be within any Realm christned; yet the said exactions of Annates, or First-Fruits, be so intolerable and importable to this

Realm, that it is considered and declared, by the whole
Body of this Realm now represented, by all the Estates of
the same assembled in this present Parliament, that the
King's Highness before Almighty God, is bound, as by the
duty of a good Christian Prince, for the conservation and
preservation of the good Estate and Common-Wealth of
this his Realm, to do all that in him is to obviate, repress,
and redress the said abusions and exactions of Annates, or
First-Fruits. And because that divers Prelates of this
Realm being now in extream Age, and in other debilities
of their Bodies, so that of likelyhood, bodily death in short
time shall or may succeed unto them; by reason whereof
great sums of Mony shall shortly after their deaths, be conveighed unto the Court of Rome, for the unreasonable and
uncharitable Causes abovesaid, to the universal damage,
prejudice, and impoverishment of this Realm, if speedy
remedy be not in due time provided: It is therefore ordained, established, and enacted, by Authority of this present Parliament, That the unlawful paiment of Annates,
or First-Fruits, and all manner Contributions for the same,
for any Arch-Bishoprick, or Bishoprick, or for any Bulls
hereafter to be obtained from the Court of Rome, to or for
the foresaid purpose and intent, shall from henceforth utterly cease, and no such hereafter to be payed for any Arch-
Bishoprick, or Bishoprick, within this Realm, other or
otherwise than hereafter in this present Act is declared;
And that no manner, Person, nor Persons hereafter to be
named, elected, presented, or postulated to any Arch-
Bishoprick, or Bishoprick, within this Realm, shall pay
the said Annates, or First-Fruits, for the said Arch-Bishoprick, or Bishoprick, nor any other manner of Sum or Sums
of Mony, Pensions or Annates for the same, or for any
other like exaction, or cause, upon pain to forfeit to our
said Sovereign Lord the King, his Heirs and Successors,
all manner his Goods and Chattels for ever, and all the
Temporal Lands and Possessions of the same Arch-Bishoprick, or Bishoprick, during the time that he or they which
shall offend, contrary to this present Act, shall have, pos-
sess, or enjoy, the Arch-Bishoprick, or Bishoprick; wherefore he shall so offend contrary to the form aforesaid. And
furthermore it is enacted, by Authority of this present Par-

liament, That if any Person hereafter named and presented
to the Court of Rome by the King, or any of his Heirs or
Successors, to be Bishop of any See or Diocess within this
Realm hereafter, shall be letted, deferred, or delayed at
the Court of Rome from any such Bishoprick, whereunto
he shall be so represented, by means of restraint of Bulls
Apostolick, and other things requisite to the same; or shall
be denied, at the Court of Rome, upon convenient suit
made, any manner Bulls requisite for any of the Causes
aforesaid, any such Person or Persons so presented, may
be, and shall be consecrated here in England by the Arch-
Bishop, in whose Province the said Bishoprick shall be, so
alway that the same Person shall be named and presented
by the King for the time being to the same Arch-Bishoprick: And if any Persons being named and presented, as
aforesaid, to any Arch-Bishoprick of this Realm, making
convenient suit, as is aforesaid, shall happen to be letted,
deferred, delayed, or otherwise disturbed from the same
Arch-Bishoprick, for lack of Pall, Bulls, or other to him
requisite, to be obtained in the Court of Rome in that behalf, that then every such Person named and presented to
be Arch-Bishop, may be, and shall be, consecrated and invested, after presentation made, as is aforesaid, by any
other two Bishops within this Realm, whom the King's
Highness, or any of his Heirs or Successors, Kings of England for the time being, will assign and appoint for the
same, according and in like manner as divers other Arch-
Bishops and Bishops have been heretofore, in ancient time
by sundry the King's most noble Progenitors, made, consecrated, and invested within this Realm: And that every
Arch-Bishop and Bishop hereafter, being named and presented by the King's Highness, his Heirs or Successors,
Kings of England, and being consecrated and invested, as
is aforesaid, shall be installed accordingly, and shall be accepted, taken, reputed, used, and obeyed, as an Arch-
Bishop or Bishop of the Dignity, See, or Place whereunto
he so shall be named, presented, and consecrated requireth;
and as other like Prelates of that Province, See, or Diocess, have been used, accepted, taken, and obeyed, which
have had, and obtained compleatly, their Bulls, and other
things requisite in that behalf from the Court of Rome.

And also shall fully and entirely have and enjoy all the Spi-
ritualities and Temporalities of the said Arch-Bishoprick
or Bishoprick, in as large, ample, and beneficial manner,
as any of his or their Predecessors had, or enjoyed in the
said Arch-Bishoprick, or Bishoprick, satisfying and yield-
ing unto the King our Sovereign Lord, and to his Heirs and
Successors, Kings of England, all such Duties, Rights, and
Interests, as before this time had been accustomed to be
paid for any such Arch-Bishoprick, or Bishoprick, according to the Ancient Laws and Customs of this Realm, and
the King's Prerogative Royal. And to the intent our said
Holy Father the Pope, and the Court of Rome, shall not
think that the pains and labours taken, and hereafter to be
taken, about the writing, sealing, obtaining, and other
businesses sustained, and hereafter to be sustained, by the
Offices of the said Court of Rome, for and about the Expedition of any Bulls hereafter to be obtained or had for
any such Arch-Bishoprick, or Bishoprick, shall be irremu-
nerated, or shall not be sufficiently and condignly recom-
pensed in that behalf. And for their more ready expedition to be had therein, it is therefore enacted by the Authority aforesaid, That every Spiritual Person of this
Realm, hereafter to be named, presented, or postulated, to
any Arch-Bishoprick or Bishoprick of this Realm, shall
and may lawfully pay for the writing and obtaining of his
or their said Bulls, at the Court of Rome, and ensealing
the same with Lead, to be had without payment of any Annates, or First-Fruits, or other charge or exaction by him
or them to be made, yielden, or paied for the same, five
pounds Sterling, for and after the rate of the clear and
whole yearly value of every hundreth pounds Sterling,
above all charges of any such Arch-Bishoprick, or Bishoprick, or other mony, to the value of the said five pounds,
for the clear yearly value of every hundreth pounds of
every such Arch-Bishoprick, or Bishoprick, and not above,
nor in any other wise, any things in this present Act before
written notwithstanding. And forasmuch as the King's
Highness, and this his High Court of Parliament, neither have, nor do intend to use in this, or any other like
cause, any manner of extremity or violence, before gentle
courtesie or friendship, ways and means first approved and

attempted, and without a very great urgent cause and occasion given to the contrary, but principally coveting to
disburden this Realm of the said great exactions, and intolerable charges of Annates, and First-Fruits, have therefore thought convenient to commit the final order and determination of the Premisses, in all things, unto the King's
Highness. So that if it may seem to his high wisdom, and
most prudent discretion, meet to move the Pope's Holiness,
and the Court of Rome, amicably, charitably, and reasonably, to compound, other to extinct and make frustrate the
payments of the said Annates, or First-Fruits; or else by
some friendly, loving, and tolerable composition to moderate the same in such wise as may be by this Realm easily
born and sustained; That then those ways and compositions
once taken, concluded, and agreed, between the Pope's
Holiness and the King's Highness, shall stand in strength,
force, and effect of Law, inviolably to be observed. And
it is also further ordained, and enacted by the Authority of
this present Parliament, That the King's Highness at any
time, or times, on this side the Feast of Easter, which shall
be in the Year of our Lord God, a thousand five hundred
and three and thirty, or at any time on this side the beginning of the next Parliament, by his Letters Patents under
his Great Seal, to be made, and to be entred of Record in
the Roll of this present Parliament, may and shall have
full power and liberty to declare, by the said Letters Patents, whether that the Premisses, or any part, clause, or
matter thereof, shall be observed, obeyed, executed, and
take place and effect, as an Act and Statute of this present
Parliament, or not. So that if his Highness, by his said
Letters Patents, before the expiration of the times above-
limited, thereby do declare his pleasure to be, That the
Premisses, or any part, clause, or matter thereof, shall not
be put in execution, observed, continued, nor obeyed, in
that case all the said Premisses, or such part, clause, or
matter, as the King's Highness so shall refuse, disaffirm, or
not ratifie, shall stand and be from henceforth utterly void
and of none effect. And in case that the King's Highness,
before the expiration of the times afore-prefixed, do declare by his said Letters Patents, his pleasure and determination to be, that the said Premisses, or every clause,

sentence, and part thereof, that is to say, the whole, or such
part thereof as the King's Highness so shall affirm, accept,
and ratifie, shall in all points stand, remain, abide, and be
put in due and effectual execution, according to the purport, tenour effect, and true meaning of the same; and to
stand and be from henceforth for ever after, as firm, sted-
fast, and available in the Law, as the same had been fully
and perfectly established, enacted, and confirmed, to be in
every part thereof, immediately, wholly, and entirely executed, in like manner, form, and effect, as other Acts and
Laws; The which being fully and determinately made,
ordained, and enacted in this present Parliament: And if
that upon the foresaid reasonable, amicable and charitable
ways and means, by the King's Highness to be experi-
mented, moved, or compounded, or otherwise approved, it
shall and may appear, or be seen unto his Grace, that this
Realm shall be continually burdened and charged with this,
and such other intolerable Exactions and Demands, as
heretofore it hath been. And that thereupon, for continuance of the same, our said Holy Father the Pope, or any
of his Successors, or the Court of Rome, will, or do, or
cause to be done at any time hereafter, so as is above
rehearsed, unjustly, uncharitably, and unreasonably vex,
inquiet, molest, trouble, or grieve our said Sovereign Lord,
his Heirs or Successors, Kings of England, or any of his or
their Spiritual or Lay-Subjects, or this his Realm, by Excommunication, Excomengement, Interdiction; or by any
other Process, Censures, Compulsories, Ways, or Means;
Be it Enacted by the Authority aforesaid, That the King's
Highness, his Heirs and Successors, Kings of England,
and all his Spiritual and Lay-Subjects of the same, without
any scruples of Conscience, shall and may lawfully, to the
honour of Almighty God, the encrease and continuance of
vertue and good example within this Realm, the said Censures, Excommunications, Interdictions, Compulsories, or
any of them notwithstanding, minister, or cause to be ministred, throughout this said Realm, and all other the Dominions or Territories belonging or appertaining thereunto; All and all manner Sacraments, Sacramentals, Ceremonies, or other Divine Services of the Holy Church, or
any other thing or things necessary for the health of the

Soul of Mankind, as they heretofore at any time or times have been vertuously used or accustomed to do within the same; and that no manner such Censures, Excommunications, Interdictions, or any other Process or Compulsories, shall be by any of the Prelates, or other Spiritual Fathers of this Region, nor by any of their Ministers or Substitutes, be at any time or times hereafter published, executed, nor divulged, nor suffered to be published, executed, or divulged in any manner of ways. *Cui quidem Billæ prædictæ et ad plenum intellectæ per dictum Dominum Regem ex assensu et Autoritate Parliamenti prædicti taliter est Responsum.*

Le Roy le Volt   *Soit Baille aux comunes*
                    A cest Bille Les comunes sont assentes.

MEMORAND. quod nono die Julii, Anno Regni Regis Henrici vicesimo quinto, idem Dominus Rex per Literas suas Patentes sub magno sigillo suo sigillat. Actum prædictum ratificavit et confirmavit, et actui illo assensum suum regium dedit, prout per easdem Literas Patentes cujus tenor sequitur in hæc verba, magis apte constat.

Here follows the King's Ratification, in which the Act is again recited and ratified.

XLII.

The King's last Letter to the Pope. A Duplicate.

To the Pope's Holiness, 1532.

Cotton
Libr.
Vitell.
B. 13.

AFTER most humble commendations, and most devout kissing of your blessed Feet. Albeit that we have hitherto differed to make answer to those Letters dated at Bonony, the 7th day of October; which Letters of late were delivered unto us by Paul of Cassali: Yet when they appear to be written for this Cause, that we deeply considering the Contents of the same, should provide for the tranquillity of our own Conscience, and should purge such Scruples and Doubts conceived of our Cause of Matrimony; We could neither neglect those Letters sent for such a purpose, nor after that we had diligently examined and perpended the effects of the same, which we did very diligently, noting, conferring, and revolving every thing in them contained, with deep study of mind, pretermit ne leave to answer unto them. For sith that your Holiness seemeth to go about that thing chiefly, which is to vanquish those Doubts, and to take away inquietations which daily do prick our Conscience; insomuch as it doth appear at the first sight to be done of Zeal, Love, and Piety, we therefore do thank you of your good will. Howbeit sith it is not performed in Deed, that ye pretend, we have thought it expedient to require your Holiness to provide us other Remedies; wherefore forasmuch as your Holiness would vouchsafe to write unto us concerning this Matter, we heartily thank you, greatly lamenting also both the chance of your Holiness, and also ours, unto whom both twain it hath chanced in so high a matter of so great moment to be frustrated and deceived; that is to say, That your Holiness not being instructed, nor having knowledg of the Matter, of your self, should be compelled to hang upon the Judgment of others, and so put forth and make answers, gathered of other Men, being variable and repugnant among themselves. And that we being so long sick, and exagitate with this same Sore, should so long time in vain look for Remedy; which when we have augmented our ægritude and distress, by delay and protracting of time, ye do so cruciate the Patient and Afflicted, as who seeth it should much avail to protract the Cause, and thorough vain hope of the end of our desire to lead us whither ye will. But to speak plainly to your Holiness; Forasmuch as we have suffered many Injuries, which with great difficulty we do sustain and digest; albeit that among all things passed by your Holiness, some cannot be laid, alledged, nor objected against your Holiness, yet in many of them some default appeareth to be in you, which I would to God we could so diminish, as it might appear no default; but it cannot be hid, which is so manifest, and tho we could say nothing, the thing it self speaketh. But as to that that is affirmed in your Letters, both of God's Law,

and Man's, otherwise than is necessary and truth, let that
be ascribed to the temerity and ignorance of your Counsellors, and your Holiness to be without all default, save only
for that ye do not admit more discreet and learned Men to
be your Counsellors, and stop the mouths of them which
liberally would speak the Truth. This truly is your default, and verily a great fault, worthy to be alienate and
abhorred of Christ's Vicar, in that ye have dealt so varia-
bly, yea rather so inconstantly and deceivably. Be ye not
angry with my words, and let it be lawful for me to speak
the Truth without displeasure; if your Holiness shall be
displeased with that we do rehearse, impute no default in
us, but in your own Deeds; which Deeds have so molested
and troubled us wrongfully, that we speak now unwillingly,
and as enforced thereunto. Never was there any Prince
so handled by a Pope, as your Holiness hath intreated us.
First; When our Cause was proponed to your Holiness,
when it was explicated and declared afore the same; when
certain Doubts in it were resolved by your Counsellors,
and all things discussed, it was required that answer might
be made thereunto by the order of the Law. There was
offered a Commission, with a promise also that the same
Commission should not be revoked; and whatsoever Sentence should be given, should streight without delay be
confirmed. The Judges were sent unto us, the Promise
was delivered to us, subscribed with your Holiness's hand;
which avouched to confirm the Sentence, and not to revoke
the Commission, nor to grant any thing else that might lett
the same; and finally to bring us in a greater hope, a certain Commission Decretal, defining the Cause, was delivered to the Judges hands. If your Holiness did grant us
all these things justly, ye did injustly revoke them; and if by
good and truth the same was granted, they were not made
frustrate nor annihilate without fraud; so as if there were
no deceit nor fraud in the Revocation, then how wrongfully and subtilly have been done those things that have
been done! Whether will your Holiness say, That ye
might do those things that ye have done, or that ye might
not do them? If ye will say that ye might do them, where
then is the Faith which becometh a Friend, yea, and much
more a Pope to have, those things not being performed,

which lawfully were promised? And if ye will say that ye might not do them, have we not then very just cause to mistrust those Medicines and Remedies with which in your Letters ye go about to heal our Conscience, especially in that we may perceive and see those Remedies to be prepared for us, not to relieve the Sickness and Disease of our Mind, but for other means, pleasures, and worldly respects? And as it should seem profitable, that we should ever continue in hope or despair, so always the Remedy is attempted; so that we being always a-healing, and never healed, should be sick still. And this truly was the chief cause why we did consult and take the advice of every Learned Man, being free, without all affection, that the Truth (which now with our labour and study we seem partly to have attained) by their judgments more manifestly divulged, we might more at large perceive; whose Judgments and Opinions it is easy to see how much they differ from that, that those few Men of yours do shew unto you, and by those your Letters is signified. Those few Men of yours do affirm the prohibition of our Marriage to be inducted only by the Law positive, as your Holiness hath also written in your Letters; but all others say the prohibition to be inducted, both by the Law of God and Nature: Those Men of yours do suggest, that it may be dispensed for avoiding of slanders; The others utterly do contend, that by no means it is lawful to dispence with that, that God and Nature hath forbidden. We do separate from our Cause the Authority of the See Apostolick, which we do perceive to be destitute of that Learning whereby it should be directed; and because your Holiness doth ever profess your ignorance, and is wont to speak of other Mens mouths, we do confer the sayings of those, with the sayings of them that be of the contrary Opinion; for to confer the Reasons it were too long. But now the Universities of Cambridg, Oxford, in our Realms; Paris, Orleance, Biturisen, Andegavon, in France; and Bonony in Italy, by one consent; and also divers other of the most famous and Learned Men, being freed from all affection, and only moved in respect of verity, partly in Italy, and partly in France, do affirm the Marriage of the Brother with the Brother's Wife, to be contrary both to the Law of God and

Nature; and also do pronounce that no Dispensation can be lawful or available to any Christian Man in that behalf; But others think the contrary, by whose Counsels your Holiness hath done that, that sithence ye have confessed ye could not do, in promising to us as we have above rehearsed, and giving that Commission to the Cardinal Campege to be shewed unto us; and after, if it so should seem profitable to burn it, as afterwards it was done indeed as we have perceived. Furthermore, those which so do moderate the Power of your Holiness, that they do affirm, That the same cannot take away the Appellation which is used by Man's Law, and yet is available to Divine Matters everywhere without distinction. No Princes heretofore have more lighly esteemed, nor honoured the See Apostolick than we have; wherefore we be the more sorry to be provoked to this contention, which to our usage and nature is most alienate and abhorred. Those things so cruel we write very heavily, and more glad would have been, to have been silent if we might, and would have left your Authority untouched with a good will, and constrained to seek the verity, we fell, against our Will, into this contention; but the sincerity of the Truth prohibited us to keep silence, and what should we do in so great and many perplexities? For truly if we should obey the Letters of your Holiness, in that they do affirm that we know to be otherwise, we should offend God and our Conscience, and we should be a great slander to them that do the contrary, which be a great number, as we have before rehearsed: Also, if we should dissent from those things which your Holiness doth pronounce, we would account it not lawful, if there were not a Cause to defend the Fact, as we now do, being compelled by necessity, lest we should seem to contemn the Authority of the See Apostolick. Therefore your Holiness ought to take it in good part, tho we do somewhat at large and more liberally speak in this Cause, which doth so oppress us, specially forasmuch as we pretend none atrocity, nor use no rethorick in the exaggerating and encreasing the indignity of the Matter; but if I speak of any thing that toucheth the quick, it proceedeth of the meer verity, which we cannot nor ought not to hide in this Cause, for it toucheth not Worldly Things but Divine, not frail but eternal;

in which things no feigned, false, nor painted Reasons, but only the Truth, shall obtain and take place: and God is the Truth to whom we are bound to obey rather than to Men; and nevertheless we cannot but obey unto Men also, as we were wont to do, unless there be an express cause why we should not; which by those our Letters we now do to your Holiness: and we do it with charity, not intending to spread it abroad, nor yet further to impugn your Authority, unless ye do compel us; albeit also, that that we do, doth not impugne your Authority, but confirmeth the same, which we revocate to its first foundations; and better it is in the middle way to return, than always to run forth head-long and do ill. Wherefore if your Holiness do regard or esteem the tranquillity of our Mind, let the same be established with verity, which hath been brought to light by the consent of so many Learned Men; So shall your Holiness reduce and bring us to a certainty and quietness, and shall deliver us from all anxiety, and shall provide both for us and our Realm, and finally shall do your Office and Duty. The residue of our Affairs we have committed to our Ambassadours to be propounded unto you, to whom we beseech your Holiness to give credence, &c.

XLIII.

A Promise made for engaging the Cardinal of Ravenna.
An Original.

Rome, Februar. 7. 1532.

EGO Willielmus Benet Serenissimi Domini mei D. Henrici Octavi Angliæ, &c. Regis, in Romana Curia Orator, habens ad inscripta ab ipso Rege potestatem et facultatem, prout constat per ipsius Majestatis Literas Patentes datas in Regia sua Greenewici die penultima Decemb. M.D.XXXI. manu sua propria suprascriptas, et secreto sigillo suo sigillatas; Quoniam in ipsius Regis arduis negotiis expertus sum singularem et præclaram operam Reverendissimi in Christo Patris et Domini D. Henrici Sancti Eusebii S. R. E. Presbyteri Cardinalis Ravennæ, quibus

Cotton
Libr.
Vitel.

et deinceps uti capio, ut eandem semper voluntatem et operam sua Dominatio Reverendissima erga ipsum regem præ-
stet, libere promitto eidem Cardinali nomine dicti mei Regis, quod sua Majestas provideri faciet eidem Cardinali, de
aliquo Monasterio seu Monasteriis aut aliis beneficiis Ecclesiasticis in Regno Galliæ primo vacaturis, usq; ad valo-
rem annuum sex millium ducatorum: Et insuper promitto
quod Rex Angliæ prædictus præsentabit, seu nominabit
eundem Cardinalem ad Ecclesiam Cathedralem primo quovis modo vacaturam, seu et ad præsens vacantem, in Regno Angliæ, et de illa ei provideri faciet; et casu quo Ecclesia primo vacatura hujusmodi, ceu ad præsens vacans,
non sit Ecclesia Eliensi, promitto etiam quod succedente
postea vacatione Ecclesiæ Eliensis, Rex Angliæ transferri
faciet eundem Cardinalem, si ipsi Cardinali magis placuerit,
ab illa alia Ecclesia de qua provisus erit, ad Ecclesiam Elien-
sem: et dictorum Monasteriorum et Beneficiorum Ecclesiasticorum in Regno Galliæ, et Ecclesiæ Cathedralis in Regno
Angliæ possessionem pacificam, cum fructuum perceptione,
ipsum Cardinalem assequi faciet: Et hæc omnia libere promitto, quod Rex meus supradictus plenissime et sine ulla
prorsus exceptione ratificabit et observabit et exequetur;
in quorum fidem præsentes manu mea propria scripsi et
subscripsi, sigilloq; munivi. Dat. Rom. die septimo Feb-
ruarii, M.D.XXXII.

XLIV.

Bonner's Letter about the proceedings at Rome. An Original.

Rome, April 29, 1532.

PLEASETH it your Highness; This is to advertise the
same that sithen we William Benet, Edward Karne, and Edmond Bonner, sent our Letters of the 7th of this present to
your Highness; There hath been two Disputations publick,
the one the 13th of this, the other the 20th day of the same,

according to the order given and assigned, which was three Conclusions to be disputed every Consistory; and what was spoken, as well by your Highness's Counsel, for the justification of the Conclusion purposed the said 13th, as also for the impugnation thereof by the Party adverse, with Answers made thereunto by your Highness's said Counsel as fully as were any wise deduced, your said Highness shall perceive by the Books sent herewithal containing the same; and also the Justifications, Objections, and Answers, made in the 6th of this present, according as I Edward Karne in my said Letters promised. The Copies of all the which Justifications, Objections, and Answers, after that they were fully noted and deduced in writing, and maturely considered by your Highness's Learned Counsel, I Edward Karne did bring to the Pope's Holiness, and to the Cardinals, for their better information; and likewise did of the first, alwise afore the Consistory, according to the order assigned at the beginning; looking in likewise that the Queen's Counsel should do this same, but as yet they have done nothing therein, tho your Ambassadors and I have called upon the Pope many times for the same. And as concerning such things as were spoken and done for either part in the Disputation of the 20th day, it is not possible for us, by reason of the shortness of time, to reduce all in good order, and to send the same to your Highness at this time; nevertheless with all speed it shall be made ready, and sent to your Highness by the next Courier. After the Disputation done, the said 13th day of this present, the Advocate of the Party adverse did alledg, That we did seek this Disputation but only to defer the Process; protesting therefore, That the Queen's Counsel would dispute no more; and desiring therefore the Pope's Holiness, and the whole Consistory, to make Process in the principal Cause. Whereunto I Edward Karne said, That the Pope's Holiness, with the whole Senate, had granted the Disputations upon the Matters, and given an order that the Conclusions published should be disputed according to the same. Whereupon I desired that forasmuch as there remained sixteen Conclusions not disputed, (which to propose and justify, with your Highness's Counsel, I would be ready at all times) that if the Party adverse knowing the

Conclusions to be Canonical, would not confess them, and
thereby avoid Disputations, that then the said Party should
dispute them, and upon the refusal of both the same, the
Matters excusatories to be admitted by his Holiness, especially because the said Party adverse hath nothing material that could be perceived to lett the same. The Pope's
Holiness answered, That he would deliberate upon the demand of both Parties. The 16th of this present, the Datary on the Pope's behalf sent unto me Edward Karne an
Intimation for disputation of the Consistory to be kept the
20 of this present, and that I should send the Conclusions
not disputed, that they might be in the said Consistory disputed; adding withal, that the said Consistory should be,
ultimus et peremptorius terminus quoad alias Disputationes.
Of the which Intimation your Highness shall receive a
Copy herewith. Upon this, with the advice of your Ambassadors and Counsel here, I repaired unto the said Datary, and brought unto him three Conclusions to be disputed, with a Protestation, *De non recedendo ab ordine
hactenus observato,* according to the Proem of the said Conclusions, the Copy whereof your Highness shall receive
herewith. Afterwards, with the same Conclusions and
Protestation, I went to Cardinal de Monte, who said, at
the beginning, That all the Consistory crieth out upon the
Disputations, and that we had been heard sufficiently, and
that it was enough that we should have the fourth Disputation; adding withal, That it was a thing never seen before after such sort; and that it stood not with the honour
of the See to have such Disputations in the Consistory, to
the great disquieting of the Pope and the Cardinals, especially considering the manner that is used, and that all the
Conclusions be touched which should content us. To this
I answered, and desired his most Reverend Lordship to
call to his remembrance, what he had promised to your
Highness's Ambassadors and me, in the Castel-Angel upon
Shrove-Sunday, the Pope being present, and allowing the
same, contented that all the Conclusions should be disputed *singulariter;* and that I should at my pleasure, from
time to time, chuse the Conclusions to be disputed. And
how also afterward, viz. 17 Febr. the Pope's Holiness,
Cardinal Ancona, and his Lordship, not going from that

promise, gave direction for three Conclusions to be disputed every Consistory; the choice whereof to be at my liberty (according to the Copy of the said Order which I sent to your Highness with my Letters, of the date of the 22 of the last): And furthermore, that what time the order to dispute three Conclusions in a Consistory was sent unto me, and I required to send the Conclusions first to be disputed according to the said order; I did, to avoid all manner of doubts, protest afore I would accept it, and in the deliverance of the said Conclusions, that I would not otherwise accept it, but that all the Conclusions, according to the order promised in Castel-Angel should be disputed and examined *singulariter*, and that standing, and not otherwise, I delivered my said Conclusions according to the Order of the 17th of February; which Order the Pope's Holiness hitherto had approved and observed, and from that I neither could nor would go from: And where he said that we had been heard sufficiently; I said, that Audience and Information of less than the one half of a Matter could not be sufficient; and if they intended to see the truth of the whole, every point must be discussed. And as for the crying out of the Cardinals, I said, They had no cause so to do, for it was more for the honour of the See Apostolick, to see such a Cause as this is, well and surely tried, so that the Truth may appear, and the Matters be well known, than to proceed *præcipitanter*, as they did at the beginning of this Matter, afore they well knew what the Matter was. And as touching the disquieting the Pope's Holiness, and the said Cardinals, I said, your Highness for their pains was much beholden unto them; nevertheless, I said, that they might on the other side ponder such pains as your Highness hath taken for them, in part declared by me; which was much more than for them to sit in their Chairs two or three hours in a week, to hear the justice of your defence in this cause. And as touching the manner used in the said Disputation, I said, his Lordship knew well that it was by the Party adverse, which all manner of ways goeth about to fatigate and make weary the Consistory of the Disputations, specially in chiding, scolding, and alledging Laws and Decisions that never were, nor spoken of by any Doctor, and vainly continuing the time, to

the intent that the Pope's Holiness, and the Cardinals,
dissolving the Consistory, and not giving audience, the said
Party, without Law, Reason, or any good ground, might
attain their desire, and keep under the Truth, that it should
not appear; and if any thing was sharply spoken of our
Party, I said it was done only for our defence, and to shew
the errors and falsity of the Queen's Advocates in their Allegations, wherein, I said, they should not be spared. And
forasmuch as on the behalf of your Highness there was nothing spoken but that which was grounded upon Law, and
declared in what place, so that it cannot be denied; I desired his Lordship that he would continue his goodness in
this Matter, as your Highness's especial trust was he would
do; and that we might always, as we were accustomed,
have recourse unto the same in all our Business for his
good help and counsel. His Lordship not yet satisfied,
said, That as concerning the Order, the Pope's Holiness
might interpretate and declare what he meaned by it; and
as touching the Conclusions, they were superfluous, impertinent, and calumnious, only proposed to defer the Matter.
I answered, and said, That to interpretate the said Order,
where it is clear out of doubt, the Pope's Holiness considering the promise made on Shrove-Sunday, with my Protestation foresaid, and the execution of the said Order to
that time, in divers Consistories observed, could not by right
interpretate the said Order, admitting disputation upon
all the Conclusions; and of this I said, That if such altera-
tions were made, without any cause given of your Highness's Party, there was little certainty to be reckoned upon
amongst them. And as touching the superfluity and im-
pertinency of the said Conclusions, I said, That that was
the saying of the Party adverse, that did not understand
the same Conclusions. And further, that such Conclusions
as were clamorously, by the Advocates of the Party adverse, alledged to be superfluous, his Lordship in the Disputation and trial thereof in the Consistory, did manifestly
perceive that it was not so. And where it was alledged the
said Conclusions to be calumnious, and laid in to defer the
Process. I answered, That we might well alledg again
the Counsel of the Party adverse, the thing against us alledged, and say truly, that we were calumniously dealed

withal, seeing the matters were so just and clear, and yet not admitted. Then his Lordship went further, and said, that *Impedimentum allegatum erat perpetuum*, because your Highness, *ex causa reipublicæ*, could not come out your Realm, and *quia dignitas vestra est perpetua*; and also *quod Causa requirit celeritatem*. To this, I said, that his Lordship mistook the Matter, for we said not in the Matters that your Highness could not go out of your Realm to no place, but we said, that the same could not go, *ad loca tam remota*, as Rome is; so that it was not *perpetuum impedimentum*. And to the other I shewed him a Text, and the common opinion of Doctors in a Cause of Matrimony, being *inter Regem et Reginam*, which took away the thing that he had said. Then his Lordship said, That it was enough that the place were sure to the Procurator by the Chapter, *Cum olim de testibus*. I said, That that Chapter did not prove that Allegation, and that they mistook the Text that so did understand it, for the Alternative that is in that Text is not referred *ad locum tutum*, but *ad ordinem Citationis inchoandæ in persona principali, aut ejus procuratore;* and so *Petrus de Anchorano* understandeth that Text; and otherwise understanding the same it should be against the Chapter, *Ex parte de appellatione*, and the common opinion there. Then he said that Aretine saith, *Quod sufficit quum locus sit tutus procuratori.* I said, that under his favour, Aretine saith the contrary, for he saith, *Quod partibus debet locus tutus assignari si poterit, et si non poterit partibus, detur procuratoribus.* Then his Lordship said to me, That I knew well he began to set forward these Disputations, and that he would do the best he could for the furtherance thereof.

The 19th of this present I went with your Highness's Ambassadors to the Pope, and delivered his Holiness in writing those things that were done in the Disputation of the 13th of this: And then your Ambassadors were in hand with the Pope to alter the Intimation, and to put out the term *peremptory*, and other that were exclusory of further Disputations to be had upon the same Conclusions. The Pope's Holiness said, That Disputations was no act Judicial requiring to be in the Consistory; and therefore he said, he would call certain Congregations of Cardinals, on Friday and Monday following, to hear the Disputations.

Then I William Benet said, That that could not stand
very well with the Decree of the Intimation, which was,
peremptory for any further Disputations after the 20th of
this present; and therefore I spake that the same term
peremptory might be put out of the Intimation, alledging
withal, that upon the said Friday or Monday it was no time
to hear the Disputation, being so nigh after; and that his.
Holiness hitherto hath observed the Consistory for the Disputations, which Consistory cannot be unto after Easter,
if the manner of the Court be observed. Then the Pope
said, he might call a Consistory when he would, as he hath,
done in making of Cardinals, an Act much more solemn
than a Disputation. To that, I said, his Holiness might so
do if he would; howbeit, it should be *præter solitum morem:* and therefore desired his Holiness to consider therein the order before assigned, and that this term *peremptory.*
would not stand with the order. His Holiness then willed
we should inform the Cardinals, Anchona, and de Monte,
and so we did; Anchona shewed himself somewhat reasonable, and was contented the term *peremptory* should be put,
out. De Monte said that the Pope would promise to hear the
Conclusions disputed in Congregations, calling thereto certain Cardinals, so that the term *peremptory* should not be
prejudicial. Then I Edward Karne desired him, that if the
said term should not be prejudicial, that it might be
stricken out, for I told him plainly that I would not stand
to words, the writing shewing the contrary; adding withal,
that I would not dispute in this term, *tanquam perempto-
rio,* but would manifestly shew and protest, That I, with
other your Highness's Counsel, were ready to defend the.
Conclusions published, according to the order given, and
hitherto observed; alledging also, that the Conclusions
being justified, the Matters ought to be admitted; and,
that if the Pope's Holiness and the Cardinals would not.
give audience to me and your Highness's said Counsel, for
the manifest trial and showing of the truth, they should
give us cause to complain upon them, and to cry out, *usque
ad Sidera,* your Highness's Ambassadors all affirming the
same. Then the said Cardinal de Monte said, that the.
Pope's Holiness would provide for the Disputations, notwithstanding the term *peremptory* assigned, and said also,.

that in the Morning he would speak with the Pope, and
give your Ambassadors and me an answer.

In the morning, which was the 20th of this present, the
said Cardinal would, that nothing of the Decree of Intimation should be manifested, because the other part had a
Copy thereof, but would the Pope's Holiness to give an order that the word *peremptory* should be only for Disputations to be had in the Consistory, and not in Congregations, in which Congregations, the Conclusions remaining
might be disputed; and tho they had drawn out this Order, yet because it was nothing plain, neither certain to
be conformable to the former Order, I would have had the
said Cardinal to speak to the said Datary for to make it as
afore: and he was then contented, howbeit the Pope's
Holiness commanded all the Cardinals to their places, so
that I could not have the said Order, and was driven thereby either to dispute and accept the term, *tanquam peremp-
torium*, or else to fly the Disputations, giving occasion to
the adverse Party to say, that I diffided in the justness of
the Matters, and defence of the Conclusions. Whereupon
your Highness's Ambassadors and we, with other your
Learned Counsel, concluded, that I Edward Karne should
protest, *De non consentiendo in termino, tanquam perempto-
rio*, and afterward to proceed to the proposing of the Conclusions, and so I did by mouth according to the tenour of a
Copy, which here withal your Highness shall receive.
When I had protested, and the Pope had spoken this
word *Acceptamus*, the Queen's Advocate began to protest
that they would dispute no more, and desired his Holiness
to proceed in the principal Cause. Then I Edward Karne
said, That the Pope's Holiness did well perceive, that the
Conclusions were published and proposed, not only for
them to dispute, but also for all other, come who would, for
the information of his Holiness, and the whole Consistory.
And therefore I said, that tho they would not dispute, yet
I was there, with other your Highness's Learned Counsel,
to propose the Conclusions, according to the Order given,
justifying them to be Canonical, and ready to defend them
against all those that would gainsay them; and thereupon
desired the Pope's Holiness, that tho the Counsel of the
Party Adverse would not dispute, yet I with your High-

ness's Learned Counsel might be heard again; against
which my desire the Queen's Advocate made great excla-
mations, till at the last the Pope commanded him to silence,
and willed us to go to the Conclusions, which we did.

And here now it is determined, That we shall have no
more Disputations in the Consistory, but the rest of the
Conclusions to be disputed in Congregations before the
Pope, purposely made for the same; and what therein
shall be determined or done, your Highness from time to
time shall thereof by us be adverised, and of all other our
doings in that behalf.

And as concerning the Letters which your Highness sent
by Francis the Courier, of the last of February, as well to
the Pope, as to me Edward Karne, for the admission of me
and the Matter excusatory, we shall, according to your
Highness's pleasure and order assigned, in the common
Letter sent unto us by your said Highness, proceed and
do therein as may be most beneficial and profitable for the
same.

And thus most humbly we commend us to your Highness, beseeching Almighty God to preserve the same in
felicity and health many years. At Rome the 28th of
March 1532.

> Your Highness's most humble Subjects,
> Servants, and Chaplains,
>
> > William Benet.
> > Edward Karne.
> > Edmond Bonner.

XLV.

Another Letter concerning the Process at Rome.
An Original.

PLEASETH it your Highness, sithen our Letters of the
28 of March, here hath been great labour, and solliciting,
to bring the Disputation publick out of the Consistory kept
once in the week, into the Congregations, to be observed

and kept before the Pope's Holiness and the Cardinals, in such place, and as oft as should please them; to the intent, as we perceived, that the said Disputation might be the sooner ended, and not take such effect as it was devised for. And upon this great importance labour, I Edward Karne, was monished oftentimes to send Conclusions to be proposed in the said Congregations, as well in Palm-Sunday week, as in Easter-week, as appeareth by the Copies of the Intimations sent herewithal to your Highness: Upon which Intimations I delivered certain Conclusions, according to the order taken at the beginning, with a Protestation devised by your Grace's Counsel here, *De non recedendo ab eodem ordine, et de proponendo easdem Conclusiones in Consistorio, juxta eundem ordinem et non aliter.* That notwithstanding the Pope's Holiness caused me to be monished again, *cum Comminatione,* that if I would not come in, *cum Advocatis,* the third day of April, *procederet ad ulteriora protestatione me a prævia non obstante.* Whereupon, with the advice of your said Learned Counsel, I conceived a Protestation, and the same delivered to the Pope's Holiness the said third day in the morning, protesting as it was therein contained, and causing it to be registred by the Datary; of the which Protestation your Highness shall also receive a Copy herewithal. This notwithstanding, the Pope's Holiness, the said third day in the afternoon made a Congregation, where the said Protestation was examined; and after the Treaty had upon the same, we were in conclusion remitted again to the Consistory, there to be heard, as much as the Consistory intendeth to hear, upon the Conclusions that are published; which was much more beneficial to us, than to have had all proposed in Congregations to have been kept, as is afore. And by this means the Matter was shifted off, and deferred unto the 10th of this month; at which time the Pope's Holiness kept the Consistory. And one Mr. Providal, a singular good Clerk, which came from Bonony for the furtherance of your Highness's Cause, very compendiously, and after good fashion and handling, to the great contentation, as appeared, of the Audience there, purposed three Conclusions, of the which two concerned the habilitation of me Edward Karne, to lay in the Matters Excusatory: And the third was, that the Cause ought to be committed, *extra curiam, ad locum tutum utrique parti:* Of the which Conclusions, and also his Sayings, the said 10th day, your Highness shall receive a Copy here-withal. And forasmuch as at the said Consistory, neither the Imperials, neither yet the Queens Counsel did appear; I, Edward Karne, with the advice of your Highness's Counsel, said to the Pope's Holiness, after the Proposition made by Mr. Providal, that his Holiness might perceive well, that if the Party adverse had any good matter to alledg, against such things as were deduced for the justification of the Conclusions, and matter Excusatory, and did not diffide of their part, they would not have absented themselves, or shrunken from the Disputations, which they afore had accepted and taken; wherefore I accused their contumacy and absence, desiring that it might be enacted, and thereupon departed from the Consistory, for that day dissolved.

The 14th of this present, the Pope's Holiness caused Intimation to be made unto me, of the Consistory to be kept the 17th of the same; willing me to be there, *cum Advocatis,* to dispute all the Conclusions not proposed and disputed: Upon the which Intimation, I delivered to the Datary three Conclusions, the 19, the 20, and the 21 in order, with a Protestation devised by your Learned Counsel, sent here-withal to your Highness: And in the said Consistory, Mr. Providel did also alledg for the justification of the Matters and conclusions; and over that answered to such Objections as he thought the Party adverse to make foundation upon, and that very compendiously, being sorry that the Imperials, and Queen's Counsel, did not come in to dispute the said Conclusions, and the sayings of the said Mr. Providel in the said Consistory, with my Protestation also, in not agreeing to the term, as *peremptory* your Highness shall perceive in writing sent here-withal.

As concerning the seven Conclusions yet remaining undisputed, we think the Pope's Holiness will hear us no further in the Consistory; saying, that the Part adverse will not abide the Disputations, nor come in to the same: Nevertheless to take otherwise out of the Consistory, with the Cardinals Information, his Holiness is well contented.

And verily, Sir, to study, labour; set forward, and call upon such things as may confer to the advancement of the Matter, and your Highness's Purpose, there shall not want, neither good will, neither diligence to the uttermost, that we can excogitate or desire, as hitherto surely neither Party hath failed; trusting in God that thereby, if Justice be not oppressed, some good effect shall follow, to the good contentation of your Highness. With these Presents, your Highness shall also receive a Copy of all things that were spoken, as well for your Highness's behalf, as by the Party adverse, in the Consistory, the 20th day of March.

And thus most humbly we commend us to your Highness, beseeching Almighty God long to continue the same in his most Royal Estate. At Rome, the 29th of April.

Your Highness's most humble Subjects,

and poor Servants,

Edward Karne.
Edmond Bonner.

XLVI.

A Letter from Benet and Cassali about the Process.

An Original.

SERENISSIME et Invictissime Domine noster Supreme, salutem. Tribus Superioribus Consistoriis ante vacationes habitis, de Causa Excusatoria actum fuit; sed quid illud fuerit quod in primo egerunt rescire non potuimus, quia Cardinales pœna Excommunicationis prohibiti fuerant quicquam revelare. Secundo etiam aliquid super eadem causa tractarunt, quod itidem nos celaverunt. Sed ultimo illo, quod die octavo Julii Congregatum fuit, ita ut inferius patebit, constituerunt. Quum ergo postero die Pontificem adivissemus, ut quod decretum foret cognosceremus, ab eo sic accepimus; nolle se ore suo, propterea quod Jurisperitus non sit, Consistorii deliberationem pronunciare; quocirca die sequenti ad ipsum rediremus, quoniam vellet

Cardinales Montem et Anconitanum id ipsum nobis proferre: Et nihilominus idem quod deinde ex ipsis Cardinalibus audivimus tunc explicavit, noluit tamen nobis esse
Responsi loco. Igitur sicut dixerat, redivimus, et nobis
duo illi Cardinales sic retulerunt summum Dominum et
Cardinales decrevisse, literas Exhortatorias cum a Pontifice, tum a Collegio Cardinalium, Majestati vestræ scri-
bendas esse, quibus vestram Majestatem adhortarentur, ut
velit hic ad Causam Procuratorem constituere, idq; per
totum Octobrem proximum facere. Pontifex præterea
suadebat ut ad idem nos Majestatem Vestram cohortare-
mur, iidemq; fecerunt Cardinales, volentes omnes ambi-
guitates et dubitationes tollere. Respondimus, velle quod
nobis injungebatur Majestati Vestræ scribere; verum illud
non posse reticere quod erga Majestatem Vestram inique
actum videbatur; quum neq; Excusator admissus, neq;
ipsius allegationes forent probatæ ac receptæ, id quod tam
sæpe instantissime petitum fuerat. Præterea non posse
nos non valde mirari, ac etiam summopere conqueri, quod
quum pro comperto haberemus juris esse id fieri, esset
nihilominus denegatum; quum præsertim petendo Mandatum procuratorium, tacite viderentur rejicere Excusatorem,
et per ipsum allegata. Sic autem illi nobis Responderunt,
neque Excusatorem fuisse rejectum, neq; per ipsum allegata, sed in eodem, quo prius, statu permanere; hoc autem
excusatorium negotium minime, ut nobis judicibus clarum,
sed dubium videri. Ibiq; Anconitanus quædam nostris
contraria adduxit, quæ D. Karne suis literis recenset. Di-
cebant quoq; in hac re favorabilius nos, quam adversarios
fuisse tractatos; illud etiam addentes, quod si procuratorium mandatum mittatur, justitia optime ministrabitur, ac
etiam quatenus fieri possit, favorabiliter; idque et Pontifex
et Cardinales ambo constanter asseverabant. Quum vero
nos sæpius diceremus, excusatorem admitti debuisse, dixerunt, si recte considerare velimus, nos idem ipsum re habuisse; si enim (aibant), Procurator hic constituatur, literæ
Remissoriæ et Compulsoriæ decernentur, ad testes in partibus examinandos. Itemq; vir aliquis probus ad id dele-
gabitur ad utramq; partem, testesque scil. examinandos,
ita ut processus in partibus fiat; Atque hoc pacto nos id
consequi quod desideramus, quoniam quod ad totius causæ

decisionem pertinet, ex eo quod de Pontificis potestate cognoscendum, et de jure Divino disceptandum sit, ac aliis etiam de causis, ipsam Decisionem Pontifici integram semper reservari nihilominus oporteret, quamvis causam alibi quam Romæ cognosci permissum fuisset. Nobis certe visum est, haud parum esse quod obtinuimus, longe enim pejora timebamus, quum nemo in urbe esset, qui non crederet Excusatorem una cum suis allegationibus rejectum iri. Hunc quidem eventum rei Cæsariani ægerrime tulerunt. Optime valeat Majestas Vestra.   Romæ die 13 Julii 1532.

BOOK II.

Vestræ Regiæ Majestatis

Hier. Episcopus Wigornien.

W. Benet.
Gregorio Cassali.

XLVII.

The Sentence of Divorce.

Anno Incarnationis millesimo quingentesimo tricesimo tertio, Indictione sexta, Clementis Papæ decimo, mensis Maii vicesimo tertio, in Ecclesia Conventuali Monasterii Sancti Petri Dunstabliæ, Ordinis Sancti Augustini Lincoln. Dioces. nostri Cantuarien. Provinciæ.

In Dei Nomine, Amen. ' Nos Thomas Permissione Divina Cantuarien. Archiepiscopus, totius Angliæ Primas, et Apostolicæ Sedis Legatus, in quadam causa inquisitionis de et super viribus Matrimonii inter Illustrissimum et Potentissimum Principem et Dominum nostrum Henricum Octavum Dei Gratia Angliæ et Franciæ Regem, Fidei Defensorem et Dominum Hiberniæ, ac Serenissimam Dominam Catharinam nobilis memoriæ Ferdinandi Hispaniarum Regis Filiam contracti et consummati, quæ coram nobis in judicio ex officio nostro mero aliquandiu vertebatur, et adhuc vertitur, et pendet indecisa, rite et legitime procedentes, visis primitus per nos et diligenter inspectis, articulis sive capitulis in dicta causa objectis et ministratis, una cum

In an Inspeximus Rot. Pat. 25. Reg. 2d Part.

BOOK
IL

responsis eis ex parte dicti Illustrissimi et Potentissimi Principis Henrici Octavi factis et redditis, visisque et similiter per nos inspectis plurimorum Nobilium et aliorum testium fide dignorum dictis et dispositionibus in eadem causa habitis et factis, visisq; praeterea et similiter per nos inspectis, quamplurium fere totius Christiani orbis Principalium Academiarum Censuris ceu Conclusionibus Magistralibus, etiam tam Theologorum quam Jurisperitorum responsis et opinionibus, utriusq; deniq; Provinciae Anglicanae Consiliorum Provincialium assertionibus et affirmationibus, aliisque salutaribus monitis et doctrinis super dicto matrimonio desuper respective habitis et factis; visisq; ulterius, et pari modo per nos inspectis, pactis seu foederibus pacis et amicitiae inter perennis famae Henricum septimum nuper Regem Angliae, et dictum nobilis memoriae Ferdinandum nuper Regem Hispaniae desuper initis et factis; visis quoque peramplius, et diligenter per nos inspectis, omnibus et singulis actis, actitatis, literis, processibus, instrumentis, scripturis, monumentis, rebusq; aliis universis in dicta causa quomodolibet gestis et factis, ac aliis omnibus et singulis per nos visis et inspectis, atq; a nobis cum diligentia et maturitate ponderatis et recensitis, servatisq; ulterius per nos in hac parte de jure servandis, necnon partibus praedictis, videlicet praefato illustrissimo et potentissimo Principe Henrico Octavo per ejus Procuratorem idoneum coram nobis in dicta causa legitime comparente, dicta vero Serenissima Domina Catharina per contumaciam absente, cujus absentia Divina repleatur praesentia, de Consilio Jurisperitorum et Theologorum, cum quibus in hac parte communicavimus, ad sententiam nostram definitivam sive finale Decretum nostrum in dicta causa ferendam sive ferendum sic duximus procedendum, et procedimus in hunc modum. Quia per acta actitata, deducta, proposita, exhibita, et allegata, probata pariter et confessata, articulataque, capitulata, partis responsa, testium depositiones, et dicta instrumenta, monumenta, literas, scripturas, censuras, conclusiones Magistrales, opiniones, consilia, assertiones, affirmationes, tractatus et foedera pacis, processus, res alias, et caetera promissa coram nobis in dicta causa respective habita, gesta, facta, exhibita et producta; Necnon ex eisdem, et diversis aliis ex causis et

considerationibus, argumentisq; et probationum generibus
variis, et multiplicibus, validis quidem et efficacibus, quibus animum nostrum hac in parte ad plenum informavimus,
plene et evidenter invenimus et comperimus dictum Matrimonium inter præfatos Illustrissimum et Potentissimum
Principem et Dominum nostrum Henricum Octavum, ac
Serenissimam Dominam Catharinam, ut præmittitur, contractum et consummatum, nullum et omnino invalidum
fuisse et esse, et Divino Jure prohibente contractum et
consummatum extitisse : Idcirco nos Thomas Archiepiscopus Primas et Legatus antedictus, Christi nomine primitus
invocato, ac solum Deum præ oculis nostris habentes, pro
nullitate et invaliditate dicti Matrimonii pronunciamus, decernimus et declaramus, ipsumq; prætensum Matrimonium fuisse et esse nullum et invalidum, ac Divino Jure prohibente contractum et consummatum, nulliusq; valoris aut
momenti esse, sed viribus et firmitate juris caruisse et carere, præfatoq; Illustrissimo et Potentissimo Principi
Henrico Octavo et Serenissimæ Dominæ Catharinæ non
licere in eodem prætenso Matrimonio remanere, et pronunciamus, decernimus et declaramus; ipsosq; Illustrissimum
et Potentissimum Principem Henricum Octavum ac Serenissimam Dominam Catharinam, quatenus de facto et non
de jure dictum prætensum Matrimonium ad invicem con-
traxerunt et consummarunt, ab invicem separamus et divor-
ciamus, atq; sic separatos et divorciatos, necnon ob omni
vinculo Matrimoniali respectu dicti prætensi Matrimonii
liberos et immunes fuisse et esse, pronunciamus, decernimus et declaramus, per hanc nostram sententiam definitivam, sive hoc nostrum finale Decretum, quam sive quod
ferimus et promulgamus in his scriptis. In quorum præmissorum fidem, et testimonium, has literas nostras testi-
moniales, sive præsens publicum sententiæ vel Decreti instrumentum, exinde fieri ac per Notarios Publicos sub-
scriptos, scribas et actuarios nostros in ea parte specialiter
assumptos, subscribi et signari, nostriq; sigilli appensione
jussimus et fecimus communiri.

He likewise passed Judgment (confirming the King's Mar-
   riage with Queen Ann) at Lambeth, May 28, 1533.
   which is in the same Inspeximus.

BOOK 11.

XLVIII.

Act 5. Anno Regni 25.

An Act concerning the Deprivations of the Bishops of Salisbury and Worcester.

WHERE before this time the Church of England, by the King's most noble Progenitors, and the Nobles of the same, have been founded, ordained, and established in the Estate and degree of Prelatie Dignities, and other Promotions Spiritual, to the intent and purpose that the said Prelates, and other Persons, having the said Dignities and Promotions Spiritual, continually should be abiding, and Reseants upon their said Promotions within this Realm; and also keep, use, and exercise Hospitality, Divine Services, teaching and preaching of the Laws of Almighty God, to such Persons as were and have been within the precinct of their Promotions or Dignities, for the Wealth of the Souls of their Givers and Founders, greatly to the honour of Almighty God. Of the which said Spiritual Persons, the King's Highness, and his most noble Progenitors, have had right honourable, and well-learned Personages, apt, meet, and convenient, for to guide and instruct his Highness, and his most noble Progenitors, in their Counsels, concerning as well their Outward as Inward Affairs, to be devised and practised for the utility and preservation of this Realm; by reason whereof the Issues, Revenues, Profits, and Treasure, rising and coming of the said Spiritual Promotions and Dignities, were and should be spent, employed, and converted within this Realm, to the great profit and commodity of the King's Subjects of the same. And where also by the laudable Laws and Provisions of this Realm, before this time made, it hath been ordained, used, and established, that no Person nor Persons, of whatsoever Estate, Degree, or Quality he or they were, should take or receive within this Realm of England, to Farm, by any Procuracy, Writ, Letter of Attorney, Administrations, by Indenture, or by any other Mean, any Benefice, or other Promotion within this Realm, of any Person or Persons, but only of the King's true and lawful Subjects, being born under the King's Dominions. And also that no Person or Persons, of what estate and degree soever he or they were, by reason of any such Farm, Procuracie, Letter of Attorney, Administration, Indenture, or by any other mean, as is aforesaid, should carry, conveigh, or cause to be carried and conveighed out of this Realm, any Gold, Silver, Treasure, or other Commodity, by Letter of Exchange, or by way of Merchandise, or otherwise, for any of the Causes aforesaid, to the profit or commodity of any Alien, or other Stranger, being born out of this Realm, having any such Promotion Spiritual within the same, without license of the King's Highness, by the advice of his Council, as by the same Laws, Statutes, and Provisions, more plainly at large it may appear; which said laudable Laws, Statutes, and Provisions, were made, devised, and ordained, by great policy and foresight of the King's most noble Progenitors, the Nobles and Commons of this Realm, for the great profit, utility, and benefit of the same, to the intent that the Gold, Silver, Treasure, Riches, and other Commodity of the same, by the occasion aforesaid, should not be exhausted, employed, converted, and otherwise transported out of this Realm and Dominions of the same, to the use, profit, and commodity of any Stranger being born out of this Realm, or the Dominions of the same; But only to be spent, and used, and bestowed within the same, to the great comfort and consolation of the Subjects of this Realm. Notwithstanding which said wholsome Laws, Statutes, and Provisions, the King's Highness being a Prince of great benignity and liberality, having no knowledg, nor other due information, or instruction of the same Laws, Statutes, and Provisions, heretofore hath nominated, and preferred, and promoted, Laurence Campegius Bishop of Sarum, with all the Spiritual and Temporal Possessions, Promotions, and other Emoluments and Commodities in any wise belonging or appertaining to the same: And also hath nominated, preferred, and promoted, Hierome, being another Stranger, born out of the King's said Realm and Dominions, to the See and Bishoprick of Worcester, with all the Spiritual and Temporal Promotions, and other Emoluments and Commodities, in any wise belonging or appertaining to the same. Which said two Bishops, and namely the Bishop of

Sarum, nothing regarding their Duties to Almighty God, nor their Cures of the said Bishopricks, eversith or for the more part of the time of their said Promotions or Profections into the same, have been, and yet be resident, dwelling and abiding at the See of Rome, or elsewhere, in other parts beyond the Sea, far out and from any of the King's said Dominions; by reason whereof, the great Hospitality, Divine Service, teaching and Preaching the Laws, and Examples of good living, and the other good and necessary effects before rehearsed, have been many years by-past, and yet continually be, not only withdrawn, decayed, hindred, and minished, but also great quantity of Gold, Silver, and Treasure, to the yearly sum and value of 3000l. at the least, have been yearly taken and conveighed out of this Realm, to the singular profit, and great enriching of the said Bishops, and daily is like to be conveighed, transported, and sent, contrary to the purport and effect of the said former wholsome Laws and Statutes, to the great impoverishing of this Realm, as well presently as for to come, if speedy remedy be not had therefore in brief time provided. In consideration whereof, be it enacted by the Authority of this present Parliament, that the said two several Sees and Bishopricks of Salisbury and Worcester, and either of them from henceforth, shall be taken, reputed, and accounted in the Law to be utterly void, vacant, and utterly destitute of any Incumbent, or Prelate, &c.

XLIX.

A Letter from Cromwel to Fisher, about the Maid of Kent, Anno 34, or end of 35.

Cotton
Libr.
Cleop.
E. 4.
My Lord, in my right hearty wise I commend me to your Lordship, doing you to understand, that I have received your Letters dated at Rochester, the 18th day of this Month; in which ye declare what craft and cunning ye have to persuade, and to set a good Countenance upon an ill Matter, drawing some Scriptures to your purpose; which

well weighed, according to the places whereout they be
taken, make not so much for your purpose as ye alledge
them for; and where in the first Leaf of your Letters ye
write, that ye doubt nothing, neither before God nor before the World, if need shall that require, so to declare
your self, whatsoever hath been said of you, that ye have
not deserved such heavy words, or terrible threats, as hath
been sent from me unto you by your Brother.

How ye can declare your self afore God and the World,
when need shall require, I cannot tell; but I think verily that
your Declaration made by these Letters, is far insufficient to
prove that ye have deserved no heavy words in this behalf.
And to say plainly, I sent you no heavy words, but words
of great comfort, willing your Brother to shew you how
benign and merciful the Prince was: And that I thought it
expedient for you to write unto his Highness, and to recognize your Offences, and desire his pardon, which his Grace
would not deny you now in your age and sickness; which
my counsel I would you had followed, rather than to have
written these Letters to me, excusing your self altho there
were no manner of default in you. But, my Lord, if it
were in an other manner of case than your own, and out of
the Matter which ye favour, Í doubt not but that ye would
think him that should have done as ye have done, not only
worthy heavy Words, but also heavy Deeds; for where
ye labour to excuse your self of your Hearing, Bribing,
and concealing of the Maiden's false and feigned Revelations, and of your manifold sending of your Chaplains
unto her, by a certain intent which ye pretend your self to
have had, to know by communing with her, or by sending
your Chaplains to her, whether her Revelations, were of
God, or no, alledging divers Scriptures that ye were bound
to prove them, and to receive them after they were proved.
My Lord, whether ye have used a due means to try her and
her Revelations, or no, it appeareth by the Process of your
own Letters. For where you write that ye had conceived
a great opinion of the holiness of this Woman, for many
considerations rehearsed in your Letters, comprised in six
Articles; whereof the first is grounded upon the bruit and
fame of her; the second, upon her entring into Religion
after her trances and disfiguration; the third, upon re-

hearsal that her Ghostly Father being Learned and Religious, should testify that she was a Woman of great holiness; the fourth, upon the report that divers other vertuous
Priests, Men of good Learning and Reputation, should so
testify of her, with which Ghostly Father, and Priests, ye
never spake, as ye confess in your Letters; the fifth, upon
the praises of my late Lord of Canterbury, which shewed
you, as ye write, that she had many great Visions; the
sixth, upon the saying of the Prophet Amos, *Non faciet
Dominus Deus Verbum, nisi revelaverit secretum suum ad
servos suos Prophetas.* By which considerations ye were
induced to the desire to know the very certainty of this
Matter, whether these Revelations which were pretended
to be shewed to her from God, were true Revelations or
not. Your Lordship in all the sequel of your Letters,
shew not that ye made no further trial upon the truth of
her and her Revelations, but only in communing with her,
and sending your Chaplains to her with idle Questions, as
of the 3 Mary Magdalens, by which your communication
and sending, ye tried out nothing of her falshood, neither
(as it is credibly supposed) intended to do as ye might have
done, in any wise more easily than with communing with
her, or sending to her; for little credence was to be given
to her, affirming her own feigned Revelations to be from
God; for if credence should be given to every such lewd
Person as would affirm himself to have Revelations from
God, what readier way were there to subvert all Common-
Weals and good orders in the World?

Verily, my Lord, if ye had intended to trace out the truth
of her, and of her Revelations, ye would have taken an
other way with you; first, you would not have been converted with the vain Voices of the People, making bruits
of her Trances and Diffiguration, but like a wise, discreet,
and circumspect Prelate, ye should have examined (as other
since) such sad and credible Persons as were present at her
Traunces and Diffigurings, not one or two, but a good
number, by whose testimony ye should have proved, whether the Bruits of her Traunces and Diffigurations were
true or not. And likewise ye should have tried by what
craft and persuasion she was made a Religious Woman;
and if ye had been so desirous, as ye pretended, to enquire

out the truth or falshood of this Woman, and of her Revelations; it is to be supposed ye would have spoken with her
good, religious, and well-learned Ghostly Father e're this
time, and also with the vertuous and well-learned Priest,
(as they were esteemed) of whose reports ye would have
been informed by them which heard them speak : or ye
would also have been minded to see the Book of her Revelations, which was offered you, of which ye might have
had more trial of her and her Revelations, than of a hundred communications with her, or of as many sendings of
your Chaplains unto her. As for the late Lord of Canterbury's saying unto you, That she had many great Visions,
it ought to move you never a deal to give credence unto
her or her Revelations; for the said Lord knew no more
certainty of her, or of her Revelations, than he did by her
own report. And as touching the saying of Amos the
Prophet, I think verily the same moved you but a little to
hearken unto her; for sithence the Consummation and the
end of the Old Testament, and sithen the Passion of Christ,
God hath done many great and notable things in the World,
whereof he shewed nothing to his Prophets that hath come
to the knowledg of Men. My Lord, all these things moved
you not to give credence unto her, but only the very matter
whereupon she made her false Prophesies; to which matter ye were so affected, as ye be noted to be in all matters
which ye enter onee into, that nothing could come amiss
that made for that purpose. And here I appeal your Conscience, and instantly desire you to answer, Whether if she
had shewed you as many Revelations for the confirmation
of the King's Graces Marriage, which he now enjoyeth, as
she did to the contrary, ye would have given as much credence to her as the same done, and would have let the trial
of her and her Revelations, to overpass those many years,
where ye dwelt not from her but twenty miles in the same
Shire where her Traunces, and Diffigurings, and Prophesies in her Traunces were surmised, and reported.
And if percase ye will say (as it not unlike but ye will say,
minded as ye were wont to be) that the matter be not like,
for the Law of God, in your opinion, standeth with the one
and not with the other : Surely, my Lord, I suppose there
had been no great cause more to trust the one more than

the other; for ye know by Scriptures of the Bible, that
God may by his Revelation dispense with his own Law, as
with the Israelites spoiling the Egyptians, and with Jacob
to have four Wives, and such other. Think you, my Lord,
that any indifferent Man, considering the quality of the
Matter, and your Affections, and also the negligent passing
over of such lawful Trials as ye might have had of the said
Maiden, and her Revelations, is so dull, that cannot perceive and discern that your communing, and often sending
to the said Maid, was rather to hear and bruit many of her
Revelations, than to try out the truth or falshood of the
same. And in this Business, I suppose, it will be hard for
you to purge your self before God, or the World, but that
ye have been in great default in hearing, believing, and
concealing such things as tended to the destruction of the
Prince; and that her Revelations were bent and purposed
to that end, it hath been duly proved afore as great Assem-
bly and Council of the Lords of this Realm, as hath been
seen many years meet out of a Parliament. And what the
said Lords deemed them worthy to suffer, which said, heard,
believed, and concealed those false Revelations, be more
terrible than any threats spoken by me to your Brother.

And where ye go about to defend, that ye be not to be
blamed for concealing the Revelations concerning the
King's Grace, because ye thought it not necessary to rehearse them to his Highness, for six Causes following in
your Letters; afore I shew you my mind concerning these
Causes, I suppose that albeit you percase thought it not
necessary to be shewed to the Prince by you, yet that your
thinking shall not be your Trial, but the Law must define
whether ye oughted to utter it or not.

And as to the first of the said seven Causes; Albeit she
told you that she had shewed her Revelations concerning
the King's Grace to the King her self; yet her saying, or
others, discharged not you, but that ye were bound, by your
fidelity, to shew to the King's Grace that thing which seemed
to concern his Grace and his Reign so nighly: for how knew
you that she shewed these Revelations to the King's Grace,
but by her own saying, to which ye should have given no
such credence, as to forbear the utterance of so great Matters concerning a King's Weal? And why should you so

sinisterly judg the Prince, that if ye had shewed the same
unto him, he would have thought that ye had brought that
tale unto him, more for the strengthening and confirmation of your Opinion, than for any other thing else.   Verily, my Lord, whatsoever your Judgment be, I see daily
such benignity and excellent humanity in his Grace, that I
doubt not but his Highness would have accepted it in good
part, if ye had shewed the same Revelations unto him, as
ye were bounden by your fidelity.

   To the second Cause; Albeit she shewed you not that
any Prince, or other Temporal Lord, should put the
King's Grace in danger of his Crown; yet there were ways
enough by which her said Revelations might have put the
King's Grace in danger, as the foresaid Council of Lords
have substantially and duly considered: And therefore
albeit she shewed you not the means whereby the danger
should ensue to the King, yet ye were nevertheless bounden
to shew him of the danger.

   To the third; Think you, my Lord, that if any Person
would come unto you, and shew you, that the King's
destruction were conspired against a certain time, and
would fully shew you that he were sent from his Master to
shew the same to the King, and will say further unto that,
he would go streight to the King; were it not yet your
duty to certify the King's Grace of this Revelation; and
also to enquire whether the said Person had done his foresaid Message or no? Yes verily, and so were ye bound,
tho the Maiden shewed you it was her Message from God
to be declared by her to the King's Grace.

   To the fourth; Here ye translate the temporal duty that
ye owe to your Prince, to the spiritual Duty of such as
be bound to declare the Word of God to the People, and
to shew unto them the ill and punishment of it in another
World; the concealment whereof pertaineth to the Judgment of God, but the concealment of this Matter pertaineth
to other Judges of this Realm.

   To the fifth; There could no blame be imputed to you,
if ye had shewed the Maidens Revelation to the King's
Grace, albeit they were afterward found false, for no Man
ought to be blamed doing his Duty: And if a Man would
shew you secretly, that there were a great Mischief in-

tended against the Prince, were ye to be blamed if ye shewed him of it; albeit it was a feigned talk, and the said mischief were never imagined.

To the sixth; Concerning an Imagination of Mr. Pary, it was known that he was beside himself, and therefore they were not blamed that made no report thereof; but it was not like in this case, for ye took not this Maiden for a mad Woman, for if ye had, ye would not have given unto her so great credence as ye did.

To the final, and seventh Cause; Where ye lay unto the charge of our Sovereign, that so hath unkindly entreated you with grievous Words, and terrible Letters, for shewing his Grace truth in his great Matter, whereby ye were discomforted to shew unto him the Maidens Revelations: I believe that I know the King's Goodness, and natural Gentleness so well, that his Grace would not so unkindly handled you, as your unkindly writings him, unless ye gave him other Causes than be expressed in your Letters. And whatsoever the King's Grace hath said or written unto you heretofore, yet notwithstanding ye were nevertheless bounden to utter to him those pernicious Revelations.

Finally; Where ye desire, for the Passion of Christ, that ye be no more twitched in this matter, for if ye be put to that strait, ye will not lose your Soul, but ye will speak as your Conscience bindeth you, with many more words of great courage. My Lord, if ye had taken my counsel sent unto you by your Brother, and followed the same, submitting your self, by your Letters, at the King's Grace, for your offences in this behalf, I would have trusted that ye should never be quykkrand in this matter more. But now, where ye take upon you to defend the whole Matter, as ye were in no default, I cannot so far promise you: And surely, my Lord, if the Matter come to trial, your own confession in this Letter, besides the Witness which be against you, will be sufficient to condemn you: Wherefore, my Lord, I will eft-soons advise you, That laying apart all such excuses as ye have alledged in your Letters, which in my opinion be of small effect, as I have declared, ye beseech the King's Grace, by your Letters, to be your Gracious Lord, and to remit unto you your negligence, over-sight, and offence, committed against his Highness in this behalf; and I dare undertake that his Highness shall benignly accept you into his gracious favour, all matters of displeasure past afore this time forgotten and forgiven. As touching the speaking of your Conscience, It is thought that ye have written and have spoken as much as ye can, and many things, as some right probably believes, against your own Conscience: and men report, that at the last Convocation, ye spake many things which ye could not well defend; and therefore it is not greatly feared what ye can say or write in that Matter, howsoever ye be qukkrane and startled. And if ye had taken, &c.

L.

A Renunciation of the Pope's Supremacy; signed by the Heads of six Religious Houses.

Quum ea sit non solum Christianæ Religionis et pietatis ratio, sed nostræ etiam obedientiæ regula, ut Domino nostro Henrico ejus nominis pro Dominio Regio Octavo, cui uni et soli post Christum Iesum Salvatorem nostrum debentur omnia, non modo omnimodam in Christo, et eandem sinceram perpetuamq; animi devotionem, fidem, observantiam, honorem, cultum, reverentiam præstemus, sed etiam de eadem fide et observantia nostra rationem quotiescunq; postulabitur reddamus, et palam omnibus si res poscat libentissime testemur: Norint universi ad quos præsens scriptum pervenit, quod nos Priores et Conventus fratrum, viz. prædicatoris Langley Regis ordinis Sancti Dominici, Minorum de Ailsbury Ordinis Sancti Francisci, prædicatorum Dunstopliæ Ordinis antedicti, Minorum de Bedford Ordinis Sancti Francisci, Fratrum Carmelitarum de Hechyng Ordinis Beatæ Mariæ, Minorum de Morea Ordinis Sancti Francisci, uno ore et voce, atque unanimi omnium et singulorum consensu et assensu, hoc scripto nostro sub sigillis nostris communibus, et in domibus nostris capitularibus dato, pro nobis et successoribus nostris omnibus singulis, in perpetuum profitemur, testamur et fideliter promittimus et spondemus, nos dictos Priores et

Conventus et Successores nostros, omnes et singulos, integram, inviolatam, sinceram perpetuamq; fidem, observantiam et obedientiam semper præstituros erga Dominum
Regem nostrum Henricum Octavum, et erga Serenissimam
Reginam Annam Uxorem ejusdem, et erga castum Sanc-
tumq; Matrimonium nuper non solum inter eosdem juste
et legitime contractum, ratum et consummatum, sed etiam
tam in duabus Convocationibus Cleri, quam in Parliamento
Dominorum Spiritualium et Temporalium atq; Commu-
nium in eodem Parliamento Congregatorum et præsentum
determinatum, et per Thomam Cantuarien.. Episcopum
solenniter confirmatum, et erga quamcunq; aliam ejusdem
Henrici Regis nostri Uxorem, post mortem prædictæ Annæ
nunc Uxoris suæ legitimæ ducendam, et erga sobolem dicti
Domini Regis Henrici ex prædicta Anna legitime tam pro-
genitam quam progignendam, et erga sobolem dicti Domini
Regis ex alia quacunq; legitima Uxore post mortem ejusdem Annæ legitime progignendam, et quod eadem populo
notificabimus, prædicabimus et suadebimus, ubicunq; da-
bitur locus et occasio. Item, quod confirmatum ratumq;
habemus semperq; perpetuo habituri sumus, quod prædictus Rex noster Henricus est Caput Ecclesiæ Anglicanæ.
Item, quod Episcopus Romanus, qui in suis Bullis Papæ
nomen usurpat et summi Pontificis Principatum sibi arro-
gat, nihilo majoris neq; Auctoritatis aut jurisdictionis
habendus sit, quam cæteri quivis Episcopi in Anglia alibi
in sua cujusq; Diocese. Item, quod soli dicto Domino
Regi et Successoribus suis adhærebimus, atq; ejus et Pro-
clamationes, insuper omnes Angliæ leges atque etiam Statuta omnia, in Parliamento et per Parliamentum decreta,
confirmata, stabilita et ratificata, perpetuo manutenebi-
mus, Episcopi Romani legibus, decretis et Canonibus, si
qui contra legem Divinam et Sacram Scripturam esse inve-
nientur, in perpetuum renunciantes. Item, quod nullus
nostrum omnium in ulla vel privata vel publica concione
quicquam ex Sacris Scripturis desumptum ad alienum sensum detorquere præsumet, sed quisquis Christum ejusq;
vera, prædicabit Catholice et Orthodoxe. Item, quod
unusquisq; in suis orationibus et comprecationibus de more
faciendis, primum omnium Regem, tanquam Supremum
Caput Ecclesiæ Anglicanæ, Deo et populi precibus com-

mendabit; deinde Reginam cum sua sobole, tum demum Archiepiscopam Cantuarien. cum cæteris Cleri Ordinibus, prout videbitur. Item, quod omnes et singuli prædicti Priores et Conventus et Successores nostri, Conscientiæ et Jurisjurandi Sacro firmiter obligamur, quod omnia et singula prædicta fideliter et in perpetuum observabimus. In cujus rei testimonium huic Instrumento, vel scripto nostro, communia sigilla nostra appendimus, et nostra nomina propria quisq; manu subscripsimus, Sacris in Domibus nostris Capitularibus, die quinto Mensis Maii, Anno Christi millesimo quingentesimo trigesimo quarto, Regni vero Regis nostri Henrici Octavi vicesimo sexto.

Ego Frater Richardus Ingerth Prior Conventus, et Prædicator Langley Regis, cum consensu omnium Fratrum Conventus prædicti, non coactus sed sponte subscribo.

Ego Frater Joannes Cotton, Prior Conventus Prædicatorum Dunstabliæ, cum assensu omnium Fratrum Conventus prædicti, non coactus sed sponte subscribo.

Ego Frater Joannes Sutler, Prior Conventus Carmelitarum Hicchiæ, cum Assensu omnium Fratrum Conventus prædicti, non coactus sed sponte subscribo.

Ego Frater Edwardus Tryley Sacræ Theologiæ Bacalaureus, et Conventus Ailsberiæ, cum assensu omnium Fratrum Conventus prædicti, non coactus sed sponte subscribo.

Ego Frater Joannes Wyatt, Sacræ Theologiæ Doctor Conventus Bed. una cum assensu omnium Fratrum, sponte hoc scribo et non coactus.

Ego Frater Joannes Chapman, Sacræ Theologiæ Bacalaureus, Magister immerito Conventus Mare, cum assensu omnium Fratrum, mea sponte subscribo.

Another Declaration to the same purpose, Mutatis Mutandis *is made by the Prioress of Bedford in Kent, of the Order of St. Dominick, May* 4. 1534. Regn. vicesimo sexto. Rot. Clausa.

LI.

A Mandate for the Consecration of a Suffragan Bishop.

Rot. Pat. 2. par. 27 Regni.

REX Reverendissimo in Christo Patri et perdilecto Consiliario nostro Thomæ Cantuariensi Episcopo salutem. Reverendus Pater et dilectus Consiliarius noster Richardus Norvicensis Episcopus nobis significavit, quod Diocesis sua Episcopi Suffraganei solatio, qui suæ sollicitudinis partem sustinere consuevit, destituta est et existit; et ideo reverendos Patres Gregorium Abbatem Monasterii Beatæ Mariæ de Leystone, et Thomam Mannynge Priorem Monasterii Beatæ Mariæ de Butley, Norvicen. Dioc. Ordine Sacerdotali rite insignitos, et legitimo Matrimonio natos, et in ætate legitima constitutos, virosq; in Spiritualibus et Temporalibus multum circumspectos, quibus de Canonicis nihil obviant instituta, quo minus (ut asserunt) ad Episcopalem Suffraganei Dignitatem admitti possint et deberent, nobis per suas literas suo magno sigillo munitas præsentavit, humiliter et devote supplicans, quatenus nos alterum ipsorum sic præsentatorum ad aliquam sedem Episcopi Suffraganei infra Provinciam Cantuariensem existentem nominare, ipsique sic nominato stylum, Titulum et Dignitatem hujusmodi sedis donare dignaremur: unde nos ex gratia nostra speciali et mero motu nostris, dictum Reverendum Patrem Thomam Mannynge Priorem Monasterii Beatæ Mariæ de Butley prædicti, alterum ex dictis, Præsentamus in Episcopum Suffraganeum Sedis Gips vici Norvicen. Dioces. antedictæ, nominamus, eique Stilum, Titulum et Dignitatem ejusdem Sedis Episcopi Suffraganei damus et conferimus. Atque hæc vobis tenore præsentamus, significamus, requirentes vos, quatenus eundem Patrem sic per nos nominatum, in Episcopum Suffraganeum ejusdem Sedis Gips vici consecretis, eique Benedictionem ac omnia Episcopalia Insignia conferatis; cæteraq; omnia et singula quæ vestro in hac parte incumbunt officio pastorali, juxta modum et formam Statuti Parliamenti in vicesimo sexto Anno Regni nostri apud Westmonasterium nuper editi peragetis.

T. R. apud Westm. 6. die Martii 27. Regn.

AD LIBRUM TERTIUM.

——————

I.

Instructions for the General Visitation of the Monasteries.

Articuli Regiæ Inquisitionis, in Monasticam vitam agentes, exponendi, et præcipue in exemptos a jurisdictione Diocœsana, jam tantum Regiæ Majestati et ejus jurisdictioni subditos et subjectos, ac hujus inclyti sui Regni Statutis et legibus, nullisq; aliis penitus, obnoxios et astrictos.

1. *In primis;* Whether Divine Service be solemnly sung, said, observed, and kept in this Monastery, according to the Number and the Abilities thereof, by Night and by Day, in due time and hours? and how many be present commonly at Mattins, and other Service, and who be absent, and so accustomed to be, without cause or sickness?

2. *Item;* How many Monks, Cannons Regulars, or Nuns, be within this Monastery, and how many there ought to be, and whether the number be compleat according to the Founder's Will, or the Statutes, Ordinances, and laudable custom of this House; and whether the number be augmented or diminished now of late?

3. *Item;* Who were the first Founders of this House?

Fundationem primam, secundam, tertiam, et quotquot habent, exhibeant.

4. *Item;* Whether this House hath had any encrease of Lands given to it sithence the first Foundation thereof? by whom? by how many? and when?

5. *Item;* To what Sum of Mony those Revenues and Rents of this House do extend and amount unto yearly?

6. *Item;* Whether this House was ever translated from one habit and order to another? by whose Authority? and for what Cause?

Translationem exhibeant.

7. *Item;* How the Lands and Possessions appertaining unto this Monastery, given by the first Founder, and all other Lands given sithence the first Foundation, were granted, given, and established, and so first brought to *Morte main?* whether by the only Authority of the Giver, or by the Authorization of the Prince for that time reigning, and by what tenour and form ye hold them?

　　, Donationem et Confirmationem exhibeant.

8. *Item;* What evidence have you to shew for all and singular your Lands, Manors, Tenements, and other your Possessions Mortisate, and given unto you, and this your Monastery?

9. *Item;* Wherefore, for what Causes and Considerations ye were exempt from your Diocesan? and what was your Suggestion and Motive at the obtaining of your said Exemption?

　　Exemptionem exhibeant.

10. *Item;* Whether ye have any private, peculiar, or local Statutes, Confirmations, Ordinances, or Rules, made only for the behoof, good order, and singular weal of this House, besides the Rules of your Profession? and whether they were made either by your Founders before your Exemption, or by the good Fathers of this House, with the whole consent of the Brethren, being sinneth your exemption: to what use they were made, and how ye observe them?

　　Statuta illa localia, et alia quotquot habent, exhibeant.

11. *Item;* By what way and form the Master of this House was elected and chosen? And whether all the Brethren having, or ought to have by the Law, Statutes, or laudable custom of this House, Voices in the Election, were present in the same Election, or lawfully called or cited to it?

12. *Item;* Whether any Persons Excommunicate, Suspended, or Interdicted, did give Voices in the same Election?

13. *Item;* Within what time after the Election was

máde and done, the Master of this House was confirmed? and by whom?

14. *Item*; Whether unto the Confirmation, all that had Interest, or that would object against the same, were lawfully cited, monished, and called?

Exhibeat Electionem, Confirmationem, et Titulum suæ Incumbentiæ.

15. *Item*; What Rule the Master of this House, and other the Brethren, do profess?

16. *Item*; How many be Professed, and how many be Novices; and whether the Novices have like Habit, or use to wear an Habit distinct from the Habit of the Brethren Professed?

17. *Item*; Whether ye do use to profess your Novices in due time, and within what time and space after they have taken the Habit upon them?

18. *Item*; Whether the Brethren of this House do know the Rule that they have professed, and whether they keep their Profession according to that their Rule, and Custom of this House; and in especial, the three substantial and principal Vows, that is to say, *Poverty, Chastity,* and *Obedience?*

19. *Item*; Whether any of the Brethren use any propriety of Mony, or of Plate, in their Chambers; or of any other manner thing unwarre of the Master, and without his knowledg and license, or by his sufferance and knowledg? and for what cause?

20. *Item*; Whether ye do keep Chastity, not using the company of any suspect Woman within this Monastery, or without? And whether the Master, or any Brother of this House be suspected upon Incontinency, or defamed for that he is much conversant with Women?

21. *Item*; Whether Women useth and resorteth much to this Monastry by back-ways, or otherwise? and whether they be accustomably, or at any time lodged within the Precinct thereof?

22. *Item*; Whether the Master, or any Brother of this House, useth to have any Boys or young Men laying with him?

23. *Item*; Whether the Brethren of this House keep

their Obedience, being ready at their Master's Commandment, in all things honest, lawful, and reasonable?

Sequuntur Regulæ Cæremoniales.

24. *Item;* Whether ye do keep silence in the Church, Cloister, Fraitrie, and Dormitorie, at the hours and time specified in your Rule?

25. *Item;* Whether ye do keep Fasting and Abstinence, according to your Rules, Statutes, Ordinances, and laudable Customs of this House?

26. *Item;* Whether ye abstain from Flesh in time of Advent, and other times declared and specified by the Law, Rules, and laudable Customs of this House?

27. *Item;* Whether ye wear Shirts and Sheets of Woollen, or that ye have any Constitution, Ordinance, or Dispensation, granted or made to the contrary, by sufficient and lawful Authority?

Profitentes Regulam Benedicti quam arctissime tenentur ad prædicta Cæremonialia observanda.

28. *Item;* Whether ye do sleep altogether in the Dormitorie, under one Roof, or not?

29. *Item;* Whether ye have all separate Beds, or any one of you doth lay with an other?

30. *Item;* Whether ye do keep the Fraitry at Meals, so that two parts, or the least, the two part of the whole Covent be always there, unless the Master at every one time dispense with you to the contrary?

31. *Item;* Whether ye do wear your Religious habit continually, and never leave it off but when ye go to bed?

32. *Item;* Whether every Brethren of this House have lightly departed hence, and hath gone to any other House of like Order and Profession, without special Letters and License of their Master?

33. *Item;* Whether the Master and Brethren of this House have received and admitted any Brother of another House, without special License and Letters of his Master and Head?

34. *Item;* Whether any of you, sithence the time of your Profession, hath gone out of this House to his Friends, or otherwise?

35. *Item;* How oftimes he did so, and how long at every time ye tarried forth ?

36. *Item;* Whether ye had special license of your Master so to go forth, or not?

37. *Item;* Whether at every time of your being forth, ye changed or left off your habit, or every part thereof?

38. *Item;* Whether ye, or any of you be, or hath been, in manifest Apostasy, that is to say, Fugitives or Vagabonds ?

39. *Item;* For what cause or occasion ye have so gone forth and been in Apostasy ? and whether the cause of your going forth was by reason of the great cruelty of your Master, or by his negligence, not calling you home to your Cloister ?

40. *Item;* Whether ye be weekly shaven, and do not nourish or suffer your Hair to be long ? and whether ye wear your Apparel according to the Rule, not too excessive, nor too exquisite ; and in like wise the trappo's of your Horses, and other your bearing Beasts ?

41. *Item;* Whether the Master and Head of this House do use his Brethren charitably, without partiality, malice, envy, grudg, or displeasure more shewed to one than to another ?

42. *Item;* Whether he do use his Disciplines, Corrections, and Punishments upon his Brethren, with mercy, pity, and charity, without cruelty, rigorousness, and enormous hurt, no more favouring one than another?

43. *Item;* Whether any Brother, or Religious Person of this House, be incorrigible ?

44. *Item;* Whether the Master of this House do use his Brethren charitably when they be sick and diseased? and whether in time of their sickness he do procure unto them Physicians, and all other necessaries ?

45. *Item;* Whether he make his Accompts (as he ought to do) once every year before his Brethren, and chiefly the Seniors and Officers, to the intent they may be made privy to the state and condition of the House, and know perfectly the due administration thereof?

46. *Item;* Whether the Prior, Subprior, Sellerar, Kitchener, Terrure, Sacristen, or any such-like Officer, having Administration of every manner Revenues of this House, do make his whole and true Accompt, according as he is

bound to do, not applying any thing by him received to his own proper use or commodity?

47. *Item*; Whether any Religious Person of this House do bear, occupy, or exercise more Offices than one, for, and to his own singular commodity, advantage, or profit, by the partial dealing of the Master?

48. *Item*; Whether all and singular the Revenues and Profits of this House be converted and employed to the behove and use thereof, and of the Brethren, and according to the Founder's mind and Giver?

49. *Item*; Whether the Master do make sufficient reparations upon his Monastery, as the Church and all other housing thereto adjoined, and also upon all other the Lands, Granges, Farms, and Tenements belonging to the same, and whether he suffer any dilapidation, decay, or ruine in any part of them?

50. *Item*; Whether there be any Inventory made of all and singular the Moveables, Goods, which from time to time have been, and yet be in this House, as of Jewels, Reliques, Ornaments, Vestiments, ready Mony, Plate, Bedding, with other Utensils; also of Corn, Chattels, and other Commodities, to the intent the state and condition of this House may be always known?

51. *Item*; That ye express truly and sincerely the whole state and condition of this House, as Mony, Plate, Cattel, Corn, and other Goods?

52. *Item*; Whether this Monastery be indebted? to whom? and for what cause?

53. *Item*; Whether any of the Lands be sold, or mortgaged? and for what Sums?

54. *Item*; Whether any be lett to Farm by the Master of this House for term of years, and for how many years? and specially whether they be letten for small Sums, or for less Sums than they were wont to be letten for, to the intent to have great sums of ready Mony before hand?

55. *Item*; Whether he do enforce, compel, or constrain his Brethren, or any of them, to consent to the sealing of any Leases, Grants, Farm-Holds, Annuities, Corrodies, or any other Alienations?

56. *Item*; Whether the Plate and Jewels, or any part or parcel thereof, or of any other moveable Goods of this

House be laid to pledg, sold, or alienated for a time, or for ever? for what cause, and to whom? or otherwise imbezled, or consumed?

57. *Item;* Whether the Master of this House be wont to give under his Seal of Office, or Covent-Seal, Farms, Corrodies, Annuities, or Offices, to his Kinsfolk, Alliances, Friends, or Acquaintance, for term of years, or otherwise, to the hurt, hindrance, dammage, and impoverishment of this House?

58. *Item;* Whether he be wont to grant any Patent, or Covent-Seal, without the consent of his Brethren?

59. *Item;* Whether the Covent-Seal of this House be surely and safely kept under three Keys; that is to say, one remaining and being in the custody of the Master, and the other two in the custody of two Seniours?

60. *Item;* Whether the Muniments and Evidences of the Lands, Rents, and Revenues of this House, be safely kept from Vermine and Moistness?

61. *Item;* Whether the Master do keep Hospitality according to the ability of his House, and in like manner as other Fathers hereof have done heretofore?

62. *Item;* Whether the Master of this House, in receiving any Novice, being of willing and toward mind to enter into Religion, hath demanded or received, or convented to receive any Mony, Rewards, or any other temporal Commodities of him so entring, or willing to enter, or of any other his Friends? and whether for not promising, granting, or giving such Rewards or Gifts, any hath been repelled and not received?

63. *Item;* Whether the Novices, and other received into Religion, have a Preceptor and Master deputed unto them to teach them Gramar and good Letters?

64. *Item;* Whether any Seniour of this House be deputed to declare, inform, and instruct them their Rules, and whereunto they shall be bounden to observe and keep, after their Profession?

65. *Item;* Whether any of you have taken upon him the Habit and Profession of your Religion, chiefly for the intent, hope, or trust to be made Head and Master of this House?

66. *Item;* Whether the Master of this House, in giving

any Advocation, Nomination, Presentation, or Collation of any Parsonage, Vicarage, Chapel, or Benefice of the Patronage and Gift this House, do take, or use to take any manner Pension, Portion, or other Commodity or Gains; or else doth make any Convention or Compaction, whereby any lucre may ensue to him in that behalf?

67. *Item;* Whether he do receive, or use to receive, the Fruits and Revenues of every such Benefice vacant, or use to borrow any Mony of him to whom he intendeth to give such Benefice unto, expresly covenanting or intending, that he so obtaining the said Benefice, shall freely and clearly remit the said Mony so borrowed?

68. *Item;* What, and how many Benefices the Master of this House doth occupy and keep in his own hands?

69. *Item:* Whether the same Benefices be appropriate and united to this House by sufficient authority?

70. *Item;* Whether the Master of this House doth make distributions amongst the Parishoners of the Benefices appropriate, and doth keep and observe all and singular other Provisions and Ordinances specified and expressed in the Appropriations of the same Benefices?

    *Exhibeant omnes et singulas Appropriationes, una cum
       Ordinationibus et Dotationibus Vicariatuum.*

71. *Item;* Whether he do promote unto such Benefices as be of his Gift, sufficient and able Persons in Learning, Manners, and Vertue?

72. *Item;* Whether any Brother of this House do serve any Parish-Church, being appropriate and united to the same, and how many Churches appropriate be so served?

73. *Item;* Whether the Master of this House hath and possesseth any Benefice with Cure, or any other Dignity with his Abbey?

    Si aliquod tale habet, Dispensationem exhibeat.

74. *Item;* Whether the Master of this House at any time since he was first made Abbot, or Master, did know or believe that he was Suspended, or Excommunicate, either by the Law, or by any Judg; and whether he knowing or supposing himself so to be, did sing Mass in the mean time, and before he was absolved?

In Visitatione Monialium ad Præmissa addantur hæc.

75. *Item;* Whether this Monastery hath good and sufficient Enclosure, and whether the Doors and Windows be diligently kept shut, so that no Man can have any entry into the same, or any part thereof, at inconvenient times?

Propter quod necessarium erit Visitatori circumire Monasterium, ac videre et rimare dispositionem ædificiorum, et an sint aliqua loca pervia per quæ secrete intrari possit; et una secum habeat Abbatissam cum duabus aut tribus senioribus Monialibus, a quibus tum interroget, an ostia Monasterii singulis quibusque noctibus sub clavibus clausa teneantur, et quæ earum Monialium senio confectarum, vel an Abbas ipsa clavium custodiam tempore nocturno habeant et teneant: nam non est tutum clavium custodiam Junioribus committere.

76. *Item;* Whether Strangers, both Men and Women, useth commonly to have communication with the Sisters of this House, without license of the Abbess or Prioress, specially in secret places, and in the absence of their Sisters?

77. *Item;* Whether any Sister of this House were professed for any manner of compulsion of her Friends and Kinsfolks, or by the Abbess or Prioress?

78. *Item;* Whether any of the Sisters of this House useth to go forth any whither out of the Precinct thereof, without special license of their Abbess or Prioress?

79. *Item;* Whether any Sister doth use her Habit continually out of her Cell?

80. *Item;* Wherein every one of you occupieth her self, beside the time of Divine Service?

81. *Item;* Whether any Sister of this House hath any familiarity with Religion Men, Secular Priests, or Lay-Men, being not near of kin unto them?

82. *Item;* Whether any Sister of this House hath been taken and found with any such accustomably so communing, and could not shew any reasonable cause why they so did?

83. *Item;* Whether any of you doth use to write any Letters of Love, or lascivious fashion to any Person, or receive any such, or have any privy Messengers coming and

resorting unto you, or any of you, with Token or Gifts, from any manner secular Person or other ?

84. *Item;* Whether any of you doth use to speak with any manner of Person, by night or by day, by Grates or back Windows, or other privy Places within this Monastry, without license of your Head ?

85. *Item;* Whether the Confessor of this House be a discreet Man, of good learning, vertue and honest behaviour, of good name and fame, and whether he hath been always so taken ?

86. *Item;* How oftimes in the year the Sisters of this House useth to be Confessed and Communicate ?

> *Restat pro Ecclesiis Collegiatis, Hospitalibus, Ecclesiis Cathedralibus, Parrochialibus, Ecclesiis, Episcopo, et Archiepiscopo, pro ordine Jerosolomitarum ?*

> *Exhibeant omnia scripta, munimenta, Inventaria, Scedulas quascunque, unde aliquid cognitionis eorum reformationi Monasteriorum, sive domorum utilitati, necessariæ explicari, aut quoquo modo colligi possit.*

II.

General Injunctions to be given on the King's Highness's behalf, in all Monastries and other Houses, of whatsoever Order or Religion they be.

FIRST; That the Abbot, Prior, or President, and all other Brethren of the Place that is visited, shall faithfully, truly, and heartily, keep and observe, and cause teach, and procure to be kept and observed of oath, as much as in them may lie, all and singular Contents, as well in the other of the King's Highness Succession, given heretofore by them, as in a certain Profession lately sealed with the Common Seal, and subscribed and Signed with their own hands: Also that they shall observe and fulfil, by all the means that they best may, the Statutes of this Realm, made, or to be made, for the suppression and taking away of the usurped and pretensed Jurisdiction of the

Bishop of Rome within this Realm : and for the assertion and confirmation of the Authority, Jurisdiction and Pre- rogative of our most noble Sovereign Lord the King, and his Successors; and that they shall diligently instruct their Juniors and Youngers, and all other committed to their Cure, That the King's Power is by the Laws of God most excellent of all under God in Earth ; and that we ought to obey him afore all other Powers, by God's Prescript; and that the Bishop of Rome's Jurisdiction or Authority here- tofore usurped, by no means is founded or established by Holy Scripture : but that the same, partly by the craft and deceit of the same Bishop of Rome, and by his evil and am- bitious Canons and Decretals ; and partly by the toleration and permission of Princes, by little and little hath grown up; and therefore now, of most right and equity, is taken away and clean expelled out of this Realm.

Also, that the Abbot, Prior, or President and Brethren, may be declared, by the King's Supream Power and Au- thority Ecclesiastical, to be absolved and loosed from all manner Obedience, Oath, and Profession by them hereto- fore perchance promised, or made, to the said Bishop of Rome, or to any other in his stead, or occupying his Au- thority ; or to any other Forreign Prince, or Person : And nevertheless let it be enjoined to them, that they shall not promise or give such Oath or Profession to any such For- reign Potentate hereafter. And if the Statutes of the said Order Religious, or Place, seem to bind them to Obedi- ence, or Subjection, or any other Recognizance of Superi- ority to the said Bishop of Rome, or to any other Forreign Power, Potentate, Person or Place. by any ways; such Statutes, by the King's Graces Visitors, be utterly annihi- late, broken, and declared void and of none effect; and that they be in no case bounden or obligate to the same, and such Statutes to be forthwith utterly put forth and abolish- ed out of the Books, or Muniments of that Religion, Order or Place, by the President and his Brethren.

Also, that no Monk, or Brother of this Monastery, by any means go forth of the Precinct of the same.

Also, that Women, of what state or degree soever they be, be utterly excluded from entring into the Limits or

Circuit of this Monastery, or place, unless they first obtain
license of the King's Highness, or his Visitor.

Also, that there be no entring into this Monastery but
one, and that by the great fore-gate of the same, which diligently shall be watched and kept by some Porter specially
appointed for that purpose, and shall be shut and opened by
the same both day and night, at convenient and accustomed
hours; which Porter shall repel all manner Women from
entrance into the said Monastery.

Also, that all and singular Brethren, and Monks of this
Monastery, take their refections altogether in a place called
the *Misericorde*, such days as they eat Flesh, and all other
days in their Refectory; and that at every Mess there sit
four of them, not of duty demanding to them any certain,
usual, or accustomed duty or portion of Meat as they were
wont to do; but that they be content with such Victuals as
is set before them, and there take their Refections soberly,
without excess, with giving due thanks to God; and that
at every such Refection, some Chapter of the New Testament, or Old, by some of the said Brethren, be read and
recited to the other, keeping silence, and giving audience
to the same.

Also, that the Abbot and President do daily prepare one
Table for himself and his Guests thither resorting, and that
not over sumptuous, and full of delicate and strange Dishes,
but honestly furnished with common Meats; At which
Table, the said Abbot, or some Senior in his stead, shall
sit to receive, and gently entertain the Strangers, the
Guests.

Also, that none of the Brethren send any part of his
Meat, or the leavings thereof to any Person, but that there
be assigned an Almoner, which shall gather the Leavings,
both of the Covent and Strangers Tables, after that the
Servants of the House have had their convenient Refections, and distribute the same to poor People; amongst
whom special consideration be had of such, before other,
as be Kinsfolk to any of the said Brethren, if they be of
like power and debility as other be; and also of those
which endeavour themselves, with all their will and labour,
to get their living with their hands, and yet cannot fully help

themselves for their chargeable Houshold, and multitude of
Children: yet let not them be so cherished, that they shall
leave labour and fall to idleness; with consideration also
specially to be had of them, which by weakness of their
Limbs and Body be so impotent that they cannot labour;
and by no means let such Alms be given to valiant mighty
and idle Beggars and Vagabonds, as commonly use to resort about such places; which rather, as drove-Beasts and
Mychers, should be driven away and compelled to labour,
than in their idleness and lewdness, against the form of the
King's Graces Statute in this behalf made, cherished, and
maintained, to the great hindrance and damage of the Common-Weal.

Also, that all other Almses or Destributions due, or accustomed to be made, by reason of the Foundation, Statutes, or customes of this place, be made and given, as
largely and as liberally as ever they were at any time heretofore.

Also, that the Abbot, Prior, or President, shall find
Wood and Fewel sufficient to make Fire in the Refectory,
from Allhallow-even to Good-Friday.

Also, that all the Brethren of this House, except the
Abbot, and such as be sick, or evil at ease, and those that
have fulfilled their Jubilee, lie together in the Dormitory,
every one by himself, in several Beds.

Also, that no Brother, or Monk, of this House, have any
Child or Boy laying, or privily accompanying with him, or
otherwise haunting unto him, other than to help him to
Mass.

Also, that the Brethren of this House, when they be
sick, or evil at ease, be seen unto, and be kept in the infir-
mary duly, as well for their sustenance of Meat and Drink,
as for their good keeping.

Also, that the Abbot, or President, keep and find in
some University, one or two of his Brothers, according to
the Ability and Possessions of this House; which Brethren, after they be learned in good and holy Letters,
when they return home, may instruct and teach their Brethren, and diligently preach the Word of God.

Also, that every day, by the space of one hour, a Lesson
of Holy Scripture be kept in this Covent, to which all, un-

der pain by this said President to be moderated, shall report; which President shall have Authority to dispense
with them, that they, with a low and treatable voice, say
their long hours, which were wont to be sung.

Also, that the Brethren of this House, after Divine Service done, read or hear somewhat of Holy Scripture, or
occupy themself in some such like honest and laudable
exercise.

Also, that all and every Brethren of this House shall
observe the Rule, Statutes, and laudable Customs of this
Religion, as far as they do agree with Holy Scripture and
the Word of God. And that the Abbot, Prior, or President of this Monastery, every day shall expound to his
Brethren, as plainly as may be, in English, a certain part
of the Rule that they have professed, and apply the same
always to the Doctrine of Christ, and not contrariwise;
and he shall teach them, that the said Rule, and other
their Principles of Religion (so far as they be laudable) be
taken out of Holy Scripture ; and he shall show them the
places from whence they were derived ; and that their Ceremonies, and other observances of Religion, be none other
things than as the first Letters or Principles, and certain
Introductions to true Christianity, or to observe an order in
the Church. And that true Religion is not contained in
Apparel, manner of going, shaven Heads, and such other
marks; nor in silence, fasting, up-rising in the night, sing-
ing, and such other kind of Ceremonies, but in cleanness
of mind, pureness of living, Christ's Faith not feigned,
and brotherly Charity, and true honouring of God in Spirit
and Verity: And that those above-said things were instituted and begun, that they being first exercised in these, in
process of time might ascend to those as by certain steps,
that is to say, to the chief point and end of Religion : and
therefore let them be diligently exhorted, that they do not
continually stick and surcease in such Ceremonies and Observances, as tho they had perfectly fulfilled the chief and
outmost of the whole true Religion ; but that when they
have once past such things, they endeavour themselves to
higher things, and convert their minds from such external
Matters, to more inward and deeper Considerations, as the
Law of God and Christian Religion doth teach and show.

And that they assure not themselves of any Reward or Commodity any wise, by reason of such Ceremonies and Observances, except they refer all such to Christ, and for his sake observe them; and for that they might thereby the more easily keep such things as he hath commanded, as well to them as to all Christian People.

Also, that the Abbot and President of this Place shall make a full and true reckoning and accompt of his Administration every year to his Brethren, as well of his Receipts as Expences; and that the said Accompt be written in a great Book remaining with the Covent.

Also, that the Abbot and President of this House shall make no waste of the Woods pertaining to this House, nor shall set out unadvisedly any Farmes or Reversions, without the consent of the more part of the Convent.

Also, that there be assigned a Book and a Register that may copy out into that Book all such Writings, word by word, as shall pass under the Convent-Seal of this House.

Also, that no Man be suffered to profess, or to wear the Habit of Religion in this House e're he be 24 years of Age compleat; And that they entice nor allure no Man with suasions and blandyments to take the Religion upon him.

Item, that they shall not shew no Reliques, or feigned Miracles, for encrease of Lucre, but that they exhort Pilgrims and Strangers to give that to the Poor, that they thought to offer to their Images or Reliques.

Also, that they shall suffer no Fairs, or Markets, to be kept or used within the limits of this House.

Also, that every Brother of this House that is a Priest, shall every day in his Mass, pray for the most happy and most prosperous estate of our Sovereign Lord the King, and his most noble and lawful Wife Queen Ann.

Also, that if either the Master, or any Brother of this House, do infringe any of the said Injunctions, any of them shall denounce the same, or procure to be denounced, as soon as may be, to the King's Majesty, or to his Visitor-General, or his Deputy. And the Abbot, or Master, shall minister spending Mony, and other Necessaries, for the way to him that shall so denounce.

Other Spiritual Injunctions may be added by the Visitor,

as the place and nature of the Comperts shall require, after
his discretion.

Reserving Power to give more Injunctions, and to examine and discuss the Comperts, to punish and reform them
that be convict of any notable Crime, to search and try the
Foundations, Charters, Donations, Appropriations and Muniments of the said Places; and to dispose all such Papistical Escripts as shall be there found, to the Right Honourable Mr. Thomas Cromwell General-Visitor to the King's
said Highness, as shall seem most expedient to his high
wisdom and discretion.

III.

Some Particulars relating to the Dissolution of Monasteries.

SECTION I.

The Preamble of the Surrender of the Monastery of Langden.

OMNIBUS Christi fidelibus, &c. Willielmus Dyer, Abbas Monasterii Beatæ Mariæ Virginis et S. Thomæ Martyris de Langden, in Com. Kent, et ejusdem loci Conventus, Ordinis Præmonstrat. capitulum dictæ domus plene
facientes, ejusdemq; domus (quæ in suis fructibus, redditi-
bus, provenien. even. et emolumen, non mediocriter deteri-
orata est, et quasi in totum diminuta, ingentiq; ære alieno
obruta, oppressa, et gravata extitit) statum usq; adeo matura deliberatione, et diligenti tractatu, considerantes, ponderantes, et pensantes, quod nisi celeri remedio, regia provisione huic Monasterio sive Prioratui (quippe quod de
ejus fundatione et personatu existit) brevi succuratur et
provideatur, funditus in Spiritualibus et Temporalibus an-
nihiletur, per præsentes damus et concedimus, &c.

*The rest follows in the ordinary form of Law: but the ordi-
nary Preamble in most Surrenders is,*

Omnibus Christi fidelibus, &c. Nos—Salutem. Sciatis
quod nos, deliberate, certa scientia, et mero motu, nostris,
ex quibusdam causis, justis, et rationabilibus, nos, animas

et conscientias nostras, specialiter moventibus, ultro et sponte dedisse et concessisse, Domino Regi, &c.

But it seems some few Houses, though they were prevailed with to surrender, yet would not do it with such a Preamble, for there are about twenty Surrenders without any Preamble at all, made to John London Clerk, *ad usum Domini Regis.*

SECTION II.

A List of Religious Houses, which by the King's Letters Patents were of new founded and preserved from the dissolution of Lesser Monasteries.

St. Mary of Betlesden, Buckinghamshire, Cistercians.
St. Mary of Huntington, Augustians.
Chertsey, Cambridg-shire, Benedict. Nuns.
St. Mary in Winton, Southamp.shire, Benedict. Nuns.
Grace-dieu, Leicester-shire, August. Nuns.

} 17. Aug.

Anno Regni 28.

St. Michael Hull, York-shire, Carthusians.	27.
St. Clare of Denby, Cambridg-shire, Nuns.	28.
Kymme, Lincoln-shire, Augustin.	2. Sept.
St. Ann Marrick, York-shire, Benedict. Nuns.	9.
St. Mary of Bindon, Dorset-shire, Cistercians.	16. Nov.
St. Mary Harpa, Westmor. Præmonstrat.	16.
St. Mary of Hynnings, Lincoln-shire, Cist. Nuns.	27.
St. Mary de-la-Pray, Northamp. shire, Nuns.	13. Dec.
St. Mary of Kelling, York-shire, Nuns.	14.
St. Mary of Cockersand, Lancash. Præmonstrat. Nuns.	19.
De-la-val, York-shire, Carthus.	2. Jan.
St. Mary Newstead, Nottinghamsh. Aug. Nuns.	2.
Wormsley, Herefordsh. August.	27.
St. Mary of Alnewick, Northumb. Præmonst.	30.
Bellalanda, Yorksh. Cisterc.	30.
St. John Bapt. Egglestone, Yorksh.	30.
St. Mary de Nith, Glamorgansh. Cisterc.	30.
St. Mary Ulnestock, Leicestersh.	30.
St. Mary of Dale, Derbysh. August.	30.
St. Katharine of Poleslo, Devon. Ben. Nuns.	30.

BOOK III.

St. Mary Lacock, Wiltsh. August. Nuns.   30. Jan.
St. Mary Chester, Nuns.   30.
St. Mary of Studley, Oxfordsh. Nuns.   30.
St. Mary of Canon Leigh, Devonsh. Nuns   12. Feb.
Cockhill, Worcestersh. August. Nuns.   5. March.
St. Bartholomew, New-Castle, Nuns.   30.
St. Mary of Wallingwells, Yorksh.   April.

The Grants for these Houses are all in the 28th year of the King, to be held in perpetuam eleemosynam, and are enrolled in the 1st, 2d, 4th, and 5th parts of the Patent Rolls for that Year.

SECTION III.

A List of all the Surrenders of Abbies, which are yet extant in the Augmentation Office.

Regni 27.

LANGDEN, Præmonst. signed by the Abbot
    and 10 Monks, Com. Kent.   13. Nov.
Folkeston, Bendict. the Prior, Kent.   15.
Dover, the Prior, 8 Monks, Kent.   16.
Merten, August. the Prior, and 5 Friers, Yorkhs. 9. Feb.
Hornby, Premonst. the Prior and two Monks.   23.
Tilty, Cisterc. the Abbot and 5 Monks, Essex.   28.
Bilsington, the Prior and two Monks, Kent.   21.

These are all enrolled Rot. Claus. Part 1st.

Regni 28.

Furnesse, the Abbot and 30 Monks, Lancashire.   9. April.
Bermondsey, the Abb. Surrey.   1. June.
Bushlisham, Bp. of St. Davids, Commendator,
    Berk.   5. July.

The Originals of these two last are lost, but enrolled Rot. Claus. Part 2d. Regn. 28.

Regni 29.

Lanthony, August. the Prior and 21 Monks,
    Glocestsh.   10. May.
Abbington, Bened. the Abbot and 25 Monks,
    Berksh.   29.
Charterhouse, the Prior, London.   10. June.
Chertsey,—the Abbot and 14 Monks.   6. July.

Wardon, Cisterc. the Abbot and 14 Monks,
   Bedfordsh.   4. Dec.

St. Austins Canterb. the Abbey-Seal.   5.

Westacre, August. the Prior and 8 Monks,
   Norfolk.   14. Jan.

Kingswood, Cisterc. Glocestsh. the Abbot
   and 13 Monks.   1. Feb.

Coxhall, Cisterc. the Abbot, Essex.   5.

St. Andrew, Bened. Northampt. the Prior and
   12 Fr.   2. March.

Holmcultrin——the Abbot and 25 Monks,
   Cumberland.   6.

Butley, August, the Commend. and 8 Monks,
   Suffolk.   7.

Stradford-Langthorn, Cisterc. the Abbot and
   14 Monks, Essex.   8.

Southwick, August. Hampsh.   7. April.

Kennelworth, Bened. the Prior and 16 Mon.
   Warwicksh.   14.

Merton, August. the Abbot and 14 Monks,
   Surrey.   16.

Pont-Robert, Cisterc. the Abbot and 8 Monks,
   Sussex.   16.

Belloloco, Cisterc. the Abbot and 19 Monks,
   Hampsh.   17.

Besides these, the following Surrenders are enrolled.

Lewes, Cluniac. Sussex, the Prior.   16. Nov.

Castle-Acre, Cluniac. Norfolk, the Prior   22.

Titchfield, Præmonst. the Commend. South-
   amptsh.   18. Dec.

Muchelling, Bened. Somersetsh. the Abbot.   3. Jan.

Boxley, Cisterc. Kent, the Abbot.   26.

Walden, Bened. Essex the Bpp. Suffr. of
   Colchester, Commend.   22. March.

*Almost all these Abbies were above the value of two hundred
   pound, so that they were not within the Statute for suppressing the lesser Abbies, but the Abbots were prevailed
   on by other Motives to surrender their Houses to the King.*

BOOK
III.

Regni.
30.

Batle, Bened. Sussex, the Abbot and 16 Monks.   27. May.

Thurgarton, August. Yorksh. the Prior and 8 Frat.   14. June.

Bushlisham, Bened. Berksh. the Abbot and 15 Monks.   19.

Axiholm, Carthus. Lincolnsh. the Prior and 8 Monks.   23.

Rupa, Cisterc. Yorksh. the Abbot and 17 Monks.   23.

Walbeck, Præmonst. Nottingsh. the Abbot and 18 Monks.   20.

Huntington Cannons, Aug. the Prior and 8 Cannons.   11. July.

Lincoln, Gilbertines the Prior, and 15 Monks.   14.

Feversham, Cluniac. Kent, the Abbot and 8 Monks.   8.

Bordesley, Cisterc. Worcestsh. the Abbot and 19 Monks.   17.

Cumbermore, August. Chesh. the Abbot.   27.

St. Austins, Canterb. Bened. the Abbot and 30 Monks.   30.

St. James, Northamptonsh. Bened. the Abbot Elect and 5 Monks.   25. Aug.

Fordham, Gilbertines, Cambridgsh. the Prior and 3 Frat.   1. Sept.

Chateras, Black-Nuns, Cambridgsh. the Abbess and 10 Nuns.   3.

Val-royal, Chesh. the Abbot and 14 Monks.   7.

Croxton, Præmonst. Leicestersh. the Abbot and 22 Monks.   8.

Haughmond, Cannons, Shropsh. the Abbot and 10 Monks.   9.

Tudburry, Bened. Staffordsh. the Prior and 8 Monks.   14.

De-la-pray, no Subscriptions, only the Common Seal.   16.

Rostiter, August. Staffordsh. the Abbot and 8 Monks.   16.

Crockesden, Cisterc. Staffordsh. the Abbot and 12 Monks.   17.

Hilton, Cisterc. Staffordsh. the Abbot and 8
Monks.   18. Sept.

Semperingham,* Gilbertines, the Prior and 8
Monks.   18.

Sulby, Præmonst. Northampsh. the Abbot
and 11 Monks.   20.

Haberholm, Gilb. Lincolnsh. the Prior and
6 Cannons.   24.

Betlesden, Cisterc. Bedfordsh. Abbot and 11
Monks.   25.

Cately, Gilb. Lincolnsh. the Prior.   25.

Bolington, Gilb. Lincolnsh. the Prior and 9
Monks.   26.

Thelsford, the Holy Trinity, Warwicksh.
Prior and 3 Mon.   20.

Sixhill, Gilb. Lincolnsh. the Commend. and
8 Monks   27.

Thetford, August. Norfolk, the Prior.   27.

Alvinghame, Gilb. Lincolnsh. the Prior and
27 Monks.   29.

Ormesby, Gilb. the Prior and 6 Frat.
Linn Carmelites,   The Prior and 10 Fra.
Linn Dominicans,   The Prior and 11 Fr. Nor. } 30.
Linn August.   The Prior and 14 Fra.

Linn, Francisc. the Warden and 9 Frat.   1. Oct.

Ailesbury, Francisc. Buckinghamsh. the Warden and 6 Frat.   1

Coventry, Carm. Warwicksh. the Prior and
13 Frat.   1.

Newstead Gilb. the Prior and 5 Monks.   2

Mattersey, Gilb. the Prior and 4 Monks.   3.

Coventry, Franc. Warden and 10 Frat.   5.

Marmond, Cannons, Cambridgsh. the Prior
and 1 Monk.   5.

Stamford, August. Lincolnsh. the Prior and 5
Frat.   6.

* In the Houses of this Order there were Cloisters for both Sexes. St. Gilbert L.
of Semperingham founded it; the Bpp. of Landaff was at this time Commendator of
the whole Order.

BOOK
III.

Stamford, Dominic. the Prior and 9 Frat.	7. Oct.
Grinsbey, Francisc. Lincolnsh. the Prior and 5 Frat.	9.
Miraval, Cisterc. Warwicksh. the Abbot and 9 Monks.	13.
Shouldham, Gilb. Norfolk, the Prior, 9 Monks, 7 Nuns.	15.
Braywood, Black-Nuns, Staffordsh. the Prioress.	16.
Lilleshull, August. Shropsh. the Abbot and 10 Monks.	16.
Stafford, August. the Prior and 5 Monks.	16.
Northampton, Dominic. the Prior and 7 Frat.	16.
Northallerton, Carmel. Yorksh. the Prior and 9 Frat.	17.
Warwick, Dominic. the Prior and 6 Frat.	20.
Northampton, Carmel. the Prior and 8 Frat.	20.
Weatheral, Dominic. Cumberland, the Prior.	20.
Chicksand, Gilb. Bedfordsh. the Prior, 6 Monks, 18 Nuns.	22.
Darley, August. Derbysh. the Abbot and 13 Monks,	22.
Dale, Premonst. Derbysh. the Abbot and 16 Monks.	24.
Repton, August. Derbysh. the Subprior and 8 Monks.	25.
Grace-dieu, August. Nuns, Leicestersh. the Prioress.	27.
Northampton, Francisc. the Warden and 10 Frat.	28.
Northampton, August. the Prior and 9 Frat.	28.
Mallen Nuns, Kent, the Abbess and 10 Nuns.	29.
Bardney, Bened. Lincolnsh. the Abbot and 13 Monks.	1. Nov.
Barnwell, August. Can. Cambridg the Prior and 6 Monks.	8.
Leicester, Francis. the Warden and 7 Frat.	10.
Dominic. the Prior.	10.
August. the Prior.	10.
London, Dominic. the Bp of Rochest. Commend. and 15 Frat.	10.

London, August. the Prior and 12 Frat.   12. Nov.
       Francis. the Warden and 25 Frat.   12.
       Cross- Friers, 6 Frat.   13.

Doncaster, Carm. Yorksh. the Prior and 6 Fr. 13.

Werksop, August. Notting.sh. the Prior and
   15 Friers.   14.

Pipewell—Lincolnsh. the Abbot and 13 Monks. 15.

Wigemore—Herefordsh. the Commend. and
   10 Friers.   18.

York, August. the Prior and 7 Friers. 18.

Doncaster. Francisc. Guardian, 6 Friers,
   3 Novices.   20.

Monkbreton, Bened. Yorksh. the Prior and
   13 Monks.   21.

St. Helens London, a Nunnery, no hands,
   only the Seal.   25.

Pomfret, Dominic. York. the Prior, 7 Friers,
   1 Novice.   26.

York, Carmel. the Prior, 9 Friers, 3 Novices 27.
       Francis. the Guardian, 15 Friers, 5
          Novices.   27.
       Dominic. the Prior, 6 Friers, 4 Novices. 27.
       Gilbertines, the Prior, 3 Monks.   28.
       August. the Prior, 9 Friers, 4 Novices. 28.

Bellalanda, Cisterc. Yorksh. the Abbot and
   24 Monks   30.

Dunnington, the Order of the Trinity, Berksh. the Minister.   30.

Ryeval, Cisterc. Yorksh. the Abbot and 23
   Monks.   3. Dec.

St. Albans, Bened. Herefordsh. the Abbot and
   37 Monks.   5.

Ansham, Bened. Oxfordsh. the Prior and
   8 Monks.   4.

Kirkham, August. Yorksh. the Prior and 17
   Friers.   8.

Notely—Yorksh. the Abbot and 17 Monks. 9.

Ellerton, Gilber. Yorksh. the Prior and 4
   Friers.   11.

York, the H. Trin. the Minister and 10 Priests.

Yarom, Dominic. the Prior, and 5 Friers,
6 Novices.

Darby, Dominic. the Prior, and 6 Friers.   3. Jan.

Semperingham, Gilber. the Commend. and
3 Monks.   6.

Newcastle, Francis. the Warden, with 8
Friers, and 2 Novices.   9.

Newcastle, August.   9.

Newcastle, Dominic. the Prior and 12 Friers.   10.

Newcastle, Carmel. the Prior, 7 Friers, and
2 Novices.   10.

Walknell, Newcastle, H. Trin. the Prior.   10.

Tinmouth, Bened. Northumberl. Prior, 15
Prebend. 3. Nov.   12.

Warwick, Bened. the Prior and 12 Monks.   15.

Coventry, Carthus. the Prior and 7 Monks.   16.

York, August. the Prior and 17 Fellows.   17.

Brednestock, Wiltsh. the Prior and 13 Monks.   18.

Richmond, Yorksh. Francis. the Prior and
14 Friers.   19.

Lacock, Wiltsh. Nunnery, the Abbess.   21.

Combe, Warwicksh. Cisterc. the *quondam*
Abbot, 13 Monks.   21.

Kenisham, Sommer.sh. August. the Abbot
and 10 Monks.   23.

Bolton, Yorksh. August. the Prior and 14
Friers.   29.

Cockersand, Land.sh. Premons. the Abbot
and 22 Monks.   29.

Pollsworth, Warwicksh. Nunnery, no Hands,
only the Seal.   31.

Nottingham, Carmel. the Prior and 6 Friers.   5. Feb.
        Francis. the Prior and 7 Friers.   5.

Athelny, Sommer.sh. Bened. the Abbot and
8 Monks.   8.

Taunton, Sommer.sh. August. the Prior and
12 Monks.   10.

Buckland, Sommer.sh. Nunnery, the Prioress.   10.

Dunkeswell, Sommer.sh. Cisterc.   12.

Polleslow, Devonsh. Nunnery, the Prioress.   14.

Witham, Sommer.sh. Carthus. the Prior and
12 Monks.   15. Feb.

Bushsham, Devonsh.   19.

Cannonleigh, Devonsh. Nunnery, no Hands
but the Seal.   19.

Hartland, Devonsh. August. the Abbot and
4 Monks.   21,

Torry, Premonst. Devonsh. the Abbot and
15 Monks.   23.

Launceston, Cornwal, August, the Prior and
8 Monks.   24.

Buckfast, Devonsh. Cister. the Abbot with
10 Monks.   25.

Buckland, Devonsh. Cister. the Abbot.   27.

Bodmyn, Cornwal, August. the Prior and
8 Monks.   27.

Edingdon, Wiltsh. August. the Rector and
12 Monks.   28.

Plimptone, Canons, August. Devonsh. the
Prior and 18 Monks.   1. March.

St. Germans, Can. Aug. Cornwal, the Prior
and 7 Monks.   2.

Ford, Cister. Devon. the Abbot and 13 Monks. 8.

Midleton, Bened. Devonsh. Abbot and Bp.
Suff. of Shafts. 12 Monks.   11.

Abbots-bury, Bened. Dorsetsh. the Prior and
10 Monks.   12.

Tarent, Nunnery, Dorsetsh. the Abbess and
18 Nuns.   13,

Bindon, Cisterc. Dorsetsh. the Abbot and
7 Monks.   14.

Cerne, Bened. Dorsetsh. the Abbot and 16
Monks.   15.

Sherburne, Bened. Dorsetsh. the Abbot and
16 Monks.   18. March,

Montecute, Cluniac. Sommer.sh. the Abbot
and 13 Monks.   20.

Tavenstock, Bened. Sommer.sh. the Abbot
and 20 Monks.   20.

Shaftsbury Nunnery, Dorsetsh. the Abbess.   23.

Willton Nunnery, Wiltsh. the Abbess.   25,

Hinton, Carthus. Sommersetsh. the Prior
and 19 Monks.   31. March.

Brutton Cannons-August. Sommer.sh. the
Abbot and 14 Monks.   1. April.

Hide, Bened. Hampsh. Bp. Bangor Commend. and 21 Mon. in April, but no date.

Without date there are four.

Francisans Cambr. the Guardian and 23 Frat.
Dominicans Cambr. the Prior and 15 Fr.
Thetford Dominic. the Prior.
Sancta Maria de Pratis, the Abbot and 19 Monks.

Hospitals resigned this Year.

St. Thomas Southwark, the Master and one
Brother.   25. July.
St. John Wells, the Master and 3 Brothers.   3. Feb.
Bridgwater, the Master and 7 Brothers.   3.
St. John Exon, the Master and 2 Brothers.   20.

> *All the former Resignations have the Covent Seals put to
> them, except those of some few Houses of Begging
> Friars, which perhaps had no Seals: they are also en-
> rolled in the 1st, 2d, 3d, and 5th Claus. Rolls of that
> Year. There are likewise some few more enrolled, of
> which the Originals are lost, which follow.*

Hales-Owen, Premonst. Sallop. the Abbot   9. June.
Clattercott. Gilbert. the Prior   22. Aug.
Bedford, Francis. the Warden.   3. Oct.
Stamford, Francis. the Warden.   8.
Derleyghs, Cisterc. Staffordsh. the Abbot.   20.
Pipeldeth, Cisterc, Northam.sh. the Abbot.   5. Nov.
De-la-pray Nunnery, Northam.sh. the Abbess.   16. Dec.
Northallerton. Carmel. Yorksh. the Prior.   20.
Pulton Gilbert. the Prior.   16. Jan.
Newburg, August. Yorksh.   22.
Bath Cathedral, Bened.   27.
Brusyard Nunnery, Suffolk, the Abbess.   17. Feb.
Newham, Cisterc. Devonsh. the Abbot.   8. March.

Here follow the Resignations made in the 31 Year of the King's Reign, of which the Originals are yet extant.

KIMME Can. August. Lincolnsh. the Prior and 9 Monks.	6. July.
Bevoll Carthus. Notting.sh. the Prior and 7 Monks.	8.
Irthforth Nunnery, Lincolnsh. the Prioress and 17 Nuns.	9.
Nuncotton Nunnery, Yorksh. without Subscriptions.	11.
Hynings Nunnery, Lincolnsh. no Subscriptions.	11.
Fosse Nunnery, Lincolnsh. the Prioress.	11.
Newstead Premonst. Notting.sh. the Prior and 11 Monks.	21.
St. Osith. Can. August. Essex. the Abbot and 16 Monks.	28.
Elistu Nunnery, Bedfordsh. the Abbess.	26. Aug.
Hamond, a Commission to the Bp. of Chester to take the Surrender of it.	31.
Swine Nunnery, Yorksh. no Subscriptions.	3. Sept.
Haughmond Can. August. Sallop. the Abbot and 10 Monks.	9.
Nunnkeling Nunnery, Yorksh. no Subscription but the Seal.	10.
Nunniton Nunnery, the Prioress, 27 Crosses for Subscript.	12.
Ulnescroft, Leicestersh. the Prior and 11 Friers.	15.
Marrick Nunnery, Yorksh. the Prioress.	15.
Burnham Nunnery, Bucks, the Abbess and 9 Nuns.	19.
St. Bartholomew Smithfield, the Prior.	25. Oct.
Edmundsbury Bened. Suffolk, the Abbot and 44 Monks.	4. Nov.
A Commission for the surrender of St. Allborrough, Chesh.	7.
Berkin Nunnery, Essex, the Abbess.	14.
Tame, Oxfordsh. Bp. Reonen.* and 16 Monks.	16.
Osney, *ibid. id.* and 12 Monks.	17.

---

* Perhaps Roanen: King, Abbot of Osney, had the title Episcopus Roanansis.

Godstow Nunnery, Oxfordsh. subscribed by
  a Notary.   17. Nov.

Studley Nunnery, Oxfordsh. signed as the
  former.   19.

Thelsford, Norfolk, the Prior and 13 Monks. 16. Feb.

Westminster Bened. the Abbot and 27 Monks. 16. Jan.

A Commission to the Arch-Bpp. of Canterb.

for taking the Surrender of Christ-Church
Canterbury.   20. March.

And another for the surrender of Rochester,
  both dated

Waltham Benedict. Essex. the Abbot and
  17 Monks.   23.

St. Mary Watte, Gilber. Bpp. of Landaffe
  Commend. 8 Friers and 14 Nuns.

*There is also in the Augmentation-Office, a Book concerning
the Resignations and Suppressions of the following Monasteries.*

St. Swithins Winchester.   15. Nov.

St. Mary Winchester.   17.

Wherewell, Hampshire.   21.

Christ's Church, Twinham, the Commendator
  thereof is called *Episcopus Neopolitanus.*   28.

Winchelcomb.   3. Dec.

Ambrose Bury.   4.

St. Austins, near Bristol.   9.

Billesswick, near Bristol.   9.

Malmesbury.   15.

Cirencester.   19.

Hales.   24.

St. Peter's Glocesterwark.   2. Jan.

Teuksbury.   9.

*There are also several other Deeds enrolled, which
follow.*

St. Mary-Overhay, in Southwark.   14. Oct.

St. Michael, near Kingston upon Hull, Carthus.   9. Nov.

Burton upon Trent. Staffordsh.	14. Nov.	
Hampol Nunnery, Yorksh.	19.	
St. Oswald, Yorksh.	20.	
Kirkstall, Yorksh.	22.	
Pomfret, Yorksh.	23.	
Kirkelles, Yorksh.	24.	
Ardyngton, Yorksh.	26.	
Fountains, Yorksh.	26.	
St. Mary York.	29.	
St. Leonard York.	1. Dec.	
Nunnapleton Nunnery, Yorksh.	5.	
St. Gelmans Selbe, Yorksh.	6.	
Melsey, Yorksh.	11.	
Malton, Yorksh.	11.	
Whitby, Yorksh.	14.	
Albalanda, Northumb.	18.	
Montgrasse Carthus. Yorksh.	18.	
Alnewick Premonstrat. Northumb.	22.	
Gisburne August. Yorksh.	22.	
Newshame, Dunelme.	29.	
St. Cuthberts Cathedral of Duresme.	31.	
St. Bartholomew Nunnery, in Newcastle.	3. Jan.	
Egeliston, Richmondsh.	5.	
St. Mary Carlile, Cumber.	9.	
Hoppa Premonst. Westmorland.	14.	
St. Werburg. Chester.	20.	
St. Mary Chester, a Nunnery.	21.	
St. Peters Shrewsbury.	24.	
St. Milburg Winlock, Salop.	26.	

SECTION IV.

It seems there was generally a Confession made with the Surrender: Of these some few are yet extant, though undoubtedly great care was taken to destroy as many as could be in Queen Mary's time. That long and full one made by the Prior of St. Andrews in Northampton, the Preamble whereof is printed by Fuller, and is at large printed by Weaver, is yet preserved in the Augmentation-Office. There are some few more also extant, six of these I have seen, one of them follows.

FORASMUCH as we Richard Green, Abbot of our Monastery of our Blessed Lady St. Mary of Betlesden, and the Convent of the said Monastery, do profoundly consider, That the whole manner and trade of living, which we and our pretensed Religion have practised, and used many days, does most principally consist in certain dumb Ceremonies, and other certain Constitutions of the Bishops of Rome, and other Forinsecal Potentates, as the Abbot of Cistins, and therein only noseled, and not taught in the true knowledg of God's Laws, procuring always Exemptions of the Bishops of Rome from our Ordinaries and Diocesans: submitting our selves principally to Forinsecal Potentates and Powers, which never came here to reform such disorders of living and abuses, as now have been found to have reigned amongst us. And therefore now assuredly knowing, that the most perfect way of living, is most principally and sufficiently declared unto us by our Master Christ, his Evangelists and Apostles, and that it is most expedient for us to be governed and ordered by our Supream Head, under God, the King's most noble Grace, with our mutual assent and consent, submit our selves, and every one of us, to the most benign Mercy of the King's Majesty; and by these presents do surrender, &c.

The Surrender follows in common form, Signed by the Abbot, Subprior, and 9 Monks, 25. Septemb. Regni 30.

There are others to the same purpose Signed by the Guardian and seven Franciscans at Alisbury, the 1st of October. By the Franciscans at Bedford the 3d of October. The Franciscans in Coventry the 5th of October. And the Franciscans in Stamford the 8th of October. And the Carmelties in Stamford on the same day, which I shall also insert, the former four agreeing to it.

FORASMUCH as we the Prior and Friers of this House of Carmelites in Stamford, commonly called the White Friers in Stamford, in the County of Lincoln, do profoundly consider that the perfection of Christian living doth not consist in some Ceremonies, wearing of a white Coat, disguising our selves after strange fashions, dockying and becking, wearing Scapulars and Hoods, and other-like Papistical

Ceremonies, wherein we have been most principally practised and noseled in times past; but the very true way to
please God, and to live a true Christian Man, without all
hypocrisy and feigned dissimulation, is sincerely declared
to us by our Master Christ, his Evangelists, and Apostles;
being minded hereafter to follow the same, conforming our
self to the Will and Pleasure of our Supream Head, under
God, on Earth, the King's Majesty; and not to follow
henceforth, the superstitious Traditions of any Forinsecal
Potentate or Power, with mutual assent and consent, do
submit our selves unto the Mercy of our said Sovereign
Lord, and with the like mutual assent and consent do surrender, &c.

Signed by the Prior and 6 Friers.

SECTION V.

Of the manner of suppressing the Monasteries after they were Surrendered.

THE Reader will best understand this by the following
account of the Suppression of the Monastery of Teuksbury, copied from a Book that is in the Augmentation-
Office, which begins thus:

THE Certificate of Robert Southwell Esquire, William
Petre, Edward Kairne, and John London, Doctors of Law;
John Ap-rice, John Kingsman, Richard Paulet, and Wil-
liam Bernars, Esquires, Commissioners assigned by the
King's Majesty, to take the Surrenders of divers Monas-
teries, by force of his Grace's Commission to them, 6, 5, 4,
or 3 of them, in that behalf directed; bearing date at his
Highness's Palace, of Westminster, the 7th day of Novemb-
in the 31 year of the Reign of our most dread Sovereign
Lord Henry the Eighth, by the Grace of God, King of
England, and of France, Defender of the Faith, Lord of
Ireland, and in Earth immediately under Christ Supreme
Head of the Church of England, of all and singular their
Proceedings, as well in and of these Monasteries by his
Majesty appointed to be altered, as of others to be dis-
solved, according to the tenour, purport, and effect of his
Graces said Commission; with Instructions to them like-
wise delivered, as hereafter ensueth.

Com. Glocester.

Tuek-
bury late
Monas-
tery.

{ Surrendred to the use of the King's Majesty, and
of his Heirs and Successors for ever made, bearing date under the Covent-Seal of the same late
Monastery, the 9th day of January, in the 31year
of the Reign of our most dread victorious Sovereign Lord, King Henry the Eighth and the said
day and year clearly dissolved and suppressed.

The clear
yearly value
of all the
Possessions
belonging to
said late Mo-
nastery.

{ As well Spiritual as Temporal,
over and besides 136*l.* 8*s.* 1*d.* in
Fees, Annuities, and Custodies,
granted to divers Persons by
Letters Patents under the Covent-Seal of the said late Monastery for term of their lives.

l.　s.　d.
1595 15 6

Pensions as-
signed to the
late Religi-
ous dispat-
ched ; that
is to say, to

l.　s.　d.

J. Wich, lateAbbotthere 266	13	4
J. Beley late Prior there 16	0	0
J. Bromesgrove late Pri-		
or of Delehurst 13	6	8
Robert Circester Prior of		
St. James 13	6	8
Will. Didcote Prior of		
Cranborne 10	0	0
Rob. Cheltenhem B. D. 10	0	0
Two Monks 8*l.* a piece 16	0	0
One Monk 7	0	0
27 Mon. 6*l.* 13*s.* 4*d.* each 180	0	0

551 6 8

And so remains clear—1044 8 10

Records and
Evidences

{ Belonging
to the late
Monastery

} Remains in the Treasury there
under the Custody of JohnWhit-
tingtonKt.theKeys whereofbeing
delivered to R. Paulet Receiver.

Houses
and
Build-
ings as-
signed
to re-
main
unde-
faced.

{ The Lodging called the Newark, leading
from the Gate to the late Abbots Lodging,with Buttery, Pantry,Cellar, Kitch-
ing, Larder, and Pastry thereto adjoining. The late Abbot's Lodging, the Hos-
tery, the great Gate entring into the
Court, with the Lodging over the same ;
the Abbot's Stable, Bakehouse, Brew-
house and Slaughterhouse, the Almry,
Barn, Derryhouse, the great Barn next
Aven, the Maltinghouse, with the Gar-
ners inthe same, the Oxhouse in theBar-
ton, the Barton-gate, and the Lodging
over the same.

Com-
mitted
to the
custo-
dy of
John
Whit-
tington
Knight

Deemed to be superfluous.	The Church, with Chappels, Cloister, Chapter-house, Misericord, the two Dormitories, the Infirmary, with Chappels and Lodgings within the same; the Workhay, with another House adjoining to the same, the Covent-Kitching, the Library, the old Hostery, the Chamberers Lodging, the new-Hall, the old Parlor adjoining to the Abbot's Lodging; the Cellarers Lodging, the Poultry-house, the Gardner, the Almary, and all other Houses and Lodgings not above reserved.	Committed as abovesaid.
Leads remaining upon	The Quire, Iles, and Chappels annext the Cloister Chapter-house, Frater, St. Michaels Chappel, Halls, Fermory, and Gate-house, esteemed to	180 Foder.
Bells remaining	In the Steple there are eight poize by estimation	14600 weight.
Jewels reserved to the use of the King's Majesty.	Miters garnished with gilt, rugged Pearls, and counterfeit Stones.	2.
Plate of Silver reserved to the same use.	Silver gilt 329 ounces. Silver parrel gilt 605 ounces. Silver white 497 ounces.	1431.
Ornaments reserved to the said use.	One Cope of Silver Tissue, with one Clesible, and one Tunicle of the same; one Cope of Gold Tissue, with one Cles. and two Tunicles of the same.	
Sum of all the Ornaments, Goods, and Chattels belonging to the said late Monastery.	Sold by the said Commissioners, as in a particular Book of Sales thereof made ready to be shewed, as more at large may appear.	*l. s. d.* 194 8 0

			l.	*s.*	*d.*
Pay-ments.	To the late Religious and Servants dispatcht	To 38 late Religious Persons of the said late Monastery of the King's Mat. reward.	80	13	4
		To an 144 late Servants of the said late Monastery, for their Wages and Liveries	75	10	0
Pay-ments.	For debts owing by the said late Mo-nastery,	To divers Persons for Vic-tuals and Necessaries of them had to the use of the said Monastery, with 10*l.* paied to the late Abbot there, for and in full paiment of 124*l.* 5*s.* 4*d.* by him to be paid to certain Creditors of the said late Monastery, by Covenants made with the aforesaid Commissioners.	18	12	0

And so remains clear—19 12 8

Then follows a List of some small Debts owing to and by the said Monastery.

Then follows a List of the Livings in their Gift.

Com. Glocest.	Four Parsonages and 10 Vicarages.
Com. Wigorn.	Two Parsonages and 2 Vicarages.
Com. Warwic.	Two Parsonages.
Com. Will. Bristol.	Five Parsonages and 1 Vicarage.
Com. Wilts.	2 Vicar.
Com. Oxon.	One Pars. and 2 Vicar.
Com. Dors.	Four Pars. and 2 Vicar.
Com. Sommers.	Three Pars.
Com. Devon.	1 Vicar.
Com. Corub.	2 Vicar.
Com. Glamorg. and Morgan.	5 Vicar.

In all 21 Parsonages and 27 Vicarages.

IV.

Queen Ann Boleyn's last letter to King Henry.

SIR,

YOUR Grace's displeasure, and my Imprisonment, are things so strange unto me, as what to write, or what to excuse, I am altogether ignorant. Whereas you send unto me (willing me to confess a Truth, and so obtain your favour) by such an one whom you know to be mine ancient professed Enemy. I no sooner received this Message by him, than I rightly conceived your meaning; and if, as you say, confessing a Truth indeed may procure my safety, I shall with all willingness and duty perform your Command.

But let not your Grace ever imagine that your poor Wife will ever be brought to acknowledg a Fault, where not so much as a thought thereof proceeded. And to speak a Truth, never Prince had Wife more loyal in all duty, and in all true affection, than you have ever found in Ann Boleyn, with which Name, and Place I could willingly have contented my self, if God, and your Grace's pleasure had been so pleased. Neither did I at any time so far forget my self in my Exaltation, or received Queenship, but that I always looked for such an alteration as now I find; for the ground of my preferment being on no surer Foundation than your Grace's Fancy, the least alteration, I knew, was fit and sufficient to draw that Fancy to some other Subject. You have chosen me, from a low estate, to be your Queen and Companion, far beyond my desert or desire. If then you found me worthy of such honour, Good your Grace let not any light Fancy, or bad counsel of mine Enemies, withdraw your Princely Favour from me; neither let that Stain, that unworthy stain of a disloyal heart towards your good Grace, ever cast so foul a blot on your most dutiful Wife, and the Infant-Princess your Daughter: Try me, good King, but let me have a lawful Trial, and let not my sworn Enemies sit as my Accusers and Judges; yea, let me receive an open Trial, for my Truth shall fear no open shame; then shall you see, either mine innocency cleared, your suspicion and Conscience satisfied, the ignominy and

Cotton
Libr.
Otho.
C. 10.

slander of the World stopped, or my Guilt openly declared. So that whatsoever God or you may determine of
me, your Grace may be freed from an open censure; and
mine Offence being so lawfully proved, your Grace is at
liberty, both before God and Man, not only to execute
worthy punishment on me as an unlawful Wife, but to follow your Affection, already settled, on that Party, for whose
sake I am now as I am, whose Name I could some good
while since have pointed unto : your Grace being not ignorant of my suspicion therein.

But if you have already determined of me, and that not
only my Death, but an infamous slander must bring you
the enjoying of your desired happiness; then I desire of
God, that he will pardon your great sin therein, and likewise mine Enemies, the Instruments thereof; and that he
will not call you to a strict account for your unprincely and
cruel usage of me, at his General Judgment-Seat, where
both you and my self must shortly appear, and in whose
Judgment I doubt not (whatsoever the World may think
of me) mine Innocence shall be openly known, and sufficiently cleared.

My last and only request shall be, That my self may only
bear the burthen of your Grace's displeasure, and that it
may not touch the innocent Souls of those poor Gentlemen, who (as I understand) are likewise in strait Imprisonment for my sake. If ever I have found favour in your
sight, if ever the Name of Ann Boleyn hath been pleasing
in your ears, then let me obtain this request; and I will
so leave to trouble your Grace any further, with mine
earnest Prayers to the Trinity to have your Grace in his
good keeping, and to direct you in all your Actions. From
my doleful Prison in the Tower this 6th of May.

Your most Loyal and ever Faithful Wife,

Ann Boleyn.

V.

The Judgment of the Convocation concerning General-Councils. Published by the L. Herbert from the Original.

As concerning General-Councils, like as we (taught by long experience) do perfectly know that there never was, nor is, any thing devised, invented, or instituted by our Fore-Fathers, more expedient or more necessary for the establishment of our faith, for the extirpation of Heresies, and the abolishing of Sects and Schisms; and finally, for the reducing of Christ's People unto one perfect unity and concord in his Religion, than by the having of General-Councils. So that the same be lawfully had and congregated in *Spiritu Sancto*, and be also conform and agreeable, as well concerning the surety and indifferency of the Places, as all other Points requisite and necessary for the same, unto that wholsome and godly Institution and usage, for the which they were at first devised and used in the Primitive Church. Even so on the other side, taught by like experience, we esteem, repute, and judg, That there is, ne can be any thing in the World more pestilent and pernicious to the Common-weal of Christendom, or whereby the Truth of God's Word hath in times past, or hereafter may be sooner defaced or subverted, or whereof hath and may ensue more contention, more discord and other devilish effects, than when such General Councils have or shall be assembled, not christianly nor charitably, but for and upon private malice and ambition, or other worldly and carnal Respects and Considerations, according to the saying of Gregory Nazianzenus, in his Epistle to one Procopius, wherein he writeth this Sentence following; *Sic sentio, si verum scribendum est, omnes Conventus Episcoporum fugiendos esse, quia nullius Synodi finem vidi bonum, neque habentem magis solutionem malorum, quam incremen-tum: Nam cupiditates contentionum, et gloria (sed ne putes me odiosum ista scribentem) vincunt rationem.* That is to say; " I think this, if I should write truly, That all General Councils be to be eschewed, for I never saw that they produced any good End or Effect, nor that any Provision or Remedy; but rather increase of Mischiefs proceeded of

P 2

them. For the desire of maintenance of Men's Opinions and ambition of Glory (but reckon not that I write this of malice) hath always in them overcomed reason." Wherefore we think that Christian Princes, especially and above all things, ought and must, with all their wills, power, and diligence, foresee and provide; *Ne Sanctissima hac in parte majorum Instituta, ad improbissimos ambitionis aut malitiæ effectus explendos, diversissimo suo fine et sceleratissimo pervertantur: Neve ad alium prætextum possint valere, et longe diversum effectum orbi producere quam Sanctissima rei facies præ se ferat.* That is to say, " Least the most noble wholsome Institutions of our Elders in this behalf be perverted to a most contrary and most wicked end and effect; that is to say, to fulfil and satisfy the wicked affections of Men's Ambition and Malice; or, lest they might prevail for any other colour, or bring forth any other effect than their most vertuous and laudable countenance doth outwardly to the World shew or pretend." And first of all we think that they ought principally to consider who hath the Authority to call together a General Council. Secondly, Whether the Causes alledged be so weighty and so urgent, that necessarily they require a General Council, nor can otherwise be remedied. Thirdly, Who ought to be Judges in the General Council. Fourthly, What order of proceeding is to be observed in the same, and how the Opinions or Judgments of the Fathers are to be consulted or asked. Fifthly, What Doctrines are to be allowed or defended, with diverse other things which in General Councils ought of reason and equity to be observed. And as unto the first Point, We think that neither the Bishop of Rome, nor any one Prince, of what estate, degree, or preheminence soever he be, may by his own Authority, call, indite, or summon any General Council without the express consent, assent, and agreement of the residue of Christian Princes, and especially such as have within their own Realms and Seigniories, *Imperium merum,* that is to say, of such as have the whole, intire, and supream Government and Authority over all their Subjects, without knowledging or recognizing of any other supream Power or Authority. And this to be true, we be induced to think, by many and sundry, as well ex-

amples as great Reasons and Authority. The which, foras- BOOK
much as it should be over-long and tedious to express here ·III.
particularly, we have thought good to omit the same for
this present.   And in witness that this is our plain and de- There
terminate Sentence, Opinion, and Judgment, touching the were
Premises, we the Prelates and Clergy under-written, being 17 Bi-
congregate together in the Convocation of the Province shops in
of Canterbury, and representing the whole Clergy of the the Pro-
same, have to these Presents subscribed our Names the Canter-
20th of July, in the Year of our Lord, 1536. 28. Hen. 8. and Rochester

Signed by   being
                                                            vacant,
       Thomas Cromwel, Thomas Cantuariensis, of the
       Johannes London, with 13 Bishops and other
       of Abbots, Priors, Arch-Deacons, Deans, did sign
       Proctors, Clerks, and other Ministers 49. this.

VI.

*Instructions for the King's Commissioners, for a new survey,
and an Inventory to be made of all the Demesnes, Lands,
Goods, and Chattels appertaining to any House of Religion of Monks, Cannons, and Nuns within their Commission, according to the Articles hereafter following. The
number of which Houses in every County limited in their
Commission, being annexed to the said Commission. An
Original.*

HENRY R.

FIRST; After the Division made, one Auditor, one parti- EiMSS
cular Receiver, one Clerk of the Register of the last Visi- Nob.
tation, with three other discreet Persons to be named by Pier-
the King in every County where any such Houses be; after point.
their repair to such House, shall declare to the Governour,
and Religious Persons of the same, the Statute of Dissolution, the Commission, and the cause and purpose of their
repair for that time.
Item; That after the Declaration made, the said Commissioners shall swear the Governors of the Houses, or

such other the Officers of the same House, or other, as ye
shall think can best declare the state and plight of the
same, to make declaration and answer to the Articles there
under-written.

Item; Of what Order, Rule, or Religion, the same
House is, and whether it be a Cell or not; and if it be a
Cell, then the Commissioners to deliver to the Governours
of the House a Privy Seal, and also to injoin him, in the
King's Name, under a great pain, to appear without delay before the Chancellor of the Augmentations of the Revenues of the King's Crown and the Council; and in the
mean time not to meddle with the same Cell, till the King's
pleasure be further known.

Item; What number of Persons of Religion be in the
same, and the conversation of their lives, and how many of
them be Priests, and how many of them will go to other
Houses of that Religion; or how many will take Capacities; and how many Servants or Hinds the same House
keepeth commonly, and what other Persons have their
living in the same House.

Item; To survey the quantity or value of the Lead and
Bells of the same House, as near as they can, with the ruin,
decay, state, and plight of the same.

Item; Incontinently to call for the Covent-Seal, with all
Writings and Charters, Evidences an Muniments concerning any of the Possessions to be delivered to them, and put
the same in sure keeping, and to take a just Inventory
betwixt them and the Governour, or other Head-Officer,
by Indenture, of the Ornaments, Plate, Jewels, Chattels,
ready Mony, Stuff of Houshold, Coin, as well signed as
not signed, Stock and Store in the Farmer's hands, and
the value thereof, as near as they can, which were appertaining to the same Houses the first day of March last
past; and what debts the House doth owe, and to what
Person; and what Debts be owing to them, and by whom.

Item; After, to cause the Covent, or Common-Seal, the
Plate, Jewels, and ready Mony, to be put in safe keeping,
and the residue of the Particulars specified in the Inventory, to be left in the keeping of the Governor, or some other
Head-Officer, without wasting or consumption of the same,
unless it be for necessary expence of the House.

Item; That they command the Governor, or other receiver of the same House, to receive no Rents of their Farms until they know further of the King's pleasure, except such Rents as must needs be had for their necessary Food or Sustenance, or for payment of their Servants Wages.

Item; To survey discreetly the Demesnes of the same House; that is to say, such as have not been commonly used to be letten out, and to certifie the clear yearly value thereof.

Item; To examine the true yearly value of all the Farms of the same House, deducting thereof Rents reserved, Pensions and Portions paied out of the same, Synodals, and proxies; Bailiffs, Receivers, Stewards, and Auditors Fees, and the Names of them to whom they be paied and due, and to none other.

Item; What Leases hath been made to any Farmer, of the Farms pertaining to the same House; and what Rent they reserved, and to whom, and for how many years, and a Copy of the Indenture if they can get it, or else the Counter-pane.

Item; To search and enquire what Woods, Parks, Forrests, Commons, or other Profit belonging to any of the Possessions of the same Houses, the Number of the Acres, the Age and Value, as near as they can.

Item; What Grants, Bargains, Sales, Gifts, Alienations, Leases of any Lands, Tenements, Woods, or Offices, hath been made by any the said Governors, of any of the said Houses, within one Year next before the 4th day of February last past, and of what things, or to what value, and to whom, and for what estate.

Item; If there be any House of the Religion aforesaid omitted and not certified in the Exchequer, then the said Commissioners to survey the same, and to make Certificate accordingly.

Item; That they straitly command every Governor of every such House limited in their Commission, to Sow and Till their Grounds as they have done before, till the King's pleasure be further known.

Item; If there be any House given by the King to any Person, in any of the said several Limits of the said Commission, the Names whereof shall be declared to the said

Commissioners, Then the said Commissioners shall immediately take the Covent from the Governor, and take an Inventory indented of the Lead, Bells, Debts, Goods, Chattels, Plate, Jewels, Ornaments, Stock and Store, to the King's use; and to make sale of the Goods, Chattels, and other Implements, Plate and Jewels only excepted.

Item; The said Commissioners in every such House, to send such of the Religious Persons that will remain in the same Religion, to some other great House of that Religion, by their discretion, with a Letter to a Governor for the receipt of them; And the residue of them that will go to the World, to send them to my Lord of Canterbury, and the Lord Chancellor for their Capacities, with the Letter of the same Commissioners.

Item; The said Commissioners to give the said Persons that will have Capacities, some reasonable Rewards, according to the distance of the place, by their discretions to be appointed.

Item; The said Commissioners to command the Governour to resort to the Chancellor of the Augmentation for his yearly Stipend and Pension.

Item; If there be any House dissolved or given up to the King by their Deed, then the Commissioners shall order themselves in every point and purpose, as the Houses given by the King to any other Person in form aforesaid.

Item; Every of the said Commissioners having in charge to survey more than one Shire within the Limits of their Commission, immediately after they have perused one Shire, parcel of their Charge, in form aforesaid, shall send to the Chancellour of the Court for the Augmentation of the Revenues of the King's Crown, a brief Certificate of all these Comperts, according to the Instructions aforesaid, what they have done in the Premisses, and in every County so surveighed, then to procced further to another County; and so as they pass the said Counties to make like Certificate, and so forth, till their Limits be surveighed, and there to remain till they know further of the King's pleasure.

Item; If the said Commissioners have but one County in charge, then to certifie the said Chancellor in form aforesaid, and there to remain till they know further of the King's pleasure.

VII.

*Injunctions given by the Authority of the King's Highness
to the Clergy of this Realm.*

In the Name of God, Amen. In the Year of our Lord God one thousand five hundred thirty six, and of the most noble Reign of our Sovereign Lord, Henry the Eighth, King of England and France, the 28 Year, and the day of   I Thomas Cromwel Knight, Lord Cromwel, Keeper of the Privy-Seal of our said Sovereign Lord the King, and Vicegerent unto the same, for and concerning all his Jurisdictions Ecclesiastical within the Realm, visiting by the King's Highness's Supream Authority Ecclesiastical, the People and Clergy of this Deanery of   by my trusty Commissary   lawfully deputed and constitute for this part, have, to the glory of Almighty God, to the King's Highness's honour, the publick Weal of this his Realm, and encrease of Vertue in the same, appointed and assigned these Injunctions ensuing to be kept and observed, of the Dean, Parsons, Vicars, Curates, and Stipendaries, resiant or having cure of Soul, or any other Spiritual Administrations within this Deanery, under the pains hereafter limited and appointed.

The first is; That the Dean, Parsons, Vicars, and other, having cure of Soul any-where within this Deanery, shall faithfully keep and observe, and as far as in them may lie, shall cause to be observed and kept of other, all and singular Laws and Statutes of this Realm, made for the abolishing and extirpation of the Bishop of Rome's pretensed and usurped Power and Jurisdiction within this Realm. And for the establishment and confirmation of the King's Authority and Jurisdiction of the same, as of the Supream Head of the Church of England; and shall, to the uttermost of their Wit, Knowledg, and Learning, purely, sincerely, and without any colour or dissimulation, declare, manifest, and open, for the space of one quarter of a year next ensuing, once every Sunday, and after that at the least-wise twice every quarter, in their Sermons and other Collations, that the Bishop of Rome's usurped Power and Jurisdiction, having no establishment nor ground by the

Register, Cranm. fol. 47.

Law of God, was of most just causes taken away and abolished; and therefore they owe unto him no manner of obedience or subjection; and that the King's Power is within his Dominion the highest Power and Potentate, under God, to whom all Men within the same Dominions, by God's Commandment, owe most loyalty and obedience, afore and above all other Powers and Potentates in Earth.

Item; Whereas certain Articles were lately devised and put forth by the King's Highness's Authority, and condescended upon by the Prelates and Clergy of this his Realm in Convocation, whereof part are necessary to be holden and believed for our Salvation, and the other part do concern and teach certain laudable Ceremonies, Rites, and Usages of the Church, meet and convenient to be kept and used for a decent and politick order in the same; the said Dean, Parsons, Vicars, and other Curates, shall so open and declare in their said Sermons, and other Collations, the said Articles unto them that be under their Cure, that they may plainly know and discern which of them be necessary to be believed and observed for their Salvation, and which be not necessary, but only do concern the decent and politick order of the said Church: according to such Commandment and Admonition as hath been given unto them heretofore, by Authority of the King's Highness in that behalf.

Moreover, That they shall declare unto all such as be under their Cure, the Articles likewise devised, put forth, and authorized of late, for and concerning the abrogation of certain superfluous Holy-days, according to the effect and purport of the same Articles: and perswade their Parishioners to keep and observe the same inviolable, as things honestly provided, decreed, and established, by common consent, and publick Authority, for the Weal, Commodity, and Profit of all this Realm.

Besides this, to the intent that all Superstition and Hypocrisie, crept into divers Mens hearts may vanish away, they shall not set forth or extol any Images, Reliques, or Miracles, for any superstition or lucre; nor allure the People by any inticements to the pilgrimages of any Saint, otherwise than is permitted in the Articles lately put forth by the Authority of the King's Majesty, and condescended upon by the Prelates and Clergy of this his Realm in Con- vocation; as though it were proper or peculiar to that Saint to give this Commodity, or that: seeing all Good- ness, Health, and Grace, ought to be both asked and looked for only of God, as of the very Author of the same, and of none other, for without him it cannot be given: But they shall exhort, as well their Parishioners as other Pilgrims, that they do rather apply themselves to the keeping of God's Commandments, and fulfilling of his Works of Charity; perswading them that they shall please God more by the true exercising of their bodily Labour, Travail, or occupa- tion, and providing for their Families, than if they went about to the said Pilgrimages; and that it shall profit more their Souls health, if they do bestow that on the Poor and Needy, which they would have bestowed upon the said Images or Reliques.

Also in the same their Sermons, and other Collations, the Parsons, Vicars, and other Curats, aforesaid, shall di- ligently admonish the Fathers and Mothers, Masters and Governors of Youth, being within their Cure, to teach, or cause to be taught, their Children and Servants, even from their Infancy, their Pater Noster, the Articles of our Faith, and the Ten Commandments, in their Mother Tongue: And the same so taught, shall cause the said Youth oft to repeat and understand. And to the intent that this may be the more easily done, the said Curats shall, in their Ser- mons, deliberately and plainly recite of the said Pater Noster, the Articles of our Faith, and the Ten Command- ments, one Clause or Article one day, and an other another day, till those be taught and learnt by little; and shall de- liver the same in writing, or shew where printed Books containing the same be to be sold, to them that can read or will desire the same. And thereto that the said Fathers and Mothers, Masters and Governors, do bestow their Children and Servants, even from their Childhood, either to Learning, or some other honest Exercise, Occupation, or Husbandry: exhorting, counselling, and by all the ways and means they may, as well in their said Sermons and Collations, as otherwise, perswading the said Fathers, Mothers, Masters, and other Governors, being under their Cure and Charge, diligently to provide and foresee that the said Youth be in no manner-wise kept or brought up in idleness, lest at any time afterwards they be driven, for lack of some Mystery or Occupation to live by, to fall to begging, stealing, or some other unthriftiness; forasmuch as we may daily see, through sloth and idleness, divers valiant Men fall, some to begging, and some to theft and murder; which after brought to calamity and misery, impute a great part thereof to their Friends and Governors, which suffered them to be brought up so idely in their Youth; where if they had been well educated and brought up in some good Literature, Occupation, or Mystery, they should, being Rulers of their own Family, have profited, as well themselves as divers other Persons, to the great commodity and ornament of the Common-weal.

Also, that the said Parsons, Vicars, and other Curats, shall diligently provide that the Sacraments and Sacramentals be duly and reverently ministred in their Parishes; and if at any time it hapned them, either in any of the Cases expressed in the Statutes of this Realm, or of special license given by the King's Majesty to be absent from their Benefices, they shall leave their Cure, not to a rude and unlearned Person, but to an honest, well learned, and expert Curate, that may teach the rude and unlearned of their Cure wholsome Doctrine, and reduce them to the right way that do err; and always let them see, that neither they, nor their Vicars, do seek more their own profit, promotion, or advantage, than the profit of the Souls that they have under their Cure, or the Glory of God.

Also, That every Parson, or Proprietary of any Parish Church within this Realm, shall on this side the Feasts of St. Peter *ad Vincula* next coming, provyde a Book of the whole Bible, both in Latin, and also in English, and lay the same in the Quire, for every Man that will to read and look therein, and shall discourage no Man from the Reading any Part of the Bible, either in Latin or in English; but rather comfort, exhort, and admonish every Man to read the same as the very word of God, and the Spiritual Food of Man's soul, whereby they may the better know the Dutys to God, to their Sovereign Lord the King, and their Neighbour: ever gently and charitably exhorting that using a sober and a modest Haviour in the Reading

and Inquisition of the true sense of the same ; they do in
no wise stiffly or eagerly contend or strive one with another about the same, but refer the Declaration of those
Places that be in Controversy to the Judgment of them
that be better Learned.

Also, the said Dean, Parsons, Vicars, Curats, and other
Priests, shall in no wise, at any unlawful time, nor for any
other cause, than for their honest necessity, haunt or resort
to any Taverns or Ale-houses ; And after their Dinner
and Supper, they shall not give themselves to Drinking or
Riot, spending their time idely, by Day or by Night, at
Tables or Cards-playing, or any other unlawful Game ;
but at such times as they shall have such leisure, they shall
read or hear somewhat of Holy Scripture, or shall occupy
themselves with some other honest Exercise ; and that they
alway do those things which appertain to good congruence
and honesty, with profit of the Common-weal, having always in mind, That they ought to excel all others in pu-
rity of life, and should be examples to all other to live well
and christianly.

Furthermore ; Because the Goods of the Church are
called the Goods of the Poor, and at these days nothing is
less seen than the Poor to be sustained with the same ; all
Parsons, Vicars, Pensionaries, Prebendaries, and other Beneficed Men within the Deanery, not being resident upon
their Benefices, which may dispend yearly 20l. or above
within this Deanry, or elsewhere, shall distribute hereafter
yearly amongst their poor Parishioners, or other Inhabitants there, in the presence of the Church-Wardens, or
some other honest Men of the Parish, the fortieth part of
the Fruits and Revenues of the said Benefices : lest they
be worthily noted of Ingratitude ; which reserving so many
parts to themselves, cannot vouchsafe to impart the fortieth
portion thereof amongst the poor People of that Parish,
that is so fruitful and profitable unto them.

And to the intent that Learned Men may hereafter
spring the more for the execution of the Premisses ; Every
Parson, Vicar, Clerk, or beneficed Man within this Deanry, having yearly to dispend in Benefices, and other promotions of the Church, an 100l. shall give competent exhibition to one Scholar ; and for as many hundred pounds

more as he may dispend, to so many Scholars more, shall
give like exhibition in the University of Oxford or Cambridg, or some Grammer-School; which after they have
profited in good Learning, may be Partners of their Pa-
trons Cure and Charge, as well in preaching as otherwise,
in the execution of their Offices; or may, when need shall
be, otherwise profit the Common-Wealth with their Counsel and Wisdom.

Also, that all Parsons, Vicars, and Clerks, having
Churches, Chappels, or Mansions within this Deanry, shall
bestow yearly hereafter upon the same Mansions, or Chan-
cels of their Churches being in decay, the fifth part of their
Benefices till they be fully repaired; and the same so repaired, shall always keep and maintain in good state.

All which and singular Injunctions shall be inviolably
observed of the said Dean, Parsons, Vicars, Curats, Stipendiaries, and other Clerks and beneficed Men, under the
pain of suspension and sequestration of the Fruits of their
Benefices, until they have done their duty according to
these Injunctions.

VIII.

*Cromwel's Letter to Shaxton, Bishop of Sarum, taken from
a Copy writ by Morison his Secretary.*

Cotton
Libr.
Cleop.
E. 4. My Lord, after hearty Commendations, I cannot but
both much marvel that you whom I have taken as mine
trusty Friend, should judg me, as I perceive by your Letters you do, and also be glad that ye so frankly utter your
Stomach to me. I would thank you for your plain writing
and free monitions, saving that you seem fuller of suspition
than it becometh a Prelate of your sort to be: and (to say
that maketh me more sorry) much worse perswaded of me
than I thought any of your Learning and Judgment could
have been. I took a Matter out of your bands to mine, if
upon considerations mine Office bind me to do so, what
cause have ye to complain? if I had done this, either upon

affection, or intending prejudice to your estimation, you might have expostulated with me ; and yet if ye then had done it after a gentler sort, I should both sooner have amended that I did amiss, and also have had better cause to judge your writing to me, to be of a friendly heart towards me. If ye be offended with my sharp Letters, how can your testy words (I had almost given them another Name) delight me ? I required you to use no extremity in your Office, *durus est hic sermo*, ye call it ; and when ye have done, ye begin again, even as tho all being said, all were still behind. If ye have used none extremity, I am, I ensure you, as glad of it as I ought to be : And though ye do not, yet upon a complaint my Office bindeth me to succour him that saith he is over-matched, and is compelled to sustain wrong. I was thus informed, and by Persons to whom I gave more credit than I intend to do hereafter, if they have abused me, as ye would make me believe they have. They thus complaining, could I do less than grant unto them such Remedies as the King's Highness and his Laws give indifferently to all his Subjects? Might I not also somewhat gather, that ye proceeded the sorer against the Reader, Roger London, when I had seen how much you desired the preferment of your Servant to that Revenue? My Lord, you had shewed your self of much more patience, I will not say of much more prudence, if ye had contented your self with their lawful Appeal, and my lawful Injunctions; and rather have written somewhat fully to instruct us in this Matter, than thus to desire to conquer me by shrewd words, to vanquish me by sharp threp of Scripture, which as I know to use travel, so I trust to God as great a Clerk as ye be, is done already. Thus out of their place, it becometh me not, neither yet I am wont to vaunt my self of well-doing, I know who worketh all that is well wrought by me; and whereas he is the whole Doer, I intend not to offer him this wrong, to labour, and I to take the thanks; yet as I do not cease to give thanks, that it hath pleased his Goodness to use me as an Instrument, and to work somewhat by me, so I trust I am as ready to serve him in my Calling, to my little power, as ye are prest to write worse of me than ye ought to think. My Prayer is, That God give me no longer life, than I shall be glad to use mine Office *in œdificationem*, and not *in de-structionem*, as ye bear me in hand I do. God, ye say, will judg such using of Authority, meaning flatly, that I do abuse such Power as hath pleased God and the King's Highness to set me in; God, I say, will judg such Judges as ye are, and charge also such thoughts as ye misuse: ye do not so well as I would ye should do, if ye so think of me as your Letters make me think ye do. The Crime that ye charge me withal, is greater than I may or ought to bear, untruer, I trust, than they that would fainest, shall be able to prove. It is a strange thing, you say, that I neither would write, nor send you word by mouth, what ye should do with the Popish Monks of Abington; and that the Abbot of Redding could get streight-way my Letters to inhibit your just doings: That was not my mind which I wrote, I did not intend to lett your just doings, but rather to require you to do justly; neither I was swift in granting my Letters to him, albeit I am much readier to help him that complains of wrong, than prest to further on him that desireth punishment of a Person whom I am not sure hath offended. I made you no answer, a strange thing! my Lord, I thought ye had better known my Business, than for such a Matter to esteem me not your Friend; you might have better judged that I was too much cumbred with other Affairs, that those which sued for the Abbot, could better espy their time than you could. Some Man will think it rather utter displeasure conceived before, than that ye have any urgent occasion here to misjudg my mind towards you. As concerning your Manor you must use your Priviledges as things lent unto you, so long as ye shall occupy them well, that is, according to the mind and pleasure of them that gave you them. I took neither the Monk's Cause, nor any other, into my hands, to be a bearer of any such whom their upright dealings is not able to bear. No, you know I think, that I love such readers of Scripture as little as ye do: would God Men of your sort were as diligent to see that in all their Dioceses good were made, as I am glad to remove things when I know them; if ye had taken even then but half the pains to send up such things against him as ye now send, neither you should have had cause, no nor occasion thus easily to divine of my good or will will towards you, nor I have been cumbred with this answer. My Lord, I pray you, while I am your Friend, take me to be so; for if I were not, or if I knew any cause why I ought not, I would not be afraid to show you what had alienated my mind from you; so you should well perceive that my displeasure should last no longer than there were cause. I pass over your *Nemo læditur niri a seipso*, I pray with you this first part, *Our Lord have pity upon me;* the other part is not in my Prayers, *That God should turn my heart*, for he is my Judg, I may err in my doings for want of knowledg, but I willingly bear no misdoers, I willingly hurt none whom honesty and the King's Laws do not refuse. Undo not you your self, I intend nothing less than to work you any displeasure. If hitherto I have shewed you any pleasure, I am glad of it : I showed it to your Qualities and not to you; if they tarry with you, my good-will cannot depart from you, except your Prayer be heard, that is, *My Heart be turned.* I assure you I am right-glad ye are in the place ye are in, and will do what shall lie in me to aid you in your Office, to maintain your Reputation, to give you credit among your Flock, and elsewhere; as long as I shall see you faithful to your Duty, according to your Calling. I will not become your good Lord, as your desire is, I am and have been your Friend, and take you to be mine; cast out vain suspition, let rash Judgment rule Men of less wit and discretion ; wilfulness becometh all Men better than a Bishop, which should always teach us to lack gladly our own Will, because you may not have your own Will. Here is *Christus paup. facit et ditat, cum Dominus dedit et Dominus abstulit*, to what purpose? *Sit nomen Domini benedictum*, can never lack his place, it becometh alwise in season; or else as great a Divine as ye are, I would say, it were not the best Placed here, except you wist better, you had rather lose all than any part of your will. I pray you teach Patience better in your Deeds, or else speak as little of it as ye can. My Lord, you might have provoked an other in my place, that would have used less patience with you, finding so little in you; but I can take your Writings, and this Heat off your Stomach, even as well as I can, I trust, beware of Flatterers. As for the Abbot of Redding, and his Monk, if I find them as ye say they are, I will order them as I shall think good; ye shall do well to do your Duty, if you so do, ye have no cause to mistrust my Friendship; if ye do not, I must tell it you, and that somewhat after the plainest sort, To take a Cause out of your hands into mine, I do but mine Office, you meddle further than your Office will bear you, thus roughly to handle me for using of mine. If ye do so no more, I let pass all that is past, and offer you such kindness as ye shall lawfully desire at my hands. Thus fare you well.

IX.

The Sentence given out by Pope Paul the third, against King Henry.

Damnatio et Excommunicatio Henrici 8. Regis Angliæ, ejusque Fautorum et Complicum, cum aliarum pœnarum adjectione.

Paulus Episcopus Servus Servorum Dei ad perpetuam rei memoriam.

Cherubini Bullariam, Tom. 2. p. 704.
Ejus qui immobilis permanens sua providentia ordine mirabili dat cuncta moveri, disponente clementia, vices, licet immeriti gerentes in terris, et in sede justitiæ constituti, juxta prophetæ quoque Hieremiæ vaticinium dicentis: Ecce te constitui super gentes et Regna, ut evellas et destruas, ædifices, plantes, præcipuum super omnes Reges Universæ Terræ cunctosq; populos obtinentes principatum: ac illum qui pius et misericors est, et vindictam ei qui illam prævenit paratam temperat, nec quos impœnitentes videt severa ultione castigat, quin prius comminetur, in assidue autem peccantes et in peccatis perseverantes, cum excessus misericordiæ fines prætereunt, ut saltem metu pœnæ ad cor reverti cogantur, justitiæ vires exercet, imitantes; ex incumbenti nobis Apostolicæ sollicitudinis studio per-urgemur, ut cunctarum personarum nostræ curæ cælitus commissarum salubri statui solertius intendamus, ac erroribus et scandalis, quæ Hostis antiqui versutia imminere

conspicimus, propensius obviemus, excessusq; et enormia ac scandalosa crimina congrua severitate coerceamus, et juxta Apostolum inobedientiam ovium promptius ulciscendo, illorum perpetratores debita correctione sic compescamus, quod eos Dei iram provocasse pœniteat, et ex hoc aliis exemplum cautelæ salutaris accedat.

Sane cum superioribus diebus nobis relatum fuisset, quod Henricus Angliæ Rex, licet tempore Pontificatus fœl. record. Leonis Papæ X. Prædecessoris nostri diversorum hæreticorum Errores, sæpe ab Apostolica Sede et Sacris Conciliis præteritis temporibus damnatos, et novissime nostra ætate per perditionis alumnum Martinum Lutherum suscitatos et innovatos, zelo Catholicæ Fidei, et erga dictam Sedem devotionis fervore inductus, non minus docte quam pie, per quendam librum per eum desuper compositum, et eidem Leoni Prædecessori ut eum examinaret et approbaret oblatum, confutasset, ob quod ad eodem Leone Prædecessore ultra dicti libri, cum magna ipsius Henrici Regis laude et commendatione, approbationem, titulum Defensoris Fidei reportaverit, a recta Fide et Apostolico tramite devians, ac propriæ salutis, famæ, et honoris immemor, postquam Charissima in Christo Filia nostra Catharina Angliæ Regina illustri sua progenie conjuge, cum qua publice in facie Ecclesiæ Matrimonium contraxerat, et per plures annos continuaverat, ac ex qua, dicto constante Matrimonio, prolem pluries susceperat; nulla legitima subsistente causa, et contra Ecclesiæ prohibitionem dimissa, cum quadam Anna Bolena, Muliere Anglica, dicta Catharina adhuc vivente, de facto Matrimonium contraxerat, ad deteriora prosiliens, quasdam leges ceu generales Constitutiones edere non erubuit, per quas subditos suos ad quosdam hæreticos et schismaticos Articulos tenendos, inter quos et hoc erat quod Romanus Pontifex Caput Ecclesiæ, et Christi Vicarius non erat, et quod ipse in Anglica Ecclesia supremum Caput existebat, sub gravibus etiam mortis pœnis cogebat. Et his non contentus, Diabolo sacrilegii crimen suadente, quamplures Prælatos, etiam Episcopos, aliasq; personas Ecclesiasticas, etiam Regulares, necnon Sæculares, sibi ut hæretico et schismatico adhærere, ac Articulos prædictos Sanctorum Patrum decretis et Sacrorum Conciliorum Statutis, imo etiam ipsi Evangelicæ veritati contrarios, tanquam tales alios damnatos approbare, et sequi nolentes, et intrepide recusantes, capi et carceribus mancipari. Hisq; similiter non contentus, mala malis accumulando, bonæ memoriæ Jo. H. S. Vitalis Presbyt. Cardinal. Roffen. quem ob fidei constantiam et vitæ Sanctimoniam ad Cardinalatus dignitatem promoveramus, cum dictis hæresibus et erroribus consentire nollet, horenda immanitate et detestanda sævitia, publice miserabili supplicio tradi et decollari mandaverat, et fecerat, Excommunicationis, et Anathematis, aliasq; gravissimas sententias censuras, et pœnas in literis et constitutionibus recolendæ mem. Bonifacii VIII. Honorii III. Roman. Pontificum prædecessorum nostrorum desuper editis contentas, et alias in tales a jure latas damnabiliter incurrendo, ac Regno Angliæ, et dominiis quæ tenebat, necnon regalis fastigii celsitudine ac præfati tituli prærogativa, et honore se indignum reddendo.

2. Nos licet ex eo, quod prout non ignorabamus, idem Henricus Rex certis censuris Ecclesiasticis, quibus a piæ memoriæ Clemente Papa VII. etiam prædecessore nostro, postquam humanissimis literis et paternis exhortationibus, multisq; nunciis et mediis, primo et postremo etiam judicialiter, ut præfatam Annam a se dimitteret, et ad prædictæ Catharinæ suæ veræ Conjugis consortium rediret, frustra monitus fuerat, innodatus extiterat, Pharaonis duritiam imitando, per longum tempus in clavium contemptum insorduerat, et insordescebat, quod ad cor rediret, vix sperare posse videremus, ob paternam tamen Charitatem, qua in minoribus constituti donec in obedientia, et reverentia Sedis prædictæ permansit, eum prosecuti fueramus, utq; clarius videre possemus, an clamor qui ad nos delatus fuerat, (quem certe etiam ipsius Henrici Regis respectu falsum esse desideramus) verus esset, statuimus ab ulteriori contra ipsum Henricum Regem processu ad tempus abstinendo, hujus rei veritatem diligentius indagare.

3. Cum autem debitis diligentiis desuper factis clamorem ad nos, ut præfertur, delatum, verum esse, simulque, quod dolenter referimus, dictum Henricum Regem ita in profundum malorum descendisse, ut de ejus resipiscentia nulla penitus videatur spes haberi posse, repererimus: Nos attendentes vetere lege, crimen adulterii notatum lapidari

mandatum, ac auctores Schismatis halitu terræ absorptos, eorumq; sequaces cœlesti igne consumptos, Elimamq; Magum viis Domini resistentem per Apostolum æterna severitate damnatum fuisse, volentesq; ne in districto examine ipsius Henrici Regis et subditorum suorum, quos secum in perditionem trahere videmus, animarum ratio a nobis exposcatur, quantum nobis ex alto conceditur, providere contra Henricum Regem, ejusque complices, fautores, adhærentes, et sequaces, et in præmissis quomodolibet culpabiles, contra quod ex eo quod excessus, et delicta prædicta adeo manifesta sunt et notoria, ut nulla possint tergiversatione celari, absq; ulteriori mora ad executionem procedere possemus, benignius agendo, decrevimus infrascripto modo procedere.

4. Habita itaq; super his cum venerabilibus fratribus nostris S. R. E. Cardinalibus deliberatione matura, et de illorum consilio et assensu, præfatum Henricum Regem, ejusq; complices, fautores, adhærentes, consultores et sequaces, ac quoscunq; alios n præmissis, ceu eorum aliquo quoque modo culpabiles, tam laicos quam Clericos, etiam regulares cujuscunq; dignitatis, status, gradus, ordinis, conditionis, præeminentiæ, et excellentiæ existant, (quorum nomina et cognomina, perinde ac si præsentibus insererentur, pro sufficienter expressis haberi volumus) per viscera misericordiæ Dei nostri hortamur, et requirimus in Domino, quatenus Henricus Rex a prædictis erroribus prorsus abstineat, et constitutiones, seu leges prædictas, sicut de facto eas fecit, revocet, casset, et annullet, et coactione subditorum suorum ad eas servandas, necnon carceratione, captura, et punitione illorum, qui ipsis constitutionibus seu legibus adhærere, aut eas servare noluerint, et ab aliis erroribus prædictis penitus, et omnino abstineat, et si quos præmissorum occasione captivos habeat, relaxet.

5. Complices vero, fautores, adhærentes, consultores, et sequaces dicti Henrici Regis in præmissis, et circa ea ipsi Henrico Regi super his de cætero non adsistant, nec adhæreant, vel faveant, nec ei consilium, auxilium, vel favorem, desuper præstent.

6. Alias si Henricus Rex, ac fautores, adhærentes, consultores, et sequaces, hortationibus et requisitionibus hujusmodi non annuerint cum effectu, Henricum Regem, fauto-

res, adhærentes, consultores et sequaces, ac alios culpabiles prædictos, auctoritate Apostolica, ac ex certa nostra
scientia, et de Apostolicæ potestatis plenitudine, tenore
præsentium, in virtute sanctæ obedientiæ, ac sub majoris
Excommunicationis lata sententia, a qua etiam prætextu
cujuscunq; privilegii, vel facultatis, etiam in forma confes-
sionalis, cum quibuscunq; efficacissimis clausulis nobis et
Sede prædicta quomodolibet concessis, et etiam iteratis
vicibus innovatis, ab alio quam a Romano Pontifice, præterquam in mortis Articulo constituti, ita tamen, quod si
aliquem absolvi contingat, qui postmodum convaluerit, nisi
post convalescentiam, monitioni et mandatis nostris hujusmodi paruerit cum effectu, in eandem Excommunicationis
sententiam reincidat, absolvi non possint.

7. Necnon rebellionis, et quoad Henricum Regem, etiam
perditionis Regni, et Dominiorum prædictorum, et tam
quoad eum, quam quod alios monitos supradictos supra et
infrascriptis pœnis, quas si dictis monitioni et mandatis, ut
præfertur, non paruerint, eos, et eorum singulos, ipso facto respective incurrere volumus, per præsentes monemus;
eisq; et eorum cuilibet districte præcipiendo mandamus,
quatenus Henricus Rex per se, vel procuratorem legitimum et sufficienti mandato suffultum, infra nonaginta, complices vero, fautores, adhærentes, consultores, et sequaces,
ac alii in præmissis quomodolibet culpabiles supradicti,
Sæculares et Ecclesiastici etiam regulares, personaliter infra sexaginta dies compareant coram nobis, ad se super
præmissis legitime excusandum et defendendum; alias videndum et audiendum contra eos et eorum singulos, etiam
nominatim, quos sic monemus, quatenus expediat, ad omnes
et singulos, actus, etiam sententiam definitivam, declarato-
riam, condemnatoriam, et privatoriam, ac mandatum exe-
cutivum procedi. Quod si Henricus Rex, et alii moniti
prædicti intra dictos terminos eis ut præfertur, respective
præfixos non comparuerint, et prædictam Excommunicationis sententiam per tres dies, post lapsum dictorum terminorum animo, quod absit, sustinuerint indurato, censuras
ipsas aggravamus, et successive reaggravamus, Henricumq;
ipsum, privationis Regni et Dominiorum prædictorum, et
tam eum quam alios monitos prædictos, et eorum singulos,
omnes et singulas alias pœnas prædictas incurrisse, ab om-

nibusq; Christi fidelibus, cum eorum bonis perpetuo dif-
fidatos esse. Et si interim ab humanis decedat, Ecclesiastica debere carere sepultura, auctoritate et potestatis plenitudine prædictis decernimus, et declaramus, eosq; anathematis, maledictionis, et damnationis æternæ mucrone per-
cutimus. .

8. Necnon quæ præfatus Henricus Rex quomodolibet, et
ex quavis causa tenet, habet, aut possidet, Quamdiu Henricus Rex, et alii moniti prædicti, et eorum singuli in aliis per
dictum Henricum Regem non tentis, habitis, aut possessis
permanserint, et triduo post eorum inde recessum, et alia
quæcunq; ad quæ Henricum Regem, et alios monitos prædictos, post lapsum dictorum terminorum declinare contigerit,
Dominia, civitates, terras, castra, villas, oppida, Metropo-
litanasque, et alias Cathedrales, cæterasq; inferiores Ecclesias, necnon Monasteria, Prioratus, Domos, Conventus,
et loca religiosa, vel pia cujuscunque, etiam S. Benedict.
Cluniacen. Cistercien. Præmonstraten. ac Prædicatorum,
Minorum, Eremitarum S. Augustini Carmelitarum, et aliorum Ordinum, ac Congregationum, et Militiarum quarum-
cunq; in ipsis Dominiis, Civitatibus, terris, castris, villis,
oppidis, et locis existentia, Ecclesiastico supponimus Interdicto, ita ut illo durante in iis etiam prætextu cujuscunque Apostolici indulti, Ecclesiis, Monasteriis, Prioratibus,
Domibus, Conventibus, locis, ordinibus, aut personis, etiam
quacunq; dignitate fulgentibus concessi, præterquam in
casibus a jùre permissis, ac etiam in illis alias quam clau-
sis januis, et Excommunicatis et interdictis exclusis, nequeant Missæ, aut alia divina officia celebrari.

9. Et Henrici Regis, complicumque, fautorum, adhærentium, consultorum, sequacium, et culpabilium prædictorum filii, pœnarum, ut hic in hoc casu par est, participes
sint, omnes et singulos ejusdem Henrici Regis ex dicta
Anna, ac singulorum aliorum prædictorum filios natos, et
nascituros, aliosq; descendentes, usq; in eum gradum, ad
quem jura pœnas in casibus hujusmodi extendunt (nemine
excepto, nullaq; minoris ætatis, aut sexus, vel ignorantiæ,
vel alterius cujusvis causæ habita ratione) dignitatibus, et
honoribus in quibus quomodolibet constituti existunt, seu
quibus gaudent, utuntur, potiuntur, aut muniti sunt, necnon privilegiis, concessionibus, gratiis, indulgentiis, im-

munitatibus, remissionibus, libertatibus, et indultis, ac dominiis, civitatibus, castris, terris, villis, oppidis, et locis,
etiam Commendatis, vel in Gubernium concessis, et quæ
in feudum, emphyteusim, vel alias a Romanis, vel aliis
Ecclesiis, Monasteriis, et locis Ecclesiasticis, ac secularibus Principibus, Dominiis, Potentatibus, etiam Regibus et
Imperatoribus, aut aliis privatis, vel publicis personis quomodolibet habent, tenent, aut possident, cæterisq; omnibus bonis, mobilibus et immobilibus, juribus et actionibus,
eis quomodolibet competentibus privatos, dictaq; bona
feudalia, vel emphyteutica, et alia quæcunq; ab aliis quomodolibet obtenta, ad directos dominos, ita ut de illis libere
disponere possint, respective devoluta, et eos qui Ecclesiastici fuerint, etiamsi religiosi existant, Ecclesiis etiam
Cathedralibus, et Metropolitanis, necnon Monasteriis et
Prioratibus, præposituris, præpositatibus, dignitatibus, personatibus, Officiis, Canonicatibus et Præbendis, aliisq; beneficiis Ecclesiasticis per eos quomodolibet obtentis privatos, et ad illa ac alia in posterum obtinenda inhabiles
esse, similiter decernimus et declaramus; eosq; sic respective privatos ad illa, et alia quæcunq; similia, ac dignitates, honores, administrationes, et officia, jura, ac feuda
in posterum obtinenda, auctoritate et scientia, ac plenitudine similibus inhabilitamus.

10. Ipsiusq; Henrici Regis, ac Regni omniumq; aliorum dominiorum, civitatum, terrarum, castrorum, villarum, fortalitiorum, arcium, oppidorum, et locorum suorum, etiam de facto obtentorum Magistratus, judices,
Castellanos, Custodes et Officiales quoscunque, necnon
Communitates, Universitates, Collegia, Feudatarios, vassallos, subditos, cives, incolas, et habitatores etiam forenses, dicto Regi de facto obedientes, tam sæculares, quam
si qui rationis alicujus temporalitatis ipsum Henricum
Regem in superiorem recognoscant, etiam Ecclesiasticos, a præfato rege, seu ejus complicibus, fautoribus,
adhærentibus, consultoribus, et sequacibus supradictis deputatis, a juramento fidelitatis, jure vassallitico, et omni erga Regem, et alios prædictos subjectione absolvimus, ac penitus liberamus. His nihilominus sub Excommunicationis pœna mandantes, ut ab ejusdem Henrici Regis, suorumq; officialium, judicum, et magistratuum quo-

rumonuq ; obedientia pœnitus et omnino recedant, nec illos
in superiores recognoscant, neque illorum mandatis obtemperent.

11. Et ut alii eorum exemplo perterriti discant ab hujusmodi excessibus abstinere, eisdem auctoritate, scientia, et plenitudine, volumus, ac decernimus, quod Henricus Rex et complices, fautores, adhærentes, consultores, sequaces, et alii in præmissis culpabiles, postquam alias pœnas prædictas, ut præfertur, respective incurrerint, necnon præfati descendentes, ex tunc infames existant, et ad testimonium non admittantur, testamenta, et codicillos, aut alias dispositiones, etiam inter vivos concedere, et facere non possint, et ad alicujus successionem ex testamento, vel ab intestato, necnon ad jurisdictionem, seu judicandi postestatem, et ad Notoriatus Officium, omnesq; actus legitimos quoscunq; ita ut eorum processus, sive instrumenta atq; alii actus quicunque, nullius sint roboris vel momenti, inhabiles existant, et nulli ipsis, sed ipsi aliis super quocunque debito et rogugu, tam civili, quam criminali, de jure respondere teneantur.

12. Et nihilominus omnes, et singulos Christi fideles, sub Excommunicationis, et aliis infrascriptis pœnis, monemus, ut monitos, Excommunicatos, aggravatos, interdictos, privatos, maledictos, et damnatos prædictos evitent, et quantum in eis est, et ab aliis evitari faciant, nec cum eisdem, seu præfati Regis Civitatum, Dominiorum, Terrarum, Castrorum, Comitatuum, Villarum, Fortalitiorum, Oppidorum, et locorum prædictorum civibus, incolis, vel habitatoribus aut subditis et vassallis, emendo, vendendo, permutando, aut quamcunque mercaturam, seu negotium exercendo, commercium, seu aliquam conversationem, seu communionem habeant ; aut vinum, granum, sal, seu alia victualia, arma, pannos, merces vel quasvis alias mercantias, vel res per mare in eorum navibus, triremibus, aut aliis navigiis, sive per terram cum mulis, vel aliis animalibus, deferre aut conducere, seu deferri aut conduci facere, vel delata per illos recipere, publice vel occulte, aut talia facientibus auxilium, consilium, favorem publice vel occulte, directe vel indirecte, quovis quæsito colore, per se, vel alium, seu alios quoqı̨o modo præstare præsumant. Quod si fecerint, ultra Excommunicationis prædictæ, etiam nulli-

tatis contractuum quos inirent, necnon perditionis merclum,
victualium, et bonorum omnium delatorum, quæ capientium fiant, pœnas similiter eo ipso incurrant.

13. Cæterum quia convenire non videtur, ut cum his qui
Ecclesiam contemnunt, dum præsertim ex eorum pertinacia spes corrigibilitatis non habetur, hi qui divinis obse-
quiis vacant, conversentur, quod etiam illos tuto facere non
posse dubitandum est, omnium et singularum Metropoli-
tanarum et aliarum Cathedralium, cæterarumq; inferio-
rum Ecclesiarum et Monasteriorum, domorum et locorum
Religiosorum, et piorum quorumcumque, etiam S. Augustini, S. Benedicti, Cluniacen. Cistercien. Præmonstraten.
ac Prædicatorum, Minorum, Carmelitarum, aliorumque
quorumcumq; ordinum, et Militiarum, etiam Hospitalis
Hierosolymitani, Prælatis, Abbatibus, Prioribus, Præ-
ceptoribus, Præpositis, Ministris, Custodibus, Guardi-
anis, Conventibus, Monachis et Canonicis, necnon Paro-
chialium Ecclesiarum Rectoribus, aliisq; quibuscunq|; per-
sonis Ecclesiasticis in Regno et Dominiis prædictis com-
morantibus, sub Excommunicationis ac privationis Administrationum et regiminum Monasteriorum, dignitatum,
personatuum, administrationum, ac officiorum, Canonica-
tuumque, et Præbendarum, Parochialium Ecclesiarum, et
aliorum beneficiorum Ecclesiasticorum quorumcumq; quomodolibet qualificatorum, per eos quomodolibet obtentorum, pœnis mandamus, quatenus infra quinq; dies, post
omnes et singulos terminos prædictos elapsos, de ipsis
Regno, et Dominiis, dimissis tamen aliquibus Presbyteris in Ecclesiis quarum curam habuerint, pro adminis-
trando baptismate parvulis, et in pœnitentia decedenti-
bus, ac aliis Sacramentis Ecclesiasticis, quæ tempore Interdicti ministrari permittuntur, exeant et discedant, neque ad Regnum, et Dominia prædicta revertantur; donec
moniti, et Excommunicati, aggravati, reaggravati, privati,
maledici, et damnati prædictis monitionibus, et mandatis
nostris hujusmodi obtemperaverint, meruerint a censuris
hujusmodi absolutionis beneficium obtinere, seu Interdictum in Regno, et Dominiis prædictis, fuerit sublatum.

14. Præterea si præmissis non obstantibus, Henricus
Rex, Complices, fautores, adhærentes, consultores, et sequaces prædicti in eorum pertinacia perseveraverint, nec

conscientiæ stimulus eos ad cor reduxerit, in eorum forte potentia, et armis confidentes, omnes et singulos Duces, Marchiones, Comites, et alios quoscunq ; tam Seculares, quam Ecclesiasticos etiam forenses, de facto dicto Henrico Regi obedientes, sub ejusdem Excommunicationis, ac perditionis bonorum suorum (quæ, ut infra dicitur, similiter capientium fiant) pœnis, requirimus et monemus, quatenus omni mora, et excusatione postposita, eos, et eorum singulos, ac ipsorum milites et stipendiarios, tam equestres quam pedestres, aliosq ; quoscumque, qui eis cum armis faverint, de Regno et Dominiis prædictis, etiam vi armorum, si opus fuerit, expellant : ac quod Henricus Rex, et ejus complices, fautores, adhærentes, consultores, et sequaces, mandatis nostris non obtemperantes prædicti, de Civitatibus, Terris, Castris, Villis Oppidis, Fortalitiis, aut aliis locis Regni et Dominii prædictorum se non intromittant, procurent : eis sub omnibus et singulis pœnis prædictis inhibentes, ne in favorem Henrici, ejusque complicum, fautorum, adhærentium, consultorum, et sequacium aliorumq ; monitorum prædictorum, mandatis nostris non obtemperantium, arma cujuslibet generis offensiva, vel defensiva, Machinas quoq ; bellicas, seu tormenta (artellarias nuncupata) sumant aut teneant, seu illis utantur, aut armatos aliquos præter consuetam familiam parent, aut ab Henrico Rege, complicibus, fautoribus, adhærentibus, consultoribus, et sequacibus, vel aliis in Regis ipsius favorem paratos, quomodolibet, quavis occasione vel causa, per se vel alium seu alios, publice vel occulte, directe vel indirecte teneant, vel receptent, aut dicto Henrico Regi, seu illius complicibus, fautoribus, adhærentibus, consultoribus, et sequacibus prædictis, consilium, auxilium, vel quomodolibet ex quavis causa, vel quovis quæsito colore sive ingenio, public vel occulte, directe vel indirecte, tacite vel expresse, per se vel alium seu alios præmissis, vel aliquo præmissorum præstent, seu præstari faciant quoquomodo.

15. Præterea ad dictum Henricum Regem facilius ad sanitatem, et præfatæ Sedis obedientiam reducendum, omnes et singulos Christianos Principes, quacumq ; etiam Imperiali et Regali dignitate fulgentes, per viscera misericordiæ Dei nostri (cujus causa agitur) hortamur et in Domino requirimus, eis nihilominus, qui Imperatore et Rege inferiores fue-

rint, quos propter excellentiam dignitatis a censuris excipimus, sub Excommunicationis pœna mandantes, ne Henrico Regi ejusq; complicibus, fautoribus, adhærentibus, consultoribus, et sequacibus, vel eorum alicui, per se vel alium seu alios, publice vel occulte, directe vel indirecte, tacite vel expresse, etiam sub prætextu confœderationum aut obligationum quocumq; etiam juramento, aut quavis alia firmitate roboratarum, et sæpius geminatarum, a quibus quidem obligationibus et juramentis omnibus, nos eos et eorum singulos eisdem auctoritate et scientia ac plenitudine per præsentes absolvimus, ipsasq; confœderationes et obligationes tam factas, quam in posterum faciendas, quas tamen (in quantum Henricus Rex et complices, fautores, adhærentes, consultores, et sequaces prædicti circa præmissa, vel eorum aliquod se directe vel indirecte juvare possent) sub eadem pœna fieri prohibemus, nullius roboris vel momenti, nullasque, irritas, cassas, inanes, ac pro infectis habendas fore decernimus et declaramus, consilium, auxilium, vel favorem quomodolibet præstent, quinimo si qui illis, aut eorum alicui ad præsens quomodolibet assistant, ab ipsis omnino et cum affectu recedant. Quod si non fecerint postquam præsentes publicatæ et executioni demandatæ fuerint, et dicti termini lapsi fuerint, omnes et singulas civitates, terras, oppida, castra, villas, et alia loca eis subjecta, simili Ecclesiastico Interdicto supponimus, volentes ipsum Interdictum donec ipsi Principes a Consilio, auxilio, et favore Henrico Regi et complicibus, fautoribus, adhærentibus, consultoribus, et sequacibus prædictis præstando destiterint, perdurare.

16. Insuper tam Principes prædictos, quam quoscumq; alios, etiam ad stipendia quorumcumq; Christi fidelium militantes, et alias quascumq; personas, tam per mare, quam per terras, armigeros habentes, similiter hortamur et requirimus, et nihilominus eis in virtute sanctæ obedientiæ mandantes, quatenus contra Henricum Regem, complices, fautores, adhærentes, consultores, et sequaces prædictos, dum in erroribus prædictis, ac adversus Sedem prædictam, rebellione permanserint, armis insurgant, eosq; et eorum singulos persequantur, ac ad unitatem Ecclesiæ, et obedientiam dictæ Sedis redire cogant et compellant; et tam eos quam ipsorum subditos et vassallos, ac civitatum, terrarum,

castrorum, oppidorum, villarum, et locorum suorum incolas,
et habitatores, aliosque omnes et singulas personas supradictis mandatis nostris, ut præfertur, non obtemperantes, et
quæ præfatum Henricum Regem, postquam censuras, et pœnas prædictas incurrerit, in Dominum quomodolibet, etiam
de facto recognoverint, vel ei quovis modo obtemperare præsumpserint, aut qui eum, ac complices, fautores, adhærentes, consultores, sequaces, ac alios non obtemperantes prædictos, ex Regno et Dominiis prædictis, ut præfertur, ex-
pellere noluerint, ubicunq; eos invenerint, eorumque bona, mobilia et immobilia, mercantias, pecunias, navigia,
credita, res, et animalia, etiam extra territorium dicti
Henrici Regis ubilibet consistentia, capiant.

17. Nos enim eis bona, mercantias, pecunias, navigia,
res, et animalia prædictá sic capta, in proprios eorum usus
convertendi, eisdem auctoritate, scientia, et potestatis plenitudine, plenariam licentiam, facultatem et auctoritatem
concedimus, illa omnia ad eosdem capientes plenarie per-
tinére, et spectare, et personas ex Regno et Dominiis prædictis originem trahentes, seu in illis domicilium habentes,
aut quomodolibet habitantes, mandatis nostris prædictis
non obtemperantes, ubicunq; eos capi contigerit, capientium servos fieri decernentes: præsentesq; literas quoad
hoc ad omnes alios cujuscunq; dignitatis, gradus, status,
ordinis, vel conditionis fuerint, qui ipsi Henrico Regi, vel
ejus complicibus, fautoribus, adhærentibus, consultoribus,
et sequacibus, aut aliis monitionibus, et mandatis nostris
hujusmodi quoad commercium non obtemperantibus, vel
eorum alicui victualia, arma, vel pecunias subministrare,
aut cum eis commercium habere, seu auxilium, consilium,
vel favorem, per se vel alium, seu alios, publice vel occulte,
directe vel indirecte, quovis modo contra tenorem præsentium præstrare præsumpserint, extendentes.

18. Et ut præmissa facilius iis quos concernunt inno-
tescant, universis et singulis Patriarchis, Archiepiscopis,
Episcopis, et Patriarchalium Metropolitan. et aliarum Cathedralium, et Collegiatarum Ecclesiarum Prælatis, Capitulis, aliisq; personis Ecclesiasticis, Sæcularibus ac quo-
rumvis ordinum Regularibus, necnon omnibus et singulis,
etiam mendicantium ordinum Professoribus, exemptis et
non exemptis, ubilibet constitutis, per easdem præsentes

sub Excommunicationis et privationis Ecclesiarum, Monasteriorum, ac aliorum Beneficiorum Ecclesiasticorum, gra-
duum quoq; et officiorum, necnon privilegiorum, et indul-
torum quorumcumq; etiam a Sede prædicta quomodolibet
emanatorum pœnis ipso facto incurrendis, præcipimus et
mandamus, quatenus ipsi ac eorum singuli, si, et postquam
vigore præsentium desuper requisiti fuerint, infra tres dies
immediate sequentes, præfatum Henricum Regem, omnesq; alios et singulos, qui supradictas censuras et pœnas
incurrerint, in eorum Ecclesiis, Dominicis et aliis festivis
diebus, dum major inibi populi multitudo ad divina conve-
nerit, cum Crucis vexillo, pulsatis campanis, et accensis, ac
demum extinctis, et in terram projectis, et conculcatis can-
delis, et aliis in similibus servari solitis cæremoniis servatis, Excommunicatos publice nuncient, et ab aliis nuntiari,
ac ab omnibus arctius evitari faciant et mandent, necnon
sub supradictis censuris et pœnis, præsentes literas, vel earum transumptum, sub forma infrascripta confectum, infra
terminum trium dierum, postquam, ut præfertur, requisiti
fuerint, in Ecclesiis, Monasteriis, Conventibus, et aliis eorum locis, publicari et affigi faciant.

19. Volentes, omnes et singulos cujuscumq; status, gradus, conditionis, præeminentiæ, dignitatis, aut excellentiæ
fuerint, qui quo minus præsentes literæ, vel earum tran-
sumpta, copiæ, seu exemplaria, in suis civitatibus, terris,
castris, oppidis, villis, et locis legi et affigi, ac publicari
possint, per se, vel alium, seu alios, publice vel occulte,
directe vel indirecte impediverint, easdem censuras et pœnas, ipso facto incurrere. Et cum fraus et dolus nemini
debeant patrocinari, ne quisquam ex his, qui alicui regi-
mini et administrationi deputati sunt, infra tempus sui re-
giminis seu administrationis prædictas sententias, censuras
et pœnas sustineat, quasi post dictum tempus sententiis,
censuris et pœnis prædictis amplius ligatus non existat,
quemcunq; qui dum in regimine, et administratione existens, monitioni et mandato nostris, quoad præmissa vel
aliquid eorum obtemperare noluerit, etiam deposito regimine, et administratione hujusmodi, nisi paruerit, eisdem
censuris et pœnis subjacere decernimus.

20. Et ne Henricus Rex ejusq; complices, et fautores,
adhærentes, consultores, et sequaces, aliiq; quos præmissa

concernunt, ignorantiam earundem præsentium literarum,
et in eis contentorum prætendere valeant, literas ipsas (in
quibus omnes et singulos, tam juris, quam facti, etiam so-
lemnitatum, et processuum, citationumq; ommissarum defectus, etiam si tales sint, de quibus specialis, et expressa
mentio facienda esset, propter notorietatem facti, auctoritate, scientia, et potestatis plenitudine similibus, supple-
mus) in Basilicæ Principis Apostolorum, et Cancellariæ
Apostolicæ de urbe, et in partibus in Collegiatæ B. Mariæ
Burgen. Tornacen. et Parochialis de Dunikerke oppidorum Morinensis diœcesis, Ecclesiarum valvis affigi, et publicari mandamus: Decernentes quod earundem literarum
publicatio sic facta, Henricum Regem, ejusq; complices,
fautores, adhærentes, consultores, et sequaces, omnesq;
alios, et singulos quos literæ ipsæ quomodolibet concernunt, perinde eos arctent, ac si literæ ipsæ eis personaliter
lectæ, et intimatæ fuissent, cum non sit verisimile, quod
ea, quæ tam patenter fiunt, debeant apud eos incognita remanere.

21. Cæterum quia difficile foret præsentes literas ad singula quæque loca, ad quæ necessarium esset deferri, singula volumus et dicta auctoritate decernimus, quod earum
transumptis manu publici Notarii confectis, vel in alma
urbe impressis, ac sigillo alicujus personæ in dignitate Ecclesiastica constitutæ munitis, ubiq; eadem fides adhibeatur, quæ originalibus adhiberetur, si essent exhibitæ vel
ostensæ.

22. Nulli ergo omnino hominum liceat hanc paginam nostræ monitionis, aggravationis, reaggravationis, declarationis, percussionis, suppositionis, inhabilitationis, absolutionis,
liberationis, requisitionis, inhibitionis, hortationis, excep-
tionis, prohibitionis, concessionis, extensionis suppletionis,
mandatorum, voluntatis, et decretorum, infringere, vel ei
ausu temerario contraire. Si quis autem hoc attentare præsumpserit, indignationem Omnipotentis Dei, ac Beatorum
Petri et Pauli Apostolorum ejus se noverit incursurum.

Datum Romæ apud Sanctum Marcum. Anno Incarnationis Domini 1535. 3 Kal. Sept. Pont. nostri
Anno I.

——— *Sequitur suspensio Executionis dictæ Bullæ, et tandem ejus*
revocatio, et Executio.

Paulus Episcopus Servus Servorum Dei, ad perpetuam
rei memoriam.

Cum Redemptor noster ideo illum qui ipsum negaverat,
Petrum, viz. Universæ Ecclesiæ præficere voluerit, ut in
sua culpa disceret aliis esse miserendum, non immerito
Romanus Pontifex qui ipsius Petri in dignitate Successor
existit, debet etiam in Officio exercendæ misericordiæ ipsius esse Successor. Sed cum in eum dirigitur misericordia,
qui ex hoc sit insolentior, et obstinatior, aliosq; secum trahit in perditionem, debet ipse Romanus Pontifex, postposita in eum misericordia, omnem severitatem adhibere,
quo membrum illud putridum ita a corpore separetur, ut
reliqua membra absq; metu contagionis salva remaneant,
præsertim cum pluribus curis adhibitis, et multo tempore
in hoc consumpto morbum quotidie magis invalescere, ipsa
experientia comprobat.

1. Alias cum nobis relatum fuisset, quod Henricus Angliæ Rex, præter ea quæ Matrimonium de facto, et contra
prohibitionem Ecclesiæ temerarie contractum concerne-
bant, quasdam leges, seu generales constitutiones subditos
suos ad hæresim, et schisma trahentes ediderat, et bonæ
memoriæ Joann. tit. Sancti Vitalis Presbyterum Cardinalem Roffen. publice damnari et capite puniri, ac alios
quamplures Prælatos, necnon alias personas Ecclesiast.
Hæresi et Schismati hujusmodi adhærere nolentes carceribus mancipari fecerat; Nos, licet illi qui talia nobis retu-
lerant tales essent, ut nullo modo de veritate suorum dictorum ambigendum esset, cupientes tamen respectu ipsius
Henrici Regis, quem antequam in has insanias incideret,
peculiari quadam charitate prosequebamur, prædicta falsa
reperiri, de eis informationem ulteriorem habere procura-
vimus, et invenientes clamorem ad nos delatum verum esse,
ne nostro Officio deessemus, contra eum procedere decrevimus, juxta formam quarundam literarum nostrarum, quarum tenor sequitur. Et est talis, &c.

Omittitur insertio, quia bulla ipsa est quæ præcedit.

2. Dum autem postea ad dictarum literarum executionem deveniendum esse statuissemus, cum nobis per nonnullos principes, et alias insignes personas persuaderetur, ut ab executione hujusmodi per aliquantum temporis supersederemus, spe nobis data, quod interim ipse Henricus Rex ad cor rediret et resipisceret; nos qui, ut hominum natura fert, facile credebamus quod desiderabamus, dictam executionem suspendimus, sperantes (ut spes nobis data erat) ex ipsa suspensione, correctionem et resipiscentiam, non autem pertinaciam et obstinationem, ac majorem delirationem, ut rei effectus edocuit, proventuram.

3. Cum itaq; resipiscentia et Correctio hujusmodi quam tribus fere annis expectavimus, non solum postea sequuta non sit, sed ipse Henricus Rex quotidie magis se in sua feritate, ac temeritate confirmans in nova etiam scelera proruperit, quippe cum non contentus vivorum Prælatorum et sacerdotum crudelissima trucidatione, etiam in mortuos, et eos quidem quos in sanctorum numerum relatos Universalis Ecclesia pluribus sæculis venerata est, feritatem exercere non expavit, Divi enim Thomæ Cantuarien. Archiepiscopi, cujus ossa, quæ in dicto Regno Angliæ potissimum, ob innumera ab omnipotenti Deo illic perpetrata miracula, summa cum veneratione in arca aurea in Civitate Cantuarien. servabantur, postquam ipsum Divum Thomam, ad majorem Religionis contemptum, in judicium vocari, et tanquam contumacem damnari ac proditorem declarari fecerat, exhumari, et comburi, ac cineres in ventum spargi jussit, omnem plane cunctarum gentium crudelitatem superans, cum ne in bello quidem hostes victores sævire in mortuorum cadavera soliti sunt; adhæc omnia ex diversorum Regum etiam Anglorum, et aliorum Principum liberalitate donaria, ipsi arcæ appensa, quæ multa, et maximi pretii erant, sibi usurpavit; nec putans ex hoc satis injuriæ religionis intulisse, Monasterium Divo illi Augustino, a quo Christianam fidem Angli acceperunt, in dicta civitate dicatum, omnibus Thesauris, qui etiam multi et magni erant, spoliavit, et sicut se in belluam transmutavit, ita etiam belluas quasi socias suas honorare voluit, feras videlicet in dicto Monasterio, expulsis Monachis, intromittendo, genus quidem sceleris non modo Christi fidelibus, sed etiam Turcis inauditum et abominandum.

4. Cum itaq; morbus iste a nullo quantumvis peritissimo medico alia cura sanari possit, quam putridi membri abscissione, nec valeret cura hujusmodi, absq; eo, quod nos apud Deum causam hanc nostram efficiamus, ulterius retardari, ad dictarum literarum (quas ad hoc ut Henricus Rex, ejusq; Complices, Fautores, adhærentes, consultores, et sequaces, etiam super excessibus per eum novissime, ut præfertur, perpetratos, intra terminum eis, quoad alia, per alias nostras literas prædictas respective præfixas, se excusare, alias pœnis ipsis literis contentas incurrant, extendimus et ampliamus) publicationem, et deinde, Deo duce, ad executionem procedere omnino statuimus. Et quia a fide dignis accepimus, quod si ipsarum et præsentium literarum publicatio Diep. Rothomagen. vel Boloniæ Ambianen. Diœc. Oppidis in Franciæ, aut Civitate Sancti Andreæ, seu in Oppido Callistren. Sancti Andreæ Diœc. in Scotiæ Regnis, vel in Thuamien. et Antiferten. Civitatibus, vel Diœc. Dominii Hiberniæ fiat, non solum tam facile, ut si in locis in dictis literis expressis fieret, sed facilius ipsarum literarum tenor, ad Henrici, et aliorum quos concernunt, præsertim Anglorum, notitiam deveniret; Nos volentes in hoc opportune providere, motu, scientia, et potestatis plenitudine prædictis decernimus, quod publicatio literarum superius insertarum, quarum insertioni superius factæ, ac ipsis Originalibus quoad validitatem publicationis, seu executionis præsentium, fidem adhiberi volumus, in duobus ex locis præsentibus literis expressis, alias juxta supra insertarum, et præsentium literarum tenore facta, etiam si in locis extra Romanam Curiam in dictis præinsertis literis specificatis, hujusmodi publicatio non fiat, perinde Henricum Regem, et alios quos concernunt præsertim Anglos afficiat, ac si Henrico Regi et aliis prædictis præsertim Anglis personaliter intimatæ fuissent.

5. Quodq; præsentium transumptis, juxta modum in præinsertis literis expressum factis, tam in judicio quam extra, eadem fides adhibeatur, quæ Originalibus adhiberetur, si forent exhibitæ, vel ostensæ.

6. Non obstantibus Constitutionibus et Ordinationibus Apostolicis, necnon omnibus illis, quæ in dictis literis voluimus non obstare, cæterisq; contrariis quibuscunque.

7. Nulli ergo omnino hominum liceat hanc paginam nos-

tri Decreti, et voluntatis infringere, vel ei ausu temerario contraire. Si quis autem hoc attentare præsumpserit, indignationem Omnipotentis Dei, ac Beatorum Petri et Pauli Apostolorum ejus se noverit incursurum.

Dat. Romæ apud S. Petrum, Anno Incarnationis Dominicæ 1538. decimo sexto Kal. Januarii, Pontificatus nostri anno quinto.

X.

The Judgment of some Bishops concerning the King's Supremacy. An Original.

THE words of St. John in his 20th Chap. *Sicut misit me* ExMSS D. Stilling- fleet. *Pater, et ego mitto vos, &c.* hath no respect to a King's or a Princes Power, but only to shew how that the Ministers of the Word of God, chosen and sent for that intent, are the Messengers of Christ, to teach the Truth of his Gospel, and to loose and bind sin, &c. as Christ was the Messenger of his Father. The words also of St. Paul, in the 20th Chap. of the Acts; *Attendite vobis et universo gregi, in qua vos Spiritus Sanctus posuit Episcopos regere Ecclesiam Dei,* were spoken to the Bishops and Priests, to be diligent Pastors of the People, both to teach them diligently, and also to be circumspect that false Preachers should not seduce the People, as followeth immediately after in the same place. Other places of Scripture declare the highness and excellency of Christian Princes Authority and Power; the which of a truth is most high, for he hath power and charge generally over all, as well Bishops, as Priests, as other. The Bishops and Priests have charge of Souls within their own Cures, power to minister Sacraments, and to teach the Word of God; to the which Word of God Christian Princes knowledg themselves subject; and in case the Bishops be negligent, it is the Christian Princes Office to see them do their duty.

T. Cantuarien.	Thomas Elien.
Joannes London.	Nicolaus Sarisburien.
Cuthbertus Dunelmen.	Hugo Wygorn.
Jo. Batwellen.	J. Roffen.

XI.

Injunctions to the Clergy made by Cromwell.

In the Name of God, Amen. By the Authority and Commission of the excellent Prince Henry, by the Grace of God, King of England and of France, Defensor of the Faith; Lord of Ireland; and in Earth Supream Head, under Christ, of the Church of England, I Thomas Lord Cromwell, Privy Seal, and Vice-gerent to the King's said Highness, for all his Jurisdiction Ecclesiastical within this Realm, do, for the advancement of the true honour of Almighty God, encrease of Vertue, and discharge of the King's Majesty, give and exhibit unto you　　·　　these Injunctions following, to be kept, observed, and fulfilled, upon the pains hereafter declared.

First; That ye shall truly observe and keep all and singular the King's Highness Injunctions, given unto you heretofore in my Name, by his Graces Authority; not only upon the pains therein expressed, but also in your default after this second monition continued, upon further punishment to be straitly extended towards you by the King's Highness Arbitriment, or his Vice-gerent aforesaid.

Item; That ye shall provide on this side the Feast of next coming, one Book of the whole Bible of the largest Volume in English, and the same set up in some convenient place within the said Church that ye have Cure of, whereas your Parishioners may most commodiously resort to the same and read it; the charge of which Book shall be ratably born between you the Parson and the Parishioners aforesaid, that is to say, the one half by you, and the other half by them.

Item; That you shall discourage no Man privily or apertly from the reading or hearing of the said Bible, but shall expresly provoke, stir, and exhort every Person to read the same, as that which is the very lively Word of God, that every Christian Man is bound to embrace, believe, and follow, if he looked to be saved; admonishing them nevertheless to avoid all contention, altercation therein, and to use an honest sobriety in the inquisition of the true sense of the same, and refer the explication of the obscure places to Men of higher judgment in Scripture.

Item; That ye shall every Sunday and Holy-day through the Year, openly and plainly recite to your Parishioners, twice or thrice together, or oftner, if need require, one particle or sentence of the Pater Noster, or Creed, in English, to the intent they may learn the same by Heart; And so from day to day, to give them one little lesson or sentence of the same, till they have learned the whole Pater Noster and Creed, in English, by rote. And as they be taught every sentence of the same by rote, ye shall expound and declare the understanding of the same unto them, exhorting all Parents and Housholders to teach their Children and Servants the same, as they are bound in Conscience to do. And that done, ye shall declare unto them the Ten Commandments, one by one every Sunday and Holy-day, till they be likewise perfect in the same.

Item; That ye shall in Confessions every Lent examine every Person that cometh to Confession unto you, whether they can recite the Articles of our Faith, and the Pater Noster in English, and hear them say the same particularly; wherein if they be not perfect, ye shall declare to the same, That every Christian Person ought to know the same before they should receive the blessed Sacrament of the Altar; and monish them to learn the same more perfectly by the next year following, or else, like-as they ought not to presume to come to God's Board, without perfect knowledg of the same, and if they do, it is to the great peril of their Souls; so ye shall declare unto them, that ye look for other Injunctions from the King's Highness by that time, to stay and repel all such from God's Board as shall be found ignorant in the Premisses; whereof ye do thus admonish them, to the intent they should both eschew the peril of their Souls, and also the worldly rebuke that they might incur after by the same.

Item; That ye shall make, or cause to be made, in the said Church, and every other Cure ye have, one Sermon every quarter of the year at least, wherein ye shall purely and sincerely declare the very Gospel of Christ, and in the same exhort your Hearers to the Works of Charity, Mer-

cy, and Faith; especially prescribed and commanded in
Scripture, and not to repose their trust or affiance in any
other Works devised by Mens fantasies besides Scripture;
as in wandering to Pilgrimages, offering of Mony, Candels,
or Tapers, to Images, or Reliques ; or kissing or licking
the same over, saying over a number of Beads, not under-
standed or minded on, or in such-like superstition ; for the
doing whereof, ye not only have no promise of reward in
Scripture, but contrariwise great threats and maledic-
tions of God, as things tending to Idolatry and Superstition, which of all other Offences God Almighty doth
most detest and abhor, for that the same diminisheth most
his honour and glory.

Item ; That such feigned Images as ye know in any of
your Cures to be so abused with Pilgrimages or Offerings
of any thing made thereunto, ye shall, for avoiding of that
most detestable offence of Idolatry, forthwith take down,
and without delay ; and shall suffer from henceforth no
Candles, Tapers, or Images of Wax to be set afore any
Image or Picture, but only the Light that commonly goeth
a-cross the Church by the Rood-loft, the Light before the
Sacrament of the Altar, and the Light about the Sepul-
chre ; which for the adorning of the Church, and Divine
Service, ye shall suffer to remain : still admonishing your
Parishioners, that Images serve for none other purpose,
but as to be Books of unlearned Men, that ken no Letters,
whereby they might be otherwise admonished of the lives
and conversation of them that the said Images do represent ; which Images if they abuse, for any other intent than
for such remembrances, they commit Idolatry in the same,
to the great danger of their Souls : And therefore the
King's Highness graciously tendering the weal of his Subjects Souls, hath in part already, and more will hereafter,
travail for the abolishing of such Images as might be an
occasion of so great an offence to God, and so great a
danger to the Souls of his loving Subjects.

Item ; That all in such Benefices, or Cures, as ye have,
whereupon ye be not your self Resident, ye shall appoint
such Curats in your stead, as can both by their ability, and
will also promptly, execute these Injunctions, and do their
duty otherwise, that ye are bounden in every behalf ac-

cordingly, and may profit them, no less with good Examples of living, than with declaration of the Word of God,
or else their lack and defaults shall be imputed unto you,
who shall straitly answer for the same if they do otherwise.

Item; That ye shall admit no Man to preach within any
your Benefices or Cures, but such as shall appear unto
you to be sufficiently licensed thereunto by the King's
Highness, or his Grace's Authority, by the Arch-Bishop of
Canterbury, or the Bishop of this Diocess; and such as
shall be so licensed, ye shall gladly receive to declare the
Word of God, without any resistance or contradiction.

Item; If ye have heretofore declared to your Parishioners any thing to the extolling or setting forth of Pilgrimages, feigned Reliques, or Images, or any such super-
stitions, that you shall now openly afore the same recant and
reprove the same, shewing them (as the truth is) that ye did
the same upon no ground of Scripture, but as one led and
seduced by a common Error and abuse crept into the
Church, through the sufferance and avarice of such as felt
profit by the same.

Item; If ye do or shall know any Man within your Parish, or elsewhere, that is a Letter of the Word of God to
be read in English, or sincerely preached, or of the execution of these Injunctions; or a favourer of the Bishop of
Rome's pretensed Power, now by the Laws of this Realm
justly rejected and extirped; ye shall detect and present
the same to the King's Highness, or his honourable Council, or to his Vice-gerent aforesaid, or the Justice of Peace
next adjoining.

Item; That you, and every Parson, Vicar, or Curat
within this Diocess, shall for every Church keep one Book
or Register, wherein he shall write the day and year of
every Wedding, Christening, and Burying, made within
your Parish for your time, and so every Man succeeding
you likewise; and also there insert every Person's Name
that shall be so wedded, christened, and buried; and for
the safe keeping of the same Book, the Parish shall be
bound to provide, of their common charges, one sure Coffer with two Locks and Keys, whereof the one to remain
with you, and the other with the Wardens of every such
Parish wherein the said Book shall be laid up; which

Book ye shall every Sunday take forth, and in the presence of the said Wardens, or one of them, write and record in the same, all the Weddings, Christenings, and Buryings, made the whole week afore; and that done, to lay up the Book in the said Coffer, as afore; And for every time that the same shall be omitted, the Party that shall be in the fault thereof, shall forfeit to the said Church 3s. 4d. to be employed on the reparation of the said Church.

Item; That ye shall every quarter of a year read these and the other former Injunctions, given unto you by the Authority of the King's Highness, open and deliberately before all your Parishioners, to the intent that both you may be the better admonished of your duty, and your said Parishioners the more incited to ensue the same for their part.

Item; Forasmuch as by a Law established, every Man is bound to pay the Tithes; no Man shall, by colour of duty, omitted by their Curats, detain their Tithes, and so re-double one wrong with another, or be his own Judg, but shall truly pay the same, as hath been accustomed, to their Parsons and Curats, without any restraint or diminution; and such lack or default as they can justly find in their Parsons and Curats to call for reformation thereof at their Ordinaries, and other Superiors hands, who, upon complaint, and due proof thereof, shall reform the same accordingly.

Item; That no Person shall from henceforth alter or change the order and manner of any Fasting-day that is commanded and indicted by the Church, nor of any Prayer, or of Divine Service, otherwise than is specified in the said Injunctions, until such time as the same shall be so ordered and transported by the King's Highness's Authority; The Eves of such Saints, whose Holy-days be abrogated be only excepted, which shall be declared henceforth to be no fasting-days; excepted also the commemoration of Thomas Becket, some-time Arch-Bishop of Canterbury, which shall be clean omitted, and in the stead thereof, the Ferial Service used.

Item; That the knolling of the Avies after Service, and certain other times, which hath been brought in and begun by the pretence of the Bishop of Rome's pardon, hence-

forth be left and omitted, lest the People do hereafter trust
to have pardon for the saying of their Avies, between the
said knolling, as they have done in times past.

Item; Where in times past Men have used in divers
places in their Processions, to sing *Ora pro nobis* to so
many Saints, that they had no time to sing the good Suffrages following, as *Parce nobis Domine,* and *Libera nos
Domine,* it must be taught and preached, that better it were
to omit *Ora pro nobis,* and to sing the other suffrages.

All which and singular Injunctions I minister unto you
and your Successors, by the King's Highness Authority to
me committed in this part, which I charge and command
you by the same Authority to observe and keep upon pain
of Deprivation, Sequestration of your Fruits, or such other
coercion as to the King's Highness, or his Vice-gerent for
the time being shall seem convenient.

*These are also in the Bp. of London's Register, Fol. 29,
30. with Bonner's Mandate to his Arch-Deacons for
observing them, 30 Sept. 1541. Anno Regn. 32.*

XII.

*Injunctions given by Thomas Arch-Bishop of Canterbury,
to the Parsons, Vicars, and other Curats in his Visitation, kept (sede vacante) within the Diocess of Hereford,
Anno Domini 1538.*

I.

FIRST; That ye, and every one of you, shall, with all
your diligence and faithful obedience, observe, and cause
to be observed, all and singular the King's Highness Injunctions, by his Graces Commissaries given in such
places as they in times past have visited.

II.

Item; That ye, and every one of you shall have, by the
first day of August next coming, as well a whole Bible in

Latin and English, or at the least a New Testament of both the same Language, as the Copies of the King's Highness Injunctions.

III.

Item; That ye shall every day study one Chapter of the said Bible, or New Testament, conferring the Latin and English together, and to begin at the first part of the Book, and so to continue until the end of the same.

IV.

Item; That ye, or none of you, shall discourage any Lay-Man from the reading of the Bible in English or Latin, but encourage them to that, admonishing them that they so read it, for reformation of their own Life, and knowledg of their Duty; and that they be not bold or presumptuous in judging of Matters afore they have perfect knowledg.

V.

Item; That ye, both in your Preaching and secret Confession, and all other works and doings, shall excite and move your Parishioners unto such Works as are commanded expresly of God, for the which God shall demand of them a strict reckoning; and all other Works which Men do of their own Will or Devotion, to teach your Parishioners that they are not to be so highly esteemed as the other; and that for the not doing of them God will not ask any accompt.

VI.

Item; That ye, nor none of you, suffer no Friar, or Religious Man, to have any Cure or Service within your Churches or Cures, except they be lawfully dispensed withal, or licensed by the Ordinary.

VII.

Item; That ye, and every one of you, do not admit any young Man or Woman to receive the Sacrament of the Altar, which never received it before, until that he or she openly in the Church, after Mass, or evening Song, upon the Holy-day, do recite, in the vulgar Tongue, the Pater Noster, the Creed, and the Ten Commandments.

VIII.

Item; That ye, and every one of you, shall two times in a quarter declare to your Parishioners the Band of Matrimony, and what great danger it is to all Men that useth their Bodies but with such Persons as they lawfully may by the Law of God. And to exhort in the said Times your Parishioners, that they make no privy Contracts, as they will avoid the extream pain of the Laws used within the King's Realm, by his Graces Authority.

XIII.

A Letter of Cromwell's to the Bishop of Landaff, directing him how to proceed in the Reformation.

An Original.

AFTER my right hearty Commendations to your Lordship, ye shall herewith receive the King's Highness Letters addressed unto you, to put you in remembrance of his Highness travels, and your duty touching order to be taken for Preaching, to the intent the People may be taught the Truth, and yet not charged at the beginning with over-many Novelties; the publication whereof, unless the same be tempered and qualified with much wisdom, do rather breed Contention, Division, and contrariety in Opinion in the unlearned Multitude, than either edify, or remove from them, and out of their hearts, such abuses as by the corrupt and unsavoury teaching of the Bishop of Rome and his Disciples have crept in the same. The effect of which Letters albeit I doubt not, but as well for the honesty of the Matter, as for your own discharge, ye will so consider and put in execution, as shall be to his Graces satisfaction in that behalf: Yet forasmuch as it hath pleased his Majesty to appoint and constitute me in the room and place of his Supream and Principal Minister, in all Matters that may touch any thing his Clergy, or their doings, I thought it also my part, for the exoneration of my Duty towards his Highness, and the rather to answer to his Graces Ex-

Cotton
Libr.
Cleop.
E. 4.

pectation, Opinion, and Trust conceived in me, and in that amongst other committed to my fidelity, to desire and pray you, in such substantial sort and manner, to travel in the execution of the Contents of his Graces said Letters; namely, for avoiding of Contrariety in preaching, of the pronunciation of Novelties, without wise and discreet qualification, and the repression of the temerity of those, that either privily, or apertly, directly or indirectly, would advance the pretended Authority of the Bishop of Rome; as I be not for my discharge enforced to complain further, and to declare what I have now written unto you for that purpose, and so to charge you with your own fault, and to devise such remedy for the same, as shall appertain: desiring your Lordship to accept my meaning herein, tending only to an honest, friendly, and Christian Reformation, for avoidage of further inconvenience, and to think none unkindness, tho in this Matter, wherein it is almost more than time to speak, I write frankly, compelled and enforced thereunto, both in respect of my private Duty, and otherwise, for my discharge; forasmuch as it pleaseth his Majesty to use me in the lieu of a Counsellour, whose Office is as an Eye to the Prince, to foresee, and in time to provide remedy for such Abuses, Enormities, and Inconveniences, as might else with a little sufferance engender more evil in his Publick Weal, than could be after recovered, with much labour, study, diligence, and travails. And thus most heartily fare you well. From the Rolls, the 7th of January.

Your Lordships Friend,

Thomas Cromwell.

XIV.

*The Commission by which Bonner held his Bishoprick of
the King.*

*Licentia Regia concessa Domino Episcopo ad exercendam
Jurisdictionem Episcopalem.*

HENRICUS Octavus, Dei Gratia Angliæ et Franciæ Rex,
Fidei Defensor, Dominus Hiberniæ, et in Terra Supremum
Ecclesiæ Anglicanæ sub Christo Caput, Reverendo in Christo Patri Edmundo Londonensi Episcopo Salutem. Quandoquidem omnis jurisdicendi Autoritas, atq; etiam juris-
dictio omnimoda, tam illa quæ Ecclesiastica dicitur quam
Sæcularis, a Regia Potestate velut a Supremo Capite, et
omnium infra Regnum nostrum Magistratuum fonte et sca-
turigine, primitus emanavit, sane illos qui jurisdictionem
hujusmodi antehac non nisi præcario fungebantur, beneficium hujusmodi sic eis ex liberalitate Regia indultum gratis animis agnoscere, idq; Regiæ Munificentiæ solummodo
acceptum referre, eique, quotiens ejus Majestati videbitur,
libenter concedere convenit. Quum itaq; nos per dilectum
Commissarium nostrum Thomam Cromwell Nobilis Ordinis
Garterii Militem, Dominum Cromwell et de Wymolden nostri privati Sigilli Custodem, nostrumq; ad quascunq; causas
Ecclesiasticas nostra Authoritate, uti Supremi Capitis dictæ Ecclesiæ Anglicanæ, quomodolibet tractand. sive ven-
tiland. Vicem gerentem, Vicarium Generalem et Officialem
Principalem, per alias Literas Patentes sigillo nostro Majori communitas, constituerimus et præfecerimus. Quia
tamen ipse Thomas Cromwell nostris et hujus Regni Angliæ tot et tam arduis negotiis adeo præpeditus existit,
quod ad omnem jurisdictionem nobis, uti Supremo Capiti
hujusmodi competentem, ubiq; locorum infra hoc Regnum
nostrum præfatum, in his quæ moram commode non patiuntur, aut sine nostrorum subditorum injuria differri non
possunt, in sua persona expediend. non sufficiet. Nos tuis
in hac parte supplicationibus humilibus inclinati, et nostrorum subditorum commodis consulere cupientes, Tibi
vices nostras sub modo et forma inferius descriptis com-
mittendas fore, Teq; licentiandum esse decernimus, ad
ordinandum igitur quoscunq; infra Dioc. tuam London.

Regist.
Bonner
fol.
primo.

ubicunq; oriundos, quos moribus et literatura prævio diligenti et rigoroso examine idoneos fore compereris, ad omnes etiam Sacros et Presbyteratus ordines promovendum, præsentatosq; ad beneficia Ecclesiastica quæcunq; infra Dioc. tuam London. constituta, si ad curam beneficiis hujusmodi imminentem sustinend. habiles reperti fuerunt et idonei, admittendum ac in et de iisdem instituendum et investigandum ; Ac etiam si res ita exigat 'destituendum, beneficiaq; ·Ecclesiastica quæcunq; ad tuam collationem sive dispositionem spectantia et pertinentia personis idoneis conferendum, atq; approbandum testamenta et ultimas voluntates quorumcunq; tuæ Diocæseos, bona, jura, sive credita non ultra summam centum librarum in bonis suis vitæ et mortis suarum temporibus habend. necnon administrationes quorumcunq; subditorum nostrorum tuæ Dioc. ab intestato decedend. quorùm bona, jura, sive credita non ultra summam prædictam vitæ et mortis suarum temporibus sese extendent, quatenus hujusmodi testatorum approbatio atq; adminstrationis commissio sive concessio per prædecessores tuos aut eorum alicujus respective Commissarios retroactis temporibus fiebat ac fieri et committi potuit, et non aliter committendum, Calculumq; ratiocinium et alia in ea parte expedienda, causasq; lites et negotia coram te aut tuis deputatis pendend. indecis. necnon alias sive alia, quascunq; sive quæcunq; ad forum Ecclesiasticum pertinentia ad te aut tuos deputatos sive deputand. per viam querelæ aut appellationis sive ex officio devolvend. sive deducend. quæ extra legum nostrarum et statutorum Regni nostri offens. còram te aut tuis Deputatis agitari, aut ad tuam sive alicujus Commissariorum per te vigore hujus Commissionis nostræ deputandorum cognitionem devolvi aut deduci valeant et possint, examinand. et decidend. Ad visitandum insuper Capitulùm Ecclesiæ tuæ Cathedral. London. civitatemq; London. necnon omnia et singula Monasteria, Abbatias et Prioratus, Collegia et alia loca pia, tam Religiosa quam Hospitalia, quæcunq; clerumq; et populum dict. Dioc. London. quatenus Ecclesiæ, Monasterii, Abbatiæ, per te sive Prædecessores tuos London. Episcopos visitatio hujusmodi temporibus retroactis exerceri potuit, ac per te sive per eosdem de legibus et statutis ac juribus Regni nostri exerceri potuit et potest, et non

aliter: Necnon ad inquirendum per te, vel alium seu alios
ad id per te deputandum sive deputandos, tam ex officio
mero mixto quam promoto super quorumcunq; excessibus,
criminibus seu delictis quibuscunq; ad forum Ecclesiasticum spectantibus infra Dioc. London. ac delinquentes sive
criminosos, juxta comperta per te in ea parte per Licita
Juris remedia pro modo culpæ, prout natura et qualitas
delicti poposcerit, coercendum et puniendum, cæteraq;
omnia et singula in Præmissis seu aliquo præmissorum,
aut circa ea necessaria seu quomodolibet opportuna, ac
alia quæcunq; Autoritatem et Jurisdictionem Episcopalem
quovismodo respiciend. et concernend. præter et ultra ea
quæ tibi ex Sacris Literis divinitus commissa esse dignos-
cantur, vice, nomine, et Autoritate nostris exequendum,
Tibi, de cujus sana doctrina, conscientiæ puritate, vitæq;
et morum integritate, ac in rebus gerendis fide et industria
plurimum confidimus, vices nostras cum potestate alium
vel alios, Commissarium vel Commissarios, ad præmissa
seu eorum aliqua surrogandi et substituendi, eosdemq; ad
placitum revocand. tenore præsentium committimus, ac
liberam facultatem concedimus; Teq; licentiam per præsentes ad nostri bene placiti duntaxat duraturas, cum cujuslibet congruæ et Ecclesiasticæ coercionis potestate quacunq; inhibitione in te datam præsentium emanata in aliquo non obstante Tuam Conscientiam coram Deo strictis-
sime onerantes, et ut summo omnium judici aliquando rationem reddere, et coram nobis tuo cum periculo corporali
respondere intendis : te admonentes ut interim tuum officium juxta Evangelii normam pie et sancte exercere stu-
deas, et ne quem ullo tempore unquam vel ad sacros ordines promoveas, vel ad curam animarum gerend. quovis
modo admittas, nisi eos duntaxat quos ad tanti et tam
venerabilis Officii functionem vitæ et morum integritas cer-
tissimis testimoniis approbata, literarum scientiæ et aliæ
qualitates requisitæ ad hoc habiles et idoneos clare et lucu-
lenter ostenderint et declaraverint; Nam ut maxime compertum cognitumq; habemus morum omnium, et Maxime
Christianæ Religionis corruptelam a malis Pastoribus in
populum emanasse, sic ut veram Christi Religionem, vitæq;
et morum emendationem a bonis Pastoribus iterum delectis
et assumptis in integrum restitutum iri haud dubie spera-

mus. In cujus rei testimonium præsentes Literas nostras
inde fieri, et Sigilli nostri quod ad Causas Ecclesiasticas
utimur appensione jussimus Communiri. Dat. 12. die mensis Novemb. Anno Dom. 1539. et Regni nostri Anno 31.

XV.

The King's Letters Patents for printing the Bible
in English.

Rot.
Pat. 31
Hea. 8.   HENRY the Eighth, &c. To all and singular Printers
and Sellers of Books within this our Realm, and all other
Officers, Ministers, and Subjects, these our Letters hearing
or seeing, Greeting. We let you wit, That being desirous
to have our People at all times convenient, give themselves
to the attaining the knowledg of God's Word, whereby they
will the better honour him, and observe and keep his Commandments; and also do their Duties better to us, being
their Prince and Sovereign Lord: And considering that
this our Zeal and Desire cannot by any mean take so good
effect, as by the granting to them the free and liberal use
of the Bible in our own natural English Tongue : so unless
it be foreseen that the same pass at the beginning by one
Translation to be perused and considered; The frailty of
Men is such, that the diversity thereof may breed and
bring forth manifold Inconveniences; as when wilful and
heady Folk shall confer upon the diversity of the said
Translations. We have therefore appointed our right trusty
and well-beloved Counsellor, the Lord Cromwell, Keeper
of our Privy-Seal, to take for us, and in our Name, special care and charge, that no manner of Person, or Persons, within this our Realm, shall enterprise, attempt, or
set in hand to print any Bible in the English Tongue of
any manner of Volum, during the space of five years next
ensuing after the Date hereof, but only all such as shall be
deputed, assigned, and admitted by the said Lord Cromwell.

The 13 Novemb. Tricesimo primo Regni.

XVI.

The Attainder of Thomas Cromwell.

*Item quædam alia petitio, formam cujusdam actus attinc-
turæ in se continens, exhibita est suæ Regiæ Majestati in
Parliamento prædicto, cujus tenor sequitur in hæc verba.*

IN their most humble-wise shewing to your most Royal
Majesty, the Lords Spiritual and Temporal, and all your
most loving and obedient Subjects, the Commons in this
your Most High Court of Parliament assembled; That
where your most Royal Majesty, our Natural Sovereign
Lord, is justly, lawfully, and really entituled to be our sole
Supream Head and Governour, of this your Realm of
England, and of the Dominions of the same; to whom,
and to none other under God, the Kingly Direction, Order,
and Governance, of your most loving and obedient Subjects, and People of this your Realm, only appertaineth
and belongeth.   And the which your most loving and obedient Subjects, your Highness prudently and quietly, without any manner of disturbance, by a long time most graciously hath preserved, sustained, and defended: And
your Highness, for the Quietness, Wealth, and Tranquillity
of your said humble and obedient Subjects, hath made,
and ordained, divers and many most godly, vertuous, and
wholsome Laws; and for due execution of the same, hath
not desisted to travel in your own most Royal Person, to
support and maintain, as well the Laws of Almighty God,
as the Laws by your Highness made and ordained, by due
and condign execution of the same Laws upon the Trans-
gressors offending contrary to the same: And your Majesty
hath always most vertuously studied and laboured, by all
ways, and all means, to and for the setting forth thereof, in
such wise as it might be most to the Honour, Glory, and
Pleasure of Almighty God; and for the common accord and
wealth of this your Realm, and other your Dominions:
And for the true execution of the same, hath elected,
chosen, and made divers, as well of your Nobles, as others
to be of your most honourable Council, as to the honour of
a Noble Prince appertaineth.   And where your Majesty
hath had a special trust and confidence in your said most

*Parlia-
ment
Rolls.*

Act 60.

*Anno
Regni
trice-
simo se-
cundo.*

trusty Counsellors, that the same your Counsellors, and
every of them, had minded and intended, and finally purposed to have followed and pursued your most Godly and
Princely Purpose, as of truth the more number hath most
faithfully done; Yet nevertheless Thomas Cromwell, now
Earl of Essex, whom your Majesty took and received into
your trusty Service, the same Thomas then being a Man of
very base and low degree, and for singular favour, trust,
and confidence, which your Majesty bare and had in him,
did not only erect and advance the same Thomas unto the
State of an Earl, and enriched him with many-fold Gifts,
as well of Goods, as of Lands and Offices, but also him,
the said Thomas Cromwell, Earl of Essex, did erect and
make one of your most trusty Counsellors, as well concerning your Grace's Supream Jurisdictions Ecclesiastical,
as your most high secret Affairs Temporal.   Nevertheless
your Majesty now of late hath found, and tried, by a large
number of Witnesses, being your faithful Subjects, and
Personages of great Honour, Worship, and Discretion, the
said Thomas Cromwell, Earl of Essex, contrary to the singular trust and confidence which your Majesty had in him,
to be the most false and corrupt Traitor, Deceiver, and
Circumventor against your most Royal Person, and the
Imperial Crown of this your Realm, that hath been known,
seen, or heard of in all the time of your most Noble Reign;
Insomuch that it is manifestly proved and declared, by the
Depositions of the Witnesses aforesaid, That the same
Thomas Cromwell, Earl of Essex, usurping upon your
Kingly Estate, Power, Authority, and Office; without your
Grace's Commandment or Assent, hath taken upon him to
set at liberty divers Persons, being convicted and attainted
of Misprision of High Treason; and divers other being
apprehended, and in Prison, for Suspection of High Treason; and over that, divers and many times, at sundry
places, in this your Realm, for manifold Sums of Mony to
him given, most traiterously hath taken upon him, by several Writings, to give and grant, as well unto Aliens, as to
your Subjects, a great number of Licenses for conveighing
and carrying of Mony, Corn, Grain, Beans, Beer, Leather,
Tallow, Bells, Mettals, Horses, and other Commodities of
this your Realm, contrary to your Highness's most Godly

and Gracious Proclamations made for the Common-Wealth
of your People of this your Realm in that behalf, and in
derogation of your Crown and Dignity. And the same
Thomas Cromwell, elated, and full of pride, contrary to
his most bounden Duty, of his own Authority and Power,
not regarding your Majesty Royal; And further, taking
upon him your Power, Sovereign Lord, in that behalf, divers and many times most traiterously hath constituted,
deputed, and assigned, many singular Persons of your
Subjects to be Commissioners in many your great, urgent,
and weighty Causes and Affairs, executed and done in this
your Realm, without the assent, knowledg, or consent of
your Highness. And further also, being a Person of as
poor and low degree, as few be within this your Realm;
pretending to have so great a stroak about you, our, and his
natural Sovereign Liege Lord, that he letted not to say pub-
lickly, and declare, That he was sure of you; which is detestable, and to be abhorred amongst all good subjects in any
Christian Realm, that any Subject should enterprize or
take upon him so to speak of his Sovereign Liege Lord and
King. And also of his own Authority and Power, without you Highness's consent, hath made, and granted, as
well to Strangers as to your own Subjects, divers and
many Pass-ports, to pass over the Seas with Horses, and
great Sums of Mony, without any search. And over that,
most Gracious Sovereign Lord, amongst divers other his
Treasons, Deceits, and Falshoods, the said Thomas Cromwell, Earl of Essex, being a detestable Heretick, and being in himself utterly disposed to sett and sow common
Sedition and Variance among your true and loving Subjects, hath secretly set forth and dispersed into all Shires,
and other Territories of this your Realm, and other your
Dominions, great numbers of false Erroneous Books,
whereof many were printed and made beyond the Seas,
and divers other within this Realm, comprising and declaring, amongst many other Evils and Errors, manifest
Matters to induce and lead your Subjects to diffidence, and
refusal of the true and sincere Faith and Belief, which
Christian Religion bindeth all Christian People to have, in
the most Holy and Blessed Sacrament of the Altar, and
other Articles of Christian Religion, most graciously de-

clared by your Majesty, by Authority of Parliament: And certain Matters comprised in some of the said Books, hath caused to be translated into our maternal and English Tongue: And upon report made unto him by the Translator thereof, that the Matter so translated hath expresly been against the said most Blessed and Holy Sacrament; Yet the same Thomas Cromwell, Earl of Essex, after he had read the same Translation, most heretically hath affirmed the same material Heresie so translated, to be good; and further hath said, that he found no fault therein; and over that, hath openly and obstinately holden Opinion, and said, That it was as lawful for every Christian Man to be a Minister of the said Sacrament, as well as a Priest. And where also your most Royal Majesty, being a Prince of Vertue, Learning, and Justice, of singular Confidence and Trust, did constitute and make the same Thomas Cromwell, Earl of Essex, your Highness's Vicegerent within this your Realm of England; and by the same, gave unto him Authority and Power, not only to redress and reform all, and all manner of Errors, and Erroneous Opinions, insurging and growing among your loving and obedient Subjects of this your Realm, and of the Dominions of the same, but also to order and direct all Ecclesiastical and Spiritual Causes within your said Realm and Dominions; the said Thomas Cromwell, Earl of Essex, not regarding his Duty to Almighty God, and to your Highness, under the Seal of your Vicegerent, hath, without your Grace's assent or knowledg, licensed and authorized divers Persons, detected and suspected of Heresies, openly to teach and preach amongst your most loving and obedient Subjects, within this your Realm of England. And under the pretence and colour of the said great Authorities and Cures, which your Majesty hath committed unto him in the Premisses, hath not only, of his corrupt and damnable Will and Mind, actually, at some time, by his own Deed and Commandment, and at many other times by his Letters, expresly written to divers worshipful Persons, being Sheriffs, in sundry Shires of this your Realm, falsly suggesting thereby your Grace's Pleasure so to have been, caused to be set at large many false Hereticks, some being there indicted, and some other being thereof apprehended, and in ward: and com-

monly, upon complaints made by credible Persons unto
the said Thomas Cromwell, Earl of Essex, of great and
most detestable Heresies committed and sprung in many
places of this your Realm, with declaration of the Specialities of the same Heresies, and the Names of the Offenders therein, the same Thomas Cromwell, Earl of Essex,
by his crafty and subtil means and inventions, hath not
only defended the same Hereticks from Punishment and
Reformation; but being a fautor, maintainer, and sup-
porter of Hereticks, divers times hath terribly rebuked divers of the said credible Persons being their Accusers, and
some others of them hath persecuted and vexed by Imprisonment and otherwise. So that thereby many of your
Grace's true and loving Subjects have been in much dread
and fear, to detect or accuse such detestable known Hereticks; the particularities and specialities of which said
abominable Heresies, Errors, and Offences, committed and
done by the said Thomas Cromwell, being over-tedious,
long, and of too great number here to be expressed, declared, or written. And to the intent to have those damnable Errors and Heresies, to be inculcated, impressed,
and infixed in the Hearts of your Subjects, as well contrary to God's Laws, as to your Laws and Ordinances.
Most Gracious Soveraign Lord, the same Thomas Cromwell, Earl of Essex, hath allured and drawn unto him
by Retainours, many of your Subjects sunderly inhabiting in every of your said Shires and territories, as well erroneously perswading and declaring to them the Contents
of the false erroneous Books, above-written, to be good, true,
and best standing with the most Holy Word and Pleasure of
God; as other his false and heretical Opinions and Errors;
whereby, and by his Confederacies therein, he hath caused
many of your faithful Subjects to be greatly infected with
Heresies, and other Errors, contrary to the right Laws and
Pleasure of Almighty God. And the same Thomas Cromwell, Earl of Essex, by the false and traiterous means
above-written, supposing himself to be fully able, by force
and strength, to maintain and defend his said abominable
Treasons, Heresies, and Errors, not regarding his most
bounden Duty to Almighty God, and his Laws, nor the natural Duty of Allegiance to your Majesty, in the last day

of March, in the 30 year of your most gracious Reign, in the Parish of St. Peter the Poor, within your City of London, upon demonstration and declaration then and there made unto him, that there were certain new Preachers, as Robert Barnes Clerk, and other, whereof part been now committed to the Tower of London for preaching and teaching of Lead Learning against your Highness's Proclamations; the same Thomas affirming the said preaching to be good, most detestably, arrogantly, erroneously, wilfully, maliciously, and traiterously, expresly against your Laws and Statutes, then and there did not lett to declare, and say, these most traiterous and detestable words ensuing, amongst other words of like matter and effect; that is to say, that " If the King would turn from it, yet I would not turn; And if the King did turn, and all his People, I would fight in the Field in mine own Person, with my Sword in my hand, against him and all others;" and then, and there, most traiterously pulled out his Dagger, and held it on high, saying these words, " Or else this Dagger thrust me to the heart, if I would not die in that Quarrel against them all: And I trust, if I live one year or two, it shall not lie in the King's Power to resist or lett it if he would." And further, then and there swearing by a great Oath, traiterously affirmed the same his traiterous saying and pronunciation of words, saying, " I will do so indeed," extending up his Arm, as though he had had a Sword in his Hand; to the most perilous, grievous, and wicked Example of all other your loving, faithful, and obedient Subjects in this your Realm, and to the peril of your most Royal Person. And moreover, our most Gracious Sovereign Lord, the said Thomas Cromwell, Earl of Essex, hath acquired and obtained into his possession, by Oppression, Bribery, Extort, Power, and false Promises made by him to your Subjects of your Realm, innumerable Sums of Mony and Treasure; and being so enriched, hath had your Nobles of your Realm in great disdain, derision, and detestation, as by express words by him most opprobriously spoken hath appeared. And being put in remembrance of others, of his estate, which your Highness hath called him unto, offending in like Treasons, the last day of January, in the 31 year of your Most noble Reign, at the Pa-

rish of St. Martin in the Field, in the County of Middlesex, BOOK III.
most arrogantly, willingly, maliciously, and traiterously,
said, published, and declared, that " If the Lords would handle him so, that he would give them such a Break-fast as never
was made in England, and that the proudest of them should
know;" to the great peril and danger, as well of your Majesty,
as of your Heirs and Successors: For the which his most detestable and abominable Heresies and Treasons, and many
other his like Offences and Treasons, over-long here to be
rehearsed and declared. Be it Enacted, Ordained, and
Established by your Majesty, with the Assent of the Lords
Spiritual and Temporal, and the Commons in this present
Parliament assembled, and by the Authority of the same,
That the said Thomas Cromwell, Earl of Essex, for his
abominable and detestable Heresies and Treasons, by him
most abominably, heretically, and traiterously practised,
committed, and done, as well against Almighty God, as
against your Majesty, and this your said Realm, shall
be, and stand, by Authority of this present Parliament,
convicted and attainted of Heresie and High Treason, and
be adjudged an abominable and detestable Heretick and
Traitor; and shall have and suffer such pains of death,
losses, and forfeitures of Goods, Debts, and Chattels, as
in cases of Heresie and High Treason, or as in cases of
either of them, at the pleasure of your most Royal Majesty.
And that the same Thomas Cromwell, Earl of Essex, shall,
by Authority abovesaid, lose, and forfeit to your Highness,
and to your Heirs and Successors, all such his Castles,
Lordships, Mannors, Mesuages, Lands, Tenements, Rents,
Reversions, Remainders, Services, Possessions, Offices,
Rights, Conditions, and all other his Hereditaments, of
what names, natures, or qualities soever they be, which he
the said Thomas Cromwell, Earl of Essex, or any other to
his use had, or ought to have had, of any Estate of Inheritance, in Fee-Simple or Fee-Tail, in Reversion or Possession, at the said last day of March, in the said thirtieth
Year of your most Gracious Reign, or at any time sith or
after, as in Cases of High Treason. And that all the said
Castles, Lordships, Mannors, Lands, Mesuages, Tenements, Rents, Reversions, Remainders, Services, Possessions, Offices, and all other the Premisses forfeited, as is

abovesaid, shall be deemed, invested, and adjudged, in the
lawful, real, and actual possession of your Highness, your
Heirs, and Successors for ever in the same, and such
estate, manner, and form, as if the said Castles, Lordships,
Mannors, Mesuages, Lands, Tenements, Rents, Reversions, Remainders, Services, Possessions, Offices, and
other the Premisses, with their Appurtenances, and every
of them, were specially or particularly founden, by Office
or Offices, Inquisition or Inquisitions, to be taken by any
Escheator, or Escheators, or any other Commissioner or
Commissioners, by virtue of any Commission or Commissions to them, or any of them, to be directed in any County
or Counties, Shire or Shires, within this your Realm of
England, where the said Castles, and other the Premisses,
or any of them, been, or do lay, and returned into any of
your Majesties Courts. Saving to all and singular, Person
and Persons, Bodies politick and corporate, their Heirs
and Successors, and their Successors and Assignees of
every of them, other than the said Thomas Cromwell, Earl
of Essex, and his Heirs, and all and every other Person
and Persons, claiming by the same Thomas Cromwell, and
to his use, all such Right, Title, Entrie, Possession, Interest, Reversions, Remainders, Lease, Leases, Conditions,
Fees, Offices, Rents, Annuities, Commons, and all other
Commodities, Profits, and Hereditaments whatsoever they
or any of them might, should, or ought to have had, if this
Act had never been had nor made. Provided always, and
be it enacted by the Authority aforesaid, that this Act of
Attainder, ne any Offence, ne other thing therein contained,
extend not unto the Deanery of Wells, in the County of
Sommerset; nor to any Mannors, Lands, Tenements, or
Hereditaments thereunto belonging; nor be in any wise
prejudicial or hurtful unto the Bishop of Bath and Wells,
nor to the Dean and Chapter of the Cathedral Church of
St. Andrew of Wells, nor to any of them, nor to any of
their Successors; but that the said Bishop, Dean, and
Chapters, and their Successors, and every of them, shall
and may have, hold, use, occupy, and enjoy, all and singular their Titles, Rights, Mannors, Lands, Tenements, Rents,
Reversions, and Services, and all and singular other their
Hereditaments, Commodities, and Profits, of what nature,

kind, or quality, or condition soever they be, in as ample and large manner and form, as tho this Act of Attainder, or any Offence therein mentioned, had never been had, committed, nor made; and that from hence-forth the Dean, and his Successors, Deans of the said Cathedral Church that hereafter shall be prefected, elected, and admitted to the same, Shall, by the Authority aforesaid, be Dean of the said Cathedral Church, fully and wholly incorporated with the Chapter of the same, in as ample, large, and like manner and form, to all intents and purposes, as the Deans before this time hath been and used to be, with the said Chapter of the said Cathedral Church of Wells. And that the same Dean and Chapter, and their Successors, shall have, occupy, and enjoy, all and singular their such Possessions, Mannors, Lands, Tenements, Rents, Reversions, and Services, and all and singular their Hereditaments, of what nature, kind, name or names they be called or known. And shall be adjudged and deemed in actual and real possession and season of, and in the same Premisses, to all intents and purposes, according to their old Corporation, as tho this Act of Attainder, or any thing, clause, or matter therein contained had never been had, committed, nor made. This said Act of Attainder, or any other Act, Provision, or any thing heretofore had or made to the contrary notwithstanding. *Cui quidem petitioni cum provisione prædict. perlect. et intellect. per dictum Dominum Regem ex Authoritate et consensu Parliamenti prædicti sic Responsum est,*

Soit faict come il est desiro.

BOOK III.

<h1 style="text-align:center;">XVII.</h1>

Cromwell's Letter to the King concerning his Marriage with Ann of Cleve. An Original.

To the King, my most Gracious Sovereign Lord his Royal Majesty.

MOST Merciful King, and most Gracious Sovereign Lord, may it please the same to be advertised, That the

Cott. Libr. Otho C. 10.

last time it pleased your benign Goodness to send unto me the Right Honourable Lord Chancellor, the Right Honourable Duke of Norff. and the Lord Admiral, to examine, and also to declare unto me divers things from your Majesty; among the which, one special thing they moved, and thereupon they charged me, as I would answer before God at the dreadful day of Judgment, and also upon the extreme danger and damnation of my Soul and Conscience, to say what I knew in the Marriage, and concerning the Marriage, between your Highness and the Queen. To the which I answered as I knew, declaring unto them the Particulars, as nigh as I then could call to remembrance. Which when they had heard, they, in your Majesty's Name, and upon like charge as they had given me before, commanded me to write to your Highness the truth, as much as I knew in that Matter; which now I do, and the very truth, as God shall save me, to the uttermost of my knowledg. First; After your Majesty heard of the Lady Ann of Cleves arrival at Dover, and that her Journies were appointed toward Greenwich, and that she should be at Rochester on New-years Even at night, your Highness declared to me, that you would privily visit her at Rochester, upon New-years-day, adding these words, " To nourish love;" which accordingly your Grace did upon New-years-day, as is above-said. And the next day, being Friday, your Grace returned to Greenwich, where I spake with your Grace, and demanded of your Majesty, How ye liked the Lady Ann: your Highness answered, as me thought, heavily, and not pleasantly, " Nothing so well as she was spoken of;" saying further, " That if your Highness had known as much before as ye then knew, she should not have come within this Realm;" saying, as by the way of lamentation, " What Remedy?" Unto the which I answered and said, I know none but was very sorry therefore; and so God knoweth I was, for I thought it a hard beginning. The next day after the receipt of the said Lady, and her entry made unto Greenwich, and after your Highness had brought her to her Chamber, I then waited upon your Highness into your Privy-Chamber; and being there, your Grace called me unto you, saying to me these words, or the like, " My Lord, is it not as I told you? say what they will, she is nothing so fair as she hath been reported; howbeit she is well and seemly." Whereunto I answered and said, By my Faith, Sir, ye say truth; adding thereunto, that I thought she had a Queenly manner; and nevertheless was sorry that your Grace was no better content: And thereupon your Grace commanded me to call together your Council, which were these by name; The Arch-Bishop of Canterbury, the Dukes of Norfolk and Suffolk, my Lord Admiral, and my Lord of Duresme, and my self, to commune of these Matters, and to know what Commissions the Agents of Cleves had brought, as well touching the performance of the Covenants sent before from hence to Dr. Wotton, to have been concluded in Cleves, as also in the declaration how the Matters stood for the Covenants of Marriage, between the Duke of Lorrain's Son, and the said Lady Ann. Whereupon Olislager and Hegeston were called, and the Matters purposed; whereby it plainly appeared, that they were much astonished and abashed, and desired that they might make answer in the next morning, which was Sunday: And upon the Sunday in the morning your said Counsellors and they met together early, and there eft-soons was proposed unto them, as well touching the Commission for the performance of the Treaty and Articles sent to Mr. Wotton, as also touching the Contracts and Covenants of Marriage between the Duke of Lorrain's Son, and the Lady Ann, and what terms they stood in. To which things so proposed, they answered as Men much perplexed, That as touching Commission, they had none to treat concerning the Articles sent to Mr. Wotton. And as to the Contract and Covenants of Marriage they could say nothing, but that a Revocation was made, and that they were but Spousals. And finally, after much reasoning, they offered themselves to remain Prisoners, until such time as they should have sent unto them from Cleves the first Articles ratified under the Duke their Masters Sign and Seal, and also the Copy of the Revocation made between the Duke of Lorrain's Son and the Lady Ann. Upon the which Answers, I was sent to your Highness by my Lords of your Council, to declare to your Highness their Answer; and came to you, by the Privy Way, into your Privy-Chamber, and declared unto the same all the Circumstances, wherewith your Grace was very much displeased, saying, "I am not well handled;" insomuch that I might well perceive that your Highness was fully determined not to have gone through with the Marriage at that time, saying unto me these words, or the like in effect; " That if it were not that she is come so far unto my Realm, and the great Preparations that my States and People have made for her, and for fear of making a ruffel in the World; that is, to mean to drive her Brother into the hands of the Emperor and the French King's hands, being now together, I would never have ne married her." So that I might well perceive your Grace was neither content with the Person, ne yet with the Proceedings of the Agents; And at after-dinner, the said Sunday, your Grace sent for all your said Counsellors in, repeating how your Highness was handled, as well touching the said Articles, as also the said Matter of the Duke of Lorrain's Son. It might, and I doubt not, did appear unto them how loth your Highness was to have married at that time. And thereupon, and upon the Considerations aforesaid, your Grace thought that it should be well done that she should make a Protestation before your said Counsellors and Notaries to be present, that she was free from all Contracts; which was done accordingly. And thereupon I repairing to your Highness, declared how that she had made her Protestation. Whereunto your Grace answered in effect these words, or much like; " Is there none other Remedy, but that I must needs, against my Will, put my Neck in the Yoke;" and so departed; leaving your Highness in a study or pensiveness. And yet your Grace determined the next morning to go through; and in the morning, which was Monday, your Majesty preparing your self towards the Ceremonies; There was one Question, Who should lead to the Church? And it was appointed that the Earl of Essex deceased, and an Earl that came with her, should lead her to the Church. And thereupon one came to your Highness, and said to you That the Earl of Essex was not come; whereupon your Grace appointed me to be one that should lead her: And so I went into her Chamber, to the intent to have done your Commandment; and shortly after I came into her Chamber, the Earl of Essex was come: Whereupon I repaired back again into your Graces Privy-Chamber, and shewed your Highness how he was come; and thereupon your Majesty advanced towards the Gallery out of your Privy-Chamber; and your Grace being in and about the midst of your Chamber of Presence, called me unto you, saying these words, or the like in sentence; " My Lord, if it were not to satisfy the World, and my Realm, I would not do that I must do this day for none earthly thing;" and therewith one brought your Grace Word that she was coming; and thereupon your Grace repaired into the Gallery towards the Closet, and there paused for her coming, being nothing content that she so long tarried as I judged then. And so consequently she came, and your Grace afterward proceeded to the Ceremonies; and they being finished, travelled the day as appertained, and the night after the custom. And in the morning, on Tuesday, I repairing to your Majesty into your Privy-Chamber, finding your Grace not so pleasant as I trusted to have done, I was so bold to ask your Grace how you liked the Queen? Whereunto your Grace soberly answered, saying, "That I was not all men, surely, as ye know, I liked her before not well; but now I like her much worse; for," quoth your Highness, " I have felt her Belly, and her Breasts, and thereby, as I can judg, she should be no Maid; which strook me so to the Heart when I felt them, that I had neither will nor courage to proceed any further in other Matters;" saying, " I have left her as good a Maid as I found her :" Which me thought then ye spake displeasantly, which made me very sorry to hear; Your Highness also after Candlemass, and before Showstie, once or twice said, " That ye were in the same case with her as ye were afore, and that your Heart could never consent to meddle with her carnally." Notwithstanding your Highness alledged, that ye for the most part used to lay nightly, or every second night by her, and yet your Majesty ever said, " That she was as good a Maid for you, as ever her Mother bare her, for any thing ye had ministred to her." Your Highness shewed to me also in Lent last passed, at such time as your Grace had some communication with her of my Lady Mary, how that she began to wax stubborn and willful, ever lamenting your fate, and ever verifying that ye never had any carnal knowledg with her: And also after Easter, your Grace likewise, at divers times, and in the Whitsun-week, in your Grace's Privy-Chamber at Greenwich, exceedingly lamented your fate, and that your greatest grief was, " That ye should surely never have any more Children for the comfort of this Realm, if ye should so continue;" assuring me, "that before God ye thought she was never your lawful Wife." At which time your Grace knoweth what answer I made; which was, that I would for my part do my utmost to comfort and deliver your Grace of your Afflictions; and how sorry I was both to see and hear your Grace God knoweth. Your Grace divers times sithen Whitsuntide, ever alleadging one thing, and also saying, " That ye had as much to do to move the consent of your Heart and Mind as ever did Man, and that you took God to witness; but ever," you said, " the obstacle could never out of your Mind." And, Gracious Prince, after that you had first seen her at Rochester, I never thought in my heart that ye were or would be contented with that Marriage. And, Sir, I know now in what case I stand, in which is only the Mercy of God and your Grace; if I have not, to the uttermost of my remembrance, said the Truth, and the whole Truth in this Matter, God never help me. I am sure there is, as I think, no Man in this your Realm that knew more in this than I did, your Highness only excepted. And I am sure, my Lord Admiral calling to his remembrance, can shew your Highness, and be my Witness what I said unto him after your Grace came from Rochester, yea, and after your Grace's Marriage: And also now of late, sithence Whitsuntide, and I doubt not but many and divers of my Lords of your Council, both before your Marriage and sithence, have right-well perceived that your Majesty hath not been well pleased with your Marriage. And as I shall answer to God, I never thought your Grace content, after you had once seen her at Rochester. And this is all that I know, most gracious and most merciful Sovereign Lord, beseeching Almighty God, who ever hath in all your Causes counselled, preserved, opened, maintained, relieved, and defended your Highness; So he will now vouchsafe to counsel you, preserve you, maintain you, remedy you, relieve and defend you, as may be most to your Honour, with Prosperity, Health, and Comfort of your Hearts desire. For the which, and for the long Life, and prosperous Reign of your most Royal Majesty, I shall, during my Life, and whiles I am here, pray to Almighty God, that he of his most abundant Goodness will help, aid, and comfort you, after your continuance of Nestor's Years: that that most noble Imp, the Princes Grace, your most dear Son, may succeed you to Reign long, prosperously, and feliciously to God's pleasure: beseeching most humbly your Grace to pardon this my rude writing, and to consider that I a most woful Prisoner, ready to take the Death, when it shall please God and your Majesty; and yet the frail flesh inciteth me continually to call to your Grace for Mercy and Grace for mine Offences; and thus Christ save, preserve, and keep you.

> Written at the Tower this Wednesday, the last of
> June, with the heavy Heart, and trembling hand, of
> your Highness's most heavy and most miserable
> Prisoner, and poor Slave,
>
> Thomas Cromwell.

Most Gracious Prince, I cry for Mercy, Mercy, Mercy.

XVIII.

The King's own Declaration concerning it.
An Original.

First; I depose and declare, That this hereafter written Cott. Libr. Otho C. 10. is meerly the verity intended, upon none sinister affection, nor yet upon none hatred nor displeasure, and herein I take God to witnesse. Now to the Matter I say and affirm; That when the first communication was had with me for the Marriage of the Lady Ann of Cleves, I was glad to hearken to it, trusting to have some assured Friend by it; I much doubting that time, both the Emperor, France, and the Bishop of Rome; and also because I heard so much, both of her excellent Beauty and vertuous Conditions, But when I saw her at Rochester, the first time that ever I saw her, it rejoiced my heart that I had kept me free from making any Pact or Bond before with her till I saw her my self; for then I adsure you I liked her so ill, and so far contrary to that she was praised, that I was woe that ever she came into England; and deliberated with my self, that if it were possible to find means to break off, I would never enter Yoke with her. Of which misliking, both the great Master, the Admiral that now is, and the Master of the Horses, can and will bear record. Then after my repair to Greenwich, the next day after I think, and doubt not, but that the Lord of Essex well examined, can, and will, or hath declared what I then said to him in that case; not doubting, but since he is a Person which knoweth himself condemned to die by Act of Parliament, will not damn his Soul, but truly declare the Truth, not only at that time spoken by me, but also continually till the day of Marriage; and also many times after, whereby my lack of consent, I doubt not, doth or shall well appear; And also lack enough of the Will and Power to consummate the same; wherein both he, my Physicians, the Lord Privy Seal that now is, Hennage and Denny can, and I doubt not will testify according to truth, which is, That I never for love to the Woman consented to marry; nor yet if she brought Maiden-head with her, took any from her by true Carnal Copulation. This is my brief, true, and perfect Declaration.

H. R.

XIX.

The Judgment of the Convocation for annulling of the Marriage with Ann of Cleve.

Regist. Cran-mer. TENOR vero Literarum Testimonialium hujusmodi sequitur, et est talis. Excellentissimo in Christo Principi, &c. Thomas Cantuarien. et Edwardus Eboracen. Archiepiscopi, ceteriq; Episcopi et reliquus vestri Regni Angliæ clerus Autoritate Literarum Commissionalium Vestræ Majestatis, Congregati ac Synodum universalem repræsentantes, cum obsequio, reverentia et honore debitis, salutem et fœlicitatem. Cum nos humillimi et Majestatis Vestræ devotissimi subditi, Convocati et Congregati sumus virtute Commissionis Vestræ magno sigillo Vestro sigillat. dat. 6 Julii Anno fœlicissimi Regni Vestri tricesimo secundo, quam accepimus in hæc quæ sequitur verba.

Henricus Octavus Dei Gratia Angliæ, &c. Archiepiscopis Cantuarien. et Eborac. ac cæteris Regni nostri Angliæ Episcopis, Decanis, Archidiaconis, et universo Clero, salutem. Egerunt apud nos Regni nostri proceres et populus, ut cum nuper quædam emerserint, quæ ut illi putant ad nos Regniq; nostri successionem pertineant, inter quæ præcipua est, causa et conditio Matrimonii quod cum Illustri et Nobili Fœmina Domina Anna Clevensi propter externam quidem conjugii speciem, perplexum alioqui etiam multis ac variis modis ambiguum videtur; Nos ad ejusdem Matrimonii disquisitionem ita procedere dignaremur ut opinionem Vestram qui in Ecclesia nostra Angliæna scientiam Verbi Dei et Doctrinam profitemini exquiramus, vobisq; discutiendum Autoritatem ita demandemus, ut si animis Vestris fuerit persuasum Matrimonium cum præfata Domina Anna minime consistere aut cohærere debere; nos ad Matrimonium contrahend. cum alia liberos esse, Vestro, Patrum ac reliquæ deinde Ecclesiæ suffragio pronuncietur et confirmetur. Nos autem qui Vestrum in reliquis Ecclesiæ hujus Anglicanæ negotiis gravioribus quæ Ecclesiasticam Oeconomiam et Religionem spectant judicium amplecti solemus, ad veritatis explicandæ testimonium omnino necessarium rati sumus Causæ hujusmodi Matrimonialis seriem et circumstantias vobis exponi et communicari curare, ut quod vos per Dei Leges licere decreveritis, id demum totius Ecclesiæ nostræ Autoritate innixi licite facere et exequi audeamus. Vos itaq; Convocari et in Synodum Universalem nostra Autoritate convenire volentes, vobis conjunctim et divisim committimus atq; mandamus ut inspecta hujus negotii veritate, ac solum Deum præ oculis habentes, quod verum, quod justum, quod honestum, quod sanctum est, id nobis de communi Concilio scripto annuncio renuncietis et de communi consensu licere definiatis : Nempe hoc unum a vobis nostro

jure postulamus, ut tanquam fida et proba Ecclesiæ membra
causæ huic Ecclesiasticæ, quæ maxima est, in justitia et
veritate adesse velitis et eam maturime juxta Commissionem vobis in hac parte factam absolvere et expedire.
In cujus rei Testimonium has Literas nostras fieri fecimus
Patentes, Teste meipso apud Westmon. sexto die Julii,
Anno Regni nostri tricesimo secundo. Nos tenorem et
effectum Vestræ Commissionis per omnia sequentes, postquam matura deliberatione perpendimus et consideravimus
omnes Matrimonii prætensi inter Vestram Majestatem Illustrissimam et Nobilem fœminam Dominam Annam Clevensem circumstantias, nobis multis modis expositas, cog-
nitas et perspectas, tandem ad definitionem et determina-
tionem sequentem, quam communi omnium consensu jus-
torumq; animorum nostrorum judicio ac recto conscientiæ
dictamine protulimus, processimus, in hunc modum et
(quod tenor Vestræ Commissionis exigit) Vestræ Nobilis-
simæ Majestati in hoc præsenti scripto referend. duximus,
et significamus prout sequitur.

Primum itaq; comperimus et consideravimus Matrimonium inter Majestatem Vestram et Nobilem fœminam Dominam Annam Clevensem prætensam præcontracto quodam sive sponsaliorum, sive Matrimonii, inter dictam Dominam Annam et Marchionem Lotharingiæ concluso ambiguum, plane impeditum et perplexum reddi; Annimad-
vertimus enim quod quamvis Vestra Majestas in prima
hujus Matrimonii prætensi tractatione præcontractus prædicti, et de quo tum sermo multus habebatur, discussionem
et declarationem ante solemnizandum cum dicta Domina
Anna Matrimonium tanta instantia exegerit, ut pro conditione contrahendi deinde Matrimonii fuisse merito existi-
mari possit, qua conditione defecta nihil ageretur; atq;
hæc cum ita se haberent tamen neque ante solemnizationem
illa de præcontractu ambiguitas expedita et declarata est,
cum id ipsum tum temporis Majestas Vestra denuo expos-
ceret et efflagitaret, cui clara jam et expedita esse omnia
falso renunciabatur, neq; postea quicquam efficax ut promissum ab Oratoribus fuerat, huc transmissum est, quo
scrupulus ille ex præcontractu natus eximeretur, tolleretur
aut amoveretur, adeo quidem ut prætensum Matrimonium
inter Majestatem Vestram et Dominam Annam prædictam.

non modo ex conditionis defectu corruerit, sed si nulla
conditio hujusmodi omnino fuisset, certe quidem Matrimonium hujusmodi prætensum ex sola præcontractus hujusmodi causa non explicata in suspenso manserit, in eum
etiam casum nullius vigoris omnino ac valoris pronuncian-
dum, quó præcontractum illum verbis de præsenti factum
fuisse constiterit, id quod multis de causis est verisimilius
et merito suspectum haberi potest.

Consideravimus præterea ex his quæ allegata, affirmata
et probata nobis fuerunt, quod prætensum Matrimonium
inter Majestatem vestram et Dominam Annam prædictam
internum, purum, perfectum et integrum consensum non
habuit: Imo contra quemadmodum inter ipsa tractationis
initia, cum de hoc Matrimonio ageretur, plurimus illece-
brarum fucus adhibitus est, et magnus laudationum acer-
vus supra fidem cumulatus, ut hic perduceretur et obtru-
deretur ignota, ita solemnizationis actus qui instabat a
Majestate Vestra animo reluctante et dissentiente exortus
est, causis maximis et gravissimis urgentibus et prementi-
bus quæ animum invitum et alienum perpellere merito
possent.

Consideravimus etiam carnalem Copulam inter Majestatem Vestram et prædictam Dominam Annam minime secu-
tam esse, nec cum ea justo impedimento intercedente consequi deinde posse. Quæ omnia ex his quas audivimus
probationibus, vera et certa esse existimamus. Postremo
illud quoq; Consideramus, quod et nobis ab aliis propositum etiam nos verum esse fatemur, agnoscimus et approba-
mus, viz. ut si Majestas Vestra (modo ne fiat divinæ jus-
sioni præjudicium) in libertate contrahendi Matrimonii
cum alia esse declaretur, maxime totius Regni beneficio id
futurum. Cum quidem Regni fœlicitas omnis et conser-
vatio, tum in Regia Vestra persona ad Dei honorem et di-
vinarum legum executionem conservandam consistit, tum
in vitandis etiam sinistris omnibus opinionibus et scandalis
quæ de Majestatis Vestræ progenie post natam nobis ex
prætenso Matrimonio sobolem suborirentur, si præcontractus ille de quo diximus, et cujus declaratio nulla secuta
est, prædictæ Dominæ Annæ objiceretur. His itaq; de
causis et considerationibus aliisq; multis non necessariis
quæ exprimantur, cum separatim singulis, tum conjunctim

T 2

omnibus consideratis et perpensis, Nos Archiepiscopi et Episcopi, cum Decanis, Archiadiaconis, et reliquo hujus Regni Clero nunc congregato, circumstantias facti ejusq; veritatem ut antedictum est considerantes, tum vero quid Ecclesia in hujusmodi casibus et possit facere et sæpenumero antehac fecerit perpendentes, tenore præsentium declaramus et definimus, Majestatem Vestram prædicto Matrimonio prætenso, utpote nullo et invalido, non alligari, sed alio desuper judicio non expectato Ecclesiæ suæ Autoritate fretam posse arbitrio suo ad contrahend. et consummand. Matrimonium cum quavis fœmina, divino jure vobiscum contrahere non prohibita, procedere, prætenso illo cum Domina Anna prædicta Matrimonio non obstante.

Similiter Dominam Annam prædictam non obstante Matrimonio prætenso cum Majestate Vestra, quod nullo pacto obstare debere Decernimus, posse arbitrio suo cum quavis alia persona divino jure non prohibita Matrimonium contrahere. Hæc Nos Clerum et doctam Ecclesiæ Anglicanæ partem repræsentantes, tum vera, justa, honesta, et sancta esse Affirmamus, tum eisdem qui perfectissime, integerrime, et efficacissime ad omnem intentionem, propositum et effectum a nobis exigi potest, Consentimus et Assentimur per præsentes. In quorum omnium et singulorum testimonium hæc scripta manuum nostrarum subscriptione, communimus, utriusq; etiam Archiepiscopi sigillo apposito. Dat. Westmon. nono die mensis Julii, Anno Dom. 1540.

XX.

*Ann of Cleve's Letter ** to her Brother.*

BROTHER,

BECAUSE I had rather ye knew the Truth by mine Advertisement, than for want thereof ye should be deceived by vain Reports, I write these present Letters unto you, by which ye shall understand, That being advertised how

* This Letter was drawn by Gardiner; but it is not certain that it was sent.

the Nobles and Commons of this Realm desired the King's **BOOK III.** Highness here to commit the examination of the Matter of Marriage, between me and his Majesty, to the determination of the Clergy: I did the more willingly consent thereunto, and since the determination made, have also allowed, approved, and agreed unto the same, wherein I have more respect, as becometh me, to Truth and good Pleasure, than any worldly Affection that might move me to the contrary. I account God pleased with that is done, and know my self to have suffered no wrong or injury; but being my Body preserved in the integrity which I brought into this Realm, and I truly discharged from all band of Consent, I find the King's Highness, whom I cannot justly have as my Husband, to be nevertheless as a most kind, loving, and friendly Father and Brother, and to use me as honourably, and with as much humanity and liberality as you, I my self, or any of our Kin or Allies could wish or desire; wherewith I am, for mine own part, so well content and satisfied, that I much desire my Mother, You, and other mine Allies so to understand it, accept, and take it; and so to use your self towards this Noble and Vertuous Prince, as he may have cause to continue his friendship towards you, which on his behalf shall nothing be empaired or altered for this Matter: for so hath it pleased his Highness to signify unto me, that like as he will shew me always a most fatherly and brotherly kindness, and has so provided for me; so will he remain with you, and other, according to such terms as have passed in the same knot of Amity which between you hath been concluded, this Matter notwithstanding, in such wise as neither I, ne you, or any of our Friends shall have just cause of miscontentment. Thus much I have thought necessary to write unto you, lest for want of true knowledg ye might otherwise take this Matter than ye ought, and in other sort care for me than ye should have cause. Only I require this of you, That ye so use your self, as for your untowardness in this Matter, I fare not the worse; whereunto I trust you will have regard.

XXI.

ExMSS
D. Stil-
lingfleet

*The Resolutions of several Bishops and Divines, of some
Questions concerning the Sacraments ; by which it will
appear with what maturity and care they proceeded in
the Reformation, taken from the Originals, under their
own hands. Only in copying them, I judged it might
be more acceptable to the Reader to see every Man's Answer set down after every Question ; and therefore they
are published in this method.*

The first Question.

What a Sacrament is by the Scripture?

Canter-
bury.

THE Scripture sheweth not what a Sacrament is, nevertheless where in the Latin Text we have *Sacramentum*,
there in the Greek we have *Mysterium ;* and so by the
Scripture, *Sacramentum* may be called *Mysterium, id est,
res occulta sive arcana.*

York.

To the first ; In Scripture we neither find Definition nor
Description of a Sacrament.

London

Without prejudice to the Truth, and saving always more
better Judgment, *Cum facultate etiam melius deliberandi
in hac parte.*

To the first Question ; I think that the Scriptures do use
this word Sacrament, in divers places, according to the
Matter it treateth upon, Tobi. 12. Rev. 1. Wisd. 2. 6. 12.
Dan. 2. Ephes. 1. 3, 5. Col. 1. 1 Tim. 10. Rev. 17. as also
it doth divers other words : Yet, what a Sacrament is by
definition, or description of Scripture, I cannot find it explicated openly. Likewise as I cannot find the definition
or description of the Trinity, nor yet such-like things.
Mary what other Men can find, being daily and of long
season exercised in Scripture, I cannot tell, referring therefore this thing to their better knowledg.

Ro-
chester.

I think that where this word, *Sacramentum,* is found in
the Scripture in the Latin Translation, there in the Greek
is found this word Μυστήριον, that is to say, a Mystery, or a
secret thing.

· What the word Sacrament betokeneth, or what is the definition, description, or notification thereof, I have found no such plainly set out by Scripture. But this I find, that it should appear by the same Scripture, that the Latin word *Sacramentum*, and the Greek word *Mysterium*, be in manner always used for one thing; as much to say as, *Absconditum, Occultatum, vel in occulto*.

Thomas Robertson. Ad Quæstiones.

Ad primam Respondeo, vocem Sacramenti, mihi in Sacris Literis non reperiri in hac significatione, nisi quatenus ad Matrimonium applicatur a Paulo, ubi tamen Græce habetur Mysterium : et proinde ex meris Scripturis expresse definiri non posse.

I find not in Scripture, the definition of a Sacrament, nor what a Sacrament is.

I find no definition in Scripture of this word *Sacramentum;* howbeit wheresoever it is found in Scripture, the same is in the Greek *Mysterium*, which signifieth a Secret, or Hid thing.

Non habetur in Scripturis, quid Sacramentum proprie sit, nisi quod subinde Mysterium dicitur: varia enim, et in Scripturis, et in Ecclesiasticis Scriptoribus reperitur ejus nominis significatio; ideoq; definiri non potest.

I find no definition of this word Sacrament, in the Scripture; nor likewise of this word *Gratia,* or *Lex*, with innumerable more; and yet what they signify, it is known; so the signification of this word Sacrament is plain, it is nothing else but a secret Hid thing, or any Mystery.

Like as *Angelus, Cœlum, Terra,* be spoken of in Scripture, yet none of them defined: So altho *Sacramentum* be spoken of in Scripture, yet it hath no definition there, but is taken divers ways, and in divers significations.

This word, Sacrament, in Scripture is not defined.

Dr.
Tre-
sham.

I say this word, Sacrament, taken in his common signification, betokeneth a Mystery, and hid, or a secret thing: But if ye understand it, in his proper signification, as we use to apply it only to the Seven Sacraments, the Scripture sheweth not what a Sacrament is. And yet lest any Man might be offended, thinking, that because the Scripture sheweth not what a Sacrament is, therefore the same is a light thing, or little to be esteemed: Here may be remembred, that there are some weighty and godly things, being also of our Belief, which the Scripture sheweth not expresly what they are. As for Example; We believe the Son is consubstantial to the Father: *Item ;* that the Father is unbegotten, yet the Scripture sheweth not what is consubstantial, nor what is unbegotten, neither maketh any mention of the words. Likewise it is true, Baptism is a Sacrament, Pennance is a Sacrament, &c. yet the Scripture sheweth not what a Sacrament is.

Edwardus Leyghton.
Responsions unto the Questions.

Dr.
Leygh-
ton.

To the first Question, I say; That in Holy Scripture I never found, and I think there is no Man that will find a definition or description of this word *Sacramentum ;* which is as much as to say in English, as, a Mystery, a secret, or a hid thing.

Dr.
Coren.

I do read no definition of this word, *Sacramentum,* in Scripture; but sometimes it is used in Scripture, to signify a thing secret or hid.

Conve-
niunt.

In primo articulo conveniunt omnes, non satis constare ex Scriptura, quid sit Sacramentum ; Pleriq; tamen dicunt Græce appellari, Mysterium, (i. e.) a secret, or a hid thing.

Agree-
ment.*

In the Answer unto the first Question, They do all agree, that it is not evident by Scripture, what a Sacrament is, but *Mysterium,* that is, a secret, or a hid thing.

---

* The agreement, at the end of these Questions, is in Cranmer's hand.—Cott. Libr. Cleopatra, E. 5.

2. Question.

What a Sacrament is by the Ancient Authors?

Answers.

THE Ancient Doctors call a Sacrament, *Sacræ rei Signum, viz. visibile Verbum, Symbolum, atque pactio qua sumus constricti.* Canterbury.

To the second; Of St. Augustin's words, this Description following of a Sacrament may be gathered; *Sacramentum est invisibilis gratiæ, visibilis forma.* And this thing, that is such visible form or sign of invisible Grace in Sacraments, we find in Scripture, altho we find not the word Sacrament, saving only in the Sacrament of Matrimony. York.

To the second; I find in Authors this Declaration, *Sacramentum est Sacræ rei signum.* Also, *Invisibilis Gratiæ Visibilis Forma.* Also, *Visibilis Forma Invisibilis Gratiæ imaginem gerens et causa existens.* And of the verity and goodness of this Description or Declaration, I refer me to the Divines, better acquainted with this Matter than I am. London

I think that this word Sacrament, as it is taken of the Old Authers, hath divers and sundry significations, for sometimes it is extended to all holy Signs, sometimes to all Mysteries, sometimes to all Alegories, &c. Rochester.

Thomas Waldensis, who writeth a solemn Work *de Sacramentis,* causeth me to say, that this word, *Sacramentum in Communi,* is defined of the Ancient Authors; who after that he had shewed how that Wycliff, and before him Berengarius hath said, that Augustine defineth *Sacramentum* thus; *Sacramentum est sacrum Signum;* and *Signum* in this wise, *Signum est res præter speciem quam sensibus ingerit aliquid aliud ex se faciens in cogitationem venire.* He himself, with Ancient Authors, as he saith, defineth it thus; *Sacramentum est invisibilis Gratiæ visibilis Forma, vel, Sa-* Carlile.

DeDoctrina Christiana.

cramentum est Sacræ rei Signum: Both these Descriptions
(saith he) be of the Ancient Fathers.

Dr. Robertson.

Sacramentum a vetustioribus, quemadmodum fert Hugo
de S. Victore, et Thomas Aquinas, nondum reperiri defi-
nitum, nisi quod Augustinus, interdum vocet Sacramenta,
Sacra signa aut signacula, interdum similitudines earum
rerum, quarum sunt Sacramenta. Et Rabanus, Sacramentum dicitur, quod sub tegumento rerum corporalium, virtus Divina secretius salutem eorundem Sacramentorum
operatur, unde et a secretis virtutibus vel Sacris Sacramenta dicuntur.

Dr. Cox

The Ancient Authors commonly say, That a Sacrament
is, *Sacræ rei Signum,* or *Sacrosanctum Signaculum;* but
they do not utterly and properly define what it is.

Dr. Day

The Ancient Doctors take this word, *Sacramentum,* di-
versly, and apply it to many things.

Dr.
Oglethorpe.

Ex Augustino et aliis colligitur, Sacramentum posse
dici, Sacræ rei Signum, vel, invisibilis gratiæ visibilis
Forma, quanquam hæc posterior definitio non conveniat
omnibus Sacramentis, scil. tantum septem istis usitatis;
sed nec his quoq; ex æquo, cum non æqualem conferant
gratiam.

Dr.
Redmayn.

Generally it is taken to signify every secret Mystery,
and *Sacramenta* be called, *Sacrarum rerum signa,* or *Sacra
signacula:* And as this word Sacrament particularly is attributed to the chief Sacraments of the Church, this definition of a Sacrament may be gathered of St. August.
Invisibilis Gratiæ visibilis Forma. And also that a Sacrament is a mystical or secret Work which consisteth
ex Verbo et elemento. And Cyprian saith, *Verborum solem-
nitas et sacri invocatio nominis, et signa institutionibus
Apostolicis Sacerdotum Ministeriis Attributa, visibile cele-
brant Sacramentum, rem vero ipsam Spiritus Sanctus for-
mat et efficit.*

Dr.
Edgeworth.

By the Ancient Authors, *Sacramentum* hath many signi-

fications, sometimes it is called a Secret Counsel. Tob. 12.
Sacramentum Regis abscondere bonum est. Nebuchad-
nezar's Dream was called *Sacramentum*, Dan. 2. The
Mystery of Christ's Incarnation, and of our Redemption,
is so called, Ephes. 3. and 1 Tim. 3. So that every secret thing having some privy sense or signification, is
called *Sacramentum*, generally extending the Vocable:
Notwithstanding in one signification, *Sacramentum* ac-
cordeth properly to them that be commonly called the
Seven Sacraments; and hath this definition taken of St.
August. and others, *Invisibilis gratiæ visibilis Forma, ut
ipsius imaginem gerat et quodammodo causa existat.*

Dr.
Symmons.

The Ancient Authors of Divinity use this word Sacrament in divers significations, for they call it *Mysterium;*
and so the Scripture useth it in many places, as 1 Tim. 3.
Tobie 12. Wisd. 2. Dan. 2. Eph. 1. and 3. The word Sacrament is also used for a Figure or a Sign of the Old Testament, signifying Christ, as the Paschal Lamb, and the
Brasen Serpent, and divers other Holy Signs. It is also
taken of the Holy Authors, to be an Holy Sign, which
maketh to the sanctification of the Soul, given of God
against sin for our Salvation, as it may be gathered of them;
for this word Sacrament is called by them, *Sacrum Signum;* but I have not read any express definition common
to all Sacraments.

Dr.
Tresham.

This word Sacrament, in the Ancient Authors, is oft-
times used in this general signification, and so (as is before-
said) it is a Mystery, or secret thing; and sometimes the
same word is used as appliable only unto the Seven Sacraments; and is thus described, A visible Form of an invisible Grace: and thus also, a thing by the which, under the
covering of visible things, the godly Power doth work our
health.

Dr.
Leyghton.

To the second, I say; That Hugo de Sancto Victore, is
one of the most Ancient Authors that I ever could perceive,
took upon him to define or describe a Sacrament: Howbeit, I suppose, that this common description which the
Schoolmen use, after the Master of the Sentences, viz. *Sa-*

*cramentum est invisibilis Gratiæ visibilis seu sensibilis For-
ma*, may be gathered of St. Austin, and divers other Ancient Author's words in many places of their Works.

Dr.
Coren.
    I do find no definition plainly set forth in old Authors,
notwithstanding this definition, *Invisibilis Gratiæ visibilis
Forma,* may be gathered out of St. Augustine.

Con.
    In secundo Articulo conveniunt omnes, Sacramentum
esse sacræ rei signum. Tresham, Oglethorpus, et Edgworth, dicunt hanc definitionem, Sacramentum est invisibilis gratiæ visibilis Forma, his septem convenire. Thurle-
beus ait, non convenire omnibus septem, et æque pluribus
posse attribui atq; septem.

Agree-
ment.
    In the second they put many Descriptions of a Sacra-
ment, as the sign of a holy Thing, a visible Word, &c.
But upon this one definition, a Sacrament is a visible Form
of invisible Grace, they do not all agree: for Doctors
Edgworth, Tresham, and Oglethorpe say, That " it is ap-
plicable only and properly unto the word Sacrament, as it
signifieth the Seven Sacraments usually received." My
Lord Elect of Westminster saith, That " it agreeth not
unto all the Seven, nor yet more specially unto the Seven,
than unto any other."

---

3. Question.

How many Sacraments there be by the Scripture?

Answers.

Canter-
bury.
    THE Scripture sheweth not how many Sacraments there
be, but *Incarnatio Christi* and *Matrimonium,* be called in
the Scripture *Mysteria,* and therefore we may call them by
the Scripture *Sacramenta.* But one *Sacramentum* the Scripture maketh mention of, which is hard to be revealed fully,
as would to God it were, and that is *Mysterium Iniquitatis,*
or *Mysterium Meretricis magnæ et Bestiæ.*

To the third; In Scripture we find no precise number of Sacraments.

To the third; I find not set forth the express number, with express declaration of this many and no more; nor yet of these expresly by Scripture which we use, especially under the name of Sacraments, saving only of Matrimony.

I think that in the Scripture be innumerable Sacraments, for all Mysteries, all Ceremonies, all the Facts of Christ, the whole Story of the Jews, and the Revelations of the Apocalypse, may be named Sacraments.

The certain number of Sacraments, or Mysteries, contained within Scripture, cannot be well expressed or assigned; for Scripture containeth more than infallibly may be rehearsed.

De istis septem, quæ usitate vocamus Sacramenta, nullum invenio nomine Sacramenti appellari, nisi Matrimonium. Matrimonium esse Sacramentum, probat Eckius, Homi. 73. et conferre gratiam, ibid.

There be divers Sacraments by the Scripture, as in Tobie 12. *Sacramentum Regis,* the King's Secret. Also Nebuchadnezars Dream, Dan. 2. is called, *Sacramentum. Incarnatio Christi, Sacramentum,* Ephes. 3. *Matrimonium, Sacramentum.*

Taking for Sacraments any thing, that this word, *Sacramentum,* doth signify, there be in Scripture a great number of Sacraments more than Seven.

Non habetur determinatus Sacramentorum numerus in Scripturis, sunt enim innumera fere illic, quæ passim vocantur Sacramenta; cum omnis allegoria, omneq; Mysterium, dicatur Sacramentum. Quin et somnia, ac secreta, subinde Sacramenta vocantur. Tobie 2. Sacramentum Regis abscondere bonum est; et Dan. 2. Imploremus misericordias Dei Cœli super Sacramento isto, et somnia.

Paulus etiam Epist. 2. vocat Mysterium Incarnationis
Christi Sacramentum: Et in Apoc. 1. vocat Sacramentum
septem Stellarum. Ac hoc præcipue observandum venit,
nullum a septem Sacramentis, receptis hoc nomine appellari, præter solum Matrimonium.

Dr.
Red-
mayn.

As many as there be Mysteries, which be innumerable;
but by Scripture, I think, the Seven which be named Sacraments, may principally bear the name.

Dr.
Edge-
worth.

Speaking of Sacraments generally, they be innumerable
spoken of in Scripture; but properly to speak of Sacraments, there be but Seven that may be so called, of which
Matrimony is expresly called *Sacramentum*, Ephes. 5. and
as I think, in the Germane and proper signification of a Sacrament; so that the indivisible knot of the Man and his
Wife in one Body, by the Sacrament of Matrimony, is the
Matter of this Sacrament; upon which, as on the literal
verity the Apostle foundeth this allegorical saying, *Ego
autem dico in Christo et in Ecclesia;* for the mystical sense
presupposeth a verity in the Letter on which that is taken.
Six more there be to which the definition doth agree, as
manifestly doth appear by the Scriptures with the exposition of the Ancient Authors.

Dr.
Sym-
mons.

In the Scripture there is no certain number of Sacraments.

Dr.
Tre-
sham.

I find no more of the seven, called expresly Sacraments,
but only Matrimony, but extending the name of Sacrament
in his most general acception; there are in Scripture a
great number of Sacraments, whereof the Apostle saith, *Si
noverint Mysteria omnia, &c.*

Dr.
Leygh-
ton.

To the third; I say, that I find not in Scripture any of
these seven which we commonly call Sacraments, called
Sacramentum, but only *Matrimonium.* But I find divers
and many other things called Sacraments in Scripture, as
in the 21 of Tobie, *Sacramentum Regis abscondere bonum
est. Item* Apoc. 17. *Dicamus tibi Sacramentum. Item,*
1 Tim. 3. *Magnum est pietatis Sacramentum, &c.*

I cannot tell how many Sacraments be, by Scripture, for they be above one hundred.

In tertio conveniunt satis: non esse certum numerum Sacramentorum per Scripturas. *Redmaynus addit,* But by Scripture I think the seven which be named Sacraments, may principally bear the name. *Idem sentit Edgworth, et septem tantum.* *Matrimonium in Scripturis haberi sub nomine Sacramenti pleriq; dicunt.*

In the third they do agree, That there is no certain number of Sacraments by Scripture, but even as many as there be Mysteries; and none of these seven called Sacraments, but only Matrimony in Scripture.

---

4. Question.

How many Sacraments there be by the Ancient Authors?

Answers.

By the Ancient Authors there be many Sacraments more than seven, for all the Figures which signifie Christ to come, or testifie that he is come, be called Sacraments, as all the Figures of the Old Law, and in the New Law; *Eucharistia, Baptismus, Pascha, Dies Dominicus, lotio Pedum, signum Crucis, Chrisma, Matrimonium, Ordo, Sabbatum, Impositio manuum, Oleum, Consecratio Olei, Lac, Mel, Aqua, Vinum, Sal, Ignis, Cinis, adapertio Aurium, vestis candida,* and all the Parables of Christ, with the Prophesies of the Apocalyps, and such others, be called by the Doctors, *Sacramenta.*

To the fourth;. There is no precise number of Sacraments mentioned by the Ancient Authors, taking the word Sacrament, in his most general signification.

To the fourth; I find that St. Austine speaketh *de Baptismo, de Eucharistia, de Matrimonio, de Ordinatione clericorum, de Sacramento Chrismatis et Unctionis:* Also I find

BOOK III.   in the said St. Austine, that in the Old Law there were many Sacraments, and in the New Law few.

Rochester.   I think that in the Doctors be found many more Sacraments than seven, viz. *Panis Catechumenorum, signum Crucis, Oleum, Lac, Sal, Mel,* &c.

Carlile.   That Scripture containeth, by the same Holy Ghost which is Author thereof, the Holy Doctors, and Ancient Fathers expoundeth; So that where in Scripture the number of Sacraments is uncertain, it cannot be among them certain.

Dr. Robertson.   Apud Augustinum lego Sacramentum Nuptiarum, Sacramentum Baptismi, Sacramentum Eucharistiæ, quod et altaris sive panis vocat; Sacramentum Ordinationis; Sacramentum Chrismatis, quod datur per manus impositionem Baptizatis; Sacramentum Unctionis.

Dr. Cox.   I find in the Ancient Authors, that Baptism is called *Sacramentum, Eucharistia Sacramentum, Matrimonium Sacramentum, Ordo Sacramentum, Chrisma Sacramentum, Impositio Manuum per Baptismum Sacramentum, Dilectio Sacramentum, Lotio pedum Sacramentum, Oleum, Mel, Lac, Sacramenta;* and many others.

Dr. Day   There be a great sort of Sacraments found in the Doctors, after the acception above-said, more than seven.

Dr. Oglethorp.   Apud Scriptores Ecclesiasticos reperiuntur multo plura Sacramenta quam hæc septem.

Dr. Redmayn.   Taking this word Sacrament universally for Mysteries, or all secret Tokens, there be more Sacraments than can be reckoned; but the seven by old Authors may specially obtain the name. *Lotio pedum* is spoken of in old Authors as a special Sacrament used then in the Church, and as it appeareth, having a great ground in the Scripture; and I think it were better to renew that again, and so to have eight Sacraments, rather than to diminish the number of the seven now used.

Even like as to the next Question before.

BOOK
III.

Dr.
Edge-
worth.
Dr.
Sym-
mons.
Dr.
Tre-
sham.

The ancient Authors acknowledg many more than seven; for they call in their Writings all Rites and Ceremonies, Sacraments.

Generally, as many as Mysteries, specially seven, and no more of like nature to them; for although I find not express mention where Penance is called a Sacrament, yet I think it may be deduced and proved by Cyprian, in his Sermon *de Passione Christi*, in these words. *Deniq; quicunq; fiunt Sacramentorum Ministri, per operationem authoritas in figura Crucis omnibus Sacramentis largitur effectum, et cuncta peragit nobis quod omnibus nominibus eminet a Sacramentorum vicariis invocatum: At licet indigni sint qui accipiunt, Sacramentorum tamen reverentia et propinquiorem ad Deum parat accessum, et ubi redierint ad cor constat ablutionis donum, et redit effectus munerum, nec alias quæri aut repeti necesse est salutiferum Sacramentum;* in these words, *redit effectus munerum;* and, *nec alias repeti necesse est salutiferum Sacramentum,* must needs be understood Penance, and also that Penance is a Sacrament: For as our first access to God is by the Sacrament Baptism, which Cyprian there following called *Ablutionem primam;* so if we fall by deadly sin, we cannot *repetere* God again, but by Penance; which repeting (*i. e.*) Penance, Cyprian calleth *Salutiferum Sacramentum.*

Dr.
Leygh-
ton.

To the fourth, I say; That I find in ancienter Authors, every one of these seven, which we call commonly Sacraments, called *Sacramentum;* as in Austin every one of them is called *Sacramentum* but only Penance, which Cyprian calleth *Sacramentum.* Also I find in the ancienter Authors divers other things (besides the seven) called Sacraments, as *Lotio Pedum* in Cyprian, &c.

More Sacraments be found in old Authors than Seven.

Dr.
Coren

In quarto conveniunt, plura esse Sacramenta quam septem apud Authores: Redman addit; But the seven, by old

Con.

Authors, may specially obtain the name. *Idem putat*
Edgworth, and Tresham. *Lotio pedum,* he thinketh were
better to be renewed, and so made eight Sacraments, than
the number of the seven to be diminished. *Treshamus*
citat Cyprianum in Serm. de Passione Christi pro pœni-
tentia, quod dicatur Sacramentum, cum alii fere omnes nus-
quam appellari aiunt Sacramentum apud Authores, et hic
locus aperte agit de Baptismo, quod vocat donum ablutionis,
et Sacramentum Salutiferum.

Agree-
ment.

In the fourth they agree, That there is no determinate
number of Sacraments spoken of in the old Authors; but
that my Lord of York, and Edgworth, Tresham, Redman,
Crayford, and Simmons, say, That those seven, by old
Authors, may specially obtain the name of Sacraments.
The Bishop of St. Davids saith, That there be but four
Sacraments in the old Doctors most chiefly spoken of, and
they be Baptism, the Sacrament of the Altar, Matrimony,
and Pennance.

---

5. Question.

Whether this word Sacrament, be and ought to be attributed
to the seven only? and whether the seven Sacraments be
found in any of the old Authors?

Answers.

Canter-
bury.

I KNOW no cause why this word, Sacrament, should be
attributed to the seven only; for the old Authors never prescribed any certain number of Sacraments, nor in all their
Books I never read these two words joined together, *viz.*
septem Sacramenta.

York.

To the fifth; To the first part of this Question, this word,
Sacrament, is used and applied in Scripture, to some things
that be none of the seven Sacraments. To the second part;

The seven Sacraments be found in some of the ancient Authors.

To the fifth, I answer; That this word, Sacrament, in our Language commonly hath been attributed to the seven customably called Sacraments, not for that yet, that the word Sacrament cannot be applied to any more, but for that the seven have been specially of very long and ancient season received, continued and taken for things of such sort.

London.

I think that the name of a Sacrament, is and may be attributed to more than seven, and that all the seven Sacraments be found in the old Authors, though all peradventure be not found in one Author. But I have not read Pennance called by the name of a Sacrament in any of them.

Rochester.

Certain it is, that this word Sacrament, neither is nor ought to be attributed to seven only, for both Scripture and ancient Authors otherwise applieth it, but yet nothing letteth, but that this word Sacrament may most especially, and in a certain due preheminence, be applied to the seven Sacraments, of most ancient name and usage among Christian Men. And that the ancient Authors have so used and applied it, affirmeth the said Thomas Walden, convincing Wycliffe and Berengarius who enforced the contrary, from Cyprian, and also Augustine, with other holy Doctors, they may so well be gathered.

Carlile.

Vocabulum, Sacramenti, in Sacris Literis, nulli Sacramentorum quod sciam tribuitur, nisi Matrimonio: a vetustis Scriptoribus tribuitur Ceremoniis et umbris legis, Incarnationi Christi, figuris, allegoriis, et festivitatibus: Apud Paulum legitur divinitatis, voluntatis divinæ, et pietatis Sacramentum. Cæterum loquendo de Sacramentis his, quæ sunt invisibilis gratiæ collatæ in Ecclesia Christi visibilia signa, opinor non plura quam septem inveniri, hisq; magis proprie quam reliquis, sub hac ratione, tribui nomen Sacramenti.

Dr. Robertson.

This word Sacrament is not, nor ought not to be attri-

Dr. Cox.

U 2

BOOK III. buted to these seven only. Those that we call seven Sacraments, be found in old Authors, although some of them be seldom found called by this name Sacrament.

Dr. Day. This word, *Sacramentum*, neither is, nor ought to be so attributed unto these seven, but that it is, and may be attributed to many more things, and so the ancienter Doctors use it. The seven Sacraments be found in ancient Doctors under the name of Sacrament, saving that I remember not that I have read in them Pennance called a Sacrament.

Dr. Oglethorpe. Nomen commune est multis aliis rebus, quam septem istis usitatis Sacramentis. Septem Sacramenta, seorsim et sparsim reperiuntur in veterum monumentis.

Dr. Redmayn. To the seven specially and principally, and in general to innumerable more. But I cannot tell whether in any old Author might be found these two words, seven Sacraments, or this number limited; but every one of the seven Sacraments, one by one, be found in the old Authors.

Dr. Edgeworth. *Sacramentum* in his proper signification, is and ought to be attributed to the seven only; and they be all seven found in the Authors.

Dr. Symmons. This word, Sacrament, is not only to be attributed to the seven, but that the seven Sacraments especially conferreth Grace, the old Authors especially accounteth them by the number of seven; and these seven are found in Authors and Scriptures, altho they be not found by the name of seven.

Dr. Tresham. I say, This word, Sacrament, is attributed to the seven; and that the seven Sacraments are found in the ancient Authors.

Dr. Leyghton. To the fifth I say, first, (as before) that this word, *Sacramentum*, is not applied or attributed in Holy Scripture to any of the seven, but only to Matrimony. But it is attributed in Scripture and ancient Authors to many other things besides these: Howbeit, taking this word, *Sacra-*

mentum, for a sensible sign of the invisible Grace of God given unto Christian People, as the Schoolmen and many late Writers take it; I think that these seven commonly called Sacraments, are to be called only and most properly Sacraments.

This word, Sacrament, may well be attributed to the seven; and so it is found in old Authors, saving that I do not read expresly in old Doctors, Pennance to be under the name of a Sacrament, unless it be in Chrysostome, in the Exposition *ad Hebræ. Homil.* 20. sect. 1. cap. 10. *in principio.*

In quinto præter Herfordens. Roffens. Dayium. Oglethorpum, Menevens. et Coxum, putant omnes nomen Sacramenti præcipue his septem convenire. Symons addit, *The seven Sacraments specially confer Grace:* Eboracens. Curren, Tresham, Symons, aiunt septem Sacramenta inveniri apud veteres, quanquam Curren et Symons mox videntur iterum negare.

In the fifth; The Bishops of Hereford and St. David, Dr. Day, Dr. Cox, say, That this word, Sacrament, in the old Authors, is not attributed unto the seven only, and ought not to be attributed. The Bishop of Carlile alledging Waldensis. Doctors Curren, Edgworth, Symons, Tresham say, That it is and may be attributed. And Dr. Curren, and Mr. Symmons, seem to vary against themselves each in their own Answers; for Dr. Curren saith, That this word, Sacrament, is attributed unto the seven in the old Doctors, and yet he cannot find that it is attributed unto Pennance. Dr. Symons saith, That the old Authors account them by the number of seven; and yet he saith, That they be not found there by the name of seven.

6. Question.

Whether the determinate number of seven Sacraments be a Doctrine, either of the Scripture, or of the old Authors, and so to be taught?

Answers.

Canterbury.
THE determinate number of seven Sacraments is no Doctrine of the Scripture, nor of the old Authors.

York.
To the sixth; The Scripture maketh no mention of the Sacraments determined to seven precisely; but the Scripture maketh mention of seven Sacraments, which be used in Christ's Church, and grounded partly in Scripture; and no more be in use of the said Church but seven so grounded; and some of the ancient Doctors make mention of seven, and of no more than seven, as used in Christ's Church so grounded; wherefore a Doctrine may be had of seven Sacraments precisely used in Christ's Church, and grounded in Scripture.

London.
To the sixth; I think it be a Doctrine set forth by the ancient Fathers, one from another, taking their matter and ground out of Scripture, as they understood it; though Scripture for all that doth not give unto all the seven, the special names by which now they are called, nor yet openly call them by the name of Sacrament, except only (as is before-said) the Sacrament of Matrimony.

Rochester.
Albeit the seven Sacraments be in effect found both in the Scripture, and in the old Authors, and may therefore be so taught; yet I have not read this precise and determinate number of seven Sacraments, neither in the Scripture, nor in the ancient Writers.

Carlile.
By what is here before-said, I think it doth well appear, that both the Scripture of God, and holy Expositors of the same, would have the seven Sacraments both taught, and

in due form exhibited to all Christian People, as it shall also better appear by what followeth.

In Scriptura tantum unum ex istis septem Sacramentum vocari invenio, nimirum Matrimonium : apud veteres reperiuntur omnia hæc septem, a nullo tamen, quod sciam, nomine 7. Sacramentorum celebrari, nisi quod Eras. ait 7. a veteribus recenseri : August. loquens de Sacramentis ad Januarium Ep. 118. ait numerum septenarium tribui Ecclesiæ proprie instar universitatis ; Item objectum fuisse Husso in Concilio Constantienti quod infideliter senserit de 7. Sacramentis. De perfectione Num. Septenarii, vide August. lib. 1. de Civ. cap. 31.

This determinate number of seven Sacraments, is no Doctrine of Scripture, nor of the old Authors, nor ought not to be taught as such a determinate number by Scripture and old Authors.

Neither the Scripture, nor the ancient Authors, do recite the determinate number of the seven Sacraments ; but the Doctrine of the seven Sacraments is grounded in Scripture, and taught by the ancient Authors, albeit not altogether.

Septenarius Sacramentorum numerus, Doctrina est recentium Theologorum; quam illi partim ex Scriptura, partim ex veterum scriptis, argute in sacrum hunc (ut aiunt) numerum, collegerunt.

I think, as I find by old Authors, the ancient Church used all these seven Sacraments ; and so I think it good to be taught.

The determinate number of seven Sacraments, is not taught in any one Process of the Scripture, nor of any one of the old Authors of purpose speaking of them altogether, or in one Process, as far as I can remember ; albeit they all seven be there, and there spoken of in Scripture manifestly, and so have the old Authors left them

BOOK III.   in sundry places of their Writings; and so it ought to be taught.

Dr. Symmons.   Forasmuch as the Scripture teacheth these seven, and sheweth special Graces given by the same, the which are not so given by others, called Sacraments, the old Authors perceiving the special Graces, have accounted them in a certain number, and so have been used by Doctors to be called seven, and without inconvenience may so be taught.

Dr. Tresham.   I say, The determinate number of seven is not expresly mentioned in the Scripture, like as the determinate number of the seven Petitions of the Prayer is not expresly mentioned; and as I think the seven Petitions to have their ground in Scripture, even so do I think of the seven Sacraments, to be grounded in Scripture.

Dr. Leyghton.   To the sixth I say as before, That the old Authors call each of these seven, Sacraments; but be it, I cannot remember that ever I read the determinate, precise, and express number of seven Sacraments in any of the ancient Authors, nor in Scripture. Howbeit we may find in Scripture, and the old Authors, also mention made, and the doctrine of each of these seven, commonly called Sacraments.

Dr. Coren.   The determinate number of seven, is a Doctrine to be taught, for every one of them be contained in Scripture, though they have not the number of seven set forth there, no more than the Petitions of the Pater Noster be called seven, nor the Articles of the Creed be called twelve.

Con.   Priori parti Quæstionis negative Respondent. Herfordens. Menevens. Roffens. Dayus, Dunelmens. Oglethorpus, Thurleby: Posteriori parti, quod sit Doctrina conveniens respondent affirmative, Eboracen. Roffen. Carliolen. Londinen. Dayus, Edgworth, Redmayn, Symmons, Curren: Londinen. et Redmanus non respondent priori parti Quæstionis, nec Oglethorpus, Tresham, Robinsonus

Posteriori. Eboracen. Londin. Symmons, Curren, volunt è
Scripturis peti Doctrinam Septem. Sacramentorum.

Agree-
ment.

In the sixth, touching the determinate number of the
seven Sacraments, the Bishop of Duresme, Hereford, St.
David, and Rochester, the Elect of Westminster, Dr. Day,
and Dr. Oglethorpe say, This prescribed number of Sacraments is not found in the old Authors. The Bishop of York,
Drs. Curren, Tresham, and Symmons, say the contrary.
Concerning the second part, whether it be a Doctrine to
be taught? The Bishops of Hereford, St. Davids, and
Dr. Cox, Think it ought.not to be so·taught as such a determinate number by Scripture. The Bishops of York, London, Carlile; Drs. Day, Curren, Tresham, Symmons, Crayford, Think it a Doctrine meet to be taught: And some of
them say, That it is founded on Scripture.

7. Question.

*What is found in Scripture of the Matter, Nature, Effect,
and Vertue of such as we call the seven Sacraments; so
as although the Name be not there, yet whether the thing
be in Scripture or no, and in what wise spoken of?*

Answers.

Canter-
bury.

I FIND not in the Scripture the Matter, Nature, and
Effect of all these which we call the seven Sacraments,
but only of certain of them, as of Baptism, in which we
be regenerated and pardoned of our sin by the Blood of
Christ: Of *Eucharistia*, in which we be concorporated
unto Christ, and made lively members of his Body, nou-
rished and fed to the Everlasting Life, if we receive it as
we ought to do, and else it is to us rather Death than Life.
Of Pennance also I find in the Scripture, whereby Sinners
after Baptism returning wholly unto God, be accepted
again unto God's Favour and Mercy. But the Scripture
speaketh not of Pennance, as we call it a Sacrament, con-

BOOK III.   sisting in three parts, Contrition, Confession, and Satisfaction; but the Scripture taketh Pennance for a pure conversion of a sinner in heart and mind from his sins unto God, making no mention of private Confession of all deadly sins to a Priest, nor of Ecclesiastical satisfaction to be enjoined by him. Of Matrimony also I find very much in Scripture, and among other things, that it is a mean whereby God doth use the infirmity of our Concupiscence to the setting forth of his Glory, and encrease of the World, thereby sanctifying the Act of Carnal commixtion between the Man and the Wife to that use; yea, although one part be an Infidel: and in this Matrimony is also a Promise of Salvation, if the Parents bring up their Children in the Faith, Love, and Fear of God. Of the Matter, Nature, and Effect of the other three, that is to say, Confirmation, Order, and extream Unction, I read nothing in the Scripture as they be taken for Sacraments.

York.   To the seventh; Of Baptism, we find in Scripture the Institution by the Word of Christ; we find also that the Matter of Baptism is Water, the Effect and Vertue is Remission of Sins. Of Confirmation, we find that the Apostles did confirm those that were baptized, by laying their hands upon them, and that the Effect then was the coming of the Holy Ghost into them, upon whom the Apostles laid their hands, in a visible sign of the Gift of divers Languages, and therewith of ghostly strength to confess Christ, following upon the same. Of the Sacrament of the Altar, we find the Institution by Christ, and the Matter thereof, Bread and Wine, the Effect, Increase of Grace. Of the Sacrament of Pennance, we find the Institution in the Gospel, the Effect Reconciliation of the Sinner, and the union of him to the Mystical Body of Christ. Of the Sacrament of Matrimony, we find the Institution both in the Old and New Testament, and the Effect thereof, Remedy against Concupiscence and discharge of sin, which otherwise should be in the Office of Generation. Of the Sacrament of Order, we find, that our Saviour gave to his Apostles power to baptize, to bind and to loose sinners, to remit sins, and to retain them, to teach and preach his Word, and to consecrate his most precious Body and Blood, which

be the highest Offices of Order; and the Effect thereof
Grace, we find in Scripture. Of extream Unction, we find
in the Epistle of the Holy Apostle St. James, and of the
Effects of the same.

To the seventh, I find, that St. Austin is of this sentence,
That " where the Sacraments of the Old Law did promise
Grace and Comfort, the Sacraments of the New Law do
give it indeed." And moreover he saith, That " the Sacraments of the New Law are, *factu faciliora, pauciora, salu-*
briora et fœliciora, more easier, more fewer, more whol-
somer, and more happy."

The Scripture teacheth of Baptism, the Sacrament of
the Altar, Matrimony, and Pennance manifestly : There be
also in the Scripture manifest examples of Confirmation,
viz. That it was done after Baptism by the Apostles, *per*
manuum Impositionem. The Scripture teacheth also of Order, that it was done, *per manuum Impositionem cum ora-*
tione et jejunio. Of the Unction of sick Men, the Epistle
of St. James teacheth manifestly.

I think verily, That of the Substance, Effect, and Vertue
of these seven usual Sacraments, that are to be taken and
esteemed above others, we have plainly and expresly by
Holy Scripture. Of Baptism, That whosoever believeth
in Christ, and is Christned, shall be saved; and except
that one be born again of Water and the Holy Ghost, he
cannot come within the Kingdom of God. Of Matrimony,
we have in Scripture, both by name, and in effect, in the
Old and New Testament, both by Christ and his Apostle
Paul. Of the Sacrament of the Altar, I find plainly expresly, both in the Holy Gospels, and other places of
Scripture. Of Pennance in like manner. Of Confirmation we have in Scripture, that when the Samaritans, by
the preaching of Philip, had received the Word of God
and were Christened; the Apostles hearing of the same,
sent Peter and John unto them; who when they came thither, they prayed for them that they might receive the Holy
Ghost : then they laid their hands upon them, and so they
received the Holy Ghost; " This, (saith Bede,) is the Office

BOOK III. and Duty only of Bishops." And " this manner and form (saith St. Hierom) as it is written in the Acts, the Church hath kept, That the Bishop should go abroad to call for the Grace of the Holy Ghost, and lay his hands upon them, who had been Christened by Priests and Deacons." Of the Sacrament of Orders, we have, That Christ made his Apostles the Teachers of his Law, and Ministers of his Sacraments, that they should duly do it, and make and ordain others likewise to do it after them. And so the Apostles ordained Matthias to be one of their number, St. Paul made and ordained Timothy and Titus, with others likewise. Of the Sacrament of Extream Unction, we have manifestly in the Gospel of Mark, and Epistle of St. James.

Dr. Robertson. Materia Sacramentorum est Verbum et Elementum, virtus quam Deus per illa digne sumentibus conferat gratiam, juxta suam promissionem, nimirum quod sint Sacra Signacula, non tantum signantia, sed etiam sanctificantia. Unde opinor constare hanc Sacramentorum vim esse in Sacris Literis.

Dr. Cox. I find in Scripture, of such things as we use to call Sacraments. First, Of Baptism manifestly. Of *Eucharistia* manifestly. Of Pennance manifestly. Of Matrimony manifestly. Of Ordering, *per manus Impositionem et Orationem* manifestly. It is also manifest, that the Apostles laid their hands upon them that were Christened. Of the Unction of the Sick with Prayer manifestly.

Dr. Day. ⸱ Albeit the seven Sacraments be not found in Scripture expressed by name, yet the thing it self, that is the Matter, Nature, Effect, and Vertue of them is found there. Of Baptism in divers places; of the most Holy Communion; of Matrimony; of Absolution; of Bishops, Priests, and Deacons, how they were ordained *per manuum Impositionem cum Oratione;* Of laying the Apostles hands on them that were Christened, which is a part of Confirmation; Of Unction of them that were sick, with Prayer joined withal.

Dr. Oglethorp. Natura, vis, effectus, ac uniuscujusq; Sacramenti proprietas, seorsim in Scriptura reperitur, ut veteres eam interpretati sunt.

As it appeareth in the Articles which be drawn of the said seven Sacraments.

In Scripture we find of the Form of the Sacraments, as the words Sacramental; and the Matter, as the Element, Oil, Chrism; and the Patient receiving the Sacrament; and of Grace and encrease of Vertue given by them as the Effects.

The things are contained in Scripture, as Baptism, Confirmation, *Eucharistia, Pœnitentia, Extrema Unctio, Ordo,* altho they have not there this name *Sacramentum,* as Matrimony hath; and every one of them hath his Matter, Nature, Effect and Vertue.

I think the Thing, the Matter, the Nature, the Effect, and Vertue of them all be in the Scripture, and all there institute by God's Authority, for I think that no one Man, neither the whole Church hath power to institute a Sacrament, but that such Institution pertaineth only to God.

To the Seventh, I say, That we may evidently find in Scripture, the substance of every one of the seven Sacraments, the Nature, Effect, and Vertue of the same; as of Baptism, Confirmation, Pennance, Matrimony, and so forth of the rest.

Of the Matter, Nature, Vertue, and Effect, of such as we call Sacraments, Scripture maketh mention: Of Baptism manifestly; of the most Holy Communion manifestly; of Absolution manifestly; of Matrimony manifestly; of Bishops, Priests, and Deacons, Scripture speaketh manifestly; for they were ordered, *per Impositiones manuum Presbyterii cum Oratione et jejunio.*

Conveniunt præter Menevens. naturam septem Sacramentorum nobis tradi in Scripturis. Eboracens. effectus singulorum enumerat, item Carliolens.

BOOK III. Londinens, non Respondet Quæstioni. Treshamus ait ideo è Scripturis tradi nobis Sacramenta, quoniam tota Ecclesia non habet Authoritatem Instituendi Sacramenta.

Agreement. In the seventh they do agree, saving this, That the Bishop of St David says, That "the Nature, Effect, and Vertue of these seven Sacraments, only Baptism, the Sacrament of the Altar, Matrimony, Pennance, are contained in the Scripture." The other say, " that the Nature and the Vertue of all the seven, be contained in the Scripture."

---

8. Question.

Whether Confirmation, cum Chrismate, of them that be Baptized, be found in Scripture?

Answers.

Canterbury. Of Confirmation with Chrism, without which it is counted no Sacrament, there is no mention in the Scripture.

York. To the eighth; We find Confirmation, *cum Impositione manuum* in Scripture, as before; *cum Chrismate* we find not in the Scripture, but yet we find Chrismation with Oil used even from the time of the Apostles, and so taken as a Tradition Apostolick.

London To the eighth; I find in Scripture, in many places, *de Impositione manuum*, which I think (considering the usage commonly and so long withal used) to be Confirmation; and that with Chrism, to supply the visible appearance of the Holy Ghost, which Holy Ghost was so visibly seen in the Primitive Church; nevertheless for the perfect declaration of the verity hereof, I refer it to the judgment of Men of higher knowledg in this Faculty.

Rochester. Altho Confirmation be found in the Scripture, by Example, as I said before, yet there is nothing written *de Chrismate.*

The Imposition of Hands, the Holy Doctors take for the same which we call Confirmation, done upon them which were christened before, whereof is written in the Acts. And as for *Chrisma*, it should seem by Cyprian, both as touching the confection and usage thereof, that it hath a great ground to be derived out of Scripture, tho it be not manifestly therein spoken of.

BOOK III. Carlile.

Res et Effectus.Confirmationis continentur in Scriptura, nempe, Impositio manuum per Apostolos Baptizatis, per quam dabatur Spiritus Sanctus. De Chrismate nihil illie legimus, quia per id tempus Spiritus Sanctus signo visibili descenderit in Baptizatos. Quod ubi fieri desierit, Ecclesia Chrismate signi externi loco uti cœpit.

Dr. Robertson.

I find not in Scripture that the Apostles laying their hands upon them that were baptized, did anoint them *Chrismate*.

Dr. Cox.

Confirmation *cum Chrismate* I read not in Scripture, but *Impositionem manuum super Baptizatos*, I find there is, which ancient Authors call Confirmation; and Inunction with *Chrisma* hath been used from the Primitive Church.

Dr. Day.

De Impositione manuum cum Oratione, expressa mentio est in Scripturis, quæ nunc usitato nomine, a Doctoribus dicitur, Confirmatio. Sacrum Chrisma, traditio est Apostolica, ut ex veteribus liquet.

Dr. Oglethorpe.

The Question is not simple, but as if it were asked, Whether *Eucharistia in infermentato*, be in the Scripture, or, *baptismus cum sale*. Imposition of the Apostles hands, in which was conferred the Holy Ghost for Confirmation of them who were baptized, is found in Scripture. *Chrisma* is a Tradition deduced from the Apostles, as may be gathered by Scripture, and by the Old Authors, and the Mystery thereof is not to be despised.

Dr. Redmayn.

This Sacrament is one, *unitate integritatis*, as some others be: Therefore it hath two parts; of which one, that is, *Impositio manuum*, is taken Heb. 6. and Act. 8.

Dr. Edgeworth.

BOOK III. The other part, that is, Chrisme, is taken of the Tradition of the Fathers, and so used from the Primitive Church. *vid. Cyp. Epist.* lib. 1. Ep. 12.

Dr. Symmons. Confirmation is found in Scripture, and Confirmation *cum Chrismate*, is gathered from the old Authors.

Dr. Tresham. I say Confirmation is found in Scripture, but this additament, *cum Chrismate*, is not of the Scripture, yet is it a very ancient Tradition, as appeareth by *Cyp. de Unct. Chrism.*

Dr. Leyghton. To the eighth Question, I say, That Confirmation of them that be baptized, is found in Scripture, but *cum Chrismate* it is not found in Scripture, but it was used *cum Chrismate* in the Church soon after the Apostles time, as it may evidently appear by the cited Authors.

Dr. Coren. The laying of the Bishops hands upon them that be christened, which is a part of Confirmation, is plainly in Scripture; and the Unction with Chrisme, which is another part, hath been observed from the Primitive Church, and is called of St. Austin, *Sacramentum Chrismatis.* Unction of the Sick with Oil, and the Prayer, is grounded expresly in Scripture.

Con. Conveniunt omnes Confirmationem cum Chrismate non haberi in Scripturis. Eboracens. Tresham, Coren, Day, Oglethorpe, Edgworth, Leighton, Symmons, Redman, Robinsonus, Confirmationem in Scripturis esse contendunt; cæterum Chrisma esse traditionem Apostolicam: addit Robertsonus, et ubi fieri desierat miraculum Consecrandi Spiritus Sancti, Ecclesia Chrismate signi externi loco uti cœpit; Convenit illi Londinens.
Carliolens. putat usum Chrismatis ex Scripturis peti posse; Putant omnes tum in hoc Articulo, tum superiori, Impositionem manuum esse Confirmationem.

Agreement. In the eighth they do agree all, except it be the Bishop of Carlile, That *Confirmatio cum Chrismate* is not found in Scripture, but only, *Confirmatio cum manuum Impositione.*

And that also my Lord of St. Davids denieth to be in
Scripture, as we call it a Sacrament. My Lord of Carlile
saith, That " *Chrisma*, as touching the confection and
usage thereof, hath a ground to be derived out of Scripture." The other say, That " it is but a Tradition."

---

9. Question.

Whether the Apostles lacking a higher Power, as in not
having a Christian King among them, made Bishops by
that necessity, or by Authority given by God?

Answers.

ALL Christian Princes have committed unto them imme- Canter-
diately of God the whole Cure of all their Subjects, as bury.
well concerning the Administration of God's Word, for
the Cure of Souls, as concerning the ministration of things
Political and Civil Governance: And in both these Ministrations, they must have sundry Ministers under them to
supply that, which is appointed to their several Offices.
The Civil Ministers under the King's Majesty, in this
Realm of England, be those whom it shall please his Highness for the time to put in Authority under him: As for Example; The Lord Chancellor, Lord Treasurer, Lord Great
Master, Lord Privy Seal, Lord Admiral, Majors, Sheriffs,
&c. The Ministers of God's Word, under his Majesty, be the
Bishops, Parsons, Vicars, and such other Priests as be appointed by his Highness to that Ministration: As for Example, the Bishop of Canterbury, the Bishop of Duresme,
the Bishop of Winchester, the Parson of Winwick, &c. All
the said Officers and Ministers, as well of that sort as the
other, be appointed, assigned, and elected, and in every
place, by the Laws and Orders of Kings and Princes.
In the admission of many of these Officers, be divers
comely Ceremonies and Solemnities used, which be not of
necessity, but only for a good order and seemly fashion;
for if such Offices and Ministrations were committed without such solemnity, they were nevertheless truly committed: And there is no more Promise of God, that Grace

is given in the committing of the Ecclesiastical Office, than it is in the committing of the Civil Office. In the Apostles time, when there was no Christian Princes, by whose Authority Ministers of God's Word might be appointed, nor Sins by the Sword corrected, there was no Remedy then for the correction of Vice, or appointing of Ministers, but only the consent of Christian Multitudes among themselves, by an uniform consent, to follow the advice and perswasion of such Persons whom God had most endued with the Spirit of Counsel and Wisdom: And at that time, forasmuch as the Christian People had no Sword, nor Governour amongst them, they were constrained of necessity to take such Curats and Priests, as either they knew themselves to be meet thereunto, or else as were commended unto them by others, that were so replete with the Spirit of God, with such knowledg in the profession of Christ, such Wisdom, such Conversation and Counsel, that they ought even of very Conscience to give credit unto them, and to accept such as by them were presented: and so sometimes the Apostles and others, unto whom God had given abundantly his Spirit, sent or appointed Ministers of God's Word; sometimes the People did choose such, as they thought meet thereunto; and when any were appointed or sent by the Apostles or others, the People of their own voluntary Will with thanks did accept them: nor for the Supremity, Empire, or Dominion, that the Apostles had over them to command, as their Princes and Masters, but as good People ready to obey the advice of good Counsellors, and to accept any thing that was necessary for their edification and benefit.

York. To the ninth; We find in Scripture, that the Apostles used the Power to make Bishops, Priests and Deacons; which Power may be grounded upon these words; *Sicut misit me vivens Pater, sic ego mitto vos*, &c. And we verily think, that they durst not have used so high Power, unless they had had Authority from Christ; but that their Power to ordain Bishops, Priests, or Deacons, by Imposition of Hands, requireth any other Authority, than Authority of God, we neither read in Scripture, nor out of Scripture,

To the ninth; I think the Apostles made Bishops by the Law of God, because, Acts 22. it is said, *In quo vos Spiritus Sanctus posuit:* Nevertheless, I think if Christian Princes had been then, they should have named by Right, and appointed the said Bishops to their Rooms and Places.

I think that the Apostles made Bishops by Authority given them from God.

That Christ made his Apostles, Priests, and Bishops, and that he gave them Power to make others like, it seemeth to be the very trade of Scripture.

Opinor Apostolos Authoritate Divina creasse Episcopos et Presbyteros, ubi Publicus Magistratus permittit.

Altho the Apostles had no authority to force any Man to be Priest, yet (they moved by the Holy Ghost) had authority of God to exhort and induce Men to set forth God's Honour, and so to make them Priests.

The Apostles made, that is to say, ordained Bishops by authority given them by God; Joh. 20. *Sicut misit me vivens Pater, ita et ego mitto vos.* Item Joan. ult. et Act. 20. and 1 Tim. 4. *Paulus ordinavit Timotheum et Titum, et præscribit quales illi debeant ordinare.* 1 Tim. I. Tit. 1.

Apostoli autoritate et mandato Dei, ordinabant ac instituebant Episcopos, petita ac obtenta prius facultate a Principe ac Magistratu (ut opinor) qui tum præerat.

Christ gave his Apostles authority to make other Bishops and Ministers in his Church, as he had received authority of the Father to make them Bishops; but if any Christian Prince had then been, the Apostles had been, and ought to have been obedient Subjects, and would nothing have attempted, but under the permission and assent of their Earthly Governors: yet was it meet that they which were special and most Elect Servants of our Saviour Christ, and were sent by him to convert the World, and having

most abundantly the Holy Ghost in them, should have
special ordering of such Ministry as pertained to the plant-
ing and encreasing of the Faith; whereunto I doubt not,
but a Christian Prince, of his godly mind, would most
lovingly have condescended. And it is to be considered,
that in this Question, with other like, this word "making
of a Bishop, or Priest," may be taken two ways: for understanding the Word, to ordain or consecrate, so it is a thing
which pertaineth to the Apostles and their Successors only;
but if by this word (Making) be understood the appointing
or naming to the Office; so, it pertaineth specially to the
Supream Heads and Governours of the Church, which be
Princes.

Dr.
Edg-
worth.
The Apostles made Bishops and Priests by authority
given them of God, and not for lack of any higher Power:
Notwithstanding where there is a Christned King or Prince,
the Election, Deputation and Assignation of them, that
shall be Priests or Bishops, belongeth to the King or
Prince, so that he may forbid any Bishop within his Kingdom, that he give no orders, for Considerations moving
him, and may assign him a time when he shall give Orders,
and to whom: Example of King David, 1 Chron. 24. di-
viding the Levites into 24 Orders, deputing over every
Order one chief Bishop, prescribing an Ordinal and Rule
how they should do their Duties, their Courses; and what
Sacrifices, Rites, and Ceremonies, they should use every
day, as the day and time required. And his Son, King Solomon, diligently executed, and commanded the same usages
to be observed in the Temple, after he had erected and
finished it, 2 Chron. 8.

Dr.
Sym-
mons.
The Apostles made Bishops and Priests, by authority
given them of God.

Dr.
Tre-
sham.
I say, That the Apostles had authority of God to make
Bishops; yet if there had been a Christian King in any
place where they made Bishops, they would, and ought,
to have desired authority also of him, for the executing of
such their godly Acts, which no Christian King would have
denied.

To the ninth, I say, That the Apostles (as I suppose)
made Bishops by authority given unto them of Christ:
Howbeit I think they would and should have required
the Christian Princes consent and license thereto, if there
had been any Christian Kings or Princes.

The Apostles made Bishops and Priests by authority
given them of God: Notwithstanding if there had been a
Christian King at that time, it had been their Duties, to
have had his License and Permission to do the same.

Omnes Conveniunt Apostolos Divinitus accepisse Potestatem creandi Episcopos; Eboracens. addit, non opus
fuisse alia authoritate Apostolis quam divina: Sic Thirleby et Edgworth, Redmanus distinguit de Institutione Presbyteri, Ordinationem et Consecrationem tribuit tantum
Apostolis et eorum Successoribus, nominationem et electionem Magistratibus: Sic Londinens. Leightonus, Redman, Tresham, Curren, aiunt petendam fuisse Potestatem
a Magistratu Christiano, si tum fuisset. Robertsonus non
respondet Quæstioni, concedit enim datam esse Apostolis
Potestatem creandi Episcopos ubi Magistratus permittit.
Oglethorpus putat eos impetrasse potestatem a principibus: Carliolens. Roffens. Dayus, non respondent ultimæ
Parti.

In the ninth, touching the Authority of the Apostles in
making Priests, the Bishop of York, the Elect of West-
minster, Dr. Edgeworth, say, That " the Apostles made
Priests by their own Power, given them by God, and that
they had no need of any other Power." The Bishop of
St. David saith, That " because they lacked a Christian
Prince, by that necessity they Ordained other Bishops."
Dr. Leighton, Curren, Tresham, and Redmayn, suppose,
That " they ought to have asked license of their Christian
Governours, if then there had been any."

10. Question.

*Whether Bishops or Priests were first? and if the Priests
were first, then the Priest made the Bishop.*

Answers.

Canter-
bury.
THE Bishops and Priests were at one time, and were no
two things, but both one Office in the beginning of Christ's
Religion.

York.
To the tenth; We think that the Apostles were Priests
before they were Bishops; and that the Divine Power
which made them Priests, made them also Bishops; and
altho their Ordination was not by all such Course as the
Church now useth, yet that they had both Visible and
Invisible Sanctification, we may gather of the Gospel,
where it is written, *Sicut misit me Pater vivens, et ego mitto
vos: et cum hæc dixit, insufflavit in eos et dixit, accipite
Spiritum Sanctum: Quorum remiseritis,* &c. And we may
well think, that then they were made Bishops, when they
had not only a Flock, but also Shepherds appointed to
them to overlook, and a Governance committed to them by
the Holy Ghost to oversee both; for the name of a Bishop,
is not properly a name of Order, but a name of Office, signifying an Overseer. And altho the inferior Shepherds
have also Cure to over-see their Flock, yet forsomuch as
the Bishops Charge is also to oversee the Shepherds, the
name of Overseer is given to the Bishops, and not to
the other; and as they be in degree higher, so in their
Consecration we find difference even from the Primitive
Church.

London
To the tenth; I think the Bishops were first, and yet I
think it is not of importance, whether the Priest then
made the Bishop, or else the Bishop the Priest; considering (after the Sentence of St. Jerome) " that in the beginning of the Church there was none (or if it were, very
small) difference, between a Bishop and a Priest, especially
touching the signification."

· I find in Scripture, That Christ being both a Priest and a Bishop, ordained his Apostles, who were both Priests and Bishops; and the same Apostles did afterwards ordain Bishops, and commanded them to ordain others.

Christ made his Apostles Exorcists, as it appeareth in the 10. Mat. Deacons, Priests, and Bishops, as partly there, and after, in the 20 of St. John, *Quorum Remiseritis*, &co. and where he said, *Hoc facite in meam Commemorationem*. In the Acts, *Cæterorum nemo audebat se conjungere illis*. So that they were all these together; and so being according to the Ordinance of Christ, who had made after them 72 other Priests, as it appeareth in the 10 of St. Luke : They made and ordained also others the seven principal Deacons, as it is shewed in the 6 of the Acts; where it is said, That they praying laid their hands upon them. In the 13 of the Acts, certain there named at the commandment of the Holy Ghost, severed Saul and Barnabas to that God had taken them, Fasting, Praying, and laying their hands upon them; the which Saul, Ananias the Disciple had baptized, laying his hand upon him, that he might be replenished with the Holy Ghost. And Paul so made, ordained Timothy and Tite, willing them to do likewise as he had done, and appointed to be done from City to City. James was ordained the Bishop of Jerusalem, by Peter, John, and James. So that Example otherwise we read not.

Incertus sum utri fuere priores, at si Apostoli in prima profectione Ordinati erant, apparet Episcopos fuisse priores, nempe Apostolos, nam postea designavit Christus alios septuaginta duos. Nec opinor absurdum esse, ut Sacerdos Episcopum Consecret, si Episcopus haberi non potest.

. Although by Scripture (as St. Hierome saith) Priests and Bishops be one, and therefore the one not before the other: Yet Bishops, as they be now, were after Priests, and therefore made of Priests

Dr. Day

The Apostles were both Bishops and Priests, and they made Bishops, and Priests, as Titus and Timotheus made Priests. *Episcopatum ejus accipiat alter*, Act. 1. *Presbyteros qui in vobis sunt, obsecro et ego Compresbyter*, 1 Pet. 5. And in the beginning of the Church, as well that word *Episcopus* as Presbyter, was common and attributed both to Bishops and Priests.

Dr. Oglethorp.

Utrique primi a Deo facti, Apostoli, Episcopi; Septuaginta discipuli (ut conjectura ducor) Sacerdotes. Unde verisimile est Episcopos præcessisse, Apostoli enim prius vocati erant.

Dr. Redmayn.

They be of like beginning, and at the beginning were both one, as St. Hierome and other old Authors shew by the Scripture, wherefore one made another indifferently.

Dr. Edgeworth.

Christ our chief Priest and Bishop, made his Apostles Priests and Bishops all at once; and they did likewise make others, some Priests, and some Bishops: and that the Priests in the Primitive Church made Bishops, I think no inconvenience; (as Jerome saith) in an *Epist. ad Evagrium.* Even like as Souldiers should choose one among themselves to be their Captain: So did Priests choose one of themselves to be their Bishop, for consideration of his learning, gravity, and good living, &c. and also for to avoid Schisms among themselves by them, that some might not draw the People one way, and others another way, if they lacked one Head among them.

Dr. Symmons.

Christ was and is the great High Bishop, and made all his Apostles Bishops; and they made Bishops and Priests after him, and so hath it ever-more continued hitherto.

Dr. Tresham.

I say, Christ made the Apostles first Priests, and then Bishops, and they by this Authority made both Priests and Bishops; but where there had been a Christian Prince, they would have desired his Authority to the same.

Dr. Leyghton.

To the Tenth. ———

BOOK
III.

Dr. Co-
ren.
Con.

The Apostles were made of Christ Bishops and Priests, both at the first; and after them, *Septuaginta duo Discipuli*, were made Priests.

Menevens. Therleby, Redmanus, Coxus, asserunt in initio eosdem fuisse Episcopos et Presbyteros. Londinens. Carliolens. Symons, putant Apostolos fuisse institutos Episcopos a Christo, et eos postea instituisse alios Episcopos et Presbyteros, et 72 Presbyteros postea fuisse Ordinatos: Sic Oglethorpus, Eboracens. et Tresham aiunt Apostolos primo fuisse Presbyteros, deinde Episcopos, cum aliorum Presbyterorum credita esset illis cura. Robertsonus incertus est utri fuere priores, non absurdum tamen esse opinatur, ut Sacerdos consecret Episcopum, si Episcopus haberi non potest. Sic Londinens. Edgworth, Dayus, putant etiam Episcopos, ut vulgo de Episcopis loquimur, fuisse ante Presbyteros. Leightonus nihil Respondet.

Agreement.

In the tenth; Where it is asked, Whether Bishops or Priests were first? The Bishop of St. David, my Lord Elect of Westminster, Dr. Cox, Dr. Redmayn, say, That " at the beginning they were all one." The Bishops of York, London, Rochester, Carlisle; Drs. Day, Tresham, Symmons, Oglethorp, be in other contrary Opinions. The Bishop of York, and Doctor Tresham, think, " That the Apostles first were Priests, and after were made Bishops, when the overseeing of other Priests was committed to them." My Lords of Duresme, London, Carlisle, Rochester, Dr. Symmons and Crayford, think, " That the Apostles first were Bishops, and they after made other Bishops and Priests." Dr. Coren and Oglethorp, say, " That the Apostles were made Bishops, and the 72 were after made Priests." Dr. Day thinks, " That Bishops, as they be now-a-days called, were before Priests." My Lord of London, Drs. Edgworth and Robertson, think " it no inconvenience, if a Priest made a Bishop in that time."

A COLLECTION

Il. Question.

Whether a Bishop hath Authority to make a Priest by the Scripture, or no? And whether any other but only a Bishop may make a Priest?

Answers.

Canter-
bury.

A BISHOP may make a Priest by the Scripture, and so may Princes and Governours also, and that by the authority of God committed to them, and the People also by their Election; for as we read that Bishops have done it, so Christian Emperors and Princes usually have done it, and the People before Christian Princes were, commonly did Elect their Bishops and Priests.

York.

To the eleventh; That a Bishop may make a Priest, may be deduced of Scripture; for so much as they have all Authority necessary for the ordering of Christ's Church, derived from the Apostles, who made Bishops and Priests, and not without Authority, as we have said before to the ninth Question; and that any other than Bishops or Priests may make a Priest, we neither find in Scripture nor out of Scripture.

Lon-
don.

To the eleventh, I think, That a Bishop duly appointed, hath authority, by Scripture, to make a Bishop, and also a Priest: because Christ being a Bishop did so make himself; and because alive, his Apostles did the like.

Ro-
chester.

The Scripture sheweth by example, that a Bishop hath authority to make a Priest; albeit no Bishop being subject to a Christian Prince, may either give Orders or Excommunicate, or use any manner of Jurisdiction, or any part of his Authority, without Commission from the King, who is Supream Head of that Church whereof he is a Member; but that any other Man may do it besides a Bishop, I find no example, either in Scripture, or in Doctors.

Carlisle

By what is said before, it appeareth, that a Bishop by

Scripture may make Deacons and Priests, and that we have none example otherwise.

Opinor Episcopum habere Authoritatem creandi Sacerdotem, modo id Magistratus publici permissu fiat. An vero ab alio quam Episcopo id rite fieri possit, haud scio, quamvis ab alio factum non memini me legisse. Ordin. conferr. gratiam. vid. Eck. homil. 60. — *Dr. Roberttson.*

Bishops have authority, as is afore-said, of the Apostles, in the tenth Question, to make Priests, except in cases of great necessity. — *Dr Cox.*

Bishops have authority by Scripture to ordain Bishops and Priests; Joh. 20. *Hujus rei gratia reliqui te Cretæ ut constituas oppidatim Presbyteros*, Tit. 1. Act. 14. — *Dr. Day.*

Autoritas ordinandi Presbyteros data est Episcopis per verbum, nullisque aliis quos lego. — *Dr. Oglethorpe.*

To the first part, I answer, Yea; for so it appeareth Tit. 1. and 1 Tim. 5. with other places of Scripture. But whether any other but only a Bishop may make a Priest, I have not read, but by singular priviledg of God; as when Moses (whom divers Authors say was not a Priest) made Aaron a Priest. Truth it is, that the Office of a Godly Prince is to over-see the Church, and the Ministers thereof; and to cause them do their duty, and also to appoint them special Charges and Offices in the Church, as may be most for the Glory of God, and edifying of the People: and thus we read of the good Kings in the Old Testament, David, Joas, Ezekias, Josias. But as for Making, that is to say, Ordaining and Consecrating of Priests, I think it specially belongeth to the Office of a Bishop, as far as can be shewed by Scripture, or any Example, as I suppose from the beginning. — *Dr. Redmayn.*

A Bishop hath authority by Scripture to make a Priest, and that any other ever made a Priest since Christ's time I read not. Albeit Moses who was not anointed Priest, made Aaron Priest and Bishop, by a special Commission — *Dr. Edgeworth.*

BOOK III,

or Revelation from God, without which he would never so have done.

Dr. Symmons.

A Bishop placed by the Higher Powers, and admitted to minister, may make a Priest; and I have not read of any other that ever made Priests.

Dr. Tresham.

I say, a Bishop hath authority by Scripture to make a Priest, and other than a Bishop, hath not power therein, but only in case of necessity.

Dr. Leyghton.

To the eleventh; I suppose that a Bishop hath authority of God, as his Minister, by Scripture to make a Priest; but he ought not to admit any Man to be Priest, and consecrate him, or to appoint him unto any ministry in the Church, without the Princes license and consent, in a Christian Region. And that any other Man hath authority to make a Priest by Scripture, I have not read, nor any example thereof.

Dr. Coren.

A Bishop being licensed by his Prince and Supream Governour, hath authority to make a Priest by the Law of God. I do not read that any Priest hath been ordered by any other than a Bishop.

Con.

Ad primam partem Quæstionis respondent omnes, et convenit omnibus præter Menevens. Episcopum habere autoritatem instituendi Presbyteros. Roffens. Leighton, Curren, Robertsonus, addunt, Modo Magistratus id permittat. Ad secundam partem Respondent Coxus et Tresham in necessitate concedi potestatem Ordinandi aliis. Eboracen. videtur omnino denegare aliis hanc autoritatem. Redmayn, Symmons, Robertson, Leighton, Thirleby, Curren. Roffen. Edgworth, Oglethorp, Carliolen. nusquam legerunt alios usos fuisse hac Potestate, quanquam (privilegio quodam) data sit Moysi, ut Redmanus arbitratur et Edgeworth. Nihil respondent ad secundam partem Quæstionis Londinensis et Dayus.

Agreement.

In the eleventh; To the former part of the Question, the Bishop of St. Davids doth answer, That " Bishops

have no authority to make Priests, without they be autho- BOOK
rized of the Christian Prince." The others, all of them do III.
say, That "they be authorized of God." Yet some of
them, as the Bishop of Rochester, Dr. Curren, Leighton,
Robertson, add, That "they cannot use this authority
without their Christian Prince doth permit them." To the
second part, the answer of the Bishop of St. Davids is,
That "Laymen have other-whiles made Priests." So doth
Dr. Edgworth and Redman say, That "Moses by a priviledg given him of God, made Aaron his Brother Priest."
Dr. Tresham, Crayford, and Cox say, That "Laymen may
make Priests in time of Necessity." The Bishops of York,
Duresme, Rochester, Carlisle, Elect of Westminster, Dr.
Curren, Leighton, Symmons, seem to deny this thing; for
they say, "They find not, nor read not any such example."

---

12. Question.

Whether in the New Testament be required any Consecration
of a Bishop and Priest, or only appointing to the Office
be sufficient ?

Answers.

In the New Testament, he that is appointed to be a Canter-
Bishop, or a Priest, needeth no Consecration by the Scrip- bury.
ture, for election or appointing thereto is sufficient.

To the twelfth Question; The Apostles ordained Priests York.
by Imposition of the Hand with Fasting and Prayer; and
so following their steps, we must needs think, that all the
foresaid things be necessarily to be used by their Successors: and therefore we do also think, that Appointment
only without visible Consecration and Invocation for the
assistance and power of the Holy Ghost, is neither convenient nor sufficient; for without the said Invocation, it be-
seemeth no Man to appoint to our Lord Ministers, as of
his own authority: whereof we have example in the Acts
of the Apostles; where we find, that when they were ga-

BOOK III. thered to choose one in the place of Judas, they appointed two of the Disciples, and commended the Election to our Lord, that he would choose which of them it pleased him, saying and praying, " Lord, thou that knowest the hearts of all Men, shew whether of these two thou dost choose to succeed in the place of Judas." And to this purpose in the Acts we read, *Dixit Spiritus Sanctus, segregate mihi Barnabam, &c.* And again, *Quos posuit Spiritus Sanctus regere Ecclesiam Dei.* And it appeareth also that in the Old Testament, in the ordering of Priests, there was both Visible and Invisible Sanctification; and therefore in the New Testament, where the Priesthood is above comparison higher than in the Old, we may not think that only appointment sufficeth without Sanctification, either Visible or Invisible.

London. To the twelfth; I think Consecration of a Bishop and Priest be required, for that in the Old Law (being yet but a shadow and figure of the New) the Consecration was required, as appears Levit. 8. yet the truth of this I leave to those of higher Judgments.

Rochester. The Scripture speaketh, *de Impositione manus et de Oratione*: and of other manner of Consecrations, I find no mention in the New Testament expresly; but the Old Authors make mention also of Inunctions.

Carlile. Upon this Text of Paul to Timothy; *Noli negligere gratiam quæ in te est, quæ data est tibi per Prophetiam cum Impositione manuum Presbyterii;* St. Anselm saith, This " Grace to be the Gift of the Bishops Office, to the which God of his meer goodness had called and preferred him. The Prophesy (he saith) was the inspiration of the Holy Ghost, by the which he knew what he had to do therein. The Imposition of the hands is that by the which he was ordained and received that Office: ' And therefore (saith St. Paul) God is my Witness, that I have discharged my self, showing you as I ought to have done. Now look you well upon it whom that ye take to Orders, lest ye lose your self thereby.'" " Let Bishops therefore, who (as saith St. Hierome) hath power to make Priests, consider well under what Law the order of Ecclesiastical Constitution is bounden; and let them not think those words of the Apostle to be his, but rather the words of Christ himself."

Opinor requiri Consecrationem quandam, hoc est impositionem manuum, Orationem, jejunium, &c. tamen nusquam hoc munere fungi posse, nisi ubi Magistratus invitet, jubeat, aut permittat.

Dr. Robertson.

By Scripture there is no Consecration of Bishops and Priests required, but only the appointing to the Office of a Priest, *cum Impositione manuum.*

Dr. Cox.

Consecration of Bishops and Priests I read not in the New Testament, but *Ordinatio per manuum Impositionem cum Oratione* is read there, as in the places above; and the only appointment, as I think, is not sufficient.

Dr. Day.

Præter vocationem, ceu designationem externam, quæ vel a Principe fiat, vel a populo per electionem et suffragia, requiritur Ordinatio alia per manuum impositionem, idque per Verbum Dei.

Dr. Oglethorpe.

Besides the appointing to the Office, it appeareth that in the Primitive Church, the Apostles used certain Consecration of the Ministers of the Church, by imposition of Hands and Prayer, Acts 6. and with Fasting, Acts 14, &c. The Office of Priesthood is too dangerous to set upon, when one is but appointed only: Therefore for the confirmation of their Faith, who take in hand such charge, and for the obtaining of farther Grace requisite in the same, Consecration was ordained by the Holy Ghost, and hath been always used from the beginning.

Dr. Redmayn.

Reputation to the Office, is not sufficient to make a Priest or a Bishop, as appeareth by David and Solomon, who deputed the 24 above-mentioned to their Offices, yet they made none of them Priests, nor any other.

Dr. Edgworth.

The appointing to the Office *per manuum Impositionem,*

Dr. Symmons.

is in Scripture, and the Consecration of them hath of long time continued in the Church.

Dr.
Tre-
sham.   There is a certain kind of Consecration required, which is imposition of the Bishops hands with Prayer, and the appointing only is not sufficient.

Dr.
Leygh-
ton.   To the twelfth; I suppose that there is a Consecration required, as by Imposition of Hands; for so we be taught by the ensample of the Apostles.

Dr. Co-
ren.   In the New Testament is required to the making of a Bishop, *Impositio manuum cum Oratione*, which I take for Consecration, and Appointment unto the Office is not sufficient; for King David, 1 Chron. 24. did appoint 24 to be Bishops, who after were consecrated; so that both the Appointment and the Consecration be requisite.

Con.   Respondent Eboracens. Londinens. Carliolens. Leighton, Tresham, Robertsonus, Edgeworth, Curren, Dayus, Oglethorp, Consecrationem esse requisitam. Redmanus ait eam receptam esse ab Apostolis, atque a Spiritu Sancto institutam ad conferendam gratiam. Dayus, Roffens. Symmons, aiunt Sacerdotium conferri per manuum impositionem, idq; è Scripturis; Consecrationem vero diu receptam in Ecclesia: Coxus Institutionem cum manuum impositione sufficere, neq; per Scripturam requiri Consecrationem. Robertsonus addit supra alios nusquam hoc munere fungi posse quempiam, nisi ubi Magistratus invitet, jubeat aut permittat.

Agree-
ment.   In the twelfth Question, where it is asked, Whether in the New Testament be required any Consecration of a Bishop, or only appointing to the Office be sufficient? The Bishop of St. Davids saith, That " only the appointing." Dr. Cox, That " only appointing, *cum manuum Impositione*, is sufficient without consecration." The Bishops of York, London, Duresme, Carlisle, Drs. Day, Curren, Leighton, Tresham, Edgworth, Oglethorp, say, That " Consecration is requisite." Dr. Redmayn saith, That " Con-

secration hath been received from the Apostles time, and
institute of the Holy Ghost to confer Grace." My Lord
of Rochester, Dr. Day, and Symmons, say, That " Priesthood is given *per manuum impositionem*, and that by Scripture; and that Consecration hath of long time been received
in the Church."

**BOOK
III.**

---

13. Question.

*Whether (if it fortuned a Christian Prince Learned, to
conquer certain Dominions of Infidels, having none but
temporal learned Men with him) if it be defended by
God's Law, that he and they should Preach and Teach
the Word of God there, or no? And also make and constitute Priests, or no?*

Answers.

IT is not against God's Law, but contrary they ought indeed so to do; and there be Histories that witnesseth, that
some Christian Princes, and other Laymen unconsecrate
have done the same.

*Canter-
bury.*

To the thirteenth; To the first part of this Question,
touching Teaching and Preaching the Word of God in case
of such need; we think that Laymen not ordered, not only
may, but must preach Christ and his Faith to Infidels, as
they shall see opportunity to do the same, and must endeavour themselves to win the Miscreants to the Kingdom
of God, if that they can; for as the Wise Man saith, "God
hath given charge to every Man of his Neighbour;" and the
Scripture of God chargeth every Man to do all the good
that he can to all Men: And surely this is the highest Alms
to draw Men from the Devil the Usurper, and bring them
to God the very Owner. Wherefore in this Case every Man
and Woman may be an Evangelist, and of this also we
have example. But touching the second part, for case of
Necessity; As we neither find Scripture, nor Example,

York.

that will bear, that any Man, being himself no Priest, may make, that is to say, may give the Order of Priesthood to another, and authority therewith to minister in the said Order, and to use such Powers and Offices, as appertaineth to Priesthood grounded in the Gospel: So we find in such case of need, what hath been done in one of the ancient Writers; altho this authority to ordain, after form afore-mentioned, be not to Laymen expresly prohibited in Scripture; yet such a prohibition is implied, in that there is no such authority given to them, either in Scripture or otherways; for so much as no Man may use this or any other authority which cometh from the Holy Ghost, unless he hath either Commission grounded in Scripture, or else Authority by Tradition, and ancient use of Christ's Church universally received over all.

London. To the thirteenth and fourteenth following; I think that necessity herein, might either be a sufficient Rule and Warrant to determine and order such Cases, considering that *tempore necessitatis mulier baptizat, et Laicus idem facit, et audit confessionem:* or else that God would inspire in the Princes heart, to provide the best and most handsome Remedy therein: And hard were it peradventure to find such great necessity, but either in the train of the said Prince, or in the Regions adjoining thereunto, there might be had some Priests for the said purposes; or, finally, That the Prince himself, godlily inspired in that behalf, might, for so good purposes and intents, set forth the Act indeed, referring yet this thing to the better judgment of others.

Rochester. To the thirteenth and fourteenth following; I never read these cases, neither in Scripture, nor in the Doctors, and therefore I cannot Answer unto them by Learning, but think this to be a good Answer for all such Questions, viz. *Necessitas non habet Legem.*

Carlile. It is to be thought, that Christ may call, as it pleaseth him, inwardly, outwardly, or by both together: So that if no Priest might be had, it cannot be thought, but that a

Christian Prince, with others learned, inwardly moved and called, might most charitably and godlily prosecute that same their Calling in the most acceptable Work, which is to bring People from the Devil to God, from Infidelity to true Faith, by whatsoever means God shall inspire.

BOOK III.

In hoc casu existimarem accersendos verbi et Sacramentorum Ministros, si qui forent vicini; quin si nulli invenirentur, Principem illum Christianum haberemus pro Apostolo, tanquam missum a Deo, licet externo Sacramento non esset commendatus, quum Deus Sacramentis suis non sit alligatus.

Dr. Robertson.

To the thirteenth, and fourteenth following; It is not against God's Law, that the Prince, and his learned temporal Men, may Preach and Teach, and in these cases of extream Necessity, make and institute Ministers.

Dr. Cox

In this case (as I think) the Prince and other temporal learned Men with him, may by God's Law, Teach and Preach the Word of God, and Baptise; and also (the same Necessity standing) elect and appoint Men to those Offices.

Dr. Day.

In summa necessitate Baptizare et prædicare possunt et debent, hæc etenim duo necessaria sunt media ad salutem; at ordinare (ut conjectura ducor) non debent, sed aliunde Sacrificos accersire, quos si habere nequeant, Deus ipse (cujus negotium agitur,) vel oraculo admonebit, quid faciendum erit, vel necessitas ipsa (quæ sibi ipsi est Lex) modum Ordinandi suggeret ac suppeditabit.

Dr. Oglethorp.

I think they might, in such case of Necessity; for in this case the Laymen made the whole Church there, and the authority of preaching and ministring the Sacraments, is given immediately to the Church; and the Church may appoint Ministers, as is thought convenient. There be two Stories good to be considered for this Question, which be written in the 10th Book of the History Ecclesiastick; the one of Frumentius, who preached in India, and was

Dr. Redmayn.

after made Priest and Bishop by Athanasius. And the other Story is of the King of the Iberians, of whom Ruffine the writer of the Story saith thus; *Et nondum initiatus Sacris fit suæ gentis Apostolus.* Yet nevertheless it is written there, That " an Ambassad was sent to Constantine the Emperor, that he would send them Priests for the further establishment of the Faith there."

Dr.
Edgeworth.
The Prince and his temporal learned Men, might and ought, in that necessity, to instruct the People in the Faith of Christ, and to baptize them, *ut idem rex sit et suæ gentis Apostolus,* and these be sufficient for the Salvation of his Subjects. But as concerning other Sacraments, he ought to abide and look for a special Commission from Almighty God, as Moses had, or else to send unto other Regions where Priests or Bishops may be had, and else not to meddle. Examples in *Eccles. Hist.* lib. 10. cap. 1. *de Frumentio.* et cap. 2. *de Ancilla captiva quæ convertit gentem Hiberorum, cujus captivæ monitis ad Imperatorem Constantinum totius gentis legatio mittitur, res gesta exponitur, Sacerdotes mittere exorantur qui cœptum erga se Dei munus implerent, &c.*

Dr.
Symmons.
I think that in such a necessity, a learned Christian Prince, and also temporal Men learned, be bound to preach and minister either Sacraments, so that the same Ministers be orderly assigned by the High Power and the Congregation.

Dr.
Tresham.
I say, to the first part, That such a King, and his temporal learned Men, not only might, but were also bound to preach God's Word in this case. And as to the second part, I say, That if there could no Bishop be had to Institute, the Prince might in that of necessity do it.

Dr.
Leyghton.
To the thirteenth: I suppose the Affirmative thereof to be true; *Quamvis potestas clavium residet præcipue in Ecclesia.*

Dr. Coren.
In such a case, I do believe that God would illumi-

nate the Prince; so that either he himself should be made **Book** a Bishop, by internal working of God (as Paul was) **III.** or some of his Subjects, or else God would send him Bishops from other Parts. And as for preaching of the Word of God, the Prince might do it himself, and other of his learned Subjects, altho they were no Priests.

In prima parte Quæstionis Conveniunt omnes, etiam **Con.** laicos, tali rerum statu, non solum posse sed debere docere. Menevens. Thirlebeus, Leightonus, Coxus, Symmons, Tresham, Redmanus, Robertsonus, etiam potestatem Ministrandi Sacramenta, et Ordinandi Ministros, concedunt illis. Eboracens. hanc prorsus potestatem denegat. Coren credit Principem Divinitus illuminandum et consecrandum fore in Episcopum interne, aut aliquem ex suis, Pauli exemplo. Simile habet Herefordensis et Carliolensis. Dayus nihil respondet de Ordinandis Presbyteris in hac necessitate.

In the thirteenth; Concerning the first part, Whether **Agree-** Laymen may Preach and Teach God's Word? They do all **ment.** agree, in such a case, " That not only they may, but they ought to teach." But in the second part, touching the Constituting of Priests of Laymen, my Lord of York, and Doctor Edgworth, doth not agree with the other; they say, That " Laymen in no wise can make Priests, or have such Authority." The Bishops of Duresme, St. Davids, Westminster, Drs. Tresham, Cox, Leighton, Crayford, Symmons, Redmayn, Robertson, say, " That Laymen in such case have authority to minister the Sacraments, and to make Priests." My Lords of London, Carlisle, and Hereford, and Dr. Coren, think, " That God in such a case would give the Prince authority, call him inwardly, and illuminate him or some of his, as he did St. Paul."

14. Question.

*Whether it be forefended by God's Law, that (if it so for-
tune that all the Bishops and Priests of a Region were
dead, and that the Word of God should remain there
unpreached, and the Sacrament of Baptism, and others
unministred) that the King of that Region should make
Bishops and Priests to supply the same, or no?*

Answers.

Canter-
bury.

IT is not forbidden by God's Law.

York.

     To the fourteenth; In this case, as we have said in the
next Articles afore, Teaching of the Word of God may be
used by any that can and would use it, to the Glory of
God; and in this case also the Sacrament of Baptism may
be ministred by those that be no Priests; which things
although we have not of Scripture, yet the universal Tradition and practice of the Church, doth teach us: And
peradventure contract of Matrimony might also be made,
the Solemnization thereof being only ordained by Law
positive, and not by any ground, either of Scripture, or of
Tradition; altho for very urgent causes, the said Solemnization is to be observed when it may be observed; but
that the Princes may not Make, that is, may not Order
Priests nor Bishops not before ordered to minister the
other Sacraments, the ministry whereof in Scripture is committed only to the Apostles, and from them derived to their
Successors, even from the Primitive Church hitherto, and
by none other used, we have answered in the thirteenth
Article.

Lon-
don.

Ut supra, Quæst. 13.——

Ro-
chester.

Ut supra, Quæst. 13.——

Carlile.

     Not only it is given of God to Supream Governours,
Kings and Princes immediate under them, to see cause,
and compel all their Subjects, Bishops, Priests, with all

others, to do truly and uprightly their bounden Duties to God, and to them, each one according to his Calling: but also if it were so, that any-where such lacked to do and fulfil that God would have done, right-well they might, by the inward moving and calling of God, supply the same.

Huic Quæstioni idem Respondendum, quod priori, arbitror.

Ut supra, Quæst. 13.

To this case, as to the first, I answer; That if there could no Bishops be had to order new Priests there, by the Princes assignation and appointment; then the Prince himself might ordain and constitute, with the consent of the Congregation, both Priests and Ministers, to Preach and Baptize, and to do other Functions in the Church.

Si ab aliis Regionibus Sacerdotes haberi non poterint, opinor ipsum Principem deputare posse etiam Laicos ad hoc Sacrum Officium; sed omnia prius tentanda essent, ut supra.

To this, I think, may be answered, as to the last Question before; howbeit the surest way, I think, were to send for some Ministers of the Church dwelling in the next Regions, if they might be conveniently had.

Likewise as to the next Question afore.

If the King be also a Bishop, as it is possible, he may appoint Bishops and Priests to minister to his People: but hitherto I have not read that ever any Christian King made Bishop or Priest.

I make the same answer, as to the 13th Question is made.

To the fourteenth; I suppose the Affirmative to be true, in case that there can no Bishops nor Priests be had forth of other Countries, conveniently.

Dr.
Coren.

In this case I make answer as before, That God will never suffer his Servants to lack that thing that is necessary: for there should, either from other parts, Priests and Bishops be called thither, or else God would call inwardly some of them that be in that Region to be Bishops and Priests.

Con.

Fatentur ut prius omnes, Laicos posse Docere. Eboracens. Symmons, Oglethorp negant posse Ordinare Presbyteros, tamen concedit Eboracens. baptizare et contrahere Matrimonia, Edgworth tantum baptizare posse; nam sufficere dicit ad salutem. Alii omnes eandem potestatem concedunt, quam prius. Roffens. non aliud respondet his duabus Quæstionibus, quam quod necessitas non habeat Legem.

Agreement.

In the fourteenth they agree for the most part as they did before, That " Lay-men in this case may teach and minister the Sacraments." My Lord of York, Dr. Symmons, and Oglethorp say, " They can make no Priests, altho Symmons said they might minister all Sacraments, in the Question before." Yet my Lord of York, and Edgworth, do grant, That " they may Christen." The Bishops of London, Rochester, and Dr. Crayford, say, That " in such a case, *Necessitas non habet Legem.*"

---

15. Question.

*Whether a Man be bound by Authority of this Scripture,
(Quorum Remiseritis) and such-like, to confess his secret
deadly sins to a Priest, if he may have him, or no?*

Answers.

Canterbury.

A Man is not bound, by the authority of this Scripture, *Quorum Remiseritis*, and such-like, to confess his secret deadly Sins to a Priest, although he may have him.

To the fifteenth; This Scripture is indifferent to secret
and open Sin; nor the authority given in the same is appointed or limited, either to the one, or to the other, but is
given commonly to both: And therefore seeing that the
Sinner is in no other place of Scripture discharged of the
confession of his secret Sins, we think, that this place
chargeth him to confess the secret Sins, as well as the
open.

To the fifteenth; I think that as the Sinner is bound by
this authority to confess his open sins, so also is he bound
to confess his secret sins, because the special end is, to
wit, *Absolutionem a peccato cujus fecit se servum*, is all one
in both cases: And that all sins as touching God are open,
and in no wise secret or hid.

I think that confession of secret deadly sins is necessary
for to attain absolution of them; but whether every Man
that hath secretly committed deadly sin, is bound by these
words to ask Absolution of the Priest therefore, it is an
hard Question, and of much controversy amongst learned
Men, and I am not able to define betwixt them; but I
think it is the surest way, to say that a Man is bound to
Confess, &c.

I think that by the mind of most ancient Authors, and
most holy Expositors, this Text, *Quorum Remiseritis peccata, &c.* with other-like, serveth well to this intent; That
Christian Folk should confess their secret deadly sins to a
Priest there to be assoiled, without which mean, there can
be none other like Assurance.

Opinor obligare, modo aliter conscientiæ illius satisfieri
nequeat.

I cannot find that a Man is bound by Scripture to confess his secret deadly sins to a Priest, unless he be so
troubled in his Conscience, that he cannot be quieted without godly Instruction.

The Matter being in controversy among learned Men,

BOOK III. and very doubtful, yet I think rather the truth is, That by authority of this Scripture, *Quorum Remiseritis, &c.* and such-like, a Man is bound to confess his secret deadly sins, which grieve his Conscience, to a Priest, if he may conveniently have him. Forasmuch as it is an ordinary way ordained by Christ in the Gospel, by Absolution to remit sins; which Absolution I never read to be given, *sine Confessione prævia.*

Dr. Oglethorpe. Confitenda sunt opinor, etiam peccata abdita ac secreta propter Absolutionem ac conscientiæ tranquillitatem, et præcique pro vitanda desperatione, ad quam plerumq; adiguntur multi in extremis, dum sibi ipsis de remissione peccatorum nimium blandiuntur, nullius (dum sani sunt) censuram subeuntes nisi propriam.

Dr. Redmayn. I think, that altho in these words Confession of privy Sins, is not expresly commanded; yet it is insinuated and shewed in these words, as a necessary Medicine or Remedy, which all Men that fall into deadly sin ought, for the quieting of their Consciences seek, if they may conveniently have such a Priest as is meet to hear their Confession.

Dr. Edgeworth. Where there be two ways to obtain remission of Sin, and to recover Grace, a Man is bound by the Law of Nature to take the surer way, or else he should seem to contemn his own Health, which is unnatural. Also because we be bound to love God above all things, we ought by the same Bond to labour for his Grace and Favour: So that because we be bound to love God, and to love our selves in an Order to God, we be bound to seek the best and surest Remedy to recover Grace for our selves. Contrition is one way; but because a Man cannot be well assured, whether his Contrition, Attrition, or Displeasure for his sin be sufficient to satisfie or content Almighty God, and able or worthy to get his Grace: Therefore it is necessary to take that way that will not fail, and by which thou mayest be sure, and that is Absolution of the Priest, which by Christ's promise will not deceive thee, so that thou put no step or bar in the way; as, if thou do not then actually sin in-

wardly nor outwardly, but intend to receive that the Church *BOOK III.*
intendeth to give thee by that Absolution, having the effi-
cacity of Christ's promise, *Quorum Remiseritis, &c.* Now
the Priest can give thee no Absolution from that sin that
he knoweth not : therefore thou art bound, for the causes
aforesaid, to confess thy sin.

This Scripture, as Ancient Doctors expound it, bindeth *Dr. Symmons.*
all Men to confess their secret deadly sins.

I say, That such Confession is a thing most consonant *Dr. Tresham.*
to the Law of God, and it is a wise point, and a wholsome
thing so for to do, and God provoketh and allureth us
thereto, in giving the active Power to Priests to assoil in
the words, *Quorum Remiseritis.* It is also a safer way for
Salvation to confess, if we may have a Priest: Yet I think
that confession is not necessarily deduced of Scripture,
nor commanded as a necessary precept of Scripture, and
yet is it much consonant to the Law of God, as a thing
willed, not commanded.

To the fifteenth; I think that only such as have not the *Dr. Leyghton.*
knowledg of the Scripture, whereby they may quiet their
Consciences, be bound to confess their secret deadly sins
unto a Priest: Howbeit no man ought to condemn such
Auricular Confession, for I suppose it to be a Tradition
Apostolical, necessary for the unlearned Multitude.

A Man whose Conscience is grieved with mortal secret *Dr. Coren.*
sins, is bound by these words, *Quorum Remiseritis, &c.* to
confess his sin to a Priest, if he may have him conveniently.

Eboracens. Londinens. Dayus, Oglethorpus, Coren, Red- *Con.*
mayn, asserunt obligari. Coxus, Tresham, et Robertsonus
dicunt non obligari, si aliter Conscientiæ illorum satisfieri
queat; Menevens. nullo modo obligari. Carliolens. et
Symmons aiunt, secundum veterum interpretationem, hac
Scriptura quemvis obligari peccatorem. Roffens. Herefordens. et Thirleby non respondent, sed dubitant. Leightonus solum indoctos obligari ad Confessionem. Edgeworth tradit duplicem modum remissionis peccatorum, per

BOOK
III.

Contritionem sive Attritionem, et per Absolutionem: et quia nemo potest certus esse, num attritio et dolor pro peccato sufficiat ad satisfaciendum Deo et obtinendam gratiam, ideo tutissimam viam deligendam, scilicet, Absolutionem a Sacerdote, quæ per promissionem Christi est certa; Absolvere non potest nisi cognoscat peccata; Ergo peccata per Confessionem sunt illi revelanda.

Agree-
ment.

In the fifteenth; Concerning Confession of our secret deadly sins. The Bishops of York, Duresme, London, Drs. Day, Curren, Oglethorp, Redmayn, Crayford, say, That " Men be bound to confess them of their secret Sins." Drs. Cox, Tresham, Robertson, say, " They be not bound, if they may quiet their Consciences otherwise." The Bishop of St. Davids also saith, That " this Text bindeth no Man." Dr. Leighton saith, That " it bindeth only such as have not the knowledg of Scripture." The Bishop of Carlisle and Symmons say, That " by ancient Doctors exposition, Men be bound, by this Text, to confess their deadly sins."

16. Question.

Whether a Bishop or a Priest may excommunicate, and for what Crimes? And whether they only may Excommunicate by God's Law?

Answers.

Canter-
bury.

A Bishop or a Priest by the Scripture, is neither commanded nor forbidden to Excommunicate, but where the Laws of any Region giveth him authority to Excommunicate, there they ought to use the same in such Crimes, as the Laws have such authority in; and where the Laws of the Region forbiddeth them, there they have no authority at all; and they that be no Priests may also Excommunicate, if the Law allow thereunto.

York.

To the sixteenth; The power to Excommunicate, that

is, to dissever the Sinner from the communion of all BOOK
Christian People, and so put them out of the Unity of the III.
Mystical Body for the time, *donec resipiscat*, is only given
to the Apostles and their Successors in the Gospel, but for
what Crimes, altho in the Gospel doth not appear, saving
only for disobedience against the Commandment of the
Church, yet we find example of Excommunication used
by the Apostles in other cases: As of the Fornicator by
Paul, of Hymeneus and Alexander for their Blasphemy by
the same; and yet of other Crimes mentioned in the Epistle
of the said Paul writing to the Corinthians. And again of
them that were disobedient to his Doctrine, 2 Thess. 3.
We find also charge given to us, by the Apostle St. John,
that we shall not commune with them, nor so much as
salute him with *Ave*, that would not receive his Doctrine.
By which it may appear that Excommunication, may be
used for many great Crimes, and yet the Church at this
day, doth not use it, but only for manifest disobedience.
And this kind of Excommunication, whereby Man is put
out of the Church, and dissevered from the Unity of Christ's
Mystical Body, which Excommunication toucheth also the
Soul, no Man may use, but they only, to whom it is given
by Christ.

To the sixteenth; I think that a Bishop may Excommu- London
nicate, taking example of St. Paul with the Corinthian;
and also of that he did to Alexander and Hymeneus. And
with the Lawyers it hath been a thing out of Question,
That to Excommunicate solemnly, appertaineth to a
Bishop, altho otherwise, both inferior Prelates and other
Officers, yea and Priests too in notorious Crimes, after
divers Mens Opinions, may Excommunicate semblably, as
all others that be appointed Governors and Rulers over
any Multitude, or Spiritual Congregation.

I answer affirmatively to the first part, in open and mani- Ro-
fest Crimes, meaning of such Priests and Bishops as be chester.
by the Church authorized to use that power. To the
second part, I answer, That it is an hard Question, wherein
I had rather hear other Men speak, than say my own Sentence; for I find not in Scripture, nor in the old Doctors,

BOOK III. that any Man hath given Sentence of Excommunication, save only Priests; but yet I think, that it is not against the Law of God, that a Lay-man should have authority to do it.

Carlile. Divers Texts of Scripture seemeth, by the Interpretation of ancient Authors, to shew, that a Bishop or a Priest may Excommunicate open deadly sinners continuing in obstinacy with contempt. I have read in Histories also, that a Prince hath done the same.

Dr. Robertson. Opinor Episcopum aut Presbyterum Excommunicare posse, tanquam ministrum et os Ecclesiæ, ab eadem mandatum habens. Utrum vero id juris nulli nisi Sacerdotibus in mandatis dari possit, non satis scio. Excommunicandum esse opinor pro hujusmodi criminibus, qualia recenset Paulus, 1 Cor. 5. si, is qui frater nominatur, est fornicator, aut avarus, aut idolis serviens, aut maledicus, aut ebriosus, aut rapax, cum hujusmodi ne cibum sumere, &c.

Dr. Cox. A Bishop or a Priest, as a publick Person appointed to that Office, may excommunicate for all publick Crimes: And yet it is not against God's Law, for others than Bishops or Priests to Excommunicate.

Dr. Day. A Bishop or a Priest may Excommunicate by God's Law for manifest and open Crimes: Also others appointed by the Church, tho they be no Priests, may exercise the power of Excommunication.

Dr. Oglethorp. Non solum Episcopus Excommunicare potest, sed etiam tota Congregatio, idq; pro lethalibus criminibus ac publicis, è quibus scandalum Ecclesiæ provenire potest. Non tamen pro re pecuniaria uti olim solebant.

Dr. Redmayn. They may Excommunicate, as appeareth 1 Cor. 5. 1 Tim. 1. and that for open and great Crimes, whereby the Church is offended: and for such Crimes as the Prince and Governours determine, and thinketh expedient, Men to be excommunicate for, as appeareth *in novellis Constitutionibus*

Justiniani. Whether any other may pronounce the Sentence of Excommunication but a Bishop or a Priest I am uncertain.

A Bishop, or a Priest only, may excommunicate a notorious and grievous Sinner, or obstinate Person from the Communion of Christian People, because it pertaineth to the Jurisdiction which is given to Priests, Jo. 26. *Quorum Remiseritis, &c. et Quorum retinetis, &c.* There is one manner of Excommunication spoken of 1 Cor. 5. which private Persons may use. *Si is qui frater nominatur inter vos est fornicator, aut avarus, aut idolis serviens, &c. cum hujusmodi ne cibum quidem capiatis.* Excluding filthy Persons, covetous Persons, Braulers and Quarrellers, out of their Company, and neither to eat nor drink with them.

Whosoever hath a place under the Higher Power, and is assigned by the same to execute his Ministry given of God, he may Excommunicate for any Crime, as it shall be seen to the High Power, if the same Crime be publick.

A Bishop and Priest may Excommunicate by Scripture: as touching, for what Crimes; I say, for every open deadly sin and disobedience. And as touching, Whether only the Priest may Excommunicate? I say, not he only, but such as the Church authorizes so to do.

To the sixteenth, I say, that a Bishop or a Priest having License and Authority of the Prince of the Realm, may excommunicate every obstinate and inobedient Person, for every notable and deadly sin. And further, I say, That not only Bishops and Priests may Excommunicate, but any other Man appointed by the Church, or such as have authority to appoint Men to that Office may Excommunicate.

A Bishop or a Priest may Excommunicate an obstinate Person for publick Sins. Forasmuch as the Keys be given to the whole Church, the whole Congregation may Excommunicate, which Excommunication may be pronounced by such a one as the Congregation does appoint, altho he be neither Bishop nor Priest.

Con.   Menevens. Herefordens. Thirleby, Dayus, Leightonus, Coxus, Symmons, Coren, concedunt authoritatem excommunicandi etiam Laicis, modo a Magistratu deputentur. Eboracens. et Edgworth prorsus negant datum Laicis, sed Apostolis et eorum successoribus tantum. Roffensis, Redmanus, et Robertsonus ambigunt, num detur Laicis. Londinens. non respondet Quæstioni: Oglethorpus et Thirleby aiunt, Ecclesiæ datam esse potestatem Excommunicandi; Idem Treshamus.

Agree-
ment.   In the sixteenth, Of Excommunication, they do not agree. The Bishops of York, Duresme, and Dr. Edgworth say, That " Lay-men have not the authority to Excommunicate, but that it was given only unto the Apostles and their Successors." The Bishops of Hereford, St. Davids, Westminster, Doctors Day, Coren, Leighton, Cox, Symmons, say, That " Lay-men may Excommunicate, if they be appointed by the High Ruler." My Lord Elect of Westminster, Dr. Tresham, and Dr. Oglethorp, say further, That " the Power of Excommunication was given to the Church, and to such as the Church shall institute."

---

17. Question.

Whether Unction of the Sick with Oil, to remit Venial Sins, as it is now used, be spoken of in the Scripture, or in any ancient Authors?

Answers.

Canter-
bury.   UNCTION of the Sick with Oil, to remit Venial Sins, as it is now used, is not spoken of in the Scripture, nor in any ancient Authors.

T. Cantuarien. This is mine Opinion and These are the Subscriptions which are at the end of every Man's Paper. Sentence at this present, which I do not temerariously define, but do remit the judgment thereof wholly unto your Majesty.

To the seventeenth; Of Unction of the Sick with Oil, York. and that Sins thereby be remitted, St. James doth teach us; but of the Holy Prayers, and like Ceremonies used in the time of the Unction, we find no special mention in Scripture, albeit the said St. James maketh also mention of Prayer to be used in the Ministry of the same.

Edward. Ebor.

To the seventeenth ; I think that albeit it appeareth not London clearly in Scripture, whether the usage in extream Unction now, be all one with that which was in the beginning of the Church: Yet of the Unction in time of Sickness, and the Oil also with Prayers and Ceremonies, the same is set forth in the Epistle of St. James, which place commonly is alledged, and so hath been received, to prove the Sacrament of extream Unction.

Ita mihi Edmundo Londinensi Episcopo pro hoc tempore dicendum videtur, salvo judicio melius sentientis, cui me prompte et humiliter subjicio.

Inunction of them that be sick with Oil, and praying Rochester. for them for remission of Sins, is plainly spoken of in the Epistle of St. James, but after what form or fashion the said Inunction was then used, the Scripture telleth not.

Written on the back of the Paper,
The Bishop of Rochester's Book.

Extream Unction is plainly set out by St. James, with Carlile. the which maketh also that is written in the 6th of St. Mark, after the mind of right good ancient Doctors.

Robert Carliolen.

BOOK III.

Dr. Robertson.

De Unctione Infirmorum nihil reperio in Scripturis, præter id quod scribitur, Marc. 6. et Jacob. 5.

Thomas Robertson.

T. Cantuarien.

Dr. Cox

Unction of the Sick with Oil consecrat, as it is now used, is not spoken of in Scripture. Richardus Cox.

Dr. Day

Unction of the Sick with praying for them is found in Scripture. George Day.

Opiniones non Assertiones.

Dr. Oglethorpe.

De Unctione Infirmorum cum oleo, adjecta Oratione, expressa mentio est in Scripturis, quanquam nunc addantur alii ritus, honestatis gratiâ (ut in aliis Sacramentis) de quibus in Scripturis nulla mentio.

Owinus Oglethorpus.

Dr. Redmayn.

Unction with Oil, adjoined with Prayer, and having promise of Remission of Sins, is spoken of in St. James, and ancient Authors; as for the use which now is, if any thing be amiss, it would be amended. J. Redmayn.

Dr. Edgeworth.

It is spoken of, in Mark 6. and James 5. Augustine and other ancient Doctors speaketh of the same.

Edgeworth.

Dr. Symmons.

The Unction of the Sick with Oil, to remit Sins, is in Scripture, and also in ancient Authors.

Symon Matthew.

Dr. Tresham.

Unction with Oil is grounded in the Scripture, and expresly spoken of; but with this Additament (as it is now used) it is not specified in Scripture, for the Ceremonies now used in Unction, I think meer Traditions of Man.

William Tresham.

Dr. Leyghton.

To the seventeenth, I say, That Unction of the Sick with Oil and Prayer to remit Sins, is manifestly spoken of in

St. James Epistle, and ancient Authors, but not with all
the Rites and Ceremonies as be now commonly used.
   T. Cantuarien.   Per me
                           Edwardum Leyghton.

Unction with Oil to remit Sins is spoken of in Scripture. Dr.
                         Richard Coren. Coren.

Menevens. et Coxus negant Unctionem Olei (ut jam est Con.
recepta) ad remittenda peccata contineri in Scripturis.
Eboracens. Carliolens. Edgworth, Coren, Redmayn, Symmons, Leightonus, Oglethorp aiunt haberi in Scripturis.
Roffens. Thirleby, Robertsonus, præterquam illud Ja-
cobi 5. et Marci 6. nihil proferunt. Herefordensis ambi-
git. Tresham vult Unctionem Olei tradi nobis è Scripturis, sed Unctionis Cæremonias traditiones esse humanas.

In the last; The Bishop of St. Davids, and Dr. Cox, Agree-
say, That " Unction of the Sick with Oil consecrate, as it ment.
is now used to remit Sin, is not spoken of in Scripture."
My Lords of York, Duresme, Carlile, Drs. Coren, Edgworth, Redman, Symmons, Leyghton, and Oglethorp, say,
That " it is found in Scripture."

XXII.

Dr. Barnes's Renunciation of some Articles informed against him.

BE it known to all Men, that I Robert Barnes, Doctor
of Divinity, have as well in Writing, as in Preaching, over-
shot my self, and been deceived, by trusting too much to
mine own heady Sentence, and giving judgment in and
touching the Articles hereafter ensuing; whereas being convented, and called before the Person of my most gracious
Soveraign Lord King Henry the Eighth, of England and of
France, Defender of the Faith, Lord of Ireland, and in
Earth Supream Head immediately under God of the Church
of England; It pleased his Highness, of his great clemency

and goodness, being assisted with sundry of his most discreet and learned Clergy, to enter such Disputation and Argument with me, upon the Points of my over-sight, as by the same was fully and perfectly confuted by Scriptures, and enforced only for Truths sake, and for want of defence of Scriptures to serve for the maintenance of my part, to yeeld, confess, and knowledg my ignorance, and with my most humble submission, do promise for ever from henceforth to abstain, and beware of such rashness: And for my further declaration therein, not only to abide such order for my doings passed, as his Grace shall appoint and assign unto me, but also with my heart to advance and set forth the said Articles ensuing, which I knowledg and confess to be most Catholick, and Christian, and necessary to be received, observed, and followed of all good Christian People. Tho it so be, that Christ by the Will of his Father, is he only which hath suffered Passion and Death for redemption of all such as will and shall come unto him, by perfect Faith and Baptism; and that also he hath taken upon him *gratis* the burden of all their sins, which as afore will, hath, or shall come to him, paying sufficient Ransom for all their sins, and so is becomed their only Redeemer and Justifier; of the which number I trust and doubt not but that many of us now-a days be of: yet I in heart do confess, that after, by the foresaid means we become right Christian Folks, yet then by not following our Master's Commandments and Laws, we do loose the benefits and fruition of the same, which in this case is irrecuperable, but by true Penance, the only Remedy left unto us by our Saviour for the same; wherefore I think it more than convenient and necessary, that whensoever Justification shall be preached of, that this deed be joined with all the fore-part, to the intent that it may teach all true Christian People a right knowledg of their Justification.

By me Robert Barnes.

Also I confess with my heart, That Almighty God is in no wise Author, causer of Sin, or any Evil; and therefore whereas Scripture saith, *Induravit Dominus Cor Pharaonis, &c.* and such other Texts of like sense, they ought to understand them, *quod Dominus permisit eum indurari*, and not otherwise; which doth accord with many of the ancient Interpreters also.

By me Robert Barnes.

Further I do confess with my heart, That whensoever I have offended my Neighbours, I must first reconcile my self unto him, e're I shall get remission of my sins, and in case he offend me, I must forgive him, e're that I can be forgiven; for this doth the *Pater Noster*, and other places of Scripture teach me.

By me Robert Barnes.

I do also confess with my heart, That good Works limited by Scripture, and done by a penitent and true reconciled Christian Man, be profitable and allowable unto him, as allowed of God for his benefit, and helping to his Salvation.

By me Robert Barnes.

Also do confess with my heart, That Laws and Ordinances made by Christian Rulers ought to be obeyed by the Inferiors and Subjects, not only for fear, but also for Conscience, for whoso breaketh them, breaketh God's Commandments.

By me Robert Barnes.

All and singular the which Articles before written, I the foresaid Robert Barnes do approve and confess to be most true and Catholick, and promise with my heart, by God's Grace, hereafter to maintain, preach, and set forth the same to the People, to the uttermost of my power, wit, and cunning.

By me Robert Barnes.
By me William Jerome.
By me Thomas Gerarde.

XXIII.

The Foundation of the Bishoprick of Westminster.

REX omnibus ad quos, &c. salutem. Cum nuper cænobium quoddam sive Monasterium, quod (dum extitit) Monasterium Sancti Petri Westmon. vulgariter vocabatur, omnia et singula ejus Maneria, Dominia, Mesuagia,

Terræ, Tenementa, Hæreditamenta, Dotationes et Possessiones, certis de causis specialibus et urgentibus, per Willielmum ipsius nuper Cænobii sive Monasterii Abbatem,
et ejusdem loci Conventum, nobis et hæredibus nostris in
perpetuum jamdudum data fuerunt et concessa, prout per
ipsorum nuper Abbatis et Conventus cartam sigillo suo
communi sive conventuali sigillatam et in Cancellar. nostram irrotulat manifeste liquet; quorum prætextu nos de
ejusdem nuper Cænobii sive Monasterii situ, septu et præ-
cinctu, ac de omnibus et singulis prædict. nuper Abbatis
et Conventus Maneriis, Dominiis et Mesuagiis, Terris, Te-
nementis, Hæreditamentis, Dotationibus et Possessioni-
bus, ad præsens pleno jure seisiti sumus in dominico nostro, ut de feodo. Nos utiq; sic de eisdem seisiti existen.
divinaq; nos clementia inspirante nihil magis ex animo af-
fectantes, quam ut vera religio verusq; Dei cultus inibi
non modo aboleatur, sed in integrum potius restituatur, et
ad primitivam sive genuinæ sinceritatis normam reforme-
tur, correctis enormitatibus in quas monachorum vita et pro-
fessio longo temporum lapsu deplorabiliter exorbitaverit,
operam dedimus, quatenus humana perspicere potest infir-
mitas, ut imposterum ibidem sacrorum eloquiorum documenta et nostræ salutiferæ Redemptionis sacramenta pure
administrentur, bonorum morum disciplina sincere obser-
vetur, Juventus in literis liberaliter instituatur, senectus
viribus defectis, eorum præsertim qui circa personam nostram, vel alioquin circa Regni nostri negotia publice bene
et fideliter nobis servierunt, rebus ad victum necessariis
condigne foveatur, et deniq; eleemosinarum in pauperes
Christi elargitiones, viarum pontiumque reparationes, et
cætera omnis generis pietatis officia illinc exuberanter in
omnia vicina loca longe lateq; dimaneant, ad Dei omnipotentis gloriam, et ad subditorum nostrorum communem utilitatem felicitatemque: Idcirco nos considerantes quod situs
dicti nuper Monasterii Sancti Petri Westmon. in quo multa
tum percharissimi patris nostri, tum aliorum Inclitorum,
quondam Regum Angliæ, præclara monumenta conduntur,
sit locus aptus, conveniens et necessarius instituendi, erigen-
di, ordinandi et stabiliendi sedem Episcopalem, et quandam
Ecclesiam Cathedralem de uno Episcopo, de uno Decano
Presbytero, et duodecim Præbendariis Presbyteris, ibidem,

· Omnipotenti Deo et in perpetuum servitium, ipsum situm dicti nuper Monast. Sancti Petri Westmon. ac locum et Ecclesiam ipsius in sedem Episcopalem ac in Ecclesiam Cathedral. creari, erigi, fundari et stabiliri decrevimus, prout per præsentes decernimus, et eandem Ecclesiam Cathedral. de uno Episcopo, de uno Decano Presbytero, et duodecim Præbendariis Presbyteris, tenore præsentium, realiter et ad plenum creamus, erigimus, fundamus, ordinamus, facimus, constituimus et stabilimus, perpetuis futuris temporibus duraturam, et sic stabiliri ac in perpetuum inviolabiliter observari volumus et jubemus per præsentes. Volumus itaq; et per præsentes Ordinamus quod Ecclesia Cathedralis prædicta sit, et deinceps in perpetuum erit Ecclesia Cathedralis et Sedes Episcopalis, ac quod tota villa nostra Westmon. ex nunc et deinceps in perpetuum sit Civitas, ipsamq; civitatem Westm. vocari et nominari volumus et decernimus, ac ipsam Civitatem et totum Comit. nostrum Midd. prout per metas et limites dignoscitur, et limitatur, tota Parochia de Fulham in eodem Comit. de Midd. tantummodo except. ab omni Jurisdictione, Autoritate et Dioc. Episcopi London. et successorum suorum pro tempore existen. separamus, dividimus, eximimus, exoneramus, et omnino per præsentes liberamus: ac omnem jurisdictionem Episcopalem infra eandem Civitatem et Comit. Midd. exceptis præexceptis, Episcopo Westmon. a nobis per has Literas nostras Patentes nominand. et eligend. et Successoribus suis Episcopis Westm. ac prædict. Episcopat. Westm. adjungimus et unimus, ac ex dictis Civitate et Com. Diocesim facimus et Ordinamus per præsentes, illamq; Diocesim Westm. in perpetuum similiter vocari, appellari, nuncupari et nominari volumus et ordinamus. Et ut hæc nostra intentio debitum et uberiorem sortiatur effectum, Nos de scientia, moribus, probitate et virtute dilecti nostri Consiliarii Thomæ Thyrlebei Clerici, Decani Capellæ nostræ plurimum confidentes, eundem Thomam Thyrleby ad Episcopatum dictæ Sedis Westm. nominamus et eligimus, ac ipsum Thomam Episcopum Westm. per præsentes eligimus, nominamus, facimus, et creamus, et volumus; ac per præsentes Concedimus et Ordinamus, quod idem Episcopatus sit corpus corporatum in re et nomine, ipsumq; ex uno corpore declaramus et acceptamus, Ordinamus, facimus et constituimus in perpetuum, habeatq; successionem perpetuam, ac quod ipse et successores sui per nomen et sub nomine Episcopi Westm. nominabitur et vocabitur, nominabuntur et vocabuntur in perpetuum, et quod ipse et successores sui per idem nomen et sub eo nomine prosequi, clamare et placitare, ac placitari, defendere et defendi, respondere et responderi, in quibuscunq; Curiis et locis legum nostrarum, ac hæredum et successorum nostrorum, et alibi, in et super omnibus et singulis causis, actionibus, sectis, brevibus, demand. et querelis, realibus, personalibus et mixtis, tam temporalibus quam spiritualibus, ac in omnibus aliis rebus, causis et materiis quibuscunque, et per idem nomen Maneria, Dominia, Terræ, Tenementa, Rectorias, Pensiones, Portiones, et alia quæcunq; Hæreditamenta, Possessiones, proficua et emolumenta, tam spiritualia sive Ecclesiastica, quam temporalia, ac alia quæcunq; per Literas Patentes præfato Episcopo et Successoribus suis, per nos seu hæredes nostros debito modo fiend. vel per quamcunq; aliam personam seu quascunq; alias personas secundum leges nostras, et hæredum sive successorum nostrorum dand. seu concedend. capere, recipere, gaudere et perquirere ac dare, alienare et dimittere possit et possint, valeat et valeant, et generaliter omnia alia et singula recipere, gaudere, et facere, prout et eisdem modo et forma quibus cæteri Episcopi infra Regnum nostrum Angliæ recipere aut facere possint, aut aliquis Episcopus infra Regnum nostrum Angliæ recipere aut facere possit, et non aliter nec ullo alio modo. Et ulterius volumus et ordinamus, quod Ecclesia Cathedralis prædicta sit, et deinceps in perpetuum erit Ecclesia Cathedralis et Sedes Episcopalis dicti Thomæ et successorum suorum Episcoporum Westm. ipsamq; Ecclesiam Cathedralem honoribus, dignitatibus, et insigniis Sedis Episcopalis per præsentes decoramus, eandemq; Sedem Episcopalem præfato Thomæ et successoribus suis Episcopis Westm. damus et concedimus per præsentes habend. et gaudend. idem Thomæ et successoribus suis in perpetuum. Ac etiam volumus et ordinamus per præsentes, quod præfatus Thomas et successores sui Episcopi Westm. prædict. omnimodam jurisdictionem, potestatem et autoritatem ordinarias et Episcopales, infra Ecclesiam Cathedralem Westm. et prædict. Dioces. exercere, fa cère, et uti possit, et debeat, possint et debeant, in tam amplis modo et forma, prout Episcopus London. infra Dioces. London. secundum leges nostras exercere, facere, et uti solet, possit aut debet. Et quod dictus Thomas Episcopus Westm. et successores sui Episcopi Westm. deinceps in perpetuum habeat sigillum authenticum, seu sigilla authentica pro rebus et negotiis suis agendis servitur, ad omnem juris effectum simili modo et forma, et non aliter nec aliquo alio modo, prout Episcopus London. habet aut habere potest. Et ut Ecclesia Cathedralis prædict. de personis congruis in singulis locis et gradibus suis perimpleatur et decoretur, dilectum nobis Willielmum Benson Sacræ Theologiæ professorem primum et originalem, et modernum Decanum dictæ Ecclesiæ Cathedralis, ac Simonem Haynes Sacræ Theologiæ professorem primum, et præsent. Presbyterum Præbendarium, ac Joannem Redman secundum Presbyterum Præbendarium, ac Edwardum Leyghton tertium Presbyterum Præbendarium, ac Antonium Belasys quartum Presbyterum Præbendarium, ac Willielmum Britten quintum Presbyterum Præbendarium, ac Dionysium Dalyon sextum Presbyterum Præbendarium, ac Humphredum Perkins septimum Presbyterum Præbendarium, ac Thomam Essex octavum Presbyterum Præbendarium, ac Thomam Ellforde nonum Presbyterum Præbendarium, ac Joannem Malvern decimum Presbyterum Præbendarium, ac Willielmum Harvey undecimum Presbyterum Præbendarium, ac Gerardum Carleton duodecimum Presbyterum Præbendarium, tenore præsentium facimus et ordinamus. Per præsentes volumus etiam et ordinamus, ac eisdem Decano et Præbendariis concedimus per præsentes, quod prædictus Decanus et duodecim Præbendarii dicti sint de se in re et nomine unum corpus corporatum, habeantq; successionem perpetuam, et se gerent, exhibebunt, et occupabunt Sedem, ordinationem, regulas et statuta, eis per nos in quadam Indentura in posterum fiend. specificand. et declarand. Et quod idem Decanus et Præbendarii et successores sui, Decanus et Capitulum Ecclesiæ Cathedralis Sancti Petri Westm. in perpetuum vocabuntur, appellabuntur; Et quod præfatus Decanus et Præbendarii Ecclesiæ Cathedralis prædictæ et successores sui sint et in perpetuum erunt Capitulum Episcopatus Westm. sitq; idem Capitulum præ-

fat. Thomæ et successoribus suis Episcopis Westm.
perpetuis futuris temporibus annexum, incorporatum et
unitum eisdem modo et forma quibus Decanus et Capitulum Ecclesiæ Cathedralis Sancti Pauli in Civitate
nostra London. Episcopo London. aut sedi Episcopali
London. annexa, incorporata et unit. exist. ipsosq; Decanum et Præbendarios unum corpus corporatum in re et
nomine facimus, creamus, et stabilimus, et eos pro uno corpore facimus, declaramus, ordinamus et acceptamus, habeantq; successionem perpetuam; Et quod ipse Decanus
et Capitulum eorumq; successores per nomen Decani et
Capitulum Ecclesiæ Cathedralis Beati Petri Westm. prosequi, clamare, placitare possint et implacitare, defendere et
defendi, respondere et responderi, in quibuscunq; tempore
et Curiis legum nostrarum et alibi, in et super omnibus et
singulis causis, actionibus, Sectis, demand. brevibus et
querelis, realibus, spiritualibus, personalibus et mixtis, et
in omnibus aliis rebus, causis et materiis, prout Decanus
et Capitulum Sancti Pauli London. agere aut facere possunt: Et per idem nomen Maneria, Dominia, Terræ, Tenementa, et cætera quæcunq; Hæreditamenta, possessiones,
proficua, et emolumenta tam Spiritualia sive Ecclesiastica
quam temporalia, et alia quæcunq; per nos per literas nostras Patentes, hæredum vel successorum nostrorum, seu per
aliquam personam vel personas quascunq; eis et successoribus suis vel aliter secundum leges nostras, vel hæredum
seu successorum nostrorum dand. seu concedend. capere,
recipere, et perquirere, dare, alienare, et dimittere possint
et valeant, et generaliter omnia alia et singula capere, recipere, perquirere, dare, alienare, et dimittere, ac facere et
exequi, prout et eisdem modo et forma, quibus Decanus et
Capitulum prædict. Cathedralis Ecclesiæ Sancti Pauli in
prædicta civitate nostra London. capere, recipere, perquirere, dare, alienare, et dimittere, ac facere aut exequi possint, et non aliter, neq; aliquo alio modo: Et quod Decanus et Capitulum Ecclesiæ Cathedralis beati Petri Westm.
et successores sui in perpetuum habebunt commune Sigillum, ad omnimodas cartas, evidentias, et cætera scripta,
vel facta sua fiend. eos vel Ecclesiam Cathedralem prædict. aliquo modo tangen. sive continend. sigilland. Et insuper volumus et per præsentes concedimus et ordinamus,

quod prædict. Episcopus Westm. et quilibet successorum **BOOK III.**
suorum pro tempore existen. et prædictus Decanus et Capitulum Ecclesiæ Cathedralis beati Petri Westm. et quilibet
successorum suorum habeant plenam potestatem et facultatem faciendi, recipiendi, dandi, alienandi, dimittendi, ex-
equendi et agendi omnia et singula quæ Episcopus London. et Decanus et Capitulum Sancti Pauli London. conjunctim et divisim facere, recipere, dare, alienare, dimittere,
exequi aut agere possint. Volumus etiam et ordinamus,
ac per præsentes Statuimus, quod Archidiaconus Midd.
qui nunc est et successores sui sunt deinceps in perpetuum
separati et exonerati et prorsus liberati a jurisdictione, potestate, jure et authoritate Episcopi London. et successorum suorum, ac ab Ecclesia Cathedrali Sancti Pauli London. ab omniq; jure, potestate et autoritate ejusdem ipsiusq;
Archidiaconi, et successores suos per præsentes separamus,
exoneramus penitus in perpetuum liberamus, eundemq; Ar-
chidiaconum et successores suos decernimus, Statuimus,
Ordinamus, ac stabilimus in simili Statu, modo, forma et
jure esse, ac deinceps in perpetuum fore, in prædicta Ecclesia Cathedrali Westm. quibus ipse aut aliquis prædecessorum suorum unquam fuit in Ecclesia Cathedrali
Sancti Pauli London. Statuimus etiam et ordinamus ac
per præsentes volumus et concedimus, quod prædictus
Thomas Episcopus Westm. et successores sui Episcopi
Westm. habeant, teneant et possideant, in omnibus et per
omnia autoritatem, potestatem, jus et jurisdictionem, de et
super Archidiaconatu Midd. et Archidiacono et successoribus suis, tam plene et integre ad omnem effectum quam
Episcopus London. qui nunc est aut aliquis prædecessorum suorum habet aut habuit, aut habere debuit vel usus
fuit. Volumus autem ac per præsentes concedimus tam
præfato Episcopo quam Decano et Capitulo, quod habeat
et habebit, habeant et habebunt, has Literas nostras Patentes sub magno sigillo nostro Angliæ debito modo factas
et sigillatas, absq; fine seu feæd. magno vel parvo nebis
in Hanaperio nostro seu alibi ad usum nostrorum, proinde
quoquo modo reddend. solvend. vel faciend. eo quod expressa mentio, et cæt. In cujus rei, &c. Teste Rege
apud Westm. decimo septimo die Decembris Anno Regni
Regis Henrici Octavi trigesimo secundo.

XXIV.

*A Proclamation ordained by the King's Majesty, with the
advice of his Honourable Council, for the Bible of the
largest and greatest Volume to be had in every Church;
devised the sixth day of May, the 33 year of the King's
most gracious Reign.*

Regist.
Bonner.
Vol. 21.
WHEREBY Injunctions heretofore set forth by the authority of the King's Royal Majesty, Supream Head of the
Church of this his Realm of England, it was ordained, and
commanded, amongst other things, That in all and singular Parish-Churches, there should be provided, by a certain
day now expired, at the costs of the Curats and Parishioners, Bibles containing the Old and New Testament in the
English Tongue, to be fixed and set up openly in every of
the said Parish Churches; the which godly Commandment
and Injunction, was to the only intent that every of the
King's Majesties loving Subjects, minding to read therein,
might, by occasion thereof, not only consider and perceive
the great and ineffable Omnipotent Power, Promise, Justice, Mercy and Goodness of Almighty God, but also to
learn thereby to observe God's Commandments, and to
obey their Sovereign Lord, and High Powers, and to exercise Godly Charity, and to use themselves according to
their Vocations, in a pure and sincere Christian Life, without murmur or grudging: By the which Injunctions, the
King's Royal Majesty intended that his loving Subjects
should have and use the commodities of the reading of the
said Bibles, for the purpose above rehearsed, humbly,
meekly, reverently, and obediently, and not that any of
them should read the said Bibles with high and loud Voices,
in time of the Celebration of the Holy Mass, and other Divine Services used in the Church; or that any his Lay-
Subjects reading the same, should presume to take upon
them any common Disputation, Argument, or Exposition
of the Mysteries therein contained; but that every such
Layman should, humbly, meekly, and reverently, read the
same for his own instruction, edification, and amendment
of his Life, according to God's Holy Word therein men-

tioned. And notwithstanding the King's said most godly BOOK
and gracious Commandment and Injunction, in form as is III.
aforesaid, his Royal Majesty is informed, That divers and
many Towns and Parishes within this his Realm, have neg-
lected their duties in the accomplishment thereof; whereof his Highness marvelleth not a little; and minding the
execution of his said former most godly and gracious Injunctions, doth straitly charge and command, That the
Curats and Parishioners of every Town and Parish within
this his Realm of England, not having already Bibles provided within their Parish Churches, shall on this side the
Feast of All-Saints next coming, buy and provide Bibles
of the largest and greatest Volume, and cause the same to
be set and fixed in every of the said Parish Churches, there
to be used as is afore-said, according to the said former
Injunctions, upon pain that the Curat and Inhabitants of
the Parishes and Towns, shall loose and forfeit to the
King's Majesty for every month that they shall lack and
want the said Bibles, after the same Feast of All-Saints,
40s. the one half of the same forfeit to be to the King's
Majesty, and the other half to him or them which shall first
find and present the same to the King's Majesties Council.
And finally, the King's Royal Majesty doth declare and
signify to all and singular his loving Subjects, that to the
intent they may have the said Bibles of the greatest Vo-
lumn, at equal and reasonable prices, his Highness, by the
advice of his Council, hath ordained and taxed, That the
Sellers thereof shall not take for any of the said Bibles
unbound, above the price of ten shillings; and for every of
the said Bibles well and sufficiently bound, trimmed and
clasped, not above twelve shillings, upon pain the Seller to
lose, for every Bible sold contrary to his Highness's Proclamation, four shillings, the one Moiety thereof to the
King's Majesty, and the other Moiety to the finder and pre-
senter of the Defaulter, as is aforesaid. And his Highness
straitly chargeth and commandeth, That all and singular
Ordinaries, having Ecclesiastical Jurisdiction within this
his Church and Realm of England, and Dominion of Wales,
that they, and every of them, shall put their effectual endeavours, that the Curats and Parishioners shall obey and
accomplish this his Majesties Proclamation and Command-

ment, as they tender the advancement of the King's most gracious and godly purpose in that behalf, and as they will answer to his Highness for the same.

God save the King.

XXV.

An Admonition and Advertisement given by the Bishop of London, to all Readers of this Bible in the English Tongue.

Register, Bonner.   To the intent that a good and wholsome thing, godly and vertuously, for honest intents and purposes, set forth for many, be not hindred or maligned at, for the abuse, default, and evil behaviour of a few, who for lack of discretion, and good advisement, commonly without respect of time, or other due circumstances, proceed rashly and unadvisedly therein; and by reason thereof, rather hinder than set forward the thing that is good of it self: It shall therefore be very expedient, that whosoever repaireth hither to read this Book, or any such-like, in any other place, he prepare himself chiefly and principally, with all devotion, humility, and quietness, to be edified and made the better thereby; adjoining thereto his perfect and most bounden duty of obedience to the King's Majesty, our most gracious and dread Soveraign Lord, and supream Head, especially in accomplishing his Graces most honorable Injunctions and Commandments given and made in that behalf. And right expedient, yea necessary it shall be also, that leaving behind him vain Glory, Hypocrisy, and all other carnal and corrupt Affections, he bring with him discretion, honest intent, charity, reverence, and quiet behaviour, to and for the edification of his own Soul, without the hindrance, lett, or disturbance of any other his Christian Brother; evermore foreseeing that no number of People be specially congregate therefore to make a multitude; and that no exposition be made thereupon otherwise than it is declared in the Book it self; and that especially regard be had no reading thereof, be used, allowed, and with noise in the time of any Divine Service, or Sermon; or that in the same, be used any Disputation, contention, or any other misdemeanour; or finally that any Man justly may reckon himself to be offended thereby, or take occasion to grudg or malign thereat.

God save the King.

XXVI.

Injunctions given by Bonner, Bishop of London, to his Clergy.

INJUNCTIONS made by the consent and authority of me Regist. Bonner. Fol. 38. Edmond Bonner Bishop of London, in the Year of our Lord God 1542, and in the 34 Year of the Reign of our Sovereign Lord Henry the Eighth, by the Grace of God, King of England, France, and Ireland, Defender of the Faith, and Supream Head here in Earth, next under God, of the Church of England and Ireland. All which and singular Injunctions, by the Authority given to me of God, and by our said Soveraign Lord the King's Majesty, I exhort, require, and also command, all and singular Parsons, Vicars, Curats, and Chantry Priests, with other of the Clergy, whatsoever they be, of my Diocess and Jurisdiction of London, to observe, keep, and perform accordingly, as it concerneth every of them, in vertue of their Obedience, and also upon pains expressed in all such Laws, Statutes, and Ordinances of this Realm, as they may incur, and be objected against them, now, or at any time hereafter, for breaking and violating of the same, or any of them.

First; That you, and every of you, shall, with all diligence, and faithful obedience, observe and keep, and cause to be observed and kept, to the outermost of your Powers, all and singular the Contents of the King's Highness most gracious and godly Ordinances and Injunctions given and set forth by his Grace's Authority; and that ye, and every of you, for the better performance thereof, shall provide to have a Copy of the same in writing, or imprinted, and so to declare them accordingly.

Item; That every Parson, Vicar, and Curat, shall read over and diligently study every day one Chapter of the Bible, and that with the gloss ordinary, or some other Doctor or Expositor, approved and allowed in this Church of England, proceeding from Chapter to Chapter, from the beginning of the Gospel of Matthew to the end of the New Testament, and the same so diligently studied to keep still and retain in memory, and to come to the rehearsal and recital thereof, at all such time and times as they, or any of them, shall be commanded thereunto by me, or any of my Officers or Deputies.

Item; That every of you do procure and provide of your own, a Book called, "The Institution of a Christian Man," otherwise called the "Bishop's Book;" and that ye, and every of you, do exercise your selves in the same, according to such Precepts as hath been given heretofore or here-after to be given.

Item; That ye being absent from your Benefices, in cases lawfully permitted by the Laws and Statutes of this Realm, do suffer no Priest to keep your Cure, unless he being first by you presented, and by me or my Officers thereunto abled and admitted. And for the more and better assurance and performance thereof to be had, by these presents I warn and monish peremptorily, all and singular Beneficed Parsons having Benefices with Cure, within my Diocess and Jurisdiction, that they and every of them, shall either be personally resident upon their Benefices and Cures, before the Feast of St. Michael the Arch-Angel now next ensuing; or else present, before the said Feast, to me the said Bishop, my Vicar-General, or other my Officers deputed in that behalf, such Curats as upon examination made by me, or my said Officers, may be found able and sufficient to serve and discharge their Cures in their absence; and also at the said Feast, or before, shall bring in and exhibite before my said Officers their sufficient Dispensations authorized by the King's Majesty, as well for non-residence, as for keeping of more Benefices with Cure than one.

Item; That every Parson, Vicar, and other Curats, once

in every quarter, shall openly in the Pulpit exhort and charge his Parishioners, that they in no wise do make any privy or secret contract of Matrimony between themselves, but that they utterly defer it until such time as they may conveniently have the Father and Mother, or some other Kinsfolks or Friends of the Person that shall make such Contract of Matrimony; or else two or three honest Persons to be present, and to hear and record the words and manner of their Contract, as they will avoid the extream pains of the Law provided in that behalf, if they presumptuously do or attempt the contrary.

Item; That in the avoiding of divers and grievous Offences and Enormities, and specially the most detestable sin of Adultery, which oft-times hath hapned by the negligence of Curats in marrying Persons together which had been married before, and making no due proof of the death of their other Husbands and Wives at the time of such Marriages, I require and command you, and monish peremptorily by these presents, all manner of Parsons, Vicars, and Curats, with other Priests, being of my Diocess and Jurisdiction, that they, nor any of them from henceforth, do presume to solemnizate Matrimony in their Churches, Chappels, or elsewhere, between any Persons that have been married before, unless the said Parson, Vicar, Curat, or Priest, be first plainly, fully, and sufficiently informed and certified of the Decease of the Wife or Husband of him or her, or of both, that he shall marry, and that in writing, under the Ordinaries Seal of the Diocess, or place where he or she inhabited or dwelt before, under pain of Excommunication, and otherwise to be punished for doing the contrary, according to the Laws provided and made in that behalf.

Item; That ye, and every of you that be Parsons, Vicars, Curats, and also Chauntry-Priests and Stipendiaries, do instruct, teach, and bring up in Learning the best ye can, all such Children of your Parishioners as shall come to you for the same; or at the least, to teach them to read English, taking moderately therefore of their Friends that be able to pay, so that they may thereby the better learn and know how to Believe, how to Pray, how to live to God's pleasure.

Item; That every Curat do at all times his best diligence to stir, move, and reduce such as be at discord to Peace, Concord, Love, Charity, and one to remit and forgive one another, as often and howsoever they shall be grieved or offended: And that the Curat shew and give example thereof, when and as often as any variance or discord shall happen to be between him and any of his Cure.

Item; Where some froward Persons, partly for malice, hatred, displeasure, and disdain, neglect contemn and despise their Curats, and such as have the Cure and Charge of their Souls, and partly to hide and cloak their lead and naughty living, as they have used all the Year before, use at length to be confessed of other Priests which have not the Cure of their Souls: Wherefore I will and require you to declare, and show to your Parishioners, That no Testimonials brought from any of them, shall stand in any effect, nor that any such Persons shall be admitted to God's Board, or receive their Communion, until they have submitted themselves to be confessed of their own Curats, (Strangers only except) or else upon arduous and urgent Causes and Considerations, they be otherwise dispensed with in that behalf, either by me or by my Officers aforesaid.

Item; That whereupon a detestable and abominable practice universally reigning in your Parishes, the young People, and other ill-disposed Persons doth use upon the Sundays and Holy-days, in time of Divine Service, and preaching the Word of God, to resort unto Ale-houses, and there exerciseth unlawful Games, with great Swearing, Blasphemy, Drunkenness, and other Enormities, so that good and devout Persons be much offended therewith: Wherefore I require and command you, to declare to such as keepeth Ale-houses, or Taverns within your Parishes, that at such times from henceforth, they shall not suffer in their Houses any such unlawful and ungodly Assemblies; neither receive such Persons to Bowling and Drinking at such Seasons, into their Houses, under pain of Excommunication, and otherwise to be punished for their so doing, according to the Laws in that behalf.

Item; That all Curats shall declare openly in the Pulpit, twice every Quarter to their Parishioners, the seven deadly

Sins, and the Ten Commandments, so that the People thereby may not only learn how to obey, honour, and serve God, their Prince, Superiors, and Parents, but also to avoid and eschew Sin and Vice, and to live vertuously, following God's Commandments and his Laws.

Item; That where I am credibly informed, that certain Priests of my Diocess and Jurisdiction, doth use to go in an unseemly and unpriestly habit and apparel, with unlawful tonsures, carrying and having upon them also Armour and Weapons, contrary to all wholsome and godly Laws and Ordinances, more like Persons of the Lay, than of the Clergy; which may and doth minister occasion to light Persons, and to Persons unknown, where such Persons come in place, to be more licentious both of their Communication, and also of their Acts, to the great slander of the Clergy: Wherefore in the avoiding of such slander and obloquy hereafter, I admonish and command all and singular Parsons, Vicars, Curats, and all other Priests whatsoever they be, dwelling, or inhabiting, or hereafter shall dwell and inhabit within my Diocess and Jurisdiction, That from henceforth they, and every of them, do use and wear meet, convenient, and decent Apparel, with their Trusstures accordingly, whereby they may be known at all times from Lay-People, and to be of the Clergy, as they intend to avoid and eschew the penalty of the Laws ordained in that behalf.

Item; That no Parson, Vicar, or other Beneficed Man, having Cure within my Diocess and Jurisdiction, do suffer any Priest to say Mass, or to have any Service within their Cure, unless they first give knowledg, and present them with the Letters of their Orders to me as Ordinary, or to my Officers deputed in that behalf; and the said Priest so presented, shall be by me, or my said Officers, found able and sufficient thereunto.

Item; That every Curat, not only in his Preachings, open Sermons, and Collations made to the People, but also at all other times necessary, do perswade, exhort, and monish the People, being of his Cure, whatsoever they be, to beware and abstain from Swearing and blaspheming of the Holy Name of God, or any part of Christ's most precious Body or Blood. And likewise to beware, and abstain from

Cursing, Banning, Chiding, Scolding, Backbiting, Slander-
ing, and Lying. And also from talking and jangling in the
Church, specially in time of Divine-Service, or Sermon-
time. And semblably to abstain from Adultery, Fornica-
tion, Gluttony and Drunkenness: And if they, or any of
them, be found notoriously faulty or infamed upon any of
the said Crimes and Offences, then to detect them at every
Visitation, or sooner, as the case shall require, so that the
said Offenders may be corrected and reformed to the example of other.

Item; That no Priest from henceforth do use any unlawful Games, or frequently use any Ale-houses, Taverns, or
any suspect place at any unlawful times, or any light Company, but only for their Necessaries, as they, and any of
them, will avoid the danger that may ensue thereupon.

Item; That in the Plague-time, no dead Bodies or
Corpses be brought into the Church, except it be brought
streight to the Grave, and immediately buried, whereby
the People may the rather avoid infection.

Item; That no Parsons, Vicars, nor Curats, permit or
suffer any manner of common Plays, Games, or Interludes,
to be played, set forth, or declared, within their Churches
or Chappels, where the Blessed Sacrament of the Altar is,
or any other Sacrament ministred, or Divine Service said
or sung; because they be Places constitute and ordained
to well disposed People for Godly Prayer, and wholesome
Consolation. And if there be any of your Parishioners,
or any other Person or Persons, that will obstinately, or
violently, inforce any such Plays, Interludes, or Games to
be declared, set forth, or played in your Churches, or Chappels, contrary to this our forbidding and Commandment;
that then you, or either of you, in whose Churches or Chappels any such Games, Plays, or Interludes shall be so used,
shall immediately thereupon make relation of the names of
the Person or Persons so obstinately and disobediently
using themselves, unto me, my Chancellor, or other my
Officers, to the intent that they may be therefore reformed
and punished according to the Laws.

Item; That all Priests shall take this order when they
Preach; first, They shall not rehearse no Sermons made
by other Men within this 200 or 300 Years; but when they

shall preach, they shall take the Gospel or Epistle of the
day, which they shall recite and declare to the people,
plainly, distinctly, and sincerely, from the beginning to the
end thereof, and then to desire the people to pray with them
for Grace, after the usage of the Church of England now
used : And that done, we will that every Preacher shall
declare the same Gospel or Epistle, or both even from the
beginning, not after his own Mind, but after the Mind of
some Catholick Doctor allowed in this Church of England,
and in no wise to affirm any thing, but that which he shall
be ready always to shew in some Ancient Writer; and in
no wise to make rehearsal of any Opinion not allowed, for
the intent to reprove the same, but to leave that for those
that are and shall be admitted to preach by the King's Majesty, or by me the Bishop of London, your Ordinary, or
by mine authority. In the which Epistle and Gospel, ye
shall note and consider diligently certain godly and devout
places, which may incense and stir the Hearers to obedience of good Works and Prayers : And in case any notable Ceremony used to be observed in the Church, shall
happen that day when any preaching shall be appointed, it
shall be meet and convenient that the Preacher declare and
set forth to the people the true meaning of the same, in
such sort that the people may perceive thereby, what is
meant and signified by such Ceremony, and also know how
to use and accept it to their own edifying. Furthermore,
That no Preacher shall rage or rail in his Sermon, but
coldly, discreetly, and charitably, open, declare, and set
forth the excellency of Vertue, and to suppress the abomination of Sin and Vice; every Preacher shall, if time
and occasion will serve, instruct and teach his Audience,
what Prayer is used in the Church that day, and for what
thing the Church prayeth, specially that day, to the intent
that all the people may pray together with one heart for the
same; and as occasion will serve, to shew and declare to
the people what the Sacraments signifieth, what strength
and efficacy they be of, how every Man should use them
reverently and devoutly at the receiving of them. And to
declare wherefore the Mass is so highly to be esteemed and
honoured, with all the Circumstances appertaining to the
same. Let every Preacher beware that he do not feed his

Audience with any Fable, or other Histories, other than he can avouch and justify to be written by some allowed Writer. And when he hath done all that he will say and utter for that time, he shall then in few words recite again the pith and effect of his whole Sermon, and add thereunto as he shall think good.

Item; That no Parson, Vicar, Curat, or other Priest, having Cure of Souls within my Diocess and Jurisdiction, shall from hence-forth permit, suffer, or admit any manner of person, of whatsoever estate or condition he be, under the degree of a Bishop, to preach, or make any Sermon or Collation openly to the people within their Churches, Chappels, or else-where within their Cures, unless he that shall so preach, have obtained before special License in that behalf, of our Sovereign Lord the King, or of me Edmund Bishop of London, your Ordinary; And the same License so obtained, shall then and there really bring forth in writing under Seal, and shew the same to the said Parson, Vicar, Curat, or Priest, before the beginning of his Sermon, as they will avoid the extream Penalties of the Laws, Statutes, and Ordinances, provided and established in that behalf, if they presumptuously do or attempt any thing to the contrary.

Item; I desire, require, exhort, and command you, and every of you, in the Name of God, That ye firmly, faithfully, and diligently, to the uttermost of your powers, do observe, fulfil, and keep all and singular these mine Injunctions. And that ye, and every of you, being Priests, and having Cure, or not Cure, as well Benefice as not Beneficed, within my Diocess and Jurisdiction, do procure to have a Copy of the same Injunctions, to the intent ye may the better observe, and cause to be observed the Contents thereof.

The Names of Books prohibited, delivered to the Curats Anno 1542. to the intent that they shall present them with the Names of the Owners, to their Ordinary, if they find any such within their Parishes.

THE Disputation between the Father and the Son.

The Supplication of Beggars; the Author Fish.

The Revelation of Antichrist.

The Practice of Prelates, written by Tindall.

The Burying of the Mass, in English Rithme.

The Book of Friar Barnes, twice printed.

The Matrimony of Tindall.

The Exposition of Tindall, upon the 7th Chap. to the Corinth.

The Exposition of Tindall upon the Epistles Canonick of St. John.

The New Testament of Tindall's Translation, with his Preface before the whole Book, and before the Epistles of St. Paul *ad Rom.*

The Preface made in the English Prymmers, by Marshall.

The Church of John Rastall.

The Table, Glosses, Marginal, and Preface before the Epistle of St. Paul *ad Romans,* of Thomas Mathews doing, and printed beyond the Sea without priviledg, set in his Bible in English.

The A. B. C. against the Clergy.

The Book made by Fryar Roys, against the Seven Sacraments.

The Wicked Mammon.

The Parable of the Wicked Mammon.

The Liberty of a Christian Man.

Ortulus Animæ, in English.

The Supper of the Lord, by G. Joye.

Frith's Disputation against Purgatory.

Tyndal's Answer to Sir T. More's Defence of Purgatory.

Prologue to Genesis, translated by Tindal.

The Prologues to the other Four Books of Moses.

The Obedience of a Christian Man.

The Book made by Sir John Oldcastle.

The Summ of Scripture.

The Preface before the Psalter, in English.

The Dialogue between the Gentleman and the Plough-man.

The Book of Jonas, in English.

The Dialogue of Goodale.

Defensorium Paris; out of Latin into English.

The Summ of Christianity.

The Mirror of them that be Sick and in Pain.

Treatise of the Supper of the Lord; by Calwyn.*

Every one of Calwyn's Works.

XXVII.

A Collection of Passages out of the Canon Law, made by Cranmer, to shew the necessity of reforming it.

An Original.

Dist. 22. *Omnes de Major. et obedien. solit. Extra.*

De Majorit. et obedient. Unam Sanctam.

Ex
MSS.
D. Stil-
lingfleet HE that knowledgeth not himself to be under the Bishop of Rome, and that the Bishop of Rome is ordained by God to have Primacy over all the World, is an Heretick, and cannot be saved, nor is not of the flock of Christ.

Dist. 10. *De Sententia Excommunicationis, Noverit* 25.
q. 11. *omne.*

Princes Laws, if they be against the Canons and De-crees of the Bishop of Rome, be of no force nor strength.

Dist. 19, 20, 24. *q.* 1. *A recta memor. Quotiens hæc est.*
25. *q.* 1. *General. violatores.*

All the Decrees of the Bishop of Rome ought to be kept perpetually of every Man, without any repugnancy, as God's Word spoken by the Mouth of Peter; and who-

* The celebrated reformer, John Calvin.

soever doth not receive them, neither availeth them the
Catholick Faith, nor the four Evangelists, but they blas-
pheme the Holy Ghost, and shall have no forgiveness.

35. *q*. 1. *Generali.*

All Kings, Bishops, and Noblemen, that believe or suffer
the Bishop of Rome's Decrees in any thing to be violate,
be accursed, and for ever culpable before God, as trans-
gressors of the Catholick Faith.

Dist. 21. *Quamvis, et 24. q. 1. A recta memor.*

The See of Rome hath neither spot nor wrinkle in it,
-nor cannot err.

35. *q*. 1. *Ideo de Senten. et re judicata, de jurejurando licet ad Apostolicæ li. 6. de jurejurando.*

The Bishop of Rome is not bound to any Decrees, but
he may compel, as well the Clergy as Lay-men, to receive
his Decrees and Canon Law.

9. *q*. *z. Ipsi cuncta. Nemo z. q. 6. dudum aliorum.* 17. *q*. 4. *Si quis de Baptis. et ejus effectu majores.*

The Bishop of Rome hath authority to judg all Men,
and specially to discern the Articles of the Faith, and that
without any Counsel, and may assoil them that the Counsel hath damned; but no Man hath authority to judg him,
nor to meddle with any thing that he hath judged, neither
Emperor, King, People, nor the Clergy: And it is not
lawful for any Man to dispute of his Power.

gr. *Duo sunt* 25. *q.* 6. *Alios Nos Sanctorum juratos in Clemen. de Hæreticis aut officium.*

The Bishop of Rome may excommunicate Emperors
and Princes, depose them from their States, and Assoil
their Subjects from their Oath and Obedience to them, and
so constrain them to rebellion.

De Major. et obedien. solit. Clement. de Sententia et re
judicata. Pastoral.

The Emperor is the Bishop of Rome's Subject, and the
Bishop of Rome may revoke the Emperor's Sentence in
temporal Causes.

De Elect. et Electi potestate Venerabilem.

It belongeth to the Bishop of Rome to allow or disallow
the Emperor after he is elected; and he may translate the
Empire from one Region to another.

De Supplenda Negligen. prælat. Grand. li. 6.

The Bishop of Rome may appoint Coadjutors unto
Princes.

*Dist. 17. Si nodam. Regula. Nec licuit multum. Concils.
96. ubinam.*

There can be no Council of Bishops without the Authority of the See of Rome; and the Emperor ought not to be
present at the Council, except when Matters of the Faith
be entreating, which belong universally to every Man.

2. q. 6.

Nothing may be done against him that appealeth unto
Rome.

1. q. 8. Aliorum Dist. 40. Si Papa. Dist. 96. Satis.

The Bishop of Rome may be judged of none but of
God only; for altho he neither regard his own Salvation,
nor no Man's else, but draw down with himself innumerable people by heaps unto Hell; yet may no mortal Man in
this World presume to reprehend him: forsomuch as he is
called God, he may not be judged of Man, for God may
be judged of no Man.

3. z. q. 5.

The Bishop of Rome may open and shut Heaven unto
Men.

Dist. 40. *Non nos.*

The See of Rome receiveth holy Men, or else maketh them holy.

De Pœnitentia. Dist. 1. *Serpens.*

He that maketh a Lye to the Bishop of Rome committeth Sacriledg.

De Consecra. Dist. 1. *De locorum præcepta. Ecclesia de Elect. et Electi potestate Fundamenta.*

To be Senator, Capitane, Patrician, Governour, or Officer of Rome, none shall be elected or pointed, without the express license and special consent of the See of Rome.

De Electione et Electi potestate Venerabilem.

It appertaineth to the Bishop of Rome to judg which Oaths ought to be kept, and which not.

De jurejurand. Si vero. 15. *q.* 6. *Authoritatem.*

And he may absolve Subjects from their Oath of Fidelity, and absolve from other Oaths that ought to be kept.

De foro competent. Ex tenore. De donat. inter Virum et Uxorem dependentia. Qui Filii sunt legittime per venerabilem. De Elect. et Electi proprietate Fundamenta. Extravag. de Majorit. et Obedient. unam Sanctam. De judiciis Novit.

The Bishop of Rome is judg in temporal things, and hath two Swords, Spiritual and Temporal.

De Hæretisis multorum.

The Bishop of Rome may give Authority to arrest Men, and imprison them in Manacles and Fetters.

Extrav. de Consuetudine super gentes.

The Bishop of Rome may compel Princes to receive his Legats.

De Truga et Pace. Trugas.

It belongeth also to him to appoint and command Peace and Truce to be observed and kept or not.

De Præbend. et dig. dilectus et li. 6. licet.

The Collation of all Spiritual Promotions appertain to the Bishop of Rome.

De Excessibus prælatorum. Sicut unire.

The Bishop of Rome may unite Bishopricks together, and put one under another at his pleasure.

Li. 6. de pœnis Felicis.

In the Chapter *Felicis li. 6. de pœnis,* is the most partial and unreasonable Decree made by Bonifacius 8. that ever was read or heard, against them that be Adversaries to any Cardinal of Rome, or to any Clerk, or Religious man of the Bishop of Rome's family.

Dist. 28. Consulendum. Dist. 96. Si Imperator. 11. q. 1. Quod Clericus. Nemo nullus. Clericum, &c. et q. 2. Quod vero de sentent. Excommunication. Si judex q. 2. q. 5. Si quis de foro competent. Nullus. Si quis. Ex transmissa. de foro compet. in 6 Seculares.

Lay-men may not be Judges to any of the Clergy, nor compel them to pay their undoubted Debts, but the Bishops only must be their Judges.

De foro Competent. Cum sit licet.

Rectors of Churches may convent such as do them wrong, whither they will, before a Spiritual Judg, or a Temporal.

Idem ex parte Dilecti.

A Lay-man being spoiled, may convent his Adversaries before a Spiritual Judg, whether the Lords of the Feod consent thereto or not.

Ibidem Significasti, et 11. q. 1. placuit.

A Lay-man may commit his Cause to a Spiritual Judg; but one of the Clergy may not commit his Cause to a Temporal Judg, without the consent of the Bishop.

Ne Clerici vel Monachi. Secundum.

Lay-men may have no Benefices to farm.

De Sententia Excommunicationis. Noverit extra. de Pænitentiis et Remiss. &c. etsi.

All they that make, or write any Statutes contrary to the Liberties of the Church; and all Princes, Rulers, and Counsellors, where such Statutes be made, or such Customs observed, and all the Judges and others that put the same in execution; and where such Statutes and Customs have been made and observed of old time, all they that put them not out of their Books be excommunicate, and that so grievously, that they cannot be assoiled but only by the Bishop of Rome.

De Immunitate Ecclesiæ. Non minus adversus.
Quia Quum et in 6. Clericis.

The Clergy, to the relief of any common necessity, can nothing confer without the consent of the Bishop of Rome; nor it is not lawful for any Lay-man to lay any Imposition of Taxes, Subsidies, or any charges upon the Clergy.

Dist. 97. Hoc capitulo et 63. Nullus et quæ sequuntur.
Non aliæ cum Laic.

Lay-men may not meddle with Elections of the Clergy, nor with any other thing that belongeth unto them.

De jurejurando. Nimis.

The Clergy ought to give no Oath of Fidelity to their Temporal Governors, except they have Temporalities of them.

Dist. 96. Bene Quidem. 12. q. 2. Apostolicos. Quisquis.

The Goods of the Church may in no wise be alienated, but whosoever receiveth or buyeth them, is bound to restitution; and if the Church have any Ground, which is little or nothing worth, yet it shall not be given to the Prince; and if the Prince will needs buy it, the Sale shall be void and of no strength.

18. q. 2. Non liceat.

It is not lawful for the Bishop of Rome to alienate or mortgage any Lands of the Church, for every manner of necessity, except it be Houses in Cities, which be very chargeable to support and maintain.

Dist. 96 Quis nunquam, 3. q. 6. Accusatio 11. q. 1. Continua nullus Testimonium Relatum Experientiæ. Si quisquam. Si quæ. Sicut Statuimus, nullus de persona. Si quis.

Princes ought to obey Bishops, and the Decrees of the Church, and to submit their Heads unto the Bishops, and not to be judg over the Bishops; for the Bishops ought to be forborn, and to be judged of no Lay-man.

De Major. et obedien. solite.

Kings and Princes ought not to set Bishops beneath them, but reverently to rise against them, and to assign them an Honourable Seat by them.

11. q. 1. Quæcunque. Relatum. Si qui omnes volumus. Placuit.

All manner of Causes, whatsoever they be, Spiritual or Temporal, ought to be determined and judged by the Clergy.

Ibidem Omnes.

No judg ought to refuse the Witness of one Bishop, although he be but alone.

De Hæreticis ad abolendam, et in Clementinis ut officium.

Whosoever teacheth or thinketh of the Sacraments otherwise than the See of Rome doth teach and observe, and all they that the same See doth judg Hereticks, be Excommunicate.

And the Bishop of Rome may compel by an Oath, all Rulers and other People, to observe, and cause to be observed, whatsoever the See of Rome shall ordain concerning Heresy, and the Fautors thereof; and who will not obey, he may deprive them of their Dignities.

Clement. de reliq. et venerat. Sanctorum. Si Dominus extravag. de relig. et venerat. Sanctorum. Cum pre excelsa: de pœnitent. et remiss. antiquorum, et Clemen. unigenitus. Quemadmodum.

We obtain Remission of Sin by observing of certain Feasts, and certain Pilgrimages in the Jubilee, and other prescribed times, by virtue of the Bishop of Rome's Pardons.

De pœnitentiis et remissionibus extravag. ca. 3. Et si Dominici.

Whosoever offendeth the Liberties of the Church, or doth violate any Interdiction that cometh from Rome, or conspireth against the Person, or Statute of the Bishop, or See of Rome; or by any ways offendeth, disobeyeth, or rebelleth against the said Bishop, or See, or that killeth a Priest, or offendeth personally against a Bishop, or other Prelate; or invadeth, spoileth, withholdeth, or wasteth Lands belonging to the Church of Rome, or to any other Church immediately subject to the same; or whosoever invadeth any Pilgrims that go to Rome, or any Suitors to the Court of Rome, or that lett the devolution of Causes unto that Court, or that put any new Charges or Impositions, real or personal upon any Church, or Ecclesiastical Person; and generally all other that offend in the Cases contained in the Bull, which is usually published by the Bishops of Rome upon Maundy Thursday; all these can be assoiled by no Priest, Bishop, Arch-Bishop, nor by none other but only by the Bishop of Rome, or by his express license.

2. 4. q. z.

Robbing of the Clergy, and poor Men, appertaineth unto the judgment of the Bishops.

23. 9. q.

He is no Man-slayer that slayeth a Man which is Excommunicate.

Dist. 63. *Tibi Domino de sententia Excommunicationis. Si judex.*

Here may be added the most tyrannical and abominal Oaths which the Bishop of Rome exacts of the Emperors; *in Clement. de jurejurando Romani dist. 6. 3, Tibi Domino.*

De Consecra. Dist. 1. *Sicut.*

It is better not to Consecrate, than to Consecrate in a place not Hallowed.

De Consecrat. Dist. 5. *De his manus, ut jejuni.*

Confirmation, if it be ministred by any other than a Bishop, is of no value, nor is no Sacrament of the Church; also Confirmation is more to be had in reverence than Baptism; and no Man by Baptism can be a Christned Man without Confirmation.

De pœniten. Dist. 1. *Multiplex.*

A penitent Person can have no remission of his Sin, but by supplication of the Priests.

XXVIII.

A Mandate for publishing and using the Prayers in the English Tongue.

Mandatum Domino Episcopo London. direct. pro publicatione Regiarum Injunctionum.

Regist.
Bonner.
Fol. 48. MOST Reverend Father in God, right trusty and right well-beloved, we greet you well, and let you wit, That calling to our remembrance the miserable state of all Christendom, being at this present, besides all other troubles, so plagued with most cruel Wars, Hatred, and Dissensions,

as no place of the same almost (being the whole reduced to a very narrow corner) remaineth in good Peace, Agreement, and Concord; the help and remedy whereof far exceeding the power of any Man, must be called for of him who only is able to grant our Petitions, and never forsaketh nor repelleth any that firmly believe and faithfully call on him; unto whom also the example of Scripture encourageth us, in all these and other our troubles and necessities, to fly and to cry for aid and succour; being therefore resolved to have continually from henceforth general Processions, in all Cities, Towns, Churches, and Parishes of this our Realm, said and sung, with such reverence and devotion as appertaineth. Forasmuch as heretofore the People, partly for lack of good Instruction and Calling, and partly for that they understood no part of such Prayers or Suffrages as were used to be sung and said, have used to come very slackly to the Procession, when the same have been commanded heretofore; We have set forth certain godly Prayers and Suffrages in our Native English Tongue, which we send you herewith, signifying unto you, That for the special trust and confidence we have of your godly mind, and earnest desire, to the setting forward of the Glory of God, and the true worshipping of his most Holy Name, within that Province committed by us unto you, we have sent unto you these Suffrages, not to be for a month or two observed, and after slenderly considered, as other our Injunctions have, to our no little marvel, been used; but to the intent that as well the same, as other our Injunctions, may be earnestly set forth by preaching good Exhortations and otherwise to the People, in such sort as they feeling the godly tast thereof, may godly and joyously, with thanks, receive, embrace, and frequent the same, as appertaineth. Wherefore we will and command you, as you will answer unto us for the contrary, not only to cause these Prayers and Suffrages aforesaid to be published, frequented, and openly used in all Towns, Churches, Villages, and Parishes of your own Diocess, but also to signify this our pleasure unto all other Bishops of your Province, willing and command them in our Name, and by virtue hereof, to do and execute the same accordingly. Unto whose Proceedings,

In the execution of this our Commandment, we will that you have a special respect, and make report unto us, if any shall not with good dexterity accomplish the same; Not failing, as our special trust is in you.

At St. James's, *Junii—Regni* 36. Directed to the Arch-Bishop of Canterbury.

XXIX.

The Articles acknowledged by Shaxton, late Bishop of Sarum.

THE First; Almighty God, by the Power of his Word, pronounced by the Priest at Mass in the Consecration, turneth the Bread and Wine into the natural Body and Blood of our Saviour Jesus Christ; so that after the Consecration, there remaineth no substance of Bread and Wine, but only the Substance of Christ, God and Man.

The Second; The said Blessed Sacrament being once Consecrate, is and remaineth still the very Body and Blood of our Saviour Christ, although it be reserved, and not presently distributed.

The Third; The same blessed Sacrament being Consecrate, is and ought to be worshipped and adored with godly honour wheresoever it is, forasmuch as it is the Body of Christ inseparably united to the Deity.

The Fourth; The Church, by the Ministration of the Priest, offereth daily at the Mass for a Sacrifice to Almighty God, the self-same Body and Blood of our Saviour Christ, under the form of Bread and Wine, in the remembrance and representation of Christ's Death and Passion.

The Fifth; The same Body and Blood which is offered in the Mass, is the very propitiation and satisfaction for the sins of the World; forasmuch as it is the self-same in Substance which was offered upon the Cross for our Redemption: And the Oblation and Action of the Priest is also a Sacrifice of Praise and Thanksgiving unto God for

his Benefits, and not the satisfaction for the Sins of the
World, for that is only to be attributed to Christ's
Passion.

The Sixth; The said Oblation, or Sacrifice, so by the
Priest offered in the Mass, is available and profitable, both
for the Quick and the Dead, although it lieth not in the
power of Man to limit how much, or in what measure the
same doth avail.

The Seventh; It is not a thing of necessity, that the Sacrament of the Altar should be ministred unto the People
under both kinds, of Bread and Wine: and it is none abuse
that the same be ministred to the People under the one kind;
forasmuch as in every of both the kinds, whole Christ, both
Body and Blood is contained.

The Eighth; It is no derogation to the vertue of the Mass,
although the Priest do receive the Sacrament alone, and
none other receive it with him.

The Ninth; The Mass used in this Realm of England, is
agreeable to the Institution of Christ; and we have in this
Church of England, the very true Sacrament, which is the
very Body and Blood of our Saviour Christ, under the form
of Bread and Wine.

The Tenth; The Church of Christ hath, doth, and may
lawfully order some Priests to be Ministers of the Sacraments, although the same do not preach, nor be not admitted thereunto.

The Eleventh; Priests being once dedicated unto God by
the Order of Priesthood, and all such Men and Women as
have advisedly made Vows unto God of Chastity or Widow-
hood, may not lawfully marry, after their said Orders received, or Vows made.

The Twelfth; Secret auricular Confession is expedient
and necessary to be retained, continued, and frequented in
the Church of Christ.

The Thirteenth; The Prescience and Predestination of
Almighty God, although in it self it be infallible, induceth
no necessity to the Action of Man, but that he may freely
use the power of his own will or choice, the said Prescience
or Predestination notwithstanding.

I Nicholas Shaxton, with my Heart, do believe, and with

my Mouth do confess all these Articles above-written to be true in every part.

Ne despicias hominem avertentem se a peccato, neque improperes ei: memento quoniam omnes in corruptione sumus, Eccles. 8.

XXX.

A Letter written by Lethington the Secretary of Scotland, to Sir William Cecil, the Queen of England's Secretary, touching the Title of the Queen of Scots to the Crown of England : By which it appears that King Henry's Will was not signed by him.

Ex MS.
D. G.
Petyt.
I CANNOT be ignorant that some do object as to her Majesties Forreign Birth, and hereby think to make her incapable of the Inheritance of England. To that you know for answer what may be said by an English Patron of my Mistriss's Cause, although I being a Scot will not affirm the same, that there ariseth amongst you a Question; Whether the Realm of Scotland be forth of the Homage and Leageance of England? And therefore you have in sundry Proclamations preceding your Wars-making, and in sundry Books at sundry times, laboured much to prove the Homage and Fealty of Scotland to England. Your Stories also be not void of this intent. What the judgment of the Fathers of your Law is, and what commonly is thought in this Matter, you know better than I, and may have better intelligence than I, the Argument being fitter for your Assertion than mine.

Another Question there is also upon this Objection of Forreign Birth; that is to say, Whether Princes inheritable to the Crown, be in case of the Crown exempted or concluded as private Persons, being Strangers born forth of the Allegiance of England? You know in this case, as divers others, the State of the Crown: the Persons inheritable to the Crown at the time of their Capacity have divers differences and prerogatives from other Persons; many Laws made for other Persons take no hold in case of the Prince, and they have such Priviledges as other Persons enjoy not: As in cases of Attainders, and other Penal Laws: Examples, Hen. 7. who being a Subject, was attainted; and Edw. 4. and his Father Richard Plantagenet were both attainted; all which notwithstanding their Attainders had right to the Crown, and two of them attained the same. Amongst many Reasons to be shewed, both for the differences, and that Forreign Birth doth not take place in the case of the Crown, as in common Persons, the many experiences before the Conquest, and since, of your King's, do plainly testify. 2. Of purpose I will name unto you Henry 2d. Maud the Empress Son, and Richard of Bourdeaux, the Black Prince's Son, the rather for that neither of the two was the King of England's Son, and so not *Enfant du Roy*, if the word be taken in this strict signification. And for the better proof, that it was always the common Law of your Realm, that in the case of the Crown, Forreign Birth was no Bar; you do remember the words of the Stat. 25. Edw. 3. where it is said, the Law was ever so: Whereupon if you can remember it, you and I fell out at a reasoning in my Lord of Leicester's Chamber, by the occasion of the Abridgment of Rastal, wherein I did shew you somewhat to this purpose; also these words, Infant and Ancestors be in *Prædicamento ad aliquid*, and so correlatives in such sort, as the meaning of the law was not to restrain the understanding of this word Infant, so strict as only to the Children of the King's Body, but to others inheritable in remainder; and if some Sophisters will needs cavil about the precise understanding of Infant, let them be answered with the scope of this word Ancestors in all Provisions, for *Filii, Nepotes* and *Liberi*, you may see there was no difference betwixt the first degree, and these that come after by the Civil Law, *Liberorum appellatione, comprehenduntur non solum Filii, verum etiam Nepotes, Pronepotes, Abnepotes*, &c. If you examine the Reason why Forreign Birth is excluded, you may see that it was not so needful in Prince's Cases, as in common Persons. Moreover, I know that England hath oftentimes married with Daughters, and married with the greatest Forreign Princes of Europe. And so I do also understand, that they all did repute the Children of them, and of the Daughters of England, inheritable in succession to that Crown, notwithstanding the Forreign Birth of their issue: And in this case I do appeal to all Chronicles, to their Contracts of Marriages, and to the opinion of all the Princes of Christendom. For though England be a noble and puissant Country, the respect of the Alliance only, and the Dowry, hath not moved the great Princes to match so often in marriage, but the possibility of the Crown in succession. I cannot be ignorant altogether in this Matter, considering that I serve my Sovereign in the room that you serve yours. The Contract of Marriage is extant betwixt the King, my Mistris's Grandfather, and Queen Margaret, Daughter to King Henry the 7th, by whose Person the Title is devolved on my Sovereign; what her Father's meaning was in bestowing of her, the World knoweth, by that which is contained in the Chronicles written by Polidorus Virgilius, before (as I think) either you or I was born; at least when it was little thought that this Matter should come in question. There is another Exception also laid against my Soveraign, which seems at the first to be of some weight, grounded upon some Statutes made in King Henry 8. time, (viz.) of the 28th, and 35th of his Reign, whereby full power and authority was given him the said King Henry, to give, dispose, appoint, assign, declare, and limit, by his Letters Patents under his Great Seal, or else by his last Will made in writing, and signed with his hand at his pleasure, from time to time thereafter the Imperial Crown of that Realm, &c. Which Imperial Crown is by some alledged and constantly affirmed to have been limited and disposed, by the last Will and Testament of the said King Henry 8. signed with his hand before his death, unto the Children of the Lady Francis; and Elenor, Daughter to Mary the French Queen, younger Daughter of Henry 7. and of Charles Brandon Duke of Suffolk; so as it is thought the Queen my Soveraign, and all others, by course of Inheritance, be by these Circumstances excluded and foreclosed: So as it does well become all Subjects, such as I am, so my liking is to speak of Princes, of their Reigns

and Proceedings modestly, and with respect; yet I cannot
abstain to say, that the Chronicles and Histories of that
Age, and your own printed Statutes being extant, do con-
taminate and disgrace greatly the Reign of that King in
that time. But to come to our purpose, what equity and
justice was that to disinherit a Race of Forreign Princes
of their possibility, and maternal right, by a municipal
Law or Statute made in that, which some would term
abrupt time, and say, that that would rule the Roast, yea,
and to exclude the right Heirs from their Title, without
calling them to answer, or any for them: well, it may be
said, that the injury of the time, and the indirect dealing
is not to be allowed; but since it is done it cannot be
avoided, unless some Circumstances material do annihilate
the said limitation and disposition of the Crown.

Now let us examine the manner and circumstances how
King Hen. 8. was by Statute inabled to dispose the Crown.
There is a form in two sorts prescribed him, which he may
not transgress, that is to say, either by his Letters Patents,
sealed with his Great Seal, or by his last Will, signed with
his hand: for in this extraordinary case he was held to an
ordinary and precise form; which being not observed, the
Letters Patents, or Will, cannot work the intent or effect
supposed. And to disprove, that the Will was signed
with his own hand; You know, that long before his death
he never used his own signing with his own hand; and in
the time of his Sickness, being divers times pressed to put
his hand to the Will written, he refused to do it. And it
seemed God would not suffer him to proceed in an Act so
injurious and prejudicial to the right Heir of the Crown,
being his Niece. Then his death approaching, some as
well known to you as to me, caused William Clarke, sometimes Servant to Thomas Henneage, to sign the supposed
Will with a stamp, (for otherwise signed it was never);
and yet notwithstanding some respecting more the satisfaction of their ambition, and others their private commodity, than just and upright dealing, procured divers honest
Gentlemen, attending in divers several Rooms about the
King's Person, to testifie with their hand-writings the Contents of the said pretended Will, surmised to be signed
with the King's own hand. To prove this dissembled and

forged signed Testament, I do refer you to such Trials as be yet left. First; The Attestation of the late Lord Paget, published in the Parliament in Queen Mary's time, for the restitution of the Duke of Norfolk. Next, I pray you, on my Sovereigns behalf, that the Depositions may be taken in this Matter of the Marquess of Winchester, Lord Treasurer of England, the Marquess of Northampton, the Earl of Pembroke, Sir William Petre then one of King Henry's Secretaries, Sir Henry Nevill, Sir Maurice Barkley, Doctor Buts, Edmond Harman Baker, John Osborn Groom of the Chamber, Sir Anthony Dennis, if he be living, Terris the Chirurgion, and such as have heard David Vincent and others speak in this case; and that their Attestations may be enrolled in the Chancery, and in the Arches, *In perpetuam rei memoriam.*

Thirdly; I do refer you to the Original Will surmised to be signed with the King's own hand, that thereby it may most clearly and evidently appear by some differences, how the same was not signed with the King's hand, but stamped as aforesaid. And albeit it is used both as an Argument and Calumniation against my Sovereign to some, that the said Original hath been embezzled in Queen Mary's time, I trust God will and hath reserved the same to be an Instrument to relieve the Truth, and to confound false Surmises, that thereby the Right may take place, notwithstanding the many Exemplifications and Transcripts, which being sealed with the great Seal, do run abroad in England, and do carry away many Mens minds, as great presumptions of great verity and validity. But, Sir, you know in cases of less importance, that the whole Realm of England, Transcripts and Exemplifications be not of so great force in Law to serve for the recovery of any thing, either real or personal: And in as much as my Sovereign's Title in this case shall be little advanced, by taking exceptions to others pretended and crased Titles, considering her precedency, I will leave it to such as are to claim after the issue of Hen. the 7th, to lay in Bar the Poligamy of Charles Brandon, the Duke of Suffolk; and also the vitiated and clandestine Contract, (if it may be so called) having no witness nor solemnization of Christian Matrimony, nor any lawful matching of the Earl of Hertford and the Lady Katharine. Lastly; The semblably compelling of Mr. Key, and the Lady Mary Sister to the Lady Katherine.

And now, Sir, I have to answer your desire said somewhat briefly to the Matter, which indeed is very little, where so much may be said; for to speak truly, the Cause speaketh for it self. I have so long forborn to deal in this matter, that I have almost forgotten many things which may be said for Roboration of her Right, which I can shortly reduce to my Remembrance, being at Edinburgh where my Notes are: So that if you be not by this satisfied, upon knowledg from you of any other Objection, I hope to satisfy you unto all things may be said against her. In the mean time I pray you so counsel the Queen, your Soveraign, as some effectual reparation may follow without delay, of the many and sundry traverses and dis-favorings committed against the Queen, my Sovereign: as the publishing of so many exemplifications of King Henry's supposed Will, the secret embracing of John Halles Books, the Books printed and not avowed the last Summer, one of the which my Mistris hath sent by Henry Killigrew to the Queen your Soveraign; The Disputes and Proceedings of Lincoln's-Inn, where the Case was ruled against the Queen my Soveraign; The Speeches of sundry in this last Session of Parliament, tending all to my Soveraigns derision, and nothing said to the contrary by any Man, but the Matter shut up with silence, most to her prejudice; and by so much the more as every Man is gone home setled and confirmed in his Error. And, Lastly, The Queen, your Soveraign's resolution to defend now by Proclamations, all Books and Writings containing any discussion of Titles, when the whole Realm hath engendred by these fond proceedings, and other favoured practises, a setled opinion against my Soveraigns, to the advancement of my Lady Katherines Title, I might also speak of an other Book lately printed and set abroad in this last Session, containing many Untruths and weak Reasons, which Mr. Wailing desired might be answered before the Defence were made by Proclamation. I trust you will so hold hand to the Reformation of all these things, as the Queen, my Soveraign, may have effectual occasion to esteem you her Friend; which doing, you shall never offend the

Queen your Mistris, your Country, nor Conscience, but be a favourer of the Truth against Errors, and yet deserve well of a Princess, who hath a good heart to recognize any good turn, when it is done her, and may hereafter have means to do you pleasure. For my particular, as I have always honoured you as my Father, so do I still remain of the same mind, as one, whom in all things not touching the State, you may direct, as your Son Thomas Cecil, and with my hearty commendations to you, and my Lady, Both, I take my leave. From Striveling, the 14th of January, 1566.

AN

APPENDIX

CONCERNING SOME OF

THE ERRORS AND FALSEHOODS

IN

SANDERS'S BOOK

OF

THE ENGLISH SCHISM.

APPENDIX.

THOSE who intend to write romances, or plays, do commonly take their plot from some true piece of history; in which they fasten such characters to persons and things, and mix such circumstances and secret passages, with those public transactions and changes, that are in other histories; as may more artificially raise these passions and affections in their readers' minds, which they intend to move, than could possibly be done, if the whole story were a mere fiction and contrivance: and though all men know those tender passages to flow only from the invention and fancy of the poet; yet by I know not what charm, the greatest part that read or hear their poems, are softened and sensibly touched.

Some such design Sanders seems to have had in his book, which he very wisely kept up as long as he lived: he intended to represent the Reformation in the foulest shape that was possible, to defame Queen Elizabeth, to stain her blood, and thereby to bring her title to the crown in question; and to magnify the authority of the See of Rome, and celebrate monastic orders, with all the praises and high characters he could devise: and therefore, after he had writ several books on these subjects, without any considerable success, they being all rather filled with foul calumnies and detracting malice, than good arguments, or strong sense, he resolved to try his skill another way; so he intended to tell a doleful tale, which should raise a detestation of heresy, an ill opinion of the Queen, cast a stain on her blood, and disparage her title, and advance the honour of the Papacy. A tragedy was fitter for these ends, since it left the deepest impressions on the graver and better affections of the mind; the scene must be laid in England, and King Henry the Eighth and his three children, with the changes that were in their times, seemed to afford very plentiful matter for a man of wit and fancy, who knew where he could dexterously shew his art, and had boldness enough to do it without shame, or the reverence due, either to crowned heads, or to persons that were dead. Yet because he knew not how he could hold up his face to the world, after these discoveries were made, which he had reason to expect, this was concealed as long as he lived: and after he had died *for his faith* (that is, in rebellion, which I shall shew is *the faith* in his style) this work of his was published. The style is generally clean, and things are told in an easy and pleasant way; only he could not use his art so decently, as to restrain that malice which boiled in his breast, and often fermented out too palpably in his pen.

The book served many ends well, and so was generally much cried up, by men who had been long accustomed to commend any thing that was useful to them, without troubling themselves with those impertinent questions, whether they were true or false; yet Rishton, and others since that time, took the pencil again in their hands, and finding there were many touches wanting, which would give much life to the whole piece, have so changed it, that it was afterwards reprinted, not only with a large continuation, that was writ by a much more unskilful poet, but with so many and great additions, scattered through the whole work, whereby it seemed so changed in the vamping, that it looked new.

If any will give themselves the trouble, to compare his fable with the History that I have written, and the certain undoubted authorities I bring in confirmation of what I assert, with the slender, and (for the most part) no authorities, he brings, they will soon be able to discern where the truth lies: but because all people have not the leisure or opportunities for laying things so critically together, I was advised, by those whose counsels directed me in this whole work, to sum up, in an Appendix, the most considerable falsehoods and mistakes of that book, with the evidences upon which I rejected them. Therefore I have drawn out the following extraction, which consists of errors of two sorts. The one is, of those in which there is indeed no malice, yet they shew the writer had no true information of

our affairs, but commits many faults, which though they
leave not such foul imputations on the author, yet tend
very much to disparage and discredit his work. But the
others are of a higher guilt, being designed forgeries, to
serve partial ends; not only without any authority, but
manifestly contrary to truth, and to such records as (in
spite of all the care they took in Q. Mary's time by destroy-
ing them, to condemn posterity to ignorance in these matters) are yet reserved, and serve to discover the falsehood of
those calumnies in which they have traded so long. I shall
pursue these errors in the series in which they are delivered
in Sanders's book, according to the impression at Colen
1628, which is that I have. I first set down his errors, and
then a short confutation of them, referring the reader for
fuller information to the foregoing History.

1. Sanders says, " That when Prince Arthur and his Page 2.
Princess were bedded, King Henry the 7th ordered a grave
matron to lie in the bed, that so they might not consummate their marriage."

This is the ground-work of the whole fable; and should
have been some way or other proved. But if we do not
take so small a circumstance upon his word, we treat him
rudely; and who will write histories, if they be bound to
say nothing but truth! But little thought our Author that
there were three depositions upon record, point blank
against this; for the Dutchess of Norfolk, the Viscount of
Fitzwater and his lady, deposed they saw them bedded together, and the bed blessed after they two were put in it;
besides that such an extravagant thing was never known
done in any place.

2. Sanders says, " Prince Arthur was not then fifteen Ibid.
years of age, and was sick of a lingering disease."

The plot goes on but scurvily, when the next thing that
is brought to confirm it is contradicted by records. Prince
Arthur was born the 20th of September in the year 1486, and
so was fifteen years old and two months passed at the 14th
of November 1501, in which he was married to the Princess,
and was then of a lively and good complexion, and did not
begin to decay till the Shrovetide following, which was imputed to his excesses in the bed, as the witnesses deposed.

3. He says, " Upon the motion for the marrying of his Ib'd.

Brother Henry to the Princess, it was agreed to by all,
that the thing was lawful."

It was perhaps agreed on at Rome, where money and
other political arts sway their counsels; but it was not
agreed to in England: for which we have no meaner author, than Warham, archbishop of Canterbury, who, when
examined upon oath, deposed, that himself then thought
the marriage was not honourable nor well-pleasing to God,
and that he had thereupon opposed it much, and that the
people murmured at it.

P. 3.   4. He says, " There was not one man in any nation under heaven, or in the whole church, that spake against it."

The common style of the Roman church, calling the See
of Rome the catholic church, must be applied to this, to
bring off our Author; otherwise I know not how to save his
reputation. Therefore by all *the nations under heaven* must
be understood only the divines at Rome, though when it
came to be examined, they could scarce find any who would
justify it: all the most famous universities, divines, and
canonists, condemned it, and Warham's testimony con-
tradicts this plainly, besides the other great authorities
that were brought against it; for which see Book II. from
page 143 to page 162.

P. 4.   5. He says, " The King once said, *He would not marry
the Queen.*"

Here is a pretty essay of our Author's art, who would
make us think it was only in a transient discourse, that the
King said he would not marry Queen Katherine; but this
was more maturely done, by a solemn protestation, which
he read himself before the Bishop of Winchester, that he
would never marry her, and that he revoked his consent
given under age: This was done when he came to be of
age, see page 56: it is also confessed by Sanders himself.

Ibid.   6. He says, " The Queen bore him three sons and two
daughters."

All the books of that time speak only of two sons, and
one daughter; but this is a flourish of his pen, to represent
her a fruitful mother.

P. 5.   7. He says, " The King had sometimes two, sometimes
three concubines at once."

It does not appear he had ever any but Elizabeth Blunt;

and if we judge of his life, by the letters the popes wrote to him, and many printed elogies that were published then, he was a prince of great piety and religion all that while.

8. He says, " The Lady Mary was first desired in mar- P. 6. riage by James the 5th of Scotland, then by Charles the 5th, the Emperor ; and then Francis asked her, first for the Dauphin, then for the Duke of Orleans, and last of all for himself."

But all this is wrong placed, for she was first contracted to the Dauphin, then to the Emperor, and then treated about to the King of Scotland ; after that it was left to Francis's choice, whether she should be married to himself, or his second son the Duke of Orleans: so little did our Poet know the public transactions of that time.

9. He says, " She was in the end contracted to the Dau- Ibid. phin:" from whence he concludes, " that all foreign princes were satisfied with the lawfulness of the marriage."

She was first of all contracted to the Dauphin. Foreign princes were so little satisfied of the lawfulness of the marriage, that though she, being heir to the crown of England, was a match of great advantage ; yet their counsellors excepted to it, on that very account, that the marriage was not good. This was done in Spain, and she was rejected, as a writer who lived in that time informs us; and Sanders confesses it was done by the French Ambassador.

10. He says, " Wolsey was first bishop of Lincoln, then P. 7. of Duresme, after that of Winchester, and last of all archbishop of York ; after that he was made chancellor, then cardinal and legate."

The order of these preferments is quite reversed ; for Wolsey, soon after he was made bishop of Lincoln, upon Cardinal Bembridge's death, was not only promoted to the See of York, but advanced to be a cardinal in the seventh year of the King's reign : and some months after that, he was made lord chancellor ; and seven years after that, he got the bishoprick of Duresme, which six years after he exchanged for Winchester. He had heard perhaps that he enjoyed all these preferments; but knowing nothing of our affairs beyond hearsay, he resolved to make him rise as poets order their heroes, by degrees, and therefore ranks his advancement not according to truth, but in the method he liked best himself.

P. 8.   11. He says, " Wolsey first designed the divorce, and made Longland, that was the King's confessor, second his motion for it."

The King not only denied this in public, saying, that he himself had first moved it to Longland in confession; and that Wolsey had opposed it all he could: but in private discourse with Grinæus, told him, he had laboured under these scruples for seven years; *septem perpetuis annis trepidatio*. Which, reckoning from the year 1531, in which Grinæus wrote this to one of his friends, will fall back to the year 1524, long before Wolsey had any provocation to tempt him to it.

P. 9,   12. He says, " In the year 1526, in which the King was first made to doubt of his marriage, he was resolved then whom to marry when he was once divorced."

But by his other story, Anne Boleyn was then but fifteen years old, and went to France at that age, where she stayed a considerable time before she came to the court of England.

Ibid.   13. He says, " The King spent a year in a private search, to see what could be found, either in the Scriptures, or the Pope's bull, to be made use of against his marriage; but they could find nothing."

In that time all the bishops of England, except Fisher, declared under their hand and seals, that they thought the marriage unlawful; for which see page 60, and upon what reasons this was grounded, has been clearly opened, page 152, &c.

Ibid.   14. He says, " If there were any ambiguities in the Pope's first letters (meaning the bull for dispensing with the marriage) they were cleared by other letters, which Ferdinand of Spain had afterwards procured."

These other letters (by which he means the breve) bear date the same day with the bull; and so were not procured afterwards. There were indeed violent presumptions of their being forged long after, even after the process had been almost a year in agitation. But though they helped the matter in some lesser particulars, yet in the main business, whether Prince Arthur did know his Princess, they did it a great prejudice; for whereas the bull bore, that by the Queen's petition her former marriage was *perhaps consummated*, the breve bears, that, in her petition, the marriage was said to be consummated, without any *perhaps*.

15. He says, "The King having seen these second let- P. 9. ters, both he and his council resolved to move no more in it."

The process was carried on, almost a year, before the breve was heard of: and the forgery of it soon appeared, so they went on notwithstanding it.

16. He says, "The Bishop of Tarby being come from P. 10. France, to conclude the match for the Lady Mary, was set on by the King and the Cardinal, to move the exception to the lawfulness of the marriage."

There is no reason to believe this; for that Bishop, though afterwards made a cardinal, never published this: which both he ought to have done as a good catholic, and certainly would have done as a true cardinal, when he saw what followed upon it, and perceived that he was trepanned to be the first mover of a thing, which ended so fatally for the interests of Rome.

17. He says, "The Bishop of Tarby, in a speech before P. 11. the King in council, said, that not he alone, but almost all learned men, thought the King's marriage unlawful and null: so that he was freed from the bond of it, and that it was against the rules of the gospel; and that all foreign nations had ever spoken very freely of it, lamenting that the King was drawn into it in his youth."

It is not ordinary for ambassadors to make speeches in King's councils: but if this be true, it agrees ill with what this Author delivers in his third page, that there was not a man in the whole church, nor under heaven, that spoke against it; otherwise the Bishop of Tarby was both an impudent and a foolish man.

18. He says, "Upon the Pope's captivity, Wolsey was P. 13. sent over to France with 300,000 crowns to procure the Pope's liberty."

Hall, Hollingshead, and Stow, say, he carried over 240,000 pounds sterling, which is more than thrice that sum.

P. 13. 19. He says, " Two colleagues were sent in this embassy with the Cardinal."

His greatness was above that, and none are mentioned in the Records.

Ibid. 20. He says, " Orders followed him to Calais, not to move any thing about the King's marriage with the French King's sister, the King having then resolved to marry Anne Boleyn."

This agrees ill with what he said page 9, that a year before the King was resolved whom to marry.

Ibid. 21. He says, " King Henry, that he might have freer access to Sir Thomas Boleyn's lady, sent him to France; where, after he had stayed two years, his lady was with child of Anne Boleyn by the King."

This story was already confuted, see pages 60, 61 ; and in it there are more than one or two lies.

1. Sir Thomas Boleyn went not ambassador to France till the seventh year of the King's reign : and if two years after that Anne was born, which was the ninth of his reign, she must then have been but ten years old at this time.

2. Though he had sent him upon his first coming to the crown, this could not be true ; for two years after, admit her to be born, that is anno 1511, then a year before this, which was anno 1526, she was fifteen years old ; in which age, Sanders says, she was corrupted in her father's house, and sent over to France, where she stayed long. But all this is false : for,

3. She was born two years before the King came to the crown, in the year 1507, and if her father was sent to France two years before, it was in the year 1505.

4. The King being then Prince, was but fourteen years old, for he was born the 28th of June, in the year 1491: in which age there is no reason to think he was so forward as to be corrupting other men's wives, for they will not allow his brother, when almost two years elder, to have known his own wife.

As for the other pieces of this story, that Sir Thomas Boleyn did sue his lady in the Spiritual Court; that upon the King's sending him word that she was with child by him, he passed it over ; that the King had also known her sister, and that she had owned it to the Queen, that at the fifteenth year of Anne's age, she had prostituted herself both to her father's butler, and chaplain; that then she was sent to France, where she was at first for some time concealed, then brought to court, where she was so notoriously lewd, that she was called a Hackney; that she afterwards was kept by the French King; that when she came over into England, Sir Thomas Wiat was admitted to base privacies with her, and offered to the King and his council, that he himself should with his own eyes see it; and, in fine, that she was ugly, misshaped, and monstrous, are such a heap of impudent lies, that none but a fool, as well as a knave, would venture on such a recital. And for all this, he cites no other authority but Rastal's Life of Sir Thomas More, a book that was seen by none but himself; and he gives no other evidence that there was any such book but his own authority. Nor is it likely that Rastal ever writ More's Life, since he did not set it out with his works, which he published in one volume, anno 1556. It is true, More's son-in-law, Roper, writ his life, which is since printed, but there is no such story in it. The whole is such a piece of lying, as if he who forged it had resolved to outdo all who had ever gone before him: for can it be so much as imagined, that a King could pursue a design for seven years together, of marrying a woman of so scandalous a life, and so disagreeable a person; and that he who was always in the other extreme of jealousy, did never try out these reports, and would not so much as see what Wiat informed? Nor were these things published in the libels that were printed at that time, either in the Emperor's court, or at Rome. All which shew, that this was a desperate contrivance of malicious traitors against their Sovereign Queen Elizabeth, to defame and disgrace her. And this I take to be the true reason, why none made any full answer to this book all her time. It was not thought for the Queen's honour to let such stuff be so much considered as to merit an answer. So that the 13, 14, 15, 16, 17, and 18th pages are one continued lie.

22. He says, " Sir Thomas Boleyn, hearing the King p. 16. intended to marry his supposed daughter, came over in all haste from France, to put him in mind that she was his own child; and that the King bade him hold his peace for

a fool, for a hundred had lain with his wife as well as he, but whosesoever daughter she was, she should be his wife: and upon that Sir Thomas instructed his daughter how she should hold the King in her toils."

Sir Thomas must have thought the King had an ill memory, if he had forgot such a story: but the one part of this makes him afraid that the King should marry his daughter, and the other part makes him afraid they should miss their hopes in it: not to mention how little likely it is, that a King of such high vanity, would have done that which the privatest person has an aversion to—I mean, the marrying the daughter of one whom they know to be a common prostitute.

P. 12. 23. He says, " Wolsey, before his return from France, sent Gambara to the Pope, desiring him to name himself Vicar of the Papacy, during his captivity."

This was not done till almost a year after this: and the motion was sent by Staphileus, dean of the Rota, for which see page 78.

P. 20. 24. He says, " None but ill men and ignorant persons wrote against the marriage, but all learned and good men wrote for it."

The whole doctors of the church, in all ages, were against it; and no doctor, ancienter than Cajetan, could ever be found to have writ for it.

Ibid. 25. He says, " That though great endeavours were used to persuade Sir Thomas More of the unlawfulness of the marriage, all was in vain."

Is it probable that the King would have made him lord chancellor, when he was so earnest in this business, if he had not known that he would have gone along with him in it? By one of his letters to Cromwell out of the Tower, it appears, that he approved the divorce, and had great hopes of success in it, as long as it was prosecuted at Rome, and founded on the defects in the bull. And in the twenty-second year of the King's reign, when the opinions of the universities, and the books of learned men were brought to England against the marriage, he carried them down to the House of Commons, and made read them there; after which he desired they would report in their country what they had heard and seen; and then all men would openly perceive that the

King had not attempted this matter of his will and pleasure, but only for the discharge of his conscience. More
was a man of greater integrity than to have said this, if he
had thought the marriage good; so that he has either afterwards changed his mind, or did at this time dissemble too
artificially with the King.

26. After a long flourish about the King's secret fears P. 32.
and apprehensions, and the perplexities the Cardinal was
in, which must pass for a piece of *his wit*, that is to say,
lying, for he knew none of their thoughts; he says, " That
Gardiner and Sir Francis Brian were sent to the Pope together, Gardiner being then secretary of state."

In this there are only three gross mistakes. First, Gardiner was not sent with the first message to the Pope; Secretary Knight carried it.

2. Sir Francis Brian went never to Rome with Gardiner. It is true, a year after the commencing the suit, Sir
Francis Brian was sent to Rome, and about a month after
him Gardiner was also sent; so though they were both together at Rome, yet they were not sent thither together.

3. Gardiner was not secretary of state, but was Wolsey's secretary, when he went first to Rome, and was made
a privy-counsellor when he was sent thither the second
time; and was not secretary of state till some months after
his return from his journey the last time.

27. He says, " They made the Pope believe that the P. 33.
Queen would willingly retire into a monastery."

This was on the contrary a contrivance of the Pope's,
who thought it the easiest way to bring the matter to a
good issue; but in England they had no hopes of it, and
so always diverted the motion when it was proposed by the
Pope.

28. He says, " The Pope said he would consult with Ibid.
some cardinals and divines, and do all that he could lawfully do to give the King satisfaction."

Upon the first motion of it, the Pope frankly granted the
King's desire; and gave a bull with a commission upon
it: and only consulted some cardinals about the methods
of doing it. And did assure the King, that he would not
only do every thing that could be granted in law or justice,
but whatsoever he could grant out *of the fulness of his power*.

It is true, afterwards when the Pope changed his measures, and resolved to agree with the Emperor, he pretended he understood not these things himself, but would needs turn it over, upon the cardinals and divines.

P. 24. 29. He says, " All the cardinals were of a mind that the marriage was good."

Cardinal Sanctorum Quatuor, by the force of that mighty argument of 4000 crowns, changed his mind. All the other cardinals were forward in granting the King's desires; for which he wrote them a letter of thanks.

P. 26. 30. He says, " The Pope granted the commission to the two Legates, not doubting but it was true, that had been told him of the Queen's readiness to go into a monastery."

The Pope knew she would not yield to any such thing; but when he granted that commission, he sent with Campegio a decretal bull, annulling the marriage: and sent afterwards a promise never to avocate the process, but to confirm what sentence the Legates should give; though soon after he broke his promise most signally. And since he had often dispensed with others for breaking their faith, he might think that it was hard to deny him the same privilege for himself.

Ibid. 31. He says, " The Pope understanding that the Queen did not consent to the propositions that were made, and that he had been abused, sent after Campegio, when he was on his journey, that he should not proceed to a sentence without a new order."

The Pope sent Campana to England after Campegio, to assure the King he would do every thing for him that he could do *out of the fulness of his power:* and ordered the same person to charge Cardinal Campegio to burn the decretal bull, which he had sent by him; in all which the Pope, as appears by the original letters, was only governed by politic maxims, and considered nothing but the dangers himself was like to fall in; though Sanders would persuade us, he was ready to run the hazard of all these.

P. 30. 32. He says, " The King by his letters to the Pope, did, at the same time that he was moving scruples about his own marriage, transact about a dispensation for a marriage betwixt his own natural son the Duke of Richmond, and his daughter the Lady Mary."

Though the whole dispatches at that time, both to and from Rome, be most happily preserved, there is not the least mention of any such design : and can any body think that if any such motion had been made, the Pope would not have taken great advantages from it, and that these letters would not have been afterwards published ? But this Sanders thought was a pretty embellishment of his fable ; and of a piece with this is his next.

33. He says, " The King did under his own hand con- P. 30. fess, he had known Anne Boleyn's sister Mary, and desired the Pope would dispense with his marrying Anne notwithstanding that."

The falsehood of this appears from the recital of it : and how came it that these letters were not published ? Nor is there any mention of this in all the dispatches I have seen. And it is not possible that in so many conferences which the English ambassadors had with the Pope, these two things should never have been discoursed of. And can it be thought credible, that at the same time when the King pretended such scruples and troubles of consciences, he could be guilty of so much folly and impudence, as to put himself thus in the Pope's mercy, by two such demands ? This was a forgery of Cardinal Pole's, which Sanders greedily catched to dress up the scene.

34. From page 34, to 42, there is a trifling account given P. 34. of the reasons brought against the marriage, which Sanders answers manfully, and fights courageously against the man of straw he had set up. But if that be compared with what has been opened in the History, it will appear how lame and defective his account is.

35. He says, " Clark, bishop of Bath and Wells, Ton- P. 42. stal, bishop of London, and West, bishop of Ely, writ for the lawfulness of the King's marriage."

All the bishops, except Fisher, had a year before this given it under their hands and seals, that the King's marriage was unlawful : and in all the memorials of that time, Fisher is the only bishop I find mentioned to have writ for it. Tonstal was also soon after translated to Duresme, which none that have considered that King's temper, will think could have been done, if he had interposed in so tender a point, against what the King so vehemently desired.

P. 42.   36. He says, "That Abell, Powel, Fetherston, and Rid-ley, also writ for the marriage."

This is not likely of the second and third, for they being afterwards attainted of treason, no such books were objected to them; but the crime charged on them, was only that they said, the King's marriage with Queen Katherine was good.

P. 43.   37. He says, "All things appeared clear in the trial before the Legates, in behalf of the marriage, so that they could give no sentence against such full evidence as was brought for it."

This is said without any regard to truth; for all the matter of fact that had been alleged, was clearly proved for the contrary side. It was proved that Prince Arthur married the Queen: violent presumptions appeared of his consummating the marriage. It was also proved that the King was under age when the bull was obtained, and that the petitions given in his name, upon which the bull was granted, were false: that the King had not desired it, but when he came of age he had protested against it: and that there was no hazard of a war between Spain and England, the preventing which was the chief reason set down in the bull that permitted it. So that all that had been informed at Rome, as to matter of fact, was fully proved before the Legates, by clear instruments, and many and noble witnesses.

Ibid.   38. He puts a long bold speech in Campegio's mouth, who was far from assuming such freedom; but lived licentiously in England, in all manner of disorders, of which both he and his bastard son were guilty. And by dissembling, and other arts, persuaded the King to delay the process, from day to day, giving him full assurances, that in conclusion he should obtain what he desired: and by such means he gained time, and drew out the trial, till the Pope had ended his treaty with the Emperor; and then he served him an Italian trick, by adjourning the court.

P. 48.   39. He says, "Some doctors, being corrupted with the King's money, declared for him; but those were none of the most learned."

The King ordered those he sent, not to give or promise any thing to any person, till they had delivered their opinion freely: upon which some of them wrote to him, that they would answer upon their heads, that they had followed his orders in that particular.

40. He says, " These determinations were published in P. 48. the names of the universities, to deceive the world by a false representation of so great authorities."

Were the public seals of the universities put to their determinations, after a long debate, all being required to deliver their consciences upon oath, and done with the unanimous consent of the whole faculty in some places, false representations? This was done in Italy, in Padua, Bononia, Ferrara, and Milan, under the Pope and the Emperor's eye, and within their dominions.

41. He says, " Endeavours were used to corrupt the Uni- P. 50. versity of Colen, and some others in Germany, for which great sums were offered, and that the King was at a vast expense in it."

Crook's accompts shew that his expense in Italy was very inconsiderable. And who can imagine, that when Paris, Padua, and Bononia, had declared for the King, he would be much concerned for Colen, or any other university in Germany? Those who will believe Sanders, and such authors as he quotes, Cochleus, and an unknown bishop of Brazil, may if they will.

42. He says, " In Oxford the King not being able to P. 51. obtain a satisfactory answer in that matter, eight students of the University broke into the place where the seal was laid, and put it to an answer, which passed for the determination of the University."

The Lord Herbert says, there was an original instrument passed, which he saw; by which the University did appoint a committee of thirty-three doctors and bachelors of divinity to examine the questions proposed by the King, and to set the seal of the University to any answer that they should agree on: and these did afterwards give a resolution against the lawfulness of the marriage.

43. " He tells a long story of the King's endeavours to P. 52. gain Reginald Pole, and that he came over to England; and being much pressed by his kindred, to comply with the King, he went to him, fully purposed to have done it.: but could not speak a word to him, till he resolved to talk to him in another style; and then he found his tongue, and

spake very freely to the King, who put his hands sometimes to his poniard, intending to have killed him; but was overcome with the simplicity and humility of his discourse: and so the King continued his pension to him, and gave him leave to go back to Padua."

This is another pretty adventure of one of the heroes of the romance, but has this misfortune in it—that it is all without any proof: for as none of the books of that time ever mention it, so neither did Pole himself pretend to have carried so, in his book, though written with the most provoking insolence that was possible. In it he mentions his going over to England, but not one word of any such discourse with the King. And King Henry was not a man of such a temper, as to permit one of Pole's quality to go out of England, and live among his enemies, and continue his pensions to him, if he had to his face opposed him in a matter he laid so much to heart.

P. 55. 44. He says, " Fisher of Rochester, and Holman, bishop of Bristol, wrote for the marriage."

There was no bishoprick, nor bishop of Bristol at that time, nor thirteen years after.

Ibid. 45. "Many are reckoned up who wrote for the marriage in all nations."

These are neither to be compared in number, nor authority, to those who wrote against it; a hundred books were shewed in parliament, written by divines, and lawyers beyond sea, besides the determinations of twelve of the most celebrated universities in Europe. The Emperor did indeed give so great rewards, and such good benefices, to those who wrote against the King, that it is a wonder there were not more writers of his side.

P. 56. 46. He says, " That upon Warham, archbishop of Canterbury's death, the Earl of Wiltshire told the King that he had a chaplain, who was at his house, that would certainly serve the King in the matter of his divorce; upon which Cranmer was promoted."

Cranmer was no stranger to the King at this time: he was first recommended by the King to the Earl of Wiltshire, to be kept in his house; but was in Germany when Warham died, and made no haste over, but delayed his journey some months. It is true, he was of the mind that

the King ought to be divorced; but this was not out of ser-
vile compliance, for when the King pressed him in other
things that were against his conscience, he expressed all
the courage and constancy of mind which became so great
a prelate.

47. He says, " That Cranmer being to swear the oath of P. 56.
obedience to the Pope, before he was consecrated, did protest to a public notary, that he took it against his will; and
that he had no mind to keep his faith to the Pope, in prejudice to the King's authority."

He did not protest that he did it unwillingly, nor was it
only to a notary, but twice at the high altar he repeated
the protestation that he made; which was to this effect, that
he intended not thereby to oblige himself to any thing, contrary to the law of God, the King's prerogative, or the laws
of the land; nor to be restrained from speaking, advising,
or consenting to any thing that should concern the reformation of the Christian faith, the government of the church of
England, and the prerogative of the crown and kingdom.

48. He says, " Cranmer did in all things so comply with P. 57.
the King's lusts, that the King was wont to say he was the
only man that had never contradicted him in any thing he
had a mind to."

Cranmer was both a good subject, and a modest and discreet man, and so would obey and submit as far as he
might, without sin: yet when his conscience charged him
to appear against any thing that the King pressed him to,
as in the matter of the six Articles, he did it with much resolution and boldness.

49. He says, " The King going over to Calais, carried P. 58.
Anne Boleyn secretly with him."

He carried her over in great state, having made her
Marchioness of Pembroke; and in the public interview between him and Francis, she appeared with all possible
splendour.

50. He says, " After the King's return from France, he P. 59.
brought the action of premunire against all the clergy."

This is an error of two years, for so long before this voyage to France was that action begun: and the clergy about
eighteen months before had made their submission, and obtained their pardon in March 1531, which appears by the

printed statutes, and the King went over to France in September, 1532; so that it is clear Sanders never looked for any verification of what he wrote.

P. 59. 51. He says, " The King by an unheard-of tyranny, and a new calumny, brought this charge against the clergy."

These laws, upon which the charge was founded, had been oft renewed: they were first made under Edward the First, by reason of the papal encroachments that gave the rise to them; they were oft confirmed by Edward the Third, Richard the Second, Henry the Fourth, and Henry the Fifth, with the concurrence of their parliaments; so the charge was neither new nor tyrannical.

Ibid. 52. He says, " The clergy submitted to the King, being betrayed by their metropolitans Cranmer and Lee."

The submission was made two years before Cranmer was archbishop, in March, 1531, and Cranmer was consecrated in March, 1533; but at that time Warham sat in Canterbury. As for Lee, he opposed it for some time.

Ibid. 53. He says, " The whole clergy petitioned the King, to forgive their crime, according to that supreme power which he had over all the clergy and laity, within this kingdom: from whence the King's counsellors took occasion afterwards to call him *Supreme Head.*"

The clergy did in the title of their submission call the King in formal terms, *Supreme Head of the Church and Clergy of England, as far as by the law of Christ is lawful:* to which Fisher, with the rest of the convocation subscribed. And all this was done when More was chancellor.

P. 62. 54. He says, " When the King went to marry Anne Boleyn, he persuaded Rowland Lee, made soon after bishop of Coventry and Litchfield, to officiate in it, assuring him he had obtained a bull for it from Rome, which was then lying in his cabinet. Upon which Lee, giving credit to what he said, did marry them."

This is another trial of Sanders's wit, to excuse Lee, who, though at this time he complied absolutely with the King, yet did afterwards turn over to the Popish party; therefore, to make him look a little clean, this story must be forged. But at that time all the world saw that the Pope and the Emperor were so linked together, that Lee could not but know that no such thing was possible. And he was so obsequious to the King, that such arts were needless to persuade him to any thing the King had a mind to.

55. For five pages he runs out in repetition of all those P. 76. foul lies concerning Anne Boleyn, by which he designed both to disgrace the reformers, who were supported by her, and to defame her daughter Queen Elizabeth, which have been before confuted: after that he says, " Queen Katherine, with three maids and a small family, retired into the country."

She had both the respect of a princess dowager, and all the jointure contracted to her by Prince Arthur; so she could not be driven to that straitness: but this must go for an ornament in the fable.

56. He says, " It was concluded, that Cranmer might P. 71. be more free to pass sentence, that there should be an oath imposed on the clergy, for paying the same obedience to the King that they had paid the Pope:" upon which he tells a long formal story, for two pages, that " it was resolved to draw Fisher into it, to swear obedience to the King in all ecclesiastical causes, with that exception, *as far as is lawful, according to the word of God;* which he did, and persuaded others to do it; and upon this Cranmer, taking the new oath, went and pronounced judgment for divorce."

There is not one tittle of this true, for there was no oath sworn about the King's supremacy at this time. The story of Fisher, is that which was done by the convocation two years before Cranmer's preferment, nor was there any oath taken then, or at this time. It is true, two years after this, Gardiner, Stokesley, and many other bishops, did of their own accord take such an oath; but there was no law for it till the twenty-eighth year of the King's reign.

57. He says, " One Richard Risey (or Rouse, according to P. 72. the Records) was hired by Anne Boleyn to poison Fisher."

Rouse was boiled alive for poisoning the Bishop's family, but did not discover any that set him on it: which none can think but he would have done, if the Queen had hired him to it, and had then deserted him to perish in so horrid a manner.

58. He says, " Cranmer being by authority of parliament P. 73. freed from his oath to the Pope, and bound by a new one to the King, went now confidently to pronounce sentence."

The parliament did not put down the Pope's authority

for eight months after this, and appointed no new oath till
three years after; for Cranmer sat in judgment as Primate
of England, and Legate of the Apostolic See.

P. 73.   59. He says, " Cranmer carried some bishops with him,
and having cited the Queen, without hearing her, he gave
sentence against the marriage."

Gardiner, Stokesley, Clark, and Longland, the Bishops of
Winchester, London, Bath, and Lincoln, went with him.
He could not hear the Queen, when she would not appear:
but he examined all the instruments and evidences that had
been brought in the whole process.

P. 75.   60. He says, " The Pope would not proceed against the
King, till he met with the French King at Marseilles; but
that the English Ambassadors did there carry so insolently,
that Francis was ashamed of their behaviour; and desired
the Pope to proceed against the King as he thought fit,
and that he should never defend him more, but should be
against him."

Here the romance goes on too grossly, for the Pope and
the French King agreed at Marseilles to bring this matter
to an issue. The Pope declared he thought the King's
cause was just and right; and promised, if the King would
send a full submission to Rome, he would give sentence
in his favour. Upon which the French King sent over
the Bishop of Paris, who prevailed with the King to do it;
though this afterwards came to nothing. It is true, Bonner,
who was always officious and forward when there was any
thing to be got by it, being sent to Marseilles by the King,
to deliver an appeal in the King's name to the Pope, to the
next general council; and perhaps knowing nothing of
' the private transactions between the Pope and the French
King, it being a secret of too great importance to be com-
, municated to such a hot-brained man, did deliver his message to the Pope in such provoking language, that the
Pope talked of throwing him into a boiling cauldron; and
he was fain to fly for it.

P. 76.   61. He says, " The Pope returning to Italy, after he
had again most carefully reviewed the whole cause, gave
sentence."

This was so precipitated, that they would not stay six
days beyond the time which they prefixed, for the return

of the messenger that was sent to England : but dispatched that, which by the forms of their court should have been done in three consistories, all in one day.

62. He says, " Upon this sentence, the King, being en- P. 78. raged, did command Queen Katherine to be only called Princess, and declared her daughter the Lady Mary a bastard."

Both these were done five months before the Pope's sentence, and soon after the sentence was pronounced by Cranmer. And these were the natural consequences of it ; for the marriage being annulled, neither could she be longer a Queen, nor her daughter Princess any more.

63. He says, " The King imprisoned F. Forest, a Fran- Ibid. ciscan observant, a most holy and learned man, for contradicting Latimer, when he was inveighing against the Pope's authority."

Concerning this Forest, I have seen an original letter of one List, a friar of the same house, a year after this, that says Forest was a great scandal to their house, and was very ignorant ; and that though he had been much against the King in his marriage, yet he had then insinuated himself into his favour, of which many of the house, who were for the King's cause, had great apprehensions. In the same letter he writes, how cruel they were against any of their brethren, who they thought discovered any thing that was done among them ; and that one Rainscroft, a brother, whom they suspected to have informed what passed among them, was cruelly used, and kept in prison till he died; which he chiefly imputes to Forest. This friar swore the King's supremacy, and yet at the same time was persuading others not to do it ; and being questioned upon it, said, he took the oath only with his outward, but not with his inward man ; and for that, and his denying the gospel, he was burnt as an obstinate heretic.

64. He says, " Abell, Powel, and Fetherston, were put P.79. in prison because they consulted with the Maid of Kent."

This is only charged upon the former of these, but the two latter are not accused of any such thing.

65. He says, " Elizabeth, being born the 8th of September, Ibid. but five months after the King had publicly married her mother, could not be the lawful issue of that marriage."

This is a malicious lie, for himself confessed that the King was married to her mother the 14th of November, the former year; between which and the 8th of September, there were ten months; nor was the King ever after that married publicly to the Queen. For what he calls a public marriage, was only the shewing her openly as Queen. But the design of this lie is so visible, that it needs not be opened.

P. 79.   66. He says, " The King's daughter Mary, who was then present, could never be induced to think she was the King's child."

In the former page he said Mary was sent to her mother, and now, forgetting himself too soon, he says, she was present when Elizabeth was born. What Mary's thoughts were, none can tell, but she publicly acknowledged her to be her sister, though she did not use her as one.

P. 80.   67. He says, " Elizabeth Barton, who was famed for her sanctity, and six with her, who thought she was inspired by the Holy Ghost, were accused in parliament."

Those six knew that she was not inspired; and that all that was given out about her, was a contrivance of their's, who had instructed her to play such tricks; as was proved by their own confessions and other evidences.

Ibid.   68. He says, " They all died very constantly;" and on the margent calls them " *seven martyrs*."

The Nun herself acknowledged the imposture at her death, and laid the heaviest weight of it on the priests that suffered with her, who had taught her the cheat; so that they died both for treason and imposture. And this being Sanders's *faith*, as appeared by *his works*, they were indeed martyrs for it.

Ibid.   69. He says, " More and Fisher, having examined her, could see no ground to think she was acted by a fanatical spirit, as it was given out."

It was not given out that she was acted by a fanatical spirit, for that had been more honest; but her spirit was cheating and knavery. More cleared himself, and looked on her as a weak woman, and commonly called her the *Silly Maid*. But Fisher did disown her when the cheat was discovered, though he had given her too much encouragement before.

70. He says, " The thing she prophesied came to pass; P. 81.
which was, that Mary should be Queen of England."

The thing for which she and her complices were attainted
of treason, was, that she said, *If the King married Anne Boleyn, he should not be a King a month longer, and not an hour
longer in the sight of God, and should die a villain's death.*
But it did not serve Sanders's ends to tell this.

71. He says, " The day she suffered, many of the nobi- Ibid.
lity came and swore to the succession of the issue of the
King's marriage with Queen Anne, before the Archbishop
of Canterbury, the Lord Chancellor, and Cromwell."

Both Houses of Parliament did in the House of Lords
take that oath, on the day of their prorogation, which was
the 30th of March, as appears by the second act of the next
session; and the Nun, with her complices, did not suffer
till the 21st of April after.

72. He says, " The Franciscans of the observance, chiefly Ibid.
two fathers in London, Elston and Payton, did, both in
their sermons and public disputes, justify the King's marriage with Queen Katherine."

Elston and Payton were not of London, but of Greenwich. They compared the King to Achab, and said, in the
pulpit, to his face, *The dogs should lick his blood;* with
many other such virulent expressions. But to rail at a
Prince with the most spiteful reproaches that could be,
was a part of Sanders's faith; and so no wonder those pass
for confessors, when Elizabeth Barton, and her complices,
are reckoned martyrs.

73. He says, " Tonstal, bishop of Duresme, was ordered P. 82.
by the King's messengers, not to come to the session of
parliament 26. regni, in which the King's supremacy was
established."

In this he is safer than in some other stories, for the
journals of that session are lost, so the falsehood of this
cannot be demonstrated : yet it is not at all likely, that he
who justified all that was done in the former session, in
which the Pope's power was put down, the nomination of
bishops annexed to the Crown, a reformation of ecclesiastical laws appointed to be made, in defence of all which
he wrote afterwards, was now so scrupulous as to be ordered to stay at home. But Tonstal suffering imprison-

ment in Edward the Sixth's time, it was fit to use some art to shew that he was unwillingly brought to comply with the King.

P. 82.

74. He, to shew God's judgments on the chief instruments that served the King, says, "That the Duke of Norfolk was by the King condemned to perpetual imprisonment."

This betrays palpable ignorance, since he was attainted of high treason the very day before the King's death, and should have suffered the next day, if the King's death had not prevented it. But since he will descant on the providence of God, he should rather have concluded that his escaping so narrowly was a sign of God's great care of him.

Ibid.

75. In the session of parliament that met the 3d of November, (as he describes it, which was the 26th year of the King's reign) he says, " Mary the King's daughter was illegitimated, and all her honours were transferred on Elizabeth, and the Pope's power put down."

This shews he never looked on our public statutes; otherwise he had seen that these acts passed in the former session.

P. 84.

76. He says, "When the King sent his ambassadors to the French court, Francis would not so much as hear them give a justification of the King's proceedings."

How true this can be, the world may judge, since these two Kings continued in a firm alliance eight years after this. And Francis did often treat, both with him and the Princes of Germany, about these things, and was inclined to do almost all that he did.

Ibid.

77. He says, " The Lutherans did so abominate the grounds of his separation from Rome, that they could never be induced to approve it ;" for which he cites Cochleus, an author of his own kidney.

They did condemn the King's first marriage as unlawful, and thought the Pope's dispensation had no force; and so far they approved it. But they had this singular opinion, that he should have continued unmarried as long as Queen Katherine lived. Yet in that they were so modest that they only desired to be excused, as to the second marriage : which, considering that Queen Anne favoured their doctrine, and that, by an absolute compliance with what the King had done, they might have secured his protection to themselves, whom otherwise they provoked highly, is an evidence of a strict adhering to what their consciences dictated, that cannot be sufficiently commended.

78. He says, "The King made many write apologies P. 85. for what he did; which some did willingly, being tainted with heresy, others unwillingly, and for fear, as Gardiner and Tonstal."

In this he shews how little judgment he had of the nature of things, when he thinks to excuse their writing for the King, as extorted by force. To have done it through error and mistake, was much the softer excuse; but to make them men of such prostituted consciences, as not only to subscribe and swear, but to write with learning and zeal, and yet against their consciences, represents them guilty of inexpressible baseness. Indeed Gardiner was a man like enough to write any thing that might please the King; but Tonstal was a man of greater probity, than to have done so unworthy a thing upon any account whatsoever. But since he mentioned writers, he should have named Longland, bishop of Lincoln, Stokesley, bishop of London, and above all Bonner, who did officiously thrust himself into the debate, by writing a preface to Gardiner's book, with the greatest vehemence that could be. But the blood he shed afterwards did so endear him to this author, that all past faults were forgiven, and to be clean forgotten.

79. He says, "Five martyrs suffered because they P. 86. would not swear the King's supremacy according to the law that was then passed."

There was no such law made at that time, nor could any such oath be then put to them. The only oath which the parliament had enacted, was the oath of the succession, and the refusing it was only misprision of treason, and was not punishable by death. But it was for denying the King's supremacy, and for writing and speaking both against it, and his marriage, that they suffered according to law.

80. He says, "Cromwell threatened the jury in the P. 87. King's name, with certain death, if they did not bring them in guilty."

Every body that knows the law of England, will soon conclude this to be a lie: for no such threatenings were ever made in trials in this nation. Nor was there any need at this time; for the law was so plain, and their facts so clearly proved, that the jury could not refuse to bring them in guilty.

P. 88, 89.

81. He says, The three Carthusians that suffered, were made to stand upright and in one place fourteen days together, with irons about their necks, arms, and legs, before they died: and then with great pomp he describes their death in all its parts, as if it had been a new-devised cruelty, it being the death which the law appoints for traitors. He tells, that Cromwell lamented that others of them had died in their cells, and so prevented his cruelty. He also adds a long story of the severities against the Franciscans.

All this he drew from his learning in the legend. The English nation knows none of these cruelties, in which the Spanish inquisitors are very expert. I find, by some original letters, that the Carthusians who were shut up in their cells, lived about a year after this; so if Cromwell had designed to take away their lives, he wanted not opportunities: but it appears from what More writ in his imprisonment, that Cromwell was not a cruel man, but, on the contrary, merciful and gentle. And for the Franciscans, though they had offended the King highly, two of them railing spitefully at him to his face, in his chapel at Greenwich: yet that was passed over with a reproof: from which it appears that he was not easily provoked against them. So all that relation which he gives, being without any authority, must pass for a part of the poem.

P. 91.

82. He says, " The Bishop of Rochester was condemned, because he would not acknowledge the King's supremacy in ecclesiastical matters."

He was never pressed to acknowledge it, but was condemned for denying it, and speaking against it: for had he kept his opinion to himself, he could not have been questioned. But the denying the King's titles, of which his being supreme head was one, was by the law treason; so he was tried for speaking against it, and not for his not acknowledging it.

P. 93.

83. He runs out in a high commendation of Fisher,

and among other things mentions his " episcopal and apostolical charity."

His charity was burning indeed. He was a merciless persecutor of heretics, so that the rigour of the law, under which he fell, was the same measure that he had measured out to others.

84. Sanders will let the world see how carefully he had P. 100. read the legend, and how skilfully he could write after that copy, in a pretty fabulous story concerning More's death; to whom I will deny none of the praises due to his memory, for his great learning, and singular probity: nor had he any blemish, but what flowed from the leaven of that cruel religion, which carried him to great severities against those that preached for a reformation. His daughter Roper was a woman of great virtue, and worthy of such a father, who needed none of Sanders's art to represent her well to the world. His story is, " That the morning her father died, she went about distributing all the money she had in alms to the poor: and at last was at her prayers in a church, when of a sudden she remembered that she had forgot to provide a winding-sheet for his body; but having no more money left, and not being well known in that place, she apprehended they would not give her credit: yet she went to a linen-draper's shop, and calling for so much cloth, she put her hand in her pocket, knowing she had nothing in it, but intending to make an excuse, and try if they would trust her. But by a miracle she found the price of the sheet, and neither more nor less was conveyed into her pocket." This is such a lively essay of the man's spirit that invented it, that I leave it without any further commentary.

85. He says, " Lee, that was not in orders, was sent to P. 105. visit the monasteries, who solicited the chastity of the nuns."

He does not mention Leighton and London, the two chief visitors, for Leighton brought in Lee: but they were of the Popish party, and Lee was Cranmer's friend, therefore all must be laid on him. He was in orders, and soon after was made dean of York. I have seen complaints of Dr. London's soliciting the nuns, yet I do not find Lee complained of. But since London was a persecutor of heretics, such a small kindness as the concealing his name, and the turning the blame over on Lee, was not to be stood on among friends, especially by a man of Sanders's ingenuity.

P.107.　　86. For the correspondence between Q. Katherine and Father Forest, and the letters that passed, since Sanders tells us not a word how he came by them, we are to look on them as a piece of the romance.

p 114.　　87. He says, " Anne Boleyn bore a monstrous and a misshaped lump of flesh, when the time of her bearing another child came."

" She bore a dead child before the time," says Hall; but there was no great reproach in that, unless made up by Sanders's wit.

P. 115.　　88. He lays out the business of Anne Boleyn with so much spite and malice, that we may easily see against whom he chiefly designed this part of his work. He says, " She was found guilty of adultery and incest."

There was no evidence against her, but only a hearsay from the Lady Wingfield: we neither know the credit of that lady, nor of the person who related it in her name. It is true, Mark Smeton did confess his adultery with the Queen: but it was generally thought he was drawn into it by some promises that were made to him, and so cheated out of his life: but for the Queen, and the other four, they attested their innocency to the last: nor would any of those unfortunate persons redeem their lives at so ignominious a rate, as to charge the Queen, whom they declared they knew to be innocent; so that all the evidence against her, was a hearsay of a woman that was dead, the confession of a poor musician, and some idle words herself spake of the discourses that had passed between her and some of those gentlemen.

P. 116.　　89. He says, " Foreigners did generally rejoice at her fall;" and to prove this, he cites Cochleus's words, that only shew that author's ill opinion of her.

The Germans had so great a value of her, that all their correspondence with the King fell to the ground with her: but he may well cite Cochleus, an author of the same honesty with himself, from whose writings we may with the like security make a judgment of foreign matters, as we may upon Sander's testimony believe the account he gives of English affairs.

90. He tells us, among other things done by the King, P. 117. and picks it out as the only instance he mentions of the King's injunctions, " That the people should be taught in churches the Lord's Prayer, the Ave, the Creed, and the Ten Commandments in English."

, It seems this author thought the giving these elements of religion to the people in the vulgar tongue, a very heinous crime, when this is singled out from all the rest.

91. " That being done," he says, " there was next a book Ibid. published, called Articles, appointed by the King's Majesty," which were the six Articles.

This shews that he either had no information of English affairs, or was sleeping when he wrote this : for the six Articles were not published soon after the Injunctions, as he makes it, by the same parliament and convocation, but three years after, by another parliament : they were never put in a book, nor published in the King's name ; they were enacted in parliament, and are neither more nor less than twenty-five lines in the first impression of that act; so far short come they of a book.

92. He reckons up very defectively the differences be- P. 119. tween the Church of Rome and the doctrine set forth by the King's authority : but in one point he shews his ordinary wit; for in the sixth particular, he says, " He retained the sacrament of order, but appointed a new form of consecrating of bishops."

This he put in out of malice, that he might annul the ordinations of that time : but the thing is false, for except that the bishops, instead of their oaths of obedience to the Pope, which they formerly swore, did now swear to the King, there was no other change made ; and that, to be sure, is no part of the form of consecration.

93. He resolved once to speak what he thought was P. 120. truth, though it be treasonable and impious : and says, " Upon these changes, many in Lincolnshire, and the northern parts, did rise for religion, and the *faith of Christ.*"

This was indeed the motive by which their seditious priests misled them; yet he is mistaken in the time, for it was not after the six Articles were published, but almost three years before it. Nor was it for the Faith of Christ, which teaches us to be humble, subject, and obedient; but because the King was removing some of the corruptions of that faith, which their false teachers did impiously call the faith of Christ.

.P. 120. 94. He says, " The King did promise most faithfully that all these things of which they complained should be amended."

This is so evidently false, that it is plain Sanders resolved dexterously to avoid the speaking of any sort of truth : for the King did fully and formally tell them, he would not be directed nor counselled by them in these points they complained of, and did only offer them an amnesty for what was past.

P. 121. 95. Then he reckons up thirty-two that died for the " defence of the *faith*."

They were attainted of treason, for being in actual rebellion against the King: and thus it appears that rebellion was the *faith* in his sense; and himself died for it, or rather in it, having been starved to death in a wood, to which he fled after one of his rebellious attempts on his Sovereign, in which he was the Pope's nuncio.

P. 122. 96. He says, " The King killed the Earl of Kildare, and five of his uncles."

By this strange way of expressing a legal attainder, and the execution of a sentence for manifest treason and rebellion, he would insinuate on the reader a fancy, that one of Bonner's cruel fits had taken the King, and that he had killed those with his own hand. The Lord Herbert has fully opened that part of the history, from the Records that he saw; and shews that a more resolved rebellion could not be, than that was, of which the Earl of Kildare and his uncles were guilty. But because they sent to the Pope and Emperor for assistance, the Earl desiring to hold the kingdom of Ireland of the Pope, since the King by his heresy had fallen from his right to it, Sanders must needs have a great kindness for their memory, who thus suffered for his *faith*.

Ibid. 97. He says, " Queen Jane Seymour being in hard labour of Prince Edward, the King ordered her body to be so opened by surgeons, that she died soon after."

All this is false, for she had a good delivery, as many original letters written by her council (that have been since printed) do shew; but she died two days after of a distemper incident to her sex.

98. He sets down some passages of Cardinal Pole's P.124. heroical constancy; which being proved by no evidence, and not being told by any other writer (whom I ever saw) are to be looked on as the flourishes of the Poet to set off his hero.

99. He would persuade the world, that the Marquis of P.125. Exeter, the Lord Montacute, and the rest that suffered at that time, died, because they were believed to dislike the King's wicked proceedings; and that the Countess of Sarum was beheaded on this single account, that she was the mother of such a son, and was sincerely addicted to the catholic faith; and that she was condemned, because she wrote to her son, and for wearing in her breast the picture of the five wounds of Christ.

The Marquis of Exeter pretended he was well satisfied with the King's proceedings, and was lord steward when the Lords Darcy and Hussy were tried, and he gave judgment against them. But it being discovered that he and other persons approved of Cardinal Pole's proceedings, who endeavoured to engage all Christian princes in a league against the King, pursuant to which they had expressed themselves, on several occasions, resolved, when a fit opportunity offered itself, to rebel; it was no wonder if the King proceeded against them according to law. And for the Countess of Sarum, though the legality of that sentence passed against her cannot be defended, yet she had given great offence; not only by her correspondence with her son, but by the bulls she had received from Rome, and by her opposing the King's injunctions, hindering all her tenants to read the New Testament, or any other books set out by the King's order. And for the picture, which was found among her clothes, it having been the standard of the rebellion, and the arms of England being found on the other side of it, there was just ground to suspect an ill design in it.

100. He says, " The images which the King destroyed, P.129.

were, by many wonderful works of God, recommended to the devotion of the nation."

All the wonder in these works was the knavery of some juggling impostors, and the simplicity of a credulous multitude, of which see page 375. which being so openly discovered, nothing that had shame in it, could speak of them as our Author does.

P. 131.　101. He says, "Six and twenty carts, drawn with oxen, were loaded with the riches taken from Thomas Becket's shrine;" whom he makes a most glorious martyr, that died for the defence of the *faith*, and was honoured by many miracles after his death.

Other writers have sufficiently shewed what a perfidious, ungrateful, and turbulent priest he was. All these were virtues in our Author's opinion, and ingredients in his faith. But he has in this account of the riches of that shrine gone beyond himself, having by a figure of speech very familiar to him, (called lying,) increased two chests (see page 378.) to twenty-six cart-loads.

P. 132.　102. He says, "The sentence which Pope Paul gave out against the King, was affixed in some towns, both in France, Flanders, and Scotland:" from which he infers, that both the Emperor, the French, and the Scotch King, did consent to that sentence.

In this he designed an eminent piece of service to the Apostolic See, to leave on record an evidence that three sovereign Princes had acknowledged the Pope's power of deposing kings. But he did ill to name the proofs of his assertion, and had done better to have said simply that it was so, than to have founded it on so ill grounds: as if the affixing papal bulls in a place, were an evidence that the princes, in whose dominions it was done, consented to it. He might with the same reason have concluded, that Queen Elizabeth consented to the sentence against herself, which it is very like will not be easily believed, though the bull was affixed in London. But all those very Princes whom he names, continuing to keep up their correspondence with the King, as well after as before this sentence, is a much clearer demonstration that they despised the Pope's sentence.

103. He says, " The King by his own authority, threw P. 134. all the begging orders out of their houses."

The falsehood of this has appeared already, for they resigned their houses to the King: and of these resignations, though many were destroyed, yet near a hundred are still extant.

104. He says, " The parliament, in the year 1539, gave Ibid. the King all the great monasteries."

The parliament passed no such act; all that they did, was only to confirm the grants made, or to be made, by these houses to the King. It was their surrenders that clothed the King with the right to them. All the tragical stories he tells us that followed upon this, are founded on a false foundation.

105. He sets down a form of a resignation, which he P. 135. says, " All the abbots, and many religious persons, were made to sign and set their seals to it."

Among all the resignations which are yet extant, there is not one in this form; for which see page 368.

106. He says, " The King's commissioners, who went P. 136. about getting hands to that form, made them believe in every house, that all the rest had signed it; and so by that, and other persuasions, prevailed with many to set their hands to it."

If all the subscriptions had been procured about the same time, such arts might be suspected: but in a thing that was three years a-doing, these tricks could not have served their turn.

107. He says, " They told the monks, that though the Ibid. King might, by virtue of the act of parliament, seize on their houses and rents, yet he desired rather to do it with their good-will."

In this there are two errors; first, most of these houses were resigned to the King before the act of parliament, see page 363, &c. and next, the act of parliament only confirmed their deeds, but did not give their houses to the King.

108. He says, " The Abbots of Glassenbury, Colches- P. 137. ter, and Reading, suffered martyrdom because they refused to set their hands to that writing."

There was no such writing ever offered to them; nor was

there any law to force them to resign: so they could not suffer on that account; but they were martyrs for Sanders's *faith*, for they were attainted by a legal trial of high treason.

P. 138.   109. " He tells a long story of Whitting abbot of Glassenbury's being brought up to London, to be prevailed with to set his hand to the surrender.   Which he still refusing to do, was sent back; and though a book against the King's divorce was found among his papers, which was laid there by those who searched for it; yet that was passed over in a chiding: but as he went home, hearing there was a meeting of the county at Wells, he went thither; and as he was going up to his place on the bench, he was called to the bar to answer some things that were to be objected to him: he was amazed at it, and asked what the matter was? But one told him he needed fear nothing, for somewhat was only to be done for form, to terrify others: upon which he was condemned and sent away to his abbey, little thinking he was so near his end; but when he came near it, a priest was sent to him to take his confession, for they told him he must die immediately; he begged a day or two's respite, but in vain: so they hanged him up in his habit, on the top of the hill near his abbey, and quartered him; and all this was done in one day."

This book came out in foreign parts, and was printed at Rome, in the reign of Sixtus the Fifth, who took great pleasure in such executions as he describes this to have been; which may fall oft out, where the lives of the subjects are wholly at the prince's mercy: but to tell such tales of England, which is so famed over the world for the safety and security the subjects enjoy, and for the regular and legal proceedings in all trials, especially of life and death, was a great error in the Poet; for the decorum of the laws and customs of a place must be observed, when any nation is made the scene of a fable.   But as nothing like this can be done by the law of England, so there was nothing of it in this case: the jury that sat on him were men of great credit in the country: when he died, he acknowledged his offences; and with appearance of repentance, begged God's pardon, and the King's: see p. 370.

P. 145.   110. After many bitter invectives against Cromwell, for which I could never see good evidence, though I cannot disprove them by any convincing arguments, he says, " That he advised the King to make a law, that persons might be convented and condemned in absence, and without being heard: and that this law first of all fell upon himself."

There was no such law ever made, only the parliament, by their supreme'authority, did attaint some in that manner, but no other court might do it. Nor was this first applied to Cromwell; for a year before his attainder, the Countess of Sarum, with a great many more, were so attainted, though she did not suffer till a year after him.

111. He tells many reasons why the King had a mind to P. 145. put away Anne of Cleve: but in this, as in other things, he betrays a profound ignorance of that time; for every body knew, that the King, from the first time he saw her, disliked her, and that he never consummated the marriage.

This is a subject not fit to be long dwelt on: but if any will compare the account I give of this matter from the Records with Sanders's tale, they will see that he wrote at random, and did not so much as know public transactions.

112. He says, " The King had promised to the Empe- P. 146. ror, that he would no longer continue in the Smalcaldick league; but Cromwell counterfeited the King's hand, to a new confirmation of it; which coming to the Emperor's knowledge, he challenged the King of it: and sent him over a copy of it; upon which the King disowned it, and cast it on Cromwell, and that this was the cause of his fall."

This I believe is one of Sanders's dreams: there is not one word of it in Cromwell's attainder; nor do I find the least shadow of this in some original letters which he wrote to the King for his pardon, in which he answers many of the things laid to his charge. Nor is it likely he would adventure on so bold a thing with such a King, nor could the Emperor have that writing in his power, as long as the King lived: for it is not to be imagined how he could come by it, till he had taken the Duke of Saxony prisoner, which was after this King's death.

113. He says, " When Cromwell was put to death, the P. 148. King proceeded to the divorce of Anne of Cleve."

The divorce was judged by the convocation eight days before Cromwell's death, and confirmed in parliament, which was dissolved before he suffered.

P. 148. **114.** He says, " The King sent to her, to tell her, he had a mind to be separated from her; and though he could proceed more severely against her, since he knew she was an heretic; yet, for her family's sake, he left it to herself to devise any reason for their divorce: upon which she came next day to the senate, (which may be either the King's council or the parliament) and confessed she had been married to another before she was married to the King; and thereupon, by the authority of parliament, he was divorced, and within eight days married Katherine Howard."

There are but six gross errors in this period. 1. The King sent not any message to her, nor came there any answer from her till the sentence of divorce was quite passed. 2. In the original letter, which those he sent to her wrote to him from Richmond, it appears that they used no threatenings to her, but barely told her what was done; to which she acquiesced. 3. She never came from Richmond in all that process, and so made no such declaration in the senate. 4. She did not say that she was married to another, but only that she had been contracted to the Prince of Lorrain when she was under age. 5. The parliament did not dissolve the marriage, but only confirmed the sentence of the convocation. 6. The King did not marry Katherine Howard before the 8th of August, and the divorce was judged the 10th of July, a month wanting two days.

P. 149. **115.** He says, " The King had consummated the marriage for seven months together."

There were but six months between his marriage and the divorce; and in all that while, as they bedded but seldom, so there were very clear evidences brought, that it was not consummated.

P. 151. **116.** He says, " The King sent the Bishop of Winchester, and Sir Henry Knevet, to the diet of the empire; who were ordered to propose to the Emperor, that the King might be again reconciled to the see of Rome; to which, he adds, his conscience did drive him: but since the King would not confess his past crimes, nor do penance for them, nor restore the goods of the church, it came to nothing."

This is another ornament of the fable, to shew the Poet's wit; but is as void of truth as any passage in Plautus or Terence is. For the King was all his life so intractable in that point, that the Popish party had no other way to maintain their interest with him, but to comply, not without affectation in that matter: and when an information was given against Gardiner, for his holding some correspondence with the Pope's legate at the diet, he got the man who had innocently discovered it, to be put in prison; and said, it was a plot against him to ruin him, which he needed not be so solicitous about, if his instructions from the King had allowed him to enter on such a treaty.

117. He runs out in a long digression, upon the King's P. 153. assuming the title of King of Ireland; to shew, that the kings of England only hold Ireland by the Pope's donation.

In this Sanders shews his art, he being to carry the standard of rebellion in that kingdom, to blast the King's right to it. He acknowledges the Crown of England had the dominion of Ireland, with the title of Lord of Ireland, about four hundred years: and certainly if so long a possession does not give a good title, and a prescription against all other pretenders, most of the royal families in Christendom will be to seek for their rights. But he says, it was given by the Pope to King Henry the Second; and yet he confesses that he had conquered some parts of it before that grant was sent him by Hadrian the Fourth. Certainly King Henry the Second had as good a right to take it, as Pope Hadrian had to give it: nor was the King's accepting the Pope's donation any prejudice to his title; for things extorted or allowed upon a public error, can have no force, when that is openly discovered. If then the superstition of those ages made, that the Pope's donation was a great help to any pretender, it was no wonder that kings made use of it; but it were a wonder indeed if they should acknowledge it, after the trick is known and seen by all.

118. After this, and a satire against Queen Elizabeth P. 162. for assuming the title, Defender of the Faith, and a long enumeration of the exactions in the last years of this reign; in which, though there is matter enough for severe

complaints, yet many of the particulars he mentions are without any proof, and must rest on the Author's credit; which, by this time, the reader will acknowledge is not very great. Another long discourse of some length follows, of the misfortunes of the Duke of Norfolk, and of all that served the King in his divorce, and in the following actions of his life: from which he infers, that these were effects of a curse from Heaven upon all that he did, and on all those that assisted him; but as the inference is bad, so he forgot to mention those noble families that were raised in his time, and have continued since in great honour; as the Seymours, from whom the Dukes of Somerset are descended; the Paulets, from whom the Marquis of Winchester derives; the Russels, Wriothslies, Herberts, Riches, and Cromwells, from whom the Earls of Bedford, Southampton, Pembroke, Essex, and Ardglass have descended; and the Browns, the Petres, the Pagets, the Norths, and the Montagues, from whom the Vice-Count Montague, the Barons Petre, Paget, North, and Montague, are descended. These families have now flourished in great wealth and honour an age and a half; and only one of them has, and that but very lately, determined in the male line: but the illustrious female branches of it are intermixed with other noble families. So that the observation is false, and the inference is weak.

P. 164.   119. He says, " When the King found his strength declining, he had again some thoughts of reconciling himself to the Church of Rome; which when it was proposed to one of the bishops, he made a flattering answer. But Gardiner moved that a parliament might be called for doing it: and that the King, for the quiet of his own conscience, would vow to do it; of which God would accept in that extremity, when more was not possible to be done. But some of his courtiers coming about him, who were very apprehensive of such a reconciliation, lest they should have been made restore the goods of the church, diverted the King from it:" and from this our Author infers, " that what the King had done was against his conscience, and that so he sinned the sin against the Holy Ghost."

I shall not examine this theological definition of the sin against the Holy Ghost, for my quarrel is not at present with his divinity, but with his history; though it were easy to shew that he is alike at both. But for this story, it is a pure dream; for not only there is no evidence for it, nor did Gardiner in the reign of Queen Mary ever own any such thing, though it had been then much for the credit of their cause, especially he being often upbraided with his compliances to this King, for which the mention of his repentance had furnished him with a good answer : but as the tale is told, the fiction appears too plainly, for a parliament was actually sitting during the King's sickness, which was dissolved by his death, and no such proposition was made in it. The King, on the contrary, destroyed the chief hopes of the Popish party, which were founded on the Duke of Norfolk's greatness, by the attainder which was passed a day before he died. And yet Sanders makes this discourse to have been between the King and Gardiner after his fall, and his son's death; between which, and the King's death, there were only nine days : but besides all this, Gardiner had lost the King's favour a considerable time before his death.

120. He says, " The King, that he might not seem P. 166. never to have done any good work in his whole life, as he was dying, founded Christ's Church Hospital in London ; which was all the restitution he ever made for the monasteries and churches he had robbed and spoiled."

If it had not already appeared, in many instances, that our Author had as little shame as honesty, here is a sufficient proof of it. I will not undertake to justify the King, as if he had done what he ought to have done, in his new foundations : but it is the height of impudence to deny things that all England knows. He founded six bishopricks; he endowed deans and prebendaries, with all the other offices belonging to a cathedral, in fourteen several sees, Canterbury, Winchester, Duresme, Ely, Norwich, Rochester, Worcester, and Carlisle; together with Westminster, Chester, Oxford, Gloucester, Peterborough; and Bristol, where he endowed bishopricks likewise. He founded many grammar-schools, as Burton, Canterbury, Coventry, Worcester, &c. He founded and endowed Trinity College in Cambridge, which is one of the noblest foundations in Christendom. He also founded professors in both Universities, for Greek, Hebrew, law, physic, and divinity. What censure then deserves our Author, for saying, that the Hospital of Christ's Church was all the restitution he ever made of the church-lands?

P. 166.   121. He gives a character of the King, which suits very well with his history, his malice in it being extravagantly ridiculous. Among other things, he says, "The King promoted always learned bishops, Cranmer only being excepted, whom he advanced to serve his lusts."

Cranmer was a man of greater learning than any that ever sat in that see before him, as appears in every thing that he writ: Tonstal was a learned man, and Gardiner was much esteemed for learning; yet if any will compare Cranmer's books of the sacrament, with those the other two writ on the same subject, there is so great a difference between the learning and solidity of the one and the other, that no man of common ingenuity can read them but he must confess it.

P. 170.   122. He says, "When the King found himself expiring he called for a bowl of white wine, and said to one that was near him, *We have lost all*: and was often heard repeating *Monks, monks,* and so he died."

This was to make the fable end as it had gone on, and it is forged without any authority or appearance of truth. The manner of his death was already told, so it needs not be repeated.

P. 172.   123. He says, " The King by his will appointed the Crown to go to his righteous heirs after his three children, and commanded his son to be bred a true catholic: but his will was changed, and another was forged, by which the line of Scotland was excluded, and they bred his son a heretic."

There was no such will ever heard of; and in all the debates that were managed in Queen Elizabeth's reign about the succession, those that pleaded for the Scottish line never alleged this; which had it been true, did put an end to the whole controversy. It was indeed said, that the will which was given out as the King's will, was not signed by his hand, nor sealed by his order, but it was never pretended that there was any other will: so this is one of our Author's forgeries.

The Conclusion.

THUS I have traced him in this history, and I hope I have said much more than was necessary, to prove him a writer of no credit, and that his book ought to have no authority, since he was not only a stranger to the public transactions, printed statutes, and the other authentic registers of that time, but was a bold and impudent asserter of the grossest and most malicious lies, that ever were contrived. I have not examined all the errors of his chronology, for there is scarce any thing told in its right order, and due place; nor have I insisted on all the passages he tells, without any proof, or appearance of truth; for as I could only deny these without any other evidence but what was negative, so there are so many of them, that I must have transcribed the greatest part of his book, if I had considered them all. I have therefore only singled out these passages, which I had in the former History demonstrated to be false: and these are both so many and so important, that I am sure enough is said to destroy the credit of that Author, and of his book, which has too long deceived the world. And what is performed in this first part, will I hope dispossess the reader of any ill impressions the following parts of that work have made on him, concerning the succeeding reigns, of which an account shall be given, as soon as it possibly can be made ready.

I shall esteem my time to have been well employed, and my pains rightly placed, if my endeavours have so good an effect, as to take off the unjust prejudices which some may have conceived at the changes that were then made in religion; or at the beginnings of them, which being represented by this Author, and upon his testimony by many other writers, in such odious characters to the world, are generally so ill looked on.

The work itself was so good, done upon so much reason, managed with such care, directed by such wisdom, and tempered with so great moderation, that those who intended to blast it, did very wisely to load it with some such prejudices: for if without these, the thing itself be examined by men of a candid temper and solid judgment, the opposers of it know well where the truth lies; and on whose side, both the Scriptures and the best ages of the primitive church have declared. But it was not fit to put a question of such importance, on so doubtful and so dangerous an issue : therefore it was well considered by them, that some popular and easily understood calumnies, to disgrace the beginnings of it, and the persons that were most employed in it, were to be fastened on them : and if these could be once generally received, then men might be alienated from it by a shorter way, than could be done by the dull and unsuccessful methods of reason. Therefore as the cause of our church hath been often vindicated, by the learned books that have been published in it; and never with more success, and a clearer victory, than of late, in the elaborate writings (which are never to be mentioned but with honour) of the renowned Dr. Stillingfleet; so I judged it might not be an unuseful and unacceptable work (which, though it be of a lower form, and so most suitable to my genius, yet will be of general use), to employ the leisure I enjoy, and the small talent committed to me, in examining and opening the transactions of those times : and if those who read it, are dispossessed of their prejudices, and inclined to consider things as they are now set before them, in a truer light, I have gained my end in it.

The truths of religion need no support from the father of lies. A religion made up of falsehoods and impostures, must be maintained by means suitable to itself: so Sanders's book might well serve the ends of that church, which has all along raised its greatness by public cheats and forgeries; such as the donation of Constantine, and the book of the Decretals; besides the vast number of miracles and visions that were for many ages made use of by them; of which even the most disingenuous of their own writers begin to be now ashamed. But the reformation of religion was a work of light, and needs none of the arts of darkness to justify it by. A full and distinct narrative of what was then done, will be its apology, as well as its history. There is no need of artifice, but only of industry and sincerity, to gather together all the remains of that time, and put them in good order.

I am now beginning to look towards the next, and indeed the best part of this work: where, in the first reign, we shall observe the active endeavours of those restorers of religion. The next reign affords a sadder prospect of that work laid in ruins, and the authors of it in ashes; but the fires that consumed them, did rather spread than extinguish that light which they had kindled. And what is fabled of the phœnix will be found true of our church, that she rose new out of these ashes, into which she seemed consumed.

Towards the perfecting this History, I hope all that love the subject of it will contribute their endeavours, and furnish every thing that is in their power, which may make it fuller or clearer: so I end with that desire which I made in the Preface, that any one who have in their hands any papers relating to these times, will be pleased to communicate them; and whatever assistance they give to it, shall be most thankfully owned and acknowledged.

The end of the Appendix.

ADDENDA.

I.

Articles about Religion, set out by the Convocation, and published by the King's Authority.   An Original.

HENRY THE EIGHT, by the Grace of God, King of England, and of France, Defender of the Faith, and Lord of Ireland, and in Earth Supream Head of the Church of England, to all and singular our most loving, faithful and obedient Subjects, greeting.   Amongst other cures committed unto this our Princely Office, whereunto it hath pleased God of his infinite mercy and goodness to call us, we have always esteemed and thought (as we also yet esteem and think) this to be most chief, most ponderous, and of most weight, that his Holy Word and Commandments may sincerely without let or hinderance, be of our Subjects truly believed and reverently kept and observed; and that unity and concord in opinions, namely, in such things as does concern our Religion, may encrease and go furthward, and all occasion of dissent and discord touching the same be repressed, and utterly extinguished; for the which cause we being of late to our great regret credibly advertised of such diversity in opinions, as have grown and sprongen in this our Realm, as well concerning certain Articles necessary to our Salvation, as also touching certain honest and commendable Ceremonies, rites, and usages in our said Church, for an honest policy, and decent order heretofore of long time used and accustomed: minding to have that unity and agreement established through our said Church concerning the premisses; and being very desirous to eschew not only the dangers of Souls, but also the outward inquietness which by

occasion of the said diversity in opinions (if remedy had
not been provided) might per chance have ensued; have
not only in our own person many times taken great pain,
study, labour and travails, but also have caused our Bishops and other the most discreet and best learned men of
our Clergy of this our whole Realm to be assembled in our
Convocation, for the full debatement and quiet determination
of the same: where after long and mature deliberation
and disputations, had of and upon the premisses, finally
they have concluded and agreed upon the said matters, as
well those which be commanded of God, and are necessary to our Salvation, as also the other touching the honest
ceremonies, and good and politick order, as is aforesaid;
which their determination, debatement and agreement, forasmuch as we think to have proceeded of a good, right
and true judgment, and to be agreeable to the Laws and
Ordinances of God, and much profitable for the establishment of that charitable concord and unity in our Church
of England, which we most desire, we have caused the
same to be published, willing, requiring and commanding
you to accept, repute, and take them accordingly; most
heartily desiring and praying Almighty God, that it may
please him so to illumin your hearts that you, and every
of you may have no less desire, zeal, and love to the said
unity and concord, in reading, divulging, and following
the same, than we have had and have, causing them to be
thus devised, set forth and published. And for because
we would the said Articles, and every of them, to be taken
and understanden of you after such sort, order, and degree as appertaineth accordingly.; We have caused by the
like assent and agreement of our said Bishops and other
Learned men, the said Articles to be divided into two
sorts, that is to say, such as are commanded expresly by
God, and are necessary to our Salvation, and such other,
as although they be not expresly commanded of God, nor
necessary to our Salvation; yet being of a long continuance for a decent order and honest policy, prudently instituted, are for that same purpose and end to be observed
in like manner; which ye following, after such sort as we
have prescribed unto you, shall not only attain that most
charitable unity and loving concord, whereof shall ensue

your incomparable commodity, profit and lucre, as well spiritual as other; but also ye conforming yourselves, and using these our said Articles as is aforesaid, shall not a little encourage us to take further travel, pains, and labours for your commodities in all such other matters, as in time to come may happen to occur, and as it shall be most to the honour of God and ours, the profit, tranquillity, and quietness of all you our most loving Subjects.

The Articles of our Faith.

FIRST, as touching the chief and principal Articles of our Faith, sith it is thus agreed as hereafter followeth by the whole Clergy of this our Realm, we will that all Bishops and Preachers shall instruct and teach our people by us committed to their spiritual Charge, that they ought and must most constantly believe and defend all those things to be true, which be comprehended in the whole body and Canon of the Bible, and also in the three Creeds or Symbols, whereof one was made by the Apostles, and is the common Creed which every man useth, the second was made in the Holy Council of Nice, and is said daily in the Mass, and the third was made by Athanasius, and is comprehended in the Psalm *Quicunque vult;* and that they ought and must take and interpret all the same things according to the selfe-same sentence and interpretation, which the words of the selfe-same Creeds or Symboles do purport, and the Holy approved Doctors of the Church do intreat and defend the same.

Item, That they ought and must repute, hold and take all the same things for the most Holy, most sure and most certain and infallible words of God, and such as neither ought nor can be altered or convelled by any contrary opinion or Authority.

Item, That they ought and must believe, repute and take all the Articles of our Faith contained in the said Creeds to be so necessary to be believed for Man's Salvation, that whosoever being taught will not believe them as is aforesaid, or will obstinately affirm the contrary of them, he or they cannot be the very members of Christ and his Spouse the Church, but be very Infidels or Hereticks, and members of the Devil, with whom they shall perpetually be damned.

Item, That they ought and must most reverently and religiously observe and keep the selfe-same words, according to the very same form and manner of speaking, as the Articles of our Faith be already conceived and expressed in the said Creeds, without altering in any wise or varying from the same.

Item, That they ought and must utterly refuse and condemn all these opinions contrary to the said Articles, which were of long time past condemned in the four Holy Councils, that is to say, in the Council of Nice, Constantinople, Ephesus, and Chalcidonense, and all other sith that time in any point consonant to the same.

The Sacrament of Baptism.

SECONDLY, As touching the Holy Sacrament of Baptism, we will that all Bishops and Preachers shall instruct and teach our people committed by us unto their Spiritual Charge, that they ought and must of necessity believe certainly all those things, which hath been always by the whole consent of the Church approved, received and used in the Sacrament of Baptism; that is to say, that the Sacrament of Baptism was instituted and ordained in the New Testament by our Saviour Jesus Christ, as a thing necessary for the attaining of everlasting life, according to the saying of Christ, *Nisi quis renatus fuerit ex aqua et Spiritu Sancto, non potest intrare in Regnum cœlorum.*

Item, That it is offered unto all men, as well Infants as such as have the use of Reason, that by Baptism they shall have remission of sins and the grace and favour of God, according to the saying of St. John, *Qui crediderit et Baptizatus fuerit Salvus erit.*

Item, That the promise of Grace and everlasting life, which promise is adjoyned unto the Sacrament of Baptism, pertaineth not only unto such as have the use of reason, but also to Infants, innocents and children; and they ought therefore and must needs be Baptised: and that by the

Sacrament of Baptism they do also obtain remission of
their sins, the grace and favour of God, and be made thereby
the very sons and children of God, insomuch as Infants
and Children dying in their Infancy shall undoubtedly be
saved thereby, or else not.

Item, That Infants must needs be Christened because
they be born in Original Sin, which sin must needs be remitted; which cannot be done but by the Sacrament of
Baptism, whereby they receive the Holy-Ghost which exerciseth his Grace and efficacy in them, and cleanseth and
purifieth them from sin by his most secret vertue and
operation.

Item, That Children or men once Baptized, can, ne ought
ever to be Baptized again.

Item, That they ought to repute, and take all the Anabaptists and the Pelagians opinions contrary to the premisses, and every other man's opinion agreeable unto the
said Anabaptists or the Pelagians opinions in this behalfe,
for detestable Heresies, and utterly to be condemned.

Item, That men or children having the use of reason,
and willing and desiring to be Baptized, shall by the vertue
of that holy Sacrament obtain the grace and remission of
all their sins, if they shall come thereunto perfectly and
truly repentant and contrite of all their sins before committed, and also perfectly and constantly confessing and
believing all the Articles of our faith, according as it was
mentioned in the Article before, or else not.

And Finally, if they shall also have firm credence and
trust in the promise of God adjoyned to the said Sacrament, that is to say, that in and by this said Sacrament
which they shall receive, God the Father giveth unto them
for his Son Jesus Christ's sake, remission of all their sins,
and the Grace of the Holy Ghost, whereby they be newly
regenerated and made the very Children of God, according
to the saying of Christ and his Apostle St. Peter, *Pænitentiam agite et Baptizetur unusquisque vestrum in nomine Jesu
Christi in remissionem peccatorum, et accipiétis donum Spiritus Sancti,* and according also to the saying of St. Paul
ad Titum 3. *Non ex operibus justitiæ quæ fecimus nos, sed
secundum suam misericordiam, salvos nos fecit per lavacrum
regenerationis et renovationis Spiritus Sancti, quem effudit*

in nos opulenter per Jesum Christum servatorem nostrum, ut justificati illius gratia hæredes efficiamur juxta spem vitæ æternæ.

The Sacrament of Penance.

THIRDLY, Concerning the Sacrament of Pennance, We will that all Bishops and Preachers shall instruct and teach our people committed by us unto their Spiritual charge, that they ought and must most constantly believe, that that Sacrament was instituted of Christ in the New Testament as a thing so necessary for man's Salvation, that no man which after his Baptism is fallen again and hath committed deadly sin, can without the same be saved or attain everlasting Life.

Item, That like-as such men which after Baptism do fall again into sin, if they do not Pennance in this Life, shall undoubtedly be damned; even so whensoever the same men shall convert themselves from the said naughty Life, and do such Pennance for the same as Christ requireth of them, they shall without doubt attain remission of their sins and shall be saved.

Item, That this Sacrament of perfect Pennance which Christ requireth of such manner of persons, consisteth of three parts, that is to say, Contrition, Confession, with the amendment of the former Life, and a new obedient reconciliation unto the Laws and will of God, that is to say, exteriour Acts in works of Charity according as they be commanded of God, which be called in Scripture, *fructus digni Pœnitentia.*

Furthermore, as touching Contrition, which is the first part, We will that all Bishops and Preachers shall instruct and teach our people committed by us unto their Spiritual charge, that the said Contrition consisteth in two special parts, which must always be conjoined together and cannot be dissevered; that is to say, the penitent and contrite man must first knowledg the filthiness and abomination of his own sin, whereunto he is brought by hearing and considering of the will of God declared in his Laws, and feeling and perceiving in his own conscience that God is angry and displeased with him for the same; he must also conceive not only great sorrow and inward shame that he hath so grievously offended God, but also great fear of God's displeasure towards him, considering he hath no works or merits of his own which he may worthily lay before God as sufficient satisfaction for his sins; which done then afterwards with this fear, shame and sorrow must needs succeed and be conjoyned, The second part, viz. a certain faith, trust and confidence of the mercy and goodness of God, whereby the penitent must conceive certain hope and faith that God will forgive him his sins, and repute him justified and of the number of his Elect children, not for the worthiness of any merit or work done by the penitent, but for the only merits of the blood and passion of our Saviour Jesus Christ.

Item, That this certain faith and hope is gotten and also confirmed, and made more strong by the applying of Christ's words and promises of his grace and favour contained in his Gospel, and the Sacraments instituted by him in the new Testament; and therefore to attain this certain faith, the second part of Pennance is necessary, that is to say, Confession to a Priest if it may be had; for the Absolution given by the Priest was institute of Christ to apply the promises of God's grace and favour to the Penitent.

Wherefore as touching Confession, We will that all Bishops and Preachers shall instruct and teach our people committed by us to their spiritual charge, that they ought and must certainly believe that the words of Absolution pronounced by the Priest, be spoken by the Authority given to him by Christ in the Gospel.

Item, That they ought and must give no less faith and credence to the same words of Absolution so pronounced by the Ministers of the Church, than they would give unto the very words and voyce of God himself if he should speak unto us out of Heaven, according to the saying of Christ, *Quorum remiseritis peccata,* &c. *et qui vos audit me audit.*

Item, That in no ways they do contemn this Auricular Confession which is made unto the Ministers of the Church, but that they ought to repute the same a verry expedient and necessary mean, whereby they may require and ask this Absolution at the Priests hands, at such time as they shall find their consciences grieved with mortal sin, and have occasion so to do, to the intent that they may thereby attain certain comfort and consolation of their consciences.

As touching the third part of Pennance, We will that all Bishops and Preachers shall instruct and teach our people committed by us to their spiritual charge, that although Christ and his death be the sufficient oblation, sacrifice, satisfaction, and recompence, for the which God the Father forgiveth and remitteth to all sinners not only their sin, but also Eternal pain due for the same; yet all men truly penitent contrite and confessed, must needs also bring forth the fruits of Penance, that is to say, Prayer, Fasting, Alms-deeds, and must make Restitution or Satisfaction in will and deed to their neighbour, in such things as they have done them wrong and injury in, and also must do all other good works of mercy and charity, and express their obedient will in the executing and fulfilling of God's Commandments outwardly, when time, power and occasion shall be Ministred unto them, or else they shall never be saved; for this is the express precept and commandment of God, *Agite fructus dignos pœnitentia;* and St. Paul saith, *Debitores sumus,* and in another place he saith, *Castigo corpus meum et in servitutem redigo.*

Item, That these precepts and works of Charity be necessary works to our Salvation, and God necessarily requireth that every penitent man shall perform the same, whensoever time, power, and occasion shall be ministred unto him so to do.

Item, That by Penance and such good works of the same, we shall not only obtain everlasting life, but also we shall deserve remission or mitigation of these present pains and afflictions in this World, according to the saying of St. Paul, *Si nos ipsi judicaremus, non judicaremur, a Domino;* and Zacharias, *Convertimini ad me et ego convertar ad vos;* and Esaias 58. *frange esurienti panem tuum, &c. tunc eris velut hortus irriguus. Hæc sunt inculcanda ecclesiis et ut exercitentur ad bene operandum, et in his ipsis operibus exerceant et confirment fidem, petentes et expectantes a Deo mitigationem præsentium calamitatum.*

The Sacrament of the Altar.

FOURTHLY, as touching the Sacrament of the Altar, We will that all Bishops and Preachers shall instruct and teach our people committed by us unto their spiritual charge, that they ought and must constantly believe that under the form and figure of bread and wine, which we there presently do see and perceive by our outward senses, is verily, substantially, and really contained and comprehended, the very selfe-same body and blood of our Saviour Jesus Christ which was born of the Virgin Mary and suffered upon the cross for our Redemption, and that under the same form and figure of bread and wine, the very selfe-same body and blood of Christ is corporally, really, and in the very substance exhibited, distributed and received of all them which receive the said Sacrament; and that therefore the said Sacrament is to be used with all due reverence and honour, and that every man ought first to prove and examine himself, and religiously to try and search his own Conscience, before he shall receive the same according to the saying of St. Paul, *Quisquis ederit panem hunc aut biberit de poculo Domini indigne, reus erit corporis et sanguinis Domini; probet autem seipsum homo, et sic de pane illo edat et de poculo illo bibat: nam qui edit aut bibit indigne, judicium sibi ipsi manducat et bibit, non dijudicans corpus Domini.*

Justification.

FIFTHLY, As touching the order and cause of our Justification, we will that all Bishops and Preachers shall instruct and teach our people committed by us unto their spiritual charge, that this word Justification signifieth remission of our sins, and our acceptation or reconciliation into the grace and favour of God, that is to say, our perfect renovation in Christ.

Item, That sinners attain this Justification by Contrition and Faith joyned with Charity, after such sort and manner as we before mentioned and declared; not as though our Contrition, or Faith, or any works proceeding thereof can worthily merit or deserve to attain the said Justification;

for the only mercy and grace of the Father, promised freely
unto us for his Sons sake Jesus Christ, and the merits of
his blood and his passion be the only sufficient and worthy
causes thereof; and yet that notwithstanding to the attaining of the said Justification, God requireth to be in us not
only inward Contrition, perfect Faith, and Charity, certain
hope and confidence, with all other spiritual graces and
motions, which as we said before must necessarily concur
in remission of our sins, that is to say, our Justification:
but also he requireth and commandeth us, that after we be
justified we must also have good works of charity and obedience towards God, in the observing and fulfilling outwardly of his Laws and Commandments; for although acceptation to everlasting life be conjoyned with Justification, yet our good works be necessarily required to the
attaining of everlasting Life, and we being justified be necessarily bound, and it is our necessary duty to do good
works, according to the saying of St. Paul, *Debitores sumus non carni ut secundum carnem vivamus, nam si secundum carnem vixerimus moriemur, sin autem spiritu facta
corporis, mortificaverimus, vivemus; etenim quicunque spiritu Dei ducuntur hi sunt filii Dei:* and Christ saith, *si vis
ad vitam ingredi serva mandata:* and St. Paul saith, *de
malis operibus, qui talia agunt Regnum Dei non posside-
bunt,* Wherefore we will that all Bishops and Preachers
shall instruct and teach our people committed by us unto
their spiritual charge, that God necessarily requireth of us
to do good works commanded by him, and that not only
outward and civil works, but also the inward spiritual motions and graces of the Holy Ghost, that is to say, to dread
and fear God, to love God, to have firm confidence and
trust in God, to invocate and call upon God, to have patience in all adversities, to hate sin, and to have certain
purpose and will not to sin again, and such other like motions and vertues; for Christ saith, *Nisi abundaverit justitia
vestra plusquam scribarum et Pharisæorum, non intrabitis
in regnum cælorum,* that is to say, we must not only do
outward civil good works, but also we must have these
foresaid inward spiritual motions consenting and agreeable
to the Law of God.

Of Images.

As touching Images, truth it is that the same have been used in the old Testament, and also for the greater abuses of them sometime destroyed and put down, and in the new Testament they have been also allowed, as good Authors do declare; wherefore we will that all Bishops and Preachers shall instruct and teach our people committed by us to their spiritual charge, how they ought and may use them. And First, that this may be attributed unto them that they be representers of vertue and good example, and that they also be by occasion the kindlers and firers of men's minds, and make men often remember and lament their sins and offences, especially the Images of Christ and our Lady; and that therefore it is meet that they should stand in the Churches, and none otherwise to be esteemed : And to the intent the rude people should not from henceforth take such superstition, as in time past it is thought that the same hath used to do, we will that our Bishops and Preachers diligently shall teach them, and according to this Doctrine reform their abuses; for else there might fortune Idolatry to ensue, which God forbid. And as for Censing of them and kneeling and offering unto them, with other like wor-shippings, although the same hath entred by devotion and fallen to custome; yet the people ought to be diligently taught, that they in no ways do it, nor think it meet to be done to the same Images, but only to be done to God and in his honour, although it be done before the Images, whether it be of Christ, of the Cross, or of our Lady, or of any other Saint besides.

Of Honouring of Saints.

As touching the honouring of Saints, we will that all Bishops and Preachers shall instruct and teach our people, committed by us unto their spiritual charge, that Saints now being with Christ in Heaven be to be honoured of Christian people in Earth; but not with that confidence and honour which are only due unto God, trusting to attain at their hands that which must be had only of God, but that they be thus to be honoured, because they be known

the Elect persons of Christ, because they be passed in
Godly Life out of this transitory World, because they already do Reign in Glory with Christ; and most specially
to laude and praise Christ in them for their excellent vertues which he planted in them, for example, of and by them
to such as are yet in this World to live in vertue and goodness, and also not to fear to dye for Christ and his cause
as some of them did; and finally to take them, in that they
may, to be the advancers of our prayers and demands unto
Christ. By these ways and such like be Saints to be honoured and had in reverence, and by none other.

Of Praying to Saints.

As touching Praying to Saints, We will that all Bishops
and Preachers shall instruct and teach our people committed by us unto their spiritual charge, that albeit grace,
remission of sin and Salvation, cannot be obtained but of
God only by the mediation of our Saviour Christ, which is
only sufficient mediator for our sins; yet it is very laudable
to pray to Saints in Heaven everlastingly living, whose
charity is ever permanent, to be intercessors and to pray
for us and with us unto Almighty God after this manner:
All holy Angels and Saints in Heaven pray for us and
with us unto the Father, that for his dear Son Jesus Christ's
sake, we may have grace of him and remission of our sins,
with an earnest purpose, not wanting Ghostly strength, to
observe and keep his holy Commandments, and never to
decline from the same again unto our lives end: And in
this manner we may pray to our Blessed Lady, to St. John
Baptist, to all and every of the Apostles, or any other
Saint particularly, as our devotion doth serve us; so that
it be done without any vain superstition, as to think that
any Saint is more merciful, or will hear us sooner than
Christ, or that any Saint doth serve for one thing more
than another, or is Patron of the same. And likewise we
must keep Holy-days unto God in memory of him and
his Saints, upon such days as the Church hath Ordained
their memories to be celebrated; except they be mitigated
and moderated by the assent or commandment of the Supream head, to the Ordinaries, and then the Subjects ought
to obey it.

Of Rites and Ceremonies.

As concerning the Rites and Ceremonies of Christ's Church, as to have such vestments in doing God service as be and have been most part used, as Sprinkling of Holy-Water to put us in remembrance of our Baptism and the blood of Christ sprinkled for our redemption upon the Cross; Giving of holy bread to put us in remembrance of the Sacrament of the Altar, that all Christen men be one body mystical of Christ, as the bread is made of many grains and yet but one Loaf, and to put us in remembrance of the receiving the holy Sacrament and body of Christ, the which we ought to receive in right Charity; which in the beginning of Christs Church, men did more often receive than they use now adays to do; Bearing of Candles on Candlemas-day in memory of Christ the spiritual light, of whom Simeon did prophesie as is read in the Church that day; Giving of ashes on Ash-Wednesday, to put in remembrance every Christen man in the beginning of Lent and Penance, that he is but ashes and earth and thereto shall return; which is right necessary to be uttered from henceforth in our mother tongue always on the same day; Bearing of Palms on Palm-Sunday in memory of receiving of Christ into Jerusalem a little before his death, that we may have the same desire to receive him into our hearts; Creeping to the Cross and humbling our selves to Christ on Good-Friday before the Cross, and offering there unto Christ before the same, and kissing of it in memory of our Redemption by Christ made upon the Cross; Setting up the Sepulture of Christ, whose body after his death was buried; the Hallowing of the Font, and other like Exorcisms and Benedictions by the Ministers of Christs Church: and all other like laudable Customs, Rites, and Ceremonies be not to be contemned and cast away, but to be used and continued as things good and laudable, to put us in remembrance of those spiritual things that they do signifie, not suffering them to be forgotten, or to be put in oblivion, but renuing them in our memories from time to time: but none of these Ceremonies have Power to remit sin, but only to stir and lift up our minds unto God, by whom only our sins be forgiven.

Of Purgatory.

FORASMUCH as due order of Charity requireth, and the book of Maccabees and divers ancient Doctors plainly shewing, that it is a very good and charitable deed to pray for Souls departed, and forasmuch also as such usage hath continued in the Church so many years even from the beginning, We will that all Bishops and Preachers shall instruct and teach our people committed by us unto their spiritual charge, that no man ought to be grieved with the continuance of the same, and that it standeth with the very due Order of Charity, for a Christen man to pray for Souls departed, and to commit them in our prayers to Gods mercy, and also to cause others to pray for them in Masses, and Exequies, and to give Alms to others to pray for them, whereby they may be relieved and holpen, of some part of their pain: But forasmuch as the place where they be, the name thereof and kind of pains there, also be to us uncertain by Scripture; therefore this with all other things we remit to God Almighty, unto whose mercy it is meet and convenient for us to commend them, trusting that God accepteth our prayers for them, referring the rest wholly to God, to whom is known their estate and condition; wherefore it is much necessary that such Abuses be clearly put away, which under the name of Purgatory hath been advanced, as to make men believe that through the Bishop of Romes Pardon Souls might clearly be delivered out of Purgatory, and all the pains of it, or that Masses said at *Scala cæli*, or otherwhere, in any place, or before any Image, might likewise deliver them from all their pain, and send them streight to Heaven, and other like Abuses.

Signed

Thomas Cromwell.

T. Cantuarien.	Joannes Roffen.
Edvardus Ebor.	Richardus Cicestren.
Joannes London.	Joannes Bathonien.
Cuthbertus Dunelmen.	Thomas Elien.
Joannes Lincoln.	Joannes Lincoln. Nomine
Joannes Lincoln Nomine	procuratorio pro Dom.
procuratorio pro Dom.	Rowlando Coven. et
Joan. Exon.	Lichfielden.
Hugo Wygornen.	Joannes Bangoren.

Nicholaus Sarisburien.
Edvardus Hereforden.
Willielmus Norwicen.
Willielmus Meneven.
Robertus Assaven.
Robertus Abbas Sancti Albani.
Willielmus Ab. Westmonaster.
Joannes Ab. Burien.
A Richardus Ab. Glasconiæ.
A Hugo Ab. Redying.
Robertus Ab. Malmesbur.
Clemens Ab. Eveshamen.
Johannes Ab. de Bello.
Willielmus Ab. S. Petri Glocest.
Richardus Ab. Winchelcombens.
Joannes Ab. de Croyland.
Robertus Ab. de Thorney.
Robertus Ab. de Waltham.
Joannes Ab. Cirencest.
Joannes Ab. Teuxburen.
Thomas Prior Coventr.

Joannes Ab. de Osney.
B Henricus Ab. de Corariis.
Anthonius Ab. de Eyntham.
Robertus Prior Elien.
Robertus Prior sive Ma-

gister ordinis de Semper-ingham.
Richardus Ab. de Notley.
Hugo Prior de Huntingtoun.
Willielmus Ab. de Stratford.
Gabriel Ab. de Buckfestriæ.
Henricus Ab. de Wardenor.
Joannes Prior de Merton.
Richardus Pr. de Walsingham.
B Thomas Ab. de
Thomas Ab. de Stanley.
Richardus Ab. de Bytlesden.
Richardus Pr. de Lanthony.
Robertus Ab. de Thame.
B Joannes Prior de Helvenham.
Radulphus Prior de Kymme.
B Richardus Ab. de Brueza.
Robertus Ab. de Welhows.
Bartholamaus Pr. de Overhey.
Willielmus Pr. de Burgaveny.
Thomas Ab. de Abendon.

Inferior Domus.

C R. Gwent Archidiaconus London, et Breck.
Robertus Alridge Archid. Colecestr. et Pro-

curator Cleri Coven. et Litchf.
Thomas Bedyl Archid. Cornub.

Richardus Street Archid.
Derbiæ.

David Pole Ar. Salop.

Richardus Doke Archid.
Sarum.

Edmundus Bonner Archid. Leycestriæ.

Thomas Baghe Archid.
Surr.

Richardus Rawson Archid. Essex.

Edmundus Cranmer Archid. Cant.

Polidorus Virgilius Archid. Wellen.

Richardus Coren Archid.
Oxon.

Henricus Morgan Procurator Cleri Lincoln.

Petrus Vannes Archid.
Wygornen.

Georgius Hennage Decanus Lincoln.

Nilo Spencer Procurator Cleri Norwicen.

Guilielmus Knight Archid.
Cestriæ.

Gamaliel Clyfton Decanus Hereford. et Proc.
Capit.

Joannes London Decanus Wallingford.

Richardus Layton Archid.
Bucks.

Hugo Coren Proc. Cleri Hereford.

Richardus Sparaheford Proc. Cleri Hereford.

Mauritius Griffith Proc.
Cleri Roffen.

Gulielmus Buckmastr. Procurator Cleri London.

Richardus Shelton Mag.
Colleg. de Melyngham.

Per me Willielmum Glyn.
Archi. An-glessen.

Robertus Evans Decan.
Bangoren.

Walterus Cretying Ar. Bathonien.

Thomas Bagard Procurator Cleri Wygornen.

Joannes Nase Proc. Cleri Bathon et Wellen.

Georgius Wyndham Archid. Norwicen.

Nicolaus Metcalfe Archid.
Roffen.

Gulielmus Hedge Procurator Cleri Norwicen.

Adam Traves Archid.
Exon.

Ricardus Woleman Dec.
Wellen.

Tho. Brerewood Archidiacan. Bar. Procur. Capituli et Cleri Exon.

Georgius Carew Archid.
Totten Proc. Capituli et Cleri Exon.

Thomas Bennet Proc. Cleri et Capit. Sarum.

Richardus Arche Proc.
Cleri et Capit. Sarum.

Petrus Lightman Proc. Cleri Cant.

Edmundus Stewart Proc.
Cleri Winton.

Joannes Rayne Proc. Cleri Lincoln.

Leonardus Savile Proc.
Cleri Archid. Lewen.

Simon Matthew Proc.
Cleri London.

LinfridOgle Archid.Salop.

Gulielmus Maye Proc.
Cleri Elien.

Rol. Philips Proc. Eccles.
St. Pauli London.

Joannes Bell Ar. Glocest.

Joannes Chambers Dec.St.
Stephani Archid. Bed-
ford.

Nicolaus Wilson.

Some Observations on the former Subscriptions.

A The Abbots of Glossenbury and Reading subscribe with
the rest: by which it appears that they complyed in the
changes that were made as readily as others did.

B The Abbots writ generally so ill that it is very hard to
read their Subscriptions. Some of them I could by no
means know what to make of.

C There are 50 of the lower house of Convocation: of
those there are 25 Archdeacons, 4 Deans of Cathedrals,
3 Deans of Collegial Churches, 17 Procurators for the
Clergy, and one Master of a Colledge.

II.

Some Queries put by Cranmer in Order to the Correcting
of several Abuses.

Cott.
Libr.
Cleop.
E. 5.

FIRST, What causes, reasons, or considerations hath or
might move any man to desire to have the Bishop of Rome
restored in any point to his pretended Monarchy, or to re-
pugn against the Laws and Statutes of this Realm made
for the setting forth of the King's Title of Supream Head?

2. Item, Whether a man offending deadly after he is Baptized, may obtain remission of his Sins, by any other way
than by Contrition, through grace?

3. Item, If the Clergy know that the common sort of men
have them in a higher estimation, because they are perswaded, that it lyeth in the will and Power of Priests to
remit, or not remit sins at their pleasure; whether in such

case the said Clergy offend if they wink at this, and voluntarily suffer the people to continue in this Opinion?

Item, Whether a sinner being sorry and contrite for his **4.** sins and forthwith dying, shall have as high a place in Heaven, as if he had never offended?

Item, Whether any, and what difference may be As- **5.** signed betwixt two men, whereof the one being very sorry and contrite for his sins dieth without Absolution of the Priest, and the other which being contrite is also absolved by the Priest and so dieth?

Item, If it may appear that the common people have a **6.** greater affiance or trust in outward Rites or Ceremonies than they ought to have, and that they esteem more vertue in Images and adorning of them, kissing their feet or offering Candles unto them, than they should esteem, and that yet the Curates knowing the same, and fearing the loss of their offerings, and such other temporal commodities, do rather encourage the people to continue after this sort, than teach them the truth in the premisses according to Scripture; what the Kings Highness and his Parliament may do, and what they are bound in conscience to do in such case?

Item, Whether now in time of the new Law the Tithes **7.** or tenth be due to Curates by the Laws of God, or of man; and if the same be due by the Laws of man, what mans Laws they be?

Item, Whether the Clergy only, and none but they ought **8.** to have voices in general Councils?

Item, Whether the 19th Canon in the Council of Calce- **9.** don, wherein is contained that one Clerk may not sue an other before any secular Judge, but only before his Bishop, and such other Canons of like effect, have been generally received or not? and whether the same be contrary to the King's Prerogative and Laws of this Realm; and whether it be expedient that it were declared by the Parliament that the said Canons being at no time received, especially within this Realm, be void and of none effect.

Item, Of the 24th Canon of the said Council, wherein is **10.** contained that Monasteries once consecrate by the Bishop, may not after be made dwelling houses for Lay-men, whether that Canon have been received and observed, and whether the same be against the Power of the King and Authority of his Parliament?

11. *Item*, If it may appear that the Bishops have not, ne yet do maturely examine and diligently inquire of the Conversation, and Learning of such as be ordered or admitted to Cures by them, but rather without examination or inquisition indistinctly admit persons, unable, whereof ensueth great peril of Souls, and innumerable inconveniences otherways, what the Kings Highness or his Parliament ought to do, or may do for reformation in the premisses?

12. *Item*, If such as have Deanries, Arch-Deaconries, Chanterships, and other Offices or promotions of the Clergy, use not themselves in their own persons after such sort as the primary institution of these Offices or Promotions require, and according to the Wills of them that endowed the same, what the King and his Parliament may do or ought to do in this case?

13. *Item*, For what causes and to what ends and purposes such Offices and promotions of the Clergy were first instituted?

14. *Item*, If Curates having Benefices with cure, for their more bodily ease, refuse to dwell upon any of their said Cures, and remain in idleness continually in Cathedral or Collegial Churches, upon their Prebends, whether it be in this case expedient, that the Kings Highness or his Parliament take any Order for the redress of the same?

15. *Item*, Of the Sacraments of Confirmation, Order, Matrimony, and extream Unction, what the external Signs and inward graces be in every of the said Sacraments, what promises be made to the receivers of them by God, and of what efficacy they be of and energy of themselves?

III.

Some Queries concerning Confirmation, with the Answers which were given to them by Cranmer, and Stokesley Bishop of London,

An Original.

Whether Confirmation be Instituted by Christ?

Respon. THERE is no place in Scripture that declareth this Sacrament to be instituted of Christ.

First, For the places alledged for the same be no Institutions but Acts and deeds of the Apostles.

Secondly, These Acts were done by a special gift given to the Apostles for the confirmation of God's Word at that time.

Thirdly, The said special gift doth not now remain with the Successors of the Apostles.

What is the External Sign?

The Church useth *Chrisma* for the exterior Sign, but the Scriptur maketh no mention thereof.

What is the Efficacy of this Sacrament?

The Bishop in the name of the Church doth invocate the Holy Ghost to give strength and constancy, with other spiritual gifts, unto the person confirmed : so that the efficacy of this Sacrament is of such value, as is the Prayer of the Bishop made in the name of the Church.

Hæc respondeo, salvo semper eruditiorum et Ecclesiæ orthodoxæ judicio.

Stokesley's Paper.

The first Question, *Whether the Sacrament of Confirmation be a Sacrament of the New Testament institute by Christ?*

To this I answer, That it is.

The second Question, *What is the outward sign, and the invisible graces which be conferred in the same?*

To this I answer, That the Words *Signo te Signo Sanctæ*

Written with Cranmer's hand. Cott. Libr. Cleop. E. 5.

crucis et confirmo te, &c. With the consignation, with the
Creame, imposition of hands of the Prelates, be the Signs:
and the increase of the gifts of the Holy Ghost, and especially of fortitude, to speak, shew, and defend the Faith,
and to suffer for the same in case need be.

The third Question, *What promises be made of the said
graces?*

I answer, That the facts and deeds that be expressed in
the Books of the Apostles, with the effects ensuing, by the
imposition of their hands, upon them that before had received Remission of their sins, joyned with the promises
of Christ, made to his Church, and the continual belief of
the university of the same Catholick Church from the time
of the Apostles hitherto, without contradiction of any man
(ignorants and suspects of Heresie only excepted) maketh
us, and in my opinion, without prejudice of other mens
opinions, ought to suffice to make all men that hath promised to believe the Catholick Church, assuredly to think
that God hath made the promises of the said grace.

*Ego Joannes London. sic respondeo, fretus autoritate et
Testimonio antiquissimorum, eorumque Doctissimorum
pariter ac Sanctissimorum virorum, et præcipue Sanctæ
matris nostræ Ecclesiæ Catholicæ, cui etiam in non expressis in sacra Scriptura, non multo minus quam scriptis, fides adhibenda est; nisi tam de baptismo parvulo-
rum, quam de perpetua Deiparæ virginis integritate, et
id genus compluribus, quibus sine salutis periculo nemo
discrepat, licebit salva fide contradicere.*

IV.

*Some Considerations offered to the King by Cranmer, to in-
duce him to proceed to a further Reformation.*

Cott.
Libr.
Cleop.
E. 4. PLEASETH it your Highness graciously to consider,
deeply to ponder and weigh by your high wisdom these Con-
siderations following.

First, How no great thing is to be determined, principally matters of Christ's Religion, without long, great, and mature deliberation.

Secondly, How evil it hath succeeded when in Provincial, yea or yet in General Councils, men have gone about to set forth any thing as in the force of Gods Law, without the manifest Word of God, or else without apparent reasons, infallibly deduced out of the Word of God.

Thirdly, How all Christened Regions are now full of Learned men in the Scripture, which can well espie out and judge how things that be, or shall be set forth are agreeable with Scripture or not.

Fourthly, Of what Audacity men be of now adays, which will not spare to write against high Princes, as well as against private persons, without any respect to their high Estates, only weighing the equity or the iniquity of the cause.

Fifthly, How not only men of the New Learning (as they be called) but also the very Papistical Authors, do allow that by the Word of God, Priests be not forbidden to Marry, although they were not ignorant that many expounders of Scripture were of the contrary judgment.

Sixthly, How that it is not possible that all Learned men should be of one mind, sentence, and opinion, as long as the cockle is mingled with the wheat, the Godly with the ungodly, which certainly shall be so long as the World endureth.

Seventhly, How variety of Opinions have been occasion of the opening of many verities heretofore taken for Heresie, yea and yet so esteemed and taken of many, in other Regions; as namely the usurped Authority of the Bishop of Rome hath by that occasion come into Light, with the effusion of the blood not of a few, such as were the first stirrers up thereof.

Lastly, There be also other opinions not spoken of, which have made, and yet will make as much variance in your Graces Realm as any of them treated of, namely, Whether the Holy Scripture teacheth any Purgatory to us after this Life or not? whether the same Scripture teacheth the Invocation of dead Saints? Whether there be any unwritten verities necessary to be believed not written in Scripture, nor deducted by infallible Arguments out of the open places of Scripture? Whether there be any satisfactions beside the satisfaction of Christ? Whether free-will by its own strength may dispose itself to grace of a conveniency (as it is said) *de congruo?* Whether it be against Scripture to kiss the Image of Christ in the Honour of him? And generally whether Images may be used any other way than your Grace setteth forth in your Injunctions?

Wherefore in consideration of the premisses it may please your Highness to suspend your judgment for a time, and not to determine the Marriage of Priests to be against Scripture, but rather to put both parts to silence, commanding them neither to preach, dispute, nor openly to talk thereof under pain of, &c. And in case these premisses do not move your Highness to stay, that then it may please the same to grant that the Article of Priests Marriage may be openly disputed in both Universities, under indifferent Judges, before it be determined. All the Arguments of the contrary party first to be delivered in writing to the defenders twelve days before the disputation; to the intent they may the more maturely and deliberately make answer to the same; and they that shall enter as defenders into this disputation, to do it under this condition, that if their Judges decern them to be overcome, they be right well contented to suffer death, therefore: And if their adversaries cannot prove their purpose, their desire is no more but that it may please your Highness to leave your most humble Subjects to the liberty that God's Word permitteth them in that behalf; and your said humble Subjects shall pray unto Almighty God for the preservation of your most Royal Estate long to continue to God's Glory and Honour.

V.

A Declaration made of the Functions and Divine Institution of Bishops and Priests.

An Original.

As touching the Sacrament of Holy Orders, we will that all Bishops and Preachers shall instruct and teach our people committed by us unto their spiritual charge,

First, How that Christ and his Apostles did institute and Ordain in the New Testament, that beside the Civil Powers and governance of Kings and Princes, which is called in Scripture, *potestas gladii*, the Power of the Sword, there should be also continually in the Church Militant, certain other Ministers or Officers, which should have Spiritual Power, Authority and commission under Christ, to Preach and teach the Word of God, unto his people, and to dispence and administer the Sacraments of God unto them; and by the same to confer and give the grace of the Holy Ghost, to consecrate the blessed body of Christ in the Sacrament of the Altar, to loose and absoil from sin, all persons which be duly penitent and sorry for the same; to bind and excommunicate such as be guilty in manifest crimes and sins, and will not amend their defaults; to order and consecrate others in the same room, Order and Office, whereunto they be called and admitted themselves; and finally to feed Christ's people like good Pastors, and Rectors, as the Apostles calleth them, with their wholsome doctrine, and by their continual exhortations and monitions to reduce them from sin and iniquity, so much as in them lyeth, and to bring them unto the perfect knowledg, the perfect love and dread of God, and unto the perfect charity of their neighbours.

Item, That this Office, this Ministration, this Power and Authority is no tyrannical Power, having no certain Laws or Limits, within the which it ought to be contained, nor yet none absolute Power, but it is a moderate Power, subject, determined, and restrained unto those certain Limits and ends for the which the same was appointed by God's Ordinance; which, as was said before, is only to admi-

Cotton Libr. Cleop. E. 5.

nister and distribute unto the members of Christ's Mystical body, spiritual and everlasting things; that is to say, the pure and heavenly doctrine of Christ's Gospel, and the graces conferred in his Sacraments : And therefore this said Power and administration is called in some places of Scripture, *donum et Gratia,* a gift and a grace; in some places it is called *Claves sive potestas clavium,* that is to say, the keys or the Power of the keys, whereby is signified a certain limited Office restrained unto the execution of a special Function or Ministration, according to the saying of St. Paul in his first Chap. of his Epistle to the Romans, and in the fourth Chap. of his first Epistle to Timothy, and also in the fourth Chap. of his Epistle to the Ephes. Where he writes in this Sentence; *Quum ascendisset Christus in altum, captivam duxit captivitatem, et dedit dona hominibus, dedit autem, alios quidem Apostolos, alios vero Prophetas, alios vero Evangelistas, alios autem pastores ac doctores, ad instaurationem sanctorum, in opus administrationis, in ædificationem corporis Christi, donec perveniamus omnes in unitatem fidei et agnitionis filii Dei, in virum perfectum, in mensuram ætatis plene adultæ Christi.* That is to say, " when Christ ascended into Heaven, he subdued and vanquished very captivity her self, and led or made her thrall and captive, and distributed and gave divers heavenly gifts and graces unto men here on earth; and among all he made some the Apostles, some Priests, some Evangelists, some Pastors and Doctors, to the intent they should execute the work and office of their administration, to the instauration, instruction, and edifying of the members of Christ's Mystical body: And that they should also not cease from the Execution of their said Office, until all the said members were not only reduced and brought unto unity of the Faith, and the knowledg of the Son of God, but also that they were come unto a perfect state, and full age therein; that is to say, until they were so established and confirmed in the same that they could no more afterwards be wavering therein, and be led or carryed like children, into any contrary doctrine, or opinion, by the craft or subtile perswasion of the false Pastors and Teachers, which go about by craft to bring them into erroneous opinions, but that they should constantly follow the true Doctrine of

Christ's Gospel, growing and encreasing continually by
charity unto a perfect member of that body, whereof Christ
is the very head, in whom if the whole body, that is to say,
if every part and member be grown and come unto his perfect estate, not all in like, but every one according to the
gift and quality which is deputed unto it, and so to be
compacted, united, and corporated together in the said
body, no doubt but that whole body and every part thereof
shall thereby be made the more perfect and the more
strong, by reason of that natural love and charity, which
one member so united in the body hath unto the other:" by
which words it appeareth evidently not only that St. Paul
accounted and numbred this said Power and Office of
the Pastors and Doctors among the proper and special
gifts of the Holy Ghost, but also it appeareth that the same
was a limited power and Office, ordained specially and
only for the causes and purposes before rehearsed.

Item, That this Power, Office, and Administration is
necessary to be preserved here in Earth for three special
and principal causes. First, for that it is the Commandment of God it should be so, as it appeareth in sundry
places of Scripture. Secondly, for that God hath instituted
and ordained none other ordinary mean or instrument,
whereby he will make us partakers of the reconciliation
which is by Christ, and confer and give the graces of his
Holy Spirit unto us, and make us the right inheritors of
everlasting Life, there to Reign with him for ever in glory,
but only his words and Sacraments; and therefore the Office and Power to Minister the said Word and Sacraments,
may in no wise be suffered to perish, or to be abolished,
according to the saying of St. Paul, *Quomodo credent in
eum de quo non audierunt? quomodo autem audient sine
prædicante? quomodo autem prædicabunt nisi missi fuerunt?
sicut scriptum est, quam speciosi super montes pedes Evan-
gelizantium pacem, annunciantium bona!* Thirdly, because
the said Power and Office or Function hath annexed unto
it assured promises of excellent and inestimable things;
for thereby is conferred and given the Holy Ghost with all
his graces, and finally our justification and everlasting life,
according to the saying of St. Paul, *Non me pudet Evangelii Jesu Christi, potentia si quidem est Dei ad salutem omni*

credenti; that is to say, I am not ashamed of the room and
Office which I have, given unto me by Christ, to preach his
Gospel, for it is the Power of God, that is to say, the elect
Organ or Instrument ordained by God and endued with
such vertue and efficacy, that it is able to give and Minister
effectually everlasting Life unto all those that will believe
and obey unto the same.

Item, That this Office, this Power and Authority was
committed and given by Christ and his Apostles unto certain persons only, that is to say, unto Priests or Bishops,
whom they did elect, call, and admit thereunto by their
Prayer and Imposition of their hands.

Secondly, We will that all Bishops and Preachers shall
instruct and teach our people committed unto their Spiritual charge, that the Sacrament of Order may worthily be
called a Sacrament, because it is a holy Rite, or ceremony
instituted by Christ and his Apostles in the New Testament, and doth consist of two parts, like as the other Sacraments of the Church do; that is to say, of a spiritual
and an invisible grace, and also of an outward and a visible Sign. The invisible gift or grace conferred in this Sacrament, is nothing else but the Power, the Office and the
Authority before mentioned: the visible and outward Sign,
is, the Prayer and Imposition of the Bishop's hands, upon
the person which receiveth the said gift or grace. And to
the intent the Church of Christ should never be destituted
of such Ministers, as should have and execute the said
power of the keys, it was also Ordained and commanded
by the Apostles, that the same Sacrament should be ap-
plyed and ministred by the Bishop from time to time, unto
such other persons as had the qualities, which the Apostles
very diligently descryve; as it appeareth evidently in the
third Chap. of the first Epistle of St. Paul to Tim. and his
Epistle unto Titus. And surely this is the whole vertue
and efficacy, and the cause also of the institution of this
Sacrament, as it is found in the New Testament; for albeit
the Holy Fathers of the Church which succeeded the Apostles, minding to beautifie and ornate the Church of Christ
with all those things, which were commendable in the Temple of the Jews, did devise not only certain other ceremonies than be before rehearsed, as Tonsures, Rasures, Unc-

tions, and such other observances to be used in the administration of the said Sacraments, but did also institute certain inferiour orders or degrees, as Janitors, Lectors, Exorcists, Acolits, and Subdeacons, and deputed to every one of those certain Offices to Execute in the Church, wherein they followed undoubtedly the example and rites used in the Old Testament; yet the truth is, that in the New Testament there is no mention made of any degrees or distinctions in Orders, but only of Deacons or Ministers, and of Priests or Bishops: nor is there any word spoken of any other ceremony used in the conferring of this Sacrament, but only of Prayer, and the Imposition of the Bishop's hands.

Thomas Cromwell.
T. Cantuarien.
Edwardus Ebor.
Joannes London.
Cuthbertus Dunelmensis.
Joannes Lincoln.
Joannes Bathoniens.
Thomas Elien.
Joannes Bangor.
Nicolaus Sarum.
Edwardus Hereforden.
Hugo Wygorn.
Joannes Roffen.
Rich. Cicestr.
Richardus Wolman.
Joannes Bell.
Willielmus Clyffe.
Robertus Aldridge.
Gilfridus Downes.

Joannes Skip.
Cuthbertus Marshall.
Marmaduke Waldeby.
Robertus Oking.
Nicolaus Heyth.
Rodolphus Bradford.
Richardus Smith.
Simon Matthew.
Joannes Prynn.
Gulielmus Buckmastre.
Willielmus Maye.
Nicolaus Wotton.
Richardus Cox.
Joannes Edmondes.
Thomas Robertson.
Thomas Baret.
Joannes Nase.
Joannes Barbar.

(Some other hands there are that cannot be Read.)

Sacræ Theologiæ, Juris Ecclesiastici et Civilis Professores.

VI.

A Letter of Melanthon's, to perswade the King to a further Reformation.

An Original.

S. D. Serenissime et Inclyte Rex, Etsi audieramus Romanum Episcopum omnibus artificiis incendere Cæsaris Caroli et Regis Gallici animos adversus Britannos et Germanos, tamen quia spero Deum hæc pericula gubernaturum esse, et defensurum tranquillitatem tuam, scripsi in alteris literis de Ecclesiarum emendatione, quam si tempora sinent rogo ut Regia Majestas tua suscipiat. Postea adjeci hanc Epistolam, non impudentia, sed optimo studio, et amore cum Ecclesiarum, cum Regiæ Majestatis tuæ incitatus: quare per Christum obtestor Regiam Majestatem tuam ut meam libertatem boni consulat. Sæpe cogito Britannicæ Ecclesiæ primordia, et cæteras laudes: hinc enim propagata est doctrina Christiana in magnam Germaniæ et Galliæ partem; imo Britannicæ Ecclesiæ beneficium fuit, quod primum Romanæ Provinciæ liberatæ sunt persecutione. Hæc primum nobis Imperatorem pium Constantinum dedit: magna hæc gloria est vestri nominis. Nunc quoque Regia Majestas tua primum heroica magnitudine animi ostendit se veritati patrocinaturum esse excussit Romani Episcopi tyrannidem, quare veterem puritatem Ecclesiæ vestræ maxime optarim restitui integram. Sed animadverto istic esse quosdam qui veteres abusus ortos aut confirmatos a Romano Episcopo adhuc mordicus tenent. Mirum est autem Autore abusuum ejecto ipsa tamen venena retineri; qua in re illud etiam periculi est, quod illi ipsi aut eorum imitatores aliquando revocaturi potestatem Romani Episcopi videntur, si populus hunc putavit esse Magistrum Ecclesiarum, incurrunt enim ritus in oculos et admonent de autore, ut Solonis memoria cum legibus Athenis et propagata et jucunda fuit.

Gaudebam igitur in Edicto recens istic proposito de Religione, promitti publicam deliberationem et emendationem de Ecclesiarum ritibus et legibus, eaque sententia mitigavit Decreti acerbitatem: quanquam enim laudo pie-tatem, quod errores prohibentur, qui pugnant cum doctrina Catholicæ Ecclesiæ quam et nos profitemur; tamen doleo ad eas causas adjectum esse articulum, in quo precipitur omnium rituum usitatorum et cælibatus observatio. Primum enim multi transferrent Edicti Autóritatem ad stabiliendos abusus Missæ. Deinde in universum confirmatur pertinacia eorum qui Doctrinæ nostræ sunt iniquiores, et debilitantur studia piorum. Augustinus queritur sua ætate jam duriorem fuisse servitutem Christianam quam Judaicam, quanto erit asperior servitus, si superstitiosiores ineptiæ, ut reptatio ad crucem aut res similes, munientur corporum suppliciis? Gerson scribit prodesse piis, qui tamen superstitiosius observant ritus, ut invitentur ad eos violandos, ut usu et exemplo dediscant superstitionem.

Sed munio tranquillitatem, dices, et nolo dissimilitudine rituum excitari discordias. Ego de piis et modestis loquor qui humanas traditiones sine tumultibus violant, non de his qui in cætu publico seditiose tranquillum populum aut concitant aut perturbant. Extant autem antea leges de seditiosis, nec statim violatio inepti et non necessarii ritus judicanda est seditiosa, attamen hac in re non solum tranquillitatis, sed etiam piarum conscientiarum ratio habenda est: est enim tenera res conscientia, facile languescit perculsa potentum judiciis.

Nec ignoro quosdam novo jam uti genere sapientiæ, excusant abusus et leniunt eos astute afflictis interpretationibus, ut habeant speciosam causam cur eos retineant; sicut nefarios abusus excusat Autor reformationis Coloniensis, ut campanarum consecrationem et similes imposturas. Quam multa sunt in fabulosis historiis sanctorum, ut Christophori, Georgii, quæ, ut poemata, continent venustissimas Allegorias; nec tamen propter has cogendæ sunt Ecclesiæ ut illas poeticas personas colant.

Erat in Egypto sacrum cum fici maturuissent, populus enim in templo edens recentes ficus, addebat canticum his verbis, Dulcis veritas. Huic ritui facile est bellam significationem addere, eumq; accommodare ad laudem Verbi Dei, nec tamen propterea hic mos in Ecclesias revocandus est; atqui hanc novam sophisticam exoriri passim videmus. Sic in Italia dicuntur abusibus patrocinari, Contarenus, Sadoletus, et Polus Cardinalis; nam hi præcipue susceperunt sibi jam has partes defendendæ Romanæ impietatis, et hanc ducunt esse magnam ingenii laudem fucos illinire vitiosis ritibus, putantq; se his ineptiis Dionysii Theologiam Mysticam renovare. Hæc Sophistica, nisi prudentes gubernatores Ecclesiarum obsistent, pariet horribilem confusionem religionum, et rursus obruet veritatem. Donec flagitantur humani ritus tanquam necessarii, confirmatur prava opinio de cultu; ideo Paulus tam vehementer non modo opinionem, sed ritus ipsos Leviticos insectatus est, prævidebat enim non excuti posse superstitionem, si ritus manerent, quare gravissime inquit, *si circumcidimini, Christus vobis nihil proderit.*

Retineatur ergo simplex et perspicua sententia de libertate in adiaphoris, et doceant concionatores quæ scandala vitanda sint; retineantur ritus divinitus instituti, et aliquæ humanæ traditiones utiles ad bonum ordinem, ut Paulus loquitur, et sit modus cæremoniarum quæ habeant conjunctam gravitatem et elegantiam; decet autem abesse ab Ecclesiis barbariem: Cæteri inutiles et inepti ritus non duriter flagitentur.

Deinde quantum periculi adfert conscientiis prohibitio conjugii, nec ignorat Regia Majestas tua, legem de cælibatu perpetuo tantum Romæ natam esse: extant Epistolæ Episcopi Tarraconensis defendentes conjugia Presbyterorum in Hispania contra Romanum Episcopum. In Germania ante annos quingentos adhuc Sacerdotes fuerunt mariti, adeoque ægre tulerunt sibi eripi hanc libertatem, ut in Episcopum Moguntinum recitantem edictum Romanum tumultuantes impetum fecerint, quare Episcopus fugere coactus recitationem omisit. Erat Autor Edicti Gregorius septimus qui cuilibet tyrannorum veterum audacia et impietate par fuit. Hic cum longo et funesto bello civili nostros Germanicos imperatores implicuisset, simul etiam Ecclesias Tyrannide oppressit. Audio et in Anglia Sacerdotes fuisse maritos: deniq; notæ sunt Historiæ, quæ exempla satis multa continent, quare miror in Edicto citari Epistolam ad Corinthios, cum hæc longe aliud tradat de conjugio, ac præcipiat conjugium iis qui non sunt idonei ad cælibatum.

Nec objicienda sunt vota quæ et expresse pugnant cum divinis mandatis, et trahunt secum multiplicem superstitionem et morum corruptionem; videmus enim qualis sit vita multorum Sacerdotum cælibum: itaq; non sine dolore aliquo legi in Edicto, quod hi qui Uxores duxerunt accusantur Levitatis, nam hoc convicio causa nostra prægravari videtur, quæ tamen Ecclesiæ necessaria est, ut conjugii dignitas clarius conspiciatur, ut superstitiosi cultus votorum reprehendantur, ut arceantur libidines. Non enim impurus cœlibatus, sed honesta et pia conjugum consuetudo, est castitas Deo grata, sicut Christus sua voce divinam conjunctionem appellat conubium, inquiens, *Quos Deus conjunxit*, &c. Discamus Dei Ordinationem in natura magnificare, eaque reverenter uti, non fingamus ipsi novos cultus sine Verbo Dei; de quo genere Paulus nominatim concionatur, cum ad Timotheum scribens duriter reprehendit eos qui prohibent nuptias.

Propheta Daniel insignes notas addidit Antichristo duas, cum ait, colet Deum Maosim argento et auro, et Deum patrum suorum non intelliget, et mulieres non curabit. Hæc quadrant maxime ad Romanos mores: Missarum abusus et Sanctorum cultus pepererunt immensas opes et Regiam potentiam. Nova numina confecta sunt, adorantur aureæ et argenteæ statuæ, et auro atque argento ornantur. Deinde accedit Lex de cœlibatu, unde magna corruptio morum orta est. Hæ notæ cui genti, cui Regno usquam competunt nisi factioni Episcopi Romani? qui cum sit Antichristus, pio et forti animo ipsius autoritati et legibus adversandum est.

Porro fæliciter cœpit Regia Majestas tua quædam emendare, sustulit aliqua idola quæ impie colebantur: Obtestor ergo Regiam Majestatem tuam, ut reliquam impietatem Romanam etiam ex Ecclesiis tollat. Exempla testantur ingentibus victoriis ornatos esse Reges qui sustulerunt Idololatriam, ac sæpe testatur Deus quantopere requirat hunc cultum ut removeantur superstitiones, et pro hoc officio ingentia præmia pollicetur: quare Deus etiam defendet Regiam Majestatem tuam, si ut Ezechias et cæteri pii Reges impios ritus sustuleris. Audit Regia Majestas tua in Belgico et alibi immanem sævitiam exerceri adversus pios; et hæc Tyrannis gignit alia multa vitia, stabilit idololatriam, delet veram invocationem, extinguit penitus veram Religionem; cumq; desint boni Doctores, multi in populo fiunt palam ἄθεοι. Constat enim pæne Ethnicam licentiam esse in Belgico, alii superstitiosi natura, alii fanaticas opiniones Anabaptistarum amplectuntur. Talis est in Belgico status, quod quidem floret pace, otio, opibus; adfluunt luxu ditiores, ita se beatos esse putant, nec interea prospiciunt quot pœnæ ipsis impendeant: Deus autem haud dubie tantam impietatem et crudelitatem atrociter puniet. Nollem igitur in Regno tuo renovari asperitatem adversus pios, quam ita prohibebit Regia Majestas tua si Edictum leniet et Ecclesias constituere perget. Deinde ut etiam ad posteritatem, animi abhorreant a Tyrannide Romani Episcopi, plurimum refert illas leges tolli, quæ sunt nervi autoritatis ipsius; magna vero adminicula potentiæ Romanorum Episcoporum fuerunt, Missarum abusus, et Cælibatus, quæ si durabunt aliquando poterunt præbere occasionem iis qui depravatæ sunt opinionis Romanæ Aulæ, ut ad eam rursus inclinationem faciant. Id caveri quantum referat, si doctrinæ puritas conservanda est, satis intelligit Regia Majestas tua. Verum adhuc est quod Juvenalis de Romana aula scripsit, *hic fiunt homines, &c.* imbuti eo loci malis artibus, contumaciam singularem adversus Reges inde referunt, ut multa exempla testantur. Hanc Epistolam loquaciorem ac liberiorem ut Regia Majestas tua boni consulat oro. Precor autem Deum et Dominum nostrum Iesum Christum, ut Regiam Majestatem tuam servet et defendat, ac gubernet ad salutem Ecclesiæ. Bene et feliciter valeat Regia Majestas tua. Ex Francofordia.

Cal. Aprilis 1539.

Regiæ Majestatis tuæ

Addictissimus

Philippus Melanthon.

Directed thus on the back;

Serenissimo et Inclyto Angliæ et Franciæ Regi D. Henrico Octavo Walliæ et Cornubiæ Principi, Capiti Anglicæ Ecclesiæ post Christum Supremo,

Principi Clementissimo.

VII.

*A Letter written by the German Ambassadors to the King,
against the taking away of the Chalice, and against private Masses, and the Celibate of the Clergie, &c.*

An Original.

SERENISSIME et Potentissime Rex, Domine Clemen- Cotton
tissime, Etsi Serenissimam Regiam Majestatem vestram Libr.
Cleop.
maximorum negotiorum mole, tum ad Regnum ac Pro- E. 5.
vincias proprias Majestatis Vestræ pertinentium, tum etiam
exterorum Regum, Principum, et Potentatuum gravissimis
causis, quæ ad Regiam Majestatem Vestram pæne quotidie
devolvuntur, obrui non ignoremus; nosque pro nostra
erga Regiam Majestatem Vestram debita observantia ut
par est, nihil minus velimus aut cogitemus, quam Serenissimam Regiam Majestatem Vestram vel mittendis literis
crebrioribus, vel ulla alia re interturbare et a Reipublicæ
curis impedire, tamen certis quibusdam dè causis, quas
Serenissimæ Regiæ Majestati Vestræ probaturos nos speramus, duximus iterum ad Serenissimam Regiam Majestatem
Vestram literas dandas esse, nihil dubitantes quin Vestra
Serenissima Regia Majestas eas pro sua insigni bonitate,
sapientia, doctrina, atque favore sincerioris Religionis, benigne acceptura sit. Cum enim ab Illustrissimis Principibus nostris nobis injuncta mandata Vestræ Serenissimæ
Majestati jampridem exposuerimus, et præterea postulante
Majestate Vestra cum quibusdam ejusdem Reverendissimis et eruditissimis Episcopis et Theologiæ Doctoribus,
de articulis Religionis Christianæ per duos pæne menses
sermones contulerimus, ac Dei beneficio res eo perducta
fuerit, ut nihil ambigamus, quin inter Serenissimam Regiam Majestatem Vestram et Principes nostros, ac eorum
in causa religionis confœderatos utrorumq; Episcopos,
Theologos et Subditos firma atq; perpetua concordia in
sinceriore Evangelii Doctrina, in laudem Dei Optimi Maximi, salutem Ecclesiæ Christianæ, ac perniciem Romani
Antichristi, secutura sit, nosque reliquam disputationem
de abusibus non expectare queamus, existimavimus non
esse alienum ab officio nostro, ut ante discessum nostrum

Serenissimæ Regiæ Majestati Vestræ, quæ per Dei Gratiam indefessa cura et diligentia sinceram Evangelii Doctrinam promotam cupit, debitam observantiam, atque perpetuum studium hostrum literis nostris testatum relinque-
remus, et Majestati Vestræ nostrorum etiam sententiam de
quibusdam Articulis abusuum, de quibus Majestas Vestra
post abitum nostrum haud dubie curabit eosdem Episcopos et Theologos pro inquirenda veritate, sermones conferre et disputare, declararemus: nihil ambigentes, quin
ea etiam in re Serenissima Regia Majestas Vestra pro
Christi gloria id præstitura sit, ut non tantum doctrinam
puram habeat, verum etiam abolitis aliquando impiis cultibus et abusibus per Romanum Episcopum in Ecclesiam
introductis, cultus ac cæremonias consentaneas Verbo Dei
constituat: facile enim Serenissima Regia Majestàs Vestra
pro sua summa sapientia perspicit, non posse unquam
Doctrinæ puritatem, vel constitui, vel conservari, nisi tollantur è medio etiam hi abusus, qui prorsus et ex diametro,
ut dici solet, cum Verbo Dei pugnant, et Romani Antichristi tyrannidem ac idololatriam, tum pepererunt, tum
etiam hactenus conservarunt; nam ut radicibus demum
resectis, necesse est arbores et herbas penitus exarescere
et perire, ita dubium non est, quin impiis Romani Episcopi abusibus et idololatria, ut fundamento stabilitatis
ipsius, labefactis et eversis, etiam Tyrannis ejusdem prorsus ruitura et interitura sit; quod nisi fiat perpetuo metu-
endum est, ne levi aliqua occasione iterum repullulescat
et tanquam a radice reviviscat.

Sunt vero hæc tria pæne capita et fundamentum Tyrannidis et Idololatriæ Pontificiæ, quibus stantibus, neque
Doctrina Religionis integra permanere, neque unquam Romani Episcopi improbissimus dominatus, penitus extirpari
poterit: nempe, Prohibitio utriusque speciei Sacramenti
in cœna Domini, Missa Privata, et Interdictio conjugii
Sacerdotum, quæ quidem usque adeo Dei Verbo adver-
santur, adeoque etiam honestati publicæ repugnant, ut
vel ex his solis apertissime intelligi possit Romanum Pontificem verum Antichristum, et omnis idololatriæ, impietatis, erroris, et turpitudinis, in Christi Ecclesiam intro-
ductæ auctorem esse; de quibus sane articulis nos pauca
quædam Serenissimæ Regiæ Majestati Vestræ optime

studio scribemus, et ejusdem ut Regis summa sapientia, acerrimo judicio, et excellenti doctrina prœditi, censurœ committemus, persuasissimum nobis habentes Vestram Majestatem Illustrissimam Principum nostrorum, et Statuum confœderatorum consilium et institutum, in hisce articulis non improbaturam esse.

Primum enim, Serenissime ac Potentissime Rex, non existimamus quenquam inficias iturum, quin Christi Doctrina, mandata, et ordinationes omnibus aliis prœceptis, traditionibus aut cœremoniis humanis prœferri debeant; hic enim cum ipse sit vita et veritas, errare non potest, humana vero omnia, prœcipue in rebus divinis, incerta et dubia sunt. Porro constat Christum ipsum utramq; speciem instituisse, cum ait, Bibite ex hoc omnes; et Paulum idem docuisse, cum inquit, 2 Cor. 11. probet seipsum homo, et sic de pane comedat et poculo bibat. Quibus sane locis, non de una parte Ecclesiœ, id est, de Sacerdotibus tantum, sed de tota Ecclesia mentio fit: Nam quod quidam ita Argumentantur solis Apostolis Christum id dixisse, eaque de causa utramq; speciem ad solos Sacerdotes pertinere, infirmum admodum est Argumentum; quia eadem ratione sequeretur, quod Laicis ne altera quidem species danda esset; neque enim alio loco Christus mandavit solum corpus laicis dari, et utramque speciem pro Sacerdotibus instituit: sed hoc fatendum est, quod illud mandatum Christi de Sacramento, aut ad omnes, hoc est, Laicos et Sacerdotes pertineat, aut Laici prorsus a Sacramento Corporis etiam arcendi fuerint, cum nusquam alibi in Evangelio, nisi tunc cum dedit Apostolis simul corpus et sanguinem, Sacramentum pro Laicis institutum reperiatur; idque ad omnes pertinere Paulus declarat, cum addit, et de poculo bibat, &c. Quod enim dicunt Sacramenti divisionem, urgentibus quibusdam causis, ab Ecclesia institutam esse, et sub una specie, non minus quam sub utraque contineri, non multum ad rem facit: Quis enim non intelligit hic de Christi instituto et mandato agi, idque humanœ auctoritati et opinionibus longe prœferendum esse; neque enim Ecclesia sumit sibi hanc libertatem ex Christi Ordinationibus res indifferentes constituendi; et rationes illœ vel de discrimine ordinum, seu dignitate Sacerdotali, vel periculo effusionis et similes, nullo modo tantam queunt vim habere,

De utraque specie.

ut propterea Divinæ Ordinationes mutandæ sint; neque
'ulla etiam consuetudo contra mandata Dei introducta,
ipsis canonibus Pontificiis attestantibus, probanda est.
Constat vero' usum utriusque speciei, et clarum habere
mandatum Christi, et adprobationem Sanctorum Patrum,
ac consuetudinem veteris Ecclesiæ; sic enim, inquit Divus
Hieronymus, Sacerdotes qui Eucharistiæ serviunt, et sanguinem Christi populis distribuunt: et Gelasius Pontifex,
Sacramenti Corporis et Sanguinis Domini divisionem prohibet, eamque grande Sacrilegium adpellat.

Adhæc, durat hodie hic mos Communionis utriusque
speciei in Græcis Ecclesiis, quæ hac in re Romani Pontificis tyrannidi semper restiterunt, neque ejus jugum recipere
voluerunt, et testantur Historiæ tum in Germania, tum in
multis aliis regionibus ac provinciis, verum Communionis
usum diu conservatum fuisse, sed tandem fulminibus Romani Antichristi, quibus totum pœne orbem terrarum con-
terruit et subjugavit, homines, ut verisimile est, victi verum
Eucharistiæ usum mutarunt, ad quem tamen, per singularem Dei Gratiam, agnita iterum veritate Evangelica cum
Principes nostri, tum alii Evangelii Doctrinam profitentes,
jam redierunt, et sese ac suos in re Universæ Ecclesiæ
maxime salutifera, tanquam in libertatem, excusso jugo
Pontificio, vendicarunt et adserverunt. Nam quæ causæ
Pontificem permoverint, ut contra Christi mandatum et institutum, contra sententiam Sanctorum Patrum, contra
consuetudinem Universæ Ecclesiæ Christianæ, Sacramentum divideret, et Laicos Sanguine Domini nefarie spolia-
ret, facile serenissima Regia Majestas Vestra perspicit.
Verisimile quidem videtur, eum voluisse suam, suique ordinis auctoritatem ac dignitatem, ea ratione augere, et hoc
discrimen inter Laicos et Sacerdotes constituere; nam
etiam nunc clamitant adversarii, laicos debere esse altera
specie contentos; quasi regnum aliquod possideant, et ita
imperare ipsis liberum sit, ut etiam Christi beneficium hominibus eripere queant, ad quod potius, si suo officio fungi
vellent, omnes invitare et pellicere deberent. Sed quid
Christo cum Belial? quid Pontifici cum Christi instituto,
cujus ipse se summum adversarium esse satis declarat,
ideoque tum in hoc, tum aliis salutaribus Religionis Christianæ Articulis oportuit ipsum a scriptura discedere, imo

Doctrinam Evangelio consentaneam damnare, ut manifestum fieret, eum esse Antichristum, de quo passim Scriptura talia prædixit.

Porro in altero Articulo, De Missa Privata, adhuc magis adparet a Romano Pontifice Religionem Christianam adeo oppressam et obscuratam, ut Christi Beneficium qui sua morte nos redemit, solusque est hostia et satisfactio pro peccatis nostris, pœnitus sustulerit, et in ejus locum idololatricum cultum pro abolendis peccatis in Ecclesiam invexerit eamque suis erroribus et prophanationibus miserabiliter implicaverit, turbaverit et deformaverit. Cum enim Missa nihil aliud sit, nec esse debeat, quam communio sive Synaxis, ut Paulus adpellat, neque etiam alius ejus usus fuerit tempore Apostolorum et veteris Ecclesiæ, quemadmodum hoc clare ex S. Patribus probari potest, plane diversum quoddam opus, prorsus pugnáns cum communione et vero Missæ usu inde factum est, quod docent ex opere operato, ut loquuntur, mereri gratiam, et tollere peccata vivorum et mortuorum. *De Missa privata.*

Hæc opinio quantopere distet a Scripturis, ac gloriam Passionis Christi lædat, Sereniss. Regia Majestas Vestra facillime judicabit. Si enim hoc verum est, quod Missa pro aliis applicari potest, quod peccata tollit et prodest tam vivis quam mortuis, sequitur Justificationem ex opere Missarum contingere, non ex fide; verum hoc omnino Scripturæ repugnat, quæ tradit nos gratis propter Christum per fidem justificari, ac peccata nobis condonari, et in gratiam nos recipi, atque ita non alieno opere, sed propria fide propter Christum, singulos justos fieri: At illi docent alienum opus pro remittendis peccatis alteri, quod quidem merum est somnium et figmentum humanum, repugnans Evangelicæ Doctrinæ; nam tunc demum adplicatur gratia per Verbum et Sacramentorum usum, cum ipsi utimur Sacramentis, sed isti pro aliis utuntur, quod perinde est ac si pro aliis Baptizarentur. Neque vero potest dici quantopere deformet Christi Gloriam opinio illa de Missa, quæ ex opere operato conferat gratiam, aut applicata pro aliis mereatur eis remissionem venialium et mortalium peccatorum culpæ et pœnæ; idque apertè adversari Scripturæ, et a vero usu Missæ sive communionis longe discedere, vel inde liquet, quia Missa sive Synaxis ideo est instituta, ut fidelis qui utitur Sacramento recordetur quæ beneficia accipiat per Christum et erigat ac soletur pavidam conscientiam; ideoque ibi porrigi debet Sacramentum, his quibus opus est consolatione, sicut Ambrosius ait, quia semper pecco, semper debeo accipere Medicinam. Atque hic usque ad tempora Gregorii in Ecclesia Missæ usus fuit, neque antea privatæ Missæ cognitæ fuerunt; quod quidem cum multis aliis Patrum Sententiis patet, tum Chrysostomi, qui inquit, Sacerdotem stare ad altare et alios ad Communionem accersere, alios arcere: Et ex veteribus Canonibus constat, unum aliquem celebrasse Missam, a quo reliqui Presbyteri et Diaconi sumpserunt corpus Domini, sic enim inquit Canon Nicenus, Accipiant Diaconi secundum Ordinem post Presbyteros ab Episcopo vel Presbytero, Sacram Communionem. Et scribit Epiphanius, in Asia Synaxim ter celebratam singulis septimanis, nec quotidianas fuisse Missas, eumque morem ab Apostolis traditum esse; qui quidem Missæ usus etiam hodie in Græcis Parochiis durare dicitur, nam tantum singulis dominicis diebus et festis, fit ibi una publica Missa, privatas vero non habent: fuitque Græca Ecclesia hoc nomine longe fœlicior quam Latina, quæ meliorem usum cœnæ Domini, Synaxis, sive Missæ retinuerit, neque vel Sacramentum Corporis et Sanguinis Domini, contra claram Evangelii Doctrinam diviserit, ut paulo ante diximus, neque etiam privatas Missas Sacræ Scripturæ acerrime repugnantes, receperit; cujus quidem rei hanc potentissimam causam fuisse arbitramur, quod Græca Ecclesia Romanum Episcopum auctorem perversæ et Idololatricæ Doctrinæ, et omnium pœne abusuum qui in Ecclesiam introducti sunt, pro summo Ecclesiæ Universalis sive Catholicæ capite, nunquam agnoverit.

Sed concedunt quidam adplicationes quæ fiunt in Missa pro vivis et mortuis, et item opiniones, quod ex opere operato gratiam mereri traduntur, non esse probandas, et disputant abolitis illis opinionibus impiis, alia ratione Missas privatas retinendas, nempe quia sunt gratiarum actiones, quæ possint ab uno vel a pluribus fieri. Hæc sane ratio videtur aliquam habere speciem, estque σοφὸν φαρμακὸν, ut inquit Sophocles, quo in causis invalidis, et ut ipse ait, morbidis, utendum sit. Si Missa tantum esset gratiarum actio, possit fortassis tali aliquo prætextu colorari; verum

constat eam principaliter institutam esse, ut sit Sacramentum quod per ministrum alteri exhibeatur, ut accipiens et
credens consequatur gratiam. Et hoc quidem principali
fine posito, accedit alter de gratiarum actione; quare nullo
modo ab institutione Christi recedere, sed modum et formam illius Institutiones, et exemplum veteris Ecclesiæ sequi et retinere debemus : Nulla enim novitas, præsertim in
Sacramentis, recipienda est, contra formam a Christo tra-
ditam, et contra exempla veteris Ecclesiæ.

Porro constat privatas Missas esse recentes, et a Romanis Pontificibus introductas, et ne hodie quidem, ut paulo
ante dictum est, in Græcis Ecclesiis esse, nisi Parochiales
diebus festis, cum quibus adhuc manet vestigium Communionis: Cum igitur contra Dei Verbum Missa privata introducta sit, eamque humanum tantum et commentitium
cultum esse adpareat, quis dubitat quin talis Missa, sine
ullo periculo omitti possit, imo debeat, cum repugnet
Evangelio? Estque pium et sanctum opus verum Missæ
sive Synaxis usum Ecclesiæ restituere ac reddere, quo per
Romanum Pontificem, hoc est Antichristum, multis jam
annis miserabiliter privata fuit, qui quidem adhuc mordicus
privatas Missas tenet, adserit, et defendit. Neque id immerito, facile enim sentit quod labefactata Missa privata,
labefactetur, imo ruat Univers umejus Regnum et Tyrannis, quæ Missis illis nititur; ut enim in seminibus causa
est Arborum et stirpium, ita hujus luctuosissimi dominatus, imperii, tyrannidis, nundinationis et idololatriæ Pontificiæ semen fuit superstitio Missarum privatarum: Nam
hæ pepererunt et sustinuerunt, veluti Atlas quidam, totum
Papatum; ad harum normam omnia redacta sunt, siquidem
nihil fuit, quod non Missa aliqua expiari posse creditum
est. His aucupatus Pontifex Romanus indulgentias, quibus immensam pecuniam ex toto orbe terrarum prædatus
est; hæ Monachorum turbas infinitas coacervarunt, cum
eorum nullus alius esset usus, quam demurmurandi Missas
privatas, et alioquin inutile terræ pondus forent. Hæ sunt
et fuerunt universa pietas, quam Pontifex Romanus profitetur, hanc solam novit ille Religionem, quæ in Missis
privatis consistit; Doctrinam enim Evangelii non modo
non habet, verum acerrime odit et prosequitur, et in summa
his Missis ipsam prædicationem Verbi Divini Pontifex

exterminavit,. ut per omnia Antichristi munere fungeretur:
Nam in loco unius concionis Verbi, amplius mille Missæ
privatæ, hoc est, humani et commentitii cultus, contra Divinum Verbum successerunt; cum non Missas fieri sed
Evangelium prædicare, et Sacramenta rite distribuere et
administrare, Christus Apostolis, quorum illi volunt esse
successores, mandaverit.

Curarunt igitur Illustrissimi Principes nostri, et alii
Evangelii Doctrinam profitentes, Principes et Status, privatas Missàs penitus aboleri, et verum Missæ usum sive
Synaxim Christi institutioni, exemplo Apostolorum, veteris Ecclesiæ ac Patrum sententiis conformem, in Ecclesiam
revocarunt et restituerunt. Quæ quidem Missa sive Synaxis summa cum reverentia celebratur, servatis pœne omnibus usitatis Cæremoniis, quæ non repugnant pietati; et
admiscentur Germanicæ sive vernaculæ cautiones ad docendum populum, præcepit enim Paulus, in Ecclesia uti
lingua intellecta a populo., Porro, quia propter communionem sive usum Sacramenti Missa instituta est, hi qui
sunt idonei et antea explorati, sacramento utuntur; ac dignitas et usus Sacramenti, summa diligentia ac cura ex
Verbo Dei populo commendatur, ut sciant et intelligant
homines, quantam consolationem pavidis conscientiis ad-
ferat, ac discant Deo credere, et optima quæque ab eo expectare et petere.

Et hunc quidem Sacramenti ·et Missæ usum, Scripturæ
consentaneum, Deo gratum, et pietati conducibilem esse,
Serenissima Regia Majestas Vestra facile agnoscit; neque
enim hic aliquid contra Dei Verbum admittitur, imo secundum Christi mandatum et ordinationem, qui hanc Sacram
Communionem ad hunc finem instituit, omnia geruntur:
Nulla est hic admixta, prava, aut impia opinio, ut in
Missa privata Papistica, cujus finis et institutio cum Evangelio pugnat. Nihil hic etiam absque summa reverentia,
ordine, et decoro, digno Ecclesiæ, fieri cernitur. Audem-
usque adfirmare, majore Religione hunc verum Missæ
usum exhiberi apud nos, quam hactenus unquam sub Pa-
patu privatæ Missæ celebratæ fuerint, provocamusque ad
testimonia doctissimorum virorum, qui a Majestate Vestra
missi in illis locis fuerunt, et hæc omnia coram fieri vide-
runt et audierunt.

Quod enim Adversarii clamitant, Nostros omnes cultus
Divinos, omnes Cæremonias, omnem denique Religionem
abolere et labefactare, ea in re Principibus nostris, et aliis
Evangelii Doctrinam profitentibus, injuriam faciunt; et
hæc eos insigni quadam malevolentia et odio plusquam
Vatiniano, ut dici solet, confingere et comminisci clare adparet, cum ex Doctrina nostrorum, quam consentientem
Sacris Literis in lucem ediderunt, et Scriptis suis universo
orbi Christiano promulgarunt, tum etiam exemplis nostrarum Ecclesiarum, in quibus nolint velint coguntur fateri,
omnia religiosius et sanctius fieri, quam apud ipsos; immo Dei beneficio universus populus non tantum in templis
est religiosior, sed in tota disciplina publica modestius se
gerit, majoremque erga Magistratum civilem, et eos qui
Ecclesiis præsunt reverentiam et honorem exhibet, quam
unquam antea factum fuerit; et hoc sinceræ Evangelii
Doctrinæ acceptum referre debemus, quæ singulos, rectius
omnibus Pontificiis constitutionibus, sui officii admonet,
et sola in quibus re vera pietas ac cultus divinus consistat,
tradit ac docet.

Porro, quod Missæ collocatæ ad quæstum, ut sub Pa-
patu accidit, turpiter prophanentur, quodque hic abusus in
omnibus pœne templis latissime pateat, non est obscurum:
Nam Christi beneficium qui nos precioso suo sanguine redemit, idque gratuito pro vili stipe et mercede vendere, et
tale etiam opus inde constituere velle, quod ex sui natura,
hoc est ex opere operato, mereatur gratiam, et possit adplicari pro peccatis aliorum, mortuorum et vivorum, quis
non videt summam esse impietatem? Quid enim est corpus
Domini indigne tractare et sumere, si hoc non esset? An
potest etiam magis impium quidquam dici, quam illi de
Missis istis docuerunt? Nempe quod Christus sua passione satisfecerit pro peccatis Originis, et instituerit Missam, in qua fieret Oblatio pro quotidianis delictis mortali-
bus et venialibus: cum Christus pœnitentiam et remissionem peccatorum prædicari mandaverit: Missam vero, hoc
est Synaxim, ad alium plane finem instituerit, viz. ut porrigatur Sacramentum his quibus opus est consolatione, et
ut per Verbum et Sacramentum credentes gratiam recipiant, et remissionem peccatorum consequantur, non ut ipsi
suum opus, quod quale quale sit, humanum figmentum,

humanus cultus est, contra Scripturam Deo offerant ac sa-
crificent. Hoc enim non placat Deum, ut Christus ipse
inquit, se frustra coli mandatis hominum : Nam Missam
non esse tale opus sive Sacrificium, quod mereatur gratiam et prosit etiam aliis, inde adparet, quia Missa sive
Synaxis ad hoc est instituta, non ut Deo aliquid offeratur,
sed ut communicantes consolationem hauriant, et veluti
pignus seu certum signum gratiæ ac bonæ voluntatis Dei
erga se recipiant, atque ita recordentur mortis Christi, hoc
est, beneficiorum quæ per Christum accipiunt, qui quidem
pro nobis mortuus est, solusque pro peccatis nostris satis-
fecit, idque probant Verba ipsa quibus et Christus et Paulus de Missa sive Synaxi usi sunt.

Primum enim inquit Christus, hoc est Corpus Meum,
quod pro vobis traditur. Hæc sunt Verba promissionis
Divinæ quæ solam fidem exigunt, quibusque offertur nobis
gratia et remissio peccatorum, ergo non est Sacrificium,
hoc est, opus quod Deo offeratur et quidem pro abolendis
peccatis. Item Paulus ait, Annunciantes mortem Domini :
Annunciare autem non est Sacrificare, hoc est tale opus
Deo reddere, quo peccata deleantur. Præterea Evangelii
textus ita sonat, Fregit et dedit Discipulis, inquiens, accipite et comedite, &c. item bibite ex hoc omnes, &c. accipere autem, comedere et bibere, non est sacrificare, quia
hæc opera ex opere operato non delent peccata.

Neque mandatur hisce verbis, ut nos Deo aliquid offera-
mus, sed potius ut ab eo accipiamus, quia addit, pro vobis
traditum, et sanguis qui pro vobis effunditur ; quæ Verba
ostendunt, non exhiberi a sumentibus Eucharistiam Deo
Sacrificium, sed donum hominibus datum. Præterea vero
nemo dicit Laicos cum sumunt Sacramentum, Sacrificare : at quantum ad hanc Sacram Communionem, Missam, sive Synaxim pertinet, nulla est ratio diversitatis,
cùm idem Christus uno eodemque tempore ac momento,
propter eundem finem et usum, hoc Sacramentum absque
differentia utentium Sacerdotum vel Laicorum instituerit.
Et quemadmodum prohibitio utriusque speciei, humanum
tantum commentum et mandatum est ; ita quod de Sacri-
ficio Missæ ex opere operato gratiam promerente traditur,
humana tantum opinio est, contra Verbum Dei, à quo in
rebus maximis, nempe ad remissionem peccatorum, salu-

tem animarum, et vitam æternam pertinentibus, nullo modo
est discedendum : Non enim frustra Paulus inquit et bis re-
petit, si nos aut Angelus de Cœlo Evangelizet vobis præter
id quod Evangelizavimus et accepistis, Anathema sit.

Præterea neo potest ratio diversitatis adsignari ex Sacris Literis, cur magis dicant eos qui Sacramento Eucharistiæ fruuntur Sacrificare, quam illos qui alio Sacramento,
ut Baptismo, utuntur, cum utrumque nihil aliud sit, quam
Sacramenta, quæ Christus horum institutor et auctor prorsus ad alium finem, quam ut sint talia Sacrificia, qualia
illi comminiscuntur, ordinavit. Sed oportuit, Romanum
Pontificem Missas privatas, ad opprimendam Christi, cum
ipse hostis est, gloriam attollere, ut populum Christianum
a veritate Evangelica et agnitione Christi, et Sacramentorum legitimo usu, prorsus abduceret, Christique bonitatem
et misericordiam obliteraret. Qui enim Missam tale Sacrificium esse cogitant, quo Deus placetur, hi non queunt
Christi beneficium expendere pro dignitate, et in terroribus
ac doloribus iræ et judicii Dei non habebunt refugium, neque bona conscientia poterunt dona et signa amoris divina
agnoscere, si alieno opere Deum placari et peccata remitti
sibi persuasum habeant: Nam illi ipsi qui nituntur impias
opiniones de Missa privata excusare, hoc prætextu, quasi
Missa ideo vocetur Sacrificium, quia sit gratiarum actio et
sacrificium laudis, hi convincuntur propriis ipsorum testimoniis et Scriptis quæ de Missis extant, hæque persua-
siones hominum animis etiam hodie de Missis privatis in-
hærent: sic enim Thomas inquit in Opusculo de Sacramento Altaris, cur Missa instituta sit? Corpus Domini
semel oblatum est in cruce, pro debito originali, sic offeratur jugiter pro quotidianis delictis in Altari, ut habeat in
hoc Ecclesia munus ad placandum sibi Deum super omnia
legis Sacrificia preciosum et acceptum.

Alexander Papa, nihil in Sacrificiis Ecclesiæ majus
esse potest, quam Corpus et Sanguis Christi, nec ulla oblatio hac potior est, sed omnes præcellit: item ipsa veritas
nos instruit, Calicem ac Panem in Sacramento offerre,
quando ait, accipite et comedite, nam crimina atq; peccata, oblatis his Domino Sacrificiis, delentur. Et rursus, inquit, talibus hostiis delectabitur et placabitur Deus, et
peccata dimittet ingentia. Gabriel de Canon. Missæ, Sa-

cramentum Eucharistiæ veluti Sacrificium summo patri oblatum, nedum veniale sed etiam mortale, non dico sumen-
tium sed omnium eorum pro quibus offertur, et quantum
ad reatum culpæ et pœnæ, plus vel minus secundum dispositionem eorum pro quibus offertur, tollit: unde Thomas
in Quarto Dist. 1, 2. q. 2. Eucharistia in quantum est Sacrificium, habet effectum etiam in aliis pro quibus offertur,
in quibus non præ-exigit vitam spiritualem in actu, sed in
potentia, et ideo si eos dispositos inveniat, eis gratiam ob-
tinet, virtute illius veri Sacrificii a quo omnis gratia in nos
fluxit, et per consequens peccata mortalia in eis delet, non
sicut causa proxima, sed in quantum gratiam contritionis
eis impetrat.

His et similibus omnes libri Scholasticorum pleni sunt,
quibus uno ore docent, Missam tale esse Sacrificium, quo
gratiam homines mereantur ex opere operato, quod ad de-
lenda aliorum peccata adplicari possit. Quæ Doctrina
aut potius perversum et impium figmentum, an pugnet cum
Saoris Literis necne? An verum Missæ seu communionis
usum tradat necne? An Christi beneficium non magis
obscuret quam illustret, imo etiam prorsus tollat? Vestræ
Serenissimæ Regiæ Majestati dijudicandum relinquimus
quæ pro sua sapientia, et non tantum in rebus politicis,
sed etiam Sacris et in omni genere doctrinarum acerrimo
judicio, facile censebit, justissimam causam habuisse Principes nostros et alios Evangelii Doctrinam profitentes, Missas privatas abrogandi, et verum Missæ sive Communionis
usum, pro Christi gloria et consolatione totius Ecclesiæ
Christianæ, restituendi et revocandi, postquam ex Dei Verbo cognoverunt, quantum privatæ Missæ à veritate Evangelica distent, quantumq; in iis insit impietatis et idololatriæ: fuit enim unicum Sacrificium propitiatorium in mundo, viz. Mors Christi, qui, ut Paulus inquit, semel est pro
nobis oblatus, et factus hostia pro peccatis nostris, quod
cætera legis Sacrificia propitiatoria significarunt, quæ si-
militudine quadam, erant satisfactioues redimentes justitiam legis, ne ex politia excluderentur illi qui peccaverant,
eaq; cessaverunt post Revelatum Evangelium: in Novo
Testamento, necesse est cultum tantum esse Spiritualem,
hoc est, justitiam fidei et fructus fidei, quia adfert justitiam et vitam spiritualem et æternam, juxta, Dabo legem

meam in cordibus eorum; et Christus ait, veri adoratores adorabunt Patrem in spiritu et veritate, id est, vero cordis adfectu, qua de causa abrogati sunt Levitici cultus, quod debeant succedere cultus Spirituales mentis, et horum fructus ac signa, ut in Epistola ad Hebræos manifeste docetur.

Ex quibus omnibus sequitur Missam non esse Sacrificium, quod ex opere operato mereatur, faciente vel aliis remissionem peccatorum, ut illi docuerunt. Et quocunq; quidam fuco nitantur excusare Missas privatas, semper eis refragatur et reclamat Doctrina ipsorum de Missa, qua eam aliis posse adplicari tradiderunt, et peccata delere hominibus persuaserunt. Hæc opinio nisi restituto vero Missæ usu, nunquam ex animis hominum delebitur, sed perpetuo manet et redit is error, quod oporteat talem esse cultum in Ecclesia, quo Deus placetur.

Et ut videatur fictione juris; ut Jureconsulti loquuntur, Missam posse vocari sacrificium memoriale sive laudis: at cum id non sit satisfactorium pro facientibus, vel adplicabile pro aliis, quo quis mereatur remissionem peccatorum, quorsum attinebit, relicto vero ejus usu et institutione, id in Ecclesiam introducere, ubi propter nullam humanam rationem, commentum, aut opinionem, à Christi mandato et ordinatione, est discedendum? Eadem enim ratione; Natalis Domini et similia festa, quæ in Christi memoriam celebrantur, sacrificia memorialia sive Eucharistica dici possent; imo talia Sacrificia verius sunt, Evangelii prædicatio, fides, invocatio, gratiarum actio, adflictiones, aut adplicationes pro aliis; et Missæ principalis finis, ut supra disseruimus, is est, ut sit Sacramentum, quod per ministrum alteri exhibeatur, quare non potest dici Sacrificium; cum nemo ignoret magnum inter Sacrificia et Sacramenta discrimen esse, his enim nos dona à Deo oblata accipimus, illis vero nostrum Deo reddimus et offerimus.

Neque vero habent privatæ Missæ alios auctores quam Pontifices, qui à tempore Gregorii, nunc hanc, nunc illam cæremoniam, cantionem, aut orationem, singuli pro sua sanctitate et opinione adjecerunt, ut historiæ uno consensu testantur, donec eandem, egregium illud opus, dignum istis auctoribus exædificarunt, et relicto vero Missæ sive Communionis usu, ac obliterata doctrina de Christo, Universa Ecclesia Missis privatis in qua sola omnem pæne sanctitatem posuerunt, repleta et obruta fuit.

Hæc Serenissime ac Potentissime Rex, nostrorum Principum et aliorum Imperii ordinum, Evangelicam Doctrinam profitentium, Theologi et Doctores, justis voluminibus explicarunt, quæ quidem hac Epistola nos breviter adtingenda duximus; non quod Serenissimam Regiam Majestatem Vestram hæc latere penitus putemus, neque enim ignoramus Serenissimæ Regiæ Majestati Vestræ et veterum et recentium scripta, de his et aliis Controversiis Ecclesiasticis diligentissime cognita esse, de quibus etiam Majestas Vestra sapientissime eruditissime sæpe cum doctis viris conferre et disputare solet: Sed hæc ideo fecimus ut Majestati Vestræ quam posset fieri brevissime, occasionem et causas quasdam abolitarum privatarum Missarum apud nos, summa cum observantia ut decet exponeremus; et adversariorum calumnias, quibus cum apud Regiam Majestatem Vestram tum alias, undecunque quæsita et arrepta occasione, variis technis et figmentis, doctrinam sinceriorem gravare et in odium omnium perducere conantur, declinaremus.

Neque vero ambigimus quin Majestas Vestra, ut Rex eruditissimus et veritatis Evangelicæ amantissimus, facillime judicabit, quod non temere privatæ Missæ apud nos abrogatæ sint, sed justissimis et firmissimis rationibus, ex Dei Verbo quod solum errare non potest, sincere et absque sophistica deductis, pro conservanda et illustranda Christi Gloria, et hominum salute id factum esse: Et opponantur qualescunque excogitari possint cavillationes et sophismata, tamen adparebit nostros hoc agere quod sit tutius, dum retinent modum et formam institutionis Christi. Ac maxima pars Sacerdotum sua sponte apud nos desiit Missas privatas celebrare, posteaquam intellexerunt ex Evangelica Doctrina, quantum in iis erroris et impietatis esset; et plurimi ac doctissimi quique, qui Sacerdotia aut Parochias sub Magistratibus alienis a sincera Evangelii Doctrina tenebant, eas deseruerunt, ne cogerentur facere contra suas conscientias, seque ad ea loca in quibus Evangelii Doctrina libere prædicatur contulerunt; gravissimum enim est quenquam in re præsertim tali, quæ Dei gloriam lædit, ac Divino Verbo repugnat, tanquam ad cultum divinum adigi, et compelli.

Sed ne Serenissimæ Regiæ Majestati Vestræ prolixitate literarum simus molesti, desinemus plura de hoc articulo inpræsentiarum disserere.

Restat tertius locus instituti Argumenti, viz. de Conju- De Con-
gio Sacerdotum, quod itidem Romanus Episcopus contra jugio
Scripturam, contra leges naturæ, et contra omnem hones- dotum.
tatem prohibuit, ac multorum peccatorum, scelerum et turpitudinis occasionem præbuit: sed fortassis ne possit du-
bitari eum esse Christi adversarium, de quo cum illam ipsam prohibitionem, tum alia quædam quæ in illum solum
adperte quadrant, Scriptura clare prædixit, oportuit eum
talem legem Cælibatus Sacerdotalis sancire, ut sicut leo
ex unguibus, ita Papa, hoc est Antichristus, ab hac prohibitione Sanctissimi et in omnibus honorabilis conjugii, ag-
nosceretur; sic enim Paulus inquit, Spiritus autem manifeste dicit, quod in novissimis temporibus discedent quidam
à fide, attendentes Spiritibus Erroris et Doctrinis Dæmo-
niorum, in hypocrisi loquentium mendacium, cauteriatam
habentium conscientiam suam, prohibentium nubere: hæc
si non in Romanum Episcopum congruunt, in quem alium
convenient? nemo enim alius quam ipse conjugium Sacerdotibus injustissime eripuit, et cælibatum impurissimum
sub specie Sanctitatis, et ut Paulus ait in Hypocrisi et per
mendacium introduxit.

Scriptura non minus Sacerdotibus, quam alterius sortis
hominibus matrimonium liberum permittit, sunt enim de
eadem carne, quæ totum genus humanum vestit et continet,
nati: non possunt igitur naturam suam mutare, non possunt carnem abjicere, nec absque singulari Dei dono cælibes vivere, nam non quilibet, ut Christus inquit, capit Verbum hoc: et Paulus, propter Fornicationem unusquisque
suam Uxorem habeat; et peculiariter de Sacerdotibus ait,
constituas per civitates Presbyteros sicut disposui tibi, si
quis sine crimine est, unius Uxoris vir, Filios habens fideles, non in accusatione luxuriæ; item, oportet Episcopum
esse irreprehensibilem, unius Uxoris virum: patet igitur
hanc prohibitionem non ex jure Divino, sed potius contra
Sacram Scripturam decretum esse.

At solet a quibusdam Pontificiis defensoribus opponi,
quod licet conjugium Sacerdotum non videatur vetitum Divinis Literis, tamen Sacerdotes a veteribus temporibus in
hunc usque diem in cælibatu vixisse, eaque de causa addunt non esse discedendum hac in re a tali exemplo, neque
permittendum conjugium Sacerdotibus. His, Serenissime
ac potentissime Rex, adperte refragantur historiæ, tum Ec-

clesiasticæ tum aliæ, ex quibus clare patet, Episcopos et
Sacerdotes veteribus temporibus conjugatos fuisse.

Primum enim Spiridion Cyprius Episcopus, vir unus ex
ordine prophetarum, ut Historia Ecclesiastica ait, Uxorem
habuit ex qua filiam nomine Irenen suscepit; deinde ordine
pene omnes Episcopi Uxorati fuerunt, quorum plurimi Filii postea, tum Romani, tum alii Episcopi creati sunt: fuit
enim Sylverius Papa Hormisdæ Episcopi Filius, Papa
Theodorus Theodori Episcopi Hierosolymitani, Papa
Adrianus secundus Talari Episcopi, Joannes decimus Papa Sergii Papæ, Gelasius Valerii Episcopi, Papa Joannes
decimus quintus Leonis Presbyteri Filius; et ne omnes
enumeremus, patet vel unica historia Polycratis, ex cujus
parentibus septem fuerunt per ordinem Episcopi, ipse vero
fuit octavus: at non est credibile omnes illos ex illegitimis
nuptiis prognatos esse, cum ipsi canones et decreta Synodorum doceant, conjugia Sacerdotum esse licita; sic enim
inquit Canon Apostolorum, si quis docuerit Sacerdotem
sub obtentu Religionis propriam Uxorem contemnere,
Anathema sit.

Item extat præclarum exemplum de Paphnutio confes-
sore, qui universæ Synodo Nicenæ prohibitionem conjugii
dissuasit, et obtinuit ne hac ex parte sancitum, sed hoc in
uniuscujusque voluntate non necessitate permissum fuerit.
Quæ Historia etiam in jure Pontificio recensetur, extatque
decretum quoddam sextæ Synodi, in quo palam damnatur
prohibitio conjugii Sacerdotalis.

Sed objicitur iterum, propter votum castitatis, quod Sacerdotes præstiterunt, non posse eis permitti nuptias. Hoc
quale votum sit, quamque obligatorium, quod sine peccato
servari non potest, Serenissima Regia Majestas Vestra pro
summa sapientia et Doctrina, facile æstimabit: neque
enim donum castitatis omnibus datum est, idque cælibatus
ipse Sacerdotum, et quotidiana experientia etiam nunc testatur; et quid de tali voto sentiendum sit, Sanctorum Patrum sententia declaravit, sic enim Augustinus ait, quidam
nubentes post votum adserunt adulteros esse, ego autem
dico vobis quod graviter peccant qui tales dividunt. Et
Cyprianus de virginibus qui continentiam voverunt, sic inquit, si perseverare nolunt, vel non possunt, melius est ut
nubant, quam ut in ignem delitiis suis cadant.

Censent itaque prædicti Sancti Patres, tale votum non

debere impedire Matrimonium, sicut revera, etiam non potest obstare quo minus hi quibus donum continentiæ non contigit, matrimonium contrahant: nam melius est nubere quam uri, ut inquit Paulus; Quid autem est impurius cœlibatu illo Sacerdotali? quam pauci vero continent? quam plurimi in fornicationibus, adulteriis, et id genus similibus ac gravioribus peccatis et flagitiis pene quotidie deprehenduntur, contra quod si leges severe animadverterent, non habituri essent, quo de illo ficto et hypocritico cœlibatu adeo gloriarentur?

Ac tradunt Historiæ in Germania triennium aut amplius, Sacerdotes acerrime restitisse Sanctioni Pontificis Hildebrandi de cælibatu, qui summa vi eis Uxores adimere conatus est, hique justissimas causas contra illam constitutionem ac tyrannidem Pontificiam, pro Matrimonio defendendo allegarunt, in qua re cum nihil æqui obtinere potuerint, tandem ingens orta est seditio contra Archiepiscopum Moguntinum, qui decretum pontificium detulat, adeo ut is ab incæpto destiterit; et vix tandem Papa post multas diras execrationes et bullas, quibus etiam cœlum ipsum expugnare conatus est, miseris Sacerdotibus facultatem liberam conjugii, contra divina et humana jura abstulerit, et omnis generis libidinis et impuritatis exercendæ occasionem præbuerit; Extat quoque Epistola ad Nicolaum Episcopum Romanum I. Divi Udalrici Episcopi Augustensis, qua is gravissimis et optimis argumentis dissuadet et damnat prohibitionem conjugii Sacerdotum.

Cum igitur Principes nostri, et alii profitentes Evangelii Doctrinam, patefacta per Dei Gratiam iterum veritate, intellexerint quid de prohibitione illa pontificia conjugii Sacerdotalis sentiendum esset, et palam viderent et experirentur, quod non posset cœlibatus ille sine peccatis et scandalis consistere, ruperunt in ea etiam vincula pontificia, ac Matrimonium Sacerdotibus, sicut hoc Scriptura Sacra et exempla Sanctorum Patrum ac veteris Ecclesiæ exigunt et testantur, liberum permiserunt. Existimarunt enim hoc quoque ad suum officium pertinere, ut infinitorum scandalorum et scelerum, quæ necessario secum trahit cælibatus Sacerdotalis, occasionem et materiam præscinderent et auferrent, publicæque honestati hac quoque in re consulerent; maxime cum animadverterent quantæ etiam abominationes, et in ordine Sacerdotali, et in Monasteriis Vestalium ac Monachorum evenerint, in quibus compertum est sæpe infantes crudeliter necatos, pharmacis fœtus depulsos, et similia nefaria crimina commissa, quos solos fructus cælibatus ille protulit: ideoque plurimi nunc sunt conjugati Sacerdotes apud nos, multi etiam cælibes, idque cujusque conscientiæ ut vel ducat uxorem, vel a conjugio abstineat, permittitur; modo ita vivat ne sit aliis offendiculo, alioqui enim non minus in Sacerdotes quam reliquum vulgus, hac quoque parte, secundum leges politicas animadvertitur. Ac per Dei Gratiam, hoc inde secutum est, quod eorum conscientiis, quibus continentiæ donum non contigit, consultum fuerit, plurimorum flagitiorum et scelerum occasio cessaverit, matronis ac puellis quibus plerique istorum sub specie pietatis sæpissime inhiabant, et laqueos nectebant, nihil ejusmodi periculi sit; et in summa, quod quum tum Officia Ecclesiastica tum politica majore reverentia et honestate tractentur, quodque ab universis in majore honore et favore habeantur Sacerdotes, quam antea in illo pleno scandalis cælibatu acciderit, id quoque magna ex parte honestum conjugium Sacerdotum præstat.

Adhæc, nulli acrius et constantius oppugnant Romanum Pontificem, et tum Matrimonii libertatem, tum sanam Doctrinam ab illo obscuratam et oppressam defendunt, quam hi qui ab ejus jugo impuri illius cælibatus liberati sunt: et honeste etiam suos liberos, quos ex conjugio suscipiunt educare solent, quibus haud dubie Deus etiam post mortem parentum, ubi in timore Domini aliti et edocti fuerint, prospiciet; gravissimum enim esset, Sacerdotes ideo a conjugio arcere, quia sua munia sive officia tantum ad vitam suam, non autem jure hæreditario tenent; eadem ratione multis aliis qui sunt aut in publicis muneribus, aut in privatis Ministeriis, Matrimonium interdicendum foret. Quod quidem si fieret, Reip. plus incommodi quam boni allaturum esset; cum et Sacrarum Literarum Auctoritate, Sanctissimorum Patrum Sententiis, legum naturæ et gentium testimonio, et omnium sapientissimorum virorum judicio ac suffragiis constet, Matrimonium semper iis qui cælibes vivere non queant, ad vitanda graviora pericula, concessum et liberum esse debere.

Hæc, Serenissime ac invictissime Rex, coram Serenissi-

ma Regia Majestate Vestra, breviter disserenda duximus, ut
Majestati Vestræ rationes quasdam commemoraremus, cur
Illustrissimi Principes nostri, et alii Evangelii Doctrinam
profitentes Principes et Status Imperii, in his tribus Articulis adeo dissentiant a Romano Pontifice, ut sicut in reliquis Doctrinæ Christianæ partibus, a veritate vel latum
digitum non discedendum esse existiment, ita in his etiam
decreverint, abjecta ejus tyrannide, pro Gloria Evangelii,
et ad vitanda infinita scelera, perdurare: neque vero hic
dicemus de aliis abusibus a Romano Pontifice introductis,
in quos imprimis Confessio Auricularis recenseri meretur,
qua ille, et Potestatem clavium tantum ad turpissimum
quæstum et tyrannidem redegit, et Confessionem ipsam,
quæ informandarum et consolandarum conscientiarum gratia salubriter instituta fuit, carnificinam tantum Conscientiarum reddidit, perque eam tum omnes Reges, Principes,
et Potentatus sub suo jugo tenuit, tum multorum malorum
auctor extitit; de qua quid nostri sentiant, ac qua reverentia
in Ecclesiis retineant, edita ipsorum scripta testantur.

Ac gratulamur nobis datam occasionem hæc Serenissimæ Regiæ Majestati Vestræ exponendi, ejusq; censuræ
committendi: Cum enim Majestas Vestra et summa Doctrina, sapientia ac studio veritatis prædita sit, et Romani
Episcopi tyrannidem (haud sine mente deum, sive numine
divum, ut Poeta inquit) itidem ex suis amplissimis Regnis
exterminari curaverit, neque amplius per Dei Gratiam illius
impiis opinionibus captiva teneatur; persuasissimum nobis habemus Vestræ Serenissimæ Regiæ Majestatis hisce
de rebus maximis, quæ ad Dei Gloriam, salutem Ecclesiæ,
et perpetuam profligationem Romani Antichristi pertinent,
æquissimum ac liberrimum fore judicium, quod sane ii,
quibus vel Doctrina aut veritatis studium deest, vel animum habent addictum Pontificiis Opinionibus, vel metu
interdum prohibentur, aut etiam ab affectibus diverse tra-
huntur, non adeo facile præstare possunt; et plurimi interdum inservientes tempori, fingunt se odiisse pontificem, si-
mulantque studium veritatis, quibus tamen revera aliud est
cordi, hi vero quum non possint nec debeant de hisce controversiis ferre sententiam, Serenissima Regia Majestas
Vestra nequaquam ignorat.

Non autem dubitamus, quin ut quisque est eruditissimus,

et veritatis Evangelicæ amantissimus, ita facillime cum causam nostram immo Christi et Ecclesiæ adprobaturum esse, neque enim ea ullum commodum aut emolumentum privatum quæritur, sed solum agitur de abolendis impiis abusibus in Christi Ecclesiam per Antichristum invectis, et Christi Gloria illustranda, ac veris cultibus restituendis, et ut hominum Conscientiæ jugo ac tyrannide pontificia liberentur, ac scandala publica, quantum fieri possit è medio tollantur. Quarum quidem rerum studium quo jure reprehendi queat, ut etiam magis favore et imitatione dignum censendum sit: Cum enim omnium bene constitutarum Rerumpub. hic præcipue finis et scopus esse debeat, ut et Dei Gloria ornetur, et publica salus, honestas, pax, et tranquillitas conservetur, quis dubitat eos qui sedent ad gubernacula Rerumpub. et ad hæc tanquam ad Cynosuram ut dici solet, cursum suum et omnem rationem regendi Rempublicam instituunt, maximis laudibus dignos esse? Et quoniam Serenissima Regia Vestra Majestas, ut Rex sapientissimus et eruditissimus, hunc quoque scopum in gubernandis amplissimis et laudatissimis Regnis et Provinciis suis, ob oculos habere luce meridiana clarius adparet, non possumus non nobisipsis, quum in hac honestissima causa promovendæ Christi gloriæ et publicæ utilitatis ad Serenissimam Regiam Majestatem Vestram Oratores missi sumus, non gratulari; non possumus etiam non fælices judicare universos subditos Majestatis Vestræ, quibus divina bonitate talis Rex et Princeps contigerit, qui cum aliis regiis virtutibus excellit, tum studio veræ pietatis et veritatis Evangelicæ omnibus modis admirandus conspicitur.

Sunt quidem illa maxima Remp. certis et justis legibus civilibus constituere, bonos tueri et juvare, improbos pœnis adficere, arcere injurias, pacem et concordiam subditorum conservare; quis enim non tanquam Deum aliquem talem Principem amplectendum et honorandum putet, a quo ista præstentur: sed adhuc sunt majora, si vera pietas accesserit, si Christi Gloria ornetur, si Dei Verbum in pretio habeatur, si cultus Divinæ voluntati consentanei instituantur, si hominum conscientiis consulatur, et publica scandala e medio tollantur; illa enim tantum hanc civilem vitam attingunt, quam unumquemq; quum tempus præfi-

nitum advenerit, deserere oportet ; hæc vero ad æternam
salutem pertinent quæ bonos et pios, cessante hac misera
conditione humanæ vitæ, expectat, quibusq; et in hoc, et
in futuro sæculo, maxima præmia proposita sunt. Hoc est
cur Deus Reges honore sui nominis ornat, cum ait, ego
dixi Dii estis, maxime ut res divinas intelligant, et veram
Religionem in mundo conservent ; huc præcipue Scriptura
hortatur, cum inquit, nunc Reges intelligite, et erudimini
qui judicatis terram, servite Domino, &c. huc invitant exempla præstantissimorum regum in Sacris Literis, qui
summa cura, opera, ac studio veram Religionem promo-
verunt, et impios cultus abrogarunt : hoc David, hoc Josias, hoc Josophat, hoc Ezechias, et deinceps omnes Sanctissimi Reges præstiterunt. Eadem cum Sereniss. R. M.
Vestra haud dubie etiam cogitet, imo jam nunc in hoc totis
viribus incumbat, ut sincera Evangelii Doctrina Papæ Tyrannide oppressa restituatur, Gloria Christi itidem a Pontifice obscurata iterum illustretur, et impii abusus ab illo
ipso Antichristo in Ecclesiam tanquam venenum quoddam
pestilentissimum sparsi et introducti aboleantur, ac veri et
Divinis Literis consentanei cultus et cæremoniæ consti-
tuantur, non dubitabimus quin Deus Opt. Max. Sereniss.
R. Majestatis Vestræ conatus et consilia, in hisce rebus
Sanctissimis et Honestissimis fortunaturus sit, et pro sua
bonitate clementer effecturus, ut inter Sereniss. R. M.
Vestram et Principes nostros, ac eorum in causa Religionis
confæderatos, talis concordia constituatur, quám et in
laudem Evangelii, et publicam totius Christiani Orbis
utilitatem cessuram, et majori exitio Romano Antichristo
futuram esse, minime ambigimus ; estque optima spes, ut
volente Deo, plures Reges, Principes, et potentatus, ad
hanc Sanctissimam causam accedant, ac Evangelicæ veritatis Doctrinam agnoscant et recipiant, sicut etiam hactenus per Dei Gratiam, maximi progressus facti sunt, et
non tantum in Germania, verum etiam extra Germaniam,
Potentissimi Reges, Principes et civitates, Divini Verbi
Doctrinam receperunt.

Adparetque homines passim agnita veritate, ex Scriptis
eorum qui Evangelii Doctrinam profitentur et docent, per
totum pene orbem terrarum sparsis, sanioris Doctrinæ admodum cupidos esse, quorum preces aliquando Deus pro

sua benignitate exaudiet, ac suum Verbum illuminatis mentibus Regum et Principum latissime propagabit, ut sit unus pastor, hoc est Dominus noster Iesus Christus, et unum ovile quod est Ecclesia Catholica, quæ profitetur sincerum Christi Evangelium, et illi consentaneum usum Sacramentorum retinet, non Papistica aut Romana, quæ utramque reprobat, odit, et oppugnat.

Quod reliquum est, Serenissime ac Potentissime Rex, Domine Clementissimo, precamur et optamus ut Sereniss. Regia Majestas Vestra in cæpto negotio veritatis Evangelicæ pro illustranda Christi Gloria et salute publica, per Dei Gratiam fortiter pergat, quod quidem Majestatem Vestram, ut Regem veræ pietatis et omnis virtutis ac Doctrinæ amantissimum, facturam nihil dubitamus: Oramusque ut Serenissima Regia Majestas Vestra dato benigno responso, ad Illustrissimos Principes nostros, quam primum fieri queat, ne commodam præsentis Navigationis occasionem negligamus, clementer nos dimittat; et ut Serenissima Regia Majestas Vestra, erga quam nostra debita officia atque servitia summa cum observantia perpetue constabunt, has nostras literas pro sua insigni humanitate, bonitate ac clementia, in optimam partem accipiat, nosque etiam clementer commendatos habeat. Bene valeat Serenissima Regia Majestas Vestra, quam Deus Opt. Max. pro illustranda et propaganda nominis sui Gloria et publica salute,¹ diu servet incolumem. Datæ Londini quinto die Augusti Anno Dom. 1538.

Vestræ Serenissimæ Regiæ
Majestatis

Addictissimi et obsequentissimi,

Franciscus Burgratus
Vicecancellarius.

Georgius a Boyneburgh
D. Oratores.

Fridericus Myconius
Ecclesiastes Gothanus.

VIII.

The King's Answer to the former Letter.

LITERAS Vestras, Egregii ac præstantissimi Oratores, per ministrum vestrum nuper ad nos missas summa humanitate plenas, atque ingentem erga nos benevolentiam spirantes, tum libenter accepimus, tum magna cum voluptate legimus; quibus significatis vos, post exposita nobis mandata, cum quibusdam Episcopis et Theologiæ Doctoribus a nobis designatis de Christianæ Religionis nonnullis articulis per duos menses contulisse; non dubitare quoque quin inter Principes vestros et nos, atq; utrorumq; Episcopos Theologos et subditos, firma perpetuaq; concordia in Evangelii Doctrina ad laudem Dei, et Romani Antichristi perniciem sit sequutura; Verum quia reliquam disputationem de abusibus expectare non potestis, cum jam naves appulerint vos in patriam deportaturæ, ante discessum vestrum existimatis vestri officii esse ut sententiam vestram de quibusdam abusuum articulis nobis declaretis, de quibus nos post discessum vestrum cum Episcopis et Theologis nostris conferre possemus. Et quia tria capita præcipua putatis, quæ fundamentum Pontificiæ Tyrannidis sustentare videntur, nempe Prohibitionem utriusque speciei in cæna Domini, Missas privatas, et Prohibitionem Conjugii Sacerdotum; de his articulis sententiam vestram ingenue aperitis, atque eam judicio nostro quantumcunq; id sit, et censuræ committitis: Quis non hanc vestram benevolentiam, Egregii Oratores, summopere amplectatur, Quis non hanc Vestram gratitudinem modis omnibus admiretur? Qui nobiscum ea communicare studetis, quæ non modo ad præsentem vitam transigendam sed ad futuram quoque assequendam conferunt? Enimvero si illos non abs re existimamus amicos, qui in Regionum commerciis ea quæ sunt grata atque commoda important, ne quid usquam desit quod ad præsentem vitam degendam pertinet, quanto magis illi sunt amici judicandi, qui quæ ad æternam vitam conferunt impertiri non gravantur! nam quæ præsentis vitæ subsidia parantur durabilia diu non sunt, quæ vero ad æternam promovent nunquam intermoriuntur; quinimo amicitia ipsa terrena, quantumvis ingens, quantumvis firma, finem habet è vita

Cott.
Libr.
Cleop.
E. 5.

excessum, charitas vero quæ nunquam excidit post hanc
vitam splendescit magis. Et quia nostrum judicium non
aspernari videmini, quod nos ipsi indignum existimamus,
ut de rebus tam arduis judicemus, atque ea proponitis quæ
putatis inprimis amplectenda, qua in re non vulgarem sed
ingentem vim erga nos amoris ostenditis, ne nos non respondere huic vestræ tantæ gratitudini videremur, si quæ
nobis ad præsens videntur vobiscum non communicare-
mus, decrevimus itidem de his tribus Articulis nonnihil at-
tingere, et pectus nostrum ingenue vobis aperire: Quo fiet
ut mutuus inter nos et Principes vestros amor eo magis
augescat, eo diutius foveatur, si nihil occultum inter amicos retentetur, sed summa sinceritate gerantur omnia, id
quod nos cum omnibus amicis semper facere consuevimus; quod nostrum perpetuum institutum in præsentia
apud Amicissimos, eosque quos habemus charissimos,
mutare nequaquam libuit. Verum de Articulis ipsis tandem agamus.

De utraque Specie.

Quod inprimis sub utraq; Specie semper Eucharistiam
populis secundum primariam Christi institutionem dandam
esse existimetis, et nullo pacto sub altera tantum, non
possumus quovis pacto adduci, egregii et præstantissimi
Oratores, ut putemus vos id ferio affirmasse, sed forsan
probandi causa nobis id protulisse, ut quid sentiamus in-
telligeretis; nam ipsa opinio tam aliena est a recta Scripturæ intelligentia, ut vix quivis id serio affirmare præsu-
meret, quod latius in hac Epistola declarabimus. Nec
nobis persuadere possumus, etsi occasio sit, vos non nobiscum credere, quod sub specie Panis sit realiter et sub-
stantialiter verum et vivum Corpus Christi, et una cum
Corpore Sanguis verus, alioqui fatendum esset Corpus ibi
exsangue esse, quod nefas esset dicere, cum Caro illa
Christi non modo viva, sed et vivificatrix sit; et quod sub
specie vini non modo vivus et verus Christi Sanguis sit,
sed etiam una cum vero Sanguine viva et vera etiam Corporis sit Caro. Quod cum ita sit, necessario consequetur
etiam eos qui sub altera specie communicant, et solum
sub specie Panis Corpus Christi sumunt, non fraudari

Communione Sanguinis Christi, atque eos etiam qui sub
specie vini Communicant non fraudari communione Corporis Domini ; Quocirca cum sub alterutra specie utrumq;
contineatur, viz. et Corpus .et Sanguis Christi, utravis solum species porrigatur populis, utrumque, id est tam Sanguis quam Corpus Christi, per hoc eisdem exhibeatur.
Nam Christus ipse sub altera specie dedisse legitur in
Evangelio Lucæ Discipulis duobus in Emaus euntibus,
quando agnitus est in fractione Panis; scribitur enim, quod
cum recumberet cum eis, accepit panem et benedixit, ac
fregit et porrigebat illis, et aperti sunt oculi eorum, et
cognoverunt eum fractione panis. Ubi de Eucharistia eum
locum vetustissimi Authores Chrysostomus, Theophylac-
tus, et Augustinus intelligunt, et tamen de vini poculo nulla
ibi fit mentio : Unde Christus qui in altera specie minis-
travit Eucharistiam, libertatem Ecclesiæ sponsæ suæ reliquisse videtur, ut imitetur sponsi sui vestigia, ac similiter sub altera specie, sicut sub utraque, communicare libere possit. Nam Christus qui sub utraq; specie Communionem docuit, etiam de Communione sub altera ipse exemplum reliquit, qui secum tamen nusquam vel in præceptis, vel in exemplis dissidet.

Simile idem Lucas in Actis Apostolorum citat, quando
post adventum Spiritus Sancti, prædicante Petro, appo-
sitæ sunt animæ circiter tria millia, inquiens, Erant autem
perseverantes in Doctrina Apostolorum et Communicatione
et fractione panis et orationibus ; Ubi similiter de Eucharistia eum locum intelligunt veteres, et de poculo nulla fit
ibi mentio. Jam si Christum ipsum Autorem, si Apostolos
ab eo ad docendum orbem missos patronos habet, Communio sub una specie nempe Panis, usitata in Ecclesia non
est tanquam Evangelicis præceptis contraria, statim repu-
dianda; nam Apostoli, qui per adventum Spiritus edocti
sunt omnem veritatem, nunquam in fractione Panis Communionem dedissent populo, si utraq; species de præcepto
Christi semper necessario fuisset porrigenda, ne Christi
jubentis parum memores institutum ejus mutasse viderentur.

Porro ipsa Christi Verba, quæ post Evangelistas Paulus
totam cœnam dominicam Corinthiis enarrans citat, nos
admonent Christum separatim de alterutra specie locutum

esse; ait enim, Dominus Iesus in qua nocte tradebatur, accepit panem et gratias agens fregit, et dixit, accipite et manducate, Hoc est Corpus meum quod pro vobis traditur, hoc facite in mei commemorationem. Ecce Christus de Corpore suo sub specie panis sumendo separatim locutus est, inquiens, Hoc facite, priusquam ullam de poculo faceret mentionem. Postea autem de Calice ait Paulus, Similiter et Calicem postquam coenavit accepit dicens, Hic calix Novum Testamentum est in meo sanguine, hoc facite quotiescunq; bibetis in mei commemorationem : Nec dixit sicut de corpore dixerat simpliciter, Hoc facite in mei commemorationem, sed dixit, Hoc facite, cum hac adjectione, nempe quotiescunq; bibetis in mei commemorationem, per hoc nobis indicans, non semper sub specie vini sumendum esse sanguinem una cum corpore sub specie Panis, sed quotiescunq; sumeretur Sanguis sub specie Vini in Commemorationem Christi, id faciendum.

Ecce rursum Christus post distributionem corporis sui, peracta coena in qua corpus suum sub specie Panis separatim prius dederat, iterum separatim sub specie Vini Sanguinem suum offert, inquiens, Hoc facite quotiescunq; bibetis in mei commemorationem, significans nobis et seorsum nonnunquam alteram porrigi posse, et tamen eum ita sit, utriusq; vim integram populis dari, alioqui suffecisset semel duntaxat de utroq; fuisse dictum, Hoc facite, nec de Calice adjecisset Hoc facite quotiescunque bibetis, cum prius de specie Panis simpliciter dixisset Hoc facite, nisi separatim ea sumi posse judicaret.

Neque quisquam negare potest Discipulos in coena sub specie panis sumpsisse Corpus Christi, nam coenantibus illis, accepit panem et benedixit ac fregit deditq; illis, dicens, Hoc est Corpus meum; Calicem autem non nisi post intervallum ac peracta coena porrexit, nisi quis adeo stupidus esset, ut crederet post sumptionem speciei panis non prius eos sumpsisse Corpus Christi, quum postquam coenavit porrexisset Calicem; quasi vero priora Verba Christi irrita fuissent, cum de specie panis diceret Hoc est Corpus meum, aut ipsa distributio facta Discipulis nullam vim haberet, priusquam de Calice peracta Coena bibissent; Quod cum impium sit sentire, tum ipsum Verbum et factum Christi, proh nefas! evacuat. Denique ipse Paulus, postquam etiam de utraque specie conjunctim locutus est, rursum de ipsis speciebus disjunctim infert, inquiens ὥστε ὃς ἂν ἐσθίει τὸν ἄρτον τοῦτον, ἢ πίνει τὸ ποτήριον τοῦ Κυρίου ἀναξίως, ἔνοχος ἐστὶ τοῦ σώματος καὶ αἵματος τοῦ Κυρίου.

Quæ verba latine sic transtulit Erasmus, Itaq; quisquis ederit panem hunc aut de Calice biberit indigne, reus erit corporis et sanguinis Domini; ubi ex Pauli verbis aperte liquet, Quisquis indigne panem hunc sumpserit, reum esse Corporis et Sanguinis Domini, aut siquis de Calice biberit indigne, similiter reum esse Sanguinis et Corporis Domini, quod tamen nullo modo crimini daretur, nisi seorsum sub specie panis esset et Corpus et Sanguis Christi, atq; itidem sub specie vini seorsum esset et Corpus et Sanguis Christi; nec disjunctim de specie panis locutus fuisset Paulus, si nunquam nisi conjunctim cum Calice sumeretur: Neq; rursum disjunctim de Calice dixisset, si nunquam nisi conjunctim cum specie panis esset sumendus. Quorsum enim ea disjunxisset si nunquam nisi conjuncta esse possent? At Verba ipsa Scripturæ singula sunt attendenda, nam Propheta inquit, Inclinate aurem vestram in Verba oris mei; et Moises in Deuteronomio ait, Ponite corda vestra in omnia verba quæ ego testificor vobis hodie, quia non incassum præcepta sunt vobis. Et iterum, non addetis ad verbum quod vobis loquor, nec auferetis ab eo. Verba igitur Domini atque ipsius Pauli, et separatim de alterutra specie primum posita, et post utriusque conjunctionem etiam iterum disjuncta, significare nobis videntur, et posse alterutram speciem seorsum porrigi secundum Verbum Christi.

Nec per hoc quod Christus dixit, Bibite ex hoc omnes, statim consequetur Christum jussisse Communionem cuilibet de populo semper sub utraq; specie et nunquam sub altera dandam esse: Nam illorum Verborum sensum non alium esse apparet, quam quem ipse Dominus Apostolum suum Paulum, qui a Domino de hoc Sacramento omnia se accepisse testatur, edocuit, nempe quod quotiescunq; de Calice hoc quisquam biberet, id in Christi memoriam faceret, sicut fecerunt Discipuli, qui tunc aderant præsentes et de eo biberunt omnes: Itaque quotiescunque Sanguis Christi bibendus a quoquam esset, in memoria Passio Christi recordanda est; sicut similiter quisquis Corpus

Christi sumpserit, ad memoriam passionem ejus revocare debet: Neque ex præcepto Christi toties bibendum esse de hoc Calice, quotiescunq; Corpus Christi sumendum est, apparet per ea quæ de verbis et de exemplo Christi supradicta sunt. Certe quicquid Christus omnino observari præcepit, non posse ulla humana sanctione prohiberi putamus, cum humana lex divinam abolere non possit. Similiter etiam existimamus, nec morem ullum, nec ullam consuetudinem tantopere apud homines valere debere, ut Dei Verbum expugnet et Christi præceptum subvertat.

Verumtamen cum Christus nobis libere reliquerit ut eum tribus modis corporaliter sumere possimus, et quarto spiritualiter, nempe primo, sub utraque specie, secundo, sub Panis specie tantum; tertio, sub Vini; quarto, voluntate et desiderio solo cum aliter necessitate coacti eum sumere nequimus; existimamus pro primo, ut siquis fidelis ardenti in Deum amore flagrans, pietateq; ingenti æstuans, magnopere desideraret Sacramentum sub utraq; specie sumere, si nullum vel valetudinis vel imbecillitatis obstaret impedimentum, ei sub utraq; specie Communio præberi possit, dummodo neq; postulans neq; ministrans Sacramentum in scandalum populi, aut in contemptum Ecclesiæ id faciat, neque suo jure leges religionis in qua degit sive Ecclesiasticas sive laicas infringere præsumat.

Pro secundo et tertio sic, Quod si impedimentum aliquod hujusmodi intervenit, ut in utraque specie absq; periculo sumi non possit, ut si quis Paralysi correptus, aut ab alio quovis naturæ aut morborum impedimento utramq; speciem recipere commode non possit, hic si desideret Sacram Communionem sumere, ei sub altera tantum specie porrigatur. Pro quarto autem, Quod si quis nausea, vel alia corporis molestia adeo sit infestatus, ut nihil in stomachum receptum non rejectet, huic si id petat, Sacramentum saltem ostendi posset, ut viso eo mortem Christi redemptoris sui citius revocans in memoriam compunctus corde spiritualiter communicet.

Plurimum igitur demiror, quod hi qui Christianæ Libertatis assertores et acerrimi propugnatores videri volunt, libertatem hanc nostram in hoc uno Corporis et Sanguinis Domini Sacramento, quo nihil superexcellentius, nihil celebrius, nihil incomparabilius, nihil deniq; ad conso-

landos fidelium animos solidius, Christus hinc abiturus
Ecclesiæ suæ reliquit, nobis tollere velint; Quid enim
majus donare potuit Christus in hoc Sacramento sumendum quam seipsum? Deinde cum ipse omnino liberum
nobis reliquerit, et posse aliquos sub utraq; specie Communionem accipere, et posse alios sub altera, nonnullos
quoq; morborum necessitate impeditos, saltem in conspec-
tum prolato Corpore Domini compuncto corde posse Spiritualiter communicare, quanta immodestia, quanta incle-
mentia esset, libertate hac fraudare Christianos? Ut quibus sub utraq; specie, ob impedimenta quæ sunt innumera,
Communio præberi non posset, his summi boni fruitione
privatis sub neutra darétur! Nec adhuc fatentur et si non
corporaliter sumatur, saltem Spiritualiter capi posse. Qua
non servitute durior esset hæc conditio, ut Christi redemptoris nostri corpus, quod ille a fidelibus sumi voluit, nobis
id summopere desiderantibus violenter eripiatur; quis ingenue Christianus libertatem fruitionis hujus sibi extortam
non omni morte intolerabiliorem putaret? Itaq; libertas hæc
a Christo nobis relicta omni conatu retinenda est, omnibus
viribus amplectenda, nec ipsis mea opinione fidendum est,
qui eam nobis tollere velint.

Præterea, quid fiat apud septentrionales populos? quid
apud populos Aphricæ et qui intra Tropicos habitant?
apud quos non ea vini copia est ut populis omnino sub
specie vini præberi possit, (nam his populis cervisia ex
frugibus est potui) an ideo quia sub utraq; specie his ministrari Sacramentum non potest, ab utraq; arcendi essent?
aut sub una non integrum Christum capere possent? id
quod absit.

Quando autem primum populus priscum morem deserere, et sub altera tantum panis specie Communionem
sacram sumere cœpit, nobis est incompertum; credibile
est majores nostros auctoritate Scripturæ motos, quæ alteram nonnunquam speciem per Christum et Apostolos
datam memorat, propter periculum effusionis in terram
Sanguinis Christi, cum liquida omnia levi membrorum
trepidante motu facile effundantur, religiosa quadam et pia
reverentia, non mediocriq; Dei timore abstinuisse in Sacramento a vini specie, nec Christum qui se cum Ecclesia
usque in finem omnibus diebus mansurum promisit, tot

sæculis eam deseruisse, ut si necessarium præceptum de utraq; specie semper ab omnibus sumenda dedisset, in re tanti momenti eam permisisset turpiter labi; sed magis Ecclesiæ suæ liberum reliquisse videtur, ut cum in alterutra specie totus et integer Christus contineatur, sub altera etiam sumi possit,

Qui vero sit mos hodie de utraq; specie in Ecclesiis Græcis, quæ Romanæ Ecclesiæ Tyrannidem nunquam admiserunt, non satis nobis est compertum, cum Græcia tota Turcarum subsit imperio, nec liberam habeant facultatem Christum ut libet profitendi, quando nec Verbum Dei publice prædicare, nec ad Campanarum sonitum populum convocare, nec publicas Litanias crucis vexillo præeunte facere, his ullo pacto est concessum,

Illud quoq; inprimis est observandum, nempe quod in Universis Ecclesiis in die Parasceves Sacerdos et omnis populus sub una tantum specie panis communicant, non sub specie Vini; ut cum is dies repræsentat mortem Christi in qua sanguis ejus pretiosus pro nostra salute effusus est et separatus a corpore, separatim illo die sub altera solum specie communicarent omnes sive Sacerdos sive populus; qui mos per universam Ecclesiam nunquam fuisset admissus, nisi sub altera tantum specie integer Christus contineretur, atq; nisi sub altera Sacramentum populis ministrari posset.

De Missa Privata.

Per Missas autem privatas multos abusus introductos esse dicitis, quas velut Atlantem quendam Papatum sustinuisse, indulgentias invexisse, orbem expilasse, utpote quæ ad quæstum pateant, monachorum turbas coacervasse, Verbum Dei exterminasse asseritis, atq; ideo Germanos Principes Synaxim veteri more reduxisse quam lingua vernacula facere, ritu satis decoro atque decenti commemoratis; privatas vero Missas apud vos in totum abolitas esse, quæ tot pepererunt abusus et fœtus malignos. Qua de re nobiscum diu multumq; cogitantes, consideramus inprimis nihil uaquam in Ecclesia sua Christum ordinasse quo malignus serpens aliquando non sit abusus, neque tamen propterea rejiciendum est quic-

quid sancte est ordinatum, alioqui Sacramenta omnia an-
tiquanda essent; quin magis reputavimus longe satius
esse abusus omnes in totum removere, quæ vero Sancte
et pie introducta sunt in Ecclesiam, illa ipsa stabilia manere.

Nam si ideo Missæ privatæ abolendæ sunt in totum,
quia de illis Thomas Aquinas, Gabriel, atque alii Doc-
trinas ut dicitis impias induxerunt, viz. Missas ex opere
operato gratiam mereri, et tollere peccata vivorum et mortuorum, et applicari posse alienum opus ad alterum,
Quicquid sit, quod illi asserunt, hoc de omni Missa asserunt, non de privata duntaxat; Qua propter si ad tollendas
illas opiniones qualescunque Missa privata esset abroganda, eadem ratione abroganda esset Synaxis et Missa
publica, quam vos ipsi retinetis nec censetis abolendam,
quicquid de ea alii opinentur. Missa vero privata, velut
privata quædam est Communio et Synaxis, quæ si recte
atque ut decet fiat, quicunque fideles illi interesse decreverint, si pœnitentes convenerint contriti de peccatis,
Deiq; implorent misericordiam cum filio prodigo dicentes,
Pater peccavi in Cœlum et coram te, haud dubie quin ipsi
Spiritualiter cum Sacerdote communicant, offerentes se et
animas suas, hostias vivas et acceptabiles Deo, tametsi
pauci fuerint, atq; a corporali Sacramenti sumptione ab-
stinuerint: ac per hoc Missa privata Ecclesiæ adeo non
obest, ut non parum et ad vitam corrigendam, et ad fidem
in Christum corroborandam prodesse videatur; quippe
Christiani per hoc peccatores se agnoscunt quotidie delinquentes, quotidie veniam postulant, quotidie per peccatum in salebroso vitæ hujus cursu cadentes, quotidie
pœnitentes resurgunt, et velut alacriores redditi, devicto
sæpius hoste, fiunt ad pugnam audentiores.

Porro statim in exordio omnis Missæ privatæ publica
est peccatorum omnium generalis Confessio, venia postu-
latur a Deo, absolutio impartitur a Sacerdote secundum
Dei Verbum, quemadmodum in Missa publica.

Et si in Missa publica et quantumcunq; solenni nemo
adsit alius præter Sacerdotem qui Communicare velit in
esu Sacramenti, quid quæso differet Missa publica a privata? An Sacerdos in solemni die populo ad Sacra con-
veniente, si nemo alius communicare velit, abstinet a

Missa publica? atque inter Græcos ipsos, ubi singulis
dominicis diebus fit una Missa publica uti asseritis, raro
admodum communicat in esu Sacramenti quisquam è populo, uti a fide dignis accepimus, qui ipsi Græcorum Sacris
interfuerunt.

Quod vero Epiphanium citatis qui singulis septimanis
ter celebratam Synaxim in Asia asserit, eumq; morem ab
Apostolis inductum, cum jam tantum in Græcia singulis
Dominicis fiat populi conventus ad Sacra, si mutari mos
potuit ab Apostolis inductus, ut rarius quam statuerunt
Apostoli populus congregaretur, cur non etiam mutari
potuit ut sæpius conveniret, quando per hoc celebrior fit
mortis Christi memoria, id quod in Missa fit etiam privata.

Jam vero si Sacramentum hoc a fidelibus exerceri Christus in mortis suæ memoriam præcepit, inquiens, Hoc facite in meam commemorationem, ne mors ejus raro admodum commemorata in oblivionem transiret, quo crebrius,
quo frequentius, memoria ejus in Sacramento repetitur, eo
mandatum ejus servatur magis: Etenim sicut raro admodum memorata oblivioni sunt obnoxia, ita crebro frequen-
tata radices in mente agunt altius, ne obliterari unquam
possint; itaq; ut mors Christi crebra memoria illustretur,
Missa etiam privata non parum confert.

Certe Paulus Apostolus singulas domos privatas, ubi
credentium numerus aliquis erat, Ecclesias vocat, membra
Majoris Ecclesiæ, civitatis illius in qua essent, sicut majores ipsas civitatum Ecclesias, membra Catholicæ et universalis Ecclesiæ appellat, scribens ad Corinthios; at quæ
Ecclesia arcenda est a Communione Corporis Domini?
Christus etiam ipse instituendo Sacramentum hoc Corporis
et Sanguinis sui, inquit, Hoc quotiescunq; facitis, facite
in meam commemorationem; nec tempus nec locum ullum cohibuit, quo fieri id non posset, quonam modo igitur
arcebimus quenquam a Missis privatis? Et ad dies festos
publicamq; Synaxim eum relegabimus? Cujus arbitrio
Christus liberum reliquit, quando et ubi id vellet decenter
exequi, dum inquit quotiescunque? nam si certa tempora
servanda essent, non indefinite locutus fuisset Christus
ipsum Dei Verbum, ipsa sapientia Patris.

Jam vero ab initio nascentis Ecclesiæ per singulas domos ubi erant fideles fiebat communio, atq; id quotidie,

teste Luca in Apostolorum Actis, ubi ait, Quotidie quoq;
perdurantes unanimiter in templo, et frangentes circa domos
panem; quem locum etiam de Communione veteres interpretes intelligunt, et tamen singulis diebus non agebant
publice dies festos, sed privatim per domos communica-
bant: Etsi terrenorum regum atq; principum ministri pleriq; omnes nullum diem transigere cupiunt, quo non fru-
antur vel solo aspectu sui Domini, tametsi propior con-
gressus non contingat, quis fidelis Christianus non omnibus
optabit votis, ut quando in hac vita Christum Regem Regum,
et Dominum Dominantium, in Majestate gloriæ regnantem
cernere mortales oculi non possunt, saltem per fidem in
Sacramento Corporis Domini, quod ille fidelibus in memoriam sui frequentandam reliquit, interim quotidie Regem
gloriæ videat?

Quod vero Chrysostomus Sacerdotem ad altare stare, et
alios ad Communionem accersere, alios arcere scribit, enar-
rat morem publicæ Communionis, qui in initio nascentis Ecclesiæ crebrius quam nunc fit frequentabatur; qui mos nunc
in Paschate, quando ubiq; communicat populus, apud omnes servatur Ecclesias: Cæterum ille ipse expostulat cum
fidelibus sui temporis, quod rarius communicent, quam vel
oporteret, vel vetus mos erat; cæterum nusquam is privatas Missas vetui.

At Canon Nicenus Diaconis in Communione publica
suum locum designat post Presbyteros; cæterum nec is
Canon, nec ullus alius Missas privatas abrogat.

Sacramentum autem Eucharistiæ Sacrificium non esse
arbitramini, quod unum Sacrificium sit propitiatorium mors
Christi, et cum is ultra non moritur, qui semel tantum pro
nobis oblatus est, nullum restat ultra Sacrificium, nisi cultus Spiritualis, hoc est, justitia fidei et fructus fidei. Quid
sibi velit justitia quæ ex fide est scimus, quippe quam
Paulus opponit Justitiæ quæ est ex lege: Cæterum qui
sunt fructus fidei, nobis ex Scripturis non satis liquet, ipsam fidem sicut charitatem, et multas alias virtutes scimus
esse fructus Spiritus. Verum enim vero non satis miramur,
cur quispiam ægre ferat Missam Sacrificium vocari, quando omnis vetustas et Græcorum et Latinorum sic eam appellare consuevit, quum ibi fiat consecratio Corporis et
Sanguinis Domini in memoriam mortis ejus, qui, ut inquit

Paulus, pro peccatis offerens hostiam, in sempiternum se-
det ad dextram Dei, una enim oblatione consummavit in
sempiternum sanctificatos; itaq; si Christus et Sacerdos
esset, et Sacrificium, et hostia, ubicunq; est Christus, ibi
est hostia nostra, ibi est sacrificium nostrum; at si in Sacramento altaris est verum Corpus Christi, et verus Sanguis Christi, quo pacto manente veritate Corporis et Sanguinis Domini, non est ibi Sacrificium nostrum?

Porro quia in Missa est Christus Sacrificium nostrum,
qui ipse ultra non moritur, ibiq; cum ipso capite nostro,
nos illius Corpus et membra nosmet ipsos Deo hostias vivas offerimus, Græci id totum ἀναίμακτον Θυσίαν, id est, Sacrificium incruentum vocant: ita veteres omnes intrepide
Missam Sacrificium vocarunt, quod ibi sit Christus Sacrificium nostrum in Sacramento.

Sic Basilius, sic Chrysostomus, sic Hieronymus, sic
Augustinus, eam appellare non dubitavit; Quocirca quid
vetat Missam, in qua consecratur Panis in Corpus Christi,
et Vinum in Sanguinem ejus, qui vere est Sacrificium nostrum, et hoc fieri in memoriam sui jussit, vocari Sacrificium: alioqui si id negabimus, non parum verendum est,
ne cum Sacramentariis quos nunc vocant, qui veritatem
Corporis et Sanguinis in Sacramento negant, et cum Ana-
baptistis consentire videamur, a qua suspicione sicut in
animo nostro nos profitemur longe abesse, ita quoq; cupimus calumniantibus adversariis omnem obtrectandi ansam
auferri: Atqui eum in Missa tum Sacerdos, tum populus
contritus de peccatis se, ut hortatur Paulus, hostiam vi-
vam, sanctam atq; Deo placentem exhibeat, laudes quas
Deo canat et in gratiarum actione versetur, quis dubitare
potest, ea quoq; ratione, Missam jure Sacrificium nominari, cum Propheta appellat Sacrificium laudis, et Paulus
omnes hortetur, ut se hostias vivas exhibeant, id quod fit
in Missa. Malachias etiam Propheta inquit, Ab ortu solis
usq; ad occasum, magnum est nomen meum in gentibus,
et in omni loco Sacrificatur, et offertur nomini meo oblatio
munda, quia magnum est nomen meum in gentibus, dicit
Dominus exercituum. At quæ alia oblatio munda in omni
loco inter gentes, nisi solus Christus, aut quod aliud Sacrificium Christianorum, nisi Missa, ubi Commemoratio mortis Christi agitur? Nam aut aliquod inter gentes Christia-

norum oportet esse Sacrificium, aut mentitus est Propheta:
quænam quæso est oblatio munda, nisi solus Christus hostia nostra, qui in Sacramento altaris est sub Panis et Vini
speciebus? quippe quantumcunq; nos ipsi nos Deo offer-
amus, hostiæ mundæ non meremur nomen, quorum omnis
justitia velut pannus est menstruatæ: Itaq; constat Missam Sacrificium vocari ex Verbo Dei per Malachiam enun-
ciato, quod cum ita sit, cur Missæ invidemus nomen Sacrificii, quod Propheta prædixit, et in qua Christus in Sacramento præsens est ipse mundi Sacrificium?

De Conjugio Sacerdotum.

Cœlibatum Sacerdotum contra Scripturam, contra leges
naturæ, contra honestatem, per Pontificem Romanum asseritis introductum, cum Scriptura Sacerdotibus, sicut cæteris hominibus, conjugium permittat, nec possint naturam
suam mutare, nec absq; singulari dono cœlibes vivere:
nam non omnes capiunt verbum hoc, et Paulus inquit,
propter fornicationem unusquisq; Uxorem suam habeat.
Hic primum ordiri juvat, ut locum illum Evangelii de
tribus Eunuchorum generibus consideremus, quandoquidem Christus alios a natura Eunuchos esse asserit, alios
per vim factos, quorum neutrum genus continentiæ virtute
splendet; quoniam alteros ad generandum natura, alteros
violentia reddidit inutiles. Tertium vero genus eorum est,
qui quanquam terrena generatione uti possunt, malunt continere, et se castrare propter Regnum Cœlorum; de quo
genere Christus statim infert, qui potest capere, capiat, id
quod nec de primo, nec de secundo Eunuchorum genere
intelligi potest, quibus continentiæ palma negata est, cum
descendere in certamen nequeunt: tertium vero genus eorum est, qui continentiæ student, et a licitis nuptiis abstinere malunt propter Regnum Cœlorum, quo Christum libe-
rius atq; expeditius sequantur, ne terrenis nuptiis impli-
cati, cogitare cogantur, ut inquit Paulus, quæ sunt mundi;
ad quod genus Christus virginitatis author homines sapientissime invitat, inquiens, Qui potest capere, capiat: per
hoc quod inquit, capiat, homines adhortans ad capescen-
dum certamen ut palmam arripiant, nempe Regnum Cœlorum, ad quod neminem hortaretur, si nemo carnem pos-

sit vincere; per hoc vero quod ait, qui potest capere, posse capi palmam indicans; alioqui si impossibile esset carnem superare, quorsum attineret dicere, Qui potest, si nemo id posset.

Præterea per ea verba, Qui potest capere, quosdam etiam esse declarat, qui non facile possunt, nam nisi aliqui non facile possent capere, cur secerneret eos qui possunt; itaq; considerandas animi vires admonet, priusquam certamen aggrediare, ne temere arrepto certamine turpiter succumbas: Nec dixisset quosdam esse, qui se castraverunt propter Regnum Cœlorum, si caro esset insuperabilis, et nemo se castrare posset. Nec dubitandum est quin is qui hortatur ad subeundum certamen, gratiam suam sine qua nihil possent, his non defuturam demonstrat, qui nomina sua in militiam ei dederunt, quorum ille ipse dux futurus est, qui non modo in periculis suos milites invocatus nunquam deserit, sed stat ante Januam et pulsat, paratus semper ad succurrendum, siquis ei aperiat: Nam Paulus tentationes superari posse nos admonet, modo Dei auxilium imploremus, inquiens, Tentatio vos non apprehendit nisi humana, fidelis autem Deus qui non patietur vos tentari supra id quod potestis, sed faciet etiam cum tentatione proventum ut possitis sustinere. Quamobrem his qui continentiam semel profitentur, et eam postea turpiter deserunt, etiam atq; etiam considerandum est, ne nomen Dei blasphemare videantur, Christum accusantes deserti auxilii, cum sint ipsi desertores militiæ, et primo statim congressu terga dantes hosti: itaq; quod Paulus liberum cuiq; facit, ut propter fornicationem Uxorem suam habeat, id de his intelligi, qui continentiam non sunt professi, Paulus ipse nos docet, inquiens, de viduis adolescentioribus, quæ cum luxuriatæ fuerunt in Christo nubere volunt, habentes damnationem quia primam fidem irritam fecerunt. Augustinus Pauli Doctrinam secutus, Psal. 83. inquit, alius ex Dei munere majus aliquid vovit, statuit nec nuptias pati, qui non damnaretur si duxisset Uxorem; post votum quod Deo promisit si duxerit damnabitur: sic virgo quæ si nuberet non peccaret, Sanctimonialis si nupserit Christi adultera reputabitur, respexit enim retro de loco quo accesserat, exemplo Uxoris Loth, et sicut canis reversus ad vomitum reputatur.

Itidem Augustinus, Psal. 75. ample asserit votum somel
emissum servandum esse. Hicronymus etiam adversus
Jovinianum inquit, virgo quæ se Deo dicavit, si nubat,
damnationem habet; atq; alio loco adversus eundem, Virgines tuæ quas prudentissimo consilio (quod nemo unquam legerat, nec audierat de Apostolo) docuisti, melius
esse nubere quam uri, occultos adulteros in apertos verte-
runt maritos; non suasit hoc Apostolus, non Electionis
vas Virgilianum consilium est, conjugium vocat, hoc præ-
texit nomine culpam. Verbum ipsum Dei palam adversatur ubique ne rumpantur vota. Propheta inquit, vovete
et reddite Domino Deo Vestro; in Deuteronomio quoq;
scribitur, cum votum voveris Domino Deo tuo, non tarda-
bis reddere, quia requiret illud Dominus Deus tuus, et si
moratus fueris, reputabitur tibi in peccatum; si nolueris
polliceri absq; peccato eris, quod autem egressum est de
labiis tuis, observabis et facies, sicut promisisti Domino
Deo tuo et propria voluntate et ore locutus es. Ecclesiastes etiam inquit, siquid vovisti ne moreris reddere, sed
quodcunq; voveris redde: Et in Numerorum libro scribitur, siquis virorum votum Domino voverit, aut se con-
strinxerit juramento, non faciat irritum Verbum suum, sed
omne quod promisit implebit. Quocirca Ecclesia a principio sicut conjugatos Sacerdotes et Episcopos, qui sine crimine essent unius Uxoris viri propter necessitatem admisit, cum tot alii quot possent ad edocendum orbem sufficere tunc non reperirentur idonei, et tamen Paulus ipse Timotheum coelibem elegit; ita quoq; siquis ad Sacerdotium coelebs accersitus, postea Uxorem duxerit, semper a
Sacerdotio deponebatur, secundum Canonem Neocæsari-
ensis Concilii, quod fuit ante Nicenum. Similiter in Cal-
cedonensi Concilio, in cujus primo capite priora Concilia
confirmantur, statuitur ut Diaconissa, si se nuptiis tradat,
maneat sub Anathemate, et Virgo Deo dicata et Monachus
jungentes se nuptiis, maneant excommunicati.

Hoc quoq; observandum est, quod in Canonibus Apostolorum habetur, tantummodo Lectores cantoresq; non
conjugatos posse Uxores ducere, cæteris vero in clerum
admissis postea Uxorem ducere nunquam licuit.

Qui vero conjugati ad Sacerdotium admissi erant, Uxores suas prætextu Religionis abjicere nequaquam pote-

rant, ut docet Canon Apostolicus ; cumque in Niceno Concilio proponeretur de Presbyterorum jam ductis Uxoribus
abjiciendis, restitit Paphnutius ne legitimæ Uxores pelle-
rentur, cujus sententiam, cum Canone Apostolorum de non
abjiciendis Uxoribus concordantem, omnes sunt secuti.

Cæterum in Niceno Concilio nihil unquam propositum
fuit, ut Sacerdotes post Sacerdotium Uxores ducerent, quod
jam ante sic erit prohibitum, ut siquis contrarium auderet,
ducens postea Uxorem, deponeretur a Sacerdotio, ut supra
dictum est ; itaq; Paphnutius de non abjiciendis jam ductis ante Sacerdotium Uxoribus, non autem deducendis post
Sacerdotium aperte locutus est.

Itaq; neq; Canon aliquis Apostolicus, neq; Concilium
Nicenum quicquam habet ejusmodi ut in Sacerdotium admissi, postea Uxores ducant, sicut vos allegatis.

His concordat sexta Synodus in qua sancitum est quod
siquis è clero vellet Uxorem ducere, ante subdiaconatum
id faceret, postea nequaquam liceret, nec ulla usquam libertas Sacerdotibus in sexta Synodo datur post Sacerdotium Uxores ducendi, sicut vos asseritis.

Itaq; a principio nascentis Ecclesiæ, plane compertum
est nullo unquam tempore licuisse Sacerdoti post Sacerdotium Uxorem ducere ; atq; ubicunq; id fuit attentatum,
id non fuit impune, nam tantum nefas ausus deponebatur a
Sacerdotio. Paulus Apostolus inquit, de conjugibus loquens, nolite fraudare invicem nisi forte ex consensu ad
tempus, ut vacetis orationi. Hieronymus in Apologia ad
Pammachium ait, Paulus Apostolus dicit, Quando coimus
cum Uxoribus nos orare non posse, si per coitum quod minus est impeditur, id est orare, quanto plus quod majus est,
id est Corpus Christi, prohibetur accipere : idque late prosequitur exemplo panum propositionis, qui non dabantur
nisi continentibus Davidi et ministris, ut scribitur in libro
Regum ; Panes enim Propositionis, quasi Corpus Christi,
de Uxorum cubilibus consurgentes edere non poterant, ut
inquit Hieronymus, atque exemplo dationis legis veteris,
ante cujus dationem filii Israel in Exodo triduo abstinere
sunt jussi ab Uxoribus.

Hieronymus etiam adversus Jovinianum inquit, si Laicus et quicunq; fidelis orare non potest, nisi careat officio
conjugali, Sacerdoti cui semper pro populo offerenda sunt

Sacrificia, semper orandum est : si semper orandum est, semper ergo careadum Matrimonio. Idem asserit Ambrosius ample in Epistola ad Timotheum prima, eum quo consentit Augustinus.

Paulus Timotheum Discipulum in Sacerdotali Officio erudiens, admonet secularia negotia fugienda esse, inquiens, Labora ut bonus miles Christi Iesu, nemo militans implicat se negotiis secularibus, ut ei placeat cui se probavit; et si Sacerdotes Uxores acciperent, curis secularibus necesse est involvantur, nam teste Paulo, qui cum Uxore est, solicitus est quæ sunt mundi, quomodo placeat Uxori; qui vero sine Uxore est, solicitus est quæ Domini sunt, quomodo placeat Deo : Ideoq ; eundem ad cœlibatum hortatur, quando ait, Teipsum castum custodi, nam castitas, ubi de conjugatie non fit sermo, cœlibatus intelligitur, suum enim Discipulum sui similem reddere cupiebat; atque quodam in loco Corinthiis scribens, omnes homines hortatur ad continentiam, ait enim, volo omnes homines esse sicut meipsum, et rursus dico non nuptis et viduis bonum est, si sic permanserint sicut et ego. Alio in loco scribens eisdem, ministros Ecclesiæ sui officii admonet, adhortans ne in vacuum Gratiam Dei recipiant, et subdit, Nemini dantes ullam offensionem, ut non vituperetur ministerium, sed in omnibus exhibeamus nosmetipsos sicut Dei Ministros, &c. in vigiliis, in jejuniis, in castitate, in scientia, in verb v eritatis. Quæ omnia ad ministros Ecclesiæ pertinent quos castitatem maxime sectari convenit, ut impuri non appropinquent altaribus, a quibus salaces ommino aréeri decet : Nam non nisi de Sacerdotibus ea intelligi possunt, quando scientia divinæ legis et populi institutio ad eos spectat, ut inquit Malachias, Labia Sacerdotis custodiunt scientiam et legem requirunt ex ore ejus. Et Paulus Timotheum vult se exhibere operarium inconfusibilem, recte tractantem verbum veritatis, viz. in Doctrina populi ; igitur Sacerdotes Domini, qui se Deo jampridem dedicaverunt, qui se castraverunt propter Regnum Cœlorum, qui pro suis et populi peccatis orare assidue debent, quonam pacto, deserto cœlibatus vexillifero Christo, novis nuptiis operam dare secularibusq; molestiis quibus scaturiunt se implicare decet ? quid enim est ad aratrum manum mittere, retroq; recipere exemplo Uxoris Loth, si

hoc non est? cujusmodi homines non aptos esse Regno
Dei, Christus ipse pronunciat, etenim si nemo potest Uxori
pariter et Philosophiæ operam dare, ut mundana prudentia
docet, quanto magis is qui se Deo dicavit, duobus Dominis
servire non poterit, nempe Deo pariter et mundo, quorum
uterq; totum hominem, non dimidiatum, ad se raptat?

Quanquam autem et conjugati et cœlibes in initio Ecclesiæ admittebantur ad Sacerdotium, id tamen non ubiq;
ita servabatur teste Hieronymo adversus Vigilantium, ubi
inquit, quid facient Orientis Ecclesiæ, quid Egypti, et
Sedis Apostolicæ, quæ aut Virgines clericos accipiunt, aut
continentes, aut si Uxores habuerint mariti esse desistunt?
Atque ad Pammachium Hieronymus inquit, Christus Virgo, Virgo Maria, utriusq; sexus virginitatem dedicaverunt, Apostoli vel Virgines, vel post nuptias continentes,
Episcopi, Presbyteri, Diaconi, aut Virgines eliguntur, aut
vidui, aut certe post Sacerdotium in æternum pudici, in morem Ecclesiæ veterem, cujus autor est haud dubie Paulus
et Scriptura ipsa. Jam vero uti Augustinum citatis, qui
ait, quidam nubentes post votum asserunt adulteros esse,
ego dico vobis quod graviter peccant qui tales dividunt : at
ille ipse Augustinus asserit, lapsus et ruinas a castitate
Sanctiori quæ vovetur Deo adulteriis esse pejores, neq;
statim legitimum est quicquid tolerat Ecclesia.

Cyprianus quoq; ipse quem citatis, in illa ipsa Epistola
de Virginibus quæ continentiam voverunt, ubi inquit, si
perseverare nolunt, vel non possint, melius est ut nubant,
quam ut in ignem delitiis suis ruant ; ex quo infertis tale
votum non impedire Matrimonium, longe aliud sentit :,
nam consultus a Pomponio Sacerdote, quid sibi videretur
de Virginibus his, quæ cum semel statum suum continenter
et firmiter tenere decreverint, detectæ sunt postea in
eodem lecto pariter mansisse cum Masculis ; ea de re altius
repetens Sermonem, periculosamq; esse Virginum et Mas-
culorum cohabitationem, confirmans per Scripturas ac
graves multorum ruinas ex hoc enatas, asserens generaliter
de omnibus Virginibus inquit, quod si ex fide Christo se
dicaverint caste et pudice sine ulla fabula perseverent, ita
fortes et stabiles præmium Virginitatis expectent ; si autem perseverare nolunt, vel non possunt, melius est ut nubant, quam ut in ignem delitiis suis cadant, certe nullum

fratribus aut sororibus scandalum faciant, cum scriptum
sit, &c. Et paulo post infert, Christus Dominus et judex
noster, cum virginem suam sibi dicatam et sanctitati suæ de-
stinatam jacere cum altero cernat, quam indignatur et iras-
citur, et quas pœnas incestis hujusmodi conjunctionibus
comminatur! Deinde ad quæsitum respondens, jubet obste-
trices adhiberi ut videatur an Virgines illæ sint corruptæ,
ubi inquit, si autem aliquæ ex eis corruptæ fuerunt depre-
hensæ, agant pœnitentiam plenam, quia quæ hoc crimen
admisit, non mariti sed Christi adultera est, et ideo æsti-
mato justo tempore et ex homologesi facta ad Ecclesiam
redeant; quod si obstinatæ perseverent, nec se ab invicem
separent, sciant se cum hac sua impudica obstinatione nunquam a nobis admitti in Ecclesiam posse, ne exemplum
cæteris ad ruinam delictis suis facere incipiant. Ecce quid
sentit Cyprianus de votis ruptis, incestuosos et Christi
Adulteros hujusmodi flagitiosos appellat, et nisi separen-
tur, nunquam admittit in Ecclesiam; quomodo ergo talia
vota non impediant Matrimonium, aut quis ad tale Matrimonium quenquam hortari audebit, quod sine violatione
voti et transgressione divini mandati, ideoq; sine gravissimo scelere contrahi non possit? Atqui quod Principes
Germaniæ, scribitis, cum viderent multa flagitia de cœlibatu Sacerdotum provenire, Matrimonia Sacerdotibus libera permisisse, si meum, Egregii Oratores, consilium re-
quisissent vestri Principes, priusquam tot Sacerdotes apud
vos ruptis vinculis ad nuptias convolassent, ad id consilii
dedissem quod vestri Principes arripuerunt, hæsito magnopere; nam si Sacerdotes qui continere nollent, erumpere
ad nuptias omnino voluissent, quanto satius forte fuisset,
exemplo veterum deposuisse tales a Sacerdotio, suæq; de
cætero Conscientiæ quenquam reliquisse, ac deinde puri-
ores altaribus admovisse, quam libere omnia permittendo
peccatis alienis auctores videri, atq; ea ratione aliena peccata nostra facere: Veruntamen nos qui in aliena Repub.
curiosi nunquam fuimus nec esse voluimus, omnia Principum vestrorum acta atq; gesta in optimam partem inter-
pretamur, non dubitantes, quin ad tollendos abusus omnes
sincerus his animus, atq; ad repurgandam Dei Ecclesiam
appositus non desit.

Porro nos qui in Regno nostro Romani Episcopi Tyran-

nidem profligare magna industria studuimus, et Christi
Gloriam sinceriter promovere curabimus Deo propitio,
quantum humano consilio fieri potest, ne quis abusus sive a
Romano Episcopo sive a quovis alio inductus non aboleatur, et si quos comperiemus tempori inservientes, fingen-
tesq; se odisse Romanum Episcopum, atq; in Sermone
simulare veritatem, quam corde non amplectuntur, ejusmodi viris consilia nostra de rebus Sacris non communica-
bimus, nec eorum vel de Sacris vel de Prophanis expecta-
bimus sententiam.

Quæ vero Christi puram atq; sinceram Doctrinam promovere, quæ Christi Evangelium dilatare, quæ ad repur-
ganda Ecclesiæ Anglicanæ vitia tendere, quæ ad extirpan-
dos abusus atq; errores omnes spectare, quæ deniq; Ecclesiæ candorem exornare posse videbuntur, ea totis viribus sectabimur, his studebimus, his Deo volente in perpetuum incumbemus.

De Articulis vero quos jam disseruimus maturius cum
Theologis nostris quamprimum vacabit agemus, atq; ea
demum statuemus quæ ad Christi Gloriam Ecclesiæque
sponsæ ejus decorem conducere existimabimus.

Vobis autem, Præstantissimi Oratores qui tot labores
terra marique perpessi estis, ut nos inviseretis, qui cum
Theologis nostris tamdiu contulistis, qui ob Evangelii
negotium a Patria abfuistis multis mensibus, immensas
atq; innumeras habemus gratias; nec miramur si dulcis
amor Patriæ, post diuturnam absentiam vestram, ad redi-
tum vos invitat. Itaque post expleta Principum vestrorum mandata, post absoluta in totum negotia vestra, si
non gravabimini nos invisere, vester ad nos accessus admodum gratus erit, vosque in Patriam non modo libenter di-
mittemus cum bona venia, sed ad Principes etiam vestros,
literas dabimus summæ diligentiæ vestræ in exequenda le-
gatione testimonium perhibentes. Valete.

IX.

*A Letter written by the King to his Bishops, directing them
how to instruct the People. An Original.*

BY THE KING.

HENRY R.

RIGHT Reverend Father in God, right trusty and well-
beloved, we greet you well: And whereas for the Vertue,
Learning, and good qualities which we saw and perceived
heretofore in you, judging you thereby a Personage that
would sincerely, devoutly, purely, and plainly set forth the
Word of God, and instruct our People in the truth of the
same, after a simple and plain sort, for their better instruction, unity, quiet, and agreement in the points thereof, we
advanced you to the room and office of a Bishop within this
our Realm ; and so endowed you with great Revenues and
Possessions ; perceiving after, by the contrariety of preaching within this our Realm, our said People were brought
into a diversity of Opinion, whereby there ensued contention amongst them ; which was only engendred by a certain
contemptuous manner of speaking, against honest, laudable, and tolerable Ceremonies, Usages, and Customs of
the Church ; we were enforced, by our sundry letters, to
admonish and command you, amongst others, to preach
God's Word sincerely; to declare abuses plainly, and in no
wise contentiously to treat of matters indifferent, which be
neither necessary to our Salvation, as the good and vertuous
Ceremonies of Holy Church, ne yet to be in any wise contemned and abrogated, for that they be incitements and
motions to Vertue, and allurements to Devotion : all
which our travail notwithstanding, so little regard was by
some taken and adhibited to our advertisements therein,
that we were constrained to put our own Pen to the Book,
and to conceive certain Articles, which were by all you
the Bishops and whole Clergy of this our Realm in Convocation agreed on, as Catholick, meet, and necessary to
be by our Authority for avoiding of all contention set forth,
read and taught to our Subjects, to bring the same in unity,
quietness, and good concord : supposing then that no Per-

2 K 2

son having Authority under us, would either have presumed to have spoken any word, that might have offended the sentence and meaning of the same, or have been any thing remiss, slack, or negligent in the plain setting forth of them as they be conceived, so as by that mean of abstinence such quiet and unity should not grow thereupon as we desired and looked for of the same; and perceiving eftsoons, by credible report, that our labours, travail and desire therein, is nevertheless defeated, and in manner by general and contemptuous words spoken, by sundry light and seditious persons, contemned and despised, so that by the abstinence of direct and plain setting-forth of the said Articles, and by the fond and contentious manner of speaking, that the said light Personages do still use against the honest Rites, Customs, Usages, and ceremonial Things of the Church, our People be much more offended than they were before; and in a manner exclaim that we will suffer that injury at any Man's hand, whereby they think both God, us, and our whole Realm highly offended, insomuch that principally upon that ground, and for the Reformation of those Follies and Abuses, they have made this commotion and insurrection, and have thereby grievously offended us, dammaged themselves, and troubled many of our good Subjects: We be now enforced, for our discharge towards God, and for the tender love and zeal we bear unto the tranquillity and loving unity of our said People and Subjects, again to readdress these our Letters to all the Bishops of our Realm, and amongst other unto you, as a peremptory warning to admonish you, to demean and use your self for the redobbying of these things as shall be hereafter declared, upon pain of deprivation from the Bishoprick, and further to be punished for your contempt, if you shall offend in the contrary, as Justice shall require for your own Trespass.

And first, we straitly charge and command you, that plainly and distinctly, without any additions, ye shall every Holy day, wheresoever ye shall be within your Diocess, when ye may so do with your health and convenient commodity, openly, in your Cathedral Church, or the Parish Church of the place where ye shall for time be, read and declare our Articles; and in no wise, in the rest of your

words which ye shall then speak of your self, if you speak
any thing, utter any word that shall make the same, or any
word in the same, doubtful to the people.

Secondly; We will and command you, That you shall in
your Person travel from place to place in all your Diocess,
as you may with your commodity, and endeavour your
selves every Holy-day to make a Collation to the People,
and in the same to set forth plainly the Texts of Scripture
that you shall treat of; and with that also as well to declare the obedience due by God's Laws to their Prince and
Soveraign Lord, against whose commandment they ought
in no wise, though the same were unjust, to use any violence, as to commend and praise honest Ceremonies of the
Church as they be to be praised, in such plain and reverent
sort, that the People may perceive they be not contemned,
and yet learn how they were instituted, and how they ought
to be observed and esteemed; using such a temperance
therein, as our said People be not corrupted, by putting
over-much affiance in them, which a part should more offend, than the clear silencing of the same, and that our
People may thereto the better know their duties to us, being
their King and Soveraign Lord.

Thirdly; We straitly charge and command you, That
neither in your private communications you shall use any
words that may sound to the contrary of this our Commandment, ne you shall keep or retain any Man of any
degree, that shall in his words privately or openly, directly
or indirectly, speak in these matters of the Ceremonies,
contentiously or contemptously; but we will that in case
ye have, or shall have towards you any such Person that
will not better temper his Tongue, you shall, as an Offender
and a Seductor of our People, send the same in sure custody to us and our Council, to be punished as shall appertain; and semblably to do with other Strangers whom ye
shall hear to be notable offenders in that part.

Fourthly; Our pleasure and commandment is, That you
shall on your behalf, give strait commandment upon like
pain of deprivation and further punishment, to all Parsons,
Vicars, Curats, and Governors of Religious Houses, Col-
ledges, and other places Ecclesiastical within your Diocess,
that they and every of them shall, touching the indifferent

praise of Ceremonies, the avoiding of contentious and contemptous Communication, concerning any of the same, and the distinct and plain reading of our said Articles, observe and perform, in their Churches, Monasteries, and other Houses Ecclesiastical aforesaid, the very same order that is before to you prescribed. And further, that you permit nor suffer any Man, of what degree soever in learning, Strangers or other, to preach in any place within your said Diocess out of his own Church, by virtue of any License by us, or any other of our Ministers, granted before the fifteenth day of this month, neither in your presence nor elsewhere, unless he be a Man of such honesty, vertue, learning, and judgment, as you shall think able for that purpose, and one whom in manner you dare answer for.

Finally; Whereas we be advertised that divers Priests have presumed to marry themselves, contrary to the custom of our Church of England, our pleasure is, Ye shall make secret enquiry within your Diocess, whether there be any such resiant within the same or not: And in case ye shall find that there be any Priests that have so presumed to marry themselves, and have sithence nevertheless used and exercised in any thing the Office of Priesthood, we charge you, as ye will answer upon the pains aforesaid, not to conceal their doings therein, but rather to signify their demeanour to our Council, or to cause them to be apprehended, and so sent up unto us accordingly. Given under our Signet at our Castle of Windsor, the 19th day of November, in the 28th Year of Our Reign.

X.

Tonstall's Arguments for the Divine Institution of Auricular Confession; with some Notes written on the Margent by King Henry's own Hand. An Original.

Quod Confessio Auricularis sit de Jure Divino.

PROBARI videtur ex illo loco Matthæi 3. ubi Joanne Baptista in deserto prædicante pœnitentiam, exibat ad eum

Hierosolyma et omnis Judæa, et baptizabantur ab eo in Jordane confitentes peccata sua; quem locum Chrysostomus ita exponit, inquiens, Confessio peccatorum est testimonium Conscientiæ confitentis Deum, qui enim timet Judicium Dei peccata sua non erubescat confiteri; qui autem erubescit non timet, perfectus enim timor solvit omnem pudorem; illic enim turpitudo confessionis aspicitur, ubi futuri judicii pœna non creditur. Nunquid nescimus quia Confessio peccatorum habet pudorem, et quia hoc ipsum erubescere pœna est gravis, sed ideo magis nos jubet Deus confiteri peccata nostra, ut verecundiam patiamur pro pœna? nam et hoc ipsum pars est Judicii, O misericordia Dei! quem toties ad iracundiam excitavimus, sufficit ei * solus pudor pro pœna.

* Nota bene de solo pudore. Fallax.

Si verecundia pro pœna est apud Deum, ea autem non contingat ex confessione facta soli Deo, nam nemo rationis compos ignorat etiam absque Confessione Deum peccata nostra scire, de Confessione facta homini necesse est intelligantur. Præterea ipsa Verba demonstrant quod Joanni Baptistæ confessi sunt peccata sua, nam dixit eis, facite ergo fructum dignum pœnitentia, quod apte dicere non poterat, nisi pœnitentes eos ex confessione sibi facta rescivisset.

Beda Marci I.

Et Baptizabantur ab illo in Jordane flumine, confitentes peccata sua. * Exemplum confitendi peccata ac meliorem vitam promittendi datur eis, qui Baptisma accipere desiderant, sicut etiam prædicante † Paulo in Epheso multi credentium veniebant, confitentes et annunciantes actus suos, quatenus abdicata vita veteri, renovari mererentur in Christo.

* Exemplum dicit non præceptum. † Non præcepto.

Scribitur quoq; in Evangelio Joannis 21. Quorum remiseritis peccata, remittuntur eis et quorum retinueritis, retenta sunt: et Matth. 18. Quæcunq; ligaveritis super terram, erunt ligata in Cœlo, et quæcunq; solveritis super terram, erunt soluta in Cœlo. Remittere autem et solvere nemo potest id quod ignorat, occulta autem peccata præter peccantem novit nisi solus Deus, quare nisi peccata aperiantur Sacerdoti, nec ea ligare nec solvere posset. Et

Huic respondendum est. Absolutio datur in remedium peccatorum petentibus tan-

* quemadmodum Sacratissima tua Majestas, si commissionem aliquibus dedisset audiendi et terminandi negotium aliquod, non possent judices rem ignorantes nisi negotio coram eis patefacto causam finire, viz. propter culpam litigatorum non comparentium coram eis; sic nec Sacerdotes ligare et solvere possunt peccata quæ ignorant. Itaq; cum Deus Sacerdotem velut medicum Spiritualem Ecclesiæ dederit, siquis enim sua vulnera celat, ipse sua culpa perit, cum tamen de salute sua deberet esse sollicitus, sicut Paulus ad Phil. 2. admonet, inquiens, cum metu et tremore Salutem vestram operamini.

Origenes in Levit. Homilia 2. loquens de Remissionibus Peccatorum.

Est adhuc et septima, licet dura et laboriosa, per pœnitentiam remissio peccatorum, cum lavat peccator lachrimis stratum suum, et fiunt ei lachrimæ suæ panis die et nocte, et cum non erubescit Sacerdoti Domini indicare peccatum suum, et quærere medicinam secundum eum qui ait, * Dixi pronunciabo adversum me injustitiam meam Domino, et tu remisisti impietatem cordis mei, in quo impletur et illud quod Jacobus Apostolus dicit, Siquis autem infirmatur, vocet Presbyteros Ecclesiæ, et imponant ei manus † ungentes eum oleo in nomine Domini, et oratio fidei salvabit infirmum, et si in peccatis fuerit remittentur ei.

Origenes Homilia 2. in Psal. 37.

Intellige mihi fidelem quidem hominem sed tamen infirmum, qui etiam vinci ab aliquo peccato potuit, et propter hoc mugientem pro delictis suis et omni modo curam vulneris sui sanitatemq; requirentem, licet præventus sit et lapsus, volentem tamen medelam ac salutem reparare; si ergo hujusmodi homo memor delicti sui, confiteatur quæ commisit, et humana confusione parvi pendat eos, qui exprobrant eum confitentem, et notant vel irrident, ille autem intelligens per hoc veniam sibi dari, et in die Resurrectionis pro his quibus nunc confunditur coram hominibus, tunc ante Angelos Dei confusionem atq; opprobria evasurum, ut nolit tegere et occultare maculam suam, sed pronunciet delictum suum, nec velit esse Sepulchrum dealbatum, quod deforis quidem appareat hominibus specio-

tum, id est ut videntibus se quasi justus appareat, intus autem sit repletus omni immunditie et ossibus mortuorum.

Et paulo post, Quoniam iniquitatem meam pronuncio. Pronunciationem iniquitatis, id est, confessionem peccati, frequentius diximus, vide ergo quid edocet nos scriptura divina, quia oportet peccatum non celare intrinsecus; fortassis enim sicut ii qui habent intus inclusam escam indigestam, aut humoris, vel flegmatis stomacho graviter et moleste imminentem, si vomuerunt relevantur; ita etiam hi qui peccarunt, si quidem occultant et retinent intra se peccatum intrinsecus urgentur, et propemodum suffocantur a phlegmate vel humore peccati: Si autem ipse sui accusator fiat, dum accusat semetipsum, simul evomit et delectum, atque omnem morbi digerit causam. Tantummodo circumspice diligentius cui debeas confiteri peccatum tuum, proba prius medicum cui debeas causam languoris exponere, qui sciat infirmari cum infirmante, flere cum flente, qui condolendi et compatiendi noverit disciplinam, ut ita demum siquid ille dixerit, qui se prius et eruditum medicum ostenderit et misericordem, siquid consilii dederit, facias et sequaris, si intellexerit et præviderit talem esse languorem tuum, qui in conventu totius Ecclesiæ exponi debeat et curari, ex quo fortassis et cæteri ædificari poterunt, et tu ipse facile sanari, multa hac deliberatione et satis perito medici illius consilio procurandum est.

Cyprianus in Sermone de Lapsis.

Denique quando et fide majore et timore meliores sunt, qui quamvis nullo Sacrificii aut libelli facinore constricti, quoniam tamen de hoc vel cogitaverunt, hoc ipsum apud Sacerdotes Dei dolenter et simpliciter confitentur, exomolegesin conscientiæ faciunt, animi sui pondus exponunt, salutarem medelam parvis licet et modicis vulneribus exquirunt, scientes scriptum esse, Deus non deridetur; derideri et circumveniri Deus non potest, nec astutia aliqua fallente deludi: plus imo delinquit qui secundum hominem Deum cogitans evadere se pœnam criminis credit, si non palam crimen admisit. Christus in præceptis suis dicit, qui confusus me fuerit, confundet eum filius hominis, et

(margin: Fateor Cyprianus Confessionem auricularem nobis non plus præcipi quam virginitatem.)

Christianum se putat qui Christianus esse aut confunditur aut veretur: Quomodo potest esse cum Christo qui ad Christum pertinere aut erubescit aut metuit? minus plane peccaverit non videndo idola, nec sub oculis circumstantis atq; insultantis populi sanctitatem fidei profanando, non polluendo manus suas funestis Sacrificiis, nec sceleratis cibis ora maculando; hoc eo proficit ut sit minor culpa, non ut innocens conscientia; facilius potest ad veniam criminis pervenire, non est tamen immunis a crimine, nec cesset in agenda poenitentia, atq; in Domini misericordia deprecanda, ne quod minus esse in qualitate delicti videtur, in neglecta satisfactione cumuletur. Confiteantur singuli, quaeso vos fratres, delictum suum, dum adhuc qui deliquit in saeculo est, dum admitti confessio ejus potest, dum satisfactio et remissio facta per Sacerdotes apud Dominum grata est; convertamur ad Dominum mente tota, et poenitentiam criminis veris doloribus exprimentes Dei misericordiam deprecemur; illi se anima prosternat, illi moestitia satisfaciat, illi spes omnis incumbat; rogare qualiter debeamus dicit ipse, Revertimini, inquit, ad me ex toto corde vestro, simulq; et jejunio, et fletu, et planctu, et scindite corda vestra et non vestimenta.

Si praeceptum haberet non persuaderet.

Praeterea Esaias peccatorem admonet Cap. 42. secundum 70. inquiens, Dic tu prior iniquitates tuas ut justificeris; et Solomon Prov. 18. ait, Justus prior est accusator sui, atq; ideo ne Satan nos in judicio coram omnibus accuset, nos illum in hac vita, per priorem confessionem delicti nostri factam aliis praevenire debemus, nam Deum praevenire in nostri accusatione nequimus qui omnia facta nostra jam novit, imo vero antequam fierent ea praescivit; quare Confessio illa necesse est, intelligatur, de extranea confessione facta Dei ministro qui id ignoravit, nam Deum nihil unquam latuit non modo jam factum, sed ne futurum quidem quicquam.

Hi omnes suadent, sed non praecipiunt.

Circa personas vero ministrorum quibus fieri doberet Confessio, atq; circa tempora Ecclesiae nonnunquam aliquid immutarunt, et varie pro regionibus statuerunt.

Cum nec cui nec tempora designantur non firmum praeceptum datur.

Et ne tuam solicitudinem, Sacratissima Majestas, circa publicam Regni tui tranquillitatem stabiliendam sanctissime occupatam, longa multorum lectione, quae praeter ista afferre possem, remorari videar, plura adjungere supersedebo, illud tantummodo precatus, ut meam hanc scribendi temeritatem boni consulat, quam ego totam perspicacissimo atq; eruditissimo Majestatis tuæ judicio considerandam pensitandamq; committo. Atq; ita fœlicissime valeat Sacratissima tua Majestas, cujus Regnum et prosperrimum et in sæculum diuturnum vobis fore precamur.

XI.

A Letter of King Henry's to Tonstall, Bishop of Duresme, against Auricular Confession being of Divine Institution. An Original:

SINCE me thought (my Lord of Durham) that both the Bishops of York, Winchester, and your Reasons and Texts were so fully answered this other day, in the House, as to my seeming and supposal, the most of the House was satisfied; I marvelled not a little why eft-soons you have sent to me this now your writing, being in a manner few other Texts or Reasons than there were declared both by the Bishop of Canterbury and me, to make smally or nothing to your intended purpose : but either I esteem that you do it to prove my simple judgment alone, which indeed doth not much use (tho not the wisest) to call in aid, the judgments of other learned Men, and so by mine ignorant answer, seem to win the Field; or else that you be too much blinded in your own fansy and judgment, to think that a Truth, which by learning you have not yet proved, nor I fear me cannot by Scriptures, nor any other Directors probable grounds, though I know mine unsufficiency in learning, if the matter were indifferent, and that the ballance stood equal, since I take the verity of the Cause rather to favorize the part I take than yours; it giveth me therefore great boldness, not presuming in Learning, but in justness of the Cause, seeing by writing you have provoked me to it, to make answer to your Arguments: Therefore I beginning now to reply to your first Allegation, shall essay to prove, if I can, that your own Author in place by you

Cott. Libr. Cleop. E. 5.

alledged, maketh plain against your Opinion; for as you
alledg him, St. Chrysostom saith, *Quod sufficit solus pudor
pro pœna*, then Auricular Confession is not by commandment necessary; for if it were, this word *(Solus)* is by your
Author ill set; therefore your Author in this place furder-
eth you but little. To your *Fallax* Argument, I deny your
consequent, founded only upon small Reason, which is the
ground of your *Fallax* Argument: which Reason I need
not take away, for your alledged Author doth shew too
plainly, in his 5. Homily, Tom. 5. that you gather wrong
sense upon his words; for he saith, with much more touching this matter, these few words, *Non hominibus peccata de-
tegere cogo;* then this other Text before rehearsed, is not
to be understood as you will by writing it. Further, me
thinketh, I need not (God thank you) too greatly study for
Authors to conclude your wrong taking of Texts, for those
your self alledg serveth me well to purpose: for all your
labour is to prove that Auricular Confession were by God
commanded, and both your Authorities of Bede and Paul,
sheweth nothing but that they did confess their sins, and
yet do not they affirm that it was by commandment; wherefore they make for mine Argument and not for yours. Your
other Texts of John 21. and Matthew 10. were so tho-
roughly answered this other day, and so manifestly declared
not to appertain to our grounded Argument, that I marvel
you be not ashamed eft-soons to put them in writing, and
to found your Argument now so fondly on them; for what
fonder Argument can be made to prove thereby a necessity
of Confession, than to say, If you confess not, I cannot
forgive? Would a Thief which committeth Felony, think
himself obliged by the Law to disclose his Felony, if the
Law say no more, but if thou confess not I cannot forgive
thee? or would theft the sooner therefore be forgiven?
This is matter so apparent, that none can but perceive except he would not see. As touching Origens places by you
alledged; as the first, in Leviticum, sheweth that we be as
much bound *lavare stratum lacrimis*, as *dicere Sacerdoti*,
which no man, I think, will affirm that we be bound to do;
and yet he affirmeth not that any of them is commanded:
the Text also whereby ye would approve his so saying,

doth not yet speak *quod pronunciabo justitiam meam Sacerdoti*, but *Domino :* The other of James seemeth better to make for extream Unction, than for Confession; for when was ever the use, that Folk coming only to Confession, were wont to be anointed with Oil, therefore this makes nothing to your Argument. As touching Origen in Psal. 37. he saith not, *quod obligamur dicere Sacerdoti*, but *si confiteantur ;* and seemeth rather to perswade Men that they should not *parvi pendere Confessionem*, (as all good Folk would) than that they were obliged to Confess them to a Priest. Though Cyprian *de Lapsis*, doth praise them which do Confess their Faults to Priests, yet doth he confess that we be not bound to do so; for he saith in the highest of his praise these words, " How much be they then higher in Faith, and better in fear of God, which though they be not bound by any deed of Sacrifice, or Book, yet be they content sorrowfully to confess to the Priest sins !" He knowledgeth no bond in us by neither fact of Sacrifice or Libel, why alledg you (tho he praise Auricular Confession) that we should be bound by God and Law thereto? This is no proof thereof, neither by Reason nor by Scripture, nor any good Authority. And whereas he saith further, *Confiteantur singuli, quæso vos fratres, delictum suum;* this doth not argue a precept : nor yet the saying of Esay, cap. 43. *secundum Septuaginta;* nor Solomon in the Proverbs 10. for these speak rather of knowledging our Offence to God in our Heart, than of Auricular Confession; after David the Prophets saying and teaching, when he said, *Tibi soli peccavi*, that was not to a Priest. By the text also which you alledg, beginning, *circa personas vero ministrorum, &c.* you do openly confess that the Church hath not accepted Auricular Confession to be by God's Commandment; or else by your saying and Allegation, they have long erred : for you confess that the Church hath divers times changed both to whom Confession should be made, and times when; and that also they have changed divers ways for divers Regions; if it were by God's Commandment they might not do thus : Wherefore, my Lord, since I hear no other Allegations, I pray you blame not me tho I be not of your Opinion; and of the both, I think that

I have more cause to think you obstinate, than you me, seeing your Authors and Allegations make so little to your purpose. And thus fare you well.

XII.

A Definition of the Church, corrected in the Margent by 'King Henry's own hand. An Original.

De Ecclesia.

Cotton Libr.Cleop. E. 5.

ECCLESIA præter alias acceptiones in Scripturis duas habet præcipuas: Unam, qua Ecclesia accipitur pro Congregatione Sanctorum et vere fidelium qui Christo capiti vere credunt, et sanctificantur Spiritu ejus hæc autem una est, et vere Sanctum Corpus Christi sed Soli Deo * cognitum, qui hominum corda solus intuetur. Altera acceptio est, qua Ecclesia accipitur pro Congregatione omnium Hominum qui baptizati sunt in Christo, et non palam abnegarint Christum, nec sunt† excommunicati : ‡ quæ Ecclesiæ acceptio congruit ejus Statui in hac vita duntaxat, ubi habet malos bonis simul admixtos,‖ et debet esse cognita per Verbum et legitimum usum Sacramentorum ut possit audiri ; sicut docet Christus, Qui Ecclesiam non audierit. Porro ad veram unitatem Ecclesiæ, requiritur ut sit consensus in recta Doctrina Fidei et administratione Sacramentorum.

Traditiones vero et ritus atq; Cæremoniæ quæ vel ad decorem, vel ordinem, vel Disciplinam Ecclesiæ ab hominibus sunt institutæ, non omnino necesse est, ut eadem sint ubiq; aut prorsus similes : hæ enim et variæ fuere et variari possunt § pro regionum atq; morum diversitate et commodo,¶ sic tamen ut sint consentientes Verbo Dei : et quamvis in Ecclesia secundum posteriorem acceptionem mali sint bonis admixti, atq; etiam Ministeriis Verbi et Sacramentorum nonnunquam præsint, tamen cum ministrent non suo sed Christi nomine, mandato et authoritate, licet eorum ministerio uti tam in

(marginal notes)

* Sponsa Christi cognita.
† Juste.
‡ Aut obstinati.
‖ Et cognitio hujus Ecclesiæ pervenit per usum Verbi et Sacramentorum, acceptione, perfecta, unitate, ac unanimi consensu acceptata.
§ Modo rectoribus placeant quibus semper obtemperandum est, tamen ut eorum institutio atq; Lex Verbo Dei non adversetur.
¶ Ista est

verbo audiendo quam recipiendis Sacramentis, juxta
illud, Qui vos audit me audit; nec per eorum maliti-
am imminuitur effectus aut gratia donorum Christi rite
accipientibus, sunt enim efficacia propter promissionem et ordinationem Christi etiamsi per malos exhibe-
antur.

Ecclesia
nostra Ca-
tholica et
Apostolica,
cum qua
nec Ponti-
fex Roma-
nus, nec
quivis ali-
quis Præ-

latus aut Pontifex, habet quicquid agere præterquam in suas Dioceses.

End of the Addenda.

A TABLE

BOOK III.

ADDENDA.

J. F. Dove, Printer, St. John's Square.

Date Loaned

Demco 292-5

Lightning Source UK Ltd.
Milton Keynes UK
UKHW02f1900080818
326964UK00006B/477/P